The Cambridge Companion to International Organizations Law

The Cambridge Companion to International Organizations Law illuminates, from a legal perspective, what international organizations are, what makes them 'tick' and how they affect the world around them. It critically discusses such classic issues as the concept of international organization and membership, as well as questions of internal relations, accountability and how they make law, set standards and otherwise affect both their member states and the world around them. The volume further discusses the role of international organizations in particular policy domains, zooming in on domains which are not often discussed through international organizations, including disarmament, energy, food security and health. Eventually, a picture emerges of international organizations as complex phenomena engaging in all sorts of activities and relationships, the operation and authority of which is underpinned by the rules and regulations of international law.

Jan Klabbers is Professor of International Law at the University of Helsinki, and a leading authority on international organizations law. He has held visiting positions at NYU, Sorbonne and the Graduate Institute in Geneva. He is currently working on an ERC-funded project on international organizations and the private sector.

Cambridge Companions to Law

Cambridge Companions to Law offers thought-provoking introductions to different legal disciplines, invaluable to both the student and the scholar. Edited by world-leading academics, each offers a collection of essays which both map out the subject and allow the reader to delve deeper. Critical and enlightening, the Companions library represents legal scholarship at its best.

The Cambridge Companion to European Union Private Law
Edited by Christian Twigg-Flesner

The Cambridge Companion to International Law
Edited by James Crawford and Martti Koskenniemi

The Cambridge Companion to Comparative Law
Edited by Mauro Bussani and Ugo Mattei

The Cambridge Companion to Human Rights Law
Edited by Conor Gearty and Costas Douzinas

The Cambridge Companion to Public Law
Edited by Mark Elliott and David Feldman

The Cambridge Companion to International Criminal Law
Edited by William A. Schabas

The Cambridge Companion to Natural Law Jurisprudence
Edited by George Duke and Robert P. George

The Cambridge Companion to Comparative Family Law
Edited by Shazia Choudhry and Jonathan Herring

The Cambridge Companion to Comparative Constitutional Law
Edited by Roger Masterman and Robert Schütze

The Cambridge Companion to the First Amendment and Religious Liberty
Edited by Michael D. Breidenbach and Owen Anderson

The Cambridge Companion to the Philosophy of Law
Edited by John Tasioulas

The Cambridge Companion to Legal Positivism
Edited by Torben Spaak and Patricia Mindus

The Cambridge Companion to Hugo Grotius
Edited by Randall Lesaffer and Janne E. Nijman

The Cambridge Companion to International Arbitration
Edited by Chin Leng Lim

The Cambridge Companion to Business & Human Rights Law
Edited by Ilias Bantekas and Michael Stein

The Cambridge Companion to International Organizations Law
Edited by Jan Klabbers

The Cambridge Companion to

International Organizations Law

Edited by

Jan Klabbers

University of Helsinki

CAMBRIDGE
UNIVERSITY PRESS

CAMBRIDGE
UNIVERSITY PRESS

University Printing House, Cambridge CB2 8BS, United Kingdom

One Liberty Plaza, 20th Floor, New York, NY 10006, USA

477 Williamstown Road, Port Melbourne, VIC 3207, Australia

314–321, 3rd Floor, Plot 3, Splendor Forum, Jasola District Centre, New Delhi – 110025, India

103 Penang Road, #05–06/07, Visioncrest Commercial, Singapore 238467

Cambridge University Press is part of the University of Cambridge.

It furthers the University's mission by disseminating knowledge in the pursuit of education, learning, and research at the highest international levels of excellence.

www.cambridge.org
Information on this title: www.cambridge.org/9781108495356
DOI: 10.1017/9781108574242

First published 2022

A catalogue record for this publication is available from the British Library.

ISBN 978-1-108-49535-6 Hardback
ISBN 978-1-108-46764-3 Paperback

Contents

Contributors

José E. Alvarez, New York University

Laurence Boisson de Chazournes, University of Geneva

Gian Luca Burci, Graduate Institute of International and Development Studies

Vincent Chetail, Graduate Institute of International and Development Studies

B. S. Chimni, Jindal Global University

Megan Donaldson, University College London

Alison Duxbury, University of Melbourne

Isabel Feichtner, University of Würzburg

Mónica García-Salmones Rovira, University of Helsinki

Matthias Goldmann, Goethe University Frankfurt

Angelo Golia Jr, Max Planck Institute for Comparative Public Law and International Law

Ian Johnstone, Tufts University

Jan Klabbers, University of Helsinki

Vassilis Pergantis, Aristotle University Thessaloniki

Anne Peters, Max Planck Institute for Comparative Public Law and International Law

Surabhi Ranganathan, University of Cambridge

Volker Roeben, University of Durham

Guy Fiti Sinclair, University of Auckland

René Urueña, Universidad de los Andes

Nigel D. White, University of Nottingham

Acknowledgements

This volume would not have come into existence without the inspiring vision of Finola O'Sullivan, the law editor at Cambridge University Press who a few years ago asked me if I thought it might be of interest to publish a *Cambridge Companion to International Organizations Law* and if so, whether I would want to be its editor. The first question struck me as an excellent idea, but I needed some time to reflect on the second. Editing often means chasing and cajoling authors, trying to get them to write what the editor wants and according to the editor's timetable, yet chasing and cajoling are not among my stronger suits. But then it dawned on me that if I were to invite the right authors and give them plenty of time, the chasing and cajoling could perhaps be kept to a bare minimum. So I agreed, and both Finola and Marianne Nield at the Press proved immensely helpful and supportive, as always.

Invitations were sent out sometime in 2017, with drafts envisaged in the summer of 2019, and final deadlines only scheduled for February 2020. Pretty much all authors I approached seemed to find this a workable idea, and accepted: I got the 'dream team' I wanted. An improvised, last-minute author's workshop took place in late 2018 at the Erik Castrén Institute of International Law and Human Rights (ECI) at the University of Helsinki, with financial support (gratefully acknowledged) from the Academy of Finland. The practical organization rested in the very calm and extremely capable hands of Anna van der Velde, ECI's coordinator. By the summer of 2019, the first drafts were coming in, received comments and were returned to their respective authors, in eager anticipation of the final texts.

And then, by the time those final versions were expected, the Covid-19 pandemic hit, and all schedules could be thrown out. Some authors had already more or less finalized their texts by then; but most had to tear up their timetables. Some have young children, and all of a sudden needed to focus on home-schooling. Some may have had elderly relatives requiring care and attention. Some have spouses working in hospitals on the Covid-

19 frontline. All needed to adapt to new demands of online teaching, attending webinars and meetings online; needed to reschedule and rethink their commitments; and all needed to come to terms with the idea that globalization (something international lawyers, no matter how critical, tend to look at with some natural affinity) may have been part of the problem. And the author of the planned chapter on international organizations working on global health became possibly the busiest international lawyer on the planet. After all, there were few others that newspapers, blogs, podcasts, and other outlets and institutions could turn to with a similar level of expertise in precisely the legal aspects of global health.

So, February 2020 came and went, and while quite a few chapters understandably came in later than anticipated, the amazing thing is that they arrived at all. None of the authors dropped out; none of them gave up. All authors remained committed, showing grace under pressure – considerably more so than the harried editor of this volume. Hence, in terms of acknowledgements, the only fitting tribute is to say a kind (but loud) word of thanks to the authors, who have all produced wonderful, informative and illuminating chapters. Covid-19 taught us (or those of us who did not realize it before) that there are more important things in life than producing academic volumes, but even so, if academic volumes must to be produced, they might as well be good. Taken together, the chapters in this volume demonstrate that international organizations are among the main institutions exercising global governance, and are worthy of considerably more attention and scrutiny than they have traditionally been given.

Cases

Arbitration

European Court of Human Rights

European Union Courts

General Court (Earlier Court of First Instance)

Court of Justice of the European Union (Earlier ECJ)

Inter-American Court of Human Rights

International Court of Justice

International Criminal Tribunal for the former Yugoslavia (ICTY)/Rwanda (ICTR)

International Labour Organization Administrative Tribunal

International Tribunal for the Law of the Sea

NATO Administrative Tribunal

Permanent Court of International Justice

Société des Nations Tribunal Administratif (League of Nations Administrative Tribunal)

Special Court for Sierra Leone

Special Tribunal for Lebanon

WTO

Panel

Appellate Body

Federal Republic of Germany

USA

Introduction

Jan Klabbers

Behind the newspaper headlines, often an international organization can be discerned. Sometimes the connection remains somewhat hidden. When the USA chides Turkey for procuring weapons from Russia, it suggests that US manufacturers should be privileged because Turkey is a member state of NATO, the US-driven Atlantic security organization. When Poland aims to withdraw from the Istanbul Convention, outlawing domestic violence, the Council of Europe expresses concern, if only because the Istanbul Convention was concluded under its auspices. And when it turns out that mailing parcels from certain countries is cheaper than mailing similar parcels domestically, it is not always immediately realized that this may have something to do with postal rates negotiated within the Universal Postal Union.

Our everyday lives owe much to international organizations, and it is probably fair to say that we are better off, overall, as a result. International air traffic is facilitated by the International Civil Aviation Organization, which ensures that aircraft are safe and pilots are well-trained. The plight of the many workers of the world has for a century been the province of the International Labour Organization. Refugees can invoke the help of the UN High Commissioner for Refugees. Migrants will sooner or later encounter the International Organization for Migration. Fishermen will do well to acquaint themselves with rules and guidelines set by regional fisheries organizations and the Food and Agricultural Organization. And since the outbreak of the Covid-19 pandemic in early 2020, few will not have heard of the World Health Organization.

Indeed, the Covid-19 pandemic may well be seen as a microcosm of the way international law operates, and how international organizations stand in the world. It is fairly obvious, for one, that a virus originating in one part of the world can rapidly spread to cover the entire globe. This owes much to international trade, travel and tourism, all of which are facilitated by international law, and subject to some form of management by international organizations. At the same time, overcoming the pandemic also needs to involve international law and international organizations. The latter can sometimes take mandatory measures (though this is still fairly rare), but also facilitate the exchange of relevant information, recommend effective medical approaches and can coordinate national or regional measures. One reason for this resides in the epistemic authority of such organizations, as repositories of relevant expertise: a declaration by the World Health Organization that the outbreak amounts to a 'public health emergency of international concern' will be taken more seriously than when the same words are spoken by, say, Kim Kardashian, or the prime ministers of Denmark or Canada.

The aim of this *Cambridge Companion to International Organizations Law* is to provide a picture of the law of international organizations as it helps to structure the work of international organizations: how they do things, in addition to what they do. In doing so, this *Companion* departs considerably from the standard approach, and does so in two ways. First, a standard approach would entail the inclusion of a chapter on the competences (powers) of international organizations; a chapter on their financing; a chapter on their privileges and immunities, et cetera. Important as these are, they do not provide a good picture of what organizations do and how they do it. The standard approach has its uses in teaching law students about international organizations, preparing them for a possible legal job within an international organization, but is less suitable for a general audience.[1]

Second, the standard approach tends to pay a disproportionate amount of attention to three organizations: the UN, the EU and the WTO. Yet all three are highly atypical. The UN is the only international organization of general jurisdiction and near-universal membership. The EU is so evolved that it comes closer to the model of a state. The WTO, unlike many other international organizations, has little or no regulatory powers: it is

[1] Readers looking for comprehensive treatment of what is generally referred to as the law of international organizations might wish to consult the monumental treatise by H. G. Schermers and N. M Blokker, *International Institutional Law: Unity within Diversity*, 6th ed. (Leiden: Martinus Nijhoff, 2018) or, less treatise and more textbook, J. Klabbers, *An Introduction to International Organizations Law*, 3rd ed. (Cambridge University Press, 2015). A textbook-like volume bringing expert authors together is J. Klabbers and Å. Wallendahl (eds.), *Research Handbook on the Law of International Organizations* (Cheltenham: Edward Elgar, 2011).

essentially a free trade agreement with a dispute settlement mechanism attached to it. By contrast, the standard approach usually pays less attention to, for example, the International Organization for Migration or the Organization for the Prohibition of Chemical Weapons, let alone the European University Institute which, its higher education mission notwithstanding, is also set up as an international organization.

In other words, this *Companion* aims to look beyond the surface level of the law of international organizations. It will focus not so much on particular legal topics or doctrines, but on the law that informs these doctrines, and it will focus not on the obvious organizations but on the patchwork of entities, clubs and networks that together make up a large chunk of the system of global governance. Put differently, if standard textbooks tend to look at the software (the specific rules often said to make up the corpus of international organizations law), the current volume aims to have an in-depth look at the operating system. This *Cambridge Companion* thus concentrates on two related issues: how organizations are legally structured, and how they themselves structure the world around them.

International organizations number at least some 300 or so, and come in all kinds of shapes and guises, dealing with all sorts of topics. Shipping? Look at the International Maritime Organization, for starters. The production of olive oil? The International Olive Council. Labour standards? The International Labour Organization. Nuclear control? The International Atomic Energy Agency. The local regulation of fisheries? The North Atlantic Fisheries Organization, among a dozen or so similar organizations from other parts of the globe. International organizations can be highly formal, solemnly created entities marking important political watersheds, as is the case with the UN arising out of World War II. They can also be set up in more modest, informal manner, such as the Paris Club (addressing debt relief), tucked away in a corner of the French Treasury Department. They can express lofty ideals, as with the UN and before it the League of Nations, or be set up for a limited period of time, with a mandate that from time to time needs to be renewed (Financial Action Task Force). They can have all the hallmarks of the rule of law, with courts and judicial review of executive action (this is rare, but it does apply to the EU), but can seemingly also be operating outside the law, as a political entity, based on what is referred to as a politically binding constituent instrument (Organization for Security and Cooperation in Europe). They can consist of states, but may also comprise other international organizations and perhaps even the private sector (GAVI, the Vaccine Alliance). In short, there is a bewildering variety, and this factor alone makes it difficult to say much of general validity and applicability about international organizations. What applies to the International Monetary Fund is unlikely to apply in quite the same way and quite the same manner to, say, the Organization of Petroleum Exporting Countries or the International Organization for Migration.[2]

This wide variety obviously limits the possibilities for comprehensive coverage, something made even more difficult by the awkward circumstance that there is no general definition of what constitutes an international organization. The absence of an authoritative definition entails that at the margins, there is considerable debate about whether an entity such as the Organization for Security and Cooperation in Europe qualifies as an international organization: it looks like one, and works like one, but is often denied to be one, claiming to have been intentionally set up as a political rather than a legal creature. That claim may never have been terribly persuasive, but cannot be dismissed out of hand.[3] Likewise, there is debate on whether the various Conferences of the Parties often established under multilateral agreements and acting much like international organizations are actually to be considered as such; or whether informal networks of states and others should be considered as such;[4] or whether international tribunals such as the International Criminal Court should be considered as such.[5]

This *Companion* starts by discussing general issues and activities, and then slowly moves on to discuss the role of international organizations in

[2] I have elsewhere suggested that there is actually no unified field of international organizations law: each organization forms its own legal order, and their relations with the world around them are governed by international law and the law of the states in which they operate. See J. Klabbers, 'The Paradox of International Institutional Law', (2008) 5 *International Organizations Law Review* 151.

[3] The OSCE seems to have turned a corner though, and reconciled itself with being part of international law. For in-depth discussion, see M. Steinbrück Platise, C. Moser and A. Peters (eds.), *The Legal Framework of the OSCE* (Cambridge University Press, 2019).

[4] An example might be the Contact Group on Piracy off the Somali Coast, legitimized by Security Council resolutions and bringing together a number of states, several international organizations, the insurance industry, seafarer's unions and others.

[5] In a way the ICC possesses most of the hallmarks identified in the literature: set up by states on the basis of a treaty to perform tasks delegated by member states. Yet, one hesitates to think of the judicial task as one controlled and delegated by states.

specific policy domains. Following a discussion by the editor on how to look at international organizations generally, subsequent chapters will include a discussion of the concept of international organization (Angelo Golia Jr and Anne Peters). This will be followed by a dissection of the accountability – *vel non* – of international organizations (Megan Donaldson and Surabhi Ranganathan). Setting up any organization inevitably involves asking who will be included and who will be excluded, as Groucho Marx already realized when famously quipping to refuse to join any club that would accept him as a member. Such issues relating to inclusion and exclusion are discussed by B. S. Chimni. In the subsequent chapter, Laurence Boisson de Chazournes and Vasileios Pergantis take an in-depth look at how international organizations are set up internally.

The *Companion* continues with a chapter on what is often considered the most relevant topic of standard-setting by international organizations, by José Alvarez. This, however, is not the only thing international organizations do. Alison Duxbury, in her contribution, makes clear that international organizations do not only set standards, but also act in the field: they undertake numerous operational activities, which are both structured by law and give rise to law. And Ian Johnstone suggests that international organizations may also be relevant, in a pluralist world, as places where states can debate with themselves and with other stakeholders. Guy Fiti Sinclair suggests a further reflexivity in that international organizations teach their members states how they should operate as states, therewith piercing the classic view that international organizations merely execute the wishes of their members. René Uruena's chapter opens up the hardly explored topic of the relations between international organizations with each other. He suggests they may collaborate with each other, influence each other and compete with each other. This is followed by a discussion by Vincent Chetail of the relationship between the work of an international organization and general international law, in the specific context of the field of migration law and focusing on the International Organization for Migration.

Here then the *Companion* has arrived at discussing specific policy domains. Their delimitation, selection and nomenclature are naturally highly arbitrary, but the main idea was to avoid the all-too-familiar, and instead focus some attention on policy domains that have been somewhat neglected or that still, as policy domains, are in development. The former applies to health, energy and disarmament; the latter to development and resources, food security and financial stability.

Gian Luca Burci provides the chapter on global health, a not-very-well-known policy domain until rather recently. When this volume was conceived, the global health regime had rarely occupied a prominent place in discussions on international organizations – and then the Covid-19 pandemic exploded. Burci's chapter is followed by a chapter on another policy domain rarely to be found in general works on international organizations: the provision of energy is the subject of Volker Roeben's chapter. Nigel White discusses the role of international organizations in disarmament, a policy domain often seen to be based on distrust rather than trust among member states – although the incidence of trust in those others may be overrated. Isabel Feichtner subsequently discusses the position of international organizations in development, while Monica Garcia-Salmones Rovira analyzes the emergence of the international regime on food security. The final chapter, by Matthias Goldmann, discusses the role of international organizations in securing global financial stability. The volume finishes with some concluding words by the editor.

1 Beyond Functionalism

International Organizations Law in Context

Jan Klabbers

1.1 Introduction

Even the most casual observer of international organizations must at times be puzzled. It is puzzling to realize, for instance, that regardless of the public outcry over nasty acts done on the watch of some international organization or another, nothing ever seems to happen: accountability is much-discussed, but rarely materializes. It is somewhat mystifying that for all the discussion of the reform of international organizations and of their policies, and for all that these are often amended, nothing much ever seems to change. Likewise, few international organizations have lawmaking powers properly so-called, and yet international organizations seem to be highly influential. By the same token, international organizations often engage in co-operation with one another without anyone noticing it, and seemingly without having strong authorization to do so. And it must be puzzling to realize that the law tends to treat all international organizations in much the same way, regardless of whether they work for the global common good or are better seen as interest groups for a particular group of states; regardless of whether they serve a global cause or manage a particular industry; and regardless also of the sort of activities they engage in – whether they occupy themselves with questions of peace, security and disarmament or are, effectively, institutions of higher learning set up as international organizations.

In most academic disciplines, when the central object of study provokes so many puzzling issues without there seemingly being much chance that any of them will receive a plausible answer, observers will start to look at whether the prevailing framework for thinking about such matters (call it 'theory') is up to its job. So too, albeit with some delay perhaps, in the law of international organizations. There is an increasing awareness that the leading theory, often referred to as functionalism (or legal functionalism, or international organizations legal functionalism), has but a limited explanatory potential, a potential that was, arguably, exhausted by the 1950s, when international organizations started to come into their own and started to act more or less independently from their member states. It is from the 1950s onwards that international organizations started to conclude treaties with outsiders; it is from the 1950s onwards that the awareness arose that, actually, the natural recipients of their work are individuals and groupings of individuals, rather than abstract member states.

In this chapter, I will briefly sketch the development and limits of functionalism (having done so extensively elsewhere);[1] and briefly sketch the contours of a different approach, building on functionalism but departing from it as well. I will call this new approach 'supra-functionalism', with a wink and a nod to earlier attempts to distinguish the EU from other organizations and because another obvious term ('post-functionalism') happens to be taken by a group of political scientists in order to describe their – radically different – approach to international organizations.[2] I thought it best to try not to add to the confusion, and thus opted for using a different label.

1.2 A Brief History of Functionalism

The legal functionalist approach to international organizations does not have an official date of birth, but it is plausible to claim that the idea may have first emerged in print in 1882, and was more or less finalized by 1919 – precisely the moment often said to mark a 'move to institutions'.[3] Since those days, the theory has been complemented and has been provided with a somewhat greater degree of sophistication and detail, but in outline it has remained remarkably recognizable: readers having a look at the seminal work published in 1911, Paul Reinsch's *Public International Unions*, could be forgiven for thinking it might just as well have been written in 1961 or even, adjusted for inflation, 2011.[4]

[1] J. Klabbers, 'The EJIL Foreword: The Transformation of International Organizations Law', (2015) 26 *European Journal of International Law* 9.

[2] L. Hooghe, T. Lenz and G. Marks, *A Theory of International Organization* (Oxford University Press, 2019).

[3] D. Kennedy, 'The Move to Institutions', (1987) 8 *Cardozo Law Review* 841.

[4] P. Reinsch, *Public International Unions, Their Work and Organization: A Study in International Administrative Law* (Boston MA: McGinn, 1911).

While the management of international rivers was experimented with in Europe since the days of Napoleon, it long remained unclear what the resulting river commissions represented, and to what extent they marked a departure from classical international law. Even after a century of experience, early twentieth-century writers were prone to regard them simply as treaties rather than institutions – the idea that there could be something 'institutional' about these creatures took a long time to form,[5] perhaps also because they tended to be run by member state representatives rather than having their own bureaucracies.[6]

Still, what had already become clear by the final third of the nineteenth century was that seemingly technical transboundary questions could well benefit from a permanent arrangement on the inter-state level. When the technology arose to make telegraphic messaging possible (involving cables for transmission, even on the seabed), it was thought useful to set up an international organization to regulate and manage the domain: this became the International Telegraphic Union, going back to 1865. Likewise, when the postmasters-general of several states realized that there was little or no uniformity in sending letters or parcels from one place to the other, thus dampening business interests, some of them pushed for an organization to regulate and manage postal relations – this became, in 1874, the Universal Postal Union. Both still exist.

The examples (river commissions, telegraphs, postal matters) suggest that a premium was placed on streamlining means of communication as well as introducing the idea that common problems could be managed, in a rational, goal-oriented manner. It is hardly a coincidence that around the same time, attempts were made to invent a global language in the form of Esperanto, and it is hardly a coincidence that statistics (even etymologically related to statecraft) started to blossom. And a few years later those ideas spread to other domains, including railway traffic, agriculture and, of great economic significance, the standardization of weights and measures.[7]

[5] W. J. M. van Eysinga, *Ontwikeling en inhoud der Nederlandsche tractaten sedert 1813* (The Hague: Martinus Nijhoff, 1916).

[6] K. Gram-Skjoldager, H. Ikonomou and T. Kahlert (eds.), *Organizing the 20th-Century World: International Organizations and the Emergence of International Public Administration, 1920–1960s* (London: Bloomsbury, 2020).

[7] M. Mazower, *Governing the World* (London: Allen Lane, 2012).

The first attempt to capture all this in legal terms was arguably undertaken by Georg Jellinek, Germany's towering nineteenth-century legal thinker. In a brief chapter published in 1882, he distinguished between unions of states aspiring to statehood (such as newly founded Italy and Germany, for example), and others, whose institutionalized co-operation would manifest what he called a *Verwaltungszweck*, an administrative goal or function.[8] This may well have been a decisive moment: once Jellinek had discussed the unions in terms of their *functions*, the tone was set, and an intellectual path-dependency created. The genie was out of the bottle, and it proved well-nigh impossible to think of unions in terms *not* related to their functions. The baton was picked up by a Russian scholar, Piotr Kazansky, who wrote most of his work in Russian but also a few articles in French, publishing as Pierre Kazansky. He did not set out a general theory, but at least he asked pertinent questions and did not treat international organizations purely as vehicles for their member states, as was customary in those days and later.[9]

The real culmination point was found in the work of Paul Reinsch, a political science professor with legal background from Wisconsin. Reinsch had written his doctoral work on the reception of English law in its American colony; had written various handbooks for the would-be colonial administrator based on in-depth comparative research; he had authored an influential textbook pioneering the discipline of international relations; and had been a delegate at various meetings of the Pan American Union.[10] Using the same comparative approach, he brought his practical experiences and reflexive insights together in a string of articles on the international unions, including in the newly established *American Journal of International Law*, and those articles were to become the basis of his book of 1911: *Public International Unions.*[11]

In it, he launches a theory (without seemingly realizing that he is theorizing) about international unions. Having looked at several dozen species, he concluded not surprisingly that they were all set up by member

[8] G. Jellinek, *Die Lehre von den Staatenverbindungen* (Berlin: Hölder, 1882).

[9] P. Kazansky, 'Les premiers éléments de l'organisation universelle', (1897) 29 *Revue de Droit International et de Législation Comparée* 238; P. Kazansky, 'Théorie de l'administration internationale', (1902) 9 *Revue Générale de Droit International Public* 353.

[10] For biographical detail, see N. Pugach, *Paul S. Reinsch: Open Door Diplomat in Action* (Millwood NY: KTO Press, 1979).

[11] Reinsch, *Public International Unions.*

states in order to perform a particular function. This entails that they are agents for their principals, the member states, and should do as their member states tell them. Thus, their creation involves no loss of sovereignty: the member states retain control. Those functions, moreover, are technical, apolitical: it is easy to think of delivery of the mail across boundaries, or the management of submarine cables or the harmonization of weights and measures, in technical and apolitical terms.[12] Indeed, to the extent that international organizations are political (no contradiction here), they were political in the good way: the unions worked for the global public good, and thus would help to achieve universal peace. And how can one disagree with that? How can one even think of that as a political goal? And not unimportant either, their costs would be limited, not just in terms of loss of sovereignty but also in sheer financial terms: Reinsch consistently pointed out that the annual contribution to any given organization remained small and manageable – in short, he could present membership of international organizations as, quite simply, a 'good deal'. And he made this perfectly clear in a speech advocating US involvement in the Pan American Union to the Milwaukee Bankers Association, in 1906: sure, the US could colonize Latin America, but the Pan American Union would be an equally effective instrument, at far lower cost.[13]

The final step towards what was to become functionalism was taken by Frank Sayre, a Harvard law professor and, as it happens, the son-in-law of US President Woodrow Wilson. Sayre wrote an enthusiastic brief study in 1919 on how to design a successful international organization, in preparation for the Versailles Conference, and while there was little remarkable about the details of what he wrote, what proved to be hugely influential was how he conceptualized international organizations.[14] If Reinsch had limited himself, a decade earlier, to studying unions with something of a recognizably public ethos, Sayre did not hesitate to include all sorts of ventures in his study, including such dubious examples as river commissions set up in China to guarantee untrammelled commerce (but without Chinese participation), or international police missions (intervention

[12] A recent study on the strategies used by international organizations (but also their member states) to depoliticize matters is M. Louis and L. Maertens, *Why International Organizations Hate Politics: Depoliticizing the World* (Abingdon: Routledge, 2021).

[13] Reported in J. Klabbers, 'The Emergence of Functionalism in International Institutional Law: Colonial Inspirations', (2014) 25 *European Journal of International Law* 645.

[14] F. B. Sayre, *Experiments in International Administration* (New York: Harper, 1919).

missions, really) aiming to safeguard trading routes in various parts of the world. As a result, the concept of international organization took on a highly formal characteristic. Since Sayre, any more or less regular (institutionalized) form of co-operation between states will count as an international organization, whether it is endowed with a public ethos or serves purely private interests.

Importantly though, the underlying idea formulated by Reinsch of international organizations serving the global good, of working in a public spirit, was retained, leading to what can only be called a gross anomaly: under Sayre's conception, an organization of states setting out to control resource exploitation for private gain would just as much be an international organization as an organization dedicated to eradicating the Covid-19 virus, or ending poverty. In retrospect, perhaps it is no coincidence that King Leopold's brutal reign over the Congo originally started as an international organization, as historian Madeleine Herren recalls,[15] and this questionable notion of its central concept has plagued international organizations law ever since.[16]

The idea of functionalism was consolidated and refined in subsequent decades, but never really further developed: it kept (and still keeps) revolving around functions delegated and (perhaps) controlled by member states, and seemingly mostly technical in nature. The world changed and, importantly, the context in which organizations operated and the way they operated changed as well, but the theory of functionalism never really caught up. Influential post–World War II scholars and practitioners such as Schermers, Seidl-Hohenveldern, Bowett and Jenks offered variations on functionalism, with the former three finding solace in comparison and the latter drifting ever so slightly towards a more constitutionalist approach, but all stayed firmly within the same broad paradigm – a paradigm still embraced by scholars of international organizations law to this day.[17]

The key to understanding functionalism as an approach to international organizations is to realize that it developed around the turn of the twentieth century and in a particular setting. International organizations, like so much

[15] M. Herren, *Internationale Organisationen seit 1865: Eine Globalgeschichte der internationalen Ordnung* (Darmstadt: WBG, 2009).

[16] J. Klabbers, 'Unity, Diversity, Accountability: The Ambivalent Concept of International Organization', (2013) 14 *Melbourne Journal of International Law* 149.

[17] As evidenced by the monumental treatise by H. G. Schermers and N. Blokker, *International Institutional Law: Unity within Diversity*, 6th ed. (Leiden: Martinus Nijhoff, 2018).

international law, were envisaged as creatures set up to solve problems that states had in common. Those problems were largely conceptualized as inter-state problems, involving state authorities, but would otherwise remain limited: like international law generally, they were not thought to address the plight of ordinary people or other actors within domestic legal orders, and they were not thought to address issues beyond the circle of member states. Against this background, it makes perfect sense that international organizations were neither granted international legal personality (not explicitly, at any rate), and were given few powers to deal with actors other than their member states. Organizations were expected to be more or less self-contained systems operating in a vacuum; creatures of their member states, set up in order to do things for or on behalf of those member states and solely affecting those member states.

The thought that there could be something like a world outside the closed universe of the international organization only started to gain ground in the 1940s, hesitantly with the creation of the UN (which, so some thought at the time, should perhaps explicitly have been given international legal personality, but never was), and with some greater urgency after the ICJ suggested in its landmark *Reparation for Injuries* opinion that there was actually a world existing outside the UN's universe, a world in which mediators could get assassinated while trying to mediate between factions which were not all part of the same universe.[18] That same UN, moreover, started to conclude treaties, and increasingly organizations appeared with some treaty-making powers, again suggesting that there was a whole world outside the universe of any particular organization, a world that could potentially be engaged with.

Still, functionalism had a hard time absorbing these developments. It could paper them over by suggesting that personality can be granted by the member states and that treaty-making by organizations is mostly a matter of whether the member states have granted treaty-making powers (in both cases reconceptualizing the matter as one of relevance solely to the relations between organization and member states, effectively excluding the

[18] The opinion arose out of the assassination of a UN-appointed mediator in the Palestine conflict, and boiled down to the legal question of whether the organization was legally capable of bringing a claim against a state that, at the relevant time, was not yet a member state. The Court answered in the affirmative, but without having much clear law to work with. See *Reparation for Injuries Suffered in the Service of the United Nations* (Advisory Opinion), [1949] ICJ Rep. 174.

outside world), but this started to show fatal cracks by the 1980s. Two incidents proved decisive. The first of these was an advisory opinion rendered in 1980 in a case involving a treaty between the World Health Organization and one of its member states: Egypt. The ICJ realized it could not decide the case on the basis only of WHO law or the WHO's interests. Egypt was not only a member state of the WHO, but also the WHO's treaty partner, and its interests as treaty partner needed to be taken into account. These were different from its interests as WHO member: as a WHO member it could have been asked to follow the organization's line; as its treaty partner, however, it was protected by the idea that treaty partners are equal and that treaties should be performed (*pacta sunt servanda*). Second, a few years later the International Tin Council, an international organization based in London, became insolvent, illustrating that organizations could actually do damage to the outside world, in this case damage to the Council's creditors. And the law, so it transpired, had no resources to address this sort of situation, precisely because the outside world had never existed in the functionalist model, which revolved around relations between the organization and its member states – the outside world, the world of creditors and treaty partners and individuals possibly being affected by an organization's work, had been *ex hypothesi* excluded.

Around the same time, it became clear that on other questions too functionalism was hard-pressed to present a plausible answer. Immunity in cases of harassment of staff members could hardly be justified by pointing out that generally, the organization performed a useful function – after all, that hardly diminishes the plight of the individual being harassed.[19] And the post-Cold War activation of the Security Council quickly resulted in calls for judicial review of its decisions, but this, understandably, was a task the ICJ was reluctant to accept, as its highly ambivalent behaviour in *Lockerbie* suggested.[20] In short, while functionalism had something to say about the relationship between the organization and its member states, it had far less to say about relations between organizations and others. This applied both to the world of non-member states, creditors or individuals affected by an organization's behaviour as

[19] See *Mendaro* v. *World Bank*, US Court of Appeals, DC Circuit, 27 September 1983, in 99 *International Law Reports* 92.

[20] Here, the Court was asked to answer whether it could review the lawfulness of Security Council resolutions, and dithered long enough for the case to be resolved by other means.

well as the world inside the organization: the relations between organization and staff members, and the relations between different organs of organizations. Here concepts such as checks and balances may play a role, but invoking an organization's function is usually not very helpful, as the ICJ had already observed, not entirely without some theoretical embarrassment perhaps, in 1962.[21]

It turned out, moreover, that even on those topics where functionalism thought it had something to say, there was not all that much it actually could say. A functionalist explanation helps explain why international organizations and their staff can claim privileges and immunities; these, after all, may be expected to facilitate the performance of the organization's function. But it cannot explain why exactly some organizations should pay service charges (e.g., to cover garbage collection), and others should not. Neither can it explain why for some, immunity is absolute, while for others it is relative; or why in some jurisdictions labour disputes fall within the 'official activities', but in others they do not. The reason should be obvious: agreements on privileges and immunities and headquarters agreements are the result of negotiations involving several parties, all of whom may entertain different ideas as to what the functions of the organization concerned may require.

Likewise, functionalist considerations may help explain why organizations have been endowed with particular powers, but already have a harder time explaining so-called 'implied powers', all the more so if and when implied powers morph into 'mission creep'. NATO observers may understand that NATO can engage in self-defence activities, but how to justify (in light of the NATO Constitution) the bombing of Belgrade by NATO when the former Yugoslavia was not a member of NATO nor threatening NATO or its member states in any direct or obvious way? Lawyers are able to answer such questions with the help of other doctrines: perhaps NATO could tap into an inherent power, or perhaps it could be suggested that NATO had, behind the scenes, changed its function, without too many people noticing. The point though is that traditional functionalist theory,

[21] In a dispute about whether peacekeeping was to be considered within the powers of the UN even if not ordained by the Security Council, it acknowledged the possibility that action could be outside the powers of a specific organ but still within the competences of the organization as such. See *Certain Expenses of the United Nations (Article 17, Paragraph 2, of the Charter)* (Advisory Opinion), [1962] ICJ Rep. 151.

insisting on functions and powers being delegated and controlled by member states, has difficulties answering such questions.

In light of functionalism's limited reach and limited explanatory potential, it should not come as a surprise that since the mid-1990s or thereabouts, functionalism as the theory underpinning the law of international organizations (its 'operating system', so to speak) has increasingly been questioned. Much of this questioning has remained somewhat incidental: many have criticized the ease with which international organizations and their policies can be seen as violating human rights, but without inquiring into the underlying theoretical framework.[22] Many have decried the existence of a remedies and accountability gap, but without questioning the underlying framework.[23] The inability of functionalism to address issues relating to intra-organizational affairs and to relations between organizations and the world around them has given rise to many projects inspired by constitutionalist or administrative law sensibilities.[24] And many have lamented the expansion of powers of international organizations (often mistakenly suggesting an 'abdication of sovereignty', therewith implying that innocent member states were deceived and are suffering as a result of organizational cunning),[25] but without questioning how the legal framework facilitates such expansion of powers. In short, the complaints have typically related to the 'software', not realizing that the choice of software is influenced, or even dictated, by what is compatible with the 'operating system'.[26] There is little point in changing organizational policies, devising sophisticated accountability mechanisms, or elaborate procedures for controlling international organizations, if these cannot be accommodated by

[22] Exemplary is J. Wouters *et al.* (eds.), *Accountability for Human Rights Violations by International Organisations* (Antwerp: Intersentia, 2010).

[23] Exemplary is C. Ferstman, *International Organizations and the Fight for Accountability: The Remedies and Reparations Gap* (Oxford University Press, 2017).

[24] See, for example, A. von Bogdandy et al. (eds.), *The Exercise of Public Authority by International Institutions: Advancing International Institutional Law* (Heidelberg: Springer, 2010); S. Cassese (ed.), *Research Handbook on Global Administrative Law* (Cheltenham: Edward Elgar, 2016); E. Morlino, *Procurement by International Organizations: A Global Administrative Law Perspective* (Cambridge University Press, 2019).

[25] Some of this infuses T. Johnson, *Organizational Progeny* (Oxford University Press, 2014).

[26] There are exceptions, including the pioneering article by M. Singer, 'Jurisdictional Immunities of International Organizations: Human Rights and Functional Necessity Concerns', (1995) 36 *Virginia Journal of International Law* 53.

the way international organizations are generally conceptualized and legally structured.

1.3 Beyond Functionalism

It seems reasonably clear then that in light of its limited explanatory power, functionalism is ripe for reconsideration: a theory that does not help in explaining or understanding its object of study runs the risk of becoming ideology, and a plausible case can be made that indeed functionalism is little more than ideology at present.[27] It is a popular tool for socializing new generations of lawyers, and a successful tool for marketing the idea of international organizations to the general public, but it does little to enhance understanding of what international organizations are, how they work and what they do.

And yet, one core insight of functionalism needs to be the starting point of any subsequent reworking: the insight that international organizations are set up to perform a function. Theirs is indeed, as Jellinek would say, a *Verwaltungszweck*, but instead of stopping here, this should be the starting point: what exactly is it that any particular international organization is supposed to do? One way of approaching this question, beyond looking at its stated function, is to abstract from the written text and explore two related, if distinct, avenues. The first of these may be termed historical, the second is more sociological perhaps. The point is not to have these replace legal thinking; the point, instead, is further to develop a way of legal thinking that is informed not just by itself.

Organizational sociologists, political economists and institutional economists are broadly in agreement that the organizational form has characteristics that do not apply to other forms of co-operation – not in quite the same way, at any rate. And thus it becomes important to understand why states, when co-operating, choose this particular form over alternative forms, and what the characteristics of organizations may

[27] J. Klabbers, 'Notes on the Ideology of International Organizations Law: The International Organization for Migration, State-making, and the Market for Migration', (2019) 32 *Leiden Journal of International Law* 383; J. Klabbers, 'What Role for International Organizations in the Promotion of Community Interests? Reflections on the Ideology of Functionalism', in E. Benvenisti and G. Nolte (eds.), *Community Interests across International Law* (Oxford University Press, 2018) 86.

include.[28] Organizations – institutions generally, whether the local fire department or the Rotary Club or the Universal Postal Union – tend to do three things, albeit in varying combinations and with varying points of emphasis. Organizations generally *regulate* within the domain of their assigned function; they *manage* what they have regulated and what might further affect them; and in doing so they inevitably *allocate* costs and benefits. And especially this third point is worthy of attention, for it raises (or should raise) an immediate question: if costs and benefits are allocated, on whom do these fall? Who gains, who loses? And what sorts of costs and benefits does it concern? The latter question warrants a broad answer: it can be tangible, financial costs and benefits, or costs and benefits more in the nature of 'social capital': legitimacy, recognition. The answer to the former, needless to say, differs from organization to organization: different organizations (or even the same organization at different moments in time) may generate different winners and losers.

This conception of organizations as regulating, managing and allocating differs strongly from traditional functionalism. Functionalism always regarded the function of the organization as its starting point but, influenced by Sayre's broad conception of international organization, never gave it much hands and feet. The function remained an abstract task which actually, in many functionalist writings, came to be associated with the adjective 'international' in international organizations. The function of any given international organization was to be 'international': a venue for, or manifestation of, co-operation between states. This was perhaps an inevitable by-product of trying to devise a separate academic discipline: international organizations have little in common (far less than states); they are set up in different ways, and they have different functions, ranging from ensuring security to providing postgraduate education. Small wonder, perhaps, that the discipline ended up, following Sayre, concentrating on the one thing organizations actually seemed to have in common: they were all, in one way or another, 'international'. They represent co-operation between states, and co-operation between states, against the acknowledged backdrop of a Hobbesian setting where life is nasty, brutish and short, is generally considered a good thing. Perhaps as a result, the

[28] See further J. Klabbers, 'International Organizations and the Problem of Privity: Towards a Supra-Functionalist Approach', in G. Politakis *et al.* (eds.), *ILO 100: Law for Social Justice* (Geneva: ILO, 2019) 629.

adjective 'international' was always deemed decisive; the particular form this co-operation takes (the *organizational* form) has generally been ignored. Yet, the organizational form is not self-evident: co-operation can also be cast in the form of a treaty regime, or in a set of international resolutions or communiqués, or the much looser Congresses known from diplomatic history.

It is, quite obviously, accurate to claim that international organizations represent co-operation between states. After all, they are typically established by states on the basis of treaties concluded between states. But this hardly exhausts the matter, if only because states are mostly abstractions with little or no interests of their own (beyond the curiously circular idea of *raison d'état*). Put differently, states represent interests prevailing in their societies, and might do so with greater or lesser accuracy, but at the end of the day international organizations typically arise and develop as someone's political project. There is, we may presume, always a reason why a particular organization is set up in a particular way by a particular constellation of actors. This is not to lapse into conspiracy theories: the political project concerned may well be benign, logical, sensible, well-intentioned, and the end result, the organization, may well be the product of different inspirations and different forces bumping into each other.[29] But the fact remains that organizations are usually someone's project, and end up allocating costs and benefits, making some better off and some worse off.

International organizations, as noted, started out in the early nineteenth century in the form of various river commissions. Rivers are media, means of communication, allowing for goods to be transported and therewith commercially relevant. The same logic would come to be applied to other means of communication as well: postal relations in 1874, and a few years earlier marine cables for telegraph communication.[30] The same year also saw the creation of the Lighthouse at Cape Spartel, which early observers already realized was using a small part of Morocco 'for the benefit of western shipping'.[31] And the various sanitary bureaux, forerunners of

[29] See, e.g., S. Pedersen, *The Guardians: The League of Nations and the Crisis of Empire* (Oxford University Press, 2015) 406.

[30] The ITU's significance in channeling the first global telecommunications revolution is well-sketched in C. Murphy, *International Organization and Industrial Revolution: Global Governance since 1850* (Cambridge: Polity, 1994).

[31] Van Eysinga, *Nederlandsche tractaten*, 17: as Morocco had no shipping of its own, it was reluctant to maintain a lighthouse by itself. Hence the creation of an organization (van

today's World Health Organization, were mainly meant to protect the western world against infectious diseases stemming from elsewhere.[32]

It turns out that quite a few international organizations can be traced to one of two (related) sentiments. Some spring from dedicated lobbies by individuals or groups (including companies) that had something to gain by sponsoring an organization-based solution. Perhaps the classic example is the Bern Union, devoted to copyright protection.[33] This owed much to the dedicated efforts of the president of the Association Littéraire et Artistique Internationale (ALAI), French author Victor Hugo, who had realized that often literary works were reproduced and translated abroad without their authors receiving financial benefits. Others spring from attempts to solve particular problems that are seen as undermining the smooth progress of commerce, and here perhaps the classic example is the creation of the Universal Postal Union in 1874, a dedicated response to the veritable jungle of rates, routes, tariffs and methodologies, initiated by the US postmaster-general at the time, Mr Montgomery Blair.[34]

It was only a matter of time before the same logic started to be applied not just to creating harmonized circumstances for use on markets, but also to markets themselves, and here too, the origins of many international organizations derive from either an inspired individual or from the realization that controlling the market and market conditions could be profitable – and needless to say, the two are not mutually exclusive. The International Sugar Union was an example of the latter, and was so *avant garde* that it was already setting market prices with binding effect around the turn of the century.[35] And the best-known example of the 'inspired individual' narrative is, no doubt, the League of Nations, inspired by the vision of US President

Eysinga actually, not yet socialized into institutional thinking, classified it as a servitude on Moroccan soil) 'ten bate der westersche scheepvaart'. See also, more extensively, D. Bederman, 'The Souls of International Organizations: Legal Personality and the Lighthouse at Cape Spartel', (1996) 36 *Virginia Journal of International Law* 275.

[32] J. Klabbers, 'The Normative Gap in International Organizations Law: The Case of the World Health Organization', (2019) 16 *International Organizations Law Review* 272.

[33] Today's version is the World Intellectual Property Union (WIPO).

[34] J. Sly, 'The Genesis of the Universal Postal Union', (1927) 233 *International Conciliation* 393.

[35] Sayre, *Experiments*; see further also M. Fakhri, *Sugar and the Making of International Trade Law* (Cambridge University Press, 2014).

Woodrow Wilson and taking on tasks going beyond economic matters – although those too were part of its remit.[36]

The pattern is repeated throughout the twentieth century, during which the number of international organizations skyrocketed. They are usually the result of an inspired visionary or a calculation of expected costs and benefits (or, often enough, both), and their structure usually reflects someone's vision on the topic at hand. This entails, in other words, that the international organization, far from being a benign, angelic creature destined by some superior power to save humanity, is usually the result of intense political struggle, and perhaps this was never more clear than with the creation of the World Bank and the International Monetary Fund, the result of an ideological battle between two different conceptions of post-war global capitalism. The UK, inspired by John Maynard Keynes, favoured a set of institutions allowing for intervention and reconstruction, and did so in large measure because that is what the UK needed – having come out of World War II in bad shape. The USA, by contrast, was keen on as much liberalization as possible, realizing very well that as global leader it could only gain from unimpeded flows of capital.[37]

Viewing international organizations as objects and sites of political struggle entail that they be lifted out of their vacuum. The traditional idea that organizations are creatures of their member states and only affect these member states has been hugely influential, but has become untenable (if it was ever tenable to begin with). Instead, states tend to operate as conduits: since they have the legal resources to set up international organizations, it is through them that entrepeneurs have to channel their political projects; and since states can enforce legal rules, it is through states that organizations aim to exercise authority. But it is a mistake to think of the member states as the only ones having a stake in international organizations. Instead, organizations affect their outside world, and are increasingly seen as autonomous actors capable of doing precisely that.

It is, for instance, notable that organizations often engage with each other, both in competition and in regulatory co-operation,[38] and often the

[36] M. MacMillan, *Paris 1919* (New York: Random House, 2001).

[37] R. Gardner, *Sterling-Dollar Diplomacy in Current Perspective: The Origins and the Prospects of Our International Economic Order* (New York: Columbia University Press, 1980).

[38] See, e.g., B. Faude, *Von Konkurrenz zu Arbeitsteilung: Komplexität und Dynamik im Zusammenspiel internationaler Institutionen* (Frankfurt am Main: Campus, 2015).

latter takes place without a very specific mandate to do so. Organizations may be given broad powers to co-operate with other organizations operating in the same domain, but that hardly exhausts the matter – still apart from the cognitive problems included in the reference to the 'same domain': if the WTO and ILO are co-operating to manage the tensions between labour issues and trade issues, they effectively create a new domain on the boundary between them. So too when the FAO and WHO set up the Codex Alimentarius Commission on food standards, or when a number of humanitarian organizations jointly operates a humanitarian assistance mission, or when regional organizations engage in missions implementing the decisions of universal organizations.[39] Competition between organizations takes place when one organization assumes jurisdiction over something occurring within the substantive domain of another, as when the Security Council deems a viral outbreak to constitute not just a public health issue but also a security issue. Or it occurs when a powerful state sets up a new entity in response to domination by an existing one representing the previous hegemon – think of the creation of the Asian Infrastructure Investment Bank, in 2015, as China's answer to the US-dominated World Bank, or earlier the European Free Trade Area as the UK-inspired response to the European Union.

Organizations typically also interact with states that are not their members. Sanctions imposed by international organizations need to be implemented also by non-member states, so as to avoid legal loopholes.[40] Likewise, the OECD's attempt to create a universal regime against tax evasion (its Base Erosion and Profit Shifting project) requires the participation of states that are not members; after all, the OECD, with thirty-seven member states, is simply too small to achieve this on its own. And should the International Criminal Court (ICC) be considered an international organization, it too depends on the co-operation of non-members, if only when it comes to gathering evidence of war crimes or handing over suspects.

And then organizations affect private actors, and have actually always done so. Early river commissions such as the Rhine Commission affected

[39] L. Boisson de Chazournes, *Interactions between Regional and Universal Organizations: A Legal Perspective* (Leiden: Martinus Nijhoff, 2017).

[40] Seminal on UN sanctions is J. M. Farrall, *United Nations Sanctions and the Rule of Law* (Cambridge University Press, 2007).

not just Germany or Switzerland, but also, and especially, the people active in inland shipping. The Universal Postal Union (UPU) affects not just Brazil or Nigeria, but businesses sending parcels to each other, and ordinary people sending postcards home from their holidays. The ILO was set up with a view to improving the lot of the working man, and to do so in order to protect capital from being either out-competed by cheap labour from the colonies, or protect it against communist sympathies.[41] And international organizations spend large sums of money in procuring goods and services, therewith affecting private companies.[42] In short, the idea that international organizations only operate at the behest of their member states, and can only affect those member states, is a fiction – and one that has successfully masked the broader political role of international organizations for well over a century.

1.4 To Conclude

This chapter has sought to argue that the dominant theoretical framework in which international organizations law is embedded, that of functionalism, is no longer up to the task (presuming it ever was), and has aimed to sketch the contours of a novel approach, an updated functionalism if you will. This concentrates not only on the 'international' but also on the 'organization', and views the organization as political actor, as both the result and the site of political struggle and as itself implicated in political struggle. Those engaged in that political struggle are not just the member states but, in addition to the organizations and their bureaucracies,[43] also other actors, whether businesses or even private persons. This different perspective aims to take relations of organizations with their environment (non-member states, other international organizations) seriously.

[41] J. Klabbers, 'An Accidental Revolution: The ILO and the Opening Up of International Law', in T. Halonen and U. Liukkunen (eds.), *International Labour Organization and Global Social Governance* (Dordrecht: Springer, 2020) 123.

[42] Morlino, *Procurement by International Organizations.*

[43] Seminal works include M. Barnett and M. Finnemore, *Rules for the World: International Organizations in Global Politics* (Ithaca, NY: Cornell University Press, 2004); G. Sarfaty, *Values in Translation: Human Rights and the Culture of the World Bank* (Stanford University Press, 2012).

To be sure, a functionalist perspective, traditionally focusing on the relation between the organization and its member states only, captures something of relevance about international organizations. But it has become increasingly clear that such a perspective also misses much of its relevance. The functionalist perspective is structurally incapable of discussing such developments as whether the UN should be held to account for spreading cholera in Haiti, or whether NATO can engage in humanitarian interventions outside the territory of its member states, or whether the ICJ can exercise judicial review over acts of the Security Council, or whether the International Monetary Fund can be held legally responsible for endorsing austerity policies or how organizations should treat their staff. In a functionalist framework, these will remain puzzling questions.

The Concept of International Organization 2

Angelo Golia Jr and Anne Peters

2.1 Introduction: The Conceptualization of the Concept

A *fil rouge* runs from the system of conferences, the river commissions and the administrative unions of the nineteenth century through the UN, its 'family' and the Bretton Woods institutions established in the mid-twentieth century, up to the most recent forms of international and transnational cooperation. The issues for which these forms of cooperation have been established range from the containment of communicable diseases to the protection of intellectual property, from the preservation of historic sites to food safety and from banking supervision to internet regulation. This phenomenon, as a whole, was analyzed as 'the legal organisation of the international society',[1] or even 'of the world'[2] at the end of the nineteenth century. Activities and patterns have further developed into what is now called global governance.[3] The entities engaged are intergovernmental organizations, treaty bodies, supervisory and expert bodies, standing secretariats, civil society actors, transnational corporations and varieties of hybrid or 'soft' actors, all of which have some 'legal life' of their own.

In the framework of traditional interstate law, these entities could never be 'original' international legal persons (as states are). But that framework no longer matches reality – if it ever did. On the one hand, even states do

[1] P. Fiore, 'L'organisation juridique de la société internationale', (1899) 2 *Revue de droit international et de législation comparée* 105, 209.

[2] W. Schücking, 'Die Organisation der Welt', in W. van Calker and P. Laband (eds.), *Staatsrechtliche Abhandlungen* (Tübingen: Mohr Siebeck, 1908) 533.

[3] See for the concept the Commission on Global Governance, *Our Global Neighborhood* (Oxford University Press, 1995) 2–3; M. Zürn, *A Theory of Global Governance* (Oxford University Press, 2018) 3–4; and K.-H. Ladeur, 'Governance, Theory of', *Max Planck Encyclopedia of Public International Law* (on-line).

not – even potentially – possess the totality of all legal positions possible in international law. For instance, they are unable to enjoy human rights. On the other hand, manifold actors are not only outcomes but themselves drivers of a global legal process. They are in historical terms *original* and in logical terms *necessary* actors of global governance; they are the 'natural' persons of global law,[4] alongside states.

Against this background, the standard focus of the discipline of 'international organizations law' (or 'international institutional law' as it is often called) seems overly narrow. Legal questions such as the contribution to international lawmaking, the interpretation of the legal basis or bases, the scope of immunities and the legal regime of the staff of the entities under scrutiny here do not necessarily hinge on legal personality (which will be discussed in Section 2.4.1). They are often not even governed exclusively by international law but by other legal orders as well, for example by the law of the host state, by contracts set up under whatever chosen law and frequently by an interaction of all these. The entanglement of various legal orders which altogether forms the 'global' legal environment and the legal inner life of the entities studied in this chapter suggest overcoming a strictly circumscribed concept of international organization. Rather, we need a legal concept of international organization that is both sufficiently specific to have an analytical value for legal examination and sufficiently broad for not missing out entities which are apt to shape the normative situation of individuals or to deploy substantial direct or indirect legal effects for the fate of nations and for the integrity of our planet. Faced with this challenge, a legal scholar seeking to conceptualize international organizations is in a dilemma: the traditional method of legal positivism does not allow him or her to integrate the factual reality of the object of study into the general legal framework, but the political and social dimension of the phenomenon is so overwhelming that it cannot be compressed into a 'pure' textual and doctrinal analysis.

Against this background, we suggest that the legal conceptualization should proceed inductively and with sociological awareness. We therefore conceive 'international organization' as a *cluster* concept and as an *open* one.[5]

[4] Here roughly defined as a regulatory mix of state-made and non-state made rules, on the domestic, local, regional and international levels.

[5] Our approach differs from the one adopted by L. Gasbarri, *The Concept of International Organization in International Law* (Oxford University Press, 2021) 5–6. See for an outstanding reflection on this open concept: C. Brölmann, *The Institutional Veil in Public*

This means that there is not one single common denominator which 'makes' an international organization. There is not even a set of fixed criteria. Although the debates have revolved around typical features, the exact content and the relative importance of these features have changed and continue to change over time and space. Some entities (such as the United Nations) are in the core of the concept because they possess many or all of the most popular features in high intensity, others (such as the International Union for Conservation of Nature – IUCN)[6] are more on the fringes. Whether a given actor is 'in' or 'out' depends on the scholarly or practical purpose and against which competitors the conceptualization is done.

2.2 Standard Definitions

2.2.1 The Traditional Trinity

The word 'organization' to designate an intergovernmental institution was first used in the peace treaties after World War I.[7] Treaties drafted from the 1960s to 1980s mentioned the attribute 'intergovernmental' as the single denominator of international organizations.[8] Notably the Vienna Convention on the Law of Treaties between States and International Organizations or between International Organizations provided that 'for

International Law: International Organisations and the Law of Treaties (Oxford: Hart, 2007) 16–22, 23. Because of the difficulty of drawing contours, it has been suggested to shift the doctrinal matrix away from the actors to the output, focussing on 'international public authority' by whomsoever exercised. See, e.g., M. Goldmann, *Internationale öffentliche Gewalt* (Heidelberg: Springer, 2015), esp. 328, 381.

6 The IUCN is an association under article 60 Swiss Civil Code. Members are governmental authorities, for example environment agencies (not states themselves) and NGOs such as the World Wildlife Fund.

7 Article 23(a) of the League of Nations Covenant; Part XIII of the Treaty of Versailles (establishing an 'Organization of Labour'); Article 67 of the PCIJ Statute.

8 See Article 2(1)(i) VCLT 1969; Article 11. (1) of the 1975 Vienna Convention on the Representation of States in their Relations with International Organizations of a Universal Character; Article 2(1)(n) of the 1978 Vienna Convention on Succession of States in Respect of Treaties. Already in 1958, the UN General Assembly Sixth Committee invited the International Law Commission to study the topic of the 'Relations between States and International Organizations' (UNGA Res. 1289 (XIII) of 5 December 1958). In 1963, the Special Rapporteur Abdullah El-Erian presented his first report where he identified three 'categories' of definitions: see ILC, 'First Report on relations between States and inter-governmental organizations by Abdullah El-Erian' (1963) UN Doc. A/CN.4/161 and Add.1; (1964) *Yearbook International Law Commission* vol. II, 164–167.

the purposes of the present Convention … "international organization" means an intergovernmental organization'.[9]

The intention of that older definition was first of all to exclude non-governmental organizations. The contemporary textbook definitions usually establish three cumulative criteria: founding document governed by public international law, intergovernmentality (state membership) and will of its own.[10] From that perspective, a given entity is an international organization only if established (1) by an instrument governed by international law, and if (2) its founders and members are states (or exceptionally other international legal persons) and (3) if it is capable of generating – through at least one organ – a 'will' distinct from that of its members (*volonté distincte*).

2.2.2 International Legal Personality as a *Conditio Sine Qua Non*?

Some more recent legal definitions have replaced the third element of 'distinct will' by 'international legal personality' and posit this as a necessary defining element of an international organization 'proper'.[11] Notably Article 2(a) of the 2011 ILC Articles on the Responsibility of International Organizations (ARIO) defines the international organization as 'an organization established by a treaty or other instrument governed by international law and possessing its own international legal personality. International organizations may include as members, in addition to States, other entities'.[12] However, this definition is only given for the narrow purpose of international legal responsibility.[13]

Similarly, the 1995 report of the Institut de Droit International (IDI) on the liability of international organizations defined international organizations as entities 'possessing an international legal personality distinct from

[9] Article 2(1)(i) VCLT IO 1986 (not in force).

[10] K. Schmalenbach, 'International Organizations or Institutions: General Aspects', *Max Planck Encyclopedia of Public International Law* (online), paras 3–11; J. Klabbers, *An Introduction to International Organizations Law*, 3rd ed. (Cambridge University Press, 2015) 9–14; H. G. Schermers and N. Blokker, *International Institutional Law*, 6th ed. (Leiden: Martinus Nijhoff, 2018) 41.

[11] See in scholarship P. Sands and P. Klein, *Bowett's Law of International Institutions*, 6th ed. (London: Sweet & Maxwell, 2009) 15.

[12] UN GA Res. 66/100 of 9 December 2011; (2011) *Yearbook International Law Commission* vol. II, Part Two, 39–104.

[13] Article 2 ARIO.

that of its members'.[14] The legal personality mentioned by the IDI as the sole feature is not overly restrictive, because it is not conceived as flowing from or needing recognition by states but as an 'objective' status.[15] The IDI-definition is usefully comprehensive and flexible and has unduly been forgotten. However, international legal personality should in the end not be seen as a *conditio sine qua non* for the existence of an international organization, for reasons discussed below (Section 2.4.1).

2.2.3 Additional Features

The traditional three elements are useful criteria. Many entities that matter for global governance do fulfil most of them most of the time. However, the elements should not be used as a checklist, because they are neither strictly necessary nor sufficient. In particular two further elements should be taken into consideration.

First, an important feature of international organizations is to fulfil tasks of global public interest or of global public relevance which could not be accomplished by any state alone.[16] This perspective is most faithful to the historical evolution of the phenomenon of international organizations which around the turn of the twentieth century mostly grew out of or in close symbiosis with industrial, professional, academic and civil society associations and were thus initially private or hybrid in form.[17] The global public interest can be roughly described as not in the private, personal or

[14] *The Legal Consequences for Member States of the Non-fulfilment by International Organizations of Their Obligations toward Third Parties*, Fifth Commission, Rapporteur Rosalyn Higgins, 66-I *Annuaire de l'Institut de droit international.*

[15] See esp. Article 2 of the original draft resolution of October 1994, *Annuaire de l'Institut de droit international* 66-I (1995), 465. See in detail on 'objective' international legal personality below Section 2.4.1.

[16] M. Virally, 'Definition and Classification: A Legal Approach', (1977) 39 *International Social Sciences Journal* 58, 61–2; M. Ruffert and C. Walter, *Institutionalised International Law* (Munich: Beck, 2015), 5; E. Lagrange, 'La catégorie "organisation internationale"', in E. Lagrange and J.-M. Sorel (eds.), *Droit des Organisations Internationales* (Paris: LGDJ, 2013) 25 (paras. 83–5). See for an excellent analysis G. Burdeau, 'Les organisations internationales: Entre gestion publique et gestion privée', in J. Makarczyk (ed.), *Essays in Honour of Krzysztof Skubiszewski* (The Hague: Kluwer, 1996) 611.

[17] A. Peters and S. Peter, 'International Organizations: Between Technocracy and Democracy', in B. Fassbender and A. Peters (eds.), *Oxford Handbook of the History of International Law* (Oxford University Press, 2012) 170, 186–8.

profit interest.[18] While an abstract definition is not necessary, we can draw on the prevalent (and of course changing) visions about services which are so basic for humans that they should not be left to markets alone. The global public interest is a key criterion because it transcends the (sometimes purely coincidental and changing) legal form of the actor. It is therefore apt, to give an example, to capture also those institutions which have been privatized such as the previously intergovernmental organizations on satellite telecommunication (INTELSAT, EUTELSAT and INMARSAT). These were dissolved around the turn of the twenty-first century, and their activities are since then run by private business enterprises, as a logical consequence of the privatization of the tasks within the member states themselves.

Second, a permanent infrastructure is important. Entities can hardly be called international organizations if they lack a seat, a functioning infrastructure and budgetary means. The bodies or organs of international organizations vary, but they typically have a permanent secretariat, a plenary body in which all members meet, a smaller executive body, and sometimes an additional assembly. The infrastructure and budget secures its permanence through time. It accounts for the organization's 'institutionalisation' in a factual sense and distinguishes it from recurring conferences and ad hoc meetings.

2.3 Embedding the Concept

The conceptualization of international organizations has been traditionally embedded in broader paradigms, merging legal theory and related approaches and assumptions in political science. Legal scholars and practitioners seem to consciously or unconsciously embrace them (which explains conflicting trends in international case law), probably in search of a way to cope with the diversity and political colouring of the facts which are otherwise difficult to integrate into a 'pure' legal analysis.

2.3.1 Realism

Realism claims that international relations (IR) predominantly reflect power struggles of states, conceived as rationally strategic actors. From

[18] Seminally J. Delbrück (ed.), *New Trends in International Lawmaking: International 'Legislation' in the Public Interest* (Berlin: Duncker & Humblot, 1997).

this perspective, international organizations are (to use the current IR terms), not 'actors' but at best 'forums' and mainly 'instruments' in the hands of the member states. Realism stresses that particular international organizations 'may be nothing more than playthings of power politics and handmaidens of national ambitions'.[19] However, realism fails to capture the normal functioning of international organizations, their normative output and the fact that states normally comply with the obligations stemming from their membership, even when they are against their own strategic interest.

2.3.2 Functionalism

Functionalism has been the most important paradigm for understanding international organizations.[20] The basic functionalist idea is that the *raison d'être* of international organizations is the fulfilment of specific tasks (functions), needed to tackle problems which concern more than one state. The functions attributed to the organization are supposed to, at the same time, set the limits and enable the expansion of its powers. However, functionalism has to some extent deteriorated into a rhetorical and even ideological device justifying ex post the expansion of the functions, and therewith powers, of organizations.[21] And because functionalism is fixated on the relationship between the organization and its members, the 'blind spot' of such approach is the organization's surrounding, notably individuals who might be negatively affected by its activities.[22] Functionalism is therefore unable to contribute to the accountability of international organizations towards outsiders. Taken together, the increase of power of international organizations, enabled but not properly constrained by functionalism as a theoretical device, has contributed to the crisis of their legitimacy.

[19] I. L. Claude, *Swords Into Plowshares: The Problems and Progress of International Organization* (New York: Random House, 1956) 449. Claude adds that 'international organization, considered as an historical process', may nevertheless make the world safer.

[20] See Jan Klabbers, Chapter 1 in this volume.

[21] See J. Klabbers, 'Notes on the Ideology of International Organizations Law: The International Organization for Migration, State-Making, and the Market for Migration', (2019) 32 *Leiden Journal of International Law* 383.

[22] J. Klabbers, 'The EJIL Foreword: The Transformation of International Organizations Law', (2015) 26 *European Journal of International Law* 9, 10–11.

2.3.3 Constitutionalism and Public Law Approaches

Various public law approaches[23] start from the premise that *every* exercise of 'public' power (or 'authority') is legitimate only if and to the extent that it is constituted, constrained and guided by (constitutional and/or administrative) law. Such approaches also provide material standards – ranging from checks and balances in the organizations over the protection of human rights and transparency and participation/inclusion in decision-making up to some form of independent review – for institutional design and reform.

The public law approaches have two merits. First, they focus not only on entities falling within the core concept of international organization, but also on less formalized institutions. Second, notably constitutionalism brings on stage the individual, the actor most sacrificed by scholarship, caught up between international institutions and states.

However, the putative constitutional and administrative obligations supposedly resting on international organizations can hardly be traced back to traditional sources of international law, and the public law approaches have so far not properly explained the gamut of legal standards they draw on.

2.3.4 Critical Approaches

Critical approaches note that the law and practice of international organizations have been strongly shaped first by colonialism and later, in the aftermath of the Second World War, by decolonization.[24] They note that

[23] With a high degree of simplification, we refer here collectively to three approaches, namely 'global constitutionalism', 'global administrative law' (GAL) and 'international public authority' (IPA). J. Klabbers, A. Peters and G. Ulfstein, *The Constitutionalization of International Law* (Oxford University Press, 2009); specifically on the 'constitutionalization' of organizations, see A. Peters, 'Constitutionalisation', in J. d'Aspremont and S. Singh (eds.), *Concepts for International Law: Contributions to Disciplinary Thought* (Cheltenham: Edward Elgar, 2019) 141; B. Kingsbury, N. Krisch and R. Stewart, 'The Emergence of Global Administrative Law', (2005) 68 *Law and Contemporary Problems* 15; S. Cassese, 'Administrative Law without the State? The Challenge of Global Regulation', (2005) 37 *New York University Journal of International Law and Politics*, 663; A. von Bogdandy *et al.* (eds.), *The Exercise of Public Authority by International Institutions: Advancing International Institutional Law* (Heidelberg: Springer, 2010).

[24] See for the following G. F. Sinclair, 'Toward a Postcolonial Genealogy of International Organizations Law', (2018) 31 *Leiden Journal of International Law* 841; B. S. Chimni,

the concerns of Asian and African states have been neglected in these processes. Especially international finance institutions such as the World Bank (WB) and the International Monetary Fund (IMF) have been accused of implementing neo-liberal policies aimed to keep postcolonial states in a condition of economic and cultural dependence serving the agenda and the interests of a hegemonic Global North.[25] Similarly, the International Criminal Court (ICC) is reproached of being a neocolonial instrument.[26] The refusal of various African states to surrender the Sudanese President Al Bashir to the ICC was justified by the African Union by denouncing 'ill-considered, self-serving decisions of the ICC' and 'double standards that become evident from the investigations, prosecutions and decisions by the ICC relating to situations in Africa'.[27] The critical approaches have the merit of uncovering Eurocentrism in the law and practice of international organizations. However, they risk overstating it and offer little guidance in terms of legal policy and reform.

2.3.5 The Need to Take the Normative Aspirations Seriously

Overall, the analytical value of the various paradigms for the resolution of legal questions such as legal interpretation, legal responsibility, revisions of the founding document and the like, is limited. However, their normative ambitions are relevant for the conceptualization of international organizations. To reach those normative objectives (for example proper consideration for the human rights of persons substantially affected by the activities of international organizations, and less favouritism towards European interests), we need a more comprehensive legal concept of international organization that can be used as a unitary point of reference by both international and domestic courts and stakeholders. We now proceed to sketch such a concept.

'International Organizations, 1945–Present', in J. Cogan, I. Hurd and I. Johnstone (eds.), *Oxford Handbook of International Organizations* (Oxford University Press, 2016) 113.

25 See A. Anghie, 'Time Present and Time Past: Globalization, International Financial Institutions, and the Third World', (2000) 32 *New York University Journal of International Law and Politics* 243.

26 Statement of Rwanda, UN SC, 7060th meeting 'Peace and Security in Africa', 15 November 2013 (UN Doc. S/PV.7060), 11; see also the statement of Kenya, *ibid.*, 14.

27 African Union, Press release No. 002/2012 of 9 January 2012, 3.

2.4 In the Concept's Core

The standard textbook definitions mention the '*volonté distincte*' as a 'fundamental' feature of an international organization.[28] The term appeared around the turn of the twentieth century in the literature on the administrative unions and the League of Nations, borrowed from the domestic commercial laws on corporations. The distinct will is seen as crucial because (only) a body forming and expressing such a will of its own is 'more than the sum of its members'.[29] The *distinct* will distinguishes the entity from treaties in which the contracting parties lay down a 'common will' which remains the parties' 'will' (in present-day terms: leads to the imputation of legal decisions to all of them jointly).[30] We suggest replacing the outdated, obscure and even 'metaphysical'[31] language of will with more modern concepts of autonomy and legal personality. Accompanied by the additional or alternative features of fulfilment of tasks in the global public interest and permanence through time, as mentioned above (in Section 2.2.3), these are useful criteria to build a (cluster) concept of international organization which is analytically and normatively adequate in the context of (de-)globalization processes.

2.4.1 International Legal Personality

Legal personality (or 'subjecthood')[32] has been only half-ironically called the 'soul' of international organizations.[33] The idea of personality under the law is highly complex.[34] Different legal orders have different meta-rules on the legal act of personification (incorporation). In international

[28] Schermers and Blokker, *International Institutional Law*, 48. [29] *Ibid.*

[30] *Ibid.*, 49. See for the seminal distinction between 'international' organs created by the entities themselves and the mere 'common organ' of states ('*staatliche Organe als gemeinsam*') G. Jellinek, *Die Lehre von den Staatenverbindungen* (Aalen: Scientia, 1969 [1882]) 171.

[31] Brölmann, *The Institutional Veil*, 21.

[32] The ICJ uses the term 'international (legal) person' interchangeably with 'subject of international law' (ICJ, *Reparation for Injuries Suffered in the Service of the United Nations* (Advisory Opinion), [1949] ICJ Rep. 174, 179.

[33] D. Bedermann, 'The Souls of International Organizations: Legal Personality and the Lighthouse at Cape Spartel', (1996) 36 *Virginia Journal of International Law* 275.

[34] See for an excellent analysis N. Naffine, 'Who Are Law's Persons? From Cheshire Cats to Responsible Subjects', (2003) 66 *Modern Law Review* 346; see also R. Portmann, *Legal Personality in International Law* (Cambridge University Press, 2010).

law, no codified norm governs the definition and attribution of international legal personality, and this is one reason for controversy and obscurity on the legal personality of international organizations.[35]

The broad function of legal personhood is to identify and circumscribe membership in a legal community. Legally speaking, personhood creates 'a point of imputability' for legal rights and obligations.[36] International legal personality is the decisive criterion for answering the doctrinal questions of which *international law-based* rights and obligations a given actor has and when it is legally responsible for violations of international law. Because the award or denial of personhood determines 'who counts' and who is legally accountable, it is an eminently important decision.[37] The 'politics of international legal personality'[38] are at the heart of the concept of international organization.

We do not share the view that the question of 'personhood' is irrelevant because – as that argument goes – what matters are the individual rights and duties (which can be verified in legal-empirical terms). In contrast to that view, we assert that personhood is rather the precondition for holding those rights and duties (as opposed to being at the mercy of objective international law, or being a legal nullity). Legal personality is – not without merit - identified with 'legal capacity'. But because in the debate on international organizations, the word 'capacity' is more often used for the *domestic* legal status of the organizations[39] we will avoid it.

The leading case which decided the question of principle whether international organizations can at all enjoy international legal personality is *Reparation for Injuries.* The question here was whether the UN could bring a claim for compensation against Israel (which at that time was not a member state) even in the absence of any mentioning of such competence in the UN Charter. The ICJ first investigated whether the UN possessed an

[35] Portmann, *Legal Personality*, 9.

[36] H. Kelsen, *Reine Rechtslehre* (Vienna: Deuticke, 1934) 53 (our translation). Kelsen changed the wording in his second edition (Tübingen: Mohr Siebeck, 1960) 313–14.

[37] Naffine, 'Law's Persons', 347.

[38] N. Blokker and R. Wessel, 'Revisiting Questions of Organisationhood, Legal Personality and Membership in the OSCE: The Interplay between Law, Politics and Practice', in M. Steinbrück Platise, C. Moser and A. Peters (eds.), *The Legal Framework of the OSCE* (Cambridge University Press, 2019) 135, 149.

[39] For example in article 104 UN Charter and article 4 of the Draft Convention on the International Legal Personality, Legal Capacity, and Privileges and Immunities of the OSCE (Annex to MC.DD/28/07 of 29 November 2007).

international legal personality which was also not explicitly mentioned in the UN Charter. After having examined various elements (attribution of legal capacity in domestic law, privileges and immunities in the territory of member states, the capacity to conclude treaties), the ICJ determined that the members had entrusted the UN with several functions, the fulfilment of which would have been impossible if the UN were not an international legal person.[40] This (implicit) legal personality in turn implied the power to bring claims for compensation.[41]

International legal personality does not automatically and in itself entail specific rights or duties. Rather it is a container; it can be loaded immediately or successively with only single rights or various sets of rights or obligations. Indeed, international legal persons can have a very different material scope of rights and duties. It is therefore often said that only states are 'full' international legal persons while international organizations are 'partial' persons. The better terminology is that the organizations's competences are limited.[42]

The legal basis of the international legal status and its personal scope (in relation to whom?) of international organizations are controversial. Many writers still opine that personality flows (explicitly or implicitly) from the founding treaty. The legal status is therefore not opposable to non-members unless these latter recognize the legal personality, either explicitly or implicitly. This voluntarist position leads to the relativity of the legal status of the organization.

The opposing and increasingly accepted view is that personality is 'objective', that the status as a legal person is not created by the founding treaty but flows from a general norm of international law, notably from a customary rule.[43] This supposed general rule says that the entity *is* a legal

[40] *Reparation*, 179: The UN 'could not carry out the intentions of its founders if it was devoid of international personality. It must be acknowledged that its Members, by entrusting certain functions to it, with the attendant duties and responsibilities, have clothed it with the competence required to enable those functions to be effectively discharged. Accordingly, the Court has come to the conclusion that the Organization is an international person'.

[41] *Ibid.*, 182. Several commentators have noted the circularity of this reasoning, see e.g. Sands and Klein, *Bowett's Law*, 476.

[42] See on the principle of conferral below Section 2.5.3.

[43] Seminally F. Seyersted, 'Objective International Personality of Intergovernmental Organizations: Do Their Capacities Really Depend upon the Conventions Establishing Them?', (1964) 34 *Nordisk Tidsskrift for International Ret* 3.

person as soon as certain 'objective' facts are present.[44] The logical consequence then is that the legal status as a person is opposable to non-members, independent of their recognition of that status; any recognition (if it takes place) would be purely 'declaratory'. In light of the normalization and consolidation of the phenomena of international organizations, and in order to avoid the awkward situation of entities which are legal persons towards some actors and non-persons towards others, it seems fair to *presume* the international legal personality of inter*governmental* organizations unless exceptional or ambiguous circumstances speak against it.[45]

Nevertheless and all things considered, non-personalized actors should not be left out of the picture for the reasons given in the introduction, notably those actors's power to shape the normative situation of humans, too. And because the ascription of legal personhood is always internal to a given legal order (an actor or an entity can be a person in the international legal order and a non-person in whatever domestic legal order),[46] international legal personality should not be seen as the crucial marker in the current situation of entanglement of legal orders that global governance is. Although actors with international legal personality are prototypical organizations, we submit that *non-personified* actors (especially intergovernmental ones) are international organizations if they possess a sufficient degree of autonomy. An example is the Organization for Security and Co-operation in Europe (OSCE).[47] Autonomy thus is a key element to which we turn now.

[44] R. Higgins, *Problems and Process: International Law and How We Use It* (Oxford: Clarendon, 1995) 47–8. This position is gaining ground in textbooks: P. d'Argent, 'La personnalité juridique internationale', in Lagrange and Sorel (eds.), *Droit des organisations internationales*, 439, 452; D. Akande, 'International Organizations', in M. Evans (ed.), *International Law*, 5th ed. (Oxford University Press, 2018) 227, 233.

[45] C. F. Amerasinghe, *Principles of the Institutional Law of International Organizations*, 2nd ed. (Cambridge University Press, 2005) 91; A. Peters and A. Petrig, *Völkerrecht*, 5th ed. (Zürich: Schulthess, 2020), ch. 8, para. 20. This presumption should not apply to entities in private law form, although these can become international legal persons based on a clear (not necessarily explicit and written) norm. This is the case for the ICRC.

[46] G. Radbruch, 'Rechtsphilosophie', 3rd ed. 1932, in G. Radbruch, *Gesamtausgabe Band 2: Rechtsphilosophie II* (Heidelberg: Müller, 1987/1993) 363–5.

[47] On the latter, see Steinbrück Platise, Moser and Peters (eds.), *Legal Framework of the OSCE*. Another case is the EU before it was explicitly awarded international personality by the Treaty of Lisbon. At that point in time, its personality could, however, already be reasonably presumed.

2.4.2 Autonomy

The ICJ stated, speaking of the WHO, that the object of the founding treaties of organizations is to create 'new subjects of law', 'endowed with a certain autonomy'.[48] 'Will' and 'autonomy' largely overlap but are not fully identical. While the *volonté distincte* may be just nominal, autonomy (which literally means self-ordering) is present only when this 'will' can in fact be deployed and leads to changes in real life. To be autonomous, the organization must not only be 'willing' but it must also be 'able'.

Importantly, the 'autonomy' of international organizations is the counterpart to the sovereignty of states.[49] Like sovereignty, it holds the prime place as the most important property of the relevant actor. And like sovereignty, autonomy is best understood not as an on/off concept but as a graded concept which does not only have a formal/legal side but needs a factual power base.

'Autonomy' cannot be properly measured by looking merely at the formal international legal personality as foreseen in the founding document but only by additionally examining the rules on the functioning of the organization (not only in the books but also in action). This concerns the scope of competences, the type of powers, especially lawmaking powers, decision-making procedures (especially majority voting or a requirement of unanimity), the procedures for amending the constituent act, the exit options for member states and more.[50] We must thus examine the rules on these points and their application in practice – which will depend not only on the law but also on the factual constellation shaped for example by the overwhelming power of some member states, the degree of independence of the staff and the financial means of the organization.

Autonomy is absent when the entity under scrutiny is not even a collective *actor* (understood as someone who can make things happen or happen differently).[51] On this understanding, regimes[52] and

[48] *Legality of the Use by a State of Nuclear Weapons in Armed Conflict* (Advisory Opinion), [1996] ICJ Rep. 66, para. 19.

[49] A. Peters, 'Membership in the Global Constitutional Community', in Klabbers, Peters and Ulfstein, *The Constitutionalization*, 153, 209.

[50] A. Peters, 'The Constitutionalisation of International Organisations', in N. Walker, J. Shaw and S. Tierney (eds.), *Europe's Constitutional Mosaic* (Oxford: Hart, 2011) 253, 258.

[51] A. Giddens, *The Constitution of Society: Outline of the Theory of Structuration* (Cambridge: Polity, 1984) 9, 14–15.

[52] Defined in the IR literature as 'principles, norms, rules, and decision-making procedures around which actor expectations converge in a given issue-area': see S. Krasner,

networks[53] do not fall under our concept of international organization. But both might contribute to processes of institutional 'thickening' of looser or more isolated entities, as a process of progressive legal autonomization which can lead to the (potentially unintended) establishment of an international organization in the broad sense suggested here (see below, Section 2.5).

We submit that 'autonomy' is a key feature of international organizations. Nevertheless, it should not be elevated to the single *differentia specifica*. For sure, the vague, multidimensional and graduated quality of the concept diminishes its analytical value. But it has an enormous normative importance: the more autonomous an international organization is, the stronger are the normative demands addressed to it. In constitutionalist language: the more autonomous an organization is, the more it needs constitutional guidance and constraints.[54]

2.4.3 The Limits and Relevance of Autonomy

Although autonomy and legal personality typically go hand in hand, and although legal personality can be an important ingredient of autonomy, both features are not fully congruent and interchangeable. While personality is an on/off concept and – as explained – an empty vessel, autonomy is – as mentioned – substantive and a matter of degree. An entity may have legal personality but may enjoy very little or no autonomy. Inversely, an entity may be quite autonomous even without international legal personality, such as the OSCE.

On the traditional premise that the sovereign will of states is the exclusive basis of all legally relevant acts of international organizations, the latter may not extend their activity beyond the tasks originally attributed. This is the principle of conferral ('*compétence d'attribution*' or 'principle of

'Structural Causes and Regime Consequences: Regimes as Intervening Variables', in S. Krasner (ed.), *International Regimes* (Ithaca NY: Cornell University Press, 1983) 1.

53 Defined as 'a pattern of regular and purposive relations among like governments units working across the borders that divide countries from one another and that demarcate the "domestic" from the "international" sphere': A.-M. Slaughter, *A New World Order* (Princeton University Press, 2004) 14. For the differences between the broader (cluster) concept of IO outlined here and a legal conceptualization of network, see A. Jr. Golia and G. Teubner, 'Networked Statehood: An Institutionalised Self-contradiction in the Process of Globalisation?', (2021) 12 *Transnational Legal Theory* 7, 19–23.

54 Peters, 'The Constitutionalisation of International Organisations', 260–1.

speciality'), as codified, for example in article 5(1) TEU, and as applied both by the PCIJ[55] and by the ICJ. While this principle can be understood in different ways, depending on the underlying – realist, functionalist, constitutionalist – broader assumptions, the ICJ explained it as follows: 'International organizations are governed by the "principle of speciality" … they are invested by the States which create them with powers, the limits of which are a function of the common interests whose promotion those States entrust to them.' On this basis, the ICJ rejected a request by the WHO for an advisory opinion on the legality of the use of nuclear weapons. The WHO mandate is about health matters and thus covers the unhealthy effects of nuclear weapons – but these are independent of the legality of their deployment.[56]

The corollary to the principle of specialty is the doctrine of *ultra vires.* This doctrine prohibits activities of the organization overstepping its competences, but is obscure about the legal effects of such transgression. When applied by domestic courts, the legal consequence is that the impugned legal act does not bind the member state or its national organs. Along that line, the German Federal Constitutional Court held that the European Central Bank's decision to establish a Public Sector Purchase Programme and the CJEU judgement upholding this decision were 'manifestly disproportionate' and thus *ultra vires*. Therefore, the judgement does not bind Germany, said the Federal Constitutional Court.[57] Or, to give another example, the current US administration reproached the WTO Appellate Body of going *ultra vires* and refused to participate in the appointment of members of the Appellate Body which led to the petering out of this body.[58] However, a group of members united to form an alternative appeal mechanism (via Article 25 DSU) which erects a new second instance and thus replaces the dysfunctional Appellate Body.[59] These events also illustrate the general proposition that an organization cannot easily be

[55] *Jurisdiction of the European Commission of the Danube between Galatz and Braila*, Publ. PCIJ Ser. B no 14, at 64.

[56] *Legality of the Use*, para. 25. *Cf.* Art. 96(2) UN Charter which allows 'specialized agencies' to 'request advisory opinions of the Court on legal questions *arising within the scope of their activities*' (emphasis added).

[57] BVerfG, judgement of the Second Senate of 5 May 2020 – 2 BvR 859/15 – paras. 117–63.

[58] See for the US critique against the Appellate Body's 'judicial activism' and 'overreach' the US 2019 Trade Policy Agenda and 2018 Annual Report of the President of the United States on the Trade Agreements Program (March 2019), 6 and 148.

[59] 'Interim Appeal Arrangement for WTO Disputes', entered into force on 30 April 2020.

captured by one, even powerful, member state alone – which is, in a way, a manifestation of the organization's autonomy and defies the realist paradigm.

Historically, the terminological and conceptual quarrels over personality and autonomy of international organizations have revolved around one key concern, namely the tension in the relationship between the organization and its members. From that perspective, autonomy is 'inversely proportional to the control and influence that members can exercise over their organisation'.[60] Along these lines, member states are considered either as the 'masters'[61] or as the 'servants'[62] of the (founding) treaty.

In reality, the relationship between the organization and its members depends on the concrete organization and on the context. It has various dimensions and it may change over time through the practice of the organization itself, too. Importantly, the distribution of power is *no zero-sum game*. Therefore, the organization can be (at different times, or even at the same time) *both* a vehicle *and* an actor. This fact is expressed by qualifying the founding document *both* as a treaty and a constitution, as 'conventional and at the same time institutional', to use the words of the ICJ.[63]

Second, and crucially, we suggest considering autonomy not exclusively in the relationship between the organization and its members, but also in relation to individuals and third parties who may be affected by an organization's actions and omissions. The principal normative reason to look beyond the membership is the fact that all organizational behaviour produces military, environmental, economic or financial externalities for humans, often independent from the latter's citizenship in a member state. Humans may therefore be the 'stakeholders' of organizations, beyond the member states, seen as the 'shareholders'. In order to delineate, in a concrete context, the circle of stakeholders, we need criteria. Without

[60] M. Steinbrück Platise, 'Legitimate Governance as a Privilege and Price for the Autonomy of International Organisations', in Steinbrück Platise, Moser and Peters (eds.), *The Legal Framework of the OSCE*, 297, 300.

[61] German Constitutional Court, *Lisbon Treaty*, judgement of 30 June 2006, 2/BvE 2/08, para. 334.

[62] *'Diener der Verträge'.* See U. Everling, 'Sind die Mitgliedstaaten der Europäischen Gemeinschaft noch Herren der Verträge? Zum Verhältnis von Europäischem Gemeinschaftsrecht und Völkerrecht', in R. Bernhardt *et al.* (eds.), *Völkerrecht als Rechtsordnung: Festschrift für Hermann Mosler* (Berlin: Springer, 1983) 173, 178.

[63] *Legality of the Use*, para. 19. The legal consequences of this quality as treaty-constitution or constitutional treaty (if any) are controversial.

seeking to definitely establish such criteria here,[64] we suggest that, as a minimum, those individuals whose normative situation is shaped by a collective actor are its stakeholders.[65] This means that, concomitantly, the actor's shaping power is crucially important. And that normative shaping power is a key manifestation of *auto*-nomy, in the literal sense of the power to make law. In conclusion, autonomy is a key feature of international organizations not only as a marker of independence from the member states but also as a marker of their power to govern individuals and, more generally, to shape reality.

2.5 At the Concept's Fringes

The fuzziness of the concept of international organization makes it difficult to draw outer boundaries. In this section, we look at phenomena which lack one or several of the three standard elements (treaty-base, state membership, autonomy) or feature them only weakly, but could be nonetheless considered international organizations, based on the further criteria we propose here.

2.5.1 Treaty Bodies as 'Mini International Organizations'

What about the diverse array of standing secretariats, experts committees, other specialized bodies and the regularized meetings of state delegates (usually called Conferences or Meetings of the Parties (CoPs and MoPs)), all somehow attached to international treaties? These bodies's composition varies from state delegates to independent experts. Their legally relevant functions range from the production and dissemination of information and knowledge over standard-setting and rule-making to compliance monitoring and dispute settlement. Very diverse examples are the Vienna Ozone Secretariat and

[64] See for an exploration J. von Bernstorff, 'New Responses to the Legitimacy Crisis of International Institutions: The Role of "Civil Society" and the Rise of the Principle of Participation of "The Most Affected" in International Institutional Law', (2021) 32 *European Journal of International Law* 125.

[65] See along similar lines G. Teubner, '*Quod Omnes Tangit*: Transnational Constitutions without Democracy?', (2018) 45 *Journal of Law and Society* 5; Goldmann, *Internationale Öffentliche Gewalt*, 360.

the International Whaling Commission, the human rights committees attached to the core universal human rights treaties and the 'subsidiary bodies for implementation' such as under Article 10 UNFCCC.

The legal nature of a body of this kind was controversial in the *Pulp Mills* case.[66] It concerned the Administrative Commission of the River Uruguay (CARU), set up in 1975 by a bilateral treaty between Argentina and Uruguay to promote the optimal use of the Uruguay River. While Uruguay argued that the CARU was merely a treaty-body, that is, 'a mechanism established to facilitate co-operation between the Parties',[67] Argentina maintained that the treaty established a proper 'institutional framework for close and ongoing co-operation'.[68] The ICJ focused on the commission's autonomy and found that '*far from being merely a transmission mechanism between the parties*, CARU has a permanent existence of its own; it *exercises rights and also bears duties* in carrying out the functions attributed to it by the 1975 Statute',[69] and it has a 'secretariat whose staff enjoys privileges and immunities'.[70] Based on these features, the ICJ qualified the Commission as an 'international organization with legal personality'.[71]

In contrast, a historic 'Administering Authority' over the territory of Nauru, established by a Trusteeship Agreement concluded in 1965 between Australia, New Zealand and the United Kingdom and which lasted until Nauru's independence in 1968, was denied an 'international legal personality distinct from those of the States thus designated' by the ICJ.[72] This was without further reasoning, probably because no party to the case had claimed otherwise.

All mentioned bodies sit – or are alleged to sit – on the blurry boundary between mere outlet of a treaty and a 'normal' international organization. One reason for doubts about their status is the lack of a specifically designated founding document. But the most important source of uncertainty is their dubious autonomy. When the case-law looks at the stability of their infrastructure and their tasks, it takes them as indicia for or against their autonomy. A particularly important manifestation of autonomy is the rule-making power which distinguishes the collective actor

[66] *Pulp Mills on the River Uruguay (Argentina* v. *Uruguay)*, [2010] ICJ Rep. 14.
[67] *Ibid.*, para. 84. [68] *Ibid.*, para. 85. [69] *Ibid.*, para. 87 (emphases added).
[70] *Ibid.*, para. 88. [71] *Ibid.*, para. 89.
[72] *Certain Phosphate Lands in Nauru (Nauru* v. *Australia)*, preliminary objections, [1992] ICJ Rep. 240, para. 47.

not only from its members but is also crucial for shaping affected individuals's normative status.[73] Depending on the degree of autonomy from the treaty parties, some of these bodies should be qualified as international organizations, others not.[74]

2.5.2 Private Law Form but Public Interest Function

The suggested criterion of global public interest tasks (Section 2.2.3) allows us to qualify entities that have been established under domestic (mostly private) law, with members other than states, and with an international treaty sitting, if at all, only in the background. For example, the Bank for International Settlement (BIS) has been incorporated as a Swiss limited company by the central banks of six states and a US-American financial institution.[75] Because the BIS is tasked to 'promote the co-operation of central banks and to provide additional facilities for international financial operations; and to act as trustee or agent in regard to international financial settlements',[76] in the public interest, it has been rightly qualified as an international organization despite its private law form.[77]

Other global actors have the form of an association under article 60 Swiss *Zivilgesetzbuch* (*ZGB*):[78] the International Committee of the Red Cross (ICRC),[79] the International Olympic Committee

[73] Brölman, *The Institutional Veil*, 24.

[74] Seminally for the qualification of CoPs as organizations, see R. Churchill and G. Ulfstein, 'Autonomous Institutional Arrangements in Multilateral Environmental Agreements: A Little-Noticed Phenomenon in International Law', (2000) 94 *American Journal of International Law* 623.

[75] Constituent Charter of the Bank for International Settlements of 20 January 1930, which is an integral part of the so-called 'Guarantee agreement' between six states on the one side, and Switzerland on the other side.

[76] Article 3 of the Statutes of the Bank for International Settlements of 20 January 1930, as amended on 7 November 2016.

[77] Partial Award on the lawfulness of the recall of the privately held shares on 8 January 2001 and the applicable standards for the valuation of the shares, award of 22 November 2002, paras. 104–18; see Permanent Court of Arbitration, Case 2000–4.

[78] ZGB of 10 December 1907 (as of 1 January 2020; AS 24 233).

[79] Article 2 of the Statutes of the International Committee of the Red Cross of 21 December 2017, entry into force on 1 January 2018: 'Legal status: 1. The ICRC is an association governed by Article 60 and following of the Swiss Civil Code. 2. In order to fulfil its humanitarian mandate and mission, the ICRC enjoys a status equivalent to that of

(IOC),[80] the IUCN[81] and the International Organization for Standardization (ISO).[82]

ISO is a prime example for a semi-private standard-setter. Although most of ISO's now 164 member institutes are part of the governmental structure of their states or mandated by their government, other members have their basis solely in the private sector and were set up by national partnerships of industry associations.[83] ISO-standards, although not as such legally binding, are referred to by international and national legal instruments and dispute settlement bodies in countless regulatory fields. Although they are not available for free, they are deeply ingrained in the regulatory infrastructure of economic globalization.[84] It is therefore fair to say that ISO autonomously performs a task of global public interest.

Because the function as opposed to the form is decisive, interstate actors based on international treaties but with a mainly commercial objective are not international organizations but rather transnational corporations. An example is the Airport Basel Mulhouse, based on an interstate treaty on the construction and operation of the airport.[85] This categorization would however not change fundamental governmental obligations. If the owners are states, they may not escape human rights obligations by resorting to a private law form.[86]

an international organization and has international legal personality in carrying out its work.'

80 Its statute is the Olympic Charter of 26 June 2019. Rule 15 No. 1 of the Charter states: 'The IOC is an international non-governmental not-for-profit organisation, of unlimited duration, in the form of an association with the status of a legal person, recognised by the Swiss Federal Council in accordance with an agreement entered into force on 1 November 2000.'

81 As discussed above, note 6.

82 Article 22(1) of the ISO Statutes (1946, 19th ed. 2018): ISO is a 'member-based association with civil personality in accordance with Article 60 et seq. of the Swiss Civil Code. It shall be not for-profit and non-governmental'. The first statutes were adopted by a Conference attended by representatives of twenty-five national standards bodies in London.

83 G. Sander, 'International Organization for Standardization (ISO)', *Max Planck Encyclopedia of Public International Law*, para. 37.

84 On the ISO website, the related section is labelled 'store' and includes a 'catalogue'. The WTO has, despite this commercial feature, accepted ISO standards to be 'international standards' (see the legal definition in Art. 1.1 of the Agreement on Technical Barriers to Trade of 1 April 1994 and its Annex 1).

85 *Convention franco-suisse relative à la construction et à l'exploitation de l'aéroport de Bâle-Mulhouse*, of 4 July 1949.

86 Cf. Principle 4 of the Guiding Principles on Business and Human Rights on business owned or controlled by States (UN Doc A/HRC/RES/17/4, 6 July 2011).

2.5.3 Intergovernmental Actors with Weak Autonomy

A third type of entities are completely or mainly intergovernmental but lack a formal treaty as founding document and are weakly institutionalized. Depending on their degree of autonomy, structure and permanence, they should be qualified as international organizations, too. The OSCE sits at the 'thick' end of the spectrum of non-personalized organizationhood, as already mentioned.[87]

At the other, 'thin', end of the spectrum we find 'coalitions of the willing' whose most characteristic feature has been described as the interplay between formal and informal structure, process and output.[88] This is similar for other interstate groups such as the G20. Here, the decision-making rests upon the participants, and no real decision, even at micro-level, can be said to be 'taken' by the entity itself. G20 operates without a permanent secretariat or staff, while the chair rotates annually among the members and is selected from a different regional grouping of countries. Proposals to establish a permanent secretariat were so far dismissed.[89] The lack of autonomy and the lack of formal and stable infrastructure are the main reasons why the G20 is, like the coalitions of the willing, not an international organization.[90]

Contrasting examples for actors in the middle of the spectrum are the Financial Action Task Force (FATF) and the Basel Committee for Banking Supervision (BCBS). The FATF emerged out of the 1989 G7 summit. The FATF is today based on an 'open-ended Mandate', adopted in 2019 by the finance ministers of its member jurisdictions.[91] It describes itself as an 'intergovernmental body' (§ 1 of its Mandate), currently comprising thirty-eight states and two regional organizations. Its standing secretariat is hosted by the OECD. FATF is entrusted

[87] See the text with note 47 in this chapter.

[88] A. Rodiles, *Coalitions of the Willing and International Law* (Cambridge University Press, 2018).

[89] F. Amtenbrink and R. Repasi, 'G7, G20 and Global Summits', in R. Wessel and J. Odermatt (eds.), *Research Handbook on the European Union and International Organizations* (Cheltenham: Edward Elgar, 2019) 338.

[90] Cf. P. Holcombe Henley and N. Blokker, 'The Group of 20: A Short Legal Anatomy from the Perspective of International Institutional Law', (2014) 14 *Melbourne Journal of International Law* 550.

[91] Financial Action Task Force Mandate, approved by the Ministers and Representatives of the Financial Action Task Force, 12 April 2019, Washington DC (www.fatf-gafi.org/media/fatf/content/images/FATF-Ministerial-Declaration-Mandate.pdf) (last accessed 7 July 2020).

with setting international standards combatting money laundering and the financing of terrorism. Although the Mandate explicitly states that it 'is *not* intended to create any legal rights or obligations',[92] the FATF participants certainly take collective decisions with public relevance at global level.

Finally, the 'standing committee of experts on banking and foreign exchange regulations and supervisory practices' (the BCBS, or 'Basel Committee') was established in 1974 by 'the central-bank Governors of the Group-of-Ten countries and of Switzerland', as noted in a BIS press communiqué at the time.[93] It took forty years to adopt the Charter that now forms its legal basis.[94] According to section 1 of the Charter, the Committee 'is the primary global standard-setter for the prudential regulation of banks and provides a forum for cooperation on banking supervisory matters', and its members include 'organisations with direct banking supervisory authority and central banks'.[95] According to section 3 '[t]he BCBS does not possess any formal supranational authority. Its decisions do not have legal force. Rather, the BCBS relies on its members' commitments ... to achieve its mandate'.

Arguably, actors such as FATF and the Basel Committee enjoy a modicum of autonomy, less in the sense of independence from the participants but rather in the sense of lawmaking capacity which may substantially affect individuals. Although their legal output cannot be formally attributed to them, it can be attributed *to the collectivity of participants* which can in consequence be held jointly accountable, too. To use the Jellinekean term further developed by Anzilotti and recently rediscovered in French scholarship, they are a 'common organ' of the participants.[96] They might therefore count among the international organizations in a broad sense.

[92] *Ibid.*, para. 48 (emphasis added).

[93] Press Communiqué of 12 February, www.bis.org/press/p19750212.pdf (last accessed 7 July 2020). The actual decision of 8 October 1974 is not public.

[94] Basel Committee on Banking Supervision Charter of 2013, last updated 5 June 2018, www.bis.org/bcbs/charter.htm (last accessed 7 July 2020).

[95] *Ibid.*, section 4.

[96] Jellinek, *Die Lehre*; Lagrange, 'La categorie', §§ 87–9; R. Rivier, *Droit international public*, 2nd ed. (Paris: PUF, 2013) 343–8; C. Santulli, 'Retour à la theorie de l'organe commun', (2012) 116 *Revue Générale de Droit International Public* 565.

2.6 Conclusion: Towards a Concept Fit for Global Governance

This chapter has sought to bring out the need for a more comprehensive concept of international organization that accommodates a wide range of actors, for both analytical and normative reasons. *Analytically*, the concept should be able to include the relevant phenomena diachronically, covering entities such as the Danube Commission[97] and the International Organization of Securities Commissions (IOSCO).[98] More importantly, a comprehensive concept is indispensable because globalization and global governance build on the very fact of these actors.[99] They are embedded in the political-legal infrastructure of globalization and therefore constitute a corollary to any emerging global law. In *normative* terms, a more comprehensive concept is desirable as an identifiable target or a touchstone of normative demands, cross-cutting different levels of governance.

Against this background, we suggest that besides actors which are interstate in form, other entities with multiple legal bases (public and private, international and domestic) and with a hybrid membership (states, civil society, even commercial) may be qualified as international organizations if they are entrusted with competences to fulfil tasks in the global public interest and feature a certain degree of autonomy.

One objection might be that the suggested conceptual move might turn against the initial intentions, actually ending up with a surplus of legal protection and legitimacy of entities whose operations do not meet material standards of the rule of law and cannot be traced back to any political (ideally democratic, deliberate, public) decision or process. However, we submit that blinding ourselves to those entities does not help. The concentration on the interstate sources of legitimacy rooted into a Westphalian world order functions as a shield against the over-legitimation of social or de facto powers only to the extent that the reality of these powers can be 'tamed' by legal categories, structures and institutions. Otherwise, the attachment to public (international) law becomes a dangerous fallacy: the normative aspiration – that only actors legitimated by means of public

[97] Qualified in its time as 'a distinct international entity possessing sovereignty over the broad waters of the Danube': G. Blackburn, 'International Control of the River Danube', (1930) 32 *Current History and Forum* 1154.

[98] Founded in 1987 under the private law of Québec; mandate defined in the *Objectives and Principles of Securities Regulation* (IOSCO Principles), last updated in May 2017.

[99] B. Auby, *Globalisation, Law and the State* (Oxford: Hart, 2017) 14–27, 106–7.

law *should be allowed* to exercise power and affect rights – slips into the conceptual assumption that only these actually *can*. Only the recognition that these entities can be legal points of reference properly called international (or global) organizations, too, will bring to light that they should be held to account, too.

A new and more comprehensive legal concept of international organization cannot and need not give an answer to every legal issue related to it. But it should encompass actors devoid of legal personality though sufficiently structured, stable and most of all autonomous, while also distinguishing them from mere networks and ad hoc cooperation. If international law fails to give a *legal* status to these entities, it would miss reality and its own ambition of contributing to order and offering normative guidance. Ultimately and more radically, international law as part and parcel of a global legal landscape necessitates the concept of a *global* organization. Further research, inspired by institutionalist and neo-institutionalist approaches as yet unduly neglected by international legal theory, is needed to find a concept fit for the emerging reality of global law and governance.

3 Accountability

Megan Donaldson and Surabhi Ranganathan

3.1 1 June 2020, the United States of America

A week into the anti-racism protests that followed the chilling murder of George Floyd by a Minnesota police officer, the co-founder of Black Lives Matter (BLM), Patrisse Cullors, appeared on ABC's *Nightline*. The show recapped the extraordinary events of that day: US President Donald Trump had announced that he was 'dispatching thousands and thousands of heavily armed soldiers, military personnel, and law enforcement officers' to quell the demonstrations. Federal police and military troops had used tear gas, rubber bullets and flash grenades on peaceful protestors gathered around the White House to clear the route to a cynical photo-op: the President posing before a church that he did not enter, holding aloft a Bible that he did not open.

Asked to react, Cullors made several points. She noted the President's record of branding local protestors and BLM activists as 'terrorists', urging the show's host to recognize that the issue at hand was, indeed, terror, but inflicted by the state on black bodies – police terror. The protestors were seeking an end to this terror. They wanted the arrest of all the officers involved, and more: 'Everybody wants to be apologized to. Everybody wants to be told, "I'm sorry. What I did was wrong. It was unacceptable. We won't do it again and, in fact, this is how we change."' But they were unlikely to get any of that: 'We barely get a sorry, we rarely get accountability and we never get change.' Black experience of police violence was not new. The foundation of policing, Cullors noted, lay in slave patrolling. Under Trump, law enforcement had been encouraged to become more brutal, 'to hurt people'.

The movement thus wanted more than words. 'We need to defund police and we need to take those resources and put them back into our communities so that we have access to healthy food, we have access to adequate health care, we have access to adequate public health system.' The demonstrations were to mourn black deaths but also 'for black life'.

The ABC headline summed up for Cullors: 'Black Lives Matter co-founder says what protesters want is simple: Accountability.'[1]

3.2 Language, Concept, Contexts

On one view, 'accountability' seems an unlikely vessel for the expectations outlined by Cullors. In its central dictionary meaning, the word denotes a liability to account for, or answer for, one's conduct. Cullors did use it in that sense when speaking of the arrest of Floyd's killers. But what about protestors's other demands, including with respect to future public spending? Those go beyond seeking legal liability, or apology, for specific past acts. They are demands for structural change, founded on a historically and politico-economically informed analysis of the conditions that enable deadly encounters between the police and the black public. They are an effort to alter the character of future engagements; in Cullors's words, they are for black life. That 'accountability' was chosen to sum up all of this tells us something about the term itself: the capaciousness of its associations, and its normative heft within popular discourse.

In the *Oxford Handbook on Public Accountability*, Melvin Dubnick describes accountability as a prominent cultural keyword: a word which, in its changing uses, bears 'witness to a general change in our characteristic ways of thinking about our common life' including 'our social, political and economic institutions'.[2] The meanings we squeeze into the term can tell us something about how, in whose interests, to which demands and to what standards of evaluation we expect our public institutions to function. We might thus expect that accountability would be a highly contested term. Yet, that does not appear to be the case. In fact, the 'push for greater accountability seems to be a point of agreement in even the most partisan

[1] A. Riegle and A. Yang, 'Black Lives Matter Co-Founder Says What Protesters Want Is Simple: Accountability', *ABC News*, 2 June 2020, https://abcnews.go.com/US/black-lives-matter-founder-protesters-simple-accountability/story?id=71008710 (all URLs current as of 23 April 2021).

[2] M. J. Dubnick, 'Accountability as a Cultural Keyword', in E. Ferlie, L. Lynn Jr and C. Pollitt (eds.), *Oxford Handbook of Public Management* (Oxford University Press, 2014) 23.

and divided political contexts'.[3] 'Accountability' is simultaneously a revealing word when placed under critical scrutiny, and obscuring in its more general uses, where it can serve to paper over differences in positions and expectations.

International organizations have been active in disseminating the term, especially since the late 1990s. The language of accountability has also been applied, with increasing vigour, to international organizations themselves. As Ruth Grant and Robert Keohane noted in an influential essay of 2005, concerns about abuses of power have operated more strongly on the international plane, because there even 'the minimal types of constraints found in domestic governments are absent'.[4] Critics of globalization have been especially concerned with the power of international organizations, regarding institutions like the World Bank and the World Trade Organization as relatively unconstrained – 'unaccountable' – compared to democratically accountable states. Grant and Keohane's suggestion, against such concerns, that international organizations *are* accountable, albeit in different ways from states, was an early marker of a now vast body of scholarship in both international law and international relations that focuses upon identifying the checks that operate upon international organizations, and the constituencies towards whom they are or should be accountable.

Of course, as renewed cycles of violence and protest on American streets remind us, accountability may be elusive even within democratic states. Nevertheless, discussions of accountability in the international organization context do present specific difficulties relative to a domestic context. In international organizations, concern for individuals' and communities' rights sits within the broadly statist structures and logics inherent in public international law. This creates a structural tension between states on one hand, and individuals or communities on the other, as persons to whom accountability is owed.

Contestation over accountability of international organizations to individuals and communities may also reinforce inequality between states. The international institutional endowment in which accountability is being crafted is a congealment of historic power relations, in which northern

[3] *Ibid.*

[4] R. W. Grant and R. O. Keohane, 'Accountability and Abuses of Power in World Politics', (2005) 99 *American Political Science Review* 29, 33.

states have played an outsized role in shaping the mandates, leadership and internal procedures of international organizations. When NGOs advocate for enhanced human rights and accountability mechanisms for people in the global south, they are usually leveraging the influence of northern governments to reform or establish international organizations – often in the direction of northern priorities. Thus, the very process of expanding protection and voice in the south can reinscribe the north's hegemonic position in the international order. While the protagonists in this pattern may be changing, the dynamic of interstate inequality remains.

A further issue is the relative insulation of international organizations from domestic procedures. International organizations typically enjoy immunity from suit in domestic courts and from domestic enforcement action. New chinks may be emerging in this immunity, but will likely not transform the general picture.[5] Of course, national laws and domestic executive action implementing international organization decisions *are* open to challenge in domestic courts. But the role of the organization itself may not be susceptible to tort or public law claims, which have been an important element of the accountability of state authorities. This is coupled with a general absence of international courts with jurisdiction over international organizations.

Perhaps most significantly, the import of accountability depends on the underlying norms against which actors are giving an account. The fact that international law obligations, concerning the protection of human rights and the environment, for example, have been crafted for states primarily, has left a certain ambiguity about whether and in what ways international organizations might be subject to their strictures. In general, these norms tend to be partially transposed into internal policies applicable to the work of the staff of international organizations. This has several implications, including that the norms may be piecemeal, with divergences between different organizations, and vis-à-vis norms applicable to states. These internal norms also may be triggered only when the institution does seek to act, neglecting instances in which it simply omits to act, and people are harmed by its inaction. Moreover, where institutions act, they often do so in tandem with states. And here, disentangling not only the norms applicable but also the roles of different actors – including within structures of organizational decision-making –

[5] *JAM et al.* v. *International Finance Corporation*, US Supreme Court, 27 February 2019, 586 US __ (2019).

poses particular difficulties, which laws on state and international organization responsibility have addressed at best imperfectly. Unsurprisingly, with legal accountability posing particular challenges, the more common measures tend to be of investigatory or informal character, and largely supplied by international organizations themselves. Even here, allocation of roles between states and international organizations, and the reach of particular mechanisms, may remain sources of friction.

In this chapter we review the institutional mechanisms and bodies of literature that have responded to and shaped discussions of the accountability of international organizations, with a particular focus on the World Bank. The Bank's activity was an iconic trigger for accountability reforms, and the Bank is both a key player within accountability discourse and an energetic narrator of its own institutional vision of accountability. We begin with a brief sketch of the emergence of accountability as a theme in the law of international organizations, zeroing in on the catalysts of the 1980s and 1990s that inspired various organizations to examine their own decision- and policy-making, and drew practitioner and scholarly attention. We sketch the variety of forms and mechanisms that organizations have used, and the spawning and generative impacts of empirically driven legal and political science literatures. Our narrative then contextualizes the Bank, and international organizations more broadly, as agentic and reflective actors within a dynamic environment, not so much attaining accountability as engaged in long-running contestation over what it entails and how to translate it into institutional processes. We close with some reflections on the politics of accountability and directions for future research and thought.

3.3 28 September 1989, Harsud, India

On a hot afternoon, in a town slated for drowning under the march of the Narmada Valley Dam Project (NVDP), 35000 people raised a now familiar chant: '*vikaas chahiye, vinaash nahi*' – 'we want development, not destruction'.[6] The Indian state has for six decades taken the view that the

[6] M. Patkar, 'Drowned and Out', *The Hindustan Times* (4 August 2004), www.countercurrents.org/en-patkar040804.htm. For more on the formation and progress of the NBA, see this oral history collection gathered by N. Oza: https://oralhistorynarmada.in/.

NVDP, with its plans for 30 major, 136 medium and 3,000 minor dams, and featuring the gigantic (and once World Bank-funded) Sardar Sarovar and Indira Sagar dams as its centrepieces, offers development, frequently rehearsing Jawaharlal Nehru's famous aphorism that dams are 'the temples of modern India'.[7] However, the people and organizations who gathered at Harsud, and after, under the banner of the Narmada Bachao Andolan (NBA), were seeing principally the destruction that dams entailed. Sardar Sarovar alone, for instance, has displaced more than 2,00,000 people and drowned hundreds of villages and thousands of hectares of farm and forest land. Such effects were anticipated: NVDP from the very outset betokened mass displacement and environmental harms.[8] Despite this, in omissions that would become central elements of the NBA's campaigning, the state made few efforts to seek the consent of those displaced or offer much by way of rehabilitation.

The critique voiced at Harsud indicted not only the government, but also the World Bank for financing and promoting destructive models of development. By the Bank's own reckoning, between 1986 and 1993, the years when its NVDP funding was operational, Bank-supported projects displaced 2.5 million people.[9] Already in 1985 the Bank had foreseen several 'massive displacement operations', including 1,00,000 people in the context of the Indira Sagar project and 70,000 in the Sardar Sarovar project.[10] It also had in place internal policies relating to displacement, tribal peoples and environmental impacts. But it failed to follow these policies in case of the NVDP; its Indian department also omitted to inform senior management fully of resettlement and environmental deficiencies, and to address serious problems even after they had become apparent. These were among the conclusions reached by an independent review commissioned by the

[7] Though Nehru himself had grown concerned about the 'disease of gigantism' afflicting these projects: S. Amrith, *Unruly Waters: How Mountain Rivers and Monsoons Have Shaped South Asia's History* (New York: Basic Books, 2018) 213.

[8] A. Kothari and R. Bhartari, 'Narmada Valley Project – Development or Destruction?', (1984) 19 *Economic and Political Weekly* 907.

[9] World Bank Environment Department, 'Resettlement and Development: The Bankwide Review of Projects Involving Involuntary Resettlement 1986–1993', 7, http://documents1.worldbank.org/curated/en/412531468766148441/pdf/multi-page.pdf.

[10] M. M. Cerna, 'Involuntary Resettlement in Bank-Assisted Projects. A Review of the Application of Bank Policies and Procedures in FY79–85 Projects', 7–8, http://documents1.worldbank.org/curated/en/879711468765928445/pdf/multi0page.pdf.

Bank itself in 1991, after the NBA had succeeded in having its criticisms amplified by international NGOs and the US Congress.[11]

The Bank's review had few consequences for the NVDP, which continued after the Bank withdrew funding and remains deeply contested today. Nor did it save Harsud from submergence. But it did have more considerable impact upon the Bank itself. The Bank's long-serving general counsel, Ibrahim Shihata, called the Narmada involvement the 'single most important case to draw public attention to the accountability issue' facing the Bank.[12] In the wake of the NBA campaign and ensuing findings, the Bank established a novel mechanism – the Inspection Panel – with powers to investigate cases in which project-affected people claim to have been harmed by the Bank's violation of its own policies and procedures, including those with respect to social and environmental impacts.

3.4 The Embrace of Accountability in the Law of International Organizations

Shihata's framing of the controversies over the NVDP as crystallizing an 'accountability issue' mirrors broader trends in the mid-1990s. 'Accountability' was already a term of choice within the Bank – part of a suite of governance reforms the Bank was promoting in borrower countries and considered neutral enough not to stray into the 'political' terrain prohibited by its founding instrument.[13] As regards global discourse more generally, political scientists do not find evidence of 'any coherent social movement or reformist ideology' propelling the acceleration of 'accountability' to prominence.[14] Its rise perhaps owed something to contrasting political currents: the collapse of the Soviet bloc and a new democratic and

[11] Vergin, 'Vergin to Preston (World Bank President), Office Memorandum: India: Sardar Sarovar (Narmada) Projects – Morse Review, May 5, World Bank Archives', https://timeline.worldbank.org/themes/timeline/pdfjs/web/viewer.html?file=//timeline.worldbank.org/sites/timeline/files/timeline/archival-pdfs/event65_SardorSarovar_2_1662724.pdf.

[12] I. Shihata, *The World Bank Inspection Panel* (Oxford University Press, 1994) 9.

[13] 'Shihata Transcript' (11 May 1994) 29, https://oralhistory.worldbank.org/transcripts/transcript-oral-history-interview-ibrahim-f-i-shihata-held-may-11-1994; G. F. Sinclair, *To Reform the World: International Organizations and the Making of Modern States* (Oxford University Press, 2017) 255–62.

[14] Dubnick, 'Cultural Keyword', 25.

grassroots impetus against autocratic or dictatorial rule on one hand, and the neoliberal turn in Atlantic democracies towards new public management and related managerial practices on the other. These represent quite different visions of holding government to account. However, a comprehensive intellectual history is beyond our scope here; what is important for our purposes is the way that 'accountability' has provided a commodious label under which to collect a range of practices and expectations, and the way this 'socially embedded, politicized, pluralistic, and value-heavy construction' has taken shape and shaped debates within the law of international organizations.[15]

Accountability language took several different channels into the discourse within and about international organizations. Some organizations had helped disseminate and popularize a notion of accountability applied to governments, particularly in the context of aid recipients's accountability for public finance (accountability as budgetary discipline and anti-corruption), and in the context of international criminal justice and human rights (accountability juxtaposed to impunity). In various respects, however, there were concerns about the extent to which international organizations themselves were answerable – for anything from managerial inefficiencies to errors of judgement to complicity in grave human rights violations. The collapse of the International Tin Council in 1985, and ensuing litigation concerning (inter alia) whether private creditors could recover directly from member states, made clear the consequences of failure for both creditors and the states. This triggered a study in the Institut de Droit International,[16] and a surge of scholarship on the obligations of international organizations and member states vis-à-vis third parties.[17] An escalation of perennial US discontent about the perceived inability of the UN to come to grips with fraud and abuse resulted in the creation of a new Office of Internal Oversight Services.[18] As

[15] E. Weisband and A. Ebrahim, 'Introduction: Forging Global Accountabilities', in A. Ebrahim and E. Weisband (eds.), *Global Accountabilities: Participation, Pluralism, and Public Ethics* (Cambridge University Press, 2007) 3.

[16] R. Higgins, 'The Legal Consequences for Member States of the Non-Fulfilment by International Organizations of Their Obligations toward Third Parties: Preliminary Exposé and Draft Questionnaire (1989)', (1995) 66 *Annuaire de l'Institut de Droit International* 251.

[17] J. Klabbers, *An Introduction to International Institutional Law*, 3rd ed. (Cambridge University Press, 2015).

[18] D. Thornburgh, 'Today's United Nations in a Changing World', (1993) 9 *American University International Law Review* 215, 222–3; UN General Assembly Resolution 48/218B (1994).

occurred in the World Bank, demands for accountability of governments to citizens were projected back onto the organizations funding and shaping development interventions.[19] There were also criticisms of the UN envoy's and Secretariat's failures to convey accurately the developing situation as Rwanda descended into genocide in 1994.

At least some of these diverse incidents may have been part of the impetus for the 1996 creation by the International Law Association (ILA) of a Committee on Accountability of International Organizations, with a mandate to 'consider what measures (legal, administrative or otherwise) should be adopted to ensure the accountability of public international organisations to their members and to third parties, and of members and third parties to public international organisations'.[20] 'Accountability' here encompassed legal forms, but extended to 'political, administrative [and] financial' forms as well. The Committee, consulting extensively with counsel to international organizations, developed a set of Recommended Rules and Procedures (RRPs), a framing chosen to avoid any assertions as to the legal status or otherwise of the stipulations.

The Committee's early work offers a glimpse of the fluidity of vocabularies and the range of issues at stake. The Committee drew out three different 'levels' of accountability: internal and external scrutiny and monitoring; tortious liability for acts or omissions not involving breach of any international or institutional law; and responsibility for acts or omissions constituting a breach of international or institutional law. By 1998 the first level – scrutiny and monitoring – was translated into a series of 'principles' resonant with public law. The most developed of these, framed as the 'principle of good governance', encompassed 'transparent and democratic decision-making process, access to information, well-functioning of the international civil service, sound financial management'.[21] The exact framing would shift a bit over time. In the 2000 report, for example, 'democratic decision-making process' was replaced by 'participation', then reinstated in subsequent versions in a watered-down way, as 'a large degree of democracy in the decision-

[19] see, e.g., J. Cahn, 'Challenging the New Imperial Authority: The World Bank and the Democratization of Development', (1993) 6 *Harvard Human Rights Journal* 159, 164–5; Shihata, *World Bank Inspection Panel*, 38.

[20] CAIO, 'Part II: Report' (1998) 68 *International Law Association Reports of Conferences* 584, 586.

[21] *Ibid.*, 599–602.

making process'.[22] And there was increasing attention to ex post facto reporting and evaluation, and remedies. But by and large the structure remained the same: the widest sense of 'accountability' was infused with a public law sensibility ('Power entails accountability, that is the duty to account for the exercise of power'), and distilled into principles with subsections, the 'principle of good governance' serving as a kind of portmanteau.[23]

Across the second and third levels of responsibility – that is, tortious liability; and responsibility for breaches of international or institutional law – the ILA Committee laid out 'primary' rules and recommended practices, and then 'secondary' rules (essentially treatment of responsibility of international organizations). Some primary rules and recommended practices, such as that international organizations should comply with basic human rights obligations, were potentially expansive on their face, but did not on closer examination depart from the usual approaches inherent in sources doctrine and theories of international organization personality. They were fleshed out particularly in connection with temporary administration of territory, imposition of non-military coercive measures and peacekeeping and peace enforcement, but remained inchoate in other contexts.

While the ILA Committee's drafting was proceeding, the International Law Commission (ILC) also took up the question of the responsibility of international organizations, delving further into issues such as attribution, and producing, ultimately, the Articles on Responsibility of International Organizations (adopted by the General Assembly in 2011). These Articles, though clearly representing a progressive development of the law, were more squarely within the four corners of law as such, unlike the ILA's focus on political, administrative and financial forms of accountability. Their coverage was significantly narrower than that of the ILA's RRPs, because responsibility only arose where there had been non-compliance with an international obligation (by definition, most likely in relations between international organizations and states rather than between organizations and third parties), and because the ILC's work did not purport to say

[22] CAIO, 'Part II: Accountability of International Organisations', (2004) 71 *International Law Association Reports of Conferences* 164.

[23] CAIO, 1998 Report, 878.

anything about the primary rules which might give rise to these obligations.

The ILA's final report in 2004 coincided with a surge in scholarship in the early to mid-2000s, that took accountability as a touchstone and focused attention on particular institutional practices which would realize it. In political science, Grant and Keohane sketched accountability – defined as the right to hold those in authority to a set of standards, judge whether the standards have been met and impose sanctions if not – as central to democracy, and discussed how accountability might be secured beyond the democratic apparatus of states. Noting the 'clear tension between the concept of a World Bank that is accountable to poor people and one that is accountable to the US Secretary of the Treasury', they mapped accountability to these different constituencies, of different 'types' (hierarchical, supervisory, fiscal, legal, market, peer, public reputational); and called for more intelligently designed accountability systems.[24]

In law, scholars were taking a range of conceptual approaches to the theme now often framed as 'global governance': how to make legal sense of the institutions and relationships wielding power globally, but not fully legible within a statist public international law paradigm. In one influential intervention, Kingsbury, Krisch and Stewart recast transnational regulatory power as 'global administration'. International organizations loomed large in this picture, albeit as only one institutional form alongside networks of national regulators and administration by hybrid intergovernmental–private or fully private arrangements. The authors discerned in existing practice an emergent 'global administrative law' consisting of 'mechanisms, principles, practices, and supporting social understandings that promote or otherwise affect the accountability of global administrative bodies, in particular by ensuring they meet adequate standards of transparency, participation, reasoned decision, and legality, and by providing effective review of the rules and decisions they make'.[25] In this re-description the keystone of accountability was both empirically assessable and imbued with normative significance. Other scholars, particularly those shaped by a continental public law

[24] Grant and Keohane, 'Abuses of Power', 33.

[25] B. Kingsbury, N. Krisch and R. Stewart, 'The Emergence of Global Administrative Law', (2005) 68 *Law and Contemporary Problems* 15, 17.

tradition, pursued similar concerns in a vocabulary of 'legitimacy' rather than accountability.[26]

These scholarly projects converged in a focus on the concrete reforms then developing across many international organizations, particularly: greater routinization of transparency and participation in decision-making; formalization of the process and substance of decision-making; and channels for ex post facto review (and sometimes redress) following decisions. These reforms sometimes entailed adjustments to existing decision-making processes within institutions, and sometimes involved the establishment of wholly new processes or entities, such as the World Bank's Inspection Panel, and, in other cases, ombudspersons, inspectors, independent experts or appeals chambers. Such mechanisms responded to diverse concerns: from conduct that was illegal, unlawful or at least not compliant with human rights, to breaches of internal institutional policy, to lawful and internally compliant but otherwise contestable policy choices. They privileged different 'accountees': from hierarchical supervisors, member states and funders, to individuals affected. In some cases, individuals affected were readily identifiable ex ante, as with refugee status determinations, the issuance of Interpol red notices or the listing of individuals subject to anti-terrorist sanctions. In others, the class of persons affected was hard to delimit in advance, as with policy decisions about priorities for institutional action, or the conduct of humanitarian and peacekeeping missions.

Scholarship in this vein, while not exclusively determining approaches to accountability,[27] has shaped the discussion in international law in three important respects. First, it has both captured and fostered an iterative relationship between scholarship and 'practice' writ large (extending beyond what would be relevant for custom-formation). In describing practice, academic commentary enlists into 'accountability' examples of institutional transformations in which the actors themselves might not have framed their concerns in those terms. For instance, one of the most-cited examples of a shift towards greater accountability in global

[26] A. von Bogdandy, P. Dann and M. Goldmann, 'Developing the Publicness of Public International Law: Towards a Legal Framework for Global Governance Activities', in A. von Bogdandy *et al.* (eds.), *The Exercise of Public Authority by International Institutions: Advancing International Institutional Law* (Heidelberg: Springer, 2010) 3, 20.

[27] See, for other literature, Weisband and Ebrahim, 'Introduction'.

governance is the ECJ's rulings in *Kadi I* and *II*,[28] which effectively precluded EU implementation of sanctions imposed by the UN Security Council on individuals on the basis that the process involved had not met EU law protections for fundamental rights. These decisions were focused on EU law and did not themselves so much as mention accountability; yet once such decisions are named as exemplars of accountability, they can be transposed as authorities for other accountability reforms, or understood as markers of an underlying shift in the international legal order.

Second, the normative engagement of this scholarship is often explicitly mediated. This is normativity for a non-ideal world, in which thicker accounts of democracy are out of reach – recall thus the ILA Committee's hesitation around the reference to 'democratic decision-making'; and the way in which GAL scholarship, at the outset, 'bracketed' democracy as for the time being illusory and unilluminating as an ideal for global administration.[29]

Third, this scholarship has opened a question about the bounds of law, and the stakes, analytical and normative, of seeing particular norms and practices as law, or generative of it. As the ILA Committee's work reflects, the accountability discussion is always in some relation to law, but not wholly legal in nature. The charge that accountability is not itself a deep-rooted legal term in either common or civil law traditions is correct,[30] and it has been an open question for many lawyers whether it is 'capable of being applied in a legal scientific discourse'.[31] The central impulse of the ILA Committee's work ('with power comes accountability') and many of the mechanisms of accountability resonate with both underlying rationales and existing institutional forms in domestic public law; yet the work sits rather uneasily in most textbooks on the law of international organizations. As some scholars have pointed out, the *naming* of diffuse and ambiguous norms as 'law' is itself an intervention,[32] and one with

[28] Case C-402/05 P, *Kadi and Al Barakaat International Foundation* v. *Council and Commission*, ECLI:EU:C:2008:461; Case T-85/09, *Kadi* v. *European Commission*, ECLI: EU:T:2010:418.

[29] Kingsbury, Krisch and Stewart, 'Global Administrative Law', 50.

[30] G. Hafner, 'Accountability of International Organizations', (2003) 97 *Proceedings of the American Society of International Law* 236.

[31] D. Curtin and A. Nollkaemper, 'Conceptualizing Accountability in International and European Law', (2005) 36 *Netherlands Yearbook of International Law* 3, 19.

[32] S. Marks, 'Naming Global Administrative Law', (2004) 37 *New York University Journal of International Law and Politics* 995.

a potentially legitimating effect on the institutional landscape in which these norms are being elaborated.[33]

3.5 14 and 21 April 2010, Georgetown University

In two interviews that form part of the World Bank's oral history archives, Edith Brown Weiss reflected on the successes of the Bank's by then well-established Inspection Panel. A former Chair of the Panel, Brown Weiss noted that it had had a 'very positive response from civil society, including from academics', and from NGOs, with a 'whole slew of writing about the Panel having emerged'. The Panel had steadily improved its inspection and outreach practices and served as a model for similar mechanisms at other financial institutions. The interviewer's questions occasionally gave voice to the perspectives of critics, and glimpses of contestation over the Panel's operation: that international NGOs might stir up disaffection among project-affected people or discourage the taking of risk in pursuing development strategies; that, conversely, the Panel might not be known or accessible to many affected communities, that requesters might be at risk of retaliation, and that, once an investigation had been conducted, it was difficult to justify showing the draft report to Bank management prior to the Board meeting at which it would be discussed, leaving the original requesters without the full report until after the Board had considered the matter. Although acknowledging that there was 'more that could be done', Brown Weiss resisted most of these criticisms, beginning and ending the interviews with the same evaluation: the Panel had provided a means of giving voice to the affected people, built confidence in economic development and helped ensure that development was effective and sustainable.[34]

[33] M. Kuo, 'The Concept of "Law" in Global Administrative Law: A Reply to Benedict Kingsbury', (2009) 20 *European Journal of International Law* 997; M. Kuo, 'Inter-Public Legality or Post-Public Legitimacy? Global Governance and the Curious Case of Global Administrative Law as a New Paradigm of Law', (2012) 10 *International Journal of Constitutional Law* 1050; B. S. Chimni, 'Co-Option and Resistance: Two Faces of Global Administrative Law', (2006) 37 *New York University Journal of International Law and Politics* 799.

[34] E. Brown Weiss, 'Brown Weiss Transcript' (14 April 2010) 9, https://oralhistory.worldbank.org/transcripts/transcript-oral-history-interview-edith-brown-weiss-held-april-14-and-21-2010.

Brown Weiss offered two examples in particular to illustrate the Panel's work. The first was its investigation into the Mumbai Urban Transport Project (2004–5), which had involved the resettlement of about 1,20,000 people displaced by the expansions in Mumbai's railway and road networks. The second was into two loans supporting a new commercial forest concession programme in the Democratic Republic of the Congo (DRC) (2005–7), which had not taken into account the interests of DRC's indigenous 'pygmy' groups. In both cases, the requests that catalyzed the investigations came directly from the affected groups, with international NGOs playing a secondary role. If that spoke well of the Panel's outreach work, Brown Weiss also emphasized the achievements of the investigations themselves. Although she did not contextualize it as such, Mumbai was an obvious counterpoint to the NVDP, where similar failures of resettlement had met with no prompt response. In the Mumbai case, however, the Panel had issued a detailed report analyzing the failures and inadequacies of the resettlement programme; it was also 'very much involved in the Mumbai follow-up'.[35] In the case of the DRC investigation, the Panel discovered that, although there were significant numbers of indigenous people living in areas to be affected, they had been effectively invisible in the work to date: early project design had not acknowledged their existence, and thus the Bank's policy on indigenous peoples had not been applied. The Panel's report catalyzed reforms in the Bank's process for determining the existence of indigenous people in Africa who stood to be affected by Bank-financed projects.

Days prior to the oral history interviews, Brown Weiss had used the same examples in a somewhat contrapuntal lecture to the annual meeting of the American Society of International Law. On this occasion, addressing these examples at greater length, she had added more qualifications; neither was a story wholly of success. In DRC, 'pygmies were given representation on the national commission reviewing the concessions although under conditions that made it hard for them to participate effectively'; moreover 'the difficulties of development in DRC remain[ed]'. In Mumbai, '[t]he results for the people are always complicated', although some improvements did follow.[36]

[35] *Ibid.*, 20.

[36] E. Brown Weiss, 'On Being Accountable in a Kaleidoscopic World', (2010) 104 *Proceedings of American Society of International Law*, 477, 485, 486.

The more sober note was appropriate. In the case of Mumbai, scholars have noted that, following the Panel's submission of the report to the Bank's Executive Board, 'Bank management failed to meet their deadline for submitting an action plan and delayed for more than a year, meaning almost none of the targets recommended by the Executive Board were met'. One of the lead requesters was imprisoned for a time, raising doubt about the efficacy of Panel measures to protect those making use of its procedure;[37] and '[d]isappointed by the lack of improvement in resettlement programmes despite the Inspection Panel having recorded serious violations of policy, citizens turned once again to the Bombay High Court'.[38] In the case of DRC, the Board, on the very occasion of taking note of the Panel's report, expressed support for (and soon after approved) 'a large road rehabilitation project that may pose new risks to forests, the environment and forest-dependent peoples'.[39]

Such developments raise questions about how accountability mechanisms are chosen, designed and reformed. The Inspection Panel, as we will see, has moved between different self-conceptions in response to conflicting expectations and criticisms. Yet even Brown Weiss, underlining the mutability, instability and interconnectedness of the world in which the Bank was operating, seems to have felt the need for more systematic approaches. Her address closed by calling for 'a fresh look' at accountability, urging the ILC to go beyond the ILA's work, and the elaboration of international organizations' personality, to, 'consider breaking out the legal concept of accountability and addressing it in the broader scope of a kaleidoscopic world'.[40]

3.6 Agents of Accountability

It is important to see adoption of the language of accountability by international organizations, and the crafting of particular mechanisms,

[37] B. Sovacool, 'Cooperative or Inoperative? Accountability and Transparency at the World Bank's Inspection Panel', (2017) 1 *Case Studies in the Environment* 900, 901.

[38] S. Randeria and C. Grunder, 'The (Un)Making of Policy in the Shadow of the World Bank: Infrastructure Development, Urban Resettlement and the Cunning State in India', in C. Shore, S. Wright and D. Però (eds.), *Policy Worlds. Anthropology and the Analysis of Contemporary Power* (New York: Berghahn Books, 2011) 201.

[39] J. Zalcberg, 'The World Bank Inspection Panel: A Tool for Ensuring the World Bank's Compliance with International Law?', (2012) 8 *Macquarie Journal of International and Comparative Environmental Law* 1, 19.

[40] Brown Weiss, 'Kaleidoscopic World', 490.

as instances of *agency*, not as some sort of organic phenomenon ('the rise of accountability') or part of a teleological 'constitutionalisation' or 'juridification' of governance. This agency is complex, with strategic efforts to shape the narrative about an organization's functioning often mixing with sincere attempts at reform. Institutional decisions are perhaps most obviously driven by the perceived stance of an institution's key interlocutors – that is, by possibilities of the stoppages of funding, member state disengagement, NGO criticism or reputational damage. In some areas there are strong iterative and comparative patterns to institutional reform: international organizations adopt and adapt mechanisms of perceived peers, sometimes under pressure from comparative assessments. Accountability initiatives may stem from the intrinsic conviction or vocational orientation of particular senior staff, influence brought to bear on individual office-holders, or internal struggles for control over particular policies or decisions (in which pressure from outside may well strengthen the hand of some within). As accountability mechanisms are adopted, states or other actors who resist these may react by drawing back or trying to forge alternate structures; a process of regime shifting which is itself inflected by differentials in power and influence.

The design of the Bank's accountability mechanisms was the outcome of considerable struggle. Protests against the NVDP, damning internal reports, together with US NGOs' lobbying for Congressional conditions on US funding for international development assistance routed through the World Bank, forced a suite of procedural reforms in 1993–4: an origin story the Bank itself now sets out in a volume marking the twenty-fifth anniversary of the Panel's creation.[41] But the precise shape of these reforms – both a new policy on Disclosure of Information and, our focus here, the Inspection Panel – was determined by a range of actors mobilizing different institutional forms for accountability as an ideal. Influential US NGOs were initially envisaging an appeal commission wholly independent from the Bank and operating something like a court. Many Executive Directors, particularly those representing borrower countries, wanted, if anything, a body more directed to internal learning.[42]

[41] World Bank, *The Inspection Panel at 25: Accountability at the World Bank* (Washington DC: World Bank, 2018).

[42] Shihata, *The World Bank Inspection Panel*, 25–7.

What emerged was a solution 'in between'.[43] An Inspection Panel of three individuals, not current staff of the Bank, would still be *part* of the Bank: independent of management but reporting to the Bank's Board. It would investigate only whether Bank staff had complied with the Bank's internal policies – policies which had sometimes been influenced by NGOs, and developed in conversation with evolving international law standards, but did not match the human rights and environmental obligations accepted by many states. (The introduction of the Panel as a means of ensuring compliance with policies in turn prompted the rationalization and systematization of the policies themselves, into categories of Operational Policies and Bank Policies (mandatory), and good practices (not mandatory)). At the insistence of borrower countries, it was clear that the focus would be on acts or omissions of the Bank, not the borrower – though acts or omissions of the Bank included failure to follow up on the borrower's breach of obligations under relevant loan agreements that incorporated Bank policies.

Radically, the Panel would receive requests for inspection directly from affected parties: any collectivity of individuals, however constituted, or a representative of such, but not from single individuals. The formalities were minimal. Requesters had to establish only that their rights or interests had been or were likely to be materially affected by the Bank's failure to follow its operational policies and procedures. On receipt of a request, the Panel was to notify the Bank's management and Board, with management obliged within twenty-one days to provide the Panel with evidence that it had in fact complied or intended to comply with relevant policies. If the Panel was satisfied that management had failed to demonstrate that it had taken adequate steps to follow policies; that the alleged violation was of a serious character; and that certain other eligibility criteria had been met, the Panel could recommend to the Board that the matter be investigated. The borrower and the Executive Director representing the country concerned were to be consulted both before the Panel's recommendation on, and during any, investigation. The Panel was to have access to all relevant Bank staff and records during its investigations, and could carry out inspection in-country with the consent of the country concerned.

[43] I. Shihata, 'Shihata Transcript' (23 May 2000) 32, https://oralhistory.worldbank.org/transcripts/transcript-oral-history-interview-ibrahim-f-i-shihata-held-may-23-and-24-2000.

For all its formal innovations, the Panel's procedure did not place requesters on equal footing with Bank management: the Panel's report following the investigation was to be provided simultaneously to management and the Board, but not, at this stage, to the affected parties. Management was required to propose a response within six weeks, notionally in consultation with affected parties, which would be considered together with the Panel report by the Bank's Executive Directors. It was after this consideration that affected parties would be given the full Panel report. Also, the Panel was not empowered to decide anything definitively, or recommend concrete steps; its role was investigatory, a catalyst of a resolution to be developed by management.

This was, again, far removed from the independent commission for which some NGOs had pressed, and from more radical demands for bottom-up participation of affected peoples. In public writings the Bank's General Counsel, Ibrahim Shihata situated the Panel as in sympathy with, but at some remove from, more expansive visions of accountability as political empowerment: 'Rather than deferring to an abstract democratic ideal of participation – though in full harmony with it – the procedural involvement of affected local people in the work of the Panel aims at two practical concerns', namely protecting the rights and interests of project-affected people, and improving the very process of development. He emphasized that the Panel was not the sole site of accountability, but only a complement to an intricate and pre-existing accountability ecosystem (of Bank staff to the President, and President to Executive Directors whose powers are delegated by a Board of Governors on which all states are represented).[44]

The Bank's internal reforms had been undertaken with a sense of the potential for sectoral leadership, and other multilateral development banks indeed formalized and expanded their information disclosure policies, and created formal 'accountability mechanisms' somewhat similar to the WBIP.[45] However, the very plasticity of 'accountability' left open prospects for further reform, and its ambiguity facilitated coalition-building in

[44] Shihata, *The World Bank Inspection Panel*, 116–24.

[45] M. Donaldson and B. Kingsbury, 'The Adoption of Transparency Policies in Global Governance Institutions: Justifications, Effects, and Implications', (2013) 9 *Annual Review of Law and Social Science* 119; E. Suzuki and S. Nanwani, 'Responsibility of International Organizations: The Accountability Mechanisms of Multilateral Development Banks', (2005) 27 *Michigan Journal of International Law* 50.

pressing for transformation. As the NGO One World Trust noted in connection with its accountability 'framework' and 'guidelines', which it considered applicable to international organizations, NGOs and corporations alike, 'the breadth of the issue provides a wide platform on which divergent groups can come together'.[46] Research on NGO lobbying at the World Bank has highlighted the convergence on accountability as a priority by NGO networks with quite different preoccupations, and sometimes also sharply different views of the Bank's optimal role in national policy-making.[47] When the One World Trust criteria and metrics, for example, translated accountability into specific institutional features, they delivered, in the eyes of some other NGOs, artificially positive accountability scores for some development banks, that could make it harder to press these banks towards deeper reform.[48]

Even within the carefully confined parameters of the 1993 resolution establishing the Panel, there were tensions over its role and the variants of accountability on offer. Initially, when the Panel was considering admissibility of requests for inspection, it would undertake extensive work, including site visits, prior to seeking Board authorization for an inspection. This sometimes resulted in Bank management seeking to pre-empt inspection by developing remedial plans. This de facto function of the Panel as a quasi-regulatory rather than quasi-adjudicative body highlighted different possible visions of accountability: on the one hand real-time 'accountability' to people seeking practical change, sometimes including engagement with the acts of the borrowing countries themselves (which were, strictly speaking, beyond the purview of the Panel's mandate); on the other the more formal ex post facto public adjudication of the Bank's adherence to its own policies.[49] The drift towards more proactive attempts to address difficulties prior to a full-blown inspection, while sometimes

[46] R. Lloyd, S. Warren and M. Hammer, 'One World Trust 2008 Global Accountability Report', 11, www.oneworldtrust.org/uploads/1/0/8/9/108989709/2008_global_accountability_report.pdf.

[47] P. Nelson, 'Agendas, Accountability, and Legitimacy among Transnational Networks Lobbying the World Bank', in S. Khagram, J. Riker and K. Sikkink (eds.), *Restructuring World Politics* (Minneapolis MN: University of Minnesota Press, 2002) 131, 144–7.

[48] R. Lloyd, 'Promoting Global Accountability: The Experiences of the Global Accountability Project', (2008) 14 *Global Governance* 273, 278.

[49] B. Kingsbury, 'Operational Policies of International Institutions as Part of the Law-Making Process: The World Bank and Indigenous Peoples', in G. Goodwin-Gill and S. Talmon (eds.), *The Reality of International Law* (Oxford University Press, 1999) 323, 333.

supported by Executive Directors representing borrower states, could also give rise to tensions where borrower states felt the Panel was intruding into de facto review of the country's decisions.[50] Following a 1999 review of the Panel's operation, in which not only the Panel and the Board but also diverse NGOs asserted a stake in the future of the Panel, the Board ultimately opted to authorize inspections whenever admissibility criteria were met, rather than leaving an opening for pre-emptive responses by management.[51] This made for a longer process for project-affected people but also a more public assessment of the Bank's decisions.

Yet the perceived need for some more punctual, less formal dispute resolution alternative to full inspection never really went away. Newer accountability mechanisms in other development banks often had, in addition to the fact-finding function, further functions of dispute resolution or grievance redress, in which the mechanism played some role in negotiating or mediating a solution to outstanding issues without proceeding to a full inspection. In 2010, a review of the World Bank's safeguard policies by its internal Independent Evaluation Group proposed the creation of a new grievance redress and conflict resolution mechanism which would operate alongside the Inspection Panel. The eventual Grievance Redress Service (GRS; created 2015) reports to management (the Operations Policy and Country Services Vice-President), in contrast to the Inspection Panel's reporting to the Board. It focuses on 'facilitat[ing] solutions agreeable to all parties as a credible and neutral broker',[52] without examining, as the Inspection Panel would, the question of compliance with the Bank's policy.

In the meantime, the Panel itself has been seeking to achieve something like a dispute resolution role. The Panel in 2014 piloted a formalized approach to 'early solutions' which they considered could be read into the 1993 resolution rather than requiring formal amendment of it, in which registration of a request for inspection would be delayed to give management and requesters an opportunity to address alleged harms. However, though this avenue offered affected peoples more immediate access to

[50] Shihata, 'Shihata Transcript', 34–5.

[51] I. Shihata, *The World Bank Inspection Panel*, 2nd ed. (Oxford University Press, 2000) 173–203.

[52] World Bank, 'Grievance Redress Service Annual Report 2017', (2018) 3, http://documents1.worldbank.org/curated/en/881351536095781539/pdf/GRS-2017AnnualReport-final-08312018.pdf.

support, NGO evaluations indicated procedural and substantive shortcomings in its application.[53]

These permutations offer a larger window on the way in which accountability mechanisms develop, including moving – sometimes uneasily – between problem-solving and investigative functions. Constituencies within and beyond international organizations seek to shape the institutional arrangements to address pressing needs, political sensitivities and pragmatic obstacles, operating under the aegis of 'accountability' but sometimes with sharply divergent results for the people most affected by their work.

3.7 9 March 2020, Washington DC

On 9 March 2020, the Bank announced a package of further reforms in a press release headed 'World Bank Enhances Its Accountability'.[54] This announcement was the culmination of several years of work, with substantive standards and accountability mechanisms being negotiated in a world markedly different from that of the 1990s: one in which NGO participation is routinized and expanded, but in which emerging powers are now less reliant on Bank for funding – and indeed have become development funders in their own right through new, rival institutions like the Asian Infrastructure Investment Bank and New Development Bank.[55] These new institutions offer, on paper at least, fewer avenues for NGO participation, more ambiguous transparency commitments, and, in some cases, weaker avenues for review of decisions,[56] though their adoption of the basic lines of these mechanisms indicates the extent to which accountability innovations of recent decades have now become part of the script of a development bank.

[53] N. Bugalski, 'An Evaluation of the Inspection Panel's Early Solutions Pilot in Lagos, Nigeria', www.inclusivedevelopment.net/wp-content/uploads/2016/06/Lagos-Early-Solutions-Evaluation.pdf.

[54] World Bank, 'World Bank Enhances Its Accountability', www.worldbank.org/en/news/press-release/2020/03/09/world-bank-enhances-its-accountability.

[55] P. Dann and M. Riegner, 'The World Bank's Environmental and Social Safeguards and the Evolution of Global Order', (2019) 32 *Leiden Journal of International Law* 537, 547–57.

[56] E. Heldt and H. Schmidtke, 'Global Democracy in Decline?: How Rising Authoritarianism Limits Democratic Control over International Institutions', (2019) 25 *Global Governance* 231.

Following an unprecedentedly open, consultative, multi-year process the Bank had reached consensus in 2017 on a new Environmental and Social Framework (ESF), supplanting earlier policies.[57] The ESF made the first explicit commitment to human rights, albeit in a prefatory vision statement only; and coverage of some of the ESF is now more aligned with the content of treaties on indigenous rights, and the minimum standards of the International Labour Organization. On the other hand, the ESF contained a more formalized Use of Country System provision – deference to a borrower state's own legal framework where this achieves outcomes materially consistent with the ESF – which, as some NGOs have feared, could herald a practical bypass of the constraints that have been worked into Bank policies over time.

The Board had commissioned an external review to examine whether the Panel required updates to operate effectively with the ESF. This review, conducted by an academic long associated with Bank reform efforts, considered inter alia: whether requesters should have access to the Panel's report prior to the Board discussion of it; and whether there should be a formal dispute resolution function in some form. On the former, the Bank had decided in 2018 to revise Panel procedure to allow earlier access to the report by requesters, going some way to level the positions of requesters and management. On the latter, the review noted some disadvantages of the 'early solutions' approach piloted in 2014: it was arguably distorting the timelines of the compliance review process and the role of the Panel vis-à-vis Bank management, involving the Panel in overseeing mediation of solutions when it might then have to conduct an inspection later.[58] In the package announced in March 2020, the Bank chose a more far-reaching option: a new Dispute Resolution Service which will sit alongside the Panel institutionally, independent of management, but focus on helping the parties (Bank, borrower state, affected peoples) resolve issues in dispute in a mutually satisfactory way. This Service was characterized by the Chair of the Bank's Board Committee on Development Effectiveness as 'bolstering the Bank's accountability framework'.[59]

[57] Dann and Riegner, 'Environmental and Social Safeguards', 550–1.

[58] D. Bradlow, 'External Review of the Inspection Panel's Toolkit', paras. 58–61, http://documents1.worldbank.org/curated/en/562131583764988998/pdf/External-Review-of-the-Inspection-Panel-s-Toolkit.pdf.

[59] World Bank, 'World Bank Enhances Its Accountability'.

3.8 Politics of Accountability

What emerges from the now twenty-five-year history of the Bank's Inspection Panel is a sense of accountability in movement, between a theoretical ideal available for deployment by both the Bank and its diverse interlocutors and critics, and a series of institutional fixes. These fixes both shape definitions of 'accountability' in intersecting institutional, doctrinal, scholarly and activist literatures, and open new frontiers for contestation of these definitions. The Bank is of course an international organization of a particular kind: a lender rather than a direct actor; and engaged in projects which by their nature can offer major benefits but entail massive dislocation and harm to those in their path. The acts for which accountability is a salient concern thus differ qualitatively from other canonical instances, such as sexual predation by peacekeepers, or corruption or financial misfeasance by officials. Nevertheless, the World Bank case brings out many aspects of accountability across international organizations.

Accountability is often accountability for compliance with an evolving array of policies internal to an international organization, informed by, but not congruent with, legal obligations of states. The interface between obligations applicable to each of the parties in any collaboration between states and international organizations is thus often a source of friction and dispute.

The question of *to whom* an international organization is accountable is rarely answerable in a simple way. As defenders of organizations are keen to point out, mechanisms for persons affected focus on those harmed by a project, not those who might stand to benefit from it. This pattern is consistent with a basic 'do no harm' rule, but in some tension with the redistributions of benefits and burdens which major transformations within states often entail. Where there is strong social or protest mobilization, project-affected people at least may speak as one; in other cases, different groups may want quite different things, and procedural requirements for engagement with affected peoples may not grapple fully with issues of representation.

In the absence of any wholesale reorientation of the approach to international organizations in international law, or revision of the immunity regime to allow wider use of litigation in domestic courts, internal forms of accountability may offer the most plausible means for affected peoples to intervene in organizational activity. How, then, might those working on the law of international organizations engage further with these mechanisms? We suggest three areas particularly ripe for further exploration.

The first is the way in which non-judicial accountability mechanisms are nestled within a particular institutional framework, and the limits and vulnerabilities this creates. Mechanisms aimed at assessing compliance with institutional policies may have limited power where international organizations decline to play any role at all, or where acute problems fall between the remits of several organizations or emerge from their interaction. Such mechanisms are also vulnerable to shifts in institutional frameworks themselves. Although, as seen with the multilateral development banks, some accountability mechanisms have become an accepted minimum, carried over in some form when new, rival organizations are established, they may be circumvented by the shifts in decision-making from formal organizations to networks of national authorities, bilateral arrangements, or private bodies which seem poised to accelerate in the near term.[60]

A second area for exploration is what might crudely be called the 'effects' of accountability mechanisms. The World Bank is among the most exhaustively researched international organizations, but the more one scrutinizes the record the more difficult it appears to draw definitive conclusions about how these mechanisms change outcomes in particular cases.[61] More systemically, mechanisms like the Panel may offer project-affected people avenues directly into Bank processes which would not otherwise be available – but there have also been suggestions that the sheer proliferation of accountability mechanisms which have built up in the Bank encapsulate the institution in its own processes, rather than making it more responsive to outside voices.[62] Panel members have, as Brown Weiss did, stressed their commitment to understanding the situation 'on the ground'. However, the Panel is often only one in an array of sites of contestation, and the social, political and economic dynamics of

[60] B. Kingsbury, 'Frontiers of Global Administrative Law in the 2020s', in J. Varuhas and S. Wilson Stark (eds.), *The Frontiers of Public Law* (Oxford: Hart, 2020), 41, 67–9.

[61] J. Fox and L. D. Brown (eds.), *The Struggle for Accountability: The World Bank, NGOs and Grassroots Movements* (Cambridge MA: MIT Press, 1998).

[62] E. Heldt, 'Lost in Internal Evaluation? Accountability and Insulation at the World Bank', (2018) 24 *Contemporary Politics* 568.

communities affected by international organizations may not be obvious. Grappling with the real effects of accountability mechanisms is going to require international lawyers (and others) to recognize the limits of knowledge generated from the centre of international organizations.

A third area for exploration is the tense but generative relationship between accountability and law. Much public international law scholarship on accountability, and the ILA Committee's efforts, involve repeated observations that accountability is not readily translatable into orthodox categories of legal obligations and rights; followed by efforts at definition and translation. Other currents of scholarship, like that on global administrative law, have seen in increasingly systematic operational policies and accountability mechanisms processes of rule-making, rule-application and rule-enforcement which could and should be assessed in legal terms.[63] Whether one finds this plausible depends on one's notion of law, and it may not be possible to judge the question in the abstract.[64] Nor are the normative implications of the judgement obvious. Too readily drawing the outcome of contingent institutional struggles under the mantle of law risks naturalizing or legitimating particular mechanisms. At the same time, maintaining a notion of law grounded deeply in a constitutionalist tradition may simply not capture the social realities of the transnational space, and the demand for redress in new sites. Privileging orthodox patterns of legal obligation and justiciability may mistake precision of threshold and (notional) possibility of adjudication for power to make change.

It may in the end be more revealing to focus on the diverse, and sometimes unpredictable, way in which claims for and against law-ness work in various agents's negotiations with mechanisms and institutions. The agents include ourselves as lawyers. Whether we embrace accountability as a conceptual category or hold it at a distance, we should keep open the question of how particular effects and institutional forms connect to 'accountability' itself. The identity of the proper accountees, and what is owed to them, are fundamental to the normativity of our current transnational governing structures, and what is conventionally accepted as a robust accountability mechanism cannot be assumed to produce 'accountability' in all its complex promise.

[63] D. Bradlow and A. Naude Fourie, 'The Operational Policies of the World Bank and the International Finance Cooperation', (2014) 10 *International Organizations Law Review* 3, 6–7; see also, e.g., Dann and Riegner, 'Environmental and Social Safeguards'.

[64] Kingsbury, 'Frontiers', 56.

4 Inclusion and Exclusion in International Organizations

B. S. Chimni

4.1 Introduction

The exclusion of an individual or entity from the membership of a club or body inevitably raises questions regarding the fairness of the criteria used to take the decision. It is no different when it comes to the exclusion of a state from the membership of an intergovernmental organization (IO) – either through denial of membership or suspension or expulsion from membership. The elementary reason is that membership brings with it certain benefits. These can include political recognition, the possibility of making claims on institutional resources, the opportunity to influence policies of other states in particular areas of international life and signalling and locking-in domestic policies.

The story of inclusion and exclusion in international organizations can be told in at least three different ways. First, it may assume the form of a straightforward description of the formal provisions relating to grant of membership in IOs or suspension and expulsion therefrom. This story is told in standard textbooks on 'international institutional law' that also offer a comparative overview of the general state of play across organizations.[1] The formal narrative offers few insights into what membership signifies in practice as 'international institutional law' remains uni-disciplinary and under-theorized.[2]

A second mode of telling the story of inclusion and exclusion is by assessing the validity of the reasons given for designing particular

[1] See, e.g., H. G. Schermers and N. Blokker, *International Institutional Law*, 6th ed. (Leiden: Martinus Nijhoff, 2018); Phillipe Sands and Pierre Klein, *Bowett's Law of International Institutions* (London: Sweet & Maxwell, 2009).

[2] J. Klabbers. 'The EJIL Foreword: The Transformation of International Organizations Law', (2015) 26 *European Journal of International Law* 9, 19.

institutional features of an international organization, including membership provisions. The effort of 'explaining major institutional features in a theoretically informed way' is of relatively recent origin.[3] But already there are distinct theoretical positions on the question why individual organizations possess particular institutional features.[4] The structural approaches 'understand institutional design as a response to the strategic, social, cultural, political, and/or economic environment in which institutions operate' and agentic approaches 'analyze institutional design as resulting from the incentives, interests, values, initiatives, and power of the actors that created the institutions'.[5] The realist approaches, on the other hand, view institutional features as being a function of the nature of the international order, that is, whether it is unipolar, bipolar or multipolar.[6] The critical approaches contend that institutional design reflects the hegemony of powerful states and social classes and stress the need to ascertain whether membership rules have in practice allowed effective participation of weak member states and social groups. Thus, for instance, critical approaches contend that the weighted voting systems in the International Monetary Fund (IMF) and World Bank deprive developing nations of an effective voice in shaping organizational policies, negatively impacting the poor, especially women.

A third way of telling the story of inclusion and exclusion from membership of international organizations is to evaluate the fairness of distributional outcomes, both at the level of states and social classes. In the academic literature functionalist and liberal approaches contend that organizations promote common good while critical approaches contest this view.[7] The first to question the sanguine view was the classical realist approach – followed

[3] B. Koremenos, Ch. Lipson and D. Snidal, 'The Rational Design of International Institutions', (2001) 55 *International Organization* 761, 764.

[4] E. Voeten, 'Making Sense of the Design of International Institutions', (2019) 22 *Annual Review of Political Science* 147. Voeten sums up (at 158): 'Each theoretical perspective sheds light on some important aspect of institutional design. For example, rational functionalism has an account of what institutions should look like to address social problems, distributive theories explain why institutions are so often skewed toward more powerful states, historical institutionalism explains institutional persistence, and structural process theories highlight that institutions are often designed similarly even if they exercise different functions'.

[5] *Ibid.*, 148.

[6] J. Mearsheimer, 'Bound to Fail: The Rise and Fall of the Liberal International Order', (2019) 43 *International Security* 7, 22.

[7] Functionalism 'is essentially a principal–agent theory, with a collective principal (the member states) assigning one or more specific tasks – functions – to their agent'. Klabbers, 'The Transformation', 10.

by its neo-realist version – which was sceptical of the possibility of organizations transcending entrenched power structures to subserve the interests of the international community. The critical approaches go further and contest the record of international organizations from class, gender, race and intersectional perspectives.[8] The question of unfair distributional outcomes has raised the larger issue of democratic deficit in international organizations as individuals and groups affected by their policies and practices do not have a voice in shaping them. In order to address this problem many international organizations allow some degree of civil society participation in their work: the UN has even adopted a set of rules on the subject.[9]

In reviewing the theme of inclusion and exclusion this chapter adopts an eclectic approach, for each mode of telling the story offers important insights. Albeit, in the final analysis its aim is to challenge the view that international organizations allow for effective participation of weak states and social classes and promote the global common good. The chapter proceeds as follows. Section 4.2 looks at the legal provisions in the constitutive acts of international organizations to illustrate rules and practices on questions of membership, including suspension, expulsion, and withdrawal. Section 4.3 reviews the theme of inclusion and exclusion from the perspective of weak states and subaltern social classes in relation to the goals of effective representation and fair outcomes. Section 4.4 contains some final reflections. The discussion in these respects is confined to formal intergovernmental organizations. The chapter does not take on board informal arrangements or nongovernmental organizations such as Basle Committee and the Internet Corporation for Assigned Names and Numbers (ICANN).

4.2 Formal Rules of Inclusion and Exclusion

4.2.1 Joining

It is routine to classify international organizations into general purpose organizations (e.g., the United Nations (UN)), specialized agencies (such as

[8] For thumbnail sketches of these approaches, see B. S. Chimni, 'History of International Organizations: 1945–2013', in J. Cogan, I. Hurd and I. Johnstone (eds.), *Oxford Handbook on International Organizations* (Oxford University Press, 2016) 113.

[9] See ECOSOC Res. 1996/31: Consultative relationship between the United Nations and non-governmental organizations.

the IMF and World Health Organization (WHO)) and regional organizations (like the African Union (AU) and European Union (EU)) which can in turn be general purpose or specialized. The formal rules of membership inevitably flow from the stated objectives and geographical scope of an international organization. The constitutive instruments not only have rules relating to membership but in most cases also rules relating to the suspension, expulsion and withdrawal from membership.

States that become members of an international organization at the time of its creation are called 'original members'. Other states become members through acceding to the treaty which establishes the organization. The decision to admit new members can either be taken by a plenary organ (e.g., in International Organization for Migration (IOM)) or by two or more organs (United Nations General Assembly (UNGA) and United Nations Security Council (UNSC) in the case of UN) or require a formal treaty of accession (as in the case of the World Trade Organization (WTO)).[10]

The question of membership can give rise to complex legal issues. One such question relates to the membership of successor states. The problem was encountered early on in the life of the UN with the decolonization of British India in August 1947. It saw the emergence of two successor states: India and Pakistan. Since India was an original member Pakistan applied afresh for membership and was so granted in September 1947.[11] This solution was accepted and recommended by the Sixth (Legal) Committee of the UN.[12] The committee however noted that where 'the legal personality of the member state had ceased to exist . . . all the emergent states would need to apply for UN membership'.[13] This was the solution adopted in the instance of Czechoslovakia in 1992 resulting in separate applications for membership by the Czech and Slovak Republics. But the question whether the personality of a state 'had ceased to exist' can give rise to conflicting views.[14] Thus, for example, it is not clear whether when a state secedes from an existing member state, the original state can be said to cease to exist. It is at least in part because of opposing views on the subject that the

[10] K. Magliveras, 'Membership in International Organizations', in J. Klabbers and Å. Wallendahl (eds.), *Research Handbook on the Law of International Organizations* (Cheltenham: Edward Elgar, 2011) 84, 90.

[11] D. Akande, 'The Partition of India and Pakistan: Lessons on UN Membership in the Event of a Break-Up of a State', 21 August 2017, www.ejiltalk.org/the-partition-of-india-and-pakistan-lessons-for-the-un-membership-in-the-event-of-emergence-of-new-states/.

[12] *Ibid.* [13] *Ibid.* [14] *Ibid.*

Republic of Kosovo is yet to become a UN member.[15] On the other hand, South Sudan, which seceded from Sudan, was admitted as member state of UN in 2011. But even non-member states like Kosovo can become a member of other international organizations, as it has become of the United Nations Educational, Scientific and Cultural Organization (UNESCO).

There may be political entities that are admitted as less than full members, including non-voting observers.[16] For example, in November 2012, in the absence of a unanimous recommendation of the UNSC, and despite the opposition of the United States and Israel, the UNGA 'in accordance with the relevant resolutions and practice' granted to Palestine a 'non-member observer State status'.[17] The other entity which has this status is the Holy See (Vatican). The non-member observer status allows Palestine to participate actively in multilateral negotiations and become a member of other international organizations.[18] Thus, it has become a member of the International Criminal Court (ICC) and UNESCO. The membership in ICC opened up the possibility of it investigating war crimes in Palestine, under belligerent occupation.[19]

The question of membership of an international organization is not merely a legal but very often a political question. This also became clear

[15] See generally L. West and A. Rexha, 'Integrating Kosovo into the UN System' (Group for Legal and Political Studies, May 2018) available at www.legalpoliticalstudies.org/wp-content/uploads/2018/05/GLPS-Policy-Report-INtegrating-Kosovo-into-the-UN-System.pdf.

[16] In the case of UNGA see UN Doc. A/DEC/49/426, 'Question of criteria for the granting of observer status in the General Assembly', 9 December 1994. It states as follows: 'Decided that the granting of observer status in the General Assembly should in the future be confined to States and to those intergovernmental organizations whose activities cover matters of interest to the Assembly'.

[17] UNGA, A/Res.67/19, 4 December 2012, Status of Palestine in the United Nations. There were 138 states in favour, 9 against and 41 abstained. The relevant UNSC document is S/2011/705, 11 November 2011, Report of the Committee on the Admission of New Members concerning the application of Palestine for admission to membership in the United Nations.

[18] J. Quigley, 'Palestine Statehood and International Law', Global Policy Essay, January 2013 available at www.globalpolicyjournal.com/sites/default/files/pdf/Quigley%20-%20Palestine%20statehood%20and%20international%20law%2001.13_0.pdf. See also J. Quigley, *The Statehood of Palestine: International Law in the Middle East Conflict* (Cambridge University Press, 2012).

[19] See 'Statement of ICC Prosecutor, Fatou Bensouda, respecting an investigation of the Situation in Palestine', available at www.icc-cpi.int/Pages/item.aspx?name=210303-prosecutor-statement-investigation-palestine.

early in the life of the UN when the question of admission of new members was 'deeply influenced by political considerations'.[20] As the Cold War set in, states on both sides of the East-West divide opposed the membership of nations that did not support their worldview. In the event only those nations came to be admitted to the membership of UN that were seen as 'neutral'. The politicization of the question of membership took place despite the Advisory Opinion of the International Court of Justice (ICJ) in the *Competence of the General Assembly for the Admission of a State to the United Nations* (1950).[21] In it the court observed that the conditions listed on membership in Article 4(1) of UN Charter were 'an exhaustive enumeration'.[22] These being that an applicant is a State, is peace-loving, accepts the obligations of the Charter and is able and willing to carry out these obligations. But the court went to add that 'all these conditions are subject to the judgment of the Organization',[23] an observation which created space for political considerations.[24] Eventually a political compromise between Western States and the Soviet Union in 1955 allowed sixteen new states to become members.[25] Thereafter, as the decolonization process accelerated, the membership of the UN rapidly expanded, touching 135 by 1973.[26] The political nature of the debate on membership was also reflected in the question whether mini- or microstates deserved full membership of the UN. Eventually, these states were granted membership with full vote. In the 1960s the difficult question arose of replacing the Nationalist Government of China by the Peoples Republic of China (PRC) as member. The ensuing debate once again reflected political considerations with Western nations seeking to keep out a communist state.[27] However, in 1971, the UNGA decided the PRC would replace the

[20] L. Goodrich, *The United Nations in a Changing World* (New York: Columbia University Press, 1974) 40.

[21] *Conditions of Admission of a State to the United Nations* (Advisory Opinion), [1948] ICJ Rep. 57.

[22] *Ibid.*, 62. [23] *Ibid.*

[24] The observation could be seen as an interpretation of Article 4(2) of the UN Charter which provides that 'the admission of any such state to membership in the United Nations will be effected by a decision of the General Assembly upon the recommendation of the Security Council'. This came to be discussed by the ICJ in *Competence of the General Assembly for the Admission of a State to the United Nations* (Advisory Opinion), [1950] ICJ Rep. 4.

[25] Goodrich, *United Nations*, 47. [26] *Ibid.*, 48.

[27] M. S. McDougal and R. Goodman, 'Chinese Participation in the United Nations: The Legal Imperative of a Negotiated Solution', (1966) 60 *American Journal of International Law* 671, 682.

representatives of Chiang Kai-shek 'as the only legitimate representatives of China to the United Nations'.[28]

The membership of regional organizations mostly follows a geographical logic. Thus, for instance, only a European state can become a member of the EU and the Council of Europe (COE) (as per Article 49 of Treaty on European Union, as amended at Lisbon and Article 3 of Statute of the Council of Europe). Likewise, only an 'independent American state' can become a member of the Organization of American States (Charter of the Organization of American States: Article 6); 'any African state' in the case of the AU (Constitutive Act of the African Union: Article 29(1)); 'any independent Arab state' in the case of the League of Arab States (Statute of the League of Arab States: Article 1); and a state located in the geographical region of Southeast Asia in the case of the Association of South East Asian Nations (ASEAN) (ASEAN Charter: Article 6).[29] There may however be different voting criteria for admitting new members. Thus, for example, in AU, membership is decided by a simple majority of the Member States but in ASEAN a decision is taken by consensus. There may also be other pre-conditions for securing membership such as, for example, the observance of the norm of democratic governance and human rights.[30] Indeed, 'the number of democratically committed IGOs' increased from eighteen in 1980 to fifty-two in 2010.[31] The existing members of international organizations may use the issue of membership to achieve extraneous objectives. Thus, for instance, the EU set the pre-condition of adhering to the EU *acquis* to become a member. It included becoming party to the 1951 UN Convention on the Status of Refugees.[32] In effect

[28] UNGA Res. 2758 (XXVI), 25 October 1971, Restoration of the Lawful Rights of the People's Republic of China at the United Nations.

[29] The geographical logic is not present in the case of cross-regional organizations such as Bay of Bengal Initiative for Multi-Sectoral Technical and Economic Cooperation (BIMSTEC).

[30] A. Duxbury, *The Participation of States in International Organizations: The Role of Human Rights and Democracy* (Cambridge University Press, 2011).

[31] I. von Borzyskowski and F. Vabulas, 'Credible Commitments? Explaining IGO Suspensions to Sanction Political Backsliding', (2019) 63 *International Studies Quarterly* 139, 141.

[32] See European Neighborhood Policy and Enlargment Negotiations: Conditions for Membership, at https://ec.europa.eu/neighbourhood-enlargement/policy/conditions-membership_en; R. Byrne, G. Noll and J. Vedsted-Hansen, 'Understanding Refugee Law in an Enlarged European Union', (2004) 15 *European Journal of International Law* 355, 356.

the idea was to shift the burden of keeping out or providing refuge to asylum seekers to new member states.

The membership of an international organization does not necessarily mean membership of each of its bodies or organs. Nor does it always translate into equal voting rights. A good example of both these limitations is the UNSC whose membership is limited to fifteen states, including five permanent members with veto rights. In instances where membership of a body is limited there is often a provision or convention for geographical representation;[33] the chosen or elected members are expected to represent the interests of states in the region.[34] In so far as different kinds of voting systems are concerned, these range from one state-one vote (as in UNGA) to weighted voting (as in the IMF and World Bank) to voting based on group classification (e.g., exporter and importer states) with weighted voting inside a group (an example of both being International Commodity Organizations).[35]

The membership of an international organization is almost always accompanied by an obligation to make a financial contribution towards meeting its expenses. In the case of the UN every member state has to contribute to its regular and peacekeeping budget. The contributions are assessed on the basis of 'the fundamental principle' that 'the expenses of the Organization shall be apportioned broadly according to capacity to pay'.[36] If the obligation is not met by a member state and arrears equal or exceed 'the amount of the contributions due from it for the preceding two full years' it can lead to the denial of voting rights (Article 19 of UN Charter). The 'capacity to pay' principle has meant that significant financial contributions to the UN are made by developed states leading to greater influence on its work. This is true of other organizations as well. For example, on 14 April 2020 the USA announced that pending a review of the WHO's management of the Covid-19 pandemic, it was halting its contribution to the organization. The move was seen as an attempt by the Trump administration to pressurize the organization into blaming China for the origin of the virus. In the case of some organizations like the United Nations High Commissioner for Refugees (UNHCR), which is

[33] Schermers and Blokker, *International Institutional Law*, 61. [34] *Ibid.*, 62.

[35] B. S. Chimni, *International Commodity Agreements: A Legal Study* (London: Croom Helm, 1986).

[36] UNGA, A/RES/73/271, 4 January 2019: Scale of assessments for the apportionment of the expenses of the United Nations.

funded principally through voluntary contributions, rich nations of the Global North have a marked influence on its policies and practices.

4.2.2 Suspension

The constituent instruments of most international organizations contain rules relating to the suspension of a member state. The purpose of suspending a member state is to prevent it from reneging on its commitments. Thus, for example, Article 5 of the UN Charter states that a member 'against which preventive or enforcement action has been taken by the Security Council may be suspended from the exercise of the rights and privileges of membership'. While no member state of the UN has been suspended, that is not the case with UN bodies. In 2011, on being permitted by a UNGA resolution, the Human Rights Council (HRC) suspended Libya from its membership.[37]

Despite being more tight-knit there are provisions on suspension in regional organizations as well. For example, Article 9 Organization of American States (OAS) Charter provides that 'a Member of the Organization whose democratically constituted government has been overthrown by force may be suspended'. Likewise, Article 30 of the constitutive act of the AU provides that any government 'which shall come to power through unconstitutional means shall not be allowed to participate in the activities of the Union'. In pursuance of this provision Egypt was suspended from membership in July 2013 when the military overthrew the duly elected government of President Mohammed Mursi.[38] The suspension was lifted in June 2014 on the election of President Abdel-Fattah El-Sisi.

There are different procedures and requirements in international organizations for the suspension of members. Under the UN Charter a member can be suspended 'by the General Assembly upon the recommendation of the Security Council'. In the case of OAS the decision is to be taken by 'an affirmative vote of two-thirds of the Member States'. In the Shanghai Cooperation Organization (SCO) membership can be suspended 'by

[37] UNGA A/RES/60/251, 3 April, 2006, Human Rights Council: it inter alia stated that by 'a two-thirds majority of the members present and voting' it 'may suspend the rights of membership in the Council of a member of the Council that commits gross and systematic violations of human rights' (para. 8).

[38] African Union, Communique, 5 July 2013, www.peaceau.org/uploads/psc-384-com-egypt-05-07-2013.pdf.

a decision of the Council of Heads of State adopted on the basis of a representation made by the Council of Ministers of Foreign Affairs' (Article 13 SCO Charter).

The act of suspension is not taken lightly in practice. It is reported that international organizations have suspended member states only ninety-five times between 1945 and 2019.[39] This number, as has been aptly observed, 'pales in comparison to the hundreds of state violations of organizations' mandates'.[40] Borzyskowski and Vabulas argue that 'geopolitics and institutional rules often insulate violators from IGO suspension'.[41] Thus, for instance, countries that are rich in oil resources are less likely to be suspended or if 'trade and security relations' of member states are going to be negatively impacted.[42] It is also the case that 'strict voting rules and membership size' reduce the possibilities of suspension.[43] The conclusion suggests itself that organizations 'are, at best, weak commitment devices'.[44] The move to suspend a member state is therefore 'highly strategic, with geopolitical factors playing a large role'.[45] In the instance of regional organizations for example it means that suspension is 'more likely when the violator has a hostile relationship with the regional power'. This was the case when the USA pressurized the OAS to suspend Cuba in 1962, a suspension which lasted until 2009.[46] In sum, while the act of suspension must have legal backing, the elements of interest, ideology and power play an important role.

When the suspension of a member state is not possible other ways may be found to make it comply with its commitments. At least three deserve mention: not allowing a member state to participate in the work of the organization; taking disputes to judicial organs; and economic sanctions. An example of the first method is when in December 1974 the UNGA strongly condemned the South African regime 'for its persistent and flagrant violations of principles contained in the Charter of the United

[39] Borzyskowski and Vabulas, 'Credible Commitments', 139. [40] *Ibid.*

[41] To reach this conclusion they use data on suspensions in relation to reneging on democratic commitments between 1980 to 2010.

[42] *Ibid.*, 142. [43] *Ibid.*

[44] *Ibid.*, 140. Thus, for instance, despite back-tracking on their democratic commitments, Hungary and Poland have not lost their membership or voting rights in EU.

[45] *Ibid.*, 143.

[46] Final Act, 8th Meeting of Consultation of Ministers of Foreign Affairs Serving as Organ of Consultation in Application of the Inter-American Treaty of Reciprocal Assistance, Punta Del Este, Uruguay, January 22–31, 1962 (OEA/Ser.C/II.8, 1962) at pp.12–14.

Nations and its continued defiance of the resolutions of the General Assembly and Security Council' and recommended that 'it be totally excluded from participation in all international organizations and conferences under the auspices of the United Nations'.[47]

An international organization may also turn to judicial organs to bring pressure on a member state. For example, the European Commission (EC) recently took Hungary, Poland and Czech Republic to the Court of Justice of the EU (CJEU) for criminalizing activities in support of asylum seekers and non-provision of food in transit zones. In April 2020, the CJEU held that these states had failed to fulfil their obligations under EU law towards asylum seekers.[48]

Finally, there are economic sanctions which 'involve the purposive threat or actual granting or withholding of economic indulgences, opportunities and benefits by one actor or group of actors in order to induce another actor or group of actors to change a policy'.[49] In the instance of the UN, articles 39–41 of Chapter VII of the Charter cover the application of economic sanctions. These provide that if a threat to peace or breach of peace is established under article 39, the UNSC can invoke article 41 to impose economic sanctions against a member State. Article 25 of the Charter makes such a decision binding on all member states. The sanctions are however expected to be in conformity with relevant international law standards. But in practice Reisman and Stevick have noted 'the Security Council's almost complete failure to consider international law standards, particularly the criteria of proportionality and discrimination, in defining and enforcing sanctions regimes'.[50] Most recently, in the wake of the Covid-19 pandemic, the UN Special Rapporteur on the Right to Food called for the lifting of 'crippling economic sanctions' against countries such as Syria, Venezuela, Iran, Cuba and Zimbabwe.[51] It has therefore been rightly

[47] UNGA Res. 3324 (XXIX) E, 16 December 1974: The Situation in South Africa.

[48] By refusing to comply with the temporary mechanism for the relocation of applicants for international protection, Poland, Hungary and the Czech Republic have failed to fulfil their obligations under European Union law. See Case C-715/17, *Commission* v. *Poland and Others*, ECLI:EU:C:2020:257.

[49] W. M. Reisman and D. Stevick, 'The Applicability of International Law Standards to United Nations Economic Sanctions Programmes', (1998) 9 *European Journal of International Law* 86, 87.

[50] *Ibid.*, 126.

[51] 'COVID-19: Economic Sanctions Should be Lifted to Prevent Hunger Crises – UN Expert', available at www.ohchr.org/EN/NewsEvents/Pages/DisplayNews.aspx?NewsID=25761&LangID=E.

urged that 'the egregious and potentially long-term social, economic and environmental consequences of uses of economic strategies must be acknowledged'.[52]

4.2.3 Expulsion from Membership

The option of expelling a member state from an international organization has been described as a 'clumsy weapon'.[53] Yet constituent instruments often provide for such an eventuality. The provisions on expulsion can be traced back to the Covenant of the League of Nations whose article 16(4) stated that any member 'which has violated any covenant of the League may be declared to be no longer a Member of the League by a vote of the Council concurred in by the Representatives of all the other Members of the League represented there on'. The principal purpose of this provision 'was to prevent a covenant-breaking member of the League from blocking any action by the League which required a unanimous vote of the Council or Assembly'.[54] In practice the selective expulsion of USSR in 1939 showed that politics informed any such move; the measure of expulsion was not pursued against Italy and Germany. In evaluating practice under the League Louis Sohn aptly observed that 'expulsion seems to be more a weapon of the politician than the statesman'.[55] Yet Article 6 of the UN Charter provides for expulsion: 'A Member of the United Nations which has persistently violated the Principles contained in the present Charter may be expelled from the Organization by the General Assembly upon the recommendation of the Security Council'.

In assessing the need for including a provision on expulsion, and actual use, a distinction may be made between different kinds of international organizations. Those with a principal focus on promoting democracy, human rights and the rule of law cannot hesitate to use the sanction of expulsion for it could otherwise do great harm to their effectiveness and legitimacy.[56] In fact, according to Dzehtsiarou and Coffey, past practice

[52] Reisman and Stevick, 'Applicability', 141.

[53] C. W. Jenks, 'Due Process of Law in International Organizations', (1965) 19 *International Organization* 163, 166.

[54] L. B. Sohn, 'Expulsion or Forced Withdrawal from an International Organization', (1964) 77 *Harvard Law Review* 1381, 1383.

[55] *Ibid.*, 1424.

[56] K. Dzehtsiarou and D. Coffey, 'Suspension and Expulsion of Members of the Council of Europe: Difficult Decision in Troubled Times', (2019) 68 *International and Comparative Law Quarterly* 443.

shows that among the principal reasons that result in the expulsion (or suspension) of a member state is 'a change of political regime from democratic to anti-democratic'.[57] The other reasons are an act of armed aggression, human rights violations and lack of cooperation.[58] In reality the tool of expulsion is used only in the most extreme circumstances as among other things it prevents future influence over the expelled state.

In case there is no provision for expulsion in the constituent instrument, there is said to be an 'implied right to expel'.[59] It is argued that 'it is a mistake – legally and otherwise – to conclude that the *default rule* for IOs and treaties should be a flat prohibition on expulsion'.[60] There is however little doubt that 'the legitimacy of expulsion is far greater where there is an explicit power to expel'.[61] This is evidenced by the fact that the practice on expulsion is 'surrounded by questions of legality'.[62]

4.2.4 Withdrawal

A member state may however voluntarily leave an organization. In fact, in recent years there has been a 'wave of dissatisfaction' leading to withdrawals from international organizations.[63] A most prominent example is the UK leaving the EU; it was dissatisfied with both symbolic and material outcomes. As a result of its departure complex legal, social, economic and political issues have arisen which continue to be debated.[64]

The constituent instruments of international organizations often provide for withdrawal by a member state. Thus, for example, Article 50(1) of the Treaty of EU states: 'Any Member State may decide to withdraw from the Union in accordance with its own constitutional requirements'. An important exception is the UN Charter which does not contain a provision on withdrawal. In instances where there is no provision for withdrawal reference is made to the 1969 Vienna Convention on Law of Treaties, which

[57] *Ibid.*, 449. [58] *Ibid.* [59] *Ibid.*, 448.

[60] J. Blocher, M. Gulati and L. Helfer, 'Can Greece be Expelled from the Eurozone? Toward a Default Rule on Expulsion from International Organizations', in F. Allen *et al.* (eds.), *Filling the Gaps in Governance: The Case of Europe* (Florence: EUI, 2016) 127, 129 (emphasis in original – BSC).

[61] Dzehtsiarou and Coffey, 'Suspension and Expulsion', 448.

[62] Magliveras, 'Membership', 96.

[63] C. Brölmann, R. Collins and R. Wessel, 'Exiting International Organizations: A Brief Introduction', (2018) 15 *International Organizations Law Review* 243, 254.

[64] *Ibid.*, 246.

sets out in Article 54 the general conditions that regulate an act of withdrawal. The provision states that withdrawal must take place 'in conformity with the provisions of the treaty' or 'at any time by consent of all the parties after consultation with the other contracting States'. As far as the UN is concerned the only time the issue of withdrawal came up was when Indonesia announced in 1965 its withdrawal from membership, but a change of regime ensured that it did not pursue this decision.

Where there is a provision for withdrawal, a notice period is often required for the decision of a member state to become effective. For example, Article XV of the Agreement Establishing the WTO prescribes a six-month written notice, Article 31 of the constitutive instrument of AU requires one-year notice, and Article 143 of OAS charter mandates two-years written notification. The reasons for insisting on a notice period include providing time for reflection and reconsideration, identifying the consequences that follow from withdrawal, and considering ways of resetting the future relationship of the withdrawing member state with the organization.[65] During the notice period the state in question is expected to continue to discharge its obligations.

An important reason why states seek to withdraw from membership of an organization is to compel it to change its orientation, policies or practices.[66] The US has used this strategy by withdrawing from membership of the International Labour Organization (ILO) (in 1977, rejoined in 1980), UNESCO (in 1985, rejoined in 2003), the United Nations Industrial Development Organization (UNIDO) (1995), the United Nations Children's Fund (UNICEF) (2017) and the WHO (2020, rejoined in the same year). The US has also threatened to walk out of the WTO. In so far as developing nations are concerned Bolivia (2007), Ecuador (2009) and Venezuela (2012) have withdrawn from the International Centre for the Settlement of Investment Disputes (ICSID) as they were dissatisfied with both the dispute settlement process and outcomes. Many developing nations have also threatened to withdraw from the ICC for targeting African leaders. Burundi (2017) and Philippines (2019) have already done so. It has been contended by critics that withdrawal from international adjudication amounts to

[65] Magliveras, 'Membership', 100–1.

[66] I. von Borzyskowski and F. Vabulas, 'Hello, Goodbye: When Do States Withdraw from International Organizations?', (2019) 14 *Review of International Organizations* 335.

undermining international rule of law.[67] This is true in so far as it goes. But when international adjudication is used to prosecute and punish individuals and leaders belonging only to some regions, continued membership in the name of an abstract commitment to international rule of law becomes difficult to sustain.

4.3 Effective Participation and Fair Outcomes

The theme of inclusion and exclusion in international organizations thus goes beyond questions of formal membership to matters relating to effective participation and fair outcomes. An assessment in these respects can be undertaken at three levels. The first level may involve a general evaluation of the role of international organizations in the global order, the second a review of the functioning and impact of an individual organization (such as the WTO) or body (such as the UNSC) and the third can comprise assessment from the perspective of social classes, a particular state or group of states.

These assessments may be undertaken using different theoretical lenses that include liberal, functionalist, social constructivist, feminist, Marxist, neo-Gramscian and third-world approaches. Broadly speaking, mainstream liberal and functionalist approaches are positive in their assessment of the design and role of international organizations in the global order. On the other hand, critical approaches are skeptical of the view that international organizations have adopted just institutional designs or promote the global common good. For instance the neo-Gramscian scholar Robert Cox contends that international organizations 'embody the rules which facilitate the expansion of hegemonic world orders' and 'ideologically legitimate ... structures that provide the conditions for capitalism'.[68] In a similar vein the Marxist political theorist Nicos Poulantzas observed that international organizations 'express and crystallize class powers' to promote dominant global class interests.[69] It is implicit in these

[67] C. McLachlan, 'The Assault on International Adjudication and the Limits of Withdrawal', (2019) 68 *International and Comparative Law Quarterly* 499.

[68] R. W. Cox, 'Gramsci, Hegemony, and International Relations: An Essay in Method', in S. Gill (ed.), *Gramsci, Historical Materialism and International Relations* (Cambridge University Press, 1993) 62; and 'Interview with Robert W. Cox', (2003) 1 *Globalisation, Societies and Education* 22.

[69] N. Poulantzas, *Classes in Contemporary Capitalism* (London: Verso, 1978) 70.

pronouncements that institutional designs are co-opted to serve parochial ends. In what follows the critical standpoint is elaborated in relation to the goals of effective participation and fair distributive outcomes.

4.3.1 Effective Participation

The question of effective participation relates among other things to access to membership of different bodies of an organization and the nature of the decision-making process. Thus, for example, the fact that only fifteen states are members of UNSC, among which five are veto-wielding permanent members, constrains the ability of both non-permanent members and non-members to effectively influence its policies and decisions. Likewise, the weighted voting system in international financial institutions has been of concern to developing nations. In 1974, at the initiative of developing nations the UNGA adopted the Charter of Economic Rights and Duties (CERDS) whose Article 10 stated that they should 'have the right to participate fully and effectively in the international decision-making process in the solution of world economic, financial and monetary problems'.[70]

Even when an international organization adopts a one nation-one vote rule, the relative ability of member states to influence decisions varies considerably. Thus, for example, the Republic of Nauru does not wield the same power as the USA in the UNGA. But this may be an acceptable situation for small or micro states because international organizations, in particular the UN, are perceived to have a protective function. These are 'considered as an instrument that guarantees independence against external aggression'.[71] However, other states may feel the need to address the power differentials by calling for the active promotion of values of participation and democratic decision-making.[72] Weak states also attempt to

[70] The text of CERDS is available at www.un.org/ga/search/view_doc.asp?symbol=a/res/3281(XXIX).

[71] Schermers and Blokker, *International Institutional Law*, 65.

[72] These values are for instance fostered by the tenets of global administrative law (GAL) which has been defined 'as comprising the mechanisms, principles, practices, and supporting social understandings that promote or otherwise affect the accountability of global administrative bodies, in particular by ensuring they meet adequate standards of transparency, participation, reasoned decision, and legality, and by providing effective review of the rules and decisions they make'. B. Kingsbury, N. Krisch and R. Stewart, 'The Emergence of Global Administrative Law', (2005) 68 *Law and Contemporary Problems* 15, 17.

ensure effective participation in decision-making through forming coalitions of states that can act as an effective counterweight to power. But there remain many obstacles to realizing the goal of effective participation. For instance, many poor nations do not even have the resources to attend and participate in the work of international organizations, necessitating the funding of their delegations. For example, in the period 2004 and 2015, 'to boost the effectiveness of their participation' in the international standard development process undertaken in the Codex Alimentarius Commission, a Food and Agriculture Organization (FAO)/WHO Project along with the Fund for Enhanced Participation in Codex (Codex Trust Fund), supported over 2300 participants from developing and transition economy countries and trained over 1200 individuals.[73]

An assessment of effective participation in international organizations can also be made from class, gender and race standpoints. Thus, for instance, feminist scholarship points to the patriarchal character of international organizations by noting, among other things, 'the absence of women at senior levels in international institutions'.[74] It is contended that 'the invisibility of women at the decision-making levels has affected the treatment not only of "women's" issues, but also the way all international concerns are understood'.[75] The same point can be made from a class perspective as international organizations do not provide for active representation of the working classes. The sole exception is the ILO. Article 3 of its constitution requires member states to send 'tripartite delegations of representatives to meetings of the International Labour Conference. The delegation must include two Government delegates, as well as one representative each of the employers and workers in the country. The government, employer and worker delegates act in full independence of one another and, in particular, vote individually'.[76] The possibility of the ILO spirit being extended, in one form or another, to other international organizations has not been sufficiently explored.

[73] See www.fao.org/fao-who-codexalimentarius/about-codex/faowho-codex-trust-fund/en/.

[74] H. Charlesworth and Ch. Chinkin, *The Boundaries of International Law: A Feminist Analysis* (Manchester: Manchester University Press, 2000) 171.

[75] *Ibid.*

[76] International Labour Organization, Constitution, article 3. ILO, Membership in the International Labour Organization: Information Guide, available at www.ilo.org/wcmsp5/groups/public/–dgreports/–jur/documents/genericdocument/wcms_441858.pdf.

The rationale for and value of effective participation of all stakeholders is in the final analysis rooted in the principles of all affected member nations (AAMN) and all affected persons (AAP). The former flows from the principle of sovereign equality of states and the latter from the simple idea that 'democracy requires that people significantly affected by a decision should be able to take part in reaching that decision'.[77] Historically speaking, AAP was at first articulated by anti-colonial movements.[78] For instance, the Indian delegates to the League of Nations lamented that despite India being an original member they could not freely articulate the concerns of the Indian people.[79] In the contemporary world AAP seeks to address the problem of democratic deficit in international organizations resulting in the interests of women, working classes, minorities and indigenous peoples being overlooked in the articulation of national interest of member states.

The gap can possibly be filled by making formal provision for the participation of non-governmental organizations (NGOs) representing different stakeholders. But even where there is such a provision, NGOs of the Global South may not have the necessary human and financial resources to effectively represent the interests of excluded constituencies. In instances where such support is accepted from institutions of Global North there is the danger of compromising the agenda. NGOs are also not familiar with the vocabulary in which views have to be expressed in official forums. But what is most worrisome is the growing influence of corporate foundations on the functioning of international organizations. It compelled some well-known NGOs to issue a statement in 2012 expressing 'strong concerns about the growing influence of major corporations and business lobby groups within the UN' and called for 'ending corporate capture of the United Nations'. It drew attention

[77] M. Koenig-Archibugi, 'How to Diagnose Democratic Deficits in Global Politics: The Use of the "All Affected Principle"', LSE Research Online, 2, available at http://eprints.lse.ac.uk/68641/.

[78] B. S. Chimni, 'The Limits of the All Affected Principle: Attending to Deep Structures', (2018) 3 *Third World Thematics: A TWQ Journal* 807; Jochen von Bernstorff, 'New Responses to the Legitimacy Crisis of International Institutions: The Role of 'Civil Society' and the Rise of the Principle of Participation of 'The Most Affected' in International Institutional Law' (2021) XX *EJIL* (2021), 1–33.

[79] Albeit at times India's representatives 'pursued a line of action independent of the wishes of the His Majesty's Government'. L. Sundaram, 'The International Status of India', (1931) 17 *Transactions of the Grotius Society* 35, 44.

to the fact that 'Corporate lobbying within UN negotiations has managed to block effective solutions for problems related to climate change, food production, the violation of human rights, water supply, health issues, poverty and deforestation'.[80] In order to address the concern of corporate lobbying, WHO for instance adopted in 2016 a 'Framework of engagement with non-State actors'. It recognizes the risks involved in dealing with non-state actors including 'conflicts of interest' and 'undue or improper influence ... especially in, but not limited to, policies, norms and standard setting'.[81] The partnership with the corporate world also has implications for other organizations such as UNICEF, UN Women and the ILO.[82]

4.3.2 Distributive Outcomes

It has been observed that the 'genius' of the mainstream functionalist approach to international organizations is that it portrays them 'as neutral and a-political, solely functional entities'.[83] But such a view disregards the fact that in the opinion of early functionalists 'both colonial governance and international organizations were seen as vehicles for paternalistic progress'.[84] By advancing a narrative of progress, what functionalists were doing was to sustain and legitimize colonialism.[85] That scenario has not substantially changed even today, the object of legitimization now being neo-colonialism.

In discussing unfair distributive outcomes, the focus of critical approaches is usually on international economic organizations (IEOs),

[80] In 2012, Friends of the Earth International, Corporate Europe Observatory, La Via Campesina, JubileeSouth/Americas, Peace and Justice in Latin America/SERPAJ-AL, Polaris Institute, The Council of Canadians, The Transnational Institute, Third World Network, World March of Women: 'Ending Corporate Capture of the United Nations: Joint Civil Society Statement', available at www.foei.org/wp-content/uploads/2012/06/Statement-on-UN-Corporate-Capture-EN.pdf. See also C. Murphy, 'Private Sector', in T. Weiss and S. Daws (eds.), *Oxford Handbook on the United Nations* (Oxford University Press, 2007) 264.

[81] Sixty-Ninth World Health Assembly, WHA 69.10, 28 May, 2016 Framework of engagement with non-State actors.

[82] C. Gregoratti, 'UN-Business Partnerships', in T. Weiss and R. Wilkinson (eds.), *International Organization and Global Governance* (Abingdon: Routledge, 2013) 309.

[83] Klabbers, 'The Transformation', 18. [84] *Ibid.*, 46.

[85] J. Tallberg and M. Zürn, 'The Legitimacy and Legitimation of International Organizations: Introduction and Framework', (2019) 14 *Review of International Organizations* 581.

whose mandate and functioning have meant a serious loss of policy space for weak nations.[86] Whether it is the WTO, IMF or World Bank, the respective regimes constrain Global South nations from adopting certain policies, laws and regulations that promote the welfare of their peoples.[87] This can result in troubling material effects. Thus, for instance, poor nations are today being deprived access to Covid-19 vaccines at least in part because of the prevailing intellectual property rights (IPR) regime in the WTO which prevents countries like India from ratcheting up the production of, and exporting, vaccines.[88]

In order to enhance their legitimacy IEOs often respond to criticisms by member states and/or civil society organizations by advancing an alternative and more acceptable narrative of their role. For instance, the first official history of the World Bank, written a quarter of a century after its creation, 'mentioned poverty only three times in its 900 pages'.[89] Today, in face of criticism that its loans and policies negatively impact the poor, the Bank has declared that 'to end extreme poverty' is one of the two principal goals. The other is to 'create sustainable economic growth', a response to a critique of its policies by environmental groups.[90] Even the IMF, whose principal objective is to advance loans to overcome a temporary balance of payments problem, contends that its goal is to 'reduce poverty around the world'.

[86] B. S. Chimni, 'International Institutions Today: An Imperial Global State in the Making', (2004) 15 *European Journal of International Law* 1.

[87] *Ibid.*

[88] India and South Africa therefore sought a waiver on the application of relevant parts of the TRIPS text to the production and distribution of the vaccine. See WTO, 2 October 2020, 'Waiver from Certain Provisions of the TRIPS Agreement for the Prevention, Containment and Treatment of Covid-19: Communication from India and South Africa', available at https://docs.wto.org/dol2fe/Pages/SS/directdoc.aspx?filename=q:/IP/C/W669.pdf&Open=True. Later a revised proposal was submitted. See WTO, Council for Trade Related Intellectual Property Rights, IP/C/W/669/Rev.1, 25 May, 2021: Waiver from Certain Provisions of the TRIPS Agreement for the Prevention, Containment and Treatment of Covid-19. Revised Decision Text, available at https://docs.wto.org/dol2fe/Pages/SS/directdoc.aspx?filename=q:/IP/C/W669R1.pdf&Open=True The waiver is yet to be granted. See in this context A. Zaitchik, 'How Bill Gates Impeded Global Access to Covid Vaccines', *The New Republic*, 12 April 2021 available at https://newrepublic.com/article/162000/bill-gates-impeded-global-access-covid-vaccines?utm_medium=Social&utm_campaign=EB_TNR&utm_source=Twitter#Echobox=1618203574.

[89] C. Murphy, *The United Nations Development Programme: A Better Way* (Cambridge University Press, 2006) 17.

[90] See World Bank, at www.worldbank.org/en/what-we-do.

In judging distributive outcomes much is often made of the voluntary membership of IOs. Such a view disregards the phenomenon of structural coercion which ensures that the costs of non-membership are high. Thus, for example, even if the economy of a developing nation is harmed by IMF conditionalities it cannot afford to lose access to loans in times of emergency. This can result in bizarre situations. For instance, the IMF has allocated $1 trillion to aid nations in their battle against the Covid-19 pandemic.[91] This move would certainly help provide needed resources to low and middle income countries to help inter alia build the necessary public health infrastructure. But in the bargain these nations are compelled to accept the conditionalities prescribed by IMF.[92] It is however precisely these policy prescriptions that in the past undermined public health infrastructure by promoting the privatization of health facilities.

At the level of marginalized groups, to continue with the Covid-19 example, the privatization of healthcare has had grave implications for the poorer sections of the population who cannot afford its costs. Likewise, the WTO regime has been charged with sustaining unfair trade with harmful consequences for particular groups such as women.[93] This fact has been acknowledged by member states through adopting in 2017 a declaration on 'Trade and Women's Economic Empowerment'.[94] In this light a troubling aspect of the functioning of international organizations is that they cannot be held accountable for their policies. The rules of responsibility drafted by the International Law Commission do not cover situations of unjust distributive outcomes.[95]

[91] For details see 'The IMF's Response to COVID-19', at www.imf.org/en/About/FAQ/imf-response-to-covid-19.

[92] 'Softening the Blow of the Pandemic: Will the International Monetary Fund and World Bank Make Things Worse?', *Lancet Global Health*, 9 April 2020; 'IMF Conditionality after the COVID-19 Pandemic', 22 March 2021, available at https://ihsmarkit.com/research-analysis/imf-conditionality-after-the-covid19-pandemic.html.

[93] UNCTAD, Gender and Trade, https://unctad.org/en/Pages/DITC/Gender-and-Trade.aspx.

[94] Joint Declaration on Trade and Women's Economic Empowerment on the Occasion of the WTO Ministerial Conference in Buenos Aires in December 2017, available at www.wto.org/english/thewto_e/minist_e/mc11_e/genderdeclarationmc11_e.pdf.

[95] See ILC Draft Articles on the Responsibility of International Organizations, available at https://legal.un.org/ilc/texts/instruments/english/draft_articles/9_11_2011.pdf.

4.4 Conclusion

In reviewing the theme of 'inclusion and exclusion' a description of the formal provisions on membership in international organizations helps identify, explain and understand the criteria on the basis of which it is granted or taken away. But deeper insights on the subject are offered by approaches that appraise the requirements of membership amidst the reality of inequalities of power and resources among states. These inequalities not only impact the design of international organizations but also distributive outcomes. Put differently, a verdict on the historical record of international organizations on the question of 'inclusion and exclusion' depends on the theoretical lens used for evaluation. Generally speaking, the mainstream functionalist and liberal approaches view international organizations as adopting rational designs and promoting the global common good. On the other hand, the critical approaches contend that membership rules, and their working in practice, often prevent effective participation by weak nations and sustain and legitimize an unequal global order. In this view the big picture has not substantially changed from the time of the League of Nations which supported the colonial order through adopting the Mandate system. While the UN has played a positive role in the decolonization process, other international organizations, including many UN specialized agencies, have come to facilitate a neo-colonial world order. It has resulted in troubling distributive outcomes for weak nations, in particular its poor and marginalized sections, whether assessed in class, gender or race terms. In the event it may be argued that weak nations and social classes should celebrate the recent rise in the forces of nationalism and populism as it has meant that multilateralism is in retreat. But in advancing this contention it is overlooked that only those aspects of the functioning of international organizations are being undermined that do not suit the interests of powerful social classes and nations. It means that weak nations and social groups may be further marginalized by ongoing changes in international organizations both in terms of the goals of effective participation and just distributional outcomes.

5 A Legal Framework on Internal Matters
Please Mind the Gap

Laurence Boisson de Chazournes and Vassilis Pergantis

5.1 Introduction

This chapter deals with the law on the internal matters of international organizations, and more particularly, with the relations between organs of an international organization. Issues include, among others, the power of self-regulation, financial relations between organs of an organization, the creation of subsidiary organs and the applicable legal rules thereto, as well as analysis of various procedures that require the collaboration between different organs of the same organization.[1] The chapter will not deal with the legal relations between an international organization and its civil servants. It will equally steer clear of the legal relationships between organizations and their member states, third parties or other international organizations.

Amid a burgeoning academic scholarship on international institutional law, the academic field pertaining to the legal relations between an international organization's organs has received comparatively rather scant attention. There are multiple plausible reasons for the paucity of analysis. First of all, there is no doubt that each organization has its own, unique structure, rendering the drafting of a uniform, comprehensive model on internal relations a daunting task.[2] Yet, this is a problem underpinning the whole of international institutional law. Besides, despite the uniqueness of each institutional model, a constant process of cross-fertilization of institutional practices can lead to

[1] P. Klein, 'International Organizations or Institutions, Internal Law and Rules', in *Max Planck Encyclopedia of Public International Law* (online), para. 8.

[2] P. Reuter, 'Principes de droit international public', (1961-II) 103 *Recueil des Cours* 425, 524–6.

the emergence of common themes in the legal relations between organs of an international organization.[3]

A second impediment for the development of this field of study relates to the binary legal nature of the rules regulating internal matters. It is a widely shared view that each international organization creates its own legal order, within which the internal matters of the organization are regulated.[4] Relevant rules include, first and foremost, the constitutive treaty, but also derivative or secondary law, such as decisions and resolutions of the organs of the organization as well as their established practices.[5] The relationship of an organization's legal order with the international legal order and the nature of the former's rules remain ambivalent. For instance, in the commentary to the *Articles on the Responsibility of International Organizations*, it is stipulated that there is a certain controversy over whether the internal law of an international organization is part of international law, thus giving rise in case of breach to an internationally wrongful act, or not, at which point its violation only concerns the internal legal order of the relevant organization.[6] Thus, there is an interplay between autonomy from, and interaction with, the international legal order that it is not easy to grasp. The preponderant view is, however, that internal matters are also subject to some norms of general international law, consisting of, at least, *jus cogens* norms, and to other international law rules prescribed through provisions in the constitutive instruments or in international agreements to which IOs are parties.[7] Consequently, regulation of the internal matters of an international organization must be in conformity with the relevant rules of its internal legal order, as well as with some rules of the international legal order.[8]

[3] E. Lauterpacht, 'The Development of the Law of International Organization by the Decisions of International Tribunals', (1976-IV) 152 *Recueil des Cours* 377, 396.

[4] *Effect of Awards of Compensation Made by the UN Administrative Tribunal* (Advisory Opinion), [1954] ICJ Rep. 47, 55–6.

[5] Article 2(1)(j) Vienna Convention on the Law of Treaties between States and International Organizations or between International Organizations.

[6] (2011) *Yearbook of the International Law Commission*, vol. II (Part Two), 39, 63 (para. 5 of the commentary to Article 10).

[7] Case T-315/01, *Kadi* v. *Council and Commission*, ECLI:EU:T:2005:332, para. 277; *Interpretation of the Agreement of 25 March 1951 between the WHO and Egypt* (Advisory Opinion), [1980] ICJ Rep. 73, para. 37.

[8] Ph. Cahier, 'L'ordre juridique interne des organisations internationales', in R.-J. Dupuy (ed.), *Manuel sur les organisations internationales* (Dordrecht: Martinus Nijhoff, 1998) 377, 378ff.

This brings us to the third reason for the limited scholarly focus on internal matters, namely, the lack of a clear, overarching, theory or logic that would shape the juridical regime on the relations between organs of an international organization. The preponderant functionalist logic has been deemed mainly inadequate for the construction of such a comprehensive legal regime, as functionalism concerns primarily the relationships between international organizations and their member states and cannot capture the internal dynamics of an organization.[9] Yet, such a view risks throwing the baby out with the bathwater: recourse to an organ's functions is necessary both in order to explain models of hierarchy or institutional balance between organs, as well as limit the remit of any power of a principal organ to create subsidiary ones.[10]

Functionalism, however, cannot explain and regulate all aspects of internal relations. References to checks and balances within an international organization or to the necessity of judicial control of an organ's activities bring to the fore a constitutionalist paradigm, in its procedural rather than normative limb.[11] The debate about the constitutionalization of the United Nations (UN) legal order, as well as similar arguments concerning the World Trade Organization (WTO), and even more pertinently, the European Union (EU), highlight the attraction of constitutional theory precepts for international institutional law, especially regarding control and accountability over organs' activities. International organizations are not, however, states and any effort to transpose lock, stock and barrel the domestic standards of separation of powers or constitutionality review when describing the relations between organs of an international organization is bound to fail; the need for flexibility and the recognition of the political nature of those organs' activities defy a strict constitutionalist rationale.[12]

[9] J. Klabbers, 'The EJIL Foreword: The Transformation of International Organizations Law', (2015) 26 *European Journal of International Law* 9, 11, 23.

[10] M. Virally, 'La notion de fonction dans la théorie de l'organisation internationale', in *Le droit international en devenir: essais écrits au fil des ans* (Paris: PUF, 1990) 271, 282–3.

[11] J. Dunoff and J. Trachtman (eds.), *Ruling the World? Constitutionalism, International Law and Global Governance* (Cambridge University Press, 2009); J. Klabbers, A. Peters and G. Ulfstein, *The Constitutionalization of International Law* (Oxford University Press, 2009).

[12] J. Klabbers, 'Contending Approaches to International Organizations: Between Functionalism and Constitutionalism', in J. Klabbers and Å. Wallendahl (eds.), *Research Handbook on the Law of International Organizations* (Cheltenham: Edward Elgar, 2011) 3, 18–9.

In reality, both functionalism and constitutionalism instil their logic in attempting to explain and regulate the relations between the organs of international organizations. Equally important, however, is to recognize that such relationships are inescapably shaped by a pragmatic streak that aims at increased efficiency in the conduct of organizational activities.[13] In the following lines, we will examine the law on internal matters by distinguishing relations between organs at the same level of institutional governance, that is, enjoying the same 'institutional rank' within an organization, from relations between organs at different levels of 'institutional rank'.

5.2 Relations between Organs at the Same Level of Institutional Governance

The expression 'organs at the same level of institutional governance' attempts to translate both the way an organ is created and its relation *vis-à-vis* other organs of the same organization. In other words, organs pertaining to this category are usually the principal or regular organs of an international organization, namely, organs established directly by the organization's constituent instrument and considered its main organs.[14] In this category must be included some further organs, which, though not established on the basis of the constitutive treaty, enjoy such characteristics or establish relations with the principal organs of such a nature as to place them at the same institutional rank as the above organs. This category primarily concerns judicial bodies set up in the framework of an international organization, which are in many respects independent from the principal organs that establish them, as the ICJ observed in the *Effect of Awards* advisory opinion with regard to the United Nations Administrative Tribunal (UNAT) *vis-à-vis* the UN General Assembly.[15] The distinction between organs at the same or different levels of institutional governance

[13] For such an approach at the inter-organizational level, see L. Boisson de Chazournes, *Interactions between Regional and Universal Organizations: A Legal Perspective* (Leiden: Martinus Nijhoff, 2017).

[14] Article 7(1) of the UN Charter; Article 13(1) of the TEU; Article 5(1) of the Constitutive Act of the African Union.

[15] *Effect of Awards*, 53. See generally C. F. Amerasinghe, *Principles of the Institutional Law of International Organizations*, 2nd ed. (Cambridge University Press, 2005) 131.

does not have a hierarchical connotation in a normative sense. Thus, relations of hierarchy or autonomy and equality develop in both categories.[16]

5.2.1 Relations of Hierarchy

Relations of hierarchy between organs of the same institutional rank can be either formally or informally established. An illustration of formal hierarchy can be found in Articles 24 and 12(1) of the UN Charter providing for the UN Security Council's primary responsibility in international peace and security, which translates into a ban on recommendations by the UN General Assembly while the Council exercises its functions with regard to a specific situation.[17] This explicit subjection of the General Assembly to the primary responsibility of the Security Council is exceptional, as normally constitutive treaties only lay down the concrete functions attributed to each organ without regulating the way these will be exercised *vis-à-vis* those of other bodies of the organization. Moreover, this case of explicit hierarchy between the Council and the Assembly has been gradually attenuated and reframed through the interpretation of Article 12(1) and the practice of both organs,[18] particularly on the basis of the *Uniting for Peace* resolution, a development repeatedly validated since by the International Court of Justice.[19]

In other instances, hierarchy mainly takes the form of checks and balances between different institutions of the same organization.[20] A case in point is the power of an International Criminal Court Pre-Trial

[16] A. von Staden, 'No Institution Is an Island: Checks and Balances in Global Governance', in J. Mendes and I. Venzke (eds.), *Allocating Authority: Who Should Do What in European and International Law?* (Oxford: Hart, 2018) 115, 120.

[17] E. Klein and S. Schmahl, 'Article 12', in B. Simma *et al.* (eds.), *The Charter of the United Nations: A Commentary*, 3rd ed. (Oxford University Press, 2012) 507, 508–9. See also Article 11(2) UN Charter.

[18] F. Vallat, 'The General Assembly and the Security Council of the United Nations', (1952) 29 *British Yearbook of International Law* 63.

[19] General Assembly Resolution 377 (V); *Certain Expenses of the United Nations* (Advisory Opinion), [1962] ICJ Rep. 151, 163, 168; *Legal Consequences of the Construction of a Wall in the Occupied Palestinian Territory* (Advisory Opinion), [2004] ICJ Rep. 136, paras. 24–35; *Accordance with International Law of the Unilateral Declaration of Independence in Respect of Kosovo* (Advisory Opinion), [2010] ICJ Rep. 403, paras. 38–45.

[20] B. Kingsbury and L. Casini, 'Global Administrative Law Dimensions of International Organizations Law', (2009) 6 *International Organizations Law Review* 319, 337.

Chamber to overrule the Prosecutor's decision not to initiate an investigation or proceed to prosecutions thereafter.[21]

The paradigm of checks and balances is pertinently represented by the doctrine of so-called 'constitutionality control' developed in the framework of the European Union, where the Court of Justice of the EU (CJEU) has been granted the power to judicially review the legality *vis-à-vis* primary EU law of the secondary law adopted by the other EU institutions,[22] gradually even in areas preserving a model of intergovernmental cooperation.[23]

Such explicitly provided mechanism of judicial control of another organ's decisions, which is a feature of a constitutional approach to internal matters, is rare in other international organizations and is conspicuously absent in both the WTO and the UN, despite attempts to cast their institutional structures in constitutional terms. In the case of the WTO, the panels and the Appellate Body (AB) have a subsidiary status to the Dispute Settlement Body, which is the political organ of the Dispute Settlement Understanding. Moreover, not only panels and the AB are bereft of any review power regarding the decisions of WTO's political organs, but their own interpretations of the WTO agreements can be overruled through the adoption of relevant authoritative interpretations by the Ministerial Conference and the General Council, WTO's member state driven organs – a power remaining untested so far.[24]

In the case of the UN, much has been said about the role of the International Court of Justice in the organization's institutional structure. While the Court is dubbed 'the principal judicial organ' of the UN,[25] there is no stipulation granting it the power to judicially review the acts of other UN organs. The only sort-of-exception could be found in the Statute of UNAT, which recognized between 1955 and 1995 the possibility to request an advisory opinion from the ICJ challenging UNAT's decisions on such limited grounds as unlawful exercise of, or failure to exercise, jurisdiction, error of law in respect of the UN Charter or fundamental procedural error

[21] Article 53(3) *Rome Statute of the International Criminal Court.*

[22] Article 263 TFEU; Case C-294/83, *Les Verts*, ECLI:EU:C:1986:166, para. 23.

[23] Case C-72/15, *Rosneft*, ECLI:EU:C:2016:381.

[24] Article IX(2) WTO Agreement. See also the observations of P.-J. Kuijper, 'WTO Institutional Aspects', in D. Bethlehem *et al.* (eds.), *Oxford Handbook of International Trade Law* (Oxford University Press, 2009) 79, 97–8.

[25] Article 92 UN Charter.

leading to denial of justice.[26] These advisory opinions were, despite the terminology, conclusive for the legal issues submitted to the ICJ, in the sense that the parties had to comply with the Court's pronouncements,[27] thus constituting in essence an instance of judicial review of UNAT's decisions.

In all other respects, the Court's role in the UN system is reflected in its terse observation that '[p]roposals made during the drafting of the Charter to place the ultimate authority to interpret the Charter in the International Court of Justice were not accepted',[28] and its conclusion on a subsequent occasion that '[u]ndoubtedly, the Court does not possess powers of judicial review or appeal in respect of the decisions taken' by the UN organs concerned.[29] Nevertheless, such clear-cut statements barely conceal a much more complex reality. Thus, the Court has incidentally reviewed (and confirmed) the validity of acts issued by other UN organs[30] and it has summarily dismissed the political question doctrine adhering instead to a theory of 'functional parallelism',[31] where the Court might be dealing with the legal aspects of a dispute also having political ones, even while other UN organs are seized of the latter aspects.[32]

This accommodating vision of 'separate but complementary' functions of the UN organs was put to a serious test in the *Lockerbie* case, where the ICJ was confronted with a Security Council resolution under Chapter VII of the UN Charter aimed at depriving the applicant State of its rights that were at the heart of the dispute before the Court.[33] In its order on provisional

[26] Article 11(1) of the UNAT Statute, as inserted therein by virtue of GA Resolution 957(X).

[27] Ibid., Article 11(3). See also, indicatively, *Application for Review of Judgment No. 158 of the United Nations Administrative Tribunal* (Advisory Opinion) [1973] ICJ Rep. 166, para. 39.

[28] *Certain Expenses*, 168.

[29] *Legal Consequences for States of the Continued Presence of South Africa in Namibia (South West Africa) Notwithstanding Security Council Resolution 276 (1970)* (Advisory Opinion), [1971] ICJ Rep. 16, para. 89.

[30] *Ibid.*

[31] A. Pellet, 'Le glaive et la balance. Remarques sur le rôle de la C.I.J. en matière de maintien de la paix et de la sécurité internationales', in Y. Dinstein (ed.), *International Law at a Time of Perplexity: Essays in Honour of Shabtai Rosenne* (Dordrecht: Kluwer, 1989) 539, 550.

[32] *Case Concerning United States Diplomatic and Consular Staff in Tehran*, [1980] ICJ Rep. 3, para. 37; *Case concerning Military and Paramilitary Activities in and against Nicaragua*, [1984] ICJ Rep. 392, para. 95.

[33] V. Gowlland-Debbas, 'The Relationship between the International Court of Justice and the Security Council in the Light of the Lockerbie Case', (1994) 88 *American Journal of International Law* 643.

measures, the ICJ gave effect to the Security Council resolution only because 'at this stage [of the proceedings, it was not] called upon to determine definitely the legal effect' of that resolution.[34] The Court's warning to eventually proceed to review Council resolutions never materialized, because the case was removed from its docket, leaving questions about the constitutional connotations of judicial review by the ICJ unanswered.[35]

The controversial nature of judicial review within the UN institutional structure is equally evident in the *Tadić* decisions on the lawfulness of the International Criminal Tribunal for Former Yugoslavia's (ICTY) establishment by the Security Council. While the Trial Chamber declared that Council actions, based on wide discretion and political considerations, were non-justiciable, or, at least the ICTY lacked competence to judicially control them,[36] the Appeals Chamber reviewed the legality of its own existence and *incidentally* the legality of Council actions, and reached the conclusion that in creating the Tribunal the Council was lawfully exercising its functions to maintain international peace and security within its power under Article 41 UN Charter.[37]

Apart from cases of hierarchy via judicial review, checks and balances among the organs of an international organization are more frequently implemented through means of informal hierarchy. A case at hand is the various reporting obligations towards an organ, to which other organs of the same organization are subjected. In the UN, for instance, all other principal organs must report, at least, annually to the General Assembly.[38] It must be borne in mind, though, that such reporting obligations serve less as a means of control of the other UN organs by the Assembly and more as a pragmatic tool for information gathering and coordination of the organization's

[34] *Case Concerning Questions of Interpretation and Application of the 1971 Montreal Convention Arising from the Aerial Incident at Lockerbie (Libya* v. *USA)*, Order, [1992] ICJ Rep. 114, para. 43.

[35] J. Crawford, '*Marbury v. Madison* at the International Level', (2004) 36 *George Washington International Law Review* 505.

[36] *Prosecutor* v. *Tadić*, Decision on Jurisdiction, Case No. IT-94-1-T, paras. 1–40.

[37] *Prosecutor* v. *Tadić*, Decision on Interlocutory Appeal, Case No. IT-94-1-AR72, paras. 11–48. See also *Prosecutory* v. *Kanyabashi*, Decision on Jurisdiction, ICTR-96-15-T.

[38] See Articles 15(1) and 24(3) UN Charter (concerning the Council), 88 (concerning the Trusteeship Council), 98 (concerning the Secretary-General) and 15(2) (general clause).

activities. In other cases, the element of hierarchy is more pronounced. For example, the Economic and Social Council of the United Nations is explicitly considered as acting under the authority of the General Assembly (Article 60 UN Charter), performing only the functions assigned to it by the latter (Article 66(3) UN Charter) and any agreements it concludes with UN specialized agencies must be approved by the Assembly (Article 63 UN Charter).[39]

In yet other instances, the subordination of one organ to another is more subtle, but equally crucial. This is the case with the determination of the organ that holds the 'power of the purse' in an international organization.[40] In the case of the UN, while the Secretariat prepares the budget and submits it to a standing committee of the General Assembly, it is the latter that considers and approves it and apportions the expenses between member states,[41] effectively setting the policy agenda of the organization by determining which projects will get the biggest piece of the 'money pie'.[42] Moreover, the ICJ has expanded the Assembly's margin of discretion by declaring in the *Certain Expenses* opinion that the term 'expenses of the Organization' included any expenses made for the fulfilment of a UN purpose and concluding that any such expenses must be presumed *intra vires* the Organization – and the resolution apportioning them valid – even if they were *ultra vires* the functions of the acting UN organ.[43]

This broad interpretation of the Assembly's budgetary powers, evidently based on a functionalist logic, has been significantly circumscribed in three ways. First, the above presumption cuts both ways in the sense that the Assembly will not have any leeway in approving expenditures on measures considered by another UN main organ as falling within its

[39] J. Klabbers, 'Checks and Balances in the Law of International Organizations', in M. Sellers (ed.), *Autonomy in the Law* (Dordrecht: Springer, 2007) 141, 148.

[40] J. Klabbers, *An Introduction to International Organizations Law*, 3rd ed. (Cambridge University Press, 2015) 113–6.

[41] Articles 17(1)–(2) UN Charter.

[42] For a similar strategy by the European Parliament, see P.-J. Kuijper, 'Recent Tendencies in the Separation of Powers in EU Foreign Relations: An Essay', in E. Neframi and M. Gatti (eds.), *Constitutional Issues of EU External Relations Law* (Baden-Baden: Nomos, 2018) 199, 203.

[43] *Certain Expenses*, 167–8. See also J. Wouters and J. Odermatt, 'Certain Expenses of the United Nations', in C. Ryngaert *et al.* (eds.), *Judicial Decisions of the Law of International Organizations* (Oxford University Press, 2016) 91, 100.

functions.[44] Secondly, the ICJ determined in *Effect of Awards* that the Assembly must honour specific expenses arising out of obligations undertaken beforehand by the organization, as in the case of awards of compensation issued by UNAT, an independent judicial body created by the Assembly and endowed with the power to issue final awards in employment disputes that would be binding upon the UN.[45] Thirdly, the Assembly itself has delegated to other organs the authority to create special budgets for specific funds and programs and apportion the expenses.[46]

Finally, an organ's power to authoritatively interpret the constituent treaty or secondary law and thus, bind the other organs of an organization, represents a form of soft hierarchy. Besides the WTO, such a mechanism exists, *inter alia*, in the US–Mexico–Canada Agreement (USMCA),[47] where on the basis of Article 30.2(2)(f) the Free Trade Commission can issue authoritative interpretations of the USMCA binding the arbitral tribunals resolving disputes between the parties to it. In the context of the North American Free Trade Agreement, USMCA's predecessor, some arbitral tribunals had criticized the Commission's interpretations as an instance of unlawful amendment of the treaty, effectively illustrating the controversial nature of authoritative interpretation as an indirect means of hierarchy.[48]

Hierarchical relations can also be established via the exercise of normative control between organs of the same 'institutional rank'. Nevertheless, it is rare for the constituent instruments of international organizations or inter-organ agreements to provide for those effects. Is, for instance, the General Assembly or the ICJ bound by a resolution of the Security Council adopted under Chapter VII of the UN Charter, and what is the impact of Article 103 UN Charter thereon?[49] Or can the general findings of the

[44] H. Schermers and N. Blokker, 'International Organizations or Institutions, Financing of', in *Max Planck Encyclopedia*, para. 59.

[45] *Effect of Awards*, 59.

[46] P. Woeste and Th. Thomma, 'Article 17', in B. Simma *et al.* (eds.), *The Charter*, 576, 591–2.

[47] Retrieved from https://ustr.gov/trade-agreements/free-trade-agreements/united-states-mexico-canada-agreement/agreement-between (accessed 27 April 2020).

[48] *Cf. Pope & Talbot, Inc.* v. *Canada*, Award in Respect of Damages, reported in (2002) 41 *International Legal Materials* 1347, paras. 46–7; *ADF Group Inc.* v. *United States of America*, ICSID Case No. ARB(AF)/00/1, Award, (2004) 6 ICSID Rep. 470, para. 177, with regard to Article 1105 NAFTA. See Notes on Interpretation of Certain Chapter 11 Provisions, NAFTA FTC, 31 July 2001, para. B(2), available at www.naftaclaims.com/commissionfiles/NAFTA_Comm_1105_Transparency.pdf (accessed 27 April 2020).

[49] See R. Kolb, 'L'article 103 de la Charte des Nations Unies', (2013) 367 *Recueil des Cours* 9, 75ff.

Committee for the Prevention of Torture (CPT) or the Venice Commission bind or decisively influence the reasoning of another Council of Europe organ, namely, the European Court of Human Rights?[50] Such questions of normative control between organs of the same international organization remain notably understudied.[51]

5.2.2 Relations of Autonomy, Complementarity and Institutional Balance

5.2.2.1 From Autonomy to Complementarity

Despite a broad spectrum of hierarchical relations that can develop between organs at the same level of institutional governance, this is not the only available regulatory model. At times, constituent instruments might endorse a 'light-touch' approach to intra-institutional relations, leaving much to be desired. In such instances, competence conflicts can be arguably contained by applying the principle of *compétence de la compétence.* Whether a general principle of law or a rule of customary international law,[52] *compétence de la compétence* provides that each organ has 'the right in the first place itself to determine the extent of its own jurisdiction',[53] thus giving rise to a presumption of legality for any act of that organ adopted in compliance with any procedural requirements and falling prima facie within its functions.[54]

This conception of organs as self-contained, autonomous systems,[55] however, is no panacea, as it simply pits one organ's competence determination against another's, concealing but not resolving actual competence disputes. That is why, at other times, constituent instruments might opt for balancing between the competing powers and interests of organs by

[50] H. Schermers and N. Blokker, *International Institutional Law: Unity within Diversity*, 6th ed. (Leiden: Martinus Nijhoff, 2018) 811–2.

[51] A leading textbook on UN law reserves a page on the various legal acts addressed by one organ to another; see B. Conforti and C. Focarelli, *The Law and Practice of the United Nations*, 5th ed. (Leiden: Martinus Nijhoff, 2016) 454.

[52] *Prosecutor* v. *El-Sayed,* Special Tribunal for Lebanon, Decision on Appeal of Pre-trial Judge's Order Regarding Jurisdiction and Standing, CH/AC/2010/02, paras. 41–9.

[53] *Interpretation of the Greco-Turkish Agreement of December 1st, 1926*, [1928] Publ. PCIJ, Series B No. 16, 4, 20.

[54] *Certain Expenses*, 167–9.

[55] *Tadić* case (Appeals Chamber), para. 11.

imposing a model of parallel and complementary exercise of their respective competences. In the framework of the World Health Organization, for example, its Director-General must, according to the International Health Regulations, obtain the advice of the Emergency Committee 'on appropriate temporary recommendations' before making the final determination on whether to declare a 'public health emergency of international concern'.[56] This is equally the case with various procedures concerning, indicatively, the admission of new member states in the UN, the suspension of member states' rights and privileges and their expulsion from the Organization, or the selection of the UN Secretary-General and ICJ judges.[57]

Article 4(2) of the UN Charter, for instance, stipulates that the admission of a state to the UN will be effected 'by a decision of the General Assembly upon the recommendation of the Security Council'.[58] The provision gave rise to a heated debate whether the General Assembly could act despite a negative Security Council recommendation or inaction due to a (threat of) veto.[59] In a 1950 advisory opinion, the ICJ observed that an *affirmative* recommendation by the Council was a precedent condition, that is, a necessary step before the Assembly could make a decision on the admission request. In doing so, it focused on the structure of the relationship between the two UN organs as reflected in the above provision arguing that any other interpretation would 'almost nullify the role of the Security Council in the exercise of one of its essential functions'.[60]

A similar discussion[61] unfolded in the 1970s in the (then) European Community in relation to what was called at the time the consultation procedure – today forming part of the special legislative procedure – providing for the adoption of a legislative act by the EC Council after consulting the European Parliament (EP).[62] More specifically, it was argued

[56] Articles 12(2) and 49(5) of the 2005 International Health Regulations.

[57] See, respectively, Articles 4–6 and 97 UN Charter, as well as Article 4(1) ICJ Statute.

[58] A similar admission procedure is provided for in Article 7 of the Charter of the Organization of American States.

[59] Th. Grant, *Admission to the United Nations: Charter Article 4 and the Rise of Universal Organization* (Leiden: Martinus Nijhoff, 2009) 13–5.

[60] *Competence of the General Assembly for the Admission of a State to the United Nations* (Advisory Opinion), [1950] ICJ Rep. 4, 8–9.

[61] See also the relation between the Assembly and the Council of the Seabed Authority concerning regulation of deep seabed mining; S. Nandan, 'Administering the Mineral Resources of the Deep Seabed', in D. Freestone, R. Barnes and D. Ong (eds.), *The Law of the Sea: Progress and Prospects* (Oxford University Press, 2006) 75, 82–3.

[62] See Article 43(2) of the Treaty of Rome, reflected, nowadays, in Article 289(2) TFEU.

that since the EP's intervention in the legislative process had an advisory and not compulsory character for the legislating body, namely the Council, it could be bypassed altogether under specific circumstances. The European Court of Justice was unimpressed by the argument, holding that '[d]ue consultation of the Parliament in the cases provided by the Treaty … constitutes an essential formality disregard of which means that the measure concerned is void' and that the formality was satisfied not by simply asking for the Parliament's opinion but only when the latter has given it.[63] The requirement of the Parliament's consultation represented, as the Court put it, 'an essential factor in the *institutional balance* intended by the Treaty'.[64]

5.2.2.2 Principle of Institutional Balance

As seen just above, an overarching theme underpinning inter-organ relations is the necessity to preserve the distribution and balance of functions as provided for in the constituent instrument of the international organization concerned and, thus, respect the volition of the member-states. This logic applied equally in the *Certain Expenses* advisory opinion, where the Court examined whether the exercise of the General Assembly's power in the field of international peace and security had affected the distribution of functions between the Assembly and the Security Council.[65] Such concerns are translated into the principle of institutional balance.

This principle should not be conflated with or assimilated to the separation of powers doctrine. While the former emphasizes the relationship between the various organs, the latter is about allocating powers in distinct lines with the purpose to form an executive, a legislative and a judicial branch.[66] Such a strict division of powers is evidently inapplicable to international institutions.[67] In the case of the UN, for instance, while the Security Council is conceived as the executive branch of the organization, it has also adopted decisions of a quasi-legislative nature, and the General

[63] Case C-138/79, *Roquette Frères*, ECLI:EU:C:1980:249, paras. 33–4.

[64] Ibid., para. 33, emphasis added. [65] *Certain Expenses*, 164.

[66] von Staden, 'No Institution is an Island', 116; C. Chevallier-Govers, 'Article 13 [The Institutions]', in H.-J. Blanke and S. Mangiameli (eds.), *The Treaty on European Union (TEU): A Commentary* (Berlin: Springer, 2013) 529, 557–8.

[67] *Nicaragua* case, para. 92; *Tadić* case (Appeals Chamber), para. 43.

Assembly, for its part, exercises executive or judicial powers too, for instance when it suspends a member state under Article 5 UN Charter.[68] In the same vein, the General Council of the WTO has both decision-making and judicial competences, the latter exercised when it convenes as the Dispute Settlement Body,[69] while in the EU the Commission combines legislative and executive powers, but also adjudicative responsibilities in competition law cases, for example. Consequently, the principle of institutional balance is not about a strict separation of powers among functionalist lines, but about respecting the institutional structure as intended by the founding member states and developed subsequently, while regulating the evolution of the relations between organs of an international organization.

The principle has been at the heart of the EU's institutional system. In order to protect the institutional balance, for instance, the CJEU has supplemented the text of the EEC Treaty by granting the European Parliament standing to bring actions for annulment, a privilege already enjoyed by the Council and the Commission. This jurisprudential development became later codified in the Treaties themselves.[70] The CJEU has also elaborated on the principle's various components.[71] First, the principle of institutional balance imposes a duty upon each EU institution to not encroach on the powers allotted to another institution and to sincerely cooperate with each other.[72] On that basis, the CJEU has imposed a series of procedural obligations upon the Council (or the Commission) towards the European Parliament on information-sharing and reporting in relation to treaty-making by the EU in the framework of the Common Foreign and Security Policy.[73] Second, the principle impedes EU organs from exercising powers beyond those stipulated in the treaties. New tasks can be added to

[68] A. Schifano, 'Distribution of Power within International Organizations', (2017) 14 *International Organizations Law Review* 346, 369–77.

[69] A. Qureshi, *Interpreting WTO Agreements: Problems and Perspectives* (Cambridge University Press, 2015) 65ff.

[70] Case C-70/88 *Parliament* v. *Council*, ECLI:EU:C:1990:217, para. 26. See, nowadays, Article 263 TFEU.

[71] P.-J. Loewenthal, 'Article 13 TEU', in M. Kellerbauer, M. Klammert, J. Tomkin (eds.), *The EU Treaties and the Charter of Fundamental Rights: A Commentary* (Oxford University Press, 2019) 126, 129–31.

[72] Article 13(2) TEU.

[73] See, indicatively, Case C-658/11 *Parliament* v. *Council*, ECLI:EU:C:2014:2025; P. Koutrakos, 'Institutional Balance and Sincere Cooperation in Treaty-Making under EU Law', (2019) 68 *International and Comparative Law Quarterly* 1, 25.

an organ's portfolio, provided those tasks do not essentially alter the nature of that organ's powers.[74] Third, and here one enters the realm of vertical intra-institutional relations, the CJEU has determined that the principle of institutional balance requires any delegation of powers to a subsidiary organ to be subject to strict review by the delegating institution and prohibits the delegation of discretionary powers involving a transfer of responsibility.[75]

Despite the rich jurisprudence on institutional balance in the EU, the principle has not gained traction in other international organizations[76], though some authors have proclaimed its particular utility regarding the UN.[77] More importantly, its applicability has been explicitly rejected by the WTO Appellate Body in the *India-Quantitative Restrictions* case. There, India tried to circumscribe the jurisdiction of the WTO panel to review certain import trade measures allegedly adopted for balance-of-payments purposes by arguing that jurisdiction over them was assigned to the Balance of Payments Committee and the General Council, and thus, the principle of institutional balance mandated the judicial organ to adopt a deferential stance so as not to usurp the competences of the political organs.[78] The AB was unfazed by this argument, rejecting the reference to the principle of institutional balance and adopting a textual approach, according to which the DSU panel could fully review such measures as it had a different function, nature and scope than the political bodies.[79]

This shying away from a constitutionalist reading on the relations between WTO organs highlights the challenges that such a mindset

[74] B. de Witte, 'The Role of the Court of Justice in Shaping the Institutional Balance in the EU', in Mendes and Venzke (eds.), *Allocating Authority*, 143, 154–6.

[75] Case C-9/56, *Meroni*, ECLI:EU:C:1958:7; J.-P. Jacqué, 'The Principle of Institutional Balance', (2004) 41 *Common Market Law Review* 383, 384–5. It must be stressed that the *Meroni* conditions have been recently loosened; see Case C-270/12, *United Kingdom* v. *European Parliament and Council*, ECLI:EU:C:2014:1.

[76] But see *The Institutional Balance at the Council of Europe*, Parliamentary Assembly, Recommendation 1763 (2006).

[77] See, respectively, R. Monaco, 'Les principes régissant la structure et le fonctionnement des organisations internationales', (1977-III) 156 *Recueil des Cours* 81, 111; C. Chaumont, 'L'équilibre des organes politiques des Nations Unies et la crise de l'Organisation', (1965) 11 *Annuaire Français de Droit International* 428.

[78] J. Dunoff, 'The Politics of International Constitutions: The Curious Case of the World Trade Organization', in Dunoff and Trachtmann (eds.), *Ruling the World*, 178, 204.

[79] *India-Quantitative Restrictions on Imports of Agricultural, Textile and Industrial Products*, WT/DS90/AB/R, 22 September 1999, paras. 98–104. See also *Turkey-Restrictions on Imports of Textile and Clothing Products*, WT/DS34/AB/R, 19 November 1999.

encounters in institutional settings beyond the EU. Nevertheless, taking into account the paucity of solutions stemming from a functionalist logic in horizontal relations between organs of an international organization, the constitutionalist narrative retains a certain attraction.

5.3 Relations between Organs at Different Levels of Institutional Governance: Oscillating between Hierarchy and Autonomy

The legal regime regulating the creation of subsidiary organs raises interesting questions regarding vertical relations between organs of an international organization. While verticality might be commonly associated with a hierarchical model of intra-institutional relations,[80] it will be shown that, even in such a setting, pockets of autonomy in relations between principal and subsidiary organs might persist. But before those models are presented, some definitional clarifications are warranted.

The term 'subsidiary organ' includes any autonomous organ, which, in accordance with the provisions and limitations set in the constituent instrument of the organization or any other relevant text, is created by an act of will of another organ (parent organ), the latter preserving an element of authority and control over the former.[81] Such an organ is autonomous in the sense that it exercises its functions and powers in a manner distinct from that of the parent organ, not in the sense of fully escaping from the latter's control. Under this definition, any organs (beyond the principal ones) provided for directly by the constituent instrument (i.e. Military Staff Committee of Article 47(2) UN Charter),[82] do not constitute 'subsidiary organs', as they are not created directly by an act of will of an organ but by state will.[83] Nevertheless, the terms of creation of those organs might reflect their secondary or auxiliary status vis-à-vis the

[80] For instance, it is argued that recommendations of principal organs create an obligation of compliance for all lower organs; see Schermers and Blokker, *International Institutional Law*, 810.

[81] *Repertory of Practice of United Nations Organs (1945–1954)*, vol. I, 228.

[82] H. Kelsen, *The Law of the United Nations: A Critical Analysis of its Fundamental Problems* (London: Stevens & Sons, 1951) 138.

[83] P. Reuter, 'Les organes subsidiaires des organisations internationales', in *Hommages d'une génération de juristes au Président Basdevant* (Paris: Pedone, 1960) 415, 421–2.

principal ones, thus subjecting them to an institutional model that shares many of the features analyzed subsequently in this part.

Subsidiary organs must be created in conformity with the provisions and limitations set out in the constituent instrument or any other relevant text. One first issue concerns the competence of organs to create subsidiary ones. Such a competence is frequently enshrined in the constituent instrument of an international organization, either generally or specifically for particular organs.[84] The importance of subsidiary organs as a means for assisting and supplementing the work of the organization has led some to suggest that each organ has the inherent capacity to create subsidiary organs.[85]

There are however limits to an organ's competence thereto. Firstly, any subsidiary organ must be endowed with functions that remain within the limits of the competence(s) of the principal organ, a limitation clearly emanating from a functionalist logic.[86] This might be explicitly recognized in the legal act establishing a subsidiary organ, as in the case of the Human Rights Council Advisory Committee, whose scope of advice is limited only to thematic issues 'pertaining to the mandate of the Council'.[87] Secondly, any subsidiary organs must respect the balance of power enunciated via the institutional structure of the organization. This issue arose when a system of consultations was established by member states via the European Parliament and the Council to assist and control the European Commission's executive function and ensure uniform implementation of EU rules, a phenomenon described as *Comitology*.[88] In that particular instance, the CJEU determined that these consultative committees did not disturb the balance of powers as laid down in the constituent instrument since they lacked proper decision-making power.[89] Thirdly, subsidiary organs can create other subsidiary organs only within the legislative parameters set out by the parent organ.[90]

[84] See, indicatively, Articles 7(2), 22, 29 and 69 UN Charter; Article 11 Convention on the International Maritime Organization; Article 53 OAS Charter.
[85] F. Seyersted, *Common Law of International Organizations* (Leiden: Martinus Nijhoff, 2008) 68, 111–2.
[86] See *Tadic* case (Appeals Chamber), paras. 38, 44.
[87] UN Doc. A/HRC/RES/5/1, 18 June 2007, para. 76. [88] See Article 291 TFEU.
[89] Case C-25/70, *Köster*, ECLI:EU:C:1970:115.
[90] *UN Juridical Yearbook* (1991) 286; R. Higgins *et al.*, *Oppenheim's International Law: United Nations* (Oxford University Press, 2017) 164.

This last condition introduces the dominant theme in the relations between parent and subsidiary organs, that of hierarchy. In broad lines, hierarchy's impact on parent/subsidiary organs' relationships depends on two parameters: a generic one, that is, whether the parent organ has delegated powers to a subsidiary one or not; and a contextual one, that is, under what terms of reference has the subsidiary organ been created.

With regard to the first parameter, the functionalist logic determines that subsidiary organs can be lawfully created only if they are necessary for the exercise of the parent organ's functions. This is evidently broader than the principle *nemo dat quod non habet* (no one can give what he does not have), which would mean that a subsidiary organ could not possess powers that the parent organ did not have, thus limiting the creation of subsidiary organs only to instances where a delegation of powers was possible.[91]

This last view has been roundly rejected in the *Effect of Awards* advisory opinion by the ICJ and its line of reasoning was largely reproduced by the ICTY in the *Tadić* case. Both situations concerned the creation of judicial bodies by political organs of the UN. In that advisory opinion, the ICJ observed that in establishing the UN Administrative Tribunal (UNAT) the General Assembly 'was not delegating its own functions', since it possessed no judicial powers. It was solely exercising its power emanating from the UN Charter to regulate staff relations under Article 101 UN Charter and the creation of UNAT was necessary for the efficient exercise of this power.[92] This institutional constellation increases the autonomy of the subsidiary organ. For instance, it has been persuasively argued that when a subsidiary organ is designed to exercise powers or functions that the parent organ does not possess, the latter cannot change or review the decisions of the former, because such a review would signify an exercise by the latter of those very powers and functions that it did not possess in the first place.[93]

This exceptional case notwithstanding, usually the creation of subsidiary organs does involve the delegation of powers by the parent organ. In this scenario, further conditions reflecting the hierarchical relation between the parent and the subsidiary organs are applicable. First of all,

[91] M. Lippold and A. Paulus, 'Article 7', in Simma *et al.* (eds.), *The Charter*, 388, 401.

[92] *Effect of Awards*, 57, 60–1. See also *Tadić* case (Appeals Chamber), paras. 38, 44.

[93] D. Sarooshi, *The United Nations and the Development of Collective Security: The Delegation by the UN Security Council of its Chapter VII Powers* (Oxford University Press, 1999) 102.

the parent/principal organ cannot delegate discretionary powers, for which it has been granted by member states' exclusive competence. A case in point is the Security Council's power to make a determination under Article 39 of the UN Charter and decide on the measures to be taken for the maintenance or restoration of international peace and security.[94]

The above limitation was analytically corroborated in the *Meroni* case, where the CJEU adjudged that by delegating to two private companies its (discretionary) power to determine the amount to be paid to a fund by companies purchasing scrap, the High Authority of the European Coal and Steel Community had acted unlawfully, as this resulted in an actual transfer of responsibility to these companies, which undermined the balance of power reflected in the institutional structure of the European Coal and Steel Community.[95]

Thus, transfer of responsibility for competences exclusively delegated by member states to a specific organ, such as the transfer of the Security Council's competence in the admission, suspension or expulsion of member states to a subsidiary organ, or the General Assembly's transfer of the competence to apportion expenses to such an organ would be undoubtedly improper.[96] It has been admitted, however, that the Assembly can delegate to a subsidiary organ the power to review the scale of assessments for determining the amount to be paid by each state.[97]

Moreover, the parent organ must withhold a level of authority and control over the subsidiary organ, such as the power to terminate the organ's mandate,[98] the capacity to issue directives that would be binding upon the subsidiary organ or the right to retract the latter's decisions.[99] For instance, the UN Secretariat deemed lawful ECOSOC's overriding of a decision by the Commission on Human Rights – which was one of its

[94] L.-A. Sicilianos, 'L'autorisation par le Conseil de sécurité de recourir à la force: une tentative d'évaluation', (2002) 106 *Revue Générale de Droit International Public* 5, 9.

[95] *Meroni*, 152-4.

[96] J. Alvarez, 'Nuremberg Revisited: The *Tadić* Case', (1996) 7 *European Journal of International Law* 245, 254.

[97] UN Doc. A/37/11, Annex I (1982) 34–5.

[98] *Effect of Awards*, 61. See also L. Burgorgue-Larsen, 'La structure institutionnelle de l'organisation internationale', in E. Lagrange and J.-M. Sorel (eds.), *Droit des organisations internationales* (Paris: LGDJ, 2013) 375, 398–9.

[99] Boisson de Chazournes, *Interactions between Regional and Universal Organizations*, 176–80.

subsidiary organs – concerning the enhancement of the effectiveness of human rights special procedures.[100]

In this framework, it has been equally determined that in the event of conflicting decisions between parent and subsidiary organs, those of the former must prevail.[101] For example, if the Security Council decides under Chapter VII to modify the ambit of a UN peacekeeping operation's mandate, the latter organ cannot continue working within the scope of its previous mandate. Such conflicts can be avoided if the subsidiary organ intending to adopt an opposing view seeks the parent organ's approval, which can be either explicit or implicit.[102] Additionally, a parent organ might be able to control a subsidiary one through the power of the purse, as has been the case with the General Assembly's subsidiary organs and their activities.[103] Of course control breeds responsibility.[104] Hence, the main organ is, in principle, accountable for the acts of the subsidiary one.

As has been pinpointed above, the level of control, and thus, of subjection to a hierarchical model of relations, also depends on the terms of reference under which the subsidiary organ was created, that is, on a combination of the principal organ's intentions and the functions endowed to the subsidiary organ. For instance, it might be that the subsidiary organ is endowed by its parent organ with the power to reach decisions that will not require the approval of the latter. In that case, the subsidiary organ enjoys a much wider autonomy than in cases where each decision of this organ must be approved by the parent one. For instance, while the Sub-Commission on the Promotion and Protection of Human Rights, a subsidiary organ of the now defunct Commission on Human Rights, could adopt thematic resolutions out of its own initiative, its successor, the Human Rights Council Advisory Committee, is explicitly granted the

[100] ECOSOC Res. 2003/58, 24 July 2003, overriding Commission on Human Rights 2003/113. See also UN *Juridical Yearbook* (2004) 340–1.

[101] *Review of the Status and Activities of the Sub-Commission and its Relationship with the Commission on Human Rights and other United Nations Bodies*, E/CN.4/Sub.2/1982/3, Annex I, 22 February 1982, para. 2, reproduced in B. Ramcharan (ed.), *The Principle of Legality in International Human Rights Institutions: Selected Legal Opinions* (Dordrecht: Martinus Nijhoff, 1997) 42.

[102] *UN Juridical Yearbook* (1983) 169.

[103] General Assembly Resolution 3351 (XXIX), 18 December 1974.

[104] C. Eagleton, 'International Organizations and the Law of Responsibility', (1950-I) 76 *Recueil des Cours* 319, 385–6.

power to merely submit proposals to the Council requiring the latter's consideration and approval for their implementation.[105]

Moreover, in case of disputes over the subsidiary organ's mandate, that organ can itself interpret in the first place the terms of reference regarding its creation on the basis of the principle of *compétence de la compétence*. If a challenge thereon persists, the parent organ can intervene. This was asserted during discussions within the aforementioned Sub-Commission, then called Sub-Commission on Prevention of Discrimination and Protection of Minorities,[106] over whether it could be given guidance by the Secretariat on a question relating to its competences. In that framework, the Director of the Division of Human Rights argued that 'in disputable cases [concerning the validity of the subsidiary organ's decisions] it is . . . for the parent organ concerned . . . to pronounce upon the issue'.[107]

Apart from instances, where the terms of reference of the subsidiary organ's creation largely depart from the hierarchical model, as in the case of the establishment of judicial bodies by political organs, the wide application of the above model in the relations between parent and subsidiary organs can be much attenuated by the subsequent practice of the interested organs resulting in a situation where the parent organ is estopped from overruling a practice of the subsidiary one, to which it has not objected for a long period of time. This was confirmed by the Office of Legal Affairs of the UN Secretariat with regard to the said Sub-Commission's practice to contact governments directly in order to gather information for the effective preparation of its studies and recommendations. More specifically, it was argued that while such action was not explicitly incorporated in the Sub-Commission's general terms of reference, it was in line with that organ's subsequent practice of expanding its scope of activity, a practice that was notably never objected to by the parent body.[108]

[105] UN Doc. A/HRC/RES/5/1, 18 June 2007, para. 77. For a comparison of the two, see L. Boisson de Chazournes and A. Gadkowski, 'A Critical Appraisal of the Human Rights Council Advisory Committee', in Ph. Alston and F. Mégret (eds.), *The United Nations and Human Rights: A Critical Appraisal* (Oxford University Press, 2020) 239, 242.

[106] See UN Doc. E/1999/INF2/Add.2, 172.

[107] Cited in B. Ramcharan, 'Lacunae in the Law of International Organizations: The Relations between Subsidiary and Parent Organs with Particular Reference to the Commission and Sub-Commission on Human Rights', in M. Nowak, D. Steurer and H. Tretter (eds.), *Progress in the Spirit of Human Rights. Festschrift Ermacora* (Kehl am Rhein: Engel, 1988) 37, 43–4.

[108] See UN Doc. E/CN.4/1413, 13 October 1980, 53.

5.4 Conclusion

The above analysis highlights the rich, but piecemeal, practice concerning the internal relations between organs of international organizations. This panorama illustrates the complexity that reigns in those relations, rendering it impossible to cast the whole body of law developed therein in exclusively functionalist or constitutionalist terms. There is undeniably a clear streak of pragmatism in those relations. This complexity is further accentuated by instances of normative control of one organ over another, as has been illustrated above. The ad hoc settlement of many questions raised throughout this chapter cannot but leave the observer with the impression that, particularly in this field, international institutional law remains at times a *bric-à-brac* rather than a fully coherent body of norms based on a sound theoretical model.

6 Standard-Setting in UN System Organizations

José E. Alvarez

6.1 Introduction

The absence of explicit lawmaking authority has not prevented international organizations from producing 'standards' that deviate from the ways the traditional sources of international law – treaties, custom, general principles – are usually understood. Despite the fact the UN was not given plenary authority to conclude treaties,[1] a functionalist 'principle of speciality' imposes subject matter limits on UN system organizations,[2] and entities charged with progressively developing or codifying the law (such as the International Law Commission (ILC)) can only make recommendations, the extent of standard-setting by international organizations vastly exceeds what might be expected from such limitations.[3]

The greatest attention has been focused on those few instances in which organs authorized by treaty to take legally binding decisions have used that power to generate de facto legal standards. The most prominent example is, of course, the UN Security Council's deployment of Chapter VII of the UN Charter to take action in response to threats to and breaches of the peace as well as acts of aggression. A voluminous literature exists on how the Council has creatively

[1] Compare Articles 43 and 63 of the UN Charter; but see *Reparation for Injuries Suffered in the Service of the United Nations* (Advisory Opinion), [1949] ICJ Rep. 174.

[2] *Legality of the Use by a State of Nuclear Weapons in Armed Conflict* (Advisory Opinion), [1996] ICJ Rep. 66.

[3] See, e.g., K. Skubiszewski, 'Enactment of Law by International Organizations', (1965–6) 41 *British Yearbook of International Law* 198, 273; F. Kirgis, Jr., 'Specialized Law-Making Processes', in O. Schachter and Ch. Joyner (eds.), *United Nations Legal Order* (Cambridge University Press, 1995) 109; P. Szasz, 'General Law-Making Processes', in *ibid.*, 35.

interpreted what constitutes a 'threat to the peace' and what it can do in response.[4] Equal (and more critical) attention has been paid to how the Council has deployed its Chapter VII powers to 'legislate' for the world with respect to counterterrorism, the handling of foreign terrorist fighters, the safe-keeping of nuclear materials and responses to piracy.[5] Despite the near-paralysis of the Security Council in the present day, the normative impact of the Council's post–Cold War creativity has been considerable. The Council has used its power to enhance the powers of other UN system organizations or of select UN members, to revive the reality of international criminal law, and to attempt to influence customary international law as well as the interpretation of the UN Charter on diverse matters, from the use of force to human rights.[6] These Council actions have generated debates about whether the Council can legitimately act as a legislative body.[7]

Considerable attention has also been paid to more 'mundane' exercises of authority by UN system organizations pursuant to delegated powers over 'technical' specialized pockets of international law[8] as well as to their capacity to generate 'international administrative law'.[9] Extensive rules of

[4] The Council has famously deployed its Chapter VII powers to 'contract out' the use of force, compel extradition, devise 'smart sanctions', establish criminal tribunals, license particular types of use of force in response to the 'responsibility to protect"', enhance the authority of other international organizations (such as the IAEA) and deviate from the traditional exercise of the veto (as in the 'Iran Deal'). See, e.g., J. E. Alvarez, *The Impact of International Organizations on International Law* (Leiden: Martinus Nijhoff, 2017) 53–141. Along the way, it has expanded the concept of 'threat to the peace' to include threats to 'human security' whether posed by refugees exposing themselves to harm, by violence against a state's own citizens, or by risks to global health such as Ebola. See *ibid.*, 135–41.

[5] *Ibid.*, 116–27 (discussing Council resolutions 1373, 1540, 2178).

[6] *Ibid.*, 69–70 (discussing Charter innovations adopted in the course of the Council's response to the invasion of Kuwait); 116–27 (discussing the Council's possible impact on customary and Charter norms use of force norms). But see M. Scharf, *Customary International Law in Times of Fundamental Change* (Cambridge University Press, 2013) 183–210 (questioning the impact of the Council's actions on the rules governing use of force).

[7] See, e.g., M. Koskenniemi, 'The Police in the Temple', (1995) 6 *European Journal of International Law* 325.

[8] For examples, see Kirgis, 'Specialized Law-Making Processes', 135–43.

[9] Standards over the operation of organizations have emerged, for example, in the course of relations with their personnel and governments' representatives deployed to these organizations. Such standards have emerged from succinct references in international organization charters to the 'independence' of the international civil service, financing, the power to establish subsidiary organs, and powers accorded their 'chief administrative officer'. See, e.g., UN Charter, articles 17, 22, 29, 97, 100.

procedure, on privileges and immunities of employees, representatives and the organizations themselves, on the provision of technical or humanitarian assistance, for the supervision, and hiring and firing of staff and for the financing of the organization's core or operational activities have emerged as a result. While these rules or standards are sometimes dismissed as having only relevance to the 'internal' functioning of these organizations, many of them have had 'external' effects on general international law.[10] UN organizations' continuous refinement of a vast body of procedural rules for the negotiation of treaties and the financing of international organizations have, to mention but two examples, contributed significantly to a turn from bilateralism to multilateral treaty making[11] and helped to determine the meaning and scope of international legal personality.[12]

This chapter focuses on examples of standard-setting by international organizations outside these well-known contexts. In line with prior attempts to describe the 'law-making' activities of international organizations,[13] it first outlines how international organization treaty-making differs from treaty-making prior to the rise of organizations. Second, it considers institutional outputs that have legal impact even though they exist on a spectrum of legally binding authority between 'soft' and 'hard'.

As this last suggests, it is important at the outset to clarify that while it remains possible to treat most of the standards addressed here as products of treaty or as forms of custom or general principles of law, attempts to fit the outputs of international organizations into these old wine bottles render less visible what makes their 'lawmaking making' unique. The difference between international organization standards and traditional sources of international law begin with terminology. International organizations generate 'decisions', hortatory 'resolutions', 'directives', 'declarations', 'guidelines', 'opinions'/'comments'/'views' (issued by a welter of subsidiary organs, general counsels, designated experts or officials, or supervisory

[10] See, e.g., Szasz, 'General Law-making Processes', 44–5, 100–6.

[11] For examples of the procedural rules, see R. Sabel, *Procedure at International Conferences*, 2nd ed. (Cambridge University Press, 2009). For contentions of their broader normative impact see S. Chesterman *et al.* (eds.), *Oxford Handbook of United Nations Treaties* (Oxford University Press, 2019).

[12] See, e.g., J. E. Alvarez, *International Organizations as Law-Makers* (Oxford University Press, 2005) 273–400.

[13] See, e.g., Chesterman et al. (eds.), *United Nations Treaties*; Szasz, 'General Law-making Processes'; N. D. White, 'Lawmaking', in J. Cogan et al. (eds.), *Oxford Handbook of International Organizations* (Oxford University Press, 2016) 559.

bodies), 'plans of action', 'summit outcomes' and 'codes of conduct'. Except for Security Council decisions accorded primacy under the UN Charter, this potpourri of standards is not usually subject to a clear hierarchy of value and, all too often, is circumspect about whether any of these outputs are meant to be 'authoritative' or legally binding. This is one reason why attempts to limit international organization 'standard-setting' to norms that have a 'recognizably legislative form' and that are issued by an authorized body that "intends" to channel state conduct are bound to fail; these characteristics are not necessarily evident in many of the examples canvassed here.[14]

Ambiguity as to the degree of legally binding effect may be the result of the fact that organizational standards emerge under the ever-present threat of sovereign backlash. The prospect that states may object rises precisely because these standards often elude the state-centricity demanded of positivist sources of international law in three respects. First, they may involve the participation of non-state actors in the standards' establishment, ongoing interpretation or enforcement. Second, the standard may purport to *affect* non-state actors – including other treaty-based organizations, public/private hybrid bodies, transnational networks of agencies inside states, private associations of industry or other experts, international courts or arbitral tribunals, international civil servants, non-governmental organizations or designated individuals and multinational enterprises. Third, even when the organizational standard results from the actions of states, they may not require their consent.[15]

There is no agreement about what to call this phenomenon. While this chapter uses the term 'soft law' to describe a considerable portion of international organizations' normative output,[16] that ill-defined concept has been viewed as an oxymoron (or worse) by those who ask, with some

[14] See, e.g., Kirgis, 'Specialized Law-Making Processes', 110.

[15] Klabbers describes organizations' efforts to involve and reach non-state actors as the problem of 'privity': J. Klabbers, 'International Organizations and the Problem of Privity: Towards a Supra-functionalist Approach', in G. Politakis *et al.* (eds.), *ILO 100: Law for Social Justice* (Geneva: ILO, 2019) 629.

[16] For purposes of exposition, this author confines the term 'soft law' to norms that are not formally binding on states and therefore do not elicit state responsibility upon breach. In the view of the author, distinctions based on level of precision – vagueness – is better captured by distinguishing 'rules' from 'principles'. Of course, both binding authority and level of precision reflect a spectrum, not an on/off switch. See, e.g., F. Schauer, 'The Convergence of Rules and Standards', (2003) *New Zealand Law Review* 303.

justice, what is meant by 'law' if everyone (public, private and in-between) is a potential 'lawmaker' and no one can be certain about whether their efforts entail legal responsibility and, if so, for whom.[17] Further, 'soft law' might be taken as implying weak or non-existent compliance pull or enforcement; this is not what is meant here. Nor should the term be taken as meaning a firm binary; as discussed at Section 6.2.2 below, international organization standards may be *intentionally* ambiguous about legal effect and intended to remain so. As illustrated by some of the examples noted below, some may treat these standards as binding for some purposes but not others. For all these reasons and more, some scholars have preferred the term 'informal law', while yet others have opted for describing forms of or components of 'global governance', including 'global administrative law' (GAL), 'global constitutionalism', 'transnational legal orders' or 'international public law'.[18] The editor's choice of a chapter devoted to 'standard-setting' attempts to deflect these terminological debates.

6.2 How International Organizations Set 'Standards'

6.2.1 Via Treaty

The most accepted vehicle by which international organizations engage in standard-setting is by (1) concluding treaties among themselves or with states and (2) serving as the venue for the negotiation of interstate agreements.[19] The typical UN Status of Forces Agreement, for example,

[17] See, e.g., J. Klabbers, 'The Undesirability of Soft Law', (1998) 67 *Nordic Journal of International Law* 381; P. Weil, 'Towards Relative Normativity in International Law?', (1983) 77 *American Journal of International Law* 413; L. Blutman, 'In the Trap of a Legal Metaphor: International Soft Law', (2010) 59 *International and Comparative Law Quarterly* 605.

[18] See, e.g., J. Pauwelyn *et al.* (eds.), *Informal International Lawmaking* (Oxford University Press, 2012); B. Kingsbury, N. Krisch and R. B. Stewart, 'The Emergence of Global Administrative Law', (2005) 68 *Law and Contemporary Problems* 15; T. Halliday and G. Shaffer (eds.), *Transnational Legal Orders* (Cambridge University Press, 2015); A. von Bogdandy *et al.* (eds.), *The Exercise of Public Authority by International Institutions* (Heidelberg: Springer, 2010).

[19] International organizations have, of course, been involved in setting standards with respect to treaty-making in general. The International Law Commission is, after all, responsible for both the Vienna Convention on the Law of Treaties and the Vienna Convention on the Law of Treaties Between States and International Organizations or

sets standards for peacekeepers, for the host state of the operation and, less directly, for troop-contributing states. The many human rights treaties concluded at the UN have set human rights standards for their relatively high number of state ratifiers. The International Labour Organization's 2006 Maritime Labour Convention establishes rules for the treatment of seafarers. These are but three examples of the thousands of treaties generated in the wake of the turn to international organizations.[20] Another example of treaties that characterize the age of international organizations are their constituent instruments. These examples are further addressed in this section.

Treaties involving international organizations as parties or those emerging from organizations as negotiating venues resemble traditional treaties insofar as they too are generated by and generally restricted to states as parties, formally bind only the international legal persons that ultimately consent to them and, absent special provision, are subject to the traditional rules governing treaty interpretation originally set out in the Vienna Convention on the Law of Treaties (VCLT).[21] On closer inspection, however, the three treaties noted previously illustrate how organization-generated treaties deviate from all of these positivist tenets to generate 'standards'.

UN Model Status of Forces agreements are the product of administrative and constitutional principles unique to international organizations. Such agreements result from institutional practice consisting, first, of an ICJ Advisory Opinion and thereafter acquiescent action by the UN General Assembly (neither of which was legally binding). Thanks to this practice, peacekeeping was accepted as a lawful activity for the UN to undertake even though it is not mentioned in the UN Charter. The ICJ and the Assembly also accepted that certain forms of peacekeeping could be authorized by the Assembly and not just the Security Council. The authority to conclude treaties needed to engage in peacekeeping in turn contributed to an emerging consensus that under customary international law UN

Between International Organizations. Moreover, organizations, as the depositories for treaties and as the venue for treaty-making conferences, continually set standards in the course of both tasks. See generally Chesterman *et al.* (eds.), *United Nations Treaties*.

[20] See S. Chesterman, D. Malone and S. Villalpando, 'Introduction', in Chesterman *et al.* (eds.), *United Nations Treaties* 1, 1–2, noting that since the adoption of the UN Charter, more than 70,000 treaties have been registered with the UN Secretariat as compared to the 8000 mostly bilateral treaties in force in 1914.

[21] See VCLT, Article 5 (extending the application of the VCLT to IO charters).

system organizations (and perhaps all organizations established by treaty) are 'international legal persons' that can exercise certain rights and owe duties not mentioned in their constitutions so long as these rights and responsibilities are consistent with their charter-defined functions.[22]

The law governing UN peacekeeping has evolved alongside these model agreements. It has been shaped over time by a dense web of institutional practices undertaken by UN bureaucrats, states that host peacekeepers, troop contributing states and UN contractors. The law relevant to UN peacekeeping operations within which these treaties operate – including the principles of international humanitarian rules applicable to peacekeepers – has emerged, in short, from both treaty and such non-treaty sources as decisions reached by UN Secretaries-General in the interpretation of frequently vague peacekeeping mandates.[23] Accordingly, peacekeeping standards include hard and soft norms arising under the UN's internal administrative law, day to day operational and interpretative decisions reached by Secretariat officials and those charged with the command of peacekeeping operations in the field, as well as institutional 'precedents' (or 'operational practice') set by all of these over time. In the view of many scholars, at least some of those standards might be regarded as customary international law.[24] For all these reasons, any particular UN Status of Forces Agreement, although bilateral in form since it consists of the UN and the peacekeeping host state, needs to be read in an institutionally rich context that readily distinguishes it from the typical bilateral contract-treaty that imposes only reciprocal duties on its parties.

Global human rights conventions negotiated at the UN are exemplars of multilateral 'legislative' compacts that differ markedly from any treaty concluded prior to the age of international organizations.[25] The 'human rights revolution' engendered by these conventions – which many see as

[22] For a more detailed account of the connection between the evolution of international personhood for organizations and their ability to generate standards, see White, 'Lawmaking', 560–7.

[23] For examples, see F. Kirgis, *International Organizations in Their Legal Setting*, 2nd ed. (Eagan MN: West, 1993) 716–850.

[24] This is the status generally accorded, for example, to the Secretary-General's proclamation that UN peacekeepers are subject to the principles of international humanitarian law. See Guidelines for UN Forces Regarding Respect for International Humanitarian Law, UN Doc. ST/SGB/1999/113 (6 August 1999).

[25] See, e.g., Szasz, 'General Law-making Processes', 39–41. See also Chesterman *et al.*, 'Introduction', 6–9.

'humanizing' diverse international legal regimes and their institutions (including dispute settlers) – is not only the product of their high rates of ratification.[26] These treaties' cross-cutting global impact stems at least partly from their origins as UN General Assembly resolutions backed by the 'international community'. The human rights standards contained in these treaties are widely cited by international organizations, human rights treaty bodies and experts, national and international courts and governments to condemn actions taken by states, often irrespective of whether the particular state has ratified the treaty in question or made a relevant reservation to it. While it is possible to attribute these characteristics to the elevation of these treaties (or particular rights within them) to the status of custom, most national and international courts take the universality of these treaties – and of human rights – for granted, without bothering to address whether the underlying rules are supported by distinct state practice and *opinio juris*.

Moreover, human rights treaties – like many international organization-generated agreements – are dynamic engines for standard-setting over time. As human rights scholars and advocates know, UN human rights treaties are subject to continuous (re)interpretation not anticipated by the traditional VCLT rules in Article 31(3) involving the subsequent acts of treaty parties. Like many such treaty products, these instruments are not merely born within institutions, they remain nestled in them.[27] The UN General Assembly periodically attempts to 'update' the meaning of global human rights treaties over time, as do the respective treaty committees established under them, along with over thirty UN special rapporteurs, the High Commissioner for Human Rights, specialized investigatory commissions, regional and international courts, the UN's Human Rights Council and experts reporting to it. Like the rights and responsibilities of peacekeepers or the content of 'fundamental labour rights' in the ILO, the meanings of human rights 'treaty' standards – from whether a particular interrogation technique constitutes 'torture' to whether human rights

[26] See, e.g., T. Meron, 'The Humanization of Humanitarian Law', (2000) 94 *American Journal of International Law* 239; R. Teitel, *Humanity's Law* (Oxford University Press, 2011).

[27] This is one reason why UN system organizations set standards. See generally L. Boisson de Chazournes, 'Relations with Other International Organizations', in Cogan *et al.* (eds.), *International Organizations* 691.

defenders are themselves protected persons[28] – evolve over time in accordance with epistemic authorities in the respective institutions.

The ILO's 2006 Maritime Labour Convention provides another example of how institutionalization can affect standard-setting by treaty and how international organization treaties can in turn affect the organizations that produce them. That Convention responds to long-established ILO concerns with compliance and the limitations imposed by the organization's tripartite structure. As is well known, the ILO's 189 conventions – the product of sometimes fragile consensus among the ILO's three stakeholders (employers, employees and governments) – have not achieved uniformly high rates of ratification or timely submission of state reports perhaps because these two things largely rely on the cooperation of only one of those stakeholders: governments. The ILO's responses to these challenges have included innovative departures from the classical form of treaty-making. These include the organization's 1998 Declaration elevating some ILO treaties over others and drawing some 'universalistic' principles from the ILO's Constitution, along with a constitutional amendment (which only came into force in 2015) making it easier for the ILO's Assembly to abrogate, without unanimous vote, obsolete ILO conventions.[29]

Its 2006 Maritime Labour Convention is in line with such 'inventive' lawyering but goes a step further. That convention supersedes thirty-seven prior ILO treaties relating to seafarers and transforms international labour law on point by 'softening' a number of formerly rigid treaty rules and replacing these with a more flexible institutionalized regime intended to be more responsive to the changing needs of the industry, its workers and technology. The convention achieves this by including, as do 'framework conventions' in other fields, only general 'rights and principles' in its core text, along with vague 'implementation and enforcement responsibilities'.[30]

[28] See, e.g., General Assembly Resolution 66/164 (19 December 2011, on human rights defenders); General Recommendations of the Special Rapporteur on Torture, available at www.ohchr.org/Documents/Issues/SRTorture/recommendations.pdf (accessed 29 April 2020).

[29] ILO Declaration on Fundamental Principles and Rights at Work, adopted by International Labour Conference, 86th Sess., Geneva (18 June 1998); Update on the status of ratification of the 1986 and 1997 Instruments for the Amendment of the Constitution of the International Labour Organization, GB.325/LILS/INF1 (noting that the 1997 amendment permitting the abrogation of obsolete ILO conventions entered into force on 8 October 2015).

[30] Maritime Labour Convention, 2006, adopted by the International Labour Conference, 94th Sess. (entered into force 2013). Article III of the Convention imposes duties on state parties

Sovereign-intrusive standard-setting is largely left to a Code that enumerates detailed regulations which are in turn divided between those that are 'mandatory' in the Code's Part A and those in Part B which are only owed 'due consideration'.[31] The regulatory burdens on states are further softened insofar as even the ostensibly 'mandatory' parts of this new Maritime Code permit those states 'not in a position to implement' to adopt measures 'which are substantially equivalent' and it is up to states to satisfy themselves that such alternative measures still achieve the general object and purpose of the Code.[32] The Maritime Labour Convention further relies on a standing 'special tripartite committee' enabled to keep that treaty under 'continuous review' and to adopt, by non-unanimous vote, amendments to the Code.[33] Moreover, the ILO's Maritime Labour Convention remains subject, as are all ILO treaties, to continuous re-visitations by the ILO's standing tripartite and expert reporting bodies – which in the future, as in the past, can be expected to produce formally non-authoritative but nonetheless influential interpretative 'case law' in response to complaints received.

The regulatory scheme established by this ILO effort furthers the impression that the ILO now produces 'transnational' labour law distinct from the traditional 'international labour code' envisioned when the ILO was established in 1919.[34] These ILO efforts can be compared to other organizations' comparable attempts to blur the line between binding and non-binding rules discussed in the next section.

While UN system processes also generate more traditional interstate treaties (including widely ratified conventions originating in UNCITRAL), the foregoing examples suggest how international organizations have

to satisfy themselves that their law and regulations respect, with respect to the maritime sector, the ILO's core 'fundamental rights' to freedom of association, elimination of forced and child labour and the elimination of labor discrimination. Its Article IV affirms core rights for seafarers with respect to a safe and secure workplace, fair terms of employment, decent working conditions on board ship, and rights to medical, welfare and social protection. That article, along with Article V, requires states to implement these general rights through national measures.

[31] Maritime Labour Convention, Article VI. [32] *Ibid.*, Article VI, paras. 3 and 4.

[33] *Ibid.*, Article XIV, providing an alternative to the more usual amendment processes for the Convention as a whole contained in Article XIII.

[34] See, e.g., A. Trebilcock, 'Why the Shift from International to Transnational Law Is Important for Labor Standards' in H. Gött (ed.), *Labour Standards in International Economic Law* (Dordrecht: Springer, 2018) 57; A. Blackett and A. Trebilcock, 'Conceptualizing Transnational Labour Law', in A. Blackett and A. Trebilcock (eds.), *Research Handbook on Transnational Labour Law* (Cheltenham: Edward Elgar, 2015) 3.

transformed some interstate pacts into continuous 'legislative' enterprises. As these examples also suggest, and as a separate chapter in this volume addresses, the operational activity of international organizations is in itself juris-generative.[35] Suffice to say that a considerable portion of international law – from the rules governing the determination of what constitutes a 'free and fair election' to those governing the allocation of food to refugees and migrants – emerges from day to day decisions taken by UN organizations in the field or at headquarters in the course of interpreting treaties concluded within such organizations. Such institutional practice, unless objected to by members, has been treated for some time as the equivalent of 'subsequent practice' worthy of constitutional sanction.[36]

As is evident from the ILO's Maritime Labour Convention, international organization-generated treaties often combine rules and principles (defined along a spectrum of specificity of obligation) with 'soft' and 'hard' rules (defined on a spectrum of binding authority). Despite the controversies associated with these two spectrums, both are familiar to any student of national regulation – which also contains vague principles, relatively more precise rules and standards that may be legally binding or are issued for the guidance of agency officials (who may still deploy them in enforcement). These realities help explain analogies to national law invoked by GAL or other 'public law' scholars.[37]

UN-generated treaties have produced sub-regimes within international law that evince many of the same characteristics. They too embrace a number of subsidiary entities charged with overseeing treaty compliance that in turn produce additional standards in the course of their oversight. Supervisory quasi-adjudicative processes within other organizations – such as the substantial number of monitoring committees in the ILO – generate standards in the course of applying (frequently vague) treaty standards to particular facts over time. When this occurs, state consent remains relevant only at the margin, as when (on rare occasion) the interpretations issued by supervisory bodies draw powerful opposition and not the usual tacit acquiescence.[38]

[35] See the chapter by Duxbury, Chapter 7 in this volume.

[36] See Statement of Committee IV/2 of the San Francisco Conference, UNCIO Doc. 933, IV/2/42(2) (12 June 1945).

[37] See Kingsbury, Krisch, and Stewart, 'Global Administrative Law'.

[38] For a rare example where a supervisory body's interpretation of a treaty has been contested, see C. La Hovary, 'The ILO's Supervisory Bodies' Soft Law Jurisprudence', in Blackett and Trebilcock (eds.), *Transnational Labour Law*, 316.

The interpretation of international organization-generated treaties over time have also helped to establish innovative hierarchies of value. Institutionalized treaty interpreters, such as the Inter-American Court of Human Rights, have sometimes elevated 'human rights' treaties above 'mere' commercial ones;[39] just as ILO committees (and the 1998 ILO Declaration) have elevated some ILO conventions over others (as previously noted). These developments are encouraged to the extent non-state actors have been welcomed into an ever-wider number of institutionalized processes for ongoing interpretation or adjudication, including through greater acceptance of *amicus* briefs.[40] Even in organizations long accustomed to dealing with non-governmental stakeholders, such as the ILO, pressures for transparency and participation have brought about the involvement of groups or interests beyond those anticipated by that organization's tripartism.[41] In other organizations formally limited to governmental participation, changes in the hermeneutics of treaty interpretation or preferred methods of enforcement have been influenced by particular epistemic communities or experts, such as public health experts in the World Health Organization (WHO),[42] aviation specialists in the International Civil Aviation Organization (ICAO)[43] or industry representatives invested in the private international rules

[39] See, e.g., *Sawhoyamaxa Indigenous Community* v. *Paraguay*, Merits, Reparations, and Costs, Inter-American Court, Judgment of 29 March 2006, Series C No. 146, para. 140.

[40] See L. Crema, 'Testing Amici Curiae in International Law: Rules and Practice', (2012) 22 *Italian Yearbook of International Law* 91.

[41] One example emerges from the ILO's response to the Rana Plaza disaster in Bangladesh. In lieu of attempting another ILO convention involving the ILO's tripartite membership, the ILO opted in that case to help establish and enforce an accord on worker safety among multinationals in global supply chains. See J. Salminen, 'The Accord on Fire and Building Safety in Bangladesh: A New Paradigm for Limiting Buyer's Liability in Global Supply Chains?', (2018) 66 *American Journal of Comparative Law* 411.

[42] The Framework Convention for Tobacco Control, the product of a joint initiative between the WHO and the World Bank, is a prominent example. Like the ILO's Maritime Convention and other UN-generated 'framework' agreements, it relies on a Committee of the Parties (COP) that has issued politically intrusive guidelines that have transformed that seemingly narrow instrument into a 'regime complex'. See, e.g., Alvarez, *The Impact*, 316–31. On regime complexes, see K. Raustiala and D. Victor, 'The Regime Complex for Plant Genetic Resources', (2004) 58 *International Organization* 277.

[43] Thus, ICAO has taken advantage of what Klabbers has called its 'epistemic authority' to become the favoured venue for negotiation of numerous highly ratified counter-terrorism conventions which, in turn, have been relied on by other bodies, such as the Security Council. See J. Klabbers, 'The Normative Gap in International Organizations Law: The Case of the World Health Organization', (2019) 16 *International Organizations Law Review* 272.

proposed by UNCITRAL.[44] In all these ways, international organization-generated treaties often break the exclusive hold governments once held on setting standards via treaty.

The constitutions of UN system organizations enable these innovations. Reporting obligations in such charters serve as another tool for treaty dynamism.[45] The ILO, as is well known, has taken requirements that members report on the status of both ratified and unratified ILO conventions and coupled those with its tripartite membership to develop a *lex specialis* approach to a number of treaty interpretation questions. It has used the special features that characterize ILO treaty-making to limit states' capacity to make treaty reservations, to require states to bring ILO conventions, once adopted by the Assembly, to the attention of domestic authorities charged with ratification, to demand explanations from states that continue to refuse to ratify those conventions or that fail to implement them once ratified and to expose members to claims of non-compliance filed by transnational associations of employees.[46] The ILO has even combined the idea that freedom of association is such an important principle within its Constitution with the requirement that members need to report on even unratified conventions to establish an elaborate Freedom of Association supervisory machinery that has enabled labour unions to bring claims against ILO members, including countries like China that have not ratified the underlying freedom of association treaties.[47]

The constitutions of international organizations also routinely deviate from the unanimity rule requiring all states to agree to binding decisions taken by the organization, including with respect to amending their constitutions.[48] Less obviously, these constitutions have been subject to de facto amendment without resort to formal voting. This has occurred through a number of institutional processes, including 'non-authoritative' interpretations issued by the organization's legal counsel, successive 'declarations' proclaimed by plenary bodies, occasional resort to ICJ advisory opinions or simply the accumulation of other forms of 'subsequent

[44] See, e.g., S. Block-Lieb and T. Halliday, *Global Lawmakers* (Cambridge University Press, 2017).

[45] See, e.g., ILO Constitution, Article 19; ICAO Convention, Article 38, WHO Constitution, Articles 20 and 62.

[46] Kirgis, 'Specialized Law-Making Processes', 112–15.

[47] Kirgis, *International Organizations*, 413–21.

[48] For a survey of formal amendment procedures, see Kirgis, *International Organizations*, 121–4.

practice' with which members have been deemed to 'acquiesce'.[49] De facto constitutional amendments have often expanded organizational mandates, along with the respective organization's capacity to engage in standard-setting.[50]

6.2.2 Via Other Forms of 'Soft' Law

A considerable literature addresses whether UN General Assembly resolutions, although only 'recommendatory' in nature, can result in legally impactful standards. Scholars continue to debate whether such resolutions can ever constitute either (or both) *opinio juris* or 'state practice' sufficient to make custom; or whether some such resolutions can serve to 'crystallize' custom or demolish it.[51] There is no need, in this chapter, to rehash debates about the merits of drawing connections between General Assembly resolutions and customary international law. There is little dispute that despite the scholarly disagreements, in fact recommendations emanating from international organizations, especially those generated by the UN General Assembly, have changed how customary international law has been identified, including in national and international courts around the world.[52]

[49] It is widely accepted, for example, that the ILO has effectively undergone three de facto charter amendments since 1919, namely through the issuance of the 1944 Philadelphia Declaration (which transformed the organization into one concerned with human rights); the 1998 Declaration on Fundamental Principles and Rights at Work (which elevated some labour rights over others and made members responsible for those rights even if they had not ratified the relevant ILO conventions); and the ILO Declaration on Social Justice for a Fair Globalization (which sought to re-calibrate the institution to address the 'social imbalances' brought on by free trade and capital flows).

[50] See, e.g., I. Johnstone, 'The UN Charter and its Evolution' in Chesterman *et al.* (eds.), *United Nations Treaties* 23. For further examples of de facto 'constitutional' evolution, see G. F. Sinclair, *To Reform the World* (Oxford University Press, 2017).

[51] Consider the controversy generated by the ILC's relatively mild suggestion that in some cases, the actions of organizations may establish rules of custom. See S. Murphy, 'Identifying the Rules for Identifying Customary International Law', (2014) 108 *AJIL Unbound* 169.

[52] Thus, according to an extensive survey of the evidence most frequently cited to support findings of customary international law by national and international courts, of the eleven most frequently cited authorities, five are associated closely with the output of organizations: multilateral treaties, the case-law produced by international tribunals, international committee reports, international organization resolutions and international organization reports. See S. Choi and M. Gulati, 'Customary International Law: How Do Courts Do It?' in C. Bradley (ed.), *Custom's Future* (Cambridge University Press, 2016) 117.

Once we escape the confines of attempting to fit UN General Assembly resolutions into the customary bucket in the ICJ's Article 38, a broad field of inquiry emerges. The General Assembly sets standards in a number of other ways. As noted above, the Assembly attempts to reinterpret human rights treaties and the Charter's own references to human rights by openly inviting UN human rights treaty bodies to adopt the Assembly's interpretations of certain rights, by condemning specific acts by states that it deems to violate those rights (or the Charter) or by, for example, refusing to seat a delegation because of alleged human rights failings.[53] Some of its actions seem intended, like those of the ILO, to suggest hierarchies of value: to suggest, for example, that Cuba's right to engage in trade and enjoy sustainable development trumps the rights of states to engage in countermeasures or retortions.[54] Some General Assembly resolutions, like its Uniting for Peace resolution, reinterpret the Charter in an attempt to exercise a 'check' on the Security Council or to nudge the Secretary-General into reinterpreting the mandate of a peacekeeping mission.[55] Others, like its decision to establish an 'independent' administrative tribunal, or its decision to affirm the ICJ's *Reparation* opinion, are key moments in the establishment of standards applicable to international civil servants and in expanding the capacity of international organizations more generally.[56] Some of its 'declaratory' resolutions – such as its condemnation of Russia's invasion of Crimea or its repeated affirmations that the West Bank remains occupied territory – are intended to buttress endangered rules of international law or give them new life.[57] And some attempt to announce new rules without specifying their Article 38 pedigree.[58] Assembly resolutions of all of these types – as well as other actions taken by UN bodies – have been cited in rulings issued by national and international courts, thereby acquiring binding effect at least with respect to the litigants involved.[59]

[53] See Alvarez, *The Impact*, 169–78. [54] *Ibid.*, 164–5. [55] *Ibid.*, 180–5.

[56] Alvarez, *International Organizations as Law-Makers*, 122–39.

[57] Alvarez, *The Impact*, 185–9.

[58] See, e.g., Basic Principles on the Use of Force and Firearms by Law Enforcement Officials, Adopted by the 8th UN congress on the Prevention of Crime and the Treatment of Offenders, 1990, available at www.ohchr.org/en/professionalinterest/pages/useofforceandfirearms.aspx (accessed 29 April 2020); General Assembly Resolution 59/576 (8 March 2005; Declaration on Human Cloning).

[59] See, e.g., *Russia – Measures Concerning Traffic in Transit*, WTO Panel, WT/DS512/R (5 April 2019), para. 7.122 e (relying on General Assembly resolutions for finding that a genuine international emergency exists between those two states and that therefore Russia was entitled under WTO Article XXI to take measures to protect its essential security). Of course, Assembly resolutions, even those adopted by close votes and not

Despite their more limited mandates, other plenary bodies have sometimes deployed their recommendatory powers to comparable effect. The ILO has repeatedly used its Assembly's recommendations to provide more concrete guidance for vague ILO conventions, to 'blaze the trail' for labour standards not yet covered by an ILO convention, or to effectively rewrite outdated ILO conventions.[60] The Assembly has encouraged ILO treaty interpreters (including reporting bodies) to engage in greater interpretative flexibility where this is needed to better respond to contemporary gender norms, respond to new technological developments or address emerging social concerns or movements.

Recommendations issued by their plenary bodies are only one form of 'soft law' that international organizations deploy. Even entities originally charged with producing treaties that states may choose to ratify – such as the ILC or UNCITRAL – increasingly short-circuit state consent by promulgating a variety of non-treaty products. The ILC, which has some notable successes with prior efforts to promulgate alternatives to treaties,[61] seems increasingly devoted to an agenda that only rarely anticipates the promulgation of a convention. Its current agenda anticipates the production of few treaties but a considerably higher number of reports, draft articles, guidelines or comparable 'soft' products.[62] Interestingly, the ILC has never clearly articulated the difference between its chosen form of 'soft' instrument. Perhaps it is aware that the final title or form of the instrument it produces is likely to be less important than the fact that it is the product of a relatively legitimate 'expert' body and that, if its product is useful to relevant stakeholders, it is capable of exercising considerable legal authority irrespective of format.

For its part, UNCITRAL's output from the 1970s through 2016 has consisted of ten conventions but also an even higher number of non-treaty alternatives, namely four rules, four recommendations, two model law provisions, eleven model laws, two legal guides, one note, seven legislative guides, three practice

consensus, are often cited as authority by other UN subsidiary organs or experts such as UN Special Rapporteurs.

60 See, e.g., Kirgis, *International Organizations*, 276–95.

61 For a prescient effort predicting the success of the ILC's Articles of State Responsibility because of and not despite their 'soft' form, see D. Caron, 'The ILC Articles of State Responsibility: The Paradoxical Relationship between Form and Authority', (2002) 96 *American Journal of International Law* 857.

62 See the report of the ILC's 71st session in 2019, available at http://legal.un.org/ilc/sessions/71/ (accessed 29 April 2020).

guides and three reports.[63] Although UNCITRAL uses these distinct instruments for different purposes and is sometimes clearer than is the ILC about why, for example, there is merit in promulgating recommendations or legal guides prior to issuing a model law, it is revealing that two scholars categorize UNCITRAL's diverse non-treaty instruments as 'legal technologies' consisting of 'rules of conduct which in principle have no binding force but which nevertheless may have practical effects'.[64]

Resort to formally non-binding standards has also been common in organizations, like the WHO, that have been more timid about resorting to law and lawyers. For much of its history, the WHO's World Health Assembly generally refrained from deploying its ample constitutional powers to promulgate legally binding health regulations or to serve as a negotiating venue for treaties, choosing instead to rely on expert-driven policy-oriented guidance. And even when the WHO expanded the reach and depth of its old international health regulations to enable the organization to respond to public health emergencies of international concern, including those posed by new diseases and even intentional threats to health, its revised International Health Regulations (IHR) of 2005 continue to rely on a considerable number of formally non-binding 'guidance' instruments that fill out the contents of global health law.[65] Moreover, the IHR, which only authorize 'temporary recommendations' even in the wake of declarations of a public health emergency of international concern, remain ambiguous about whether they impose legal obligations on WHO members.[66] Like other technocratic UN system organizations such as ICAO, the WHO relies on a form of 'managerial' cooperation which relies on states being persuaded into compliance.[67]

63 Lieb and Halliday, *Global Lawmakers*, 82, Table 2.1.

64 *Ibid.*, 229, note 3 (citing F. Snyder).

65 See, e.g., WHO Guidance for the Use of Annex 2 of the International Health Regulations (2005) 6, available at www.who.int/ihr/publications/annex_2_guidance/en/</int_u> (accessed 29 April 2020).

66 International Health Regulations (2005), Articles 43 and 15, available at www.who.int/ihr/publications/9789241580496/en/_u> (accessed 29 April 2020). Although the IHR do not make it clear that WHO members must comply with WHO policy advice in response to emergencies, leading public health lawyers argue that states cannot legally defy the WHO's temporary recommendations. See, e.g., R. Habibi *et al.*, 'Do not Violate the International Health Regulations during the COVID-19 Outbreak', 395 *The Lancet* 664, 29 February 2020.

67 See, e.g., Kirgis, 'Specialized Law-Making Processes', 135–6, 143–54 (describing instances, including ICAO's Standards and Recommended Practices (SARPs) in which organizations

6.2.3 Via Institutionalized Adjudication

As noted, quasi-judicial bodies within international organizations charged with examining and responding to state reports are another source of potential standards. Today, those bodies – which usually can issue only non-binding opinions even when they are authorized to receive complaints about a state's lack of compliance – are complemented by some twenty permanent international courts or tribunals capable of issuing either advisory or binding opinions or both. Together, these bodies have inspired talk of an 'international judiciary' capable of not only resolving disputes but also of generating standards in the course of adjudication. Some have suggested that the new abundance of international adjudicatory activity has shifted the very 'terrain' of international law and deeply affected the political constraints imposed on states.[68]

In regimes where judges or arbitrators are authorized to impose legally binding judgments on individuals, states or companies the relevant law is 'case law'.[69] Entire sub-regimes of international law, including those governing international criminal law, trade, investment and human rights, now resemble common law regimes insofar as they are dominated by references to rulings that while they do not constitute the *stare decisis* familiar to students of the common law, nonetheless constitute a kind of 'jurisprudence constante'. In a number of regimes, the most highly cited source of authority within any judicial ruling is prior judicial rulings issued by that same court or tribunal or other international adjudicators.[70] No one subscribes to the fiction that these adjudications only engage in 'dispute settlement' bereft of wider normative consequence.[71] Even without a doctrine of

do not treat the distinction between binding and non-binding as particularly important since states are expected to see it in their interest to comply).

68 K. Alter, *The New Terrain of International Law* (Princeton University Press, 2014).

69 See, e.g., S. Schill, 'Sources of International Investment Law: Multilateralization, Arbitral Precedent, Comparativism, Soft Law', in S. Besson and J. d'Aspremont (eds.), *Oxford Handbook on the Sources of International Law* (Oxford University Press, 2017) 1095. See more generally A. von Bogdandy and I. Venzke, 'Beyond Dispute: International Judicial Institutions as Lawmakers', (2011) 12 *German Law Journal* 979.

70 Compare ICJ Statute, Article 38(1)(d) (mentioning 'judicial opinions', along with the views of scholars as only 'subsidiary' to the actual sources in Article 38 (1)(a–c)).

71 See generally I. Venzke, *How Interpretation Makes International Law* (Oxford University Press, 2012).

stare decisis, powerful reasons drive international adjudicators' reliance on case law 'precedent'.[72]

The impact institutionalized international adjudicators now have on international law have further propelled debates about the relative merits of soft, informal, or hard law or forms of 'governance'. There is no greater agreement among international lawyers about the merits of adjudicative 'standard-setting' than there is with respect to whether the Security Council ought to be able to enact 'global legislation'. Not everyone agrees with how international adjudicators have used international organization standards, even 'soft' ones, in the course of developing them. International judges and arbitrators have been criticized, for example, for findings of customary international law that appear to rely on the products of organizations (whether multilateral treaties or declarations) or on prior rulings issued by other national or international adjudicators, rather than engaging in a search for state practice and *opinio juris*.[73] International criminal tribunals, which ought to be constrained by the principle of legality, have drawn censure for relying on international organization standards – including General Assembly resolutions and even statements by prominent UN officials or experts – to ground findings that a particular international customary crime or general principle of law exists.[74]

And yet adjudicative standard-setting regularly occurs even in jurisprudentially conservative forums like the ICJ. Although the ICJ has had limited opportunities to intercede in the work of international organizations, its advisory jurisdiction has generally been deployed as a constitutional enabler of the UN.[75] While the ICJ has the potential to 'check' the powers of UN organs

[72] See, e.g., A. von Bogdandy and I. Venzke, 'The Spell of Precedents: Lawmaking by International Courts and Tribunals' in C. Romano et al. (eds.), *Oxford Handbook of International Adjudication* (Oxford University Press, 2014) 503.

[73] Indeed, many assume that the ILC's recently completed project on the proper identification of customary law was intended as a corrective to adjudicative 'shortcuts' with respect to finding custom.

[74] See, e.g., *Prosecutor* v. *San Hinga Norman*, Special Court for Sierra Leone, Decision on Preliminary Motion Based on Lack of Jurisdiction (Child Recruitment), (2004) 43 *International Legal Materials* 1129 (especially dissenting opinion of Justice Robertson); Interlocutory Decision on Applicable Law, Special Tribunal for Lebanon, Case No. STL-11-01 (Feb. 16, 2011). See B. Saul, 'Legislating from a Radical Hague: The United Nations Special Tribunal for Lebanon Invents an International Crime of Transnational Terrorism', (2011) 24 *Leiden Journal of International Law* 677; N. Jain, 'Judicial Lawmaking and General Principles of Law in International Criminal Law', (2016) 57 *Harvard International Law Journal* 111.

[75] For examples, see Alvarez, *The Impact*, 320–1.

(including the Security Council), it has generally stayed its hand and has never opined that anything that the organization has done has been ultravires.[76] Even the conservative ICJ has aided and abetted the 'missioncreep' of the UN, including its expanding standard-setting through the use of concepts such as 'implied powers' and the 'principle of effectiveness'.[77] Judicial efforts implying 'checks' on the power of the Security Council have been left to other international and national courts, including the European Court of Justice and the International Criminal Tribunal for the Former Yugoslavia.[78]

Much work remains to be done with respect to how international judges and arbitrators handle 'precedent', whether their own or that produced by other international or national courts. There are no accepted rules on, for example, when one international court should or must rely on or needs to distinguish another's rulings or whether 'boundary crossings' among international tribunals ought to be encouraged to avoid 'fragmentation' or best avoided.[79] There is no agreement on when if ever the case law produced by international courts and tribunals should be treated not as the mere 'subsidiary evidence' suggested by the ICJ Statute's Article 38, but as itself a form of 'soft law' that may, as is said of national judicial rulings in common law jurisdictions, harden over time despite the absence of a doctrine of *stare decisis*.[80] It would not be surprising, in other words, if the next wave of adjudicative standard-setting addresses how adjudicators ought to engage in setting standards in the course of deciding disputes before them.

International adjudication is another way that the standard-setting capacities of particular international organizations may be strengthened or weakened over time. While the finding of one international criminal court that a customary transnational crime of terrorism exists would appear to buttress, for example, the Council's frequent statements to the same effect, judicial criticisms of the Council's smart sanctions point in the opposite

[76] But see J. Alvarez, 'Judging the Security Council', (1996) 90 *American Journal of International Law* 1 (finding clues to implicit Security Council review in the *Lockerbie* cases).

[77] See generally Alvarez, *International Organizations as Law-Makers*, 122–39.

[78] See Joined Cases C-402/05 P & C-415/05 P, *Kadi* v. *Council and Commission* (*Kadi* I) ECLI:EU:C:2008:461; Joined Cases C-584/10 P, C-593/10 P, *Commission and others* v. *Kadi* (*Kadi* II) ECLI:EU:C:2013:518; *Prosecutor* v. *Tadić*, Case No. IT-94–1–1, Decision on Jurisdiction.

[79] See, e.g., R. Chen, 'Precedent and Dialogue in Investment Treaty Arbitration', (2019) 60 *Harvard International Law Journal* 47; J. Alvarez, *The Boundaries of Investment Arbitration* (Huntington: JurisNet, 2018).

[80] A. Guzman, 'International Common Law: The Soft Law of International Tribunals', (2009) 9 *Chicago Journal of International Law* 515.

direction.[81] The establishment of the International Criminal Court provides another two-sided example with respect to the powers of the Council. Thanks to the Rome Statute, the Security Council now has the power to engage in standard-setting with respect to international criminal law merely by launching investigations at the ICC, precluding such investigations (at least for limited and renewable periods of time), or otherwise tampering with that Court's jurisdiction.[82] At the same time, the Rome Statute's Kampala Amendment, adding aggression to the ICC's jurisdiction, has the potential to weaken the Council's formerly exclusive power to determine what constitutes aggression.[83] Of course, the standards adjudicators set may relate to their own powers. Adjudicators may sometimes enhance their own (and possibly other adjudicators') powers in the course of settling disputes.[84]

6.3 Consequences

International organization standard-setting elicits complaints about horizontal inequities among sovereign equals and 'democratic' or vertical disconnects between lawmaking at the national and international levels; it also triggers charges that international organization standards are ideologically biased or violate the rule of law.[85] International organization standards – particularly those that deviate from 'one-state, one-vote' or permit action without unanimity – elevate the power of some states over others. When standards are issued in such settings (as by the Security Council) and purport to directly affect individuals, sovereignty-based objections may combine with human rights concerns. Moreover, the proliferation of international organization standard-setters permits powerful state and sometimes non-state actors (if authorized to bring claims) to

[81] Compare criticisms of the Lebanon Tribunal's terrorism determination (Saul, 'Legislating from a Radical Hague'), to *Kadi* I and *Kadi* II.

[82] See, e.g., Alvarez, *The Impact*, 127–35.

[83] See generally, H. Koh and T. Buckwald, 'The Crime of Aggression: The United States' Perspective', (2015) 109 *American Journal of International Law* 257; B. B. Jia, 'The Crime of Aggression as Custom and the Mechanisms for Determining Acts of Aggression', (2015) 109 *American Journal of International Law* 569.

[84] Thus, investor-state tribunals have found that they have implicit or inherent powers, including under their *compétence de la compétence*, to issue binding interim measures, admit *amicus* briefs, or introduce issues not presented by the litigants before them.

[85] Alvarez, *International Organizations as Law-Makers*, 627–50.

prioritize venues for the making, interpretation or enforcement of the rules that they prefer.[86] Standards that emerge from treaty-making (which tend to privilege the executive branch of governments who initiate and dominate such negotiations) and, even more so, standards that emerge without the intermediation of treaty ratification and legislative implementation are all too easy to criticize on 'democracy' grounds, that is, as imposing, top-down, rules that elude consideration by duly elected representatives or that omit administrative checks such as notice and comment. International organization standards – whether or not horizontally or vertically deficient – may also reify the views of powerful non-state actors who may be involved behind the scenes in their creation or ongoing interpretation, from 'experts' given elevated status to select industry insiders. The product of increasingly specialized distinct forms of expertise, international organization norms may combine the 'epistemic authority' *and* the ideological baggage or blind spots of certain expert groups.[87] The authority of security or intelligence 'experts' reporting to the Council make it more credible, for example, to treat only some persons as sanctionable terrorists; the legitimacy of economists working for international financial institutions may 'blue-wash' standards that defer to the market or denigrate the role of regulation. International organization standards may be subject to capture, including by the very industries that they purport to regulate. Finally, international organization standards, particularly to the extent they are 'soft' in terms of binding authority, overly vague in terms of precision of obligation or subject to no clear limits in terms of application, may violate fundamental requisites of the rule of law.[88]

These legitimacy deficits suggest the trilemma schematically represented by the governance triangle below.

International organizations (and state and non-actors that influence them) turn to standards with certain informal characteristics to resolve endemic problems of interdependence associated with globalization even when they are not expressly authorized by states to legislate (standard-setting, apex). The functionalist rationales for standards increasingly require these entities to 'unshackle' themselves from the state-centric constraints of traditional sources

[86] E. Benvenisti and G. Downs, 'The Empire's New Clothes: Political Economy and the Fragmentation of International Law', (2007) 60 *Stanford Law Review* 595.

[87] Klabbers, 'The Normative Gap'. See generally D. Kennedy, *A World of Struggle* (Princeton University Press, 2016).

[88] T. Bingham, *The Rule of Law* (London: Penguin, 2010).

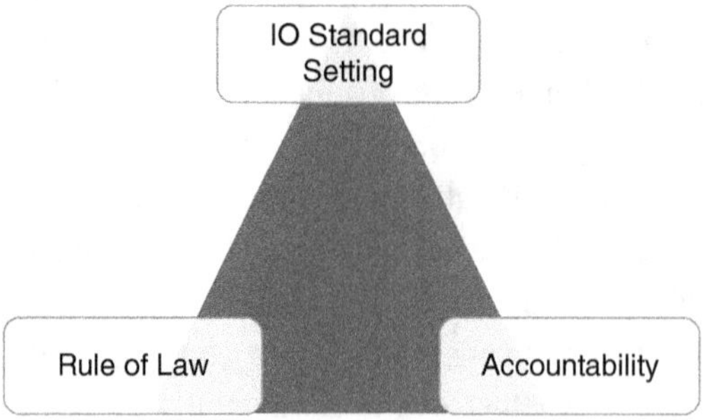

Figure 6.1 Governance triangle

of law.[89] Unlike the ICJ's Article 38 sources, such standards need not wait for explicit state consent. They are also seen as preferable to traditional sources insofar as they may reduce the ex ante costs of negotiation, lower the perceived 'sovereignty' costs, permit greater flexibility to respond to uncertainties and to changing technology, allow the targets of governance to be 'managed' into compliance over time, cope better with the diversity of states and can engage and affect non-state actors. Turning to this form of regulation advances the domain of law in terms of geography, subject matter and actors.

By extending the reach of law international organizations advance the rule of law nationally and internationally (rule of law, left leg). Standard-setting efforts to promote the rule of law underpin the idea that international organizations are purveyors of governance.[90] The line connecting the left side of the triangle (connecting standard-setting to rule of law) simultaneously empowers and disempowers international organizations: while the assumption that they can and should promote the rule of law enables organizations to gain greater authority to issue standards over matters that once might have been seen as solely within states' domestic jurisdiction, the same turn exposes organizations to expectations that those who issue such intrusive standards should themselves be limited by the rule of law.

The third leg of the triangle is precisely a key demand imposed by the rule of law: insistence on accountability. The more standard-setting occurs

[89] See, e.g., J. Pauwelyn, R. Wessel and J. Wouters, 'When Structures Become Shackles: Stagnation and Dynamics in International Lawmaking', (2014) 25 *European Journal of International Law* 733.

[90] Thus, expanding missions to promote 'good governance' (as in the World Bank) or 'rule of law' (as in manifold UN peacekeeping operations) are themselves engines for standard setting. See generally Sinclair, *To Reform the World*, 236–82.

and the more organizations encourage states to adopt such standards consistent with the rule of law, the more they are seen *and see themselves* as rule-givers who must be accountable (accountability, at the right leg).[91] 'Accountability', like 'rule of law', may be variously defined. It can include or be limited to 'representative' accountability (that is, democratic controls), 'political' accountability (that is, subject to checks and balances as between distinct parts of government), or 'legal responsibility' (that is, subject to judicial accounting to those injured by the lawmaker).[92] For some, all three forms of accountability are essential to being 'subject to the rule of law' or to achieving 'democratic governance'.[93]

The trilemma arises because, first, not everyone agrees, as previously noted, that the apex of the triangle ought to include standards that deviate from the traditional positivist sources of international law. For critics of 'soft' or 'informal' law or vaguely defined forms of 'global governance', this objection feeds into failure to attain the second leg: rule of law. Standard-setting of this kind, in their view, violates national and international rule of law expectations for predictable and stable rules about what the legal rules are. Reliance on 'informal' or 'soft' law or forms of 'governance' leaves relevant stakeholders uncertain about whether or when legal responsibility arises. As early critics of 'soft law', such as Weil, put it, resort to soft law, irrespective of its alleged benefits, fails the test of all law (and perforce the rule of law): it does not distinguish law from politics and worse still, enables those with power to turn to it when they want to confuse the issue or do not want to address the underlying problem.[94] For defenders of legal positivism,

[91] See, e.g., Report of the Secretary-General, Rule of Law and Transitional Justice in Conflict and Post-Conflict Societies, section 6, UN Doc. S/2004/616. See generally A. Peters, 'International Organizations and International Law', in Cogan *et al.* (eds.), *International Organizations* 33; M. Koenig-Archibugi, 'Accountability' in *ibid.*, 1146.

[92] See R. Grant and R. Keohane, 'Accountability and Abuses of Power in World Politics', (2005) 99 *American Political Science Review* 29, 37 (defining 'accountability' as including seven distinct modes and concluding that intergovernmental organizations, since they are subject to most of these, are among the most accountable entities in world politics). See also Donaldson and Ranganathan, Chapter 3 in this volume.

[93] See, e.g., Kingsbury, Krisch, and Stewart, 'Global Administrative Law'; R. Keohane, 'Global Governance and Democratic Accountability', 4 ('[t]he legitimacy of an official action in a democracy depends in part on whether the official is accountable'), available at https://pdfs.semanticscholar.org/c655/86769213f78c67fc447e9594393e2ffb2c2f.pdf?_ga=2.217361682.$ 568910884.1573670955-1003337852.1573670955</int_u> (accessed 29 April 2020).

[94] Weil, 'Relative Normativity'. The defence of 'soft law' offered by some does little to respond to these issues: e.g., Kirgis, 'Specialized Law-Making Processes'. The prospect that reliance on 'soft law' (and its usual companion, managerial compliance) may lead to routine

achieving 'accountability' in accordance with the third leg is equally foreclosed for the same reasons. If it is impossible to define precisely who the lawmakers are, it is not possible to render these representationally accountable or subject them to legal limits. And, without agreement on what the precise and obligatory primary or secondary rules are that apply to international organizations as standard-setters and ostensible promoters of the rule of law, it is not feasible to make these entities legally accountable.[95]

Moreover, while the governance trilemma is most apparent to legal positivists, achieving the goals suggested by the rule of law and accountability legs of the triangle is difficult even for those willing to accept the legitimacy and efficacy of standard-setting outside the confines of traditional 'Article 38' sources. Even those who accept or even praise international organization 'governance' efforts recognize that unless corrective actions are possible against mistaken international organization standards, such modes of 'law-making' will exacerbate long-standing vertical, horizontal, ideological and rule of law critiques of international law. The sovereign and public backlash generated by uncorrected and uncorrectable standards may render attainment of the second and third legs of the trilemma more difficult if not impossible. Recognition of these difficulties explains why, for example, GAL proponents propose structural reforms to governance institutions to better adhere to their vision of the requirements of the rule of law. It is why they propose enhancing the transparency of international organizations, increasing the level of participation (particularly by non-state actors and less developed states), enabling greater reason-giving (including when they turn to adjudication) and incorporating mechanisms for review and for ensuring accountability to those adversely affected by their actions.[96] Such reforms are also sold on the premise that they will relieve the 'democratic deficits' of international organizations.[97]

defiance of international organization standards is, in the age of the coronavirus, a front and center concern with respect to WHO standards. See, e.g., G. L. Burci, 'The Legal Response to Pandemics', (2020) *Journal of International Humanitarian Legal Studies* 1 (discussing major weaknesses with the WHO's IHR).

[95] See, e.g., P. Klein, 'Responsibility', in Cogan *et al.* (eds.), *International Organizations*, 1026.

[96] Kingsbury, Krisch and Stewart, 'Global Administrative Law'; R. B. Stewart, 'Remedying Disregard in Global Regulatory Governance: Accountability, Participation, and Responsiveness', (2014) 108 *American Journal of International Law* 211. See also J. Tallberg, 'Transparency', in Cogan *et al.* (eds.), *International Organizations*, 1170.

[97] See, e.g., K. Dingwerth and P. Nanz, 'Participation', in Cogan *et al.* (eds.), *International Organizations*, 1126.

The governance trilemma is not impossible to resolve.[98] An international organization might be able simultaneously to resort to soft/informal law, be able to promote the rule of law, and yet remain itself subject to the rule of law and be accountable. This is possible where, for each example, each leg of the triangle supports or reinforces the other. But in the absence of deep structural change in global politics, for this to occur in the world of today's UN system – for the trilemma to become a virtuous self-fulfilling circle – one has to be willing to relax expectations with respect to each point of the triangle. Crucially, one has to be willing to accept that imprecise and non-authoritative principles and standards can be consistent with the national rule of law and the expectations of international lawyers and their clients, that the international rule of law need not evince all of the 'thick' qualities associated with the national rule of law and that organizations can be held 'accountable' through mechanisms that do not generate binding determinations of breach or mandate compensation to those who suffer damage.[99]

Whether or not the governance trilemma can be resolved is a fundamental challenge of our time. While even self-described 'positivists' appear increasingly comfortable with 'enlightened' forms of legal positivism that embrace informal or soft law or standards,[100] achieving the goals suggested by the two bases of the triangle may prove far more difficult. It remains to be seen whether the solutions on offer to resolve rule of law, accountability and democracy deficits in international organizations – such as increasing transparency, participation, reason-giving, review and correction – will work as anticipated.[101] Such reforms may not produce the intended results. Increasing the visibility of international organization standard-setting efforts may increase dissatisfaction with them as their ad hoc nature becomes more subject to public scrutiny while, at the same time, undermining some of the pragmatic justifications offered for their 'informality'. Increasing the

98 Compare J. Dunoff and M. Pollack, 'The Judicial Trilemma', (2017) 111 *American Journal of International Law* 225.

99 J. Alvarez, 'International Organizations and the Rule of Law', (2016) 14 *New Zealand Journal of Public and International Law* 3. See also Grant and Keohane, 'Accountability and Abuses'.

100 See, e.g., B. Simma and A. Paulus, 'The Responsibility of Individuals for Human Rights Abuses in Internal Conflicts: A Positivist View', (1999) 93 *American Journal of International Law* 93.

101 For a critique that reform agendas for international organizations evince 'isomorphic mimicry' that is more symbolic than real, see D. Zaum, 'Legitimacy', in Cogan *et al.* (eds.), *International Organizations*, 1107.

participation of non-state actors may raise questions about which actors to include, the extent of their participation, the weight to be given their views and whether the answers given to the preceding questions need to be consistently applied by all adjudicators charged with, for example, admitting *amicus* briefs submitted by NGOs. Increased reason-giving or review by international adjudicators is likely to raise questions about whether such efforts enhance or limit judicial lawmaking. Some may require clearer answers about how adjudicators ought to engage in standard-setting, that is, about when it is appropriate for judges or arbitrators to fill legal gaps and about whether they need to do so consistently with prior rulings by other courts or tribunals.

In the end, whether one finds international organization standard-setting legitimate may turn on one's jurisprudential premises – whether one is, to adapt the words of Gilbert and Sullivan in another context, inclined to be more pragmatist than positivist and therefore more tolerant of an 'international rule of law' that departs significantly from how the term is used with respect to national law and whether one accepts the meagre and imperfect accountability mechanisms that now apply to international organizations.

7 Operational Activities

Alison Duxbury

7.1 Introduction

International organizations engage in a vast range of activities that can be classified as 'operational'. The United Nations' administration of East Timor and Kosovo; inspections by the International Atomic Energy Agency (IAEA); election observation by institutions such as the Commonwealth and the Organization for Security and Co-operation in Europe (OSCE); the deployment of troops on peacekeeping operations by the United Nations (UN), the African Union (AU) and the Economic Community of West African States (ECOWAS); the assessment of refugee status and the management of refugee camps by the UN High Commissioner for Refugees (UNHCR); the distribution of food aid by the World Food Programme (WFP); the deployment of experts by the World Health Organization (WHO) during a disease outbreak; and the conduct of Environmental Impact Assessments for development projects by the Food and Agricultural Organization (FAO) all fall within this description. Consequently, the term operational activities encompasses an extraordinary range of 'on the ground'[1] work by the approximately 285 – depending on how you

[1] Writers describe several activities as 'operational'. Johnstone differentiates between organizations' programmatic (operational) and normative functions, whereas Rittberger, Zangl and Kruck set out a broad range of activities as falling within this description: specifying norms, implementing norms and rules, monitoring the implementation of policies, adjudicating disputes and imposing sanctions: see I. Johnstone, 'Law-making through the Operational Activities of International Organizations', (2008) 40 *George Washington International Law Review* 87, 94; V. Rittberger, B. Zangl and A. Kruck, *International Organization*, 2nd edn (New York: Palgrave Macmillan, 2012) 124. This chapter will focus on the role of international organizations in implementing and monitoring norms and policies, including where an organization engages with other actors to fulfil its functions.

cut the numbers[2] – international organizations around the world. This chapter will examine the legal principles governing these activities, including treaties, customary international law, domestic law and the role of 'internal laws' and guidelines and will conclude by considering whether there is one legal framework that governs these diverse activities.

7.2 What Are the Legal Principles Governing Operational Activities?

The starting point for analysis is the statement by the International Court of Justice in *Interpretation of the Agreement of 25 March 1951 Between the WHO and Egypt* that '[i]nternational organizations are subjects of international law and, as such, are bound by any obligations incumbent upon them under general rules of international law, under their constitutions or under international agreements to which they are parties'.[3] This statement has been the subject of much discussion – some writers adopt it unquestioningly, others critique its lack of clarity.[4] More recently, the idea that international organizations can violate international law and therefore must be bound by (at least some of) its principles, is fundamental to the definition of 'an internationally wrongful act of an international organization' in the International Law Commission's Articles on the Responsibility of International Organizations (ARIO).[5]

[2] This figure is taken from the category 'conventional international bodies (intergovernmental)' in the *Yearbook of International Organizations*. See Union of International Associations (ed.), 'Number of International Organizations by Type', (2018–19) 4 *Yearbook of International Organizations* xxxiv.

[3] *Interpretation of the Agreement of 25 March 1951 between the WHO and Egypt* (Advisory Opinion), [1980] ICJ Rep. 73, 89–90.

[4] For critiques, see K. Daugirdas, 'How and Why International Law Binds International Organizations', (2016) 57 *Harvard International Law Journal* 325, 331–5; J. Klabbers, 'Sources of International Organisations' Law: Reflections on Accountability', in S. Besson and J. D'Aspremont (eds.), *Oxford Handbook on the Sources of International Law* (Oxford University Press, 2017) 987.

[5] International Law Commission, *Draft Articles on the Responsibility of International Organizations* (ARIO), UN Doc. A/66/10 (2011), Article 4 provides that '[t]here is an internationally wrongful act of an international organization when conduct consisting of an act or omission: (a) is attributable to that organization under international law; and (b) constitutes a breach of an international obligation of that organization'.

Starting with the second element of the ICJ's statement in *WHO-Egypt*, it is well-accepted that an organization's constituent instrument 'sets the pattern for the legal order of the international organization'.[6] Consequently, an organization is bound by the terms of its founding treaty although it is not a party to that document.[7] Such is the effect of the ruling in *Reparation for Injuries* that the UN's rights and duties 'will depend upon its purposes and functions as specified or implied in its constituent documents and developed in practice'.[8] It is also the assumption behind the ICJ's detailed analysis of the provisions of the UN Charter in *Certain Expenses* when it considered whether the General Assembly could authorize expenditure for two peacekeeping operations.[9] Debates remain as to the correct method of interpreting treaties establishing international organizations, with the ICJ repeating the mantra that, as multilateral treaties, they should be interpreted in accordance with the ordinary principles of treaty interpretation.[10] At the same time, the Court has recognized that constituent instruments are 'treaties of a particular type; their object is to create new subjects of law endowed with a certain autonomy, to which the parties entrust the task of realizing common goals'.[11] The correct approach to interpreting constituent instruments is a matter of some discussion,[12] as is the question of the extent to which an organization can rely upon implied powers as a basis for its activities. *Reparation for Injuries*, as well as subsequent cases, confirmed the possibility of international organizations possessing implied powers, although there are differing views as to the source and extent of permissible implication.[13]

[6] H. G. Schermers and N. Blokker, *International Institutional Law: Unity within Diversity*, 5th edn (Leiden: Martinus Nijhoff, 2011) 726.

[7] For discussion, see C. Chinkin, *Third Parties in International Law* (Oxford University Press, 1993) 94–5.

[8] *Reparation for Injuries Suffered in the Service of the United Nations*, (Advisory Opinion), [1949] ICJ Rep. 174, 180.

[9] *Certain Expenses of the United Nations (Article 17, Paragraph 2 of the Charter)*, (Advisory Opinion), [1962] ICJ Rep. 151, 157–65.

[10] *Ibid.*, 157; *Legality of the Use by a State of Nuclear Weapons in Armed Conflict*, (Advisory Opinion), [1996] ICJ Rep. 66, 74.

[11] *Ibid.*, 75.

[12] See, for example, T. Sato, 'Constituent Instruments of International Organizations and Their Interpretative Framework – Introduction to the Principal Doctrines and Bibliography', (1986) 14 *Hitotsubashi Journal of Law and Politics* 1.

[13] See discussion in Schermers and Blokker, *International Institutional Law*, 182–4; J. Alvarez, *International Organizations as Law-Makers* (Oxford University Press, 2005) 93–4.

The third element of the ICJ's statement in 1980 – that organizations must abide by the 'international agreements to which they are parties' – also appears relatively uncontroversial. In *Reparation for Injuries* the ICJ referenced the UN's practice in concluding treaties as confirming its international legal personality.[14] The ILC, in its work on international organizations and treaty-making, stated that organizations have the capacity to enter into agreements, and are bound to perform their obligations pursuant to those treaties in good faith (*pacta sunt servanda*).[15] The ability of international organizations to sign treaties is more limited than states – an organization's treaty-making capacity is subject to its 'rules'[16] – but, for the most part, the legal principles that govern treaties between states also apply to agreements entered into by international organizations.[17] However, as both Klabbers and Reinisch highlight, leaving aside headquarters agreements and the practice of the European Union (EU), international organizations have not been particularly active treaty-makers.[18]

More controversial is the first clause of the sentence in *WHO-Egypt* – that international organizations 'are bound by any obligations incumbent upon them under general rules of international law'.[19] Discussions have focused on whether the phrase 'general rules of international law' is merely an alternative term for customary international law or whether the Court was referring to a more limited set of principles.[20] While claims that

[14] *Reparation for Injuries*, 179.

[15] The ILC's work resulted in the adoption of the Vienna Convention on the Law of Treaties between States and International Organizations or between International Organizations (1986) (not yet in force). Article 26 provides that: '[e]very treaty in force is binding upon the parties to it and must be performed by them in good faith'.

[16] 1986 VCLT, article 6. Article 2(1)(j) of the 1986 VCLT defines the rules of an organization as 'in particular, the constituent instruments, decisions and resolutions adopted in accordance with them, and established practice of the organization'.

[17] For a comparison of the 1969 VCLT and the 1986 VCLT see O. Elias, 'Who Can Make Treaties? International Organizations', in D. Hollis (ed.), *The Oxford Guide to Treaties* (Oxford University Press, 2012) 73, 77–81.

[18] Klabbers, 'Sources of International Organizations' Law', 994–5; A. Reinisch, 'Sources of International Organizations' Law: Why Custom and General Principles are Crucial', in Besson and D'Aspremont (eds.), *Sources of International Law*, 1007, 1015.

[19] *WHO-Egypt*, 89.

[20] G. Verdirame, *The UN and Human Rights: Who Guards the Guardians?* (Cambridge University Press, 2011) 71. Amerasinghe assumed that the ICJ was referring to customary international law obligations: C. F. Amerasinghe, *Principles of the Institutional Law of International Organizations*, 2nd ed. (Cambridge University Press, 2005) 400. Klabbers

international organizations are bound by customary international law are common,[21] this position has been doubted on the basis that international organizations are not involved in the relevant 'political community' that makes custom.[22] Consequently, just as international organizations are said to be bound by treaties to which they are not parties (constituent instruments) they may also be bound by customary rules that they did not participate in creating.

The Court's statement in *WHO-Egypt* leaves open the question whether international organizations are bound by general principles of law or the domestic law of a particular state. The reference to 'general rules of international law' could be interpreted to include 'general principles of law' pursuant to Article 38(1)(c) of the Statute of the ICJ.[23] Questions then arise as to which principles of domestic law have attained this status and are also relevant to the activities of international organizations. The domestic law of a specific state may also bind international organizations when they form legal relationships with private persons. For example, international organizations may enter into agreements with third parties, including procurement or construction contracts, to fulfil their functions.[24] While immunity precludes the possibility of domestic courts adjudicating on the legality of acts of international organizations in most circumstances,[25] this does not mean that organizations do not have obligations under domestic law.

Aside from applicable domestic law, an international organization and its staff are governed by the organization's 'internal law'.[26] This phrase has been used to denote a range of provisions, including an organization's

suggests that it is possible that the Court in *WHO-Egypt* was referring to secondary rules of international law, that is, 'rules related to the making, application, and enforcement of primary rules': see Klabbers, 'Sources of International Organisations' Law', 999.

21 For example, Schermers and Blokker, *International Institutional Law*, 835; Verdirame, *The UN and Human Rights*, 72.

22 Klabbers, 'Sources of International Organizations' Law', 997; Reinisch, 'Sources of International Organizations' Law', 1016–17.

23 This suggestion is made in I. Brownlie, *Principles of Public International Law*, 7th ed. (Oxford University Press, 2008) 688. See also Amerasinghe, *Institutional Law*, 21; Schermers and Blokker, *International Institutional* Law, 834–5; Reinisch, 'Sources of International Organizations' Law', 1022.

24 Amerasinghe, *Institutional Law*, 407.

25 Treaties usually grant international organizations absolute immunity from the jurisdiction of domestic courts: see, for example, Convention on the Privileges and Immunities of the United Nations (1946), Article II, section 2.

26 Seyersted credits an early use of the phrase 'internal law' to the first decision of the Administrative Tribunal of the League of Nations in 1929 when it stated that the

constituent instrument,[27] raising questions as to the distinction between an organization's internal law and international law and the relationship between internal law and the 'rules of the organization'.[28] The status of Security Council resolutions highlights the difficulty with these distinctions. On the one hand, as resolutions of a UN organ adopted in accordance with its constituent instrument, Security Council resolutions are examples of UN internal law. On the other hand, the binding force of Chapter VII resolutions on all UN members demonstrates that they are more than internal legal provisions governing relationships within the organization.[29] This chapter will distinguish between resolutions of organs that govern operational activities and instruments such as the rules of procedure, guidelines, policies and staff regulations that apply to the work of the organization and its staff. Both types of instrument define the way in which organizations and their staff function on operations, although their legal basis and, potentially, their legal effect may be different.

7.3 How Does the Legal Framework Apply to Operational Activities?

The one-sentence statement in *WHO-Egypt* provides a starting point for analyzing the laws that govern operational activities, but the ICJ did not provide a context or examples as to the way in which the sources of international (and domestic) law apply to different activities. This section will consider the legal principles that apply to operations, while also acknowledging that an activity's legal basis may not always be attributable to one source. This problem is illustrated by debates regarding the

Tribunal 'Qu'il est tenu d'appliquer le droit interne de la Société des Nations, formulé, soit par un statut général, soit par des décisiôns et textes envisageant tels cas déterminés, ainsi que les stipulations intervenues entre l'administration et ses fonctionnaires'. [The Tribunal 'is bound to apply the internal law of the League of Nations, formulated either by a general statute, or by decisions and texts considering specific cases, as well as the terms of employment between the administration and its officials']. See Société des Nations, Tribunal Administratif, Judgment No. 1, 4; F. Seyersted, 'Applicable Law in Relations between Intergovernmental Organizations and Private Parties', (1967) 122 *Recueil des Cours* 529.

27 See Société des Nations, Tribunal Administratif, Judgment No. 1, 4.

28 See 1986 VCLT, Article 2(1)(j); ARIO, Article 2(b).

29 Verdirame notes that it is 'important to distinguish acts that are merely internal from those that have effects on the international plane': Verdirame, *The UN and Human Rights*, 83.

application of human rights law to UN operations. Mégret and Hoffman suggest three ways in which the UN is bound by human rights obligations: first, as a subject of international law it is bound as a matter of customary international law (the 'external conception'); second, the UN is bound as a matter of internal law due to the obligation to uphold human rights in the Charter (the 'internal conception'); and third, the UN cannot be allowed to escape its members' obligations (the 'hybrid conception').[30] Clapham adds a fourth reason: 'because [the UN] has unilaterally declared that it expects its personnel to act in accordance with the Universal Declaration of Human Rights and acts as if it were itself bound'.[31] These four justifications highlight a range of approaches to binding the UN to human rights obligations. Attributing a legal obligation to any one source is also complicated by the convergence of customary international law and treaty law in particular fields, for example, international humanitarian law, resulting in difficulties in discerning the basis for applying a specific principle.[32] The discussion below illustrates some of these complexities.

7.3.1 Treaties and Agreements

When determining whether it is lawful for an international organization to engage in any activity – operational or otherwise – the constituent instrument is the first point of reference. Consequently, when the General Assembly formulated the question to be answered in *Certain Expenses* it asked the ICJ to consider whether the expenses for operations in the Congo and Middle East were 'within the meaning of Article 17, paragraph 2, of the Charter of the United Nations'.[33] The Court determined the legality of the expenses by undertaking a detailed analysis of the Charter, starting with the text of Article 17 before moving to the 'general structure and scheme of the Charter'[34] and the practice of the organization.[35] This focus on ensuring compliance with the constituent instrument is evident in discussions of the

[30] F. Mégret and F. Hoffman, 'The UN as a Human Rights Violator? Some Reflections on the United Nations Changing Human Rights Responsibilities', (2003) 25 *Human Rights Quarterly* 314, 317–18.

[31] A. Clapham, *Human Rights Obligations of Non-State Actors* (Oxford University Press, 2006) 127.

[32] See G. Porretto and S. Vité, 'The Application of International Humanitarian Law and Human Rights Law to International Organisations', University Centre for International Humanitarian Law, Research Paper No. 1 (2006) 24.

[33] *Certain Expenses*, 156. [34] *Ibid.*, 162. [35] *Ibid.*, 165.

legal arrangements for a range of operations. For example, when commentators have examined the UN's ability to undertake one of its more controversial activities – the administration of territory in places such as Kosovo and East Timor – they highlight provisions of the UN Charter, including Chapter VII, Articles 36 and 81, as well as the doctrine of implied powers.[36] They also acknowledge there is no express power to administer territory in the Charter and yet a lack of obvious restraints on the organization's ability to undertake this activity.[37] As Chesterman has stated, the practice of the UN in territorial administration demonstrates the flexible nature of the Charter as a legal instrument.[38] The practice also highlights that liberal methods of treaty interpretation and the doctrine of implied powers ensure that operational activities are rarely viewed as *ultra vires* an organization's founding document.

For the most part, constituent instruments contain general statements of goals, rather than specifics as to the way an organization's activities should be conducted. When operations are established an agreement is usually signed between the organization and the host state. These agreements can take a variety of different forms, but it is not always clear that they constitute treaties governed by international law. In the category of treaties can be placed headquarters or host state agreements, which facilitate the ability of an organization to set up offices in-country. These documents generally provide for an organization's independence and freedom of action, its juridical personality, its privileges and immunities (and those of its staff) and an exemption from local taxation.[39] For example, UNHCR's in-country programmes are facilitated by 'cooperation agreements' with host states, signed in accordance with Article 16 of its Statute, and

[36] C. Stahn, *The Law and Practice of International Territorial Administration* (Cambridge University Press, 2008) 423; M. Ruffert, 'The Administration of Kosovo and East Timor by the International Community', (2001) 50 *International and Comparative Law Quarterly* 613, 615–16; T. Irmscher, 'The Legal Framework for the Activities of the United Nations Interim Administration Mission in Kosovo: The Charter, Human Rights, and the Law of Occupation', (2001) 44 *German Yearbook of International Law*, 353, 362–6.

[37] S. Chesterman, *You, the People: The United Nations, Transitional Administration, and State-Building* (Oxford University Press, 2004) 48; Stahn, *International Territorial Administration*, 423. Irmscher writes that the UN Secretariat and its sub-units, including the United Nations Mission in Kosovo (UNMIK) are 'clearly bound by the principles and purposes of the organization in performing its tasks': Irmscher, 'Legal Framework', 363.

[38] Chesterman, *You, the People*, 48.

[39] For example, World Health Organization, *Agreement with the Government of India*, WHO Doc. A2/51 (9 June 1949) annex A; International Criminal Court, *Headquarters Agreement between the International Criminal Court and the Host State*, Doc No. ICC-BD/04-01-08).

registered as treaties with the UN Secretariat.[40] Similar issues are covered in Status of Force Agreements (SOFAs) and Status of Mission Agreements (SOMAs), which govern the presence of military and civilian personnel on peacekeeping and other types of operations.[41]

Headquarters or host state agreements, whatever their designation, facilitate the activities of international organizations in a host state, but do not necessarily provide details of an organization's in-country activities. In some organizations this information is contained in non-treaty documents, in others it may be provided in instruments governed by international law. International organizations charged with inspecting states' facilities for the production of unlawful weapons, including the IAEA and the Organization for the Prohibition of Chemical Weapons (OPCW), enter into treaties with states to enable access. The IAEA has developed a Model Additional Protocol for access to nuclear facilities[42] and the OPCW can inspect members' chemical facilities pursuant to agreements covering matters such as health and safety, confidentiality and inspector equipment.[43] These types of agreements are all signed with the state where the operation takes place. In addition, international organizations may sign agreements with third states to assist with their activities. The Model Memorandum of Understanding between the UN and relevant contributing governments for the provision of resources to UN peacekeeping

[40] M. Zieck, *UNHCR's Worldwide Presence in the Field: A Legal Analysis of UNHCR's Cooperation Agreements* (Nijmegen: Wolf, 2006) 78; M. Janmyr, *Protecting Civilians in Refugee Camps: Unable and Unwilling States, UNHCR and International Responsibility* (Leiden: Martinus Nijhoff, 2014) 263. An example of a UNHCR cooperation agreement is the Headquarters Cooperation Agreement between the Office of the United Nations High Commissioner for Refugees (UNHCR) and the Government of Niger. Geneva, 8 May 2014, [2014] *United Nations Juridical Yearbook* 66.

[41] For example, *Comprehensive Review of the Whole Question of Peacekeeping Operations in All Their Aspects: Model Status-of-Forces Agreement for Peace-Keeping Operations*, General Assembly Resolution 45/594, (9 October 1990) annex (UN Model SOFA). SOMAs are signed when an operation does not include a military force: see B. Oswald, H. Durham and A. Bates, *Documents on the Law of UN Peace Operations*, 2nd ed. (Oxford University Press, 2019) 45.

[42] This applies when a state has entered into a comprehensive safeguards agreement pursuant to the Non-Proliferation Treaty. See L. Rockwood, *Legal Framework for IAEA Safeguards* (Vienna: IAEA, 2013) 13; and *Model Protocol Additional to the Agreement(s) between State(s) and the International Atomic Energy Agency for the Application of Safeguards*, IAEA Doc INFCIRC/540, Article 4.

[43] The OPCW inspects members' chemical facilities pursuant to the Chemical Weapons Convention and its Verification Annex: OPCW CSP, *Decision: Model Facility Agreement for Chemical Weapons Destruction Facilities*, C-V/DEC.23 (19 May 2000) annex.

operations contains sections on compliance with UN standards of conduct, the discipline of troops and investigations in the event of an allegation of misconduct.[44] The UN may also sign agreements with a state to facilitate peacekeeping operations in another state – for example, a 2006 Memorandum of Understanding (MOU) between Uganda and the UN enables the UN Mission in Sudan (UNMIS) to deploy personnel and provide logistical support to Sudan via Uganda.[45] The use of the terminology of MOU raises questions as to whether such instruments – commonly used to set out operational arrangements[46] – have the force of law. This will depend on whether the relevant MOU fulfils the definition of a treaty or whether the intention of the parties was to create commitments of a non-binding character.[47] The UN has indicated that it considers MOUs entered into by the organization as binding.[48]

This short description of the treaties and agreements that facilitate the operations of an organization highlights a complex web of provisions. This proliferation of agreements can lead to the possibility of conflict. The IAEA has recognized this problem by providing that if there is a conflict between the IAEA's Safeguards Agreement and an Additional Protocol, the latter agreement shall prevail.[49] Another layer of complexity is added by the application of multilateral treaties to operational activities. These include treaties that govern privileges and immunities, such as the Convention on the Privileges and Immunities of the United Nations[50] and the Convention on the Safety of United Nations and Associated Personnel.[51] It could also include treaties governing substantive areas, such as human rights. As highlighted earlier, the major problem when applying the provisions of

[44] 'Memorandum of Understanding between the United Nations and [participating State] contributing resources to [the United Nations Peacekeeping Operation] (*Extracts*)', Articles 7 *bis*, 7 *ter*, 7 *quarter*, reproduced in Oswald *et al.*, *UN Peace Operations*, 68–82.

[45] Memorandum of Understanding between the United Nations and the Government of the Republic of Uganda concerning the Activities of the United Nations Mission in Sudan in the Republic of Uganda. New York, 27 January 2006, [2006] *United Nations Juridical Yearbook* 5, Preamble, para. 3.

[46] Treaty Section of the Office of Legal Affairs (UN), *Treaty Handbook*, rev. ed. (United Nations Publications, 2012) 68.

[47] See I. Roberts, *Satow's Diplomatic Practice*, 7th ed. (Oxford University Press, 2016) 616, para. 33.20.

[48] *UN Treaty Handbook*, 68. [49] Model Additional Protocol, Article 1.

[50] Convention on the Privileges and Immunities of the United Nations (1946).

[51] Convention on the Safety of United Nations and Associated Personnel (1994).

multilateral treaties to operational activities is that organizations are not parties to the treaties. One possible response is that as member states are parties to such treaties then an organization is also bound.[52] In the context of UNHCR's refugee camps, Wilde has argued that the UNHCR is bound to uphold the human rights obligations entered into by the host state, including treaty obligations, as an exercise of delegated authority.[53] Another possibility is that a multilateral treaty's terms are incorporated by reference into the legal framework governing an operation. For example, the Special Representative of the Secretary General for Kosovo promulgated a series of regulations to govern the activities of UNMIK. Regulation 1999/24 on the law applicable in Kosovo provided that '[i]n exercising their functions, all persons undertaking public duties or holding public office in Kosovo shall observe internationally recognized human rights standards' as reflected in a long list of human rights treaties, including the European Convention on Human Rights and the International Covenant on Civil and Political Rights.[54] The Joint Action Plan covering the activities of the European Union Naval Force ATALANTA (EU NAVFOR), a naval operation that counters Somali-based piracy, refers to applicable international law, including the United Nations Convention on the Law of the Sea.[55] Through such instruments, the terms of multilateral treaties can be incorporated into an organization's operational activities.

International organizations may also apply treaty law to their activities, even where there is doubt as to whether they are bound *de jure*. The UN is not a party to the four Geneva Conventions, but contingents in UN-mandated operations have employed the provisions governing occupation in Geneva Convention IV to structure their activities. In 1993 the Australian contingent of the United Task Force (UNITAF), a US-led

[52] Mégret and Hoffmann, 'Human Rights Violator', 318.

[53] R. Wilde, '*Quis Custodiet Ipos Custodes?*: Why and How UNHCR Governance of 'Development' Refugee Camps Should be Subject to Human Rights Law', (1998) 1 *Yale Human Rights and Development Law Journal* 107, 119–20.

[54] *UNMIK Regulation 1999/24 on the Law Applicable in Kosovo*, UN Doc. UNMIK/REG/1999/24 (12 December 1999) section 1.3.

[55] *Council Joint Action 2008/851/CFSP of 10 November 2008*, [2008] OJ L 301/33, Articles 1–2 (Council Joint Action). For discussion, see F. Naert, *International Law Aspects of the EU's Security and Defence Policy, with a Particular Focus on the Law of Armed Conflict and Human Rights* (Antwerp: Intersentia, 2010) 184–5.

operation authorized by the Security Council pursuant to Security Council resolution 794, relied upon Geneva Convention IV to engage in a range of activities in southern Somalia pursuant to its mandate.[56] The Australian view was that in the absence of a government in Somalia, the Australian contingent as part of UNITAF was bound by Geneva Convention IV as a High Contracting Party that was in partial occupation of the territory of another.[57] In a UN-mandated operation that is commanded by a party to the Geneva Conventions, the appropriateness of a state applying its existing treaty obligations to the operation is understandable. However, Kelly has also argued that UNITAF's successor, the United Nations Operation in Somalia II (UNOSOM II), a UN-commanded operation that assumed responsibility in May 1993, continued to be an occupying power at least while it had effective control of territory.[58] On that approach the laws of occupation effectively become 'the proper frame of reference' for the UN's activities, although the UN is not a party to Geneva Convention IV.[59] Consequently, some treaties may be viewed as the appropriate de facto legal framework for an operational activity, even where there is doubt as to whether they apply *de jure*.

7.3.2 Customary International Law

Another response to the lack of explicit consent by international organizations to the major multilateral treaties is to state that, as international legal persons, international organizations are bound by those principles that are recognized as customary international law. This is the 'external conception', which focuses on international organizations as subjects of international law.[60] Whatever the legal basis for the application of

[56] Geneva Convention relative to the Protection of Civilian Persons in Time of War (1949). Such activities included establishing a claims regime, the re-establishment of a police force and restoring prisons, police cells, the courts and the judiciary: see M. Kelly, *Restoring and Maintaining Order in Complex Peace Operations* (The Hague: Kluwer, 1999) 38–46.

[57] Kelly, *Complex Peace Operations*, 37–8.

[58] *Ibid.*, 68, 181. Kelly highlights that the relevant Security Council resolutions only provided a general mandate, not 'clear guidance', for dealing with specific issues, such as the handling of detainees, at 70.

[59] *Ibid.*, 70. The appropriateness of applying the laws of occupation to the UN's administration of territories is widely discussed: see for example, E. Benvenisti, *The International Law of Occupation*, 2nd ed. (Oxford University Press, 2012) 276–98; Chesterman, *You, the People*, 145.

[60] Mégret and Hoffman, 'Human Rights Violator', 317.

custom, as Verdirame observes, '[o]nly those rules of customary international law that are relevant to the activities of the international organisation will matter in practice'.[61] Principles of custom may give rise to both rights and obligations for international organizations.[62] In the category of rights can be placed customary immunity rules.[63] An example of an obligation is the statement in the UN Secretary-General's Bulletin on the Observance of International Humanitarian Law that 'the fundamental principles and rules of international humanitarian law' apply to UN forces engaged in armed conflict.[64] Included within the principles of custom that are relevant to international organizations are *jus cogens* norms, one argument being that states should not be able to establish organizations to evade central rules of the legal order to which they are bound.[65] The significance of *jus cogens* to the UN was recognized by *ad hoc* Judge Lauterpacht in his separate opinion in *Application of the Convention on the Prevention and Punishment of Genocide*,[66] when he considered whether the Security Council's arms embargo imposed on Bosnia-Herzegovina violated the prohibition against genocide. Judge Lauterpacht accepted that the relevance of the *jus cogens* norm should be 'drawn to the attention of the Security Council'.[67] More recently, the ILC's Special Rapporteur on peremptory norms of general international law (*jus cogens*) proposed a draft conclusion that resolutions of international organizations, including those

[61] Verdirame, *The UN and Human Rights*, 72.

[62] N. Blokker, 'International Organizations and Customary International Law – Is the International Law Commission Taking International Organizations Seriously?', (2017) 14 *International Organizations Law Review* 1, 1.

[63] See Blokker's discussion of a Dutch court's recognition that NATO was immune from jurisdiction on the basis of customary international law: Blokker, 'International Organizations and Customary International Law', 1–2. Blokker notes that it is not generally accepted that the immunity of international organizations is a principle of custom.

[64] *Secretary-General's Bulletin: Observance by United Nations Forces of International Humanitarian Law*, UN Doc. ST/SGB/1999/13 (6 August 1999), para. 1.1. For an earlier view on this question, see F. Seyersted, *United Nations Forces in the Law of Peace and War* (Leiden: Sijthoff, 1966), 196.

[65] See International Law Commission, 'Draft Articles on the Law of Treaties between States and International Organizations or between International Organizations' [1982] II(2) *Yearbook of the International Law Commission* 17, 56 commenting on Draft Article 53. See also Daugirdas, 'How and Why', 346.

[66] *Application of the Convention on the Prevention and Punishment of Genocide Bosnia and Herzegovina* v. *Serbia and Montenegro*, Provisional Measures, Order, [1993] ICJ Rep. 325.

[67] *Ibid.*, 441.

of the Security Council, 'do not establish binding obligations if they conflict with a peremptory norm of general international law'.[68]

In practice, most debate on the extent to which custom binds international organizations concerns the application of international humanitarian law and international human rights law to UN peacekeeping forces and the application of human rights law to the activities of the international financial institutions.[69] While it is generally acknowledged that the UN and its organs must comply with human rights obligations, it is less clear what those obligations entail.[70] In this respect, customary principles may be relevant when interpreting references to human rights standards in constituent instruments.[71] More broadly, even where there is no explicit reference to human rights in a constituent instrument, it has been asserted that customary human rights law is relevant to its interpretation in accordance with Article 31(3)(c) of the 1969 VCLT.[72] In addition, customary principles may be codified in other documents that govern an organization's operations. Thus, the Secretary-General's Bulletin on the Observance of International Humanitarian Law has been said to incorporate most customary international humanitarian law rules.[73] Rule 5 of 'Ten Rules: Code of Personal Conduct for Blue Helmets' states that UN peacekeepers must '[r]espect and regard the human rights of all'.[74] This can be viewed as encompassing 'the applicable portions of the Universal Declaration of Human Rights'.[75] Greater specificity on relevant obligations is found in the Joint Action Plan for EU NAVFOR and the exchange of letters between the EU and Kenya regarding the transfer of detainees from naval vessels to Kenya for trial. EU NAVFOR must act 'in

68 *Third Report on Peremptory Norms of General International Law (Jus Cogens) by Dire Tladi, Special Rapporteur*, UN Doc. A/CN.4/714 (12 February 2018) 61–5, paras. 150–9, 67 (Draft Conclusion 17).

69 See, for example, Verdirame, *The UN and Human Rights*; M. Darrow, *Between Light and Shadow: The World Bank, the International Monetary Fund and International Human Rights Law* (Oxford: Hart, 2003); Sigrun Skogly, *The Human Rights Obligations of the World Bank and the International Monetary Fund* (Abingdon: Routledge, 2001).

70 Janmyr, *Protecting Civilians in Refugee Camps*, 238.

71 R. Wolfrum, 'Chapter I: Purposes and Principles', in B. Simma *et al.* (eds.), *The Charter of the United Nations: A Commentary, Volume I*, 3rd ed. (Oxford University Press, 2012) 107, 108–9.

72 Darrow, *Between Light and Shadow*, 129–30 (in the context of the Articles of Agreement of the international financial institutions).

73 S. Mathias, 'UN Peacekeeping Today: Legal Challenges and Uncertainties', (2017) 17 *Melbourne Journal of International Law* 138, 142.

74 UN, *Ten Rules: Code of Personal Conduct for Blue Helmets* (1999), rule 5.

75 Oswald *et al.*, *UN Peace Operations*, 523.

accordance with international human rights obligations', including the prohibition against torture and the prohibition on arbitrary detention.[76]

7.3.3 General Principles of Law and Domestic Law

Whether international organizations are bound by general principles of law as recognized in Article 38(1)(c) of the Statute of the ICJ, and what those general principles encompass for international organizations, are contentious issues.[77] Leaving aside those debates, agreements between international organizations and third parties may explicitly incorporate general principles as a source of law. Such instruments include the standard programme cooperation agreement between the United Nations Children's Fund (UNICEF) and civil society partners implementing an in-country programme.[78] The agreement provides that in the event of a dispute an arbitral tribunal should apply 'general principles of international commercial law',[79] effectively making these principles the proper law of the agreement. Similarly, the FAO's standard General Terms and Conditions for Services are subject to 'general principles of law to the exclusion of any single national system of law'.[80] Cases in employment tribunals established by organizations to hear complaints by staff members have also referenced general principles, such as equity and the prohibition on discrimination.[81] Appellants and respondents before the NATO Administrative Tribunal have cited general principles of international administrative law, principles of good or sound administration, and legitimate expectations in their arguments.[82] Such references to international

[76] *Council Decision 2009/293/CFSP of 26 February 2009,* [2009] OJ L 79/49, annex, Article 2(c).

[77] Reinisch, 'Sources of International Organizations' Law', 1022.

[78] UNICEF, Programme Cooperation Agreement, located in UNICEF, *Guidance for Civil Society Organizations on Partnership with UNICEF* (February 2020) 15, available at www.unicef.org/about/partnerships/files/Guidance-for-CSOs-on-Partnership-with-UNICEF.pdf (accessed 2 May 2020).

[79] *Ibid.*, Article XII(3).

[80] Food and Agriculture Organization, General Terms and Conditions for Services, clause 21.2, available at www.fao.org/fileadmin/user_upload/FAO-countries/Bangladesh/Procurement/FAO_GENERAL_TERMS_AND_CONDITIONS_FOR_SERVICES.pdf (accessed 2 May 2020) (FAO General Terms and Conditions for Services). The clause deems that general principles of law include the UNIDROIT Principles of International Commercial Contracts 2010.

[81] Amerasinghe, *Institutional Law*, 292–3.

[82] See, for example, *PK* v. *NATO Support Agency* (NATO Administrative Tribunal, Case No 2014/1028, 23 March 2015), para. 44; *JF* v. *NATO Airborne Early Warning and Control Force Geilenkirchen* (NATO Administrative Tribunal, Case No 2017/1113, 20 February 2018), paras. 19–20; *MS* v. *NATO International Staff* (NATO Administrative Tribunal, Case No

administrative law are derived from domestic legal principles, however, national law is not being applied as such by these tribunals – 'general principles of law are the true source of law'.[83]

International organizations may be bound by the domestic law of a specific state through a variety of mechanisms. First, organizations may enter into agreements with private parties to assist with operational activities, including contracts for goods or services. The procurement division of the OSCE has contracted with a range of third parties to provide services as diverse as security for the OSCE Special Monitoring Mission in the Ukraine (SMM) and the OSCE Mission in Kosovo (OMIK), vehicle maintenance and repair for the SMM, and the supply of equipment such as unexploded ordnance (UXO) detectors.[84] The OSCE's standard form contracts for goods and services are governed by the laws of Austria and any disputes are to be settled by negotiation or arbitration in accordance with the rules of the United Nations Commission on International Trade Law (UNCITRAL).[85] The WHO contracts with third parties in a number of different circumstances, including with companies that provide products during an influenza pandemic.[86] The WHO's contract with Sanofi in the Pandemic Influenza Preparedness Framework, which commits Sanofi to donating and reserving, at affordable prices, a certain percentage of vaccine production to the WHO, is to be interpreted according to its terms or otherwise in conformity with Swiss law.[87] Disputes under the contract are to be resolved by an arbitral tribunal in accordance with the rules of the International Chamber of Commerce.[88] Where the proper law of an agreement entered into between an organization and a private party is not explicit, the applicable law will depend on the conflict

2017/1104, 31 October 2017), paras. 34, 49; *PP* v. *NATO Communications and Information Agency* AT-J(2018)0007 (NATO Administrative Tribunal, Case No 2017/1112, 6 June 2018), paras. 23–4, 34.

[83] Amerasinghe, *Institutional Law*, 294.

[84] See OSCE, 'Contracts Awarded in 2018 (>50,000 EUR)', available at https://procurement.osce.org/resources/document/contract-awards-2018-0 (accessed 2 May 2020).

[85] OSCE, General Conditions of Contract (Services), Articles 39, 41; OSCE, General Conditions of Contract (Goods), Articles 41, 43.

[86] For example, World Health Organization, 'Standard Materials Transfer Agreements 2 (SMTA2)', available at www.who.int/influenza/pip/smta2/en/ (accessed 2 May 2020).

[87] World Health Organization, *Pandemic Influenza Preparedness Framework for the Sharing of Influenza Virus and Access to Vaccines and Other Benefits (PIP Framework): Standard Materials Transfer Agreement 2* (between Sanofi Pasteur SA and the World Health Organization), Article 7.2.

[88] *Ibid*., Article 7.1.

of law rules of the forum.[89] Overall, while international organizations are willing to have their contracts governed by a state's domestic law, they are less willing to give jurisdiction to that state's courts.

Second, international organizations may be governed by the law of the place where they undertake their activities. While organizations are usually immune from the jurisdiction of domestic courts this does not mean that they are not liable for injury caused to third parties.[90] Liability for tort is most likely governed by the place of injury, with the possibility of a court applying a different law subject to the relevant conflict of law principles.[91] Treaties can specify the applicability of local law in the event of a civil claim – for example, the Headquarters Agreement between the Organization of American States and the Government of the US applies US law to the resolution of disputes to which the OAS is a party.[92] International organizations may also be subject to domestic administrative provisions; for example, the OAS-US Headquarters Agreement requires the organization to observe local fire protection regulations.[93] In the event that the fire protection regulations are inconsistent with the internal law of the OAS, US regulations prevail.[94] Annual reports by the UN Secretary-General on the strategic heritage plan for the UN office in Geneva – a project involving the construction of new buildings and the renovation of the Palais des Nations – emphasize compliance with local development, planning and fire regulations and building codes.[95] International organizations have also applied domestic law on operations where there is no obvious territorial connection – notably on the high seas. When EU

89 Seyersted, 'Applicable Law', 474.

90 Schermers and Blokker, *International Institutional Law*, 1038.

91 C. W. Jenks, *The Proper Law of International Organisations* (London: Stevens and Co., 1962) 211; J. Crawford, *Brownlie's Principles of Public International Law*, 9th ed. (Oxford University Press, 2019) 180.

92 *Headquarters Agreement between the Organization of American States and the Government of the United States of America*, 1992, Article VIII(1).

93 *Ibid.*, Article XII(3)(a). 94 *Ibid.*

95 *Strategic Heritage Plan of the United Nations Office at Geneva: Report of the Secretary-General*, UN Doc. A/69/417 (12 July 2018) para. 98; *Third Annual Progress Report on the Strategic Heritage Plan of the United Nations Office at Geneva: Report of the Secretary-General*, UN Doc. A/71/403 (26 September 2016) para. 28 (referring to the submission of a 'voluntary construction permit application' with Swiss cantonal authorities); *Fourth Annual Progress Report on the Strategic Heritage Plan of the United Nations Office at Geneva: Report of the Secretary-General*, UN Doc. A/72/521 (9 October 2017) para. 47; *Sixth Annual Progress Report on the Strategic Heritage Plan of the United Nations Office at Geneva: Report of the Secretary-General*, UN Doc. A/74/452 (25 September 2019) para. 37.

NAVFOR detains suspected pirates in operations off the coast of Somalia, the law of the flag state of the vessel used in the operation applies – this would likely include the extraterritorial application of the European Convention on Human Rights.[96]

Third, the personnel of international organizations on operations may be bound by the domestic law of the host state or the country of their nationality. The UN Model SOFA provides that 'the United Nations peace-keeping operation and its members shall respect all local laws and regulations'.[97] This is despite the fact that those personnel may be immune from the jurisdiction of local courts. The personnel of troop contributing countries (TCCs) are subject to the exclusive criminal jurisdiction of the relevant TCC and therefore exempt from the criminal jurisdiction of the courts of the place of operation.[98] This means that service personnel will be bound by the military justice systems and criminal laws of their national state. The 'Standards of Conduct' section of the UN Peacekeeping website has a list of relevant domestic laws that apply to the military contingents of TCCs, with an emphasis on preventing and prosecuting sexual exploitation and abuse.[99] Civilian personnel on UN missions may not be entitled to immunity from the host states' criminal jurisdiction, and, consequently, may be subject to the jurisdiction of local courts with appropriate guarantees of due process.[100]

[96] See Council Joint Action, article 13; D. Guilfoyle, 'Counter-Piracy Law Enforcement and Human Rights', (2010) 59 *International and Comparatively Law Quarterly* 141, 154–8.

[97] UN Model SOFA, para. IV(6).

[98] *Ibid.*, Article VI(47)(b). See also United Nations Peacekeeping Law Reform Project, School of Law University of Essex, 'UN Peacekeeping and the Model Status of Forces Agreement: Background Paper Prepared for the Experts' Workshop, 26 August 2019, London, UK, Hosted by the New Zealand High Commission', para. 73.

[99] UN Peacekeeping, 'Standards of Conduct', available at https://peacekeeping.un.org/en/standards-of-conduct (accessed 2 May 2020).

[100] UN Model SOFA, para. 47(a). For example, the agreement between the UN and the Central African Republic (CAR) on the Status of the United Nations Integrated Peacebuilding Office in the CAR (BINUCA) provides that criminal proceedings may be instituted against a BINUCA member with certain guarantees for due process rights and non-imposition of the death penalty: the text is reproduced in (2010) *United Nations Juridical Yearbook* 19, Article 18. See also Status of Forces Agreement between the United Nations and the Government of the Republic of South Sudan concerning the United Nations Missions in South Sudan ('SOFA'). Juba, 8 August 11, (2011) *United Nations Juridical Yearbook* 50, Article 51(a).

7.3.4 Internal Law

Leaving aside these formal sources of law, the activities of international organizations in operational environments are regulated by a range of instruments that can be described as internal law, although the use of this language is something of a misnomer. These include institutional acts that have binding force as a matter of international law, such as Security Council resolutions (and documents that gain their authority from such resolutions), instruments promulgated by the executive head of an organization, for example the bulletins of the UN Secretary-General and a plethora of other administrative documents which may or may not be strictly 'legal'.[101] This section is divided into binding instruments under international law and other internal documents, although this division is not a precise one.

7.3.4.1 Instruments under International Law

As well as treaties and custom, international organizations may be bound by institutional acts under international law. Security Council resolutions are clear examples of acts of an organ that are binding by virtue of the UN Charter.[102] Although Security Council resolutions are usually directed to states, the Office of Legal Affairs, in the context of the UN's operations in Afghanistan, has expressed the view that 'such resolutions are nevertheless binding by implication on the United Nations'.[103] Security Council resolutions may be situation-specific or may be directed at UN members or organs more generally. In terms of operations already discussed in this chapter, the establishment of UNOSOM and UNOSOM II in Somalia and UNMIK in Kosovo were all authorized by Security Council resolutions.[104] The Security Council may also authorize other organizations to undertake activities under Chapter VII of the UN Charter. EU NAVFOR's mandate for its activities off the coast of Somalia derives from Security Council resolutions, including resolution 1816 (2008). Although this resolution does not name the EU, it refers to states and 'interested organizations' and authorizes states cooperating with the transitional Somali government to enter

[101] Verdirame, *The UN and Human Rights*, 83–6. [102] United Nations Charter, Article 25.

[103] Note to the Under-Secretary-General for Peacekeeping Operations relating to the Applicability of Security Council Decisions to the United Nations Organizations Operating in Afghanistan, (2006) *United Nations Juridical Yearbook* 471, 472.

[104] SC Res. 751, UN Doc. S/RES/751 (24 April 1992) (UNOSOM); SC Res. 814, UN Doc. S/RES/814 (26 March 1993) (UNOSOM II); SC Res. 1244, UN Doc. S/RES/1244 (10 June 1999) (UNMIK).

Somali waters 'to repress piracy and acts of armed robbery'.[105] The Security Council also authorized and delineated the scope of the African Union's mission in Somalia (AMISOM) – a mission that was designed to support the Transitional Federal Institutions in Somalia by providing protection and security.[106]

Security Council resolutions may enable other UN bodies to adopt instruments that bind the UN on operations. The Security Council's authorization to UNMIK to perform 'basic civilian administrative functions' was interpreted broadly and resulted in the Special Representative of the Secretary-General adopting a regulation vesting legislative and executive authority in UNMIK.[107] The ICJ held in the *Kosovo Advisory Opinion* that at least one of the Special Representative's regulations, the Constitutional Framework, had the force of international law.[108] Similarly, after the Security Council established UNTAET with 'overall responsibility for the administration of East Timor',[109] the Special Representative of the Secretary-General in East Timor adopted regulations that were described as 'legislative acts' and were to remain in force until repealed by the Transitional Administrator or superseded by the transfer of functions to East Timor.[110]

Other organs of the UN can make decisions that impact on UN operations even if such decisions are not binding by virtue of the Charter. As discussed previously, the UN Secretary-General has promulgated bulletins, including the bulletin on the observance of international humanitarian law (applicable to UN forces engaged in armed conflict) and the bulletin on the prohibition of sexual exploitation and sexual abuse (applicable to all UN staff).[111] The authority to issue these bulletins – and their force – is based on the Secretary-General's role as the chief administrative officer of the

[105] SC Res. 1816, UN Doc. S/RES/1816 (2 June 2008) para. 7.

[106] SC Res 1744, UN Doc. S/RES/1744 (21 February 2007) para. 4.

[107] SC Res. 1244, para. 11(b). See *UNMIK Regulation 1999/1*, para. 1.1. See Stahn, *International Territorial Administration*, 317–18.

[108] *Accordance with International Law of the Unilateral Declaration of Independence in Respect of Kosovo* (Advisory Opinion), [2010] ICJ Rep. 403, 440. See also Verdirame, *The UN and Human Rights*, 84.

[109] Security Council Resolution 1272, (15 October 1999) para. 1.

[110] *Regulation No. 1999/1 on the Authority of the Transitional Administration in East Timor*, UN Doc. UNTAET/REG/1991/1 (27 November 1999) section 4.

[111] *Secretary-General's Bulletin: Special Measures for Protection from Sexual Exploitation and Sexual Abuse*, UN Doc. ST/SGB/2003/13 (9 October 2003).

organization under Article 97 of the UN Charter.[112] General Assembly resolutions may also have 'prescriptive force' as a matter of the internal law of the UN.[113] In the context of the detention of individuals during peacekeeping operations, relevant General Assembly resolutions include the Universal Declaration of Human Rights, the Body of Principles for the Protection of Persons Under Any Form of Detention or Imprisonment annexed to General Assembly resolution 43/173 and the United Nations Standard Minimum Rules for the Treatment of Prisoners (the Nelson Mandela Rules) annexed to General Assembly resolution 70/175. The latter two instruments, together with relevant human rights treaties, have been described as a framework for UN peacekeeping operations to ensure 'that persons deprived of their liberty have their fundamental human rights protected'.[114]

7.3.4.2 Internal Documents

The range of other internal documents regulating the activity of personnel employed by, or contracting with, an international organization, is extensive. They include self-described 'guidelines', 'handbooks', 'frameworks' or 'policies' for the conduct of activities, as well as staff regulations, codes of conduct and the rules of engagement for peacekeeping operations. In some organizations compliance with these documents is designated as mandatory, while in others their status is not always clear. For example, the World Bank management team issues Directives, Procedures and Guidances – with the first two classes of documents being designated as mandatory.[115] Two Directives are included in the World Bank's Environmental and Social Framework, which sets out the requirements for the Bank and borrowers:[116] the Environmental and Social Directive for Investment Project Financing, which articulates 'the mandatory requirements for the

[112] See Oswald *et al.*, *UN Peace Operations*, 14–15; Porretto and Vité, 'The Application', 23–4. For a discussion of the difficulty of binding military members of national contingents, as well as UN staff, to the bulletin on international humanitarian law, see Oswald *et al.*, *UN Peace Operations*, 252–3.

[113] Verdirame, *The UN and Human Rights*, 84–5 (citing UN Charter, Article 60).

[114] Oswald *et al.*, *UN Peace Operations*, 191.

[115] World Bank, 'Bank Directive: Policy and Procedure Framework', LEG4.01DIR.01 (8 January 2014) sections II(1), III(1)(b).

[116] World Bank, 'The World Bank Environmental and Social Framework' (2017), available at http://pubdocs.worldbank.org/en/837721522762050108/Environmental-and-Social-Framework.pdf (accessed 2 May 2020).

implementation of the Environmental and Social Policy for Investment Project Financing' and the Directive on Addressing Risks and Impacts on Disadvantaged or Vulnerable Individuals or Groups.[117] These Directives have been described as 'legal acts'[118] although this status derives from the Bank's internal legal order rather than the Articles of Agreement of the International Bank for Reconstruction and Development or the International Development Association.

The legal status of other instruments, including guidelines and handbooks, is more ambiguous. The conduct of Commonwealth Election Observer Groups is governed by the 'Revised Commonwealth Guidelines for Election Observation in Member Countries'.[119] Similarly, the term 'guidelines' is used in the title of the FAO's document for conducting environmental impact assessments of field projects.[120] The EIA process is designed to '*ensure* that FAO's field operations *adhere* to [certain] governing principles'.[121] The process to be followed by employees of international organizations on operations may also be set out in handbooks for staff, such as the OSCE *Election Observation Handbook*.[122] The term 'policy' is used to describe the United Nations Human Rights Due Diligence Policy on United Nations Support to Non-United Nations Security Forces – a document which provides that UN entities supporting non-UN entities '*must* . . . pursue a policy of due diligence' to ensure that the non-UN entity is not involved in violations of human rights law, refugee law or international humanitarian law.[123] The need for compliance with this policy has

[117] World Bank, 'Bank Directive: Environmental and Social Directive for Investment Project Financing', OPS5.03-DIR.112 (28 January 2020) section I(1); World Bank, 'Bank Directive: Addressing Risks and Impacts on Disadvantaged or Vulnerable Individuals or Groups', EXC5.07-DIR.117 (4 August 2016) section I(1).

[118] Ph. Dann and M. Riegner, 'The World Bank's Environmental and Social Safeguards and the Evolution of Global Order', (2019) 32 *Leiden Journal of International Law* 537, 540–1, 551 n. 92.

[119] Revised Commonwealth Guidelines for Election Observation in Member Countries, 12 April 2018, available at https://thecommonwealth.org/sites/default/files/inline/CommonwealthGuidelinesfortheConductofElectionObservationinMemberCountries_1.pdf (accessed 2 May 2020).

[120] Food and Agriculture Organization, *Environmental Impact Assessment: Guidelines for FAO Field Projects* (Rome: FAO, 2011).

[121] *Ibid.*, 26 (emphasis added).

[122] OSCE/ODIHR, *Election Observation Handbook* (6th ed., 2000) 7–8.

[123] UN, 'Human Rights Due Diligence Policy on United Nations Support to Non-United Nations Security Forces' (Guidance Note, 2015) 43 (emphasis added).

been given weight by Security Council mandates for peacekeeping operations.[124]

Although it is not always clear whether an organization is legally bound by these documents pursuant to international or domestic law, staff members may be obliged to adhere to standards and guidelines via employment contracts, staff regulations and codes of conduct. The Staff Regulations and Rules of the United Nations set out the general rights and obligations of staff, including loyalty to the 'aims, principles and purposes of the United Nations', their accountability to the Secretary-General for the discharge of their functions, as well as specific instances of prohibited conduct, including sexual exploitation and abuse.[125] In the event that staff members fail to comply with their obligations or fail to observe the standards of conduct expected, they may be subject to disciplinary action.[126] A breach of the UN's Code of Conduct for Blue Helmets may result in disciplinary measures or criminal sanctions by either the UN or a state, depending on whether the act is committed by civilian or military personnel.[127] The UN Secretary-General requires staff to report any breach of the staff rules and regulations, with a failure to do so potentially constituting misconduct.[128] This obligation has been repeatedly highlighted in the context of allegations of sexual misconduct on peacekeeping operations.[129]

International organizations may also require their suppliers of goods and services to fulfil certain standards. The UN obliges members to screen nationals before nominating them for service with the organization to ensure that those individuals 'meet the highest standards of integrity, including respect for and commitment to human rights'.[130] As part of this process, individuals have to certify that they have not committed violations of international humanitarian law or human

[124] For example, Security Council Resolution 2459, (15 March 2019) para. 7(vii).

[125] *Staff Regulations and Rules of the United Nations: Secretary-General's Bulletin*, UN Doc. ST/SGB/2018/1 (1 January 2018) regulations 1.1, 1.2(e), 1.3(a), rule 1.2(e).

[126] *Ibid.*, regulation 10.1, rule 10.1.

[127] See UN, 'Disciplinary Process', available at https://conduct.unmissions.org/enforcement-disciplinary (accessed 2 May 2020).

[128] *Staff Regulations and Rules of the United Nations*, rule 1.2(c).

[129] See *Special Measures for Protection from Sexual Exploitation and Abuse: A New Approach: Report of the Secretary-General*, UN Doc. A/71/818 (28 February 2017) para. 44; *Special Measures for Protection from Sexual Exploitation and Abuse: Report of the Secretary-General*, UN Doc. A/72/751 (15 February 2018) para. 9.

[130] *United Nations Policy: Human Rights Screening of United Nations Personnel* (11 December 2012) para. 3.2.

rights law.[131] In the event of a false statement by a state or individual, the UN may 'take appropriate action in compliance with established procedures and the applicable regulatory framework'.[132] In order to register as a potential supplier of goods and services on the United Nations Global Marketplace, companies must acknowledge the UN Supplier Code of Conduct.[133] Contracts between international organizations and third parties may incorporate such codes in their standard terms and conditions. For example, the FAO's General Terms and Conditions for Services provides that the '[c]ontractor expressly agrees to abide by the UN Supplier Code of Conduct'.[134] These examples demonstrate that international organizations are seeking to ensure that those who provide goods and services (whether states, corporations or individuals) meet specified standards when engaged on operations.

7.4 Conclusion

The above analysis of the many different types and layers of laws – international, domestic and internal – suggests a complex web of provisions governing the operations of international organizations. Constituent instruments, treaties, customary international law principles (whether directly applicable or incorporated by reference), general principles of law, domestic laws and internal rules and regulations all operate to regulate the activities of organizations. This diverse range of instruments means it is difficult to conclude that there is one legal framework that applies to the operational activities of international organizations, or even that there is one set of laws that apply to the activities of a single organization. Complexity rather than cohesion is the result of this discussion of the laws that apply to operational activities.

The plethora of legal instruments and principles detailed in this chapter can also obscure another problem – that 'there are not all that many rules of

[131] *Ibid.*, para. 5.2. [132] *Ibid.*, para. 10.1.

[133] UN Supplier Code of Conduct – Rev.06 December 2017, available at www.un.org/Depts/ptd/about-us/un-supplier-code-conduct (accessed 2 May 2020); UNGM Registration Process, available at www.ungm.org/Public/Pages/RegistrationProcess (accessed 2 May 2020).

[134] See FAO General Terms and Conditions for Services, clause 34.1.

international law that are binding on international organisations'.[135] Organizations are not a party to their constituent instruments, they do not often enter into treaties (and may prefer the form of an MOU), the basis for applying customary international law directly to their activities is uncertain, and, in any event, they cannot participate in the formation of custom or general principles of law.[136] Indeed, any suggestion that the resolutions and activities of international organizations are relevant to the creation of custom – and could therefore bind other members of the international community – has proven controversial.[137] International organizations may be bound by domestic law through contract or tort, although they are usually immune from the jurisdiction of national courts. The internal law of organizations may prove a more certain way of applying legal principles to the activities of an organization and its staff members, although the binding force of these instruments is not always clear.

While acknowledging these problems, the proposition that an organization with international legal personality is not bound by international law is unattractive.[138] One response to this dilemma is to point to the relevance of a moral obligation on international organizations.[139] Another is to see this as an example of the decline of consent as the basis for the binding force of international law. Writers have referred to the ability of international organizations to obligate states through their lawmaking functions as evidence of the need to rethink the importance of consent.[140] Guzman writes that '[a]ny time an IO creates rules, norms, or guidelines without the consent of all members, it is attempting to influence state conduct in the absence of state consent'.[141] Similarly, Krisch has stated that 'institutions with lawmaking and adjudicatory powers act at one remove from states' consent'.[142] These writers view the 'consent problem' from the perspective of the lawmaking activities of international organizations and their ability to bind states. But, perhaps, the multiple legal frameworks

[135] Klabbers, 'Sources of International Organizations' Law', 1000. [136] *Ibid.*, 1005.

[137] For example, see the United States' comments in *Identification of Customary International law: Comments and Observations Received from Governments*, UN Doc. A/CN.4/716 (14 February 2018).

[138] See also Klabbers, 'Sources of International Organizations' Law', 1000.

[139] *Ibid.*, 1005.

[140] A. Guzman, 'Against Consent', (2012) 52 *Virginia Journal of International Law* 747.

[141] *Ibid.*, 783.

[142] N. Krisch, 'The Decay of Consent: International Law in an Age of Global Public Goods', (2014) 108 *American Journal of International Law* 1, 3.

governing the operational activities of international organizations also evidence the decline of the importance of consent from another perspective. International organizations are subjects of international law and, as such, they are bound by the sources of law even if they did not (and could not) participate in their creation and even if they did not formally consent to their terms. The multiplicity of laws that govern the operational activities of international organizations may fall short of demonstrating the existence of one legal framework that governs international organizations. However, the application of these many legal sources to international organizations provides further evidence of a move away from a purely consent-based system of international law.

Deliberation 8

Ian Johnstone

8.1 Introduction

International organizations (IOs) are sometimes derided as 'mere' talk-shops. This is unfair for two reasons. The first and most obvious is that international organizations do more than serve as venues for government representatives to speak to (or at) one another – they act. The European Union and, to a lesser extent, other organizations have governing powers. The United Nations, African Union and NATO conduct peace operations. The World Bank and regional development banks finance development projects. The Office of the UN High Commissioner for Refugees and multiple humanitarian organizations run refugee camps and massive aid programmes.

The second reason the word 'mere' before talk is unfair is because talk can be valuable. It serves instrumental purposes: enabling states and other actors to coordinate their relations and, on occasion, resolve disputes. It also serves non-instrumental purposes – what Jan Klabbers has called the 'agora' function.[1] Public deliberation has inherent value, quite apart from the instrumental benefits it may deliver. Even if the participants fail to reach agreement on an outcome, their diplomatic cajoling and berating can channel conflict away from the battlefield: as Churchill said, 'meeting jaw to jaw is better than war'.[2] Moreover, deliberative democrats see making it easier to live with disagreement as one of the principal virtues of deliberation. More fundamentally, deliberation beyond the level of the nation state can foster

[1] J. Klabbers, 'Two Concepts of International Organization', (2005) 2 *International Organizations Law Review* 94. The agora concept is rooted in Greek antiquity, a central meeting place where ideas were exchanged and discussed.

[2] Churchill as quoted in M. Gilbert, *Official Biography of Winston Churchill: Never Despair* (Vol. 8) (London: Heinemann, 1988) 1004.

a 'public sphere' for transnational politics – a virtual space where opinions are developed and exchanged on matters of mutual concern.[3]

In this chapter, I focus on deliberation in international organizations and argue that an important effect (if not necessarily the intended purpose) is to manage pluralism. I use the term broadly to connote five ways in which the international system is pluralistic. It is characterized by: multiple states and regions; multiple legal fields; multiple levels of governance; multiple actors and stakeholders; and multiple normative orders. Each dimension of pluralism has spawned a body of literature, as well as hand-wringing about the implications. I do not join those debates directly, but rather take the position that pluralism is a fact of international life that manifests itself through deliberation in international organizations.

The chapter starts with a brief section that defines deliberation as a core democratic principle, which is finding its way into transnational politics. I then turn to the elements of international organizations law that relate most directly to the phenomenon. The heart of the chapter is the third section, which describes the five dimensions of pluralism and identifies intersecting bodies of scholarly literature that address each: comparative international law; legal fragmentation; multilevel governance; multi-stakeholder governance; and normative pluralism.[4] The chapter concludes with a case study of COVID-19 as a way of illustrating how the various dimensions of pluralism are exhibited in international organizations that deliberate on global health.

8.2 Deliberation Defined

Deliberation is best understood as principled or reasoned argumentation. This is rooted in the theory of deliberative democracy, which situates deliberation alongside voting and bargaining as elements of public policy decision-making.[5] In a well-functioning democracy, politicians do not simply make trade-offs and then move to a vote; they feel compelled to

[3] J. Habermas, *Between Facts and Norms* (Cambridge MA: MIT Press, 1996); J. Dryzek, *Deliberative Global Politics: Discourse and Democracy in a Divided World* (Cambridge: Polity, 2006).

[4] I will avoid the term 'global legal pluralism' because this notoriously vague concept has been applied loosely to all five dimensions I identify.

[5] I. Johnstone, *The Power of Deliberation: International Law, Politics and Organizations* (New York: Oxford University Press, 2011) 15.

justify their decisions in terms their audiences can understand. The justifications for and against a particular policy do not always lead to consensus; in the end legislators vote and the voting is often driven by hard bargaining. But the bargains struck and the outcome of the votes are shaped by the exchange of reasons in a public debate.[6] According to the theory, the felt need to engage in principled argumentation – to exchange reasons for a policy or programme – is both a normative ideal and a description of how democracies actually work. By winning support for a position and legitimating it through deliberation, less coercion and fewer pay-offs are required to make it stick.

Some deliberative democrats question the sharp distinction made between legal and political argumentation, between courts as forums for principled adjudication and legislatures as forums for deal-making.[7] In both, decisions should be and sometimes are made for good reasons. What constitutes a 'good' reason varies from setting to setting, but as a general matter it means impartial as opposed to purely self-serving, and cast in terms that the intended audience understands to be relevant to the nature and purpose of the enterprise.[8] That is important when we consider deliberation in international organizations. A relatively small percentage of disputes between states is settled in courts. Rather, much of the disputation occurs in the political organs of international organizations.[9] In these disputes, law is a resource for producing good arguments. That is because (most) law is based on consent (at least in theory) and therefore, almost by definition, provides a shared frame of reference – a shared language. An appeal to the law is a way of signalling 'we have agreed to a principle or norm or standard, and yet you refuse to act in accordance with it now'. This is not to say that all or even most deliberation in international organizations is based on law, but simply that appealing to legal norms is a form of impartial reasoning that is not categorically different from the political argumentation that permeates international organizations.

Deliberative democrats for the most part write about deliberation in democratic or quasi-democratic societies. Transposing the theory to

6 A. Gutmann and D. Thompson, *Why Deliberative Democracy?* (Princeton University Press, 2004) 98–102.

7 A. Gutmann and D. Thompson, *Democracy and Disagreement* (Cambridge MA: Harvard University Press, 1998) 46.

8 Johnstone, *Power of Deliberation*, 5.

9 See generally, I. Johnstone and S. Ratner eds, Talking International Law: Legal Argumentation Outside the Courtroom (New York: Oxford University Press, 2021).

international society is challenging because no global 'demos' exists. Yet many have considered the possibility of transnational democratic deliberation and see evidence of it in various spheres – certainly in Europe, but also in issue areas such as the environment, human rights and security.[10] An animating theme of this literature is the notion of a 'public sphere', a space where ideas are debated and information is exchanged on matters of public concern. International organizations are a modest instantiation of this public sphere, places where transnational deliberation occurs and transnational 'public reason' may emerge.[11]

8.3 Elements of International Organizations Law That Structure Deliberation

This section outlines the main elements of international organizations law as it structures deliberations. The first part looks at the constitutive rules of an organization and how they determine *what* is deliberated about and *how*. The second part examines *who* gets to participate and *who* is their audience.

8.3.1 Constitutive and Voting Rules

What participants deliberate about in international organizations is determined first by the mission of the organization. The constitutive acts of multipurpose organizations such as the United Nations (UN), European Union (EU) and African Union (AU) authorize them to discuss almost any matter of international or regional concern. Other organizations have mandates that cover more limited ground, such as security (the North Atlantic Treaty Organization (NATO)), development (the World Bank and United Nations Development Programme (UNDP)), social well-being (the World Health Organization (WHO) and United Nations Education, Scientific and Cultural Organization (UNESCO)) and technical standards (the International Civil Aviation Organization (ICAO) and the International Telecommunication Union (ITU)). It is not unusual to see debates in these

[10] M. Zürn, 'Democratic Governance Beyond the Nation-State: The EU and Other International Institutions', (2000) 6 *European Journal of International Relations* 183; C. Bjola, 'Legitimizing the Use of Force in International Politics', (2005) 11 *European Journal of International Relations* 266.

[11] J. Cohen, 'Democracy's Reason, Global Reason', Tanner Lecture on Human Values II, 2007.

organizations about the limits of their competence – for example, when the World Health Assembly sought an International Court of Justice (ICJ) Advisory Opinion on the legality of nuclear weapons.

The same holds true for the various organs of international organizations. Most organizations have non-plenary councils as well as plenary organs and there are often struggles about what falls within the competence of each. In the UN, the numerical majority of members in the General Assembly (GA), most of whom rarely hold seats on the Security Council (SC), often oppose over-reaching by the Council. The Secretariats and executive heads of international organizations are, to varying degrees, expected or allowed to participate in deliberations. Some Secretariats are purely administrative, while others have substantive responsibilities and independent authority. The UN Secretary-General (SG) is an influential voice in intergovernmental deliberations.[12] The executive heads and professional staff of the specialized agencies, paradoxically, may have even more influence due to their perceived expertise. The staff of the World Bank and International Monetary Fund (IMF), for example, have substantial power not because they are formally granted it but because it is hard for the government representatives who oversee them to second-guess the judgement calls they make.[13]

One other important though rare type of organ is parliamentary bodies. The European Parliament, which is directly elected, is the most powerful such body. The Council of Europe and Organization for Security and Co-operation in Europe (OSCE) have parliamentary Assemblies composed of parliamentarians of member states. The AU Parliament has consultative and advisory powers, and may someday assume legislative powers.[14] These parliamentary bodies can be vehicles for bringing down the democratic deficit in international organizations as they are venues for deliberation among representatives other than the executive branches of member states.

[12] See generally S. Chesterman (ed.), *Secretary or General? The UN Secretary-General in World Politics* (Cambridge University Press, 2017); M. Fröhlich and A. Williams (eds.), *The UN Secretary-General and Security Council: A Dynamic Relationship* (Oxford University Press, 2018).

[13] For a critical perspective on the power of expertise, see D. Kennedy, *A World of Struggle: How Power, Law and Expertise Shape Global Political Economy* (Princeton University Press, 2016).

[14] Established in 2004, it has yet to assume those legislative powers, leading at least one observer to dismiss it as an expensive talk shop. See B. Fagbayibo, 'Why the Pan-African Parliament Must Clean Up Its Act if It Wants To Survive', *The Conversation*, 24 May 2018.

Most international organizations have a multitude of commissions and committees. Deliberations here tend to be at the 'working level', often among experts or diplomats who are immersed in the subject matter. In the EU, 'comitology' committees provide a forum in which state representatives engage with the European Commission on the implementation of EU law. Rational choice theorists view these committees as mechanisms for member states to supervise and control the Commission.[15] Other theorists see them as mechanisms for deliberation, where regional, national and sub-national experts engage in dialogue.[16]

As suggested above, deliberation in IOs is typically not a substitute for voting but a complement to it. Voting rules – whether by consensus, qualified majority or simple majority – have implications for the nature of deliberations. For example, when consensus is the practice, but a majority vote is possible (as in the World Trade Organization (WTO) or EU), rather than risk being outvoted, states may be more inclined to compromise. In fora where states have the veto power (as in the SC), they may feel less pressure to justify their positions or subject them to public scrutiny. When voting is weighted, those with greater voting power may feel less compelled to deliberate, while those with less voting power may feel less vested in the system if not engaged through deliberation.

8.3.2 Participation

Determining who gets to participate in international organizations starts with membership criteria. The UN is open to 'peace-loving states which accept the obligations contained in the . . . Charter and, in the judgment of the Organization, are able and willing to carry out these obligations' (Article 4(1)). The EU ostensibly applies the Copenhagen Criteria, which require candidate countries to be democratic and human rights-respecting, have a market economy, and 'the ability to take on the obligations of membership'. The Association of South-East Asian Nations (ASEAN) is open to states in the region who subscribe to the aims and purposes of

[15] M. Pollack, *The Engines of European Integration: Delegation, Agency and Agenda-Setting in the EU* (Oxford University Press, 2003); F. Franchino, *The Powers of the Union: Delegation in the EU* (Cambridge University Press, 2007).

[16] C. Joerges and J. Neyer, 'From Inter-governmental Bargaining to Deliberative Political Process: The Constitutionalization of Comitology', (2002) 3 *European Law Journal* 273.

the organization. The Arab League is open only to Arab states. The Organization of Islamic Cooperation is open only to Islamic countries.

Of course even the 'statehood' criterion can be an obstacle to aspirants, as the cases of Palestine, Taiwan and Kosovo demonstrate. Dissolution of a state has been used to prevent representatives of certain states from participating in the work of the organization, as Yugoslavia learned during the Balkan wars of the early 1990s.[17] The credential procedures have been used to deny a government the right to participate in the UN General Assembly, such as South Africa during the apartheid years, the military regime in Myanmar in early 2021, and the Taliban in Afghanistan in the late 1990s and again after its takeover in 2021.

Who, other than members of the organization, can participate in its deliberations? The European Parliament allows observers from countries aspiring to membership. NATO invites non-member aspirants to certain North Atlantic Council meetings as well as lower-level meetings and workshops. A long list of non-African states are accredited to the African Union. The UN has had non-member states as permanent observers for many years, such as Switzerland prior to formally joining in 2002.

In 1974 the Palestine Liberation Organization (PLO) was granted observer status in the UN, not as a 'state' but as an 'entity'. That gave it access to meetings in the GA and, from 1988, the right to circulate documents, but not the right to speak or vote. From 1998, Palestine has been allowed to participate more fully in the organization, but still without the right to vote. In 2011, having been blocked in its attempt to gain full membership by the threat of a US veto in the SC, it won a vote in the GA to upgrade its status to 'non-member observer *state*'. Palestine's incremental accretion of rights in the UN meant it was able to keep political pressure on both its adversaries and those of its allies who might otherwise have been reluctant to expend political capital in the UN on its behalf.

Even more noteworthy from the point of view of intergovernmental deliberations is the opening up to civil society groups and NGOs.[18]

[17] Yugoslavia was never formally expelled from the UN, but it was required to re-apply for membership. A compromise solution denied it the right to participate in General Assembly meetings, but allowed it to speak in the Security Council as a non-member when Yugoslav issues were being discussed.

[18] J. Tallberg *et al.*, *The Opening Up of International Organizations: Transnational Access in Global Governance* (Cambridge University Press, 2013).

Employee and business groups having voting rights in the ILO. The OSCE allows access to 'all interested parties'.[19] The World Intellectual Property Organization has accredited 262 international and 98 national NGOs as observers. Article 71 of the UN Charter entitles NGOs to apply for consultative status, giving them access to the Economic and Social Council (ECOSOC), its many subsidiary bodies and various human rights mechanisms. Most have 'special status', allowing them to make written and oral statements in meetings and to host side events. One hundred and forty international NGOs have 'general status', entitling them to place items on the agenda of ECOSOC and subsidiary bodies, as well as participate in meetings.[20]

Many other international organizations provide for formalized consultations with NGOs and civil society. The World Bank and IMF accredit NGOs to their annual meetings, which often end up being protest exercises. The OECD engages through its Business and Industry Advisory Committee and its Trade Union Advisory Committee. UNDP has a Civil Society Advisory Committee. The WTO does not allow for direct participation in meetings but urges the Secretariat to maintain contact with NGOs 'who ... can contribute to the accuracy and richness of the public debate'.[21]

The EU has been the most innovative organization in cultivating public participation. The European Citizen's Consultation was in effect a Europe-wide town hall meeting, combining techniques for gathering citizen opinions on a wide scale with moderated face-to-face meetings with randomly selected citizens. These experiments were eventually replaced by the more modest European Citizen's Initiative, which is aimed at gathering the wishes of organized groups rather than fostering pan-European deliberation among average citizens.[22]

A close cousin to participation in international organizations is transparency. Empirical research has uncovered not only that organizations have become more transparent, but that the transparency has brought functional benefits and enhanced the social legitimacy of the

[19] P. Mayer, 'Civil Society Participation in International Security Organizations: The Cases of NATO and the OSCE', in J. Steffek *et al.* (eds.), *Civil Society Participation in European and Global Governance: A Cure for the Democratic Deficit?* (New York: Palgrave MacMillan, 2008) 116.

[20] In December 2021, the 140 who had General Status included CARE, Greenpeace, Oxfam and Rotary International.

[21] WTO, *Guidelines for Arrangements with Non-Governmental Organizations, Decision adopted by the General Council*, 18 July 1996.

[22] K. Dingwerth and P. Nanz, 'Participation', in J. Cogan, I. Hurd and I. Johnstone (eds.), *Oxford Handbook of International Organizations* (Oxford University Press, 2016) 1126, 1143.

organizations.[23] The 'audience effect' means that even if the participants in deliberations are limited, those who actually participate do so differently if subjected to broad public scrutiny. They feel under greater pressure to explain their positions in terms that valued constituencies and stakeholders consider reasonable. This partly explains the decades-long effort to make the proceedings of the SC more transparent, for example with more public meetings and the circulation of draft resolutions in advance. Even without formal transparency mechanisms, it is difficult to keep secrets in intergovernmental deliberations: positions are often leaked or threatened to be leaked. During informal consultations of the SC, with fifteen representatives, plus aides and Secretariat staff present, rarely is a word uttered that the speaker would not want to be known publicly. Since there are no official records of the meetings, the utterances can always be denied, but the glare of publicity does find its way into even informal consultations and thereby shapes the discussions behind closed doors.[24]

8.4 The Many Dimensions of Pluralism

For some, pluralism signifies a lack of coherence, clarity and certainty in the law, which translates into a lack of compliance. For others, pluralism is to be embraced: a counter to hegemony and technocracy, allowing for multiple perspectives and values to be given expression. In this section, I discuss five dimensions of pluralism that have been the subject of distinct bodies of academic literature: multiple states and regions; multiple legal fields; multiple layers of governance; multiple actors and stakeholders; and multiple normative orders. All are exhibited in international organizations, typically as a source of tension but often mediated through deliberation.

8.4.1 Multiple States and Regions

The most obvious form of pluralism in the international system is the multiplicity of states who, in principle, are sovereign equals. Each brings

[23] Tallberg *et al.*, *The Opening Up*; F. Scharpf, *Governing in Europe: Effective and Democratic?* (Oxford University Press, 1999).

[24] I. Johnstone, 'Security Council Deliberations: The Power of the Better Argument', (2002) 14 *European Journal of International Law* 437, 463.

a unique perspective to the development and application of international law, and each brings a distinctive set of expectations about what international organizations can and should do. Sometimes these perspectives and understandings converge within a region or among a like-minded grouping of states. Thus many European states share a broad vision of the values the EU should be promoting in global affairs; Southeast Asian states subscribe loosely to the ASEAN Way, characterized by consultation, consensus and non-interference; members of the African Union are increasingly determined to find 'African solutions to African problems'. The existence of different traditions is embodied in the Statute of the International Law Commission, which calls for representation on the Commission from 'the main forms of civilization and the principal legal systems of the world'.[25]

The emerging field of 'comparative international law' (CIL) takes the study of this kind of pluralism a step further.[26] In direct response to Oscar Schachter's notion of an 'invisible college of international lawyers',[27] CIL scholars see a 'divisible college' in which international law is 'understood, interpreted, applied and approached' differently in different places.[28] Some claim that the approaches are so fundamentally different it is not accurate to speak of a single international law.[29] While CIL as a field purportedly has no normative agenda, Paul Stephan claims a 'distributed, localized and relativistic system of international law' better serves diverse communities than a universal normative system because the latter puts too much power in the hands of the 'self-appointed visionaries and arbiters of humanity's needs'.[30]

[25] Statute of the International Law Commission, 1947, Article 8.

[26] As the name would suggest, the comparative international law literature has roots in comparative domestic law. M. Delmas-Marty, 'Comparative Law and International Law: Methods of Ordering Pluralism', (2006) 3 *University of Tokyo Journal of Law and Politics* 44. See generally A. Roberts *et al.*, (eds.), *Comparative International Law* (Oxford University Press, 2018).

[27] O. Schachter, 'The Invisible College of International Lawyers', (1977) 72 *Northwestern University Law Review* 217–26.

[28] Roberts *et al.*, 'Conceptualizing Comparative International Law', in Roberts *et al.* (eds.), *Comparative International Law* 3; D. Kennedy, 'One, Two, Three, Many Legal Orders: Legal Pluralism and the Cosmopolitan Dream', (2007) 31 *New York University Review of Law and Social Change* 641, 656.

[29] A. Roberts, *Is International Law International?* (Oxford University Press, 2017) 2.

[30] P. Stephan, 'Comparative International Law, Foreign Relations Law and Fragmentation: Can the Center Hold?', in Roberts *et al.* (eds.), *Comparative International Law* 53, 66, 68.

One can question CIL's conflation of different interpretations of international law, with different 'approaches'. It is one thing to say the USA and China, or France and Russia, or even the global 'north' and 'south' interpret and apply some norms of international law differently. It is another to claim their very conceptions of international law are different. Nevertheless, the CIL literature highlights a dimension of pluralism present since the founding of the nation-state. Different states and grouping of states co-habit the international legal system and the tensions between them play out in international organizations. That kind of pluralism is here to stay.

8.4.2 Multiple Legal Fields

A second face of pluralism is among different areas of law: trade, investment, environment, human rights, law of the sea, etcetera. This has produced concerns about the so-called fragmentation of international law. As expressed in the report on fragmentation to the International Law Commission:

> such specialized law-making and institution-building tends to take place with relative ignorance of legislative and institutional activities in the adjoining fields and of the general principles and practices of international law. The result is conflicts between rules or rule-systems, deviating institutional practices and, possibly, the loss of an overall perspective on the law.[31]

The ILC study group focused on the *substance* of international law. Fragmentation also has an *institutional* dimension, mainly in the form of the proliferation of tribunals: the ICJ, the WTO dispute settlement mechanism, the International Criminal Court, the Law of the Sea Tribunal, all operating alongside multiple judicial and quasi-judicial bodies at regional and sub-regional levels.[32] Some have broad jurisdiction and others are more specialized, but even the specialized tribunals are continually being

[31] Report of the Study Group of the International Law Commission, 'Fragmentation of International Law: Difficulties Arising from the Diversification and Expansion of International Law', para. 8. UN General Assembly document A/CN.4/L682 (13 April 2006).

[32] On the proliferation of tribunals, see K. Alter, C. Romano and Y. Shany (eds.), *Oxford Handbook of International Adjudication* (Oxford University Press, 2014). On the proliferation of international institutions generally, see K. Raustiala, 'Institutional Proliferation and the International Legal Order', in J. Dunoff and M. Pollack (eds.), *Interdisciplinary Perspectives on International Law and International Relations: The State of the Art* (Cambridge University Press, 2013) 293.

confronted with disputes that encompass more than one area of law, an example being environmental issues arising in a case before the WTO.

The lack of coherence and unity is problematic from the point of view of legal certainty and the basic idea that like cases be treated alike. If the divergences and conflicts between the discrete bodies become so great, not only are those virtues undermined, but one worries whether 'the concept of international law retains any meaning' at all.[33] Yet the ILC study concludes that the need for coherence must be balanced against the reality of pluralism:

> Coherence is . . . a formal and abstract virtue. For a legal system that is regarded in some respects as unjust or unworkable, no added value is brought by the fact of its being coherently so. Therefore, alongside coherence, pluralism should be understood as a constitutive value of the system. Indeed, in a world of plural sovereignties, this has always been so.[34]

Conflicts among different areas of law are inevitable in a pluralistic society and there is no hierarchical meta-system available to do away with them – they can only be managed.

8.4.3 Multiple Levels of Governance

A third face of pluralism is multiple levels of governance. Two bodies of literature address this: studies of multilayered governance that began with the European Union have been extended to global governance generally; and the literature on 'legal pluralism', which encompasses different legal and quasi-legal regimes governing the same people in the same territory. In the 1980s, European integration prompted studies of how authority was coming to be shared between national governments, the EU above, and subnational levels of government below.[35] These layers of governance are non-hierarchical. Power is exercised at all levels and the channels between them flow in multiple directions. States are an integral part of the EU, 'but

[33] Stephan, 'Can the Center Hold?', 63.

[34] ILC para. 491. See also T. Broude, 'Keep Calm and Carry On: Martti Koskenniemi and the Fragmentation of International Law', (2013) 27 *Temple International and Comparative Law Journal* 279–92; H. G. Cohen, 'Fragmentation', in J. d'Aspremont and S. Singh (eds.), *Concepts of International Law: Contributions to Disciplinary Thought* (Cheltenham: Edward Elgar, 2019) 315.

[35] G. Marks, L. Hooghe and K. Black, 'European Integration for the 1980s: State-Centric and Multi-level Governance', (1996) 34 *Journal of Common Market Studies* 341.

they no longer provide the sole interface between supranational and subnational arenas, and they share rather than monopolize control over many activities that take place in their respective territories'.[36] The targeted sanctions regimes imposed by the SC and that prompted a series of court challenges to EU implementing regulations illustrate how multilevel governance extends to the global level.[37]

The term legal pluralism connotes the idea that different legal systems can co-exist in one place, for example colonial law and the indigenous law of colonized communities, or other forms of 'official' and 'unofficial' law.[38] As with the fragmentation literature, some scholars applaud this kind of pluralism. Berman argues that it provides alternative ideas and generates discourse among multiple community affiliations.[39] Krisch sees it as creating space for weaker actors to contest the law of their more powerful counterparts, thereby building checks and balances into the international legal order. As he states, 'the plural, divided identities, loyalties and allegiances that characterize postnational society are better reflected in a multiplicity of orders than in an overarching framework that implies ultimate authority'.[40] The relationships between them are fluid and left to be determined through political, not formal legal processes. In other words, this non-hierarchical model of decision-making encourages deliberation.[41]

What these strands of literature suggest is that the multiplicity of layers of law and governance cannot be wished away. Rather than seeking to

[36] *Ibid.*, 347.

[37] See generally A. Follesdal, R. Wessel and J. Wouters (eds.), *Multi-level Regulation and the EU: The Interplay between Global, European and National Normative Processes* (Leiden: Martinus Nijhoff, 2008).

[38] For an overview of different uses, see R. Michaels, 'Global Legal Pluralism', (2009) 5 *Annual Review of Law and Social Sciences* 243.

[39] Berman, 'Global Legal Pluralism'. See also P. S. Berman, 'Can Global Legal Pluralism Be Both "Global" and "Pluralist"', (2019) 29 *Duke Journal of Comparative and International Law* 381.

[40] N. Krisch, *Beyond Constitutionalism: The Pluralist Structure of Postnational Law* (Oxford University Press, 2010) 78–89, 103.

[41] S. Hix, 'The Study of the European Union II: The "New Governance" Agenda and Its Rival', (1998) 5 *Journal of European Public Policy* 38; T. Risse, *A Community of Europeans: Transnational Identities and Public Spheres* (Ithaca NY: Cornell University Press, 2010); M. Zürn, 'Democratic Governance Beyond the Nation-State'; Johnstone, *Power of Deliberation*.

harmonize them in a unified legal system, it is better to resolve or manage the tensions between the layers through deliberative transnational politics carried out in international organizations.

8.4.4 Multiple Actors and Stakeholders

A fourth dimension of pluralism concerns the multiple actors and stakeholders who participate in the making, interpretation and implementation of international law.[42] While national governments are the key players, international civil servants, trans-governmental networks, non-governmental organizations, business associations, philanthropies, academics, and organs of civil society also play a role.

NGOs sometimes participate in national delegations to treaty-making processes, but many keep their distance from governments, preferring to act as watchdogs, advocates and norm entrepreneurs. International civil servants and associated experts play similar roles. They may participate directly in the drafting of treaties, or indirectly in the interpretation and implementation of the law. Both NGO and international organization staff engage in operational activities, such as humanitarian action and election monitoring, that can have a lawmaking effect by giving content to inchoate norms.[43]

Transnational networks also participate in deliberations with and within international organizations. The most salient of these are tri-sectoral alliances of government agencies, international bureaucracies, and non-states actors (both corporations and elements of civil society). These networks benefit from 'the strength of weak ties': precisely because the participants are not closely tied to one another, they bring diverse perspectives and expertise.[44] Gavi, the Vaccine Alliance (formerly the Global Alliance for Vaccines and Immunization) is a good example. It is governed by a board composed of representatives from ten governments, three international

[42] I. Johnstone, 'Law-Making by International Organizations: Perspectives from International Law/International Relations Theory', in Dunoff and Pollack (eds.), *Interdisciplinary Perspectives* 266, 270.

[43] I. Johnstone, 'Law-making through the Operational Activities of International Organizations', (2009) 40 *George Washington International Law Review* 87. See also Duxbury, Chapter 7 in this volume.

[44] W. Reinicke, 'The Other World Wide Web: Global Public Policy Networks', (1999) 117 *Foreign Policy* 44, 55.

organizations, two pharmaceutical companies, one health institute, one civil society organization, the Gates Foundation and nine individuals with expertise in medicine, health policy, business management, finance and other fields.

What are the implications of allowing non-state actors to participate? An important line of scholarship sees this as a way of reducing the democratic deficit in international organizations, on the theory that inclusiveness lends legitimacy.[45] At the international level, the participation of NGOs is thought to enhance the quality of deliberations by amplifying the voices of groups whose interests would not otherwise be accounted for.[46] Moreover, the ability of NGOs to monitor what government representatives say and do – how they deliberate – in international organizations creates a 'transnational civil society channel of accountability'.[47] Participation by civil society actors can also enhance so-called output legitimacy. The tripartite membership of the ILO is thought to produce better law and better prospects for compliance. For similar reasons, broad-based participation by citizen groups and public authorities in environmental negotiations has been fostered through the Aarhus Convention.[48]

Of course, the participation of non-state actors in international organization deliberations is not an unqualified good. Large well-funded NGOs from the Global North tend to have greater capacity to participate than those from the Global South. Moreover, it is not obvious they represent anyone but themselves.[49] Some NGOs derive legitimacy from their broad-based membership, but that does not apply to smaller, single-issue NGOs funded by a few large donors. More mundanely, NGOs can be as turf-oriented as international organization agencies, concerned as much about their own institutional interests as the communities they purport to serve.

45 As Charnovitz puts it, 'more open and inclusive processes of decision-making can help to overcome the allegedly attenuated democratic legitimacy of international governance'. S. Charnovitz, 'Nongovernmental Organizations and International Law', (2006) 100 *American Journal of International Law* 348, 365.

46 Dingwerth and Nanz, 'Participation', 1139.

47 A. Buchanan and R. Keohane, 'The Legitimacy of Global Governance Institutions', (2006) 20 *Ethics and International Affairs* 405, 406.

48 UN Economic Commission for Europe, *Convention on Access to Information, Public Participation in Decision-Making and Access to Justice in Environmental Matters*, 25 June 1998.

49 M. Karns and A. Mingst, *International Organizations: The Politics and Processes of Global Governance*, 3rd ed. (Boulder CO: Lynne Rienner, 2015) 275–6.

When for-profit entities are brought into the equation, it raises even more troubling questions about motivations.

8.4.5 Multiple Normative Orders

Willian Twining defines a normative order as 'a set of norms or social practices oriented towards ordering relations between members of a community or group where this set is more or less established, more or less integrated, with more or less defined boundaries'.[50] Law is one species of normative order. There are others: social norms, religious norms, traditional customs and morality to name a few.[51] The norms stem from a multitude of sources, some more easily identified than others.[52] The Bible or Quran are evident sources of religious orders. What constitutes a social norm is harder to pinpoint; what constitutes morality, even harder.[53] We think we know what the sources of law are, but if one includes soft law, it becomes fuzzier.

In any case, it is easy to see that international law is not the only order that informs deliberations in international organizations. There is the internal law of the organization (for example, rules on the independence of international civil servants); professional codes of conduct (for example, ethical obligations of lawyers); institutional practices (for example equitable geographical distribution in working groups); and there is morality. In some institutions, the Organisation of Islamic Cooperation (OIC) for example, religious norms matter. In others, the norms of the marketplace dominate (the WTO and regional trade regimes).

Normative orders often come into conflict. An influential commission determined that NATO's intervention in Kosovo in 1999 was illegal but 'legitimate'.[54] The lack of intervention in Rwanda in 1994 was criticized as

50 W. Twining, 'Normative and Legal Pluralism: A Global Perspective', (2010) 20 *Duke Journal of Comparative and International Law* 473, 475.

51 See further B. Tamanaha, 'Understanding Legal Pluralism: Past and Present, Local to Global', (2008) 30 *Sydney Law Review* 375, 399.

52 Klabbers and Piiparinen define a normative order as 'a set of related commands, injunctions, "dos and don'ts" that stem from the same source or a multitude of similar sources'. J. Klabbers and T. Piiparinen, 'Normative Pluralism: An Explanation', in J. Klabbers and T. Piiparinen (eds.) *Normative Pluralism and International Law: Exploring Global Governance* (Cambridge University Press, 2013) 13, 21.

53 *Ibid.*, 21.

54 International Commission on Intervention in Kosovo. See B. Simma, 'NATO, the UN and the Use of Force: Legal Aspects', (1999) 10 *European Journal of International Law* 1.

blind adherence to outdated peacekeeping norms in the face of genocide.[55] In peace-making processes, the rights of women are often given short shrift when they bump up against traditional norms of patriarchal societies. In the World Bank and IMF, especially in the heyday of structural adjustments, market-driven economics typically trump human rights.[56] For better or worse, international law often gets 'overruled' by other normative orders.[57]

In some ways, all other forms of pluralism are subsumed by normative pluralism. When multiple states and legal systems are represented in an international organization (from the global East, West, North and South), when multiple legal fields and layers of authority are implicated (from 'soft' human rights norms to hard security concerns), and when the actors range from the foreign ministers of great powers, to secretariat experts to activists from fragile states, the dynamics of deliberation can be complex indeed. The result, often, is cacophony. But sometimes an institutional culture is forged that smoothens the edges and makes reasoned deliberation within and between normative orders possible.

8.4.6 Deliberation among the Many Dimensions of Pluralism

Pluralism in all its guises inevitably generates tension. Power dynamics have an impact on how those tensions play out in deliberations in international organizations. Weaker voices can be silenced or co-opted. The power of expertise can override democratic values, subjecting deeply political issues to technocratic solutions. Or, if the pluralism pits equally powerful actors against each other, 'talk' can exacerbate tensions, making it impossible to reach decisions or take action.

However, inclusive deliberation can also serve to manage the tensions. It can facilitate agreement on complex issues. It can produce better outcomes by ensuring that a broad range of perspectives and interests are considered. It can improve the prospects of those outcomes being implemented by engaging multiple stakeholders. In addition to these instrumental

[55] The UN's Independent Inquiry on Rwanda spoke of an 'an institutional ideology of impartiality, even when confronted with genocide'. UN Security Council Report 1257, Conclusion 19, S/1999/1257, 15 December 1999.

[56] Galit Sarfaty, 'Why Culture Matters in International Institutions: The Marginality of Human Rights at the World Bank', (2009) 103 *American Journal of International Law* 647.

[57] Klabbers and Piiparinen, 'An Explanation', 28.

purposes, it can serve the agora function. Learning to live with disagreement in pluralistic societies is a virtue of democratic deliberation. Citizens (and politicians) do not always get the leaders or policies they vote for. In well-functioning democracies, they accept the loss without resorting to violent conflict.[58] To the extent that it is truly inclusive and meaningful (an ideal no state lives up to), deliberation signals that the interests and perspectives of all stakeholders have been considered before moving to a vote. Transposing this to the realm of international organizations, meaningful deliberation makes it a little more likely that those on the losing end will continue to participate in the institution rather than pull up stakes and go home.

More abstractly, deliberation within international organizations can create a public sphere. Drawing on Habermas's theory of communicative action, members of the SC – a highly polarized and deeply unequal body – occupy a thin 'common lifeworld'.[59] Having met on an almost daily basis since the end of the Cold War, the five permanent members have forged a relationship in which they share some common understandings about the nature of the enterprise in which they are engaged – the maintenance of international peace and security. They may not share values and policy orientations, and they often disagree on particular issues, but they inhabit an 'institutional lifeworld'[60] that makes it possible for them to speak to rather than past each other.

The 'lifeworld' is thin not only because the permanent members and the ten elected members are – by design – heterogenous, but also because the Council does not engage fully with all dimensions of pluralism. Its mandate spans a relatively narrow range of issues; most of its members do not feel obliged to consider other layers of governance; non-state actors have minimal access to its proceedings; and *realpolitik* among its members means it studiously avoids the rhetoric of morality and religion. Even so, it is not hard for close observers to spot ways in which the many faces of pluralism appear in the Council, albeit contested.[61] Moreover, focusing on

[58] In post-conflict societies where democracy is fragile, elections sometimes produce a return to violence.

[59] I. Johnstone, 'US-UN Relations after Iraq: The End of the World (Order) As We Know It', (2004) 15 *European Journal of International Relations* 813.

[60] Bjola, 'Legitimizing the Use of Force'.

[61] It deals with non-traditional security issues; the US and other federal states have to be conscious of the limits of executive authority at home; non-state actors are participating in

one international organization is deceptive. Most matters of international concern are dealt with in multiple international organizations. Just like there are many faces of pluralism, there are many places where the pluralism is manifest in deliberations. The COVID-19 pandemic illustrates the point.

8.5 COVID-19

Managing pluralism is not stated explicitly in the constituent instruments of any international organization. Nor is it necessarily implicit in their mandates. Indeed, most international organizations are thought of as venues for reducing the tensions inherent in pluralism, not for embracing it. Yet because pluralism cannot be willed away, that is what many organizations do. This section will describe how each of the five dimensions of pluralism are implicated in responses to COVID-19. It is too soon to draw firm conclusions about the impact of the IO deliberations, but a good case can be made that both instrumental and agora functions are being served.

8.5.1 State and Regions

There has been wide variation in the response to COVID among states and regions. The variations are based on different attitudes towards the expertise of health professionals, the balance between health and economic concerns, the efficacy of international institutions, the authority of the International Health Regulations (IHR) of the WHO, and the importance of civil liberties. They are also based on different leadership styles. A quick comparison of Asia and the Transatlantic is illustrative. China began by downplaying the nature of the disease and suppressing information about its spread, then became more transparent and cooperative with the WHO, even offering its heavy-handed approach as a model for how to deal with the pandemic. Several East Asian countries (South Korea, Singapore and Taiwan) acted quickly and effectively, but more intrusively on civil liberties than in Western democracies. The US federal government response was lacklustre at home and, when it became obvious that the disease was more serious than

and listening attentively to Council deliberations; and moral considerations are sometimes invoked by elected Council members that lack material power.

President Trump was willing to admit, highly critical of international actors – especially China and the WHO. The response of most European countries fell somewhere between that of China and the USA.

The rivalry between the USA and China had a major impact on deliberations in international organizations. It paralyzed the SC for several months.[62] It inhibited a collective response among the G-20. And it put the WHO in a quandary.[63] In the May 2020 annual meeting of the World Health Assembly (WHA), two issues pitted the USA and China against each other: the participation of Taiwan as an observer, and the call for an inquiry into the origins of COVID-19 and the performance of the WHO. Taiwan's attempts to join the WHO (like the UN) have been stymied by China's opposition for decades. From 2009 to 2016 it was invited to participate as an observer, but the invitation was not extended in 2017. The USA led calls for a renewed invitation in 2020, with the US Secretary of State even suggesting that the WHO Director-General issue a personal invitation, which he is not authorized to do without a vote in the WHA.[64] The matter was never put to a vote because Taiwan, announcing it did not want to take time away from discussing COVID-19 in the shortened Assembly, agreed to delay debate on its participation to meetings later in the year. As Minister of Health Joseph Wu put it: 'After careful deliberation, we have accepted the suggestion from our allies and like-minded nations to wait until the resumed session before further promoting our bid'.[65]

On the call for an inquiry on the response to the pandemic, the USA wanted to focus on China's role and the WHO Director-General's overly deferential attitude. China opposed any kind of inquiry. The EU brokered a compromise resolution co-sponsored by 130 states and adopted by consensus that called for an independent evaluation of the global response,

[62] Security Council Resolution 2532, 1 July 2020.

[63] C. Lynch, 'WHO Becomes Battleground as Trump Chooses Pandemic Confrontation over Cooperation', *Foreign Policy*, 29 April 2020; J. S. Morrison, 'The Trump Administration's Ignominious Exit at the 2020 World Health Assembly', *Center for Strategic and International Studies*, 20 May 2020.

[64] E. R. Fletcher, 'Swelling Bloc of WHO Member States Propose Invitation to Taiwan for May 18 World Health Assembly', *Health Policy Watch*, 11 May 2020.

[65] 'Taiwan: Won't Press for World Health Assembly Participation', Associated Press, 18 May 2020, https://abcnews.go.com/Health/wireStory/taiwan-press-wha-participation-70738350. As of December 2021, Taiwan had still not been invited back to the World Health Assembly.

including, but not limited to, the WHO's performance. China was not mentioned by name in the resolution. The deliberations before and during the WHA served an instrumental purpose – concretely in the form of the outcome document that, in addition to the inquiry, calls for intensification of efforts to control the pandemic and for equitable access to essential health technologies and products to combat the virus. The deliberations also served non-instrumental purposes. The views of key players about the participation of Taiwan were aired, culminating in an agreement to disagree. The rancour around assigning blame for the pandemic was somewhat diminished, at least temporarily. Most tellingly, the deliberations kickstarted a movement to label the vaccines a 'global public good',[66] discussed further below.

8.5.2 Fields of Law

The response to COVID-19 illustrates the intersection of multiple fields of infectious disease-related law. The IHR is the centrepiece. It imposes a number of binding obligations on WHO members, including the requirement to notify the WHO of all 'unexpected or unusual' health events on their territories that could pose a risk of the spread of disease to other states, and to share information about the risk (Article 6). It also imposes a more long-term obligation on states to build core capacity in their health systems both to detect infectious disease outbreaks and to be able to respond effectively (Articles 5 and 13). Parties to the IHR are expected though not obliged to follow WHO recommendations, but can take 'additional measures' they deem necessary (Article 43).

Various human rights are also integral. The right to health requires at a minimum that a state use the 'maximum available material resources' to provide adequate health care to its citizens during an infectious disease outbreak. Civil liberties are impinged upon by lockdowns, travel restrictions and contact tracing. Human rights law permits some curtailment of these civil liberties during a public health emergency, but only to the extent necessary to meet the public health objective and in a non-discriminatory manner. The response to COVID-19 – in democratic and non-democratic countries alike – generated a fear that 'emergency powers' were being invoked for ulterior motives and would not be relinquished when the emergency is over.

[66] P. Villarreal, 'Pandemic Intrigue in Geneva: COVID-19 and the 73rd World Health Assembly', *EJIL:Talk!*, 22 May 2020.

In addition to the IHR and human rights law, many other areas of law are implicated by COVID-19: trade and intellectual property law, refugee law, wildlife law, aviation and maritime transportation law, the law of state responsibility and the defences thereto (*force majeur*, necessity and distress).[67]

Clearly global health law is pluralistic. Is it also fragmented? One of the major criticisms of the global response to COVID-19 is that there is no coordinating mechanism.[68] Some of the legal issues may be addressed in a court (either domestic, regional or global), but most will not. Certainly, no single court will address them all, let alone reconcile the conflicts among them. Meanwhile, deliberations will continue in the WHO, the UN, G-20 and other venues. If a pandemic treaty (or other international instrument) comes out of them, that may bring some coherence, but legal pluralism will likely persist,[69] perhaps managed through a coordinating council.[70]

8.5.3 Levels of Governance

The SC, the highest level of governance in the international system, has dealt with health crises in the past. It addressed HIV/AIDS in 2000 (over the objections of China) and declared the West Africa Ebola outbreak a threat to international peace and security in 2014. COVID-19 clearly has security implications: it can aggravate conflicts, hurt peace-keeping efforts and add to the vulnerability of already desperate groups. It can also create opportunities for peace (as illustrated by the SG's call for a global ceasefire) and it highlights the importance of building resilient and equitable health care systems in peace-building efforts. Yet the SC was missing in action for a full 111 days after COVID-19 was declared a global pandemic, before it

67 Center for International Law and Governance, *International Law and Pandemics: A Primer* (The Fletcher School of Law and Diplomacy, 2021).

68 'WHO Let the Bats Out?', *EJIL: The Podcast!*, 5 May 2020.

69 A G20 Leaders' Statement on COVID19 touched on the health, humanitarian, financial, employment and trade implications (though not human rights) of the pandemic, without once using the word 'law'. G20, 'G20 Leaders' Statement, G20 Extraordinary Meeting on COVID19', 2020 Riyadh Summit, 26 March 2020.

70 David Nabarro, Special Envoy of the WHO Director-General has called for Pandemic Emergency Coordination Council, led by the UN, WHO, IMF and WB and connected to the G20 and other platforms that bring together leaders from local authorities, business, civil society. David Nabarro and John Atkinson, 'World Leadership Now', 4SD, 4 April 2020.

finally adopted two resolutions supporting the SG's ceasefire call and demanding a humanitarian pause to allow for the delivery of vaccines.[71]

Other governing bodies at the global level include the WHO, the WTO and the Human Rights Council. At the regional level, the EU has been an actor in crafting a response to both the health and socio-economic crises in Europe. The African Union has done the same in Africa, including through the much-admired work of its African Centers on Disease Control and Prevention.

The authority of all of these intergovernmental organizations is fairly weak in relation to national authorities, and that of national governments is often weak in relation to local authorities. In the USA, over 2684 governing bodies have public health responsibilities – from the federal government down to city councils.[72] India is similar.

The distribution of authority among the various levels of governance has been a topic of conversation in and around international organizations. After former US President Trump condemned the WHO for lacking 'teeth', Australia's Prime Minister suggested that the WHO should have the power to deploy investigators like the weapons inspectors the SC sent to Iraq.[73] The UN's human rights experts issued a statement on the use and abuse of emergency powers,[74] a topic also discussed in the European Parliament,[75] the Council of Europe,[76] and the Inter-American Commission of Human Rights.[77]

[71] UN Security Council Resolution 2532 (2020). UN Security Council Resolution 2565 (2021) These came after multiple appeals to the Security Council to act, including from a group of about thirty women's leaders, spearheaded by Madeleine Albright. 'Women Leaders Call on UN Security Council to Address Covid-19 Crisis', Letter to the President of the Security Council, 8 April 2020.

[72] Polly Price, 'A Coronavirus Quarantine in America Could be a Giant Legal Mess', *The Atlantic*, 16 February 2020.

[73] Malcolm Farr, 'Australian PM Pushes for WHO overhaul, including the power to send investigators akin to weapons inspectors', *The Guardian*, 22 April 2020. www.theguardian.com/australia-news/2020/apr/22/australian-pm-pushes-for-who-overhaul-including-power-to-send-in-investigators.

[74] 'COVID-19: States should not abuse emergency powers to suppress human rights – UN Experts', UN Office of the High Commissioner for Human Rights, 16 March 2020. www.ohchr.org/EN/NewsEvents/Pages/DisplayNews.aspx?NewsID=25722&LangID=E.

[75] 'The Impact of Covid-19 Measures on Democracy the Rule of Law and Fundamental Rights in the EU', European Parliament LIBE Committee, 23 April 2020. www.europarl.europa.eu/RegData/etudes/BRIE/2020/651343/IPOL_BRI(2020)651343_EN.pdf.

[76] 'The impact of the COVID-19 pandemic on human rights and the rule of law – Our action', Council of Europe, Directorate General, Human Rights and the Rule of Law. www.coe.int/en/web/human-rights-rule-of-law/covid19.

[77] 'Pandemic and Human Rights in America', (2020) Inter-American Commission on Human Rights/OAS. www.oas.org/en/iachr/decisions/pdf/Resolution-1-20-en.pdf.

8.5.4 Actors and Stakeholders

Related to the multiple levels of governance, many actors are involved in preventing and responding to COVID-19 pandemics: elected politicians at the national level, as well as the ministries and health institutes that manage the response; and state governors, provincial leaders, city mayors and the professionals who support them. At the international level, we see the diplomats in international organizations, and the secretariats and health professionals who manage the day-to-day work. NGOs are significant actors, as implementing partners and advocates. Large philanthropies, pharmaceutical companies, medical equipment manufacturers and other health industry representatives have a seat at the table, figuratively or – in the case of Gavi – literally.

Deliberations around development of and access to a vaccine have involved all of these stakeholders. Consider the Access to COVID-19 Tools Accelerator initiative:

> an initial group of global health actors (BMGF, CEPI, Gavi, Global Fund, UNITAID, Wellcome Trust, WHO) and private sector partners and other stakeholders, are launching a landmark, global and time-limited collaboration to accelerate the development, production and equitable global access to new COVID-19 essential health technologies . . . We need to work together in unprecedented and inclusive partnership with all stakeholders – political leaders, public and private sector partners, civil society, academia, and all other stakeholders across society – jointly leveraging our comparative strengths and respective voices to drive towards collective solutions, an accelerated path, and access for all.[78]

At a launch event on 25 April 2020, the initial group was joined by other large federations, including the International Red Cross and Red Crescent Movement and the International Federation of Pharmaceutical Manufacturers. Two Special Envoys were asked to lead it: Ngozi Okonjo-Iweala, who was Gavi Board Chair at the time, and Sir Andrew Witty, former chief executive of GlaxoSmithKline. At an online pledging conference sponsored by the European Commission, the UK, Norway and Saudi Arabia, several countries and philanthropies pledged support for the $8.2 billion campaign, including Germany, France, Japan, Canada, Israel,

[78] WHO, 'Access to COVID-19 Tools (ACT) Accelerator: A Global Collaboration to Accelerate the Development, Production and Equitable Access to New COVID-19 Diagnostics, Therapeutics and vaccines', 24 April 2020.

Turkey, South Africa, Malaysia and the Gates Foundation.[79] The US, Russia and India did not attend. China was represented by a low-level official.

In various fora since then, there has been much discussion about whether to deem global health to be a public good, implying the vaccine should be made available to all those in need.[80] The term has been used repeatedly by government leaders, as well as the leaders of the WHO, the UN and the AU.[81] It has become part of the rhetoric of the European Commission. And as noted above, it was endorsed at the WHA. This buzz of multi-stakeholder activity suggests that the notion of deepening the public sphere for global health discourse is not fanciful.

8.5.5 Normative Orders

Finally, international law is just one of the normative orders that informs global health governance. Social distancing and mask wearing (and the sense of collective responsibility that goes along with them) are social norms. To the extent that a social norm is respected, there is less need for a legal mandate. Beyond the broad injunction implied in the right to health, equitable distribution of vaccines is a question of morality (as well as self-interest). Religious norms were certainly impacted: in Senegal, the 95 per cent Muslim population was told not to go to the mosque on Fridays, to pray at home; in the USA, restrictions on public gatherings prompted church services in parking lots. Economic norms, ranging from

[79] William Booth, Carolyn Y. Johnson, Carol Morello, 'The world came together for a virtual vaccine summit. The US was conspicuously absent'. *Washington Post*, 4 May 2020. www.washingtonpost.com/world/europe/the-world-comes-together-for-a-virtual-vaccine-summit-the-us-is-conspicuously-absent/2020/05/04/ac5b6754-8a5c-11ea-80df-d24b35a568ae_story.html.

[80] On the implications of treating the vaccine as a global public good, see generally, Ngozi Okonjo-Iweala, 'Finding a Vaccine is only the first step: no-one will be safe without the whole world being safe', *Foreign Affairs*, 30 April 2020. See also Priti Panaik, 'A strong call for COVID-19 treatments and vaccines to be global public goods – World Health Assembly', *International Health Policies*, 20 May 2020.

[81] For example, at the Africa Dialogue Series organized in collaboration with the AU, the UN SG noted that African countries should also have quick, equal and affordable access to any eventual vaccines and treatment, as these should be considered as global public goods. UN Press Release, SG/SM/22089, 20 May 2020. At an AU virtual conference, African Ministers of Health invoked the concept by insisting that the vaccine should be accessible to all. AU/African CDCs, 'Covid-19 Vaccine Develpoment and Access Virtual Conference', 24–25 June 2020. https://africacdc.org/news-item/covid-19-vaccine-development-and-access-virtual-conference/.www.un.org/press/en/2020/sgsm20089.doc.htm.

the strictures of global supply chains to the dignity of work to the practices of the informal economy, are part of the equation. The notion of the vaccine as a global public good is rooted in economics, but can also be traced to international law and has religious connotations. Institutional culture matters as well: the WHO Secretariat is acculturated to think of itself as a technical, non-political body, not in the habit of naming and shaming states. Calling out China for its apparent violation of Article 6 of the IHR, or the USA for its initial shambolic response to the pandemic, are not in the culture of the organization.

8.6 Conclusion

Deliberation, defined as principled argumentation, matters. The pluralism of the international system both complicates efforts at principled argumentation and makes those efforts especially important. It complicates because those who engage in the deliberation often have little in common. Yet joining an international organization and participating in its activities, even if only by paying lip service to its constitutive act, can generate enough of a shared frame of reference to make reasoned deliberation possible. This does not eradicate pluralism. It may even exacerbate the tensions inherent in it. But deliberation helps to manage the tensions in a manner that makes it easier for actors with different values, perspective, interests and ideologies, to co-exist.

9 Teaching Statehood

Guy Fiti Sinclair

9.1 Introduction

Scholarship on international organizations law, like most approaches in international law and international relations (IR), is dominated by state-centric, functionalist and rational choice frameworks. According to these mainstream approaches, states are axiomatically the principal actors in international affairs, which pre-exist and create international organizations to serve their own interests and needs. To realists, international relations are structured by competition, the search for security and the struggle for power among rational, self-interested states. In this view, international organizations are epiphenomenal, reflecting extant power relations and having only a marginal impact on state behaviour.[1] To IR scholars and international lawyers of a more liberal-institutionalist orientation, international organizations are designed and created by states to pursue shared goals, solve coordination problems and produce public goods.[2]

According to the functionalist assumptions underlying these approaches, states delegate authority and tasks to international organizations which they, acting as the agents of states, may be more or less efficient and faithful in carrying out.[3] International organizations law scholars are, of course, conscious of the principal-agent problem and acknowledge the possibility – even likelihood – that organizations will

[1] See, e.g., J. Mearsheimer, 'The False Promise of International Institutions', (1994–5) 19 *International Security* 5.

[2] See, e.g., K. W. Abbott and D. Snidal, 'Why States Act through Formal International Organizations', (1998) 42 *Journal of Conflict Resolution* 3.

[3] J. Klabbers, 'The Emergence of Functionalism in International Institutional Law: Colonial Inspirations', (2014) 25 *European Journal of International Law* 645.

take on a life of their own and exceed their mandates. They also increasingly recognize that international organizations have become important lawmakers in their own right, in addition to exercising a range of other powers in relation to states.[4] And yet this body of scholarship, by and large, continues to mark a sharp ontological separation between states and international organizations, assigning primacy to the former and viewing the latter as (at best) secondary, supporting actors.

The rationalist, functionalist and state-centred assumptions underpinning mainstream approaches to international organizations and international organizations law have come under challenge in recent years from a variety of disciplinary perspectives. This chapter proposes an alternative framework through which international organizations may be understood, not principally as the creatures and servants of states, but rather as engaged in an enterprise of teaching statehood – and thereby continuously constructing and transforming states. The next section begins by identifying a number of theoretical resources for developing such a framework. The following section distinguishes a series of techniques through which international organizations engage in teaching statehood. The final section of the chapter then sketches a brief history of how these techniques have evolved over the past 150 years in relation to shifting models of the state.

9.2 Resources for Rethinking International Organizations and Statehood

Resources for thinking about international organizations as teachers of statehood can be drawn from several disciplines adjacent to international law. One of the longest-standing challenges to the rationalist and functionalist assumptions underpinning mainstream approaches to international organizations has issued from the sociological institutionalist school, sometimes also called 'world polity theory' or 'world society theory'.[5] Although frequently more interested in the activities of

[4] See generally J. E. Alvarez, *International Organizations as Law-Makers* (Oxford University Press, 2005).

[5] See, e.g., J. W. Meyer *et al.*, 'World Society and the Nation-State', (1997) 103 *American Journal of Sociology* 144.

international non-governmental organizations, scholars in this school have also given considerable attention to the role of international organizations in diffusing a putative 'world culture' originating in Western Christianity and capitalism.[6] Sociological institutionalists emphasize 'rationalization, universalism, belief in progress, and individualism as foundational cultural assumptions'.[7] It is this shared culture, they argue, transmitted through international organizations as well as by other means, which explains the surprising isomorphism in state structures and practices. However, world society theory has been criticized for emphasizing structure at the expense of agency, coercion and politics.[8]

Closely related to sociological institutionalism, constructivist approaches in political science likewise give significant attention to questions of identity that are usually overlooked by rationalists.[9] In doing so, they have opened up new insights into the internal lives of international organizations and their role in the production and diffusion of cultural norms and values among states. IR constructivists have also attended to individual and institutional actors, the divergent sources of authority on which they draw, the forms of power they exercise and their mutual interactions.[10] For example, Barnett and Finnemore draw on Weberian insights to show how international organizations wield bureaucratic power through knowledge and information – by classifying objects (including problems, actors and action), fixing social meanings and articulating and diffusing norms and values.[11] Building on their distinction between the regulative and constitutive powers of international organizations, Barnett elsewhere further distinguishes between direct and diffuse forms of these

[6] See, e.g., C. L. McNeely, *Constructing the Nation-State: International Organization and Prescriptive Action* (Westport CT: Greenwood Press, 1995).

[7] E. Schofer *et al.*, 'Sociological Institutionalism and World Society', in E. Amenta *et al.* (eds.), *The Wiley-Blackwell Companion to Political Sociology* (Hoboken NJ: Blackwell, 2012) 57, 59–60.

[8] *Ibid.*; M. Finnemore, 'Norms, Culture, and World Politics: Insights from Sociology's Institutionalism', (1996) 50 *International Organization* 325.

[9] See, e.g., M. Finnemore, *National Interests in International Society* (Ithaca NY: Cornell University Press, 1996); M. Barnett and M. Finnemore, *Rules for the World* (Ithaca NY: Cornell University Press, 2004); J. Chwieroth, *Capital Ideas: The IMF and the Rise of Financial Liberalization* (Princeton University Press, 2010).

[10] See generally D. D. Avant, M. Finnemore, and S. Sell (eds.), *Who Governs the Globe?* (Cambridge University Press, 2010).

[11] Barnett and Finnemore, *Rules for the World*, 29–34.

powers, to build a typology of compulsory, institutional, structural and productive power.[12]

Other approaches in IR and international political sociology have explored how international organizations exercise all these forms of power, often in combination, with particular state-making effects. Neo-Gramscian scholars have emphasized the role of international organizations in constructing a capitalist world economy, and the particular structures and ideologies connecting state, economy and society.[13] Foucault-inspired studies of global governmentality include international organizations as vehicles for the production and dissemination of techniques of governance to states, with particular attention to the interplay of disciplinary mechanisms directed towards individuals, biopolitical regulation of populations and management of the economy.[14] These studies tend to exhibit a methodological interest in the minute details of quotidian practices, which has been taken up – with additional theoretical inputs from Bourdieusian, actor-network and performativity theory, among others – in a burgeoning literature on international practices, including those of international organizations in relation to states.[15]

Lastly, recent decades have seen a new wave of historiographic studies that have complicated existing understandings of the origins and evolution of international organizations, casting light on their relationship to state-making. Interest in the origins of contemporary forms of global governance has prompted re-evaluations of the lesser-known activities of the League of Nations, illuminating its role in shaping the global economy generally,[16] and more specifically in colonized territories subject to its Mandates system.[17] Similarly, the growing body of scholarship on the history of development and modernization, particularly in relation to the

[12] M. Barnett and R. Duvall (eds.), *Power in Global Governance* (Cambridge University Press, 2005) 8–22.

[13] See, e.g., C. Murphy, *International Organization and Industrial Change* (Cambridge: Polity, 1994); R. W. Cox, 'Gramsci, Hegemony and International Relations: An Essay in Method', (1983) 12 *Millennium* 162.

[14] See, e.g., W. Larner and W. Walters (eds.), *Global Governmentality: Governing International Spaces* (Abingdon: Routledge, 2004); J. Joseph, *The Social in the Global: Social Theory, Governmentality and Global Politics* (Cambridge University Press, 2012).

[15] See, e.g., C. Bueger and F. Gadinger, *International Practice Theory*, 2nd ed. (New York: Palgrave Macmillan, 2018); E. Adler and V. Pouliot (eds.), *International Practices* (Cambridge University Press, 2011).

[16] P. Clavin, *Securing the World Economy* (Oxford University Press, 2013).

[17] S. Pedersen, *The Guardians* (Oxford University Press, 2015).

Cold War and decolonization, has yielded fresh insights into the work of international organizations such as the United Nations (UN),[18] the World Bank and International Monetary Fund (IMF),[19] the International Labour Organization (ILO)[20] and others.[21]

This scholarship in adjacent disciplines has influenced international lawyers' thinking on the relationship between international organizations and state formation in different ways. One broad stream draws on IR constructivism and related approaches in sociology and political science. To take an influential example, Koh analyzes how the repeated interactions involved in transnational legal processes 'create patterns of behavior and generate norms of external conduct' which states internalize, shaping their identities and interests.[22] Partly building on this work, Shaffer identifies five dimensions of the state that may be impacted by processes of transnational legal ordering, including the work of international organizations: national law and practice; the boundaries between state, market and other forms of social ordering; the allocation of authority among state institutions; the role of expertise in governance; and associational patterns and normative frames.[23] With a complementary but narrower focus on international human rights, Goodman and Jinks distinguish 'three distinct mechanisms of social influence that drive state behaviour: material inducement, persuasion, and acculturation',[24] the last of which involves 'varying degrees of identification with a reference group' which in turn 'generate varying degrees of cognitive and social pressures to conform'.[25]

[18] M. Mazower, *No Enchanted Palace: The End of Empire and the Ideological Origins of the United Nations* (Princeton University Press, 2009).

[19] E. Helleiner, *Forgotten Foundations of Bretton Woods* (Ithaca NY: Cornell University Press, 2014); P. Sharma, *Robert McNamara's Other War: The World Bank and International Development* (Philadelphia PA: University of Pennsylvania Press, 2017).

[20] D. Maul, *Human Rights, Development and Decolonization: The International Labour Organization, 1940–1970* (New York: Palgrave Macmillan, 2012).

[21] For studies embracing multiple international organizations, see M. Frey, S. Kunkel and C. R. Unger (eds.), *International Organizations and Development, 1945–1990* (New York: Palgrave Macmillan, 2014).

[22] H. H. Koh, 'Transnational Legal Process', (1996) 75 *Nebraska Law Review* 181, 204.

[23] G. Shaffer, *Transnational Legal Ordering and State Change* (Cambridge University Press, 2013) 23–33.

[24] R. Goodman and D. Jinks, *Socializing States: Promoting Human Rights through International Law* (Oxford University Press, 2013) 22.

[25] *Ibid.*, 26.

A second stream of international law scholarship views the state-making work of international organizations through a more critical lens. Scholarship in this stream draws on a range of historiographical and anthropological methods and sources to explore the normative dimensions of international organizations, giving particular attention to their role in colonized (or semi-colonized) territories and decolonized states, and often noting the ways in which international organizations institutionalize or otherwise express international law's 'civilizing mission'.[26] Much of this work incorporates insights from Gramscian and Foucauldian scholarship, permitting consideration of structural and productive, as well as compulsory and institutional forms of power – the 'conduct of conduct', through both coercion and consent – as well as the incorporation of resistance from below.[27] The next section surveys an array of techniques used by international organizations to teach statehood, before turning to an episodic history of how these techniques have evolved and combined in various ways over time.

9.3 Techniques of Teaching Statehood

The theoretical approaches surveyed in the previous section can be usefully supplemented by thinking about state formation as an ongoing cultural process. According to a growing body of scholarship, 'the state' has no essence and is not a self-producing source of power.[28] Rather, each state is produced and reproduced imaginatively by the banal and technical routines of bureaucracies; by 'images, metaphors, and representational practices' through which a state may 'come to be understood as a concrete,

[26] See especially A. Anghie, *Imperialism, Sovereignty and the Making of International Law* (Cambridge University Press, 2004); A. Orford, *International Authority and the Responsibility to Protect* (Cambridge University Press, 2011); M. Fakhri, *Sugar and the Making of International Trade Law* (Cambridge University Press, 2011); S. Pahuja, *Decolonising International Law* (Cambridge University Press, 2011); L. Eslava, *Local Space, Global Life: The Everyday Operation of International Law and Development* (Cambridge University Press, 2015).

[27] See, e.g., B. Rajagopal, *International Law from Below* (Cambridge University Press, 2003).

[28] See generally G. Steinmetz (ed.), *State/Culture: State-Formation after the Cultural Turn* (Ithaca NY: Cornell University Press, 1999); T. Hansen and F. Stepputat (eds.), *States of Imagination* (Durham NC: Duke University Press, 2001); A. Sharma and A. Gupta (eds.), *The Anthropology of the State: A Reader* (Hoboken NJ: Blackwell, 2006).

overarching, spatially encompassing reality';[29] and by the aggregation of manifold dealings and exchanges in multiple settings that generate a 'powerful, apparently metaphysical effect'.[30] The meaning and limits of the state continue to be constructed and contested on a daily basis in an ongoing and disorderly process of social interaction, all of which paradoxically reinforces the sense of the state's 'reality'. It is thus possible to study the assemblage of rationalities and technologies – the 'practices, techniques, programmes, knowledges, rationales and interventions'[31] – through which international organizations teach statehood on a continuous basis.[32]

From this perspective, entry into membership in an international organization can itself provide opportunities to induct states into particular normative frameworks, structures and policies. As is widely recognized, membership in international organizations – particularly in the most universal, such as the UN – has become a potent signifier of statehood and sovereignty.[33] In the League of Nations, the controversy over membership criteria and their application to Ethiopia, which was seen as possessing marginal sovereignty, was thus resolved by 'recast[ing] membership as a process of reform, possibly overseen by the League (or European empires operating through the League), rather than as recognition of a status already achieved'.[34] Membership in the UN has been approached in a similarly pragmatic fashion, permitting the inclusion of states that might not strictly meet all criteria, in the hope that membership might serve to socialize these states into the organization's values. By

[29] J. Ferguson and A. Gupta (eds.), 'Spatializing States: Toward an Ethnography of Neoliberal Governmentality', (2002) 29 *American Ethnologist* 981.

[30] T. Mitchell, 'Society, Economy, and the State Effect', in Steinmetz (ed.), *State/Culture* 76, at 89.

[31] P. Miller, 'On the Interrelations between Accounting and the State', (1990) 15 *Accounting, Organizations and Society* 317.

[32] For more detailed examinations of this theme, see generally G. F. Sinclair, *To Reform the World: International Organizations and the Making of Modern States* (Oxford University Press, 2017); G. F. Sinclair, 'State Formation, Liberal Reform and the Growth of International Organizations', (2015) 26 *European Journal of International Law* 445; and N. Bhuta and G. F. Sinclair (eds.), dossier on *Technologies of Stateness: International Organizations and the Making of States* (2020) 11 *Humanity Journal.*

[33] A. Chayes and A. Handler Chayes, *The New Sovereignty: Compliance with International Regulatory Agreements* (Cambridge MA: Harvard University Press, 1995).

[34] M. Donaldson, 'The League of Nations, Ethiopia and the Making of States', (2020) 11 *Humanity Journal* 6.

contrast, accession to World Trade Organization (WTO) membership frequently involves far-reaching concessions on the part of acceding states, including policy changes and the establishment of new administrative units, standards and processes, as demanded by existing members.

Another obvious way that international organizations teach statehood is through their standard-setting activities. Such standards take different forms, from draft conventions to recommendations, codes, regulations, standards, 'best practices', declarations, guidelines and more, along an uneven continuum of normativity.[35] Of course, many of these activities can be understood as regulatory in nature, involving the exercise of a form of institutional power to change the behaviour of (pre-constituted) states.[36] But standard-setting also has a constitutive effect in shaping states' identities and interests – in other words, in instructing them in what it means to be a state. This is an effect of the reiterative interactions among international organizations and states, as well as other transnational actors, in the *processes* of standard-setting which take place within international organizations, as much as in the *content* of the standards themselves. To the extent that standard-setting organizations act as nodes of intergovernmental networks – whether comprising ministers (as in the WTO and IMF) or civil servants (as in many of the 'technical' institutions) – they therefore serve as powerful vehicles for socialization into statehood.[37]

Once agreed, such standards – whether in formally binding or non-binding instruments – then undergo further repeated cycles of interaction, interpretation and internalization through a diversity of implementation, reporting and enforcement mechanisms. Think, for example, of the reiterative acculturation processes involved in the interlinked mechanisms of the ILO's regular system of supervision and special procedures, the WTO's Trade Policy Review Mechanism and Dispute Settlement System, the UN Human Rights Council's Universal Periodic Review and special procedures mechanisms, or IMF surveillance. Another significant example is the flexible peer review process of the Organization for Economic Cooperation and Development (OECD), which examines the performance of states in a wide range of areas – economics, education, health, environment, governance and more – against assorted standards, including national legislation, OECD

[35] See also Alvarez, Chapter 6 in this volume.
[36] Barnett and Duvall, *Power in Global Governance*, 15–17.
[37] See generally A.-M. Slaughter, *A New World Order* (Princeton University Press, 2004).

codes and other international instruments. Even complaints procedures which appear to be aimed at enhancing the accountability of international organizations or other non-state actors, such as the World Bank's Inspection Panel, may be used in practice to influence the conduct and policies of member states.[38]

Many of the most routine and conspicuous operational activities of international organizations involve techniques of teaching statehood. Consider, for example, the complex state-making work of contemporary UN peace operations, which takes place along multiple, intersecting dimensions, including policing (external) physical borders, defining (internal) ethnic boundaries, protecting the human rights of civilian populations and supervising democratic elections. Consider, likewise, how the services provided by organizations such as the International Organization for Migration (IOM) or the UN High Commissioner for Refugees (UNHCR) aid in the performance of statehood, inscribing and reinforcing the key dimensions of territory, population and security, even – or perhaps especially – when enacting exceptions to the rule.[39] Another set of educative functions can be seen in the work of the special procedure mechanisms of the UN Human Rights Council. Or, to take a very different example, the projects and programs financed by loans from (or guaranteed by) international financial institutions reflect particular, if inchoate, models of statehood, which borrowing members internalize in the process of implementing those projects and programs.

A major area of activity carried out by many international organizations with an explicit instructive purpose is technical assistance. Often undertaken in conjunction with other operational activities, technical assistance is a capacious term that encompasses a variety of offerings, including expert advisory services; the funding of fellowships and scholarships; the establishment of training institutes, seminars, conferences and working groups; and the provision of technical publications. Technical assistance might aim to support the establishment and operation of government departments and agencies, or the drafting of new laws, regulations and constitutions. Each of these aspects of technical assistance provides

[38] R. Wade, 'Accountability Gone Wrong: The World Bank, Non-Governmental Organisations and the US Government in a Fight over China', (2009) 14 *New Political Economy* 25.

[39] J. Klabbers, 'Notes on the Ideology of International Organizations Law: The International Organization for Migration, State-Making, and the Market for Migration', (2019) 32 *Leiden Journal of International Law* 383.

avenues for international organizations to educate civil servants and government officials in the ways of statehood. Moreover, the subject matter of such assistance can vary enormously, covering fields as disparate as trade, development, agriculture, labour, aeronautics, nuclear energy, finance, justice, police and security – that is to say, all conceivable aspects of state functioning.

All these activities are underpinned and made possible by a wide array of knowledge and information practices, which themselves serve as potent techniques of teaching statehood. International organizations gather information of all kinds from their members, which feeds into and informs their operational planning and decision-making. Before gathering any information, however, some determination must be made, more or less consciously, about what information is important, revealing and useful. This determination requires, in turn, a definition of specific problems to which an international organization can offer solutions. Defining such problems and solutions is an inherently normative exercise, involving judgements about the way the world is – and, in particular, how states are – and ought to be governed. These judgements are built into the questionnaires and surveys which gather information from member states. In the process of periodically reporting information to institutions within the categories and according to the standards set by those institutions – whether relating to human rights, economic development, labour protections, environmental goals or otherwise – states gradually internalize the normative positions reflected in those categories and standards, adjusting their behaviour and aligning their practices and institutional structures to better meet their criteria.

The collection of vast amounts of information engenders a further series of knowledge practices and normative effects. First, international organizations collate and publish the information they have collected about state practices, often in a readily comparative form, in a plethora of reports and bulletins which are disseminated to their members. Second, on the basis of this information, interpreted through particular cognitive frameworks, organizations formulate descriptions of 'best practices', often in the form of published standards or guidelines. Third, the comparative presentation of data entails (at least implicitly but often explicitly) an exercise in ranking states' performances against these standards. Even when not legally binding and couched in generalised terms with numerous exceptions and caveats, the knowledge claims and prescriptions promulgated by international organizations exercise a qualitative normative influence as they are translated and enrolled into the networks of governmental bureaucracies. As an archive of expertise that synthesizes a medley of complex practices and experiences, while also necessarily abstracting and simplifying them, these claims and prescriptions contribute towards the construction of a kind of distributed global knowledge that amounts to an internationalized 'science of the state'.[40]

As the foregoing discussion suggests, international organizations are constantly engaged in a non-linear, looping series of practices involving problematization, classification, information-gathering, standardization, planning and operational activities. Of course, the actual consequences or effects of these practices vary greatly and are highly contingent on dynamic, recursive interactions among both endogenous and exogenous factors.[41] Nonetheless, it is possible to trace how the expansion of statehood-teaching techniques has occurred in tandem, and been deeply co-constituted, with the rise of particular forms of expertise. Most notably, international organizations have drawn on and contributed to the evolution of the disciplines of statistics and demography, economics, public administration and management. The next section of this chapter focuses on these expert practices as key elements of statecraft in presenting a brief history of the evolving techniques of teaching statehood.

9.4 A Brief Episodic History

To grasp how international organizations have taught statehood, it is helpful to take a view of their activities over the *longue durée*. During the past 150 years, institutions have proliferated and expanded their powers along with shifting conceptions of what constitutes a 'modern' state. Underlying all these conceptions has been a broadly European model of liberal government which takes individual freedom as principle and limit of state action, carving out certain domains of non-interference but nevertheless legitimating interventions at the level of economy and society (for the purposes of ensuring social security) and the individual (through

[40] Thanks to Nehal Bhuta for help in articulating this point.

[41] Avant, Finnemore, and Sell (eds.), *Who Governs the Globe?*; Shaffer, *Transnational Legal Ordering*.

disciplinary techniques that instil desirable capacities for autonomous action and self-mastery). These contradictory pulls produce an endlessly recursive, reiterative dynamic of liberal reform which international organizations support through the sundry statehood-teaching techniques outlined in the previous section. Thinking of state formation in this way makes it possible to identify a number of dominant transnational configurations or 'forms' of the state – associated with absolutism, laissez-faire liberalism, colonialism, Keynesian welfarism, post-colonial developmentalism, neoliberalism and so on – which have been viewed as 'modern' in their own time and place, and which have served as models for the statehood-teaching activities of international organizations.

The following episodic account sketches the evolution of international organizations and normative models of statehood in four periods of uneven lengths. The first corresponds to the century between the Congress of Vienna and the outbreak of the First World War, during which the first proto-organizations emerged as teachers of statehood in both Western societies and colonial territories. The second covers the crucial interwar period, often viewed as marking the 'move to institutions' in international law, during which institutions began to shift their focus from supporting laissez-faire liberalism to constructing welfare states.[42] The third focuses on the decades following the end of the Second World War, during which the nation-state form was effectively universalized through decolonization with the support of a new system of organizations largely centred on the UN. Finally, the fourth addresses the last four decades, which have witnessed an increasingly fragmented and diverse landscape of international organizations and statehood-teaching activities. The point is not to suggest that the statehood-teaching techniques used by organizations have changed radically in each of these periods. Rather, the episodic approach adopted here is intended to show how those techniques have been added to, layered, refined and deployed in increasingly complex ways, and to different ends, over time.

9.4.1 Liberal Political Economy, the Social and Colonial Government

Several techniques of teaching statehood can be observed already in the international bodies established under the auspices of the Concert of

[42] D. Kennedy, 'The Move to Institutions', (1987) 8 *Cardozo Law Review* 841.

Europe at the end of the Napoleonic wars. These international bodies were understood from the start to be necessary adjuncts to the promotion and consolidation of liberal government, linking together the new liberal political economy and the potential for unlimited commercial expansion by European states. Public international unions such as the International Telegraph Union, the Universal Postal Union and the International Association of Railway Congresses, were established to support the governmental institutions necessary for the international circulation of capital, goods and ideas. Similar unions for the Protection of Industrial Property and of Literary and Artistic Works, together with the Hague Conference on Private International Law, aimed to universalise property rights in all states. The International Bureau of Weights and Measures and the International Bureau of Commercial Statistics drew on the new social sciences linked to political economy to achieve a greater degree of standardization, while the International Union for the Publication of Customs Tariffs and the 'Sugar Union' institutionalized the principle of free trade by collecting and disseminating information that made state subsidies and surcharges visible to their members, and thus susceptible to negotiation and pressure.[43]

A second focus of statehood-teaching techniques in the nineteenth century concerned the rising concern with the 'social question', associated with the multiple interlinked problems arising from a large, underemployed proletariat. The decades immediately following the Congress of Vienna witnessed a dramatic increase in the use of expert technologies to widen and deepen the powers of European states. Here again, international bodies played a key role in transmitting the rationalities and technologies of social government: penal policy through the International Penitentiary Commission; public health through the International Office of Public Hygiene and the International Association of Public Baths and Cleanliness; and more broadly the International Institute of Administrative Sciences, which circulated information about 'the most efficient ways to carry out and further extend the expanding functions of the state'.[44] Perhaps most significant of all was the International Labour Office – forerunner of the ILO – which promoted social legislation as an alternative to violent revolution and exemplified the internationalization of concerns regarding the assurance of individual freedom in the conditions of modern, industrial society. As a contemporary observer

[43] Fakhri, *Sugar*. [44] Murphy, *International Organization and Industrial Change*, 100.

noted, all of this burgeoning international activity, far from detracting from state sovereignty, directly bolstered and extended it:[45]

> The process of international organization frequently favors the expansion of the sphere of the national government. When interests are organized upon an international basis, the persons and associations concerned begin to see more clearly how their purposes may be furthered through state action. They consequently demand new legislation as well as the expansion of the administrative sphere . . . [I]n every way the state is encouraged to make the fullest use of its powers.

In territories outside Europe, too, new international bodies undertook a wide range of activities that taught states to carry out the tasks necessary to meet the contradictory demands of modern government. The international sanitary councils established in Istanbul, Alexandria and Teheran, for example, introduced and applied disciplinary techniques of separation, inspection and surveillance, at once to defend European civilization at its frontiers, enhance the welfare of local populations and modernize the administration of countries in the Near East. Modernization meant more centralized institutions, standardized practices, professionalization and legalization: the work of 'civilizing' meant 'structuring and establishing what was perceived to be a "European-style" order'.[46] River commissions – such as those on the Danube, Congo, and Niger rivers and the Suez Canal – likewise came to be seen as vehicles for administrative reform in non-European societies and for the projection of European rationales and techniques of government as universally normative. International commissions were formed to address cases of 'serious disorganization in the financial system of the state' in Egypt, Turkey and elsewhere on the European periphery.[47] Regional organizations which served to extend Western influence and commercial interests were also legitimated by the goal of teaching statehood: the forerunner of the present-day Organization of American States was thus defended as 'an efficient agent in assisting the internal development of the American republics'.[48]

[45] P. S. Reinsch, *Public International Unions* (Boston MA and London: Ginn and Company, 1911) 140.

[46] M. Chahrour, '"A Civilizing Mission"? Austrian Medicine and the Reform of Medical Structures in the Ottoman Empire, 1838–1850', (2007) 38 *Studies in History and Philosophy of Biological and Biomedical Sciences* 687, 688.

[47] Reinsch, *Public International Unions*, 75. [48] *Ibid.*, 99.

9.4.2 From Laissez-Faire to the Welfare State

The 'move to institutions' at the end of the First World War marked the inauguration of a new set of experiments in teaching statehood that were now centred, at least nominally, on the League of Nations.[49] Though committed to a policy of laissez-faire liberalism at the outset, the upheavals of the following two decades prompted a 'reinvention' of the League and a redirection of its resources to address social and economic issues.[50] The expansion of the League's remit was in part achieved through an array of new organs – technical organizations, permanent and temporary advisory committees, preparatory and administrative commissions and institutes – with responsibility for, among other things, matters relating to education, health, emigration, nutrition, economics and finance, science and culture. Together, these organs helped to foster and promote among its members ideas and practices understood to be central to modern states, including industrialization, international trade, social government and economic development.[51]

Many of the techniques used by present-day international organizations for teaching statehood can be observed, albeit in embryonic form, in the activities of the League of Nations. Within its economic organs, the collection and circulation of national statistics were carried out on a vast scale, with all the effects of standardization and norm-setting discussed above.[52] The League's 'social questions' organs educated states on the nature of specific problems – such as human trafficking, narcotics and immorality – and presented solutions that deepened the League's influence over how states regulated their populations and shaped the subjectivity of individuals.[53] Efforts to reconcile the principle of national self-determination and the protection of minorities within international law led to institutional measures to adjust the boundaries, populations and

[49] See Article 24 of the Covenant of the League of Nations, which was more often than not honoured in the breach.

[50] Clavin, *Securing the World Economy.*

[51] *Ibid.*; M. Dubin, 'Transgovernmental Processes in the League of Nations', (1983) 37 *International Organization* 469; Y. Decorzant, 'Internationalism in the Economic and Financial Organization of the League of Nations', in D. Laqua (ed.), *Internationalism Reconfigured* (London: Tauris, 2011) 115.

[52] Clavin, *Securing the World Economy.*

[53] See, e.g., S. Legg, '"The Life of Individuals as well as of Nations": International Law and the League of Nations' Anti-Trafficking Governmentalities', (2012) 25 *Leiden Journal of International Law* 647.

constitutional orders of European states.[54] Programmes of technical cooperation provided occasions for League experts to transfer European know-how and technology to non-Western states, reorganizing and modernizing them along the lines of Western economic and social models.[55] And present-day peacekeeping and democracy promotion practices were prefigured in the League's techniques of deploying military commissions, administering territory *ad interim*, resolving disputes and holding plebiscites.[56]

Colonial territories continued to supply highly productive 'laboratories' for experimentation with techniques of teaching statehood under the auspices of the League of Nations. Through a system of Mandates that reported to a Permanent Commission in Geneva, the scope of the League's undertakings widened to include territories in Asia, Africa and the Pacific, reinforcing colonialism in certain respects but also serving to undermine it and encourage the rise of nationalist movements.[57] As Antony Anghie has argued, the Commission's functions extended beyond the 'strictly legal approach' of studying and ensuring that the obligations undertaken by each mandatory power were discharged, to also exercising 'an administrative function and control over the mandatory'.[58] By bringing problems of colonial administration directly under the purview of the Mandate system – including questions of 'native welfare' and progress towards self-government – the Commission was empowered to develop 'new techniques of monitoring and management', gathering 'an unprecedented volume of information' and establishing 'novel forms of control by creating, in effect, new sciences of social and economic development'. In doing so, Anghie argues, the Mandate system 'contemplated nothing less than the creation of the social, political, and economic conditions thought necessary to support a functioning nation-state'.[59]

The ILO was another centrally important site for the emergence of techniques connected with a changing model of statehood. From its humble beginnings in Part XIII of the Treaty of Versailles, the ILO grew over the next

[54] See, e.g., N. Berman, '"But the Alternative Is Despair": European Nationalism and the Modernist Renewal of International Law', (1993) 106 *Harvard Law Review* 1792; U. Özsu, *Formalizing Displacement: International Law and Population Transfers* (Oxford University Press, 2014).

[55] M. Zanasi, 'Exporting Development: The League of Nations and Republican China', (2007) 49 *Comparative Studies in Society and History* 143.

[56] A. James, 'The Peacekeeping Role of the League of Nations', (1999) 6 *International Peacekeeping* 154.

[57] Anghie, *Imperialism*, ch. 3; Pedersen, *The Guardians*.

[58] Anghie, *Imperialism*, 51.

[59] *Ibid.*, 182, 184 and 177.

two decades into an autonomous organization engaged in a set of activities going well beyond the standard-setting functions envisaged by its founders. Like the League of the Nations, the ILO built a reputation as a 'great clearing house of information', collecting data, compiling labour statistics and distributing a variety of published materials from and to member and non-member countries.[60] Its relatively expansive network – with overseas branch offices, national correspondents and regular missions abroad – created opportunities for its experts to provide technical assistance on drafting and implementing labour and social insurance laws. Following the economic slump of the 1930s, and inspired by the promises of scientific management and rationalization, ILO officials promoted techniques of national (as well as international) economic planning and management associated with the welfare state. Extending these activities to states and territories outside Europe and North America, the ILO served as a critically important vehicle for the emergence and circulation of development discourses and practices in the interwar period.[61]

9.4.3 Modernizing Postcolonial States

The idea and goal of development became a central theme of the statehood-teaching activities undertaken by international organizations in the decades immediately following the end of the Second World War. The social welfare principles championed by the ILO, restated and linked to development in its 1944 Philadelphia Declaration, were espoused in the UN Charter and even in the General Agreement on Tariffs and Trade. What the founders of the UN and other institutions created at the end of the war could not have anticipated, however, was how quickly decolonization would transform their membership, goals and operations. As a consequence, these organizations immediately became sites of struggle over the meaning of statehood and instruments for the construction of states, and especially in the decolonized global South. The state-making activities of the Mandate system were extended and accelerated in the UN through the work of the Trusteeship Council and the mechanisms for non-self-governing territories established under chapter 11 of the Charter. And a Technical Assistance Board was

[60] P. Périgord, *The International Labor Organization* (New York: Appleton and Co., 1926) 180.

[61] See generally G. F. Sinclair, 'A "Civilizing Task": The International Labour Organization, Social Reform, and the Genealogy of Development', (2018) 20 *Journal of the History of International Law* 145.

established to coordinate the UN's work with that of seven specialized agencies in an Expanded Program of Technical Assistance (EPTA).[62]

This collective (albeit sometimes contested) enterprise was strongly shaped by the ideology of modernization, which posited a universal developmental path for all states, based broadly on a welfare state model. Within this theoretical frame, the success of modernization in any society depended upon the state, seen as both the vehicle and the telos of progress. Moreover, modernization required a certain level of social engineering and 'education' to instil the appropriate attitudes, overcome psychological and cultural impediments to progress and shape individual subjects suited to the conditions of modern life. The UN and related organizations played a significant role in diffusing the norms and practices of modernization. In UN development thinking, as in modernization theory generally, the state performed a crucial function in establishing the necessary conditions for economic growth. A 1951 UN expert report on economic development in 'underdeveloped' countries thus argued that economic progress depended 'to a large extent upon the adoption by governments of appropriate administrative and legislative action'.[63] Central planning – at least of an indicative kind – was universally prescribed, and governments could legitimately intervene in economic development through a variety of approved means.

International organizations aimed to support all aspects of government and statecraft in 'underdeveloped' countries, beginning with the collection of numerical data. The UN Statistics Division performed an important function in creating a 'universally acknowledged statistical system and ... a general framework guiding the collection and compilation of data' in individual states, providing 'essential information' about the size and densities of national populations, agriculture, industry, housing, earnings, age groups and available skills.[64] From the late 1950s, the Division took further steps to devolve its operations to the regional level, providing training in

[62] See generally G. F. Sinclair, 'A Battlefield Transformed: The United Nations and the Struggle over Postcolonial Statehood', in J. von Bernstorff and P. Dann (eds.), *The Battle for International Law: South–North Perspectives on the Decolonization Era* (Oxford University Press, 2019) 257.

[63] UN Department of Economic Affairs, *Measures for the Economic Development of Under-Developed Countries* (1951) 17.

[64] UNOPI, 'What Is Economic Development? IV. The Role of International Organizations', (May 1959) 5 *UN Review* 11, 13–14; 'Statistical Questions', (1961) *United Nations Yearbook* 290, 291; M. Ward, *Quantifying the World: UN Ideas and Statistics* (Bloomington IN: Indiana University Press, 2004).

conducting field surveys, population census techniques and household budget surveys. By facilitating the collection of 'knowledge of the state in its different elements, dimensions, and the factors of its strength',[65] the UN helped to endow new states with a certain solidity, making them calculable and governable. International organizations were also instrumental in devising and universalizing standardized systems of national accounts by which states could be measured, accelerating the 'avalanche of numbers' that had begun a century earlier and transforming it into a universal science of the state, undergirding and defining the art of government.[66]

A major area of technical assistance provided by the UN concerned the construction of systems of public administration.[67] A division of the EPTA had the functions, among others, of providing 'advice and assistance to governments in the improvement of public administration and in the establishment or reform of national and regional training systems and institutions in underdeveloped areas'; collecting technical information 'with a view to the selection and development of effective methods for technical assistance in the field of public administration', stimulating the facilitating the exchange of information; and analyzing problems of public administration with particular reference to 'underdeveloped areas'. Drawing on networks established between the World Wars, the UN's public administration division published a series of reports and booklets summarizing the most important principles and practices, broadly mirroring the values and functions of Western administrative states.[68] Under the presidency of Robert McNamara, the World Bank adopted new managerial practices, which it in turn sought to transfer and project onto its borrower members through an array of statistical and demographic techniques.[69] Likewise, the UN Educational, Scientific and Cultural Organization (UNESCO) contributed to

[65] M. Foucault, *Security, Territory, Population* (New York: Palgrave Macmillan, 2007, Burchell tr.) 100.

[66] I. Hacking, *The Taming of Chance* (Cambridge University Press, 1990) 27–34.

[67] See generally G. F. Sinclair, 'Forging Modern States with Imperfect Tools: United Nations Technical Assistance for Public Administration in Decolonized States', (2020) 11 *Humanity Journal.*

[68] See, e.g., Report by the Special Committee on Public Administration Problems, *Standards and Techniques of Public Administration with special reference to Technical Assistance for Underdeveloped Countries* (UN Technical Assistance Administration, 1951); United Nations Technical Assistance Programme, *A Handbook of Public Administration: Current Concepts and Practice with Special Reference to Developing Countries* (United Nations, 1961).

[69] C. Unger, 'Development Projections: The World Bank in Calcutta in the 1970s', (2020) 11 *Humanity Journal*; Sinclair, *To Reform the World*, ch. 6.

teaching states to embrace particular norms and institutions of public administration.[70]

Other operational activities further expanded the repertoire of statehood-teaching techniques deployed by international organizations during this period. Within the UN, peacekeeping operations emerged as a complex technology which aimed simultaneously at facilitating decolonization, enhancing the role of small and medium-sized nations on the world stage and constructing modern states on a broadly Western model. In the World Bank, comprehensive surveys of borrower countries led to the preparation of national development programmes, under which new long-term policies and laws were adopted, and new state institutions – such as national economic councils, central banks and development planning offices – were established. In 1968, the Bank instituted Country Program Papers (CPPs) to provide regular comprehensive reviews of each country's social and political conditions, economy, external investment and loans. Based on these reviews, a five-year lending programme could be formulated for each borrower; in practice, CPPs gave the World Bank wide scope for incentivizing (or discouraging) particular behaviours by states. Even the Bank's lending for specific projects was motivated by a 'tutelary' concern to educate borrowing countries in the best practices of development project management, fiscal discipline and the appropriate skills, attitudes and cultures for a modern state bureaucracy.[71]

9.4.4 From Washington Consensus to Global Governance

Structural changes associated with globalization, privatization, deregulation and the rise of new technologies, as well as a series of economic and geopolitical shocks, have transformed the activities of international organizations over the past four decades. The Third World project to establish a 'New International Economic Order', which reached a climax in the 1970s, coincided with a long period of stagflation in Western economies that in turn helped to bring a series of conservative governments to power at the end of the decade. These and other political changes ushered in a new, 'neoliberal' economic orthodoxy and rhetoric of small government which was taken up, adopted and adapted in distinct ways in a number of organizations. The end of the Cold War launched an epoch of unprecedented

[70] Finnemore, *National Interests*, ch. 2.

[71] See generally Sinclair, *To Reform the World*, chs. 5–6.

optimism and normative dynamism in international organizations, resulting in an interlinked series of international actions focused on peacekeeping, humanitarian intervention, the prosecution of international crimes, the promotion of 'good governance' anti-corruption programmes, the rule of law and international sanctions. In the first decades of the new century, the activities of many institutions proliferated further in response to the global war on terror, the global financial crisis and increasingly complex scenarios involving climate change, internal state conflicts and migration.

These activities have involved a further layering of statehood-teaching techniques, often by combining novel knowledge and information practices with existing operational activities. Take, for example, the massive expansion in the World Bank's operations during this period. Beginning in the early 1980s, the Bank (as well as the IMF) increasingly attached conditionalities to its loans that required far-reaching structural adjustments in borrower states: dramatic reductions in government services, balanced budgets, privatization, deregulation and the reduction of barriers to international trade. A decade later, the Bank began promoting reforms that went even deeper, touching on matters of 'good governance', accountability and participation that reached beyond the state *policy* to address questions of *process* in government. The Bank's annual *World Development Report* (WDR), launched in 1978, has served as a powerful instrument to influence knowledge on development and the evolving role of the state.[72] In the decades since then the Bank has become a productive source of informational and planning tools, including ambitious efforts to manage the overall process of constructing modern states in developing countries, such as through Country Assistance Strategies, the Comprehensive Development Framework and Poverty Reduction Strategy Papers.

Similar techniques can be seen in the evolving activities of other international organizations over the same period. Global survey publications – such as the OECD's *Economic Outlook*, the IMF's *World Economic Outlook* or the WHO's *World Health Statistics* – influence state behaviour in a manner not unlike the WDR, as do individual country reports.[73] Ideas and values associated with New Public Management, which organizations

[72] See, e.g., World Bank, *World Development Report 1997: The State in a Changing World* (Oxford University Press, 1997).

[73] S. Pahuja, 'Technologies of Empire: IMF Conditionality and the Reinscription of the North/South Divide', (2000) 13 *Leiden Journal of International Law* 749.

like the World Bank, OECD and the UN Development Programme (UNDP) have been instrumental in diffusing worldwide,[74] have also encouraged the abandonment of 'grand development paradigms' and the adoption instead of 'microlevel, evidence-based development interventions' and experimental, participatory, approaches which emphasize mutual interaction and learning.[75] In this vein, we might include the OECD's peer review mechanisms and the European Union's Open Method of Coordination.[76]

The production and publication of indicators by international organizations have grown rapidly over the past few decades as a technique for influencing state behaviour and identity. Annexed to every WDR are the World Development Indicators, a series of comparative tables listing and ranking the economic features of states along a set of dimensions which, although ostensibly neutral and scientific, nevertheless construct a particular normative image of the state and exert a subtle pressure for reform. Other well-known examples include the Doing Business indicators, produced by the World Bank Group's International Finance Corporation (IFC); the UNDP's Human Development Index; the World Bank's Worldwide Governance Indicators; the OECD's Programme for International Student Assessment (PISA); and, perhaps most complex and ambitious of all, the UN Sustainable Development Goals (SDG) indicators, which gather together more than 230 unique indicators.[77] Through processes of data collection, simplification, ranking and evaluation, each of these instruments produces a series of effects: setting standards, influencing decision-making (including by donors), and otherwise incentivizing or disincentivizing particular sets of state practices.

A feature of these and other statehood-teaching techniques which have emerged over the past several decades has been the extent to which they involve interactions among multiple organizations. The SDG indicators –

[74] R. Common, 'The New Public Management and Policy Transfer: The Role of International Organizations', in M. Minogue, Ch. Polidano and D. Hulme (eds.), *Beyond the New Public Management* (Cheltenham: Edward Elgar, 1998) 59.

[75] S. Babb and N. Chorev, 'International Organizations: Loose and Tight Coupling in the Development Regime', (2016) 51 *Studies in Comparative International Development* 81, 91.

[76] A. Schäfer, 'A New Form of Governance? Comparing the Open Method of Coordination to Multilateral Surveillance by the IMF and the OECD', (2006) 13 *Journal of European Public Policy* 70.

[77] See generally K. Davis *et al.* (eds.), *Governance by Indicators* (Oxford University Press, 2012); S. E. Merry, K. Davis and B. Kingsbury (eds.), *The Quiet Power of Indicators* (Cambridge University Press, 2015).

and the SDG project more broadly – offer an example involving the coordination of multiple institutions, both within and outside the UN system. International organizations have collaborated to provide technical assistance for a long time, as noted above, but new mechanisms of coordination have emerged, such as the Enhanced Integrated Framework, which was established as a joint venture by the WTO, the IMF, the World Bank, the UNDP, the UN Conference on Trade and Development (UNCTAD) and others. And in the specific area of post-conflict peacebuilding and recovery, which inevitably involves considerable aspects of state-building, the UN's Peacebuilding Commission has provided a framework for collaboration with the World Bank, the IMF, regional development banks and other regional organizations such as the European Union and the African Union.

9.5 Conclusion

This chapter has outlined a framework within which international organizations can be understood as engaged in an ongoing enterprise of teaching statehood. In surveying the evolution of statehood-teaching techniques used by organizations, as the previous section suggests, it is possible to identify certain models of statehood which they have promoted at different times. However, it would be a mistake to reify these models or assume they can be distributed along a single, 'true' path of modernization. Rather, what it means to be a 'modern' state is constantly open to debate – within and among international organizations, within states, and between international organizations and states – and thus always susceptible to change. This chapter has demonstrated how new and emerging techniques used by organizations have layered with existing techniques, rather than displaced them. In addition, the interactions among different institutions' activities, in more or less tightly coupled arrangements, have produced ever more complex effects in their statehood-teaching activities.[78] Paying closer attention to these dynamics promises to reveal greater insights into how the legal powers of international organizations have evolved and expanded, and to what extent they may be constrained.

[78] Babb and Chorev, 'Loose and Tight Coupling'; J. Klabbers, 'Transforming Institutions: Autonomous International Organisations in Institutional Theory', (2017) 6 *Cambridge International Law Journal* 105.

10 Interaction between International Organizations

Rene Urueña

10.1 A Dense and Varied Landscape

International governance is increasingly characterized by the decline of formal intergovernmental organizations as the preferred sites of rule-making, as the growth rate of intergovernmental organization has declined by 20 per cent since the beginning of the twenty-first century.[1] More than a decade after the debates about fragmentation[2] and regime-collision in international law,[3] it now seems clear that the key question is not that, as a professional experience, international law seems divided in sometimes incoherent specialized regimes, but that international lawyers have a more *dense* and *diverse* institutional landscape to deal with.

Numerically, even if traditional international organizations seem to be in decline, numerous new transnational regulatory arrangements seem to be emerging constantly. Regulatory networks, such as the Basel Committee on Banking Supervision, have grown in importance, while public-private entities, such as the International Organization for Standardization (ISO) are also crucial players in certain industries. And, perhaps most importantly, the private sector is having a deep impact in international governance. From purely private entities, such as FIFA and its enormous impact on the global football field, to public-private partnerships, such as the GAVI Vaccine Alliance and its important role in managing the COVID-19 pandemic, the

[1] K. Abbott, J. Green and R. Keohane, 'Organizational Ecology in World Politics: Institutional Density and Organizational Strategies', (2016) 70 *International Organization* 247.

[2] M. Koskenniemi, *Fragmentation of International Law: Difficulties Arising from the Diversification and Expansion of International Law* (Helsinki: Erik Castrén Institute, 2007).

[3] G. Teubner and A. Fischer-Lescano, 'Regime-Collisions: The Vain Search for Legal Unity in the Fragmentation of Global Law', (2004) 25 *Michigan Journal of International Law* 999.

logic of private actors is quickly penetrating the world of international organizations.

Such a varied and dense ecosystem poses important challenges for the law of international organizations. Its variety, that is, the fact that it features public and private institutions, formal and informal (and everything in between), puts enormous pressure on the traditional doctrines of international organizations law – particularly on its choice of interstate public international law instruments as its preferred vehicle of regulation.

Moreover, the growing variety of international institutions means that the experience of international institutional governance is changing beyond what international institutional law is able to describe. Thus, even the scholarship that considers institutional density from the perspective of international law,[4] still places its focus on legal implications of the interaction between organizations (its *horizontal* dimension, if you will), and not on the effects of such interaction on those being subject to international institutional governance.

Something similar can be said regarding the *density* of international institutional governance, that is, the amount of institutions with potentially overlapping jurisdictions that exist at a single moment in time. Institutions do not appear or act in a vacuum; their default status is interaction with other institutions, which implies that international organizations are not self-standing actors that act independently. This somehow prosaic observation points to a crucial blind spot in international institutional law, which has been mostly focused on regulating the relation between member states and their respective organizations – but lacks a vocabulary to legally discuss the relations *between* organizations.

Part of the challenge is the theoretical underpinnings of international institutional law. As Klabbers has pointed out, most of the law of international organizations is implicitly premised on a principal-agent model, in which the main source of organizational competences is the delegation by member states.[5] In this model, loosely called 'functionalist', legal and political

[4] J. Klabbers, 'Transforming Institutions: Autonomous international Organisations in Institutional Theory', (2017) 6 *Cambridge International Law Journal* 105; L. Boisson de Chazournes, 'Relations with Other International Organizations', in J. Cogan, I. Hurd and I. Johnstone (eds.), *Oxford Handbook of International Organizations* (Oxford University Press, 2016) 691; J. Dunoff, 'A New Approach to Regime Interaction', in M. Young (ed.), *Regime Interaction in International Law: Facing Fragmentation* (Cambridge University Press, 2012) 136.

[5] J. Klabbers, 'The EJIL Foreword: The Transformation of International Organizations Law', (2015) 26 *European Journal of International Law* 9.

accountability for the organization's actions and, more generally, the understanding of its 'function' (hence its label), derives from the narrow definition of the member states' will. However, such a theory fails to account for the wider dynamics of institutional governance that can be observed any given day: even in the narrowest understanding of delegation, it seems counterintuitive to believe that the only threshold to evaluate the UN's role in the world is whether it is following its members' directions. If anything, we could say that, sometimes, fulfilling its true mandate would require the UN as an international organization to act *against* (some of its) members' will. And therein lie functionalism's limits for thinking of institutional interaction: once active in a densely populated regulatory space, organizations engage in legally relevant interactions with each other – a dimension that international institutional law provides little guidance for, focused as it is on the link between member states and the organization.

Given this context, this chapter seeks to describe interaction among international organizations as part of the texture of the global regulatory space. The descriptive agenda is, therefore, to highlight specific instances of interaction, and trace them to the specific experience of those being governed. This chapter is, therefore, not interested in presenting yet another taxonomy of the interaction among international organizations, but is rather concerned with developing a vocabulary to legally address the effects of such interaction on those on the receiving end of governance.

The global regulatory space, though, is more than mere aggregate interaction: these organizations bump into each other because they are 'public' (in the sense of inter-publicness). Their engagement with each other is thus normatively inspired, but we have no vocabulary to assess their relative 'weight'. The normative agenda is, therefore, to propose a 'theory of weights', which is sketched briefly at the end.

10.2 Interaction and the Experience of International Institutional Governance

Interaction among international organizations is a relatively recent phenomenon. When first established in the nineteenth century, international organizations 'were seen as self-contained entities .... The idea of such organizations entering into arrangements with other organizations ... was long considered anathema'.[6] However, as the number of institutions increased in the post-war period, interaction logically increased exponentially.

How to start thinking about such an interaction? One way is to map the different modes of interaction, from full complementarity, on one end, to full competition, on the other.[7] A different approach has been to use the metaphor of an 'ecosystem', and think of the interaction as a problem of evolution and competition among institutions for scarce resources.[8] Others, in turn, have tried to make sense of regime complexity,[9] or to read institutional interaction as a function of the collision among legal regimes.[10]

A general taxonomy of ideal types of interaction seems of limited use, though, if there is no exploration of the trajectories of institutions as they influence each other, and thereby affect the specific addressees of institutional governance. In a way, such an approach to interaction seems just fitting, following the overall 'regulatory' turn of international institutions, characterized by the creation, through international norms, of public authoritative obligations on non-state actors, or the establishment of authoritative measures to enforce such duties.[11]

Now, in the context of such a regulatory turn, power is affecting peoples' lives in transnational fashion, without being subject to significant legal controls. Of course, such exercises of power are oblivious of the strict separation between domestic and international law; as a consequence, the rule of *domestic* law will not be enough to control the exercise of this transnational power, and the rule of *international* law (understood as inter-state law), will be unable to do so as well. Thus, taking interaction seriously means that international institutional governance is wholly decentralized – while there

[6] J. Klabbers, *An Introduction to International Organizations Law*, 3rd ed. (Cambridge University Press, 2015) 286.

[7] S. Oberthür and T. Gehring, 'Institutional Interaction: Ten Years of Scholarly Development', in S. Oberthür and O. Stokke (eds.), *Managing Institutional Complexity: Regime Interplay and Global Environmental Change* (Cambridge MA: MIT Press, 2011) 25.

[8] Abbott, Green and Keohane, 'Organizational Ecology'.

[9] K. Alter and S. Meunier, 'The Politics of International Regime Complexity', (2009) 7 *Perspectives on Politics* 13; R. Keohane and D. Victor, 'The Regime Complex for Climate Change', (2011) 9 *Perspectives on Politics* 7.

[10] G. Teubner and P. Korth, 'Two Kinds of Legal Pluralism: Collisions of Transnational Regimes in the Double Fragmentation of World Society', in Young (ed.), *Facing Fragmentation* 23.

[11] J. Cogan, 'The Regulatory Turn in International Law', (2011) 52 *Harvard International Law Journal* 322.

are certain nodes of power that carry more weight than others, the fact is that there is no objective vantage point from which to observe interaction. Observation of interaction needs to be done, therefore, from the bottom up, in the specific sites where interaction transforms the experiences, lives or policies of those subject to international institutional governance.

From the receiving end of governance, it is possible to posit that institutional interaction might boost the power of a particular institution, and thus boost the experience of being governed. It might also undermine the power of the institution, and thus create an experience of non-governance, or open an opportunity for forum-shopping, and for the strategic positioning of the governed. We now turn to see examples of each these dynamics, in order to understand their particular characteristics, and see how the effects of interaction highlight the need for a different normative agenda in international institutional law (a normative theory of weights) that is outlined in the last section of this chapter.

10.2.1 Boosting Institutional Power

Institutions often cooperate with an aim to better achieve their mandates. This process might boost the powers of a particular institution, also reinforcing the experience of being governed in a particular way. Consider, for example, the close cooperation between the International Monetary Fund (IMF) with the World Trade Organization (WTO) on issues of monetary policy and trade, which is a highly regulated form of cooperation, legally mandatory for the WTO.

The basic challenge is that gains of free trade can be undermined by monetary policy (particularly, by currency exchange measures), and that trade liberalization may offset monetary policy, as foreign currency flows in or out of its economy. Particularly important in this context is the balance of payments – that is, the balance of one country's economic transactions with the other world economies. Under the GATT,[12] a country facing sharp disequilibrium in its balance of payments (if it imports much more than it exports) is allowed to apply import restrictions to 'safeguard its external financial position' (article XII), and to 'ensure a level of reserves adequate for the implementation of its program of

[12] GATT, for the record, is the General Agreement on Tariffs and Trade, effectively the substantive core of the world trading regime, around which the WTO is built.

economic development', in the case of a low-income country (article XVIII).

But this, of course, is necessarily trade-restrictive. So, when countries decide to impose such restrictions, they are required to notify the WTO's Committee of Balance of Payment Restrictions (CBPR), which then decides whether the measure fulfils the requirements put forward in the GATT. The Committee must in turn consult with the IMF, which makes a statement on the country's balance of payments situation – a crucial input for the WTO to decide whether the trade restriction was justified.[13]

This issue is distinctively relevant for poor economies. While in theory available to everyone, trade-restrictive measures for solving balance of payment issues are, in practice, a problem of developing countries. In the 1970s, most rich countries adopted a free-floating exchange rate, which should automatically correct balance of payments disequilibria, since a country with more imports than exports would see its currency lose value, making its exports cheaper, until the balance of payments is again in equilibrium. This is not always the case but, in general, this rationale made trade restrictions as an answer to disequilibrium of payments an essentially moot problem for rich economies. Developing countries, by contrast, entered the 1990s with the monetary framework of an import substitution economy, which meant fixed currency rates, in one way or another. Thus, in the interaction between the WTO and the IMF in terms of balance of payments consultation, the underlying geopolitics is one-sided, with poor economies as clear addressees of the resulting inter-actual process of governance.

When signalling its position at the WTO, the IMF often rejects the use of trade measures to solve balance of payment problems,[14] which has been controversial in the Global South.[15] For example, like many developing countries transitioning from import substitution economies, India had in the early 1990s a fixed exchange rate, and suffered massive inflation that

[13] IMF Independent Evaluation Office, *Background Document 2: Executive Board Guidance on Exchange Rate Surveillance, 1999–2005* (Washington DC: IMF, 2007).

[14] V. Thorstensen, D. Ramos and C. Muller, 'The "Missing Link" between the WTO and the IMF', (2013) 16 *Journal of International Economic Law* 353, 357–69; M. Garritsen de Vries and J. K. Horsefield, *The International Monetary Fund 1945–1965: Twenty Years of International Monetary Cooperation* (Washington DC: IMF, 1969).

[15] See generally U. C. Ukpabi, 'Juridical Substance or Myth over Balance-of-Payment: Developing Countries and the Role of the International Monetary Fund in the World Trade Organization', (2004) 26 *Michigan Journal of International Law* 701.

led to disequilibrium of its balance of payment. It imposed restrictions on imports that were then reported to the WTO's CBPR. The IMF issued its statement, arguing that India had an overall comfortable reserve situation. The Committee was unable to reach an agreement (most developing countries siding with India),[16] and the United States requested a WTO panel to settle the dispute. Ultimately, India argued that the Fund's expansive interpretation of its statement overstepped its original mandate,[17] but it had very little leverage to push the matter forward within the WTO – let alone before the IMF.

The balance of payments example shows that when organizations interact, their interaction might boost their own individual powers. From the perspective of those being governed, though, such an interaction might compound the experience of inevitability of governance, and even reduce the flexibilities that one of the institutions create. This was one of India's arguments: while the GATT gives states the right to adopt restrictive measures given certain circumstances, the IMF's high threshold for accepting the necessity of such measures ends up limiting the possibility of effectively using this right.[18]

This dynamic is even clearer when IMF packages create an incentive to go beyond WTO obligations. The Fund is careful to avoid cross-conditionality; that is, it is careful not to require countries to extend their WTO obligations in order to comply with IMF packages – a fear voiced often by developing countries in trade negotiations.[19] However, the fact is that the packages often do include tariff conditionality. More than half of IMF packages agreed from 1996 to 2007 with WTO members included tariff conditionality – and more than 70 per cent in the case of WTO accession members.[20]

From the perspective of states that are on the receiving end of trade rules, the interaction between the IMF and the WTO creates a single front of

[16] WT/BOP/R/11, WTO Committee on Balance of Payments Restrictions, *Report on the Consultation with India* (Geneva: WTO, 1998).

[17] WT/BOP/R/65, WTO Committee on Balance of Payments Restrictions, Note on the Meeting of 2 October (Geneva: WTO, 1999).

[18] *Ibid.* See also WT/DS90//R, *India – Quantitative Restrictions on Imports of Agricultural, Textile and Industrial Products*, as modified by the Appellate Body (WT/DS90/AB/R). On *India-Textile* from the perspective of international organizations law, see J. Wouters and D. Coppens, 'International Economic Policy-Making: Exploring the Legal Linkages between the World Trade Organization and the Bretton Woods Institutions', (2006) 3 *International Organizations Law Review* 267, 311–15.

[19] D. Ahn, 'Linkages between International Financial and Trade Institutions', (2000) 34 *Journal of World Trade* 1, 6.

[20] IMF, *Background Document 2*.

governance – one that pushes for lower tariffs. While formal cross-conditionality is carefully avoided in the IMF's staff directives, the practical effect is that the IMF's intervention makes WTO commitments seems more inevitable, lending them the financial urgency that made IMF packages acceptable for borrowing countries in the first place. Ultimately, the net effect of cooperation between organizations might be that the experience of international institutional governance as a top-down and inflexible process is compounded, making it feel less contingent than it really is.

10.2.2 Undermining Institutional Powers

Inter-institutional interaction might also undermine the experience of being subject to international institutional governance. Interaction might create competition among institutions, thus undermining institutional commitments and organizational effectiveness.[21] Therefore, from the perspective of those being governed, the experience can be one of incoherence and contradictory demands. This was the case, for instance, during the international administration in Kosovo after the failed peace talks of the late 1990s, when the interaction between UNMIK, KFOR, EU LEX and the International Civilian Office lead to such contradictory demands on the governed that each institution had to develop niche competences to avoid competition.[22]

However, the experience can also be one of strategic opportunity, creating the possibility of cross-institutional political strategies. A clear example is the interaction between the Office of the Prosecutor of the International Criminal Court (OTP) and the Inter-American System of Human Rights at the occasion of the Colombian peace process with its right-wing paramilitaries, in 2004–7 (not to be confused with the peace deal with the left-wing FARC guerrillas, of 2016).

In that case, and considering long-entrenched limitations in terms of prosecutorial capacity of the Colombian state, a central legal problem was whether the transitional justice process would be in breach of international law by devoting scarce judicial resources to selecting and prosecuting some of the worst crimes, while giving sharply reduced sentences to war criminals, or

[21] D. Drezner, 'The Power and Peril of International Regime Complexity', (2009) 7 *Perspectives on Politics* 65.

[22] M. Brosig, 'The Interplay of International Institutions in Kosovo between Convergence, Confusion and Niche Capabilities', (2011) 20 *European Security* 185.

perpetrators of crimes against humanity, who confessed and provided some level of truth and reparation to the victims.[23] Following its well-known jurisprudence that essentially prohibited giving amnesties to gross human rights violations, the Inter-American System of Human Rights had a clear answer to Colombia's question: international human rights in the Americas required a 'maximalist' model, that required *all* perpetrators to be prosecuted and sentenced. No possible selection or prioritization was allowed.[24]

Colombian authorities did try to comply with the ambitious threshold imposed by the Inter-American approach. However, prosecutions of thousands of war criminals proved extremely difficult. Colombia's peace process with the paramilitaries was bound to be seen as a façade for impunity, hiding a breach of Inter-American human rights law. Enter thus the ICC's OTP, represented by then-prosecutor Luis Moreno-Ocampo. In 2007, the Prosecutor delivered his first specific, substantive signal: while he stressed that there could not be amnesties for those responsible for grave human rights violations – even as part of a peace process – he urged Colombian prosecutors to focus their efforts on paramilitary leaders rather than rank-and-file members.[25] This was a crucial message. The Colombian prosecution unit charged with carrying out the Inter-American maximalist vision – that all perpetrators had to be prosecuted – was proving itself unable to perform. And now the ICC Prosecutor, whose intervention was the actual deterrent for both the government and the paramilitaries, was indicating that the principle of complementarity only required that the most important perpetrators be prosecuted. To be sure, Moreno-Ocampo's suggestion to target only high-level paramilitary operatives seemed a much more attainable goal, compared with the strict Inter-American standard.

Eventually, the OTP seemed to carry the day. The discussion drifted away from the maximalist model, and towards prosecution of the most important perpetrators. The OTP represented a competing standard, different from that developed by the Inter-American System of Human Rights, thus creating space for the emergence of new domestic strategies for complying with international legal obligations vis-à-vis the conflict.

[23] R. Urueña, 'Prosecutorial Politics: The ICC's Influence in Colombian Peace Processes, 2003–2017', (2017) 111 *American Journal of International Law* 104.

[24] C. Binder, 'The Prohibition of Amnesties by the Inter-American Court of Human Rights', (2011) 12 *German Law Journal* 1203.

[25] Urueña, 'Prosecutorial Politics'.

As the Colombian example shows, interaction might undermine the effectiveness of international institutions on the ground, which might, in turn, create spaces of opportunity, opportunism and emancipations for those governed. There is a deep correlation between political dynamics at the domestic level and international regulatory practices. Consequently, the function of the organization is not all-decisive: from the domestic vantage point, international organization are all the time interacting – for example, from the perspective of Colombia, the Inter-American Court and the ICC are not functionally distinctive, but cater to the same problem. From the domestic perspective, interaction among international institutions is the norm, and not the exception.

10.3 Interaction in the Global Regulatory Space

Institutions do not appear in a vacuum; they are not discrete utterances of law.[26] They are expressions, and form part, of a changing global regulatory space, in which they interact. The notion of a 'regulatory space' was suggested as a reaction to the narrow reading of the (domestic) regulatory process in terms of a conflict between public authority and private interests.[27] Against this view, the regulatory process within the nation state can be better understood as a 'space', where it becomes possible to explore the 'complex and shifting relationships between and within organizations at the heart of economic regulation'.[28] The key is 'to understand the nature of this shared space: the rules of admission, the relations between occupants, and the variations introduced by differences in markets and issue arenas'.[29] To be sure, these dynamics can be observed in global governance. Global interactions can be seen as part of an emergent 'global administrative space', which has been defined as 'a space, distinct from the space of inter-state relations governed by international law and the domestic regulatory space governed by domestic administrative law, although encompassing elements of each'.[30]

[26] The following discussion of the global regulatory space is based on R. Urueña, 'Temporariness and Space in Global Governance', (2014) 45 *Netherlands Yearbook of International Law* 19.

[27] L. Hancher and M. Moran, 'Organizing Regulatory Space', in L. Hancher and M. Moran (eds.), *Capitalism, Culture, and Economic Regulation* (Oxford: Clarendon, 1989) 271.

[28] *Ibid.*, 277. [29] *Ibid.*, 276.

[30] B. Kingsbury, N. Krisch and R. Stewart, 'The Emergence of Global Administrative Law', (2005) 68 *Law and Contemporary Problems* 15, 26.

This image of a 'regulatory space' aptly captures some of the dynamic interactions between international institutions that characterize global governance. To do so, we must engage in a thought experiment: imagine for a minute that institutions exist in the global regulatory space, much like planets and other great masses exist in the actual physical space.[31] To be sure, we can think of each planet independently; we often do, and such is our usual practice. However, many of the realities that affect our daily life are not just the mere product of our independent planet but are rather a function of *other* planets and masses in space. For instance, think of seasons, or sea tides: earth spins in one way and not another, at a certain angle and not the other, not only because of events that happen on Earth, but rather due to the relative equilibrium of gravitational forces around it, which include, of course, its own mass and gravitational force.

This is just an image. My argument is not that the global regulatory space is an actual space with actual forces.[32] It is useful, though, to illustrate the kind of dynamics triggered by institutional interaction.[33] International institutions seem to have a 'mass' that exerts a certain pull towards them. This 'pull' has been observed before. A similar 'pull', exerted by international norms, was famously discussed by Thomas Franck, in his classic theory of legitimacy.[34] Similarly, each institution draws towards it whatever is around: it exerts a sort of 'gravitational pull' that attracts other institutions. The situation of institutions in the global regulatory space is, therefore, the result of a relative equilibrium of all the 'gravitational pulls', as exerted by each and all norms or institutions.

Unlike the language of fragmentation, thinking of the global regulatory space allows to think about interaction when collusions occur, and also when collusions are *not* occurring. Most of legal scholarship that factors in the challenges of the multiplicity of legal orders in international law seems to be biased towards focusing on conflict; that is, when two international norms provide conflicting solutions to similar cases, or when two

[31] Urueña, 'Temporariness and Change'.

[32] But see D. Hornstein, 'Complexity Theory, Adaptation and Administrative Law', (2005) 54 *Duke Law Journal* 913.

[33] B. Simma and D. Pulkowski, 'Of Planets and the Universe: Self-Contained Regimes in International Law', (2006) 17 *European Journal of International Law* 483.

[34] Th. Franck, *The Power of Legitimacy among Nations* (Oxford University Press, 1990).

institutions collide when exercising their powers.[35] It assumes that the principle is non-interaction, and the exception is interaction, which triggers collision and incoherence. This bias is understandable, as instances of collision are clearer, and seem more politically important. But the opposite is true: international institutions are *all the time* in interaction with each other. While collisions do exist, they tell us little of the day-to-day workings of the institution. In contrast, thinking in terms of a global regulatory space allows us to consider the interactions that result, not in conflict, but rather in the practice of international institutional governance.

10.4 Institutional Interactions and the Law

The law of international organizations has little vocabulary to speak of interaction – let alone of the impact of such interaction on the governed. Part of the challenge is that the law of international organizations, as was mentioned earlier, derives its normative horizon from a principal/agent model, in which the main criterion to decide on legality of organizational behaviour is the mandate of member states. In that sense, the 'function' of the organization becomes key, as it defines the horizon of what the organization should be doing, and thus provides the normative underpinning to justify most doctrines of international institutional law.

But, as we have seen, when organizations interact, they are not rational actors guided by function. Organizational scholars have observed since the 1970s that external pressure (for example, through regulation, or civil society activism) leads organizations to be more attentive to their external environments. However, their internal organizational culture is not so responsive to change. Therefore, a 'decoupling' occurs: organizations adopt policies to conform to external expectations regarding formally stated goals, but in practice fail to change their behaviour.[36] Interaction may trigger decoupling, as it is through such interaction that the pressures of the environment enter the organization; interaction often forms a sense

35 J. Pauwelyn, *Conflict of Norms in Public International Law: How WTO Law Relates to Other Rules of International Law* (Cambridge University Press, 2003).

36 P. Bromley and W. Powell, 'From Smoke and Mirrors to Walking the Talk: Decoupling in the Contemporary World', (2012) 6 *Academy of Management Annals* 483.

of identity and appropriateness that guides the actions of staff that goes beyond the institution's 'function', or its stated policies.

While a standard insight of organizational sociology, decoupling has been less studied in international organizations. However, recent work on the UN Security Council[37] and, particularly, two key studies in the field of international financial institutions provide some evidence that the phenomenon is readily visible in international governance. Reviewing all policy conditionality in IMF loan agreements between 1985 and 2014, Kentikelenis, Stubbs and King found that, despite nominally aiming to allow borrowers more space for the protection of labour and social policies, particularly after the 2008 financial crisis, in fact the organization's programmes reincorporated many of the mandated reforms that the organization claimed to no longer advocate.[38] Similarly, Sarfaty's ethnographic field research at the World Bank has shown that, despite formally adopting an indigenous population policy organizational culture, the organization's organizational culture failed to buy into the human rights mindset and, rhetorical flourishes notwithstanding, still sees the protection of human rights as marginal to the Bank's mandate.[39]

Decoupling implies that an organization's function, expressed through a legal mandate, is only partially useful to think of the normative horizon of its actions. Put shortly, decoupling means that organizations often do different things than those defined in their mandate, not as a breach of their institutional law, but as behaviour that is somehow not prohibited by it. This is not to say that organizations go beyond their mandate to exert their inherent powers, as Seyersted's seminal work would have it.[40] In fact, the opposite process is at play: decoupling means that external pressures, and not inherent powers, bring the organization to go beyond their mandate: instead of turning their gaze within, to their institutional essence,

[37] M. Stephen, 'Legitimacy Deficits of International Organizations: Design, Drift, and Decoupling at the UN Security Council', (2018) 31 *Cambridge Review of International Affairs* 96.

[38] A. Kentikelenis, Th. Stubbs and L. King, 'IMF Conditionality and Development Policy Space', (2016) 23 *Review of International Political Economy* 543.

[39] G. Sarfaty, *Values in Translation: Human Rights and the Culture of the World Bank* (Stanford University Press, 2012).

[40] See F. Seyersted, *Common Law of International Organizations* (Leiden: Martinus Nijhoff, 2008) 65–70, 359–62. See, furthermore, the dissenting opinion of Judge Cancado Trindade in *Certain Activities Carried Out by Nicaragua in the Border Area (Costa Rica* v. *Nicaragua)*, [2013] ICJ Rep. 166, 173–4.

they have to look out, to what other institutions do, and act accordingly. In that context, international institutional law, with its focus on state delegation, provides a particularly poor map of institutional power, and of the effects of such a power on those governed.

So, how to think of an international institutional law that accounts for these diverging processes? Going back to the global regulatory space seems useful. The regulatory space is, by definition, inter-actional, in the sense that it exists only as a function of the interaction among the institutions that populate it, and influences them in turn. However, when thinking about the pull that one institution exerts over others, one is simply describing such movement. This view provides no vocabulary to perform a critique of the reasons behind such a powerful pull, or a normative standard to discuss whether the fact that one institution or norm carries so much weight is appropriate or not – which is precisely what, facing the failure of the 'function', international institutional law is supposed to do.

10.4.1 Two Normative Challenges

The description of 'gravitational pull' offered here could be subject to critique in terms of ideology, understood as 'the ways in which meaning serves to establish and sustain relations of domination'.[41] Indeed, the idea could sustain an unequal distribution of power by occluding the normative dimensions of the 'gravitational pull'. Specifically, there are at least two normative challenges in thinking in terms of institutional interaction in the global regulatory space: tunnel vision on the one hand, and regulatory capture by private interests, on the other[42] – both of which provide, in turn, the basis for the rethinking of the law of international institutions that is suggested in the final section of this chapter.

First, the suggested view of interaction seems to lack an overarching narrative of the public good in the global regulatory space. Perhaps the main challenge is the issue of 'tunnel vision'.[43] Under international institutional law, each institution in the global regulatory space has a particular mandate; that is, it is concerned with that specific issue, and not necessarily

[41] S. Marks, 'Big Brother Is Bleeping Us – With the Message that Ideology Doesn't Matter', (2001) 12 *European Journal of International Law* 109, 110.

[42] Urueña, 'Temporariness and Change'.

[43] Teubner and Korth, 'Two Kinds of Legal Pluralism'.

with wider societal concerns. Human rights regime institutions, for instance, will be focused on that specific issue, and not on economic development, or the environment. Each of these institutions may talk in terms of 'common good'; however, when these norms and institutions 'pull' towards them, they pull towards their own structural bias[44] – leaving the common good to be sorted out by the competition among norms and institutions in the global regulatory space. Talking in terms of a 'gravitational force' creates the risk of losing sight of an overarching narrative of a 'good' society.

Moreover, international institutions are not static objects to be found in nature. Instead, they are put together in order to achieve a goal that is not given by the norm or institutions in itself, but rather by external political forces that see international law as one more of their tools to achieve their needs.[45] An international institution might play the part intended for it by the powerful. What is more, institutions themselves may have hegemonic ambitions, in the sense that they seek to expand their worldview, placing their goal as more important (or universal) to the detriment of the goals of others.[46] Thus, thinking of interaction in these terms could obscure important differences of power and, in fact, could perpetuate as neutral the structure of the global regulatory space, which is a specific creation of those in power. This move, in turn, could end up empowering the narrowly defined experts that decide what the objective of the norm or institutions is. Because the mindset of regimes is wholly instrumental, a certain transnational elite that acts outside democratic or legal checks of accountability could end up being empowered by global specialized regimes.[47] Thus, the idea of neutral 'gravitational forces' could play into this expert-power base, legitimizing as mere 'interaction' what is only the result of the (functional) agenda of domination.

A second normative challenge is regulatory capture by private interests.[48] Framing the dynamics of interaction in terms of 'gravitational pulls' in the global regulatory space opens spots for private parties to

[44] M. Koskenniemi, *From Apology to Utopia: The Structure of International Legal Argument*, 2nd ed. (Cambridge University Press, 2005).

[45] R. Urueña, *No Citizens Here: Global Subjects and Participation in International Law* (Leiden: Martinus Nijhoff, 2012).

[46] M. Koskenniemi, 'Hegemonic Regimes', in Young (ed.), *Facing Fragmentation* 305.

[47] D. Kennedy, *A World of Struggle: How Power, Law, and Expertise Shape Global Political Economy* (Princeton University Press, 2016).

[48] Urueña, 'Temporariness and Change'.

engage actively with the decision-making process in the regulatory space. Private parties will use the different patterns of interaction among institutions as a tool to achieve their goal. This, in turn, could have normatively desirable results, or could further empower global actors that are already mighty, as they hold the expertise to read the patterns of influence and 'gravitational pulls' described in this contribution.

An example of a desirable outcome is the engagement of activists with the human rights regulatory space. As has been explored by Kathryn Sikkink, transnational networks of activists have played a fundamental role in the transformation of human rights governance in Latin America.[49] During the era of massive human rights violations and authoritarian regimes, Sikkink explains, local activists learned to use a 'boomerang effect' where non-state actors, faced with repression at home, would seek help from international courts and organizations, in order to bring pressure to their respective governments from above. The goal of activism in this context was to bypass the failed domestic judiciary, and get a hierarchically superior order by the Inter-American Court of Human Rights (IACtHR) against a state.[50] In this way, global human rights activists achieve their desired political output, and they also transform the structure of the regulatory space applicable to human rights, bringing new layers of complexity and opportunity.

Equally though, thinking in terms of change and the 'gravitational pull' could end up opening spaces for powerful private actors to take over the regulatory process. An example is dairy regulation. Dairy regulation is an exercise of global governance, characterized by interaction between several institution, and bodies of norms: the WTO, the Organization for Economic Cooperation and Development (OECD), the World Health Organization (WHO), the International Organization for Standardization (ISO), the World Organization for Animal Health (OIE), among many others. Each of these institutions carries a particular weight, exerting

[49] K. Sikkink, 'Human Rights Advocacy Networks and the Social Construction of Legal Rules', in Y. Dezalay and B. Garth (eds.), *Global Prescriptions: The Production, Exportation and Importation of a New Legal Orthodoxy* (Ann Arbor MI: University of Michigan Press, 2002) 37; K. Sikkink and C. Walling, 'The Justice Cascade and the Impact of Human Rights Trials in Latin America', (2007) 44 *Journal of Peace Research* 427.

[50] K. Sikkink and M. Keck, *Activists beyond Borders* (Ithaca NY: Cornell University Press, 1998); K. Sikkink and Th. Risse, 'The Socialization of International Human Rights Norms into Domestic Practices', in Th. Risse, M. Sikkink and S. Ropp (eds.), *The Power of Human Rights: International Norms and Domestic Politics* (Cambridge University Press, 1999) 1.

a particular pull over the others. The International Dairy Federation (IDF), in turn, is a private industrial organization that represents the dairy sector worldwide, by providing a source of scientific expertise in support of the development of quality milk and dairy products. IDF is well known for its scientific expertise, and often provides background information and scientific support to different international organizations.

In the universe of possibilities, the IDF engages with several institutions in different ways. However, the key issue in regulation is food standards. Thus, when the IDF entered the space of global dairy regulation, it was attracted by the Codex Alimentarius Commission, which is the institution that carries more weight in that area of regulation.[51] The attraction grew to be quite close, and the IDF ended up embedded into the Codex itself. The purpose of the Codex is to protect consumers and facilitate fair practices in the trade of food through the definition of detailed product specifications and minimum requirements. The governing body of the Codex is the Codex Alimentarius Commission, which features an Executive Committee, seven Commodity Committees and nine General Subject Committees. The point of entry for the IDF to the regulatory space was the Codex Committee on Milk and Milk Products, hosted by New Zealand. The IDF became the only private organization formally recognized in the Codex Procedural Manual as being responsible for providing first drafts of Codex standards for a group of food commodities; similarly, it also contributes expert input throughout the development of new standards until their final adoption and monitors all the other Codex Committees that influence the dairy sector. The IDF thus became an integral part of the global space of dairy regulation.

Neither of these examples shows a particularly exceptional dynamic: the IDF is an industrial organization seeking to influence regulatory standards applicable to its sector. In turn, human rights activists are trying to achieve

[51] Part of the Codex's 'weight' derives, in turn, from its close contact with the World Trade Organization. Article 3 of the WTO's SPS Agreement provides, in essence, that domestic food regulations that conform to international standards are presumed to be in compliance with that Agreement and GATT. Section 3(a) of Annex A of the SPS Agreement, in turn, defines international standards for food safety as those created by Codex Alimentarius, among others. Therefore, member states of the WTO that comply with the (voluntary) standards of the Codex are presumed to comply with the (mandatory) dispositions of the SPS Agreement and the GATT. See, generally, M. A. Livermore, 'Authority and Legitimacy in Global Governance: Deliberation, Institutional Differentiation, and the Codex Alimentarius', (2006) 81 *New York University Law Review* 766.

their own goal. But consider these examples from the perspective of the architecture of regulation applicable to dairy, or to human rights. From that perspective, we see a group of different institutions that have overlapping power over a particular issue, or a particular set of products. Private parties then enter the regulatory space – first as target to the regulation, but then becoming part of the regulatory process. This dynamic is not only a matter of lobbyists, but also transforms the architecture of the regulatory process that is being influenced. Private parties are trying to influence such institutions but, by doing so, they lend more weight to some institution over the others. At the end, the weight of each institution or set of norms (the Codex Commission, or the Inter-American System of Human Rights) is changed, boosted by the 'gravitational pull' of private institutions such as of the IDF or human rights NGOs.

10.4.2 International Institutional Law As a Normative Theory of Weight*s*

All of these are important challenges. A way to address them is to think of an overarching normative criterion to assess the patterns of certain 'gravitational' pulls. This approach would use the advantages of thinking in dynamic terms about change in international institutional law, and at the same time steer clear of a reading that simply perpetuates the status quo.

One example of such normative criteria could come from Franck's work, for whom the normative pull that characterizes legitimacy in the community of states features four indicators: (a) determinacy, meaning the literary (text-based) quality of a rule that 'makes its message clear';[52] (b) symbolic validation, that occurs when 'a signal is used as cue to elicit compliance with a command';[53] (c) coherence, meaning the attribution whereby 'distinctions in the treatment of "likes" be justifiable in principled terms';[54] and, finally, (d) adherence, referring to the 'quality of being validated by an infrastructure of rules about rules'.[55] Or we could consider Kingsbury's attempt to fill a parallel void, by arguing that not all practices of global governance can be interpreted as 'law'. Instead, only those practices that fulfil the requirement of 'publicness' can be considered law, and thus entitled to the benefits of using such language (publicness, for his purpose, is 'the claim made for law that it has been wrought by the whole society, by

[52] Franck, *The Power of Legitimacy*, 52. [53] *Ibid.*, 92. [54] *Ibid.*, 144. [55] *Ibid.*, 184.

the public, and the connected claim that law addresses matters of concern to the society as such').[56] Finally, one last strategy could be along the lines of global constitutionalism; that is, evaluating interaction among institutions and their 'gravitational pull' through the prism of certain core legal standards, just as a national constitution limits the exercise of authority in a domestic setting.

Many other options are available. It is useful to note, though, that this normative standard need not to be the source of validity of the other norms or institutions in the global regulatory space – it is not a *Grundnorm*. It just needs to carry enough weight, and thus enough 'gravitational pull'. The greater the weight it carries, the more successful it will be in serving as true normative standards in global governance.

10.4.3 International Institutional Law and Communities of Practice

Thinking in terms of a regulatory space allows us to see that a central challenge for international institutional law is to establish a normative theory of weights, according to which it is possible to establish the relative 'weight' that institutions should have in the global regulatory space. But this is a paradoxical task. It seems impossible to derive a theory of weights from a criterion that exists outside the practice of the very institutions that are interacting. This task somehow presupposes a point of view that is external to the interaction, which would allow an external observer to apply a threshold of legality, thus defining what international institutional law is. In fact, the opposite is true. International organizations law is the result of interaction, thus turning paradoxical its task of creating a legal framework for that very interaction.

A possible alternative to think of this task is to focus on the *practice* of the institutions that are interacting, and derive a normative theory of weights from such practice. Such was Brunnée and Toope's effort to insert the notion of a community of practice in the creation of international legal obligation[57] and, with different emphasis, also Klabbers and Palombella's

[56] B. Kingsbury, 'The Concept of "Law" in Global Administrative Law', (2009) 20 *European Journal of International Law* 23, 31.

[57] J. Brunnée and S. Toope, *Legitimacy and Legality in International Law: An Interactional Account* (Cambridge University Press, 2010).

call for a contextualized process of adjudication in the context of 'inter-legality', requiring highly practical wisdom, and not high-minded abstractions of system making.[58]

What these two approaches have in common is their focus on practical reasoning, and the necessary community that accompanies such reasoning: after all, it seems extremely hard to reason practically if one is completely isolated from others. From this perspective, the most important role of international organizations is not that of lawmakers, but as nodes of interaction of communities of legal practice. Around them, communities gather to create meaning, which in turn creates international institutional law and, with it, a plausible normative theory of institutional weights. The normative criterion emerges not from the outside, but from within: an acceptable theory institutional weight in the global regulatory space will result from the acceptance of the relevant community of practice.

Now, the concept of a community of practice originates in education research. In 1991, anthropologist Jean Lave and computer scientist Etienne Wenger proposed the notion of situated learning; learning, they argued, is fundamentally a social process and implies socialization.[59] A community of practice, then, denotes a group of people that is defined by mutual engagement, a joint enterprise and a shared repertoire, meaning 'routines, words, tools, ways of doing things, stories, gestures, symbols, genres, actions, or concepts that the community has produced or adopted in the course of its existence and which have become part of its practice'.[60] This notion was later taken up by international relations scholar Emanuel Adler, who suggests that

> there is no reason ... why we should not be able to identify transnational or even global communities of practice. The closer we get to the level of practices, in fact, the more we can take the international system as a collection of communities of practice – for example, communities of diplomats, of traders, of environmentalists, and of human-rights activists. Communities of practice cut across state boundaries and mediate between states, individuals, and

[58] J. Klabbers and G. Palombella (eds.), *The Challenge of Inter-Legality* (Cambridge University Press, 2019).

[59] J. Lave and E. Wenger, *Situated learning: Legitimate Peripheral Participation* (Cambridge University Press, 1991).

[60] E. Wenger, *Communities of Practice: Learning, Meaning, and Identity* (Cambridge University Press, 1998), 83.

human agency, on one hand, and social structures and systems, on the other.[61]

A community of practice does not imply homogeneity. Its members often have different, even conflicting, projects and views. This is crucially important in a theory of weight in international institutional law: a community of practice is not constituted by a single goal, but requires common practices as well as a shared understanding of the social meaning of those practices. Such disagreements, though, do not undermine the claim that a community emerges around the institutional interaction. The added value of the community of practice approach is that it underscores the fact that, for all the differences in approach and interpretation, all actors in the community shared a minimal understanding, a mutual agreement, on the kind of practice they are engaging with. As Terry Eagleton put it in his introduction to ideology: 'conflict presupposes a degree of mutual agreement: we are not politically conflicting if you hold that patriarchy is an objectionable social system and I hold that it is small town in upper New York state'.[62] It is such a basic level of understanding that the community of practice is built upon, which is not in contradiction with heated controversy over which institution should be given more normative weight by international institutional law.

Viewed through this prism, a top-down approach that posits international institutional law as some sort of global constitution would become inaccurate. International organizations, in their interaction, are at the centre of a community of practice that includes both domestic and international actors. Iterative interactions and learning are crucial for this practice. Iteration creates an interaction that is qualitatively different from that of discrete contact, as the constant process of interaction and learning shapes the behaviour and expectations of international institutions, which feeds back to the law.

10.5 Conclusion

Interaction among international institutions is the default status of global governance today. Private interests are crucial in this process, as are more

[61] E. Adler, *Communitarian International Relations: The Epistemic Foundations of International Relations* (Abingdon: Routledge, 2005) 15.

[62] T. Eagleton, *Ideology: An Introduction* (London: Verso, 2007) 13.

informal arrangements of transnational governance. Institutions, though, are not only rational actors fulfilling a 'function'; they are, rather, ever-changing, learning and adapting – a process that deeply transforms the experience of being governed.

International institutional law has a very limited vocabulary to address this process. But this void is more than a mere academic problem, because those subject to interactional forms of institutional power have nowhere else to turn to. If a public law mindset is to be applied to the interaction among institutions, be they public or private (or both), then such mindset must come from the law of international organizations. A theory of relative weights, supported by a bottom-up emphasis on communities of legal practice, seems one promising way to go. This chapter is an effort to mark some of the sites where future work can be done.

11 The International Organization for Migration and the Duty to Protect Migrants

Revisiting the Law of International Organizations

Vincent Chetail

11.1 Introduction

The International Organization for Migration (IOM) is a strange creature within the constellation of international organizations involved in migration matters. It is both a leader and an outsider, within the system and outside it. The reasons for its ambiguous stance are numerous, be they political, legal, institutional or cultural. The agility of the IOM and its perpetual adaptation to its changing environment are a legacy of its turbulent history. Still today, its hybrid nature represents a key marker of its elusive mandate and its ambivalent relations with the United Nations (UN).

Its reputation as a US-led club of Western states dates back to its early history. The IOM's predecessor – the Provisional Intergovernmental Committee for the Movement of Migrants from Europe (PICMME) – was founded in December 1951 outside the UN as an operational organization.[1] Its initial design was heavily influenced by the USA with the twofold purpose of excluding Communist states from its membership and acknowledging the admission of immigrants as a matter of domestic jurisdiction. While the current Constitution of IOM still reflects the early objectives of the USA,[2] the priority at that time was to facilitate the emigration of

[1] On IOM's history, see especially L. Venturas (ed.), *International 'Migration Management' in the Early Cold War: The Intergovernmental Committee for European Migration* (Corinth: University of the Peloponnese, 2015); M. Ducasse-Rogier, *The International Organization for Migration 1951–2001* (Geneva: IOM, 2002); R. Perruchoud, 'From the Intergovernmental Committee for European Migration to the International Organization for Migration', (1989) 1 *International Journal of Refugee Law* 501.

[2] According to Article 2(b) of the Constitution, member states must have a 'demonstrated interest in the principle of free movement of persons'. This requirement was specifically

Europeans in the aftermath of the Second World War and the beginning of the Cold War. Following the US agenda, the IOM's predecessor was established as both an antithesis of and competitor to the United Nations High Commissioner for Refugees (UNHCR) and International Labour Organization (ILO), to work outside the UN with a purely operational mandate, including migrant workers and refugees alike. After several changes, in 1989 it finally became a permanent institution, renamed the International Organization for Migration.[3]

The end of the Cold War and the subsequent rise of migration at the forefront of the domestic and international agenda initiated a new turn in the development of the IOM, which moved from a logistics agency to a global organization. As a result of its dramatic expansion, the IOM is now among the most prominent international organizations with over 13,800 staff members and 30 million beneficiaries across the world.[4] Its membership has quickly grown to become universal with a significant number of countries from the Global South: its member states have expanded from 67 in 1998 to 173 in 2019.[5] Its budget increased sevenfold between 1998 and 2018 from US$ 242.2 million to US$ 1.8 billion.[6] Meanwhile, the permissive provisions of the IOM Constitution have enabled the organization to engage in a wide range of activities, such as humanitarian assistance in post-conflict and natural disaster situations, resettlement programmes and voluntary returns, capacity-building measures in combatting human trafficking, devising migration policies and facilitating international cooperation.

After sixty-five years outside the UN, IOM has eventually joined the UN family in 2016 as a related organization.[7] This change in its legal status

introduced in order to preclude the membership of communist states. Likewise, the organization explicitly recognizes in Article 1(3) of the Constitution that 'control of standards of admission and the number of immigrants to be admitted are matters within the domestic jurisdiction of States'.

3 PICMME changed its name in 1953 as the Intergovernmental Committee for European Migration (ICEM) and the reference to Europe was then abandoned in 1980 to become the Intergovernmental Committee for Migration with a broader geographical coverage. The current IOM Constitution incorporates the ICEM Constitution of 1953, the amendments adopted in 1987 and entered into force in 1989, when the organization was renamed IOM, as well as subsequent amendments adopted in 1998 (entered into force in 2013) and more recently those adopted on 28 October 2020 and entered into force the same day.

4 IOM, *IOM Snapshot 2019* (Geneva: IOM, 2019), 2. 5 *Ibid.* 6 *Ibid.*

7 Agreement concerning the relationship between the United Nations (UN) and the International Organization for Migration (IOM). A/RES/70/296, Article 2(5). The parties had previously cooperated on the basis of an agreement concluded on 25 June 1996.

represents an important step forward in establishing close cooperation with the UN which, in turn, recognizes the IOM as 'an organization with a global leading role in the field of migration'.[8] It is an evolution, not a revolution, for its Constitution, mandate and governing structure remain unaffected.[9] While a continuing source of ambiguity and contestation, its hybrid status has raised polarized interpretations within and outside the organization: since 2016, IOM proclaims itself as the 'UN migration agency',[10] whereas several commentators criticized its relations with the UN as an 'unfinished business'[11] and a 'missed opportunity'.[12]

In fact, the ambivalent stance of the IOM and its complex relations with the UN are inherent to its status as a related organization. As such, the IOM is both within and outside the UN. As a related organization, it is part of the UN system, but it is not a specialized agency. The IOM is far from the only international organization with such a hybrid status: the International Atomic Energy Agency, the World Trade Organization and the Organization for the Prohibition of Chemical Weapons are also related organizations. Nonetheless, the law of international organizations is of little help in elucidating the ambiguity inherent to this legal status. The difference between specialized agencies and related organizations is, indeed, a question of degree, not of nature. Both entities are independent international organizations that keep their own mandate, legal personality, membership, organs and financial resources, and, as such, they shall equally conclude an agreement of cooperation with the UN.[13]

[8] *Ibid.*, Article 2(1). [9] *Ibid.*, Article 2(3).

[10] See, inter alia, the IOM website: www.iom.int/ and the press release announcing the signature of its agreement with the UN: IOM, 'Summit on Refugees and Migrants Begins as IOM Joins the United Nations, www.iom.int/news/summit-refugees-and-migrants-begins-iom-joins-united-nations (both visited 13 March 2021).

[11] E. Guild, S. Grant and K. Groenendijk, 'IOM and the UN: Unfinished Business', Queen Mary School of Law Legal Studies Research Paper No 255/2017.

[12] N. Micinski and T. Weiss, 'International Organization for Migration and the UN System: A Missed Opportunity', (2016) 42 *Future United Nations Development System Briefing* 4.

[13] N. Sybesma-Knol, *The United Nations* (The Hague: Kluwer, 2012) 158–65; Ph. Sands and P. Klein, *Bowett's Law of International Institutions*, 5th ed. (London: Sweet and Maxwell, 2001) 77–86. The difference in legal status is nonetheless clear-cut with the UN programmes (like UNHCR) which are an integral part of the UN per se. The legal status of the IOM may change in the future, for the UN Secretary-General proposed in 2017 to transform it into a specialized agency, but no concrete steps have been taken so far. For further discussion, see V. Chetail, *International Migration Law* (Oxford University Press, 2019) 341–5, 360–97.

The constructive ambiguity inherent to the hybrid status of IOM, as a related organization of the UN, is exacerbated by the elusive and open-ended terms of its Constitution. Its constituent instrument broadly assigns the organization to work as a service provider and a forum of cooperation in the field of migration.[14] Likewise, the Constitution refers in generic terms to 'migrants', 'refugees', 'displaced persons' and 'other individuals in need of international migration services',[15] without specifying further the different groups of persons falling under its mandate. The versatility of its constituent instrument gives considerable flexibility and discretion to the organization and has been instrumental in expanding the activities and influence of the IOM worldwide.

When compared to other key international organisations working in this cross-cutting area (ILO, UNHCR, Office of the High Commissioner for Human Rights and UN Office on Drugs and Crime), the IOM is the only one with a specific and exclusive mandate on migration, in the widest sense of the word. Alongside its broad and evasive Constitution, the IOM has adopted an extensive and factual definition of the term 'migrant' as 'an umbrella term, not defined under international law, reflecting the common lay understanding of a person who moves away from his or her place of usual residence, whether within a country or across an international border, temporarily or permanently, and for a variety of reasons'.[16] While heralding its wide-encompassing mandate, this definition virtually covers any persons on the move, across an international border and, more controversially, within the territory of a state. In practice, however, the IOM is far from exploiting the full potential of its broad and inclusive mandate on migrants, because it primarily works as a service provider for its Member States on specific projects funded by them.

The loosely defined terms of its mandate has created a hiatus, if not a gulf, between what the IOM can do and what it must do. Although international lawyers have long paid little attention to this particular organization, burgeoning legal literature has critically pinpointed the limits of its Constitution and the lack of a formal protection mandate.[17]

[14] Article 1(1) of the IOM Constitution, available at www.iom.int/constitution. [15] *Ibid.*

[16] This working definition continues by explaining that '[T]he term includes a number of well-defined legal categories of people, such as migrant workers; persons whose particular types of movements are legally-defined, such as smuggled migrants; as well as those whose status or means of movement are not specifically defined under international law, such as international students': IOM, *Glossary on Migration*, IML Series No. 34, 2019, 132.

[17] See e.g. J. Klabbers 'Notes on the Ideology of International Organizations Law: The International Organization for Migration, State-Making, and the Market for Migration', (2019) 32 *Leiden Journal of International Law* 383, and F. Crépeau and I. Atak, 'Global

The deafening silence of the IOM Constitution about the protection of migrants and their human rights is, indeed, disturbing. It is a historical anomaly that is no longer compatible with the profound transformation of the IOM, its new responsibilities as a UN-related organization and, more broadly, the renewed commitment towards the human rights of migrants as acknowledged in the Global Compact for Migration.[18]

Although international lawyers are used to lamenting this situation and calling for a revision of the Constitution, the potential of the law of international organizations has not yet been fully explored. While expanding and refining my arguments developed in *International Migration Law*,[19] I move from the conventional belief that the IOM has no protection mandate simply because it is not explicitly enshrined in its Constitution. When assessed from the broader perspective of international law, the provisions of the IOM Constitution are not the only source of legal commitments for the organization.

This chapter accordingly revisits the law of international organizations as an avenue of legally binding commitments for IOM and contributes to the growing demand for accountability. As subjects of international law, international organizations are not exempt from legal obligations and correlative responsibilities. The International Court of Justice (ICJ) acknowledged in its 1980 *WHO–Egypt* advisory opinion that: 'International organizations are subjects of international law and, as such, are bound by any obligations incumbent upon them under general

Migration Governance. Avoiding Commitments on Human Rights, Yet Tracing a Course for Cooperation', (2016) 34 *Netherlands Quarterly of Human Rights* 113. The literature is more prolific outside the field of international law and converges in pinpointing the same limitation of the IOM mandate. See among many others: A. Pécoud, 'What Do We Know about the International Organization for Migration?', (2017) 44 *Journal of Ethnic and Migration Studies* 1621; A. Hirsch and C. Doig, 'Outsourcing Control: The International Organization for Migration in Indonesia', (2018) 22 *International Journal of Human Rights* 681; R. Andrijasevic and W. Walters, 'The International Organization for Migration and the International Government of Borders', (2010) 28 *Society and Space* 977.

[18] Global Compact for Safe, Orderly and Regular Migration, UN General Assembly Resolution 73/195 (19 December 2018). For further discussion about its legal stance as a soft law instrument and its relevance on legally binding human rights of migrants, see V. Chetail, 'The Global Compact for Safe, Orderly and Regular Migration: A Kaleidoscope of International Law', (2020) 16 *International Journal of Law in Context* 253.

[19] Chetail, *International Migration Law*, 372–8.

rules of international law, under their constitutions or under international agreements to which they are parties'.[20]

Following this stance, I will demonstrate that the IOM is bound by international law to respect human rights and protect migrants on three mutually reinforcing legal bases. First, this legal obligation derives from the internal law of the IOM, as implied from its constituent instrument and reinforced by the subsequent practice of the organization. Second, the 2016 agreement concluded with the UN has further sanctioned and, in fact, codified the obligation of the IOM to carry out its activities in accordance with international human rights law. Third, this legal duty is reinforced by the general rules of international law.

11.2 The Internal Law of the Organization

Contrary to common belief, the fact that the human rights of migrants are not explicitly mentioned in the Constitution of IOM does not mean that the organization is not bound to respect them. Even if it has long been neglected in scholarship, the law of international organizations sheds new light on the longstanding controversies surrounding the IOM. From this broader perspective, it is well known that the mandate of any international organization cannot be reduced to the provisions of its constituent instrument. The purposes and functions may be implied from it and these are further informed by the subsequent practice of the relevant international organization. This was long acknowledged by the ICJ in relation to the UN: 'the rights and duties of an entity such as the Organization must depend upon its purposes and functions as specified or implied in its constituent documents and developed in practice'.[21]

Following this stance, I argue that protecting migrants is both implicit and explicit to the mandate of IOM. It is inherent to the purposes and functions of this organization under its Constitution

[20] See *Interpretation of the Agreement of 25 March 1951 between the WHO and Egypt*, (Advisory Opinion), [1980] ICJ Rep. 73, para. 37.

[21] See *Reparation for Injuries Suffered in the Service of the United Nations* (Advisory Opinion), [1949] ICJ Rep. 174, 180.

and, more importantly, it is an explicit duty deriving from the subsequent practice and interpretation of the IOM governing body.

11.2.1 The Implied Mandate

Protecting migrants is a necessary and intrinsic component of IOM's mandate in carrying out the tasks assigned by its Constitution to deliver assistance and migration services. This relies on the well-known doctrine of implied powers under the law of international organizations. According to this notion, every intergovernmental organization possesses implied powers that are additional to those explicitly granted by its constituent instrument and essential to fulfilling the purposes and functions of the organization. Although its exact scope and justifications are not free from ambiguities,[22] the notion of implied powers has been acknowledged by a longstanding jurisprudence of the ICJ. The Court endorsed it on several occasions[23] and reaffirmed in the *Reparation* case that: 'Under international law, the Organization must be deemed to have those powers which, though not expressly provided in the Charter, are conferred upon it by necessary implication as being essential to the performance of its duties'.[24]

Accordingly, the mandate of the IOM cannot be circumscribed by the explicit powers listed in its Constitution. In fact, the role assigned to it by its Constitution is broadly understood. Under its article 1, the purposes and functions of IOM are threefold: (1) to make arrangements for the organized transfer of migrants in need of special assistance; (2) to provide migration services at the request of states on a broad range of areas (including recruitment, selection, placement and assistance); (3) to act as a multilateral forum to promote international cooperation among states, international and other organizations.

The ordinary meaning of the Constitution, as interpreted in accordance with its context, object and purpose, necessarily implies the protection of

[22] J. Klabbers, *An Introduction to International Institutional Law*, 2nd ed. (Cambridge University Press, 2009) 59–73.

[23] See, e.g., *Certain Expenses of the United Nations* (Advisory Opinion), [1962] ICJ Rep. 151, 168; *Effect of Awards of Compensation Made by the UN Administrative Tribunal* (Advisory Opinion), [1954] ICJ Rep. 47, 57.

[24] ICJ, *Reparation*, 182. See also *Legality of Use by a State of Nuclear Weapons in Armed Conflicts* (Advisory Opinion), [1996] ICJ Rep. 66, 79.

migrants in fulfilling the functions assigned to the IOM. This conclusion is reinforced by the preamble of its Constitution: it explicitly mentions that due regard must be paid to 'the specific situation and needs of the migrant as an individual human being'. The preamble further stresses the need to promote cooperation with a view 'to facilitating emigration of persons who desire to migrate to countries where they may . . . live with their families in dignity and self-respect'. It also acknowledges that a central purpose of providing migration services is 'to facilitate, under the most favourable conditions, the settlement and integration of the migrants into the economic and social structure of the country of reception'.

Against this background, there is no doubt that protecting migrants is inherent in and essential to the activities carried out by IOM. This is especially the case when the organization provides assistance to migrants in organizing their transfer or in carrying out migration services. Delivering assistance without protecting migrants is not only an oxymoron. It is, also and above all, in blatant contradiction with the aims of the organization, its constituent instrument and the implied power deriving thereof. Nonetheless asserting that the IOM is entitled to exercise an implied power of protection is one thing. Establishing that it is legally bound to do so is another one. The remaining and critical question is to assert the existence of a legal obligation to protect migrants and respect their human rights.

11.2.2 The Explicit Duty

Ensuring due respect for the human rights of migrants is not only an implied power of the organization. It is also and above all an explicit duty of the IOM deriving from the authoritative interpretation of its governing body, its own resolutions and the subsequent practice of the organization. Here again, the law of international organizations provides valuable insights.

As codified by the ILC in the Articles on the Responsibility of International Organizations (ARIO), the binding rules of an international organization derive from a broad range of sources encompassing 'in particular, the constituent instruments, decisions, resolutions and other acts of the international organization adopted in accordance with those instruments, and established practice of the organization'.[25] Thus, an

[25] ILC, UN Doc. A/CN.4/SER.A/2011, article 2(b). For previous acknowledgements, see also Article 2(1)(j) of the Vienna Convention on the Law of Treaties between States and

international organization is not only bound by its constituent instrument, but also by its own resolutions and established practice that, in turn, constitute an integral part of its mandate.

From this perspective, the subsequent interpretation of the IOM mandate by its Council is binding for the whole organization, as its governing body determines the policies and activities of the organization under Article 6 of the Constitution. As demonstrated below in this section, the IOM Council makes it clear that the organization is committed to ensure full respect for the human rights of migrants. This subsequent interpretation and practice have accordingly informed the mandate of IOM and established a legal duty for the organization.

Since at least the 1990s, the IOM Council has formally acknowledged that one of the self-declared objectives of the organization is 'to work towards effective respect of the human dignity and well-being of migrants'.[26] The IOM Strategy adopted by the Council in 2007 is even more straightforward. It explicitly endorses 'the effective respect for the human rights of migrants in accordance with international law' as a priority of the organization in carrying out its activities.[27] Interestingly, effective respect for migrant's rights is ranked second among the twelve priorities of the IOM Strategy, the first one being 'to provide secure, reliable, flexible and cost-effective services for persons who require international migration assistance', as provided for in its Constitution. As stressed by the IOM Strategy, providing migration services in emergency or post-crisis situations also 'relates to the needs of individuals, thereby contributing to their protection'.[28]

The rationale of this last assertion has been refined in a 2010 background document entitled *Review of the IOM Strategy*: '[w]hile IOM does not have a mandate for the development and setting of norms, the Organization focuses on practical, problem-solving approaches to ensure full respect for the human rights of migrants'.[29] This purposive interpretation of the IOM

International Organizations and between International Organizations; ICJ, *Reparation*, 180.

[26] IOM, 'Council Resolution No 923 (LXXI) of 29 November 1995' (1995) para. 2; 'IOM Strategic Planning: Toward the Twenty-First Century' (1995) MC/1842 para. 27.

[27] IOM, 'Council Resolution No 1150 (XCIII) of 7 June 2007' (2007) para. 2 and its Annex.

[28] *Ibid.*

[29] IOM, 'Review of the IOM Strategy' 99th Session (12 October 2010) MC/IN/302, para. 24.

mandate relies on a broad and pragmatic understanding of the very notion of protection:

> While certain intergovernmental organizations have a legal protection function based on mandate (such as UNHCR and ICRC), the concept and indeed application of protection is not restricted to legal mandate, but also extends to *de facto* protection, where an organization's activities in effect extend protection to persons benefiting from the services of the organization. In other words, the actual assistance rendered constitutes a form of protection, especially where it protects the life and physical well-being of persons at risk.[30]

The IOM has long claimed indeed that 'protection and assistance are inextricably linked. IOM recognizes its responsibility to ensure that, when providing assistance to migrants, its activities must obtain full respect for the rights of the individual'.[31] Although this last acknowledgement was not formally done by the Council itself, it carries an important weight in acknowledging the responsibility of the organization to ensure due respect for migrants' rights in the exercise of its mandate.

Providing protection while carrying out assistance is, however, the very minimum one should expect from an international organization as a subject of international law. The enduring question is whether protection *tout court* is part of the IOM mandate. Although the organization conflates assistance with protection, a noticeable evolution can be observed from the *IOM Principles for Humanitarian Action* adopted by its Council in 2015. This policy framework acknowledges protection as an integral component of the role and responsibilities of the organization. It affirms, in clear and straightforward terms, that '[p]rotection is at the centre of IOM's humanitarian action'.[32]

The IOM *Principles for Humanitarian Action* further endorse the definition of protection provided by the Inter-Agency Standing Committee.[33]

30 IOM, 'Protection of Persons involved in Migration: Note on IOM's Role' (2007) paras. 5 and 6. See also IOM, 'The Human Rights of Migrants – IOM Policy and Activities' (2009) MC/INF/298, paras. 8 and 9.

31 IOM, 'IOM Policy on the Human Rights of Migrants', (2002) MC/INF/259, para. 4. See also R. Perruchoud, 'Persons Falling under the Mandate of the International Organization for Migration (IOM) and to whom the Organization may provide Migration Services', (1992) 4 *International Journal of Refugee Law* 205, 211–12.

32 IOM, 'IOM's Humanitarian Policy – Principles for Humanitarian Action' Council 106th Session (12 October 2015) C/106/CRP/20, section IV.1.

33 *Ibid.* See also Inter-Agency Standing Committee (IASC), 'Protection of Internally Displaced Persons' Inter-Agency Standing Committee Policy Paper (December 1999) 4.

Protection is accordingly defined as encompassing 'all activities aimed at ensuring full respect for the rights of the individual in accordance with the letter and the spirit of the relevant bodies of law'.[34] Hence, protection is not only understood by the IOM as a core element of its action and, by extension, its mandate as interpreted by the IOM Council. It is also defined in reference to the full respect of human rights under international law.

Even more significantly, the IOM commits itself to be bound by the relevant bodies of international law governing the protection of migrants. Its *Principles for Humanitarian Action* formally acknowledge that 'IOM adheres to the applicable provisions of international humanitarian law [and] also adheres to human rights law and refugee law'.[35] Such unilateral endorsement represents the most clear-cut legal ground for establishing the IOM's duty to protect migrants with due respect for their rights.

11.3 Treaty Law

As demonstrated above, the internal law of the organization itself clearly establishes the IOM's obligation to protect migrants and respect their human rights. This obligation is further sanctioned by treaty law: it is codified by the Agreement concerning the relationship between the UN and the IOM and reinforced, albeit in an ancillary and oblique way, by the treaty obligations of the IOM's member states.

[34] *Ibid.* The relevant bodies of law mentioned in the definition of the Inter-Agency Standing Committee include inter alia humanitarian law, human rights and refugee law, while the IOM's Humanitarian Policy adds to this non-exhaustive list that 'for the protection of migrants, other bodies of law may be relevant as well, e.g. labour law, maritime law and consular law'.

[35] *Ibid.*, section VI.6. See also section II.8: 'IOM is committed to providing humanitarian assistance and protection in accordance with international law and norms, where it is needed and where IOM has an added value.' For previous commitments of IOM to be bound by international law, see also IOM, 'Migration Crisis Operational Framework' (2012) MC/2355, para. 12: 'IOM is further bound and committed to the existing legal and institutional frameworks contributing to the effective delivery of assistance and protection and ultimately to the respect and promotion of human rights and humanitarian principles.'

11.3.1 The Agreement Concerning the Relationship between the UN and the IOM

The duty of the IOM to protect migrants has been formally endorsed by the agreement concluded in 2016 with the UN. According to its Article 2(2), the IOM is explicitly acknowledged 'as an essential contributor … in the protection of migrants'. As a contracting party to this agreement, the IOM is thus legally bound to protect migrants and to carry out its activities accordingly. Hence, despite the silence of its Constitution, the mandate of the IOM has been amended by the 2016 agreement and, in fact, codified alongside the practice and interpretation of its governing body.

Article 2(5) of the agreement further confirms that the IOM 'undertakes to conduct its activities in accordance with the Purposes and Principles of the Charter of the United Nations and with due regard to the policies of the United Nations furthering those Purposes and Principles and to other relevant instruments in the international migration, refugee and human rights fields'. This explicit reference to the UN Charter and other relevant instruments dissipates any doubt about the IOM's duty to respect the human rights of migrants without any discrimination. Article 1(3) of the UN Charter endorses the duty to 'promot[e] and encourag[e] respect for human rights and for fundamental freedoms for all without distinction'.

The 'other relevant instruments', moreover, include all general human rights treaties (such as the two UN Covenants and the Convention on the Rights of the Child) – which are generally applicable to everyone without regard to nationality and immigration status – as well as more specialized conventions dedicated to refugee protection and labour migration, like the Refugee Convention of 1951 as amended by its Protocol of 1967 as well as the International Convention on the Rights of Migrants Workers and the Members of their Families. These UN conventions are not directly binding on IOM, which is not a party to them. Nonetheless, the agreement of 2016 obliges the organization to carry out its activities in line with these instruments and this obligation of diligence is reinforced by the general duty to protect migrants under article 2(2) of the same agreement.

11.3.2 The UN Treaties of IOM Member States

The duty of IOM to protect migrants and respect their rights, as sanctioned in the 2016 agreement, is underpinned by the fact that the vast majority of its member states are equally bound by the same UN treaties in the fields of migration, refugee protection and human rights. In 2020, all of them (with the well-known exception of the USA) have ratified the Convention on the Rights of the Child, while respectively 157 and 153 IOM member states have ratified the International Covenant on Civil and Political Rights (ICCPR) and International Covenant on Economic, Social and Cultural Rights (ICESCR). Likewise, 142 IOM member states have ratified the Refugee Convention and/or its Protocol. Although the Migrant Workers Convention has been ratified by the fairly limited number of fifty-six states, most of them are members of the IOM, with the only exceptions of Indonesia and Syria.

Legally speaking, UN treaties ratified by its member states are not *ipso facto* binding for the IOM, for any international organization has its own international legal personality, which is distinct and autonomous from the personality of its member states. Whether an international organization is indirectly bound by the treaty obligations of its member states has raised longstanding debates among scholars.[36] Although intellectually attractive, the idea of such indirect obligations was not acknowledged in the ILC Articles on the Responsibility of International Organizations.

Nonetheless, the treaty obligations of its member states are still relevant for IOM activities at two significant levels. On the one hand, member states cannot evade their treaty obligations by resorting to IOM in carrying out activities that are contrary to international law. As a matter of principle, the continuing opposability of states' duties under human rights law is well acknowledged in international jurisprudence. For instance, in the *Waite and Kennedy* case, the European Court of Human Rights held that:

> where States establish international Organisations in order to pursue or strengthen their cooperation in certain fields of activities, and where they attribute to these Organisations certain competences and accord them immunities, there may be implications as to the protection of fundamental rights. It would be incompatible with the purpose and object of the Convention, however, if the Contracting States were thereby absolved from their responsibility under the convention in relation to the field of activity covered by such attribution.[37]

[36] See, e.g., F. Mégret and F. Hoffmann, 'The UN as Human Rights Violator? Some Reflections on the United Nations Changing Human Rights Responsibilities', (2003) 25 *Human Rights Quarterly* 314; H. G. Schermers and N. M. Blokker, *International Institutional Law*, 4th ed. (Dordrecht: Martinus Nijhoff, 2003) 995.

[37] *Waite and Kennedy* v. *Germany* (application no. 26083/94), European Court of Human Rights, 18 February 1999, para. 67.

On the other hand, the responsibility of an international organization may be engaged when it provides its assistance to a state in the commission of an internationally wrongful act. According to Article 14 ARIO, an international organization that aids or assists a state in the commission of an internationally wrongful act is internationally responsible for doing so if: (a) the organization does so with knowledge of the circumstances of the internationally wrongful act; and (b) the act would be internationally wrongful if committed by that organization.

As exemplified below, the treaty obligations of states represent an important, albeit neglected, avenue for reinforcing IOM accountability. They are bound to play a prominent role with the growing practice of Western States in outsourcing migration controls to IOM, as notably evidenced by its highly criticized involvement in the extraterritorial strategy of containment carried out by Australia in Indonesia.[38]

11.4 The General Rules of International Law

While the IOM's duty to protect migrants and respect their rights is clearly established under its internal law and codified in the agreement concluded with the UN, a third avenue of binding commitments for international organizations may be found in the general rules of international law. According to the ICJ's *WHO-Egypt* advisory opinion of 1980, 'International organizations ... are bound by any obligations incumbent upon them under general rules of international law.'[39] Many scholars have inferred from this rather elusive reference to 'general rules of international law' that international organizations are bound by 'customary international law'.[40]

[38] For further discussion about the controversial cooperation of IOM with Australia in Indonesia see, e.g., A. Dastyari and A. Hirsch, 'The Ring of Steel: Extraterritorial Migration Controls in Indonesia and Libya and the Complicity of Australia and Italy', (2019) 19 *Human Rights Law Review* 435; Hirsch and Doig, 'Outsourcing Control'; Antje Missbach, *Troubled Transit: Asylum Seekers Stuck in Indonesia* (Singapore: ISEAS Yusof Ishak Institute, 2015.

[39] *WHO-Egypt* opinion, para. 37.

[40] See among many others: A. Reinisch, 'Sources of International Organizations' Law: Why Custom and General Principles are Crucial', in S. Besson and J. d'Aspremont (eds.), *Oxford Handbook of the Sources of International Law* (Oxford University Press, 2017) 1016; K. Daugirdas, 'How and Why International Law Binds International Organizations',

Even assuming that this interpretation is correct,[41] which customary obligations are incumbent upon international organizations remains more controversial. It is a truism that international organizations are not bound by all rules of customary international law. As a matter of fact, 'a large number of rules of international law are not relevant for international organizations, which have no territory, confer no nationality and do not exercise jurisdiction in the same sense as states. But some rules may be relevant'.[42] Hence, only a subset of general international law binds international organizations.

Against such a background, inquiring into the IOM duty of protection under customary international law raises two questions: are the human rights of migrants part of customary international law? And to what extent are they incumbent upon IOM? The first question calls for a clear-cut answer, whereas the second one remains more intricate.

11.4.1 The Customary International Human Rights of Migrants

The human rights of migrants are firmly anchored in customary international law, as inherited from the centuries-old law of state responsibility for injuries to aliens and further embedded in the modern development of human rights law.[43] Historically, the protection of foreigners in their host states crystallized through the notion of the international minimum standard at the end of the nineteenth century and in the first half of the twentieth century.[44] From a conceptual and normative angle, the minimum standard of treatment was the forerunner of human rights law at the international level. Indeed, the duty of the host state to respect foreigners, as nationals of

(2016) 57 *Harvard International Law Journal* 325; H. G. Schermers and N. M. Blokker, *International Institutional Law*, 5th ed. (Dordrecht: Martinus Nijhoff, 2011), §§ 1339 and 1579.

41 Contra: J. Klabbers, 'Sources of International Organizations' Law: Reflections on Accountability', in Besson and d'Aspremont (eds.), *Sources of International Law* 987.

42 Schermers and Blokker, *International Institutional Law*, 5th ed., § 1572.

43 See generally V. Chetail, 'The Transnational Movement of Persons Under General International Law: Mapping the Customary Law Foundations of International Migration Law', in V. Chetail and C. Bauloz (eds.), *Research Handbook on International Law and Migration* (Cheltenham: Edward Elgar, 2014) 1.

44 For a general overview of the traditional law of aliens under the law of state responsibility, see V. Chetail, 'The Human Rights of Migrants in General International Law: From Minimum Standards to Fundamental Rights', (2013) 28 *Georgetown Immigration Law Journal* 225.

their own states, progressively moved from a purely interstate logic to a human rights-based approach premised on the idea that some fundamental rights are inalienable to every human being.

During the second half of the twentieth century, the traditional law of aliens was then reframed by the normative expansion of human rights law. As a result of this long evolution, human rights law has become the main source of migrant protection under a broad range of widely ratified conventions at the universal and regional level and further endorsed in state practice and intergovernmental resolutions.[45]

A significant number of migrants' rights are nowadays an integral part of customary international law. They include, most notably, the right to leave any country and the right to enter one's own country; the principle of non-refoulement when there is a real risk of torture, inhuman or degrading treatment; the prohibition of collective expulsion and due process guarantees; the prohibition of arbitrary detention and the correlative duty to provide an alternative to immigration detention; the best interest of the child and the principle of non-discrimination.[46]

11.4.2 International Organizations and the Quest for Customary Law Obligations

While the human rights of migrants are enshrined in customary international law, the more controversial issue is to what extent they are incumbent upon the IOM. This enduring question has been answered by scholars in two opposite ways. On the one hand, many authors assume from the above-mentioned dictum of the ICJ advisory opinion that international customary law is binding per se for any international organizations in the exercise of their activities.[47]

This seems to be the view of the ILC in ARIO. According to its Article 10, the international obligation of an international organization is understood in a broad sense 'regardless of the origin or character of the obligation concerned'. The accompanying commentary underlines, by analogy to the

[45] For further discussion, see Chetail, *International Migration Law*, 59–75.

[46] *Ibid.*, 119–64.

[47] See, e.g., Reinisch, 'Sources of International Organizations' Law'; A. Clapham, *Human Rights Obligations of Non-State Actors* (Oxford University Press, 2006) 82–7.

responsibility of states, that such an international obligation 'may be established by a customary rule of international law'.[48]

On the other hand, the ILC position on this issue has been viewed as 'a rather hypothetical development of international law' which does not recognize sufficiently the differences between states and international organizations.[49] Likewise, the assumption that international customary law is *ipso facto* applicable to international organizations has been criticized because it over-interprets the *WHO-Egypt* opinion and is not supported by a well-established practice of states and international organizations.[50] Furthermore, on a methodological plane, the formal source of a given rule shall not be confused with the addressees of such a rule. In other words, the very fact that a rule is part of international customary law does not necessarily entail that it is automatically binding for any types of subjects of international law.

Given the controversies surrounding this vexed issue, it is fair to say that the legal basis for applying customary law to international organizations raises more questions than answers. There is a growing recognition of the customary law duties of international organizations, but this progressive development is not yet clearly endorsed in the current stage of international law. Nonetheless, such indeterminacy calls for two substantive caveats.

First, an international organization can be bound by an internal custom resulting from the established practice of the organization. The ICJ acknowledged in the 1971 *Namibia* opinion that an established body of practice forms an integral part of the rules of the organization when considering the effect of abstentions by permanent members of the Security Council in the voting procedure.[51] From this angle, the reiterated commitment of the IOM to ensure full respect for the human rights of migrants may be viewed as an internal custom based on the established practice of the organization.

[48] UN Doc. A/CN.4/SER.A/2011.

[49] Legal Responsibility of International Organisations in International Law, Summary of the International Law Discussion Group meeting held at Chatham House on Thursday, 10 February 2011, available at www.chathamhouse.org/sites/default/files/field/field_document/il100211summary.pdf (visited 13 March 2021).

[50] See, e.g., Klabbers, 'Sources of International Organizations' Law', 993–1000; Daugirdas, 'How and Why', 331–5.

[51] See *Legal Consequences for States of the Continued Presence of South Africa in Namibia (South West Africa)* (Advisory Opinion), [1971] ICJ Rep. 16, para. 22.

Second, and in contrast to the longstanding debates about customary international law, the plain applicability of *jus cogens* norms to international organizations is well acknowledged as reflecting the current state of international law in legal scholarship, international jurisprudence and the ARIO.[52] Such peremptory norms of general international law are hierarchically superior to any other rules of international law and they are utterly binding for all subjects of international law because they endorse the fundamental values of the international community.[53]

Without reopening here the Pandora's box concerning which human rights have reached the status of *jus cogens* norms, the peremptory nature of the prohibition of racial discrimination and of torture is beyond any doubt.[54] Obviously, these two legal norms are sadly relevant in the field of migration. Additionally, the prohibition of *refoulement* where there is a real risk of torture should be considered as a norm of *jus cogens*, as a positive duty inherent to the peremptory prohibition of torture. In sum, although the customary law duties of international organizations are not clearly settled, the IOM is bound under general international law by the peremptory prohibition of torture and of racial discrimination as both negative and positive obligations.

11.5 Conclusion: From Rhetoric to Action

While having long been neglected in the specialized literature on the IOM, the law of international organizations offers a critical avenue to revisit and illuminate the IOM's mandate and the duties attached to it. The common complaint among scholars about the limits of its Constitution is not only ineffective but also misleading, as it fails to capture the potential of international law in addressing the legal duties of IOM towards migrants

[52] This view has been endorsed by all the authors quoted above. See also Article 26 ARIO and Judgment of 21 September 2005, Case T-315/01, [2005] ECR II-3649, para. 230.

[53] They thus prevail over any other contrary treaties or customs, and, contrary to the latter, these norms are not only a formal source but also a material one that is non-derogable by essence.

[54] See, e.g., *Case Concerning Armed Activities on the Territory of the Congo (Democratic Republic of the Congo* v. *Rwanda)*, Jurisdiction and Admissibility, [2006] ICJ Rep. 6, para. 78; *Application of the International Convention on the Elimination of All Forms of Racial Discrimination (Georgia* v. *Russian Federation)*, [2011] ICJ Rep. 70, dissenting opinion by Judge Cancado Trindade, para. 180.

and its correlative responsibility. This chapter has demonstrated that the IOM is legally bound to protect migrants and respect their human rights under the current state of international law, even without any change in its Constitution. The obligation of the IOM stems from a threefold legal basis: the internal law of the organization, as informed by the practice of its governing body; the international agreement concluded in 2016 with the UN; and the general rules of international law, including *jus cogens* norms.

This insight from the law of international organization may provide, in turn, a new critical step for both scholars and activists to move from a posture of IOM-bashing to a more incisive and efficient engagement with a view to ensuring its accountability on the basis of its existing legal commitments. Further scrutiny into the legal implications of its duties and its compliance in practice is needed regarding, in particular, the long decried voluntary assisted returns.[55]

Inversely, one should acknowledge several positive developments, which have occurred since 2018 after the adoption of the Global Compact for Migration and the election of a new Director General. The Compact offers an instrumental vehicle for the organization to be better aligned with its responsibility to protect migrants and respect their rights. While not formally binding and primarily addressed to states, the Compact reaffirms the 'effective respect for and protection and fulfilment of the human rights of all migrants, regardless of their migration status, across all stages of the migration cycle'.[56]

Ironically, this soft law instrument may succeed where hard law has failed so far, in bringing a change within the organization. The Compact has been formally endorsed by the organization as 'a reference document for IOM',[57] providing a significant avenue for internalizing the human rights of migrants. This is further aligned with the new responsibility of IOM to serve as the coordinator and secretariat of the UN Migration

55 Among the longstanding critics addressed against the IOM assisted voluntary returns, see e.g. A. Maâ, 'Manufacturing Collaboration in the Deportation Field: Intermediation and the Institutionalisation of the International Organisation for Migration's "Voluntary Return" Programmes in Morocco', (2020) 25 *Journal of North African Studies* 1; A. Koch, 'The Politics and Discourse of Migrant Return: The Role of UNHCR and IOM in the Governance of Return', (2014) 40 *Journal of Ethnic and Migration Studies* 905; F. Webber, 'How Voluntary are Voluntary Returns?', (2011) 52 *Race and Class* 98.

56 Global Compact for Safe, Orderly and Regular Migration, para. 15(f).

57 *Strategic Vision. Setting a Course for IOM* (IOM, 25 November 2019) 5.

Network, whose primary purpose is to ensure effective and coherent implementation of the Compact across the whole UN system.[58]

Since the adoption of the Compact, IOM has also become more vocal than ever in promoting migrants' rights. Although it long abstained from denouncing violations of migrants' rights by its member states, a more critical approach towards states may be observed during recent years. This change of attitude is perceptible in the Strategic Vision of the IOM Director General[59] and is more explicit in the 2019 annual report of the organization. According to this report, 'adherence to international standards and fulfilment of migrant's rights' is acknowledged as the very first principle informing the activities of IOM.[60] Although this task is primarily done through assistance and advise to governments to strengthen adherence to international law in their legislation and policies, the report noticeably mentions that '61 offices of IOM submitted information to the international or regional human rights monitoring bodies or supported a national human rights commission to advance the protection of migrants' rights'.[61] Likewise, in stark contrast with the past practice of the organization, IOM is more inclined to publicly condemn violations of migrants' rights, as exemplified by its call on the EU and its member states to end pushbacks, collective expulsions and the use of violence against migrants and refugees.[62]

Whether this new critical stance towards states will signal a turn towards a cultural revolution of the organization or merely represent another rhetoric device is difficult to predict. One should further concede that, in both law and practice, protection remains a marginal part of its activities, mainly unfolding at the edge of its operational work. The resulting tension between its legal commitment and actual practice underpins the need for a long-overdue reform,

[58] Global Compact for Safe, Orderly and Regular Migration, para. 45.

[59] While reaffirming that 'respect for the rights, dignity and well-being of migrants remains paramount', the Strategic Vision highlights that 'the Organization will remind governments and publics of the rights of all human beings, including migrants, in line with the values enshrined in its Constitution'. See *Strategic Vision*, 10–11.

[60] IOM, *Annual Report for 2019*, C/111/5 (25 June 2020) 2–3. [61] *Ibid.*, 3.

[62] 'IOM Calls for End to Pushbacks and Violence against Migrants at EU External Borders', available at www.iom.int/news/iom-calls-end-pushbacks-and-violence-against-migrants-eu-external-borders (visited 13 March 2021). See also, in the context of border closure and COVID-19, IOM & UNHCR, *COVID-19: Access Challenges and the Implications of Border Restrictions* (27 April 2020).

whether through a revision of its Constitution or its transformation into a UN specialized agency. It remains the case, however, that even under the current status quo the violation of its existing obligation to respect the human rights of migrants entails the international responsibility of IOM.

Global Health 12

Gian Luca Burci

12.1 Introduction

Global health is a very institutionalized field of governance, with diverse international institutions contributing in various ways to promote and protect human health (or negatively affecting it, depending on whom you ask). Such institutions include global international organizations such as the United Nations (UN) and the World Health Organization (WHO), regional organizations such as the European Union (EU), hybrid institutions comprising public agencies and corporate bodies such as the International Standardization Organization (ISO) and, more recently, public-private partnerships and networks showing a similar structure. This proliferation is not surprising conceptually if we consider that health is an intrinsic and essential dimension of human beings and communities, both from a biomedical point of view as well as from a public health and social perspectives. So many transnational factors, processes and policies have a direct or indirect impact on health that not only existing international organizations have integrated or upgraded health considerations in their agendas, but new ones have been established to address neglected aspects of global health governance.

12.2 Health and Global Governance

Historically, health was considered for a long time an essentially domestic affair revolving around health care and public health policies. The main exception was 'colonial medicine' to protect the economic and political interests of colonial and trading powers and, by extension, their own protection against infectious diseases originating mostly from Asia. In a post-colonial setting, transnational issues or collective action problems requiring institutionalized cooperation consisted mainly of the fight against specific diseases (e.g. tuberculosis, malaria, influenza), harmonization of standards to facilitate research and development of new medicines as well as the internationalization of the pharmaceutical market, as well as policy guidance for health problems of developing countries such as child and maternal mortality and humanitarian assistance. The WHO was the central authority to perform most of those functions both as a forum for consensus-building and as a technical and epistemic authority in its own right.

The systemic factors that have led to a reframing of the role of health in global governance and the emergence in policy and academic discourse of the concepts of 'global health', 'global health governance' and 'global governance for health' are fundamentally three. They coalesced together in complex ways during the 1990s, the decade that in my view fundamentally changed the role of health in global governance and consequently the institutional landscape around it.

The first factor is globalization as a largely economic and cultural phenomenon driven by a neo-liberal agenda and leading to the spread of western cultural models as well as growing inequalities between and within countries. The attention of policy-makers shifts as a result from a biomedical approach to addressing the economic and political determinants of health, including environmental factors as well as the risk factors (unhealthy diets, alcohol and tobacco use) at the root of the staggering pandemic of non-communicable diseases that dwarfs the human toll of COVID-19. Such spread is facilitated in part by the constraining effects of international trade and investment law over the authority of states to regulate private economic activities for the protection of health. It was inevitable that the newly established World Trade Organization (WTO) would be seen by activists and many developing countries as part of the problem and health protection would become the object of controversial discussions and litigation as a legitimate limit to trade and intellectual property law. Another effect of globalization that influences the institutional landscape of global health is the rapid and aggressive emergence of non-state actors, ranging from non-governmental organizations (NGOs) and philanthropic foundations to industry associations, the media and transnational corporations, and their claim to directly influence decision-making and the governance of health. The latter factor has had a profound effect on state-centred intergovernmental organizations, in particular the WHO, caught between preserving the primacy of public authority while finding ways to engage with a growing number of influential actors and their diverse agendas.[1] It has also coincided with a crisis of multilateralism, or at least a rethinking of the rationale and modalities for organized international cooperation. From a health perspective, the latter trend is in good part behind the recent proliferation of public-private partnerships and other institutional experiments that diverge from classical multilateralist doctrines.

The second factor is the HIV/AIDS pandemic and the unprecedented international mobilization against it, which raised in turn a number of important governance implications. The first such implication is the deliberate use for the first time of a human rights frame to assess and guide public health interventions, in particular those with criminalizing and discriminatory effects against vulnerable but marginalized groups in the name of health protection. This cosmopolitan principle leads to the reassessment of the 'right to health' as an operational frame to guide public health policies as well as to the increasing presence of health issues on the agenda of the Human Rights Council. The second implication is the increasing perception of life-saving antiretroviral medicines as public goods essential to promote the right to life and health, in opposition to the aggressive behaviour of pharmaceutical companies and developed countries supporting their interests, as well as the crippling effects of intellectual property law on access to life-saving medicines. The same framing has been increasingly used with regard to essential medicines in general, and we can see it at play in the discussions around the allocation of COVID-19 vaccines. This controversial and emotional situation continues to influence and at times complicate consensus-building in the international organizations most involved, in particular the WHO, WTO and the World Intellectual Property Organization (WIPO). Another relevant consequence of the HIV/AIDS crisis is the powerful political role played by activist movements and organizations that shamed governments and international organizations into action with their spectacular and aggressive advocacy. It also generated the 'dogma' of community representation in international decision-making forums and explains the governance of

[1] G. L. Burci and A. Cassels, 'Health', in J. Cogan, I. Hurd and I. Johnstone (eds.), *Oxford Handbook of International Organizations* (Oxford University Press, 2016) 447.

institutions such as UNAIDS (the first UN program giving direct representation to communities living with HIV/AIDS in its policy-setting organ), the Global Fund to Fight AIDS, Tuberculosis and Malaria (Global Fund) and the UNITAID public-private partnership. It is no exaggeration to state that HIV/AIDS 'made global health'[2] and explains the overriding concern for equity, fairness and justice in both academic and policy discourse.

A parallel development originating from the HIV/AIDS crisis consists of the increasing perception of the international spread of infectious diseases as national and international security threats besides public health problems. The 'securitization of health' originated in academic and policy thinking in the USA in the 1990s in response to the spread of HIV/AIDS. Such an approach reorients power distribution and funding towards the military and security establishment nationally and internationally, reflecting their interests; this perception explains why the Security Council has placed diseases such as HIV/AIDS, Ebola and COVID-19 on its agenda,[3] and why HIV/AIDS prevention became part of the mandate of peace-keeping operations such as MONUSCO in the Democratic Republic of the Congo.[4]

The third factor is the evolution of development thinking and governance, where health is increasingly positioned as an input, output and indicator of development and poverty reduction policies. This positioning goes back to the inclusion of health programmes in World Bank lending since the 1970s, but was consolidated by the WHO under the leadership of Director-General Gro Harlem Brundtland as well as, most importantly, by the dominance of the Millennium and subsequently Sustainable Development Goals in UN-system policies. This, in turn, has many consequences of relevance for the present chapter, such as the exponential increase in development financing directed to health problems, the proliferation of international actors and initiatives and the resulting governance fragmentation, as well as the inability of the WHO to play a coordinating and rationalizing role in this context.[5] It also contributes to the increased political profile of health and its uptake by a number of political entities, in particular the UN as well as influential networks such as the G7 and G20.

[2] S. Moon, 'Global Health: A Centralized Network Searching for Hierarchy', in M. Barnett, J. Pevehouse and K. Raustiala (eds.), *Global Governance in a World of Change* (2021 Cambridge University Press) 234.

[3] G. L. Burci, 'Ebola, the Security Council and the Securitization of Health', (2014) 20 *Questions of International Law* 27.

[4] UN Security Council Resolution, S/RES/1983 (2011).

[5] Burci and Cassels, 'Health', 470.

The foregoing political developments, which are of course only summarily reviewed here, have led to a reconceptualization of global health, the systems of governance affecting it and the functions that should be performed by the participants in those systems. 'Global health' shifts from being identified with the protection from epidemics or the health challenges of developing countries to 'the health of the global population, with a focus on the dense relationships of interdependence across national and sectors that have arisen with globalization'.[6] The emphasis in this definition is on the interdependences and shared vulnerabilities created by globalization, which render even traditionally domestic health issues a matter of legitimate international concern; the effects of the privatization of health care systems in Western European countries and the United States (USA) on the quick international spread of COVID-19 in early 2020 is a graphic example of the cogency of that vision.

To the notion of 'global health governance' – intended as the set of actors and institutions whose primary intent is the protection of health and the corresponding functions performed by them – is increasingly associated the concept of 'global governance for health' which refers mainly to those non-health institutions and processes of global governance which have a direct and indirect impact on health. Many of those institutions are related to the determinants of health; the WTO and the so-called 'commercial determinants of health' are often used as examples. The latter notion has a definite normative intent, encapsulated in the concept coined within the WHO of 'health in all policies', that is, advocating for health and equity in all major policy agendas.[7] Global health governance has been conceptualized in constructivist terms in recent scholarship as a 'complex adaptive system'. It still shows the characteristics of a 'traditional' intergovernmental system centred around the WHO but at the same time points to a shift towards networked models of governance where many autonomous actors interact across multiple scales and across sectors, shape each other's thinking and adopt innovative strategies to pursue their agendas.[8] The rise of private authority, hybrid forms of governance and informal lawmaking coexists with the jealous retention by states of their

[6] J. Frenk, O. Dantés and S. Moon, 'From Sovereignty to Solidarity: A Renewed Concept of Global Health for an Era of Complex Interdependence', (2014) 383 *The Lancet* 94.

[7] WHO, Social Determinants of Health, www.who.int/health-topics/social-determinants-of-health#tab=tab_1 (visited 1 February 2021).

[8] Moon, 'Global Health', 13.

primacy in formal rule-making through the WHO. As Suerie Moon has noted, 'the new has not replaced the old, but rather has grown up around it – sometimes complementing, sometimes competing, but not yet overtaking it'.[9]

As noted above, we cannot talk of a 'global health architecture', hinting towards accepted structures of hierarchy, coordination and intentional design that are simply not present.[10] Still, even in its current transitional and disorganized state, there are expectations about the functions that global health governance, like any governance system, should perform. Different categorizations have been proposed in this connection, reflecting methodological positions rather than deep conceptual divides. In a seminal and oft-cited article, for example, Julio Frenk and Suerie Moon[11] offer a four-pronged vision of what the actors in health governance should produce:

- Global public goods, including notably normative instruments, information and analyses as well as research and development of new health technologies. This notion comes with expectations about the role of governments in regulating, limiting and if necessary remedying market-based policies;
- The management of externalities 'to prevent or mitigate the negative health effects that situations or decisions originating in one country might have on others';[12]
- The mobilization of global solidarity as a reaction to inequalities and vulnerabilities, with particular emphasis on sustainable financing for international organizations and developing countries;
- Stewardship, consisting mainly of the 'overall strategic direction to the global health system so that all other functions can be performed adequately'.[13]

While other scholars have used different approaches to the functional aspects of global health governance,[14] the foregoing taxonomy well encapsulates current thinking on health governance and the roles played

[9] *Ibid.*

[10] D. Fidler, 'Architecture Amidst Anarchy: Global Health's Quest for Governance', (2007) 1 *Global Health Governance* 1.

[11] J. Frenk and S. Moon, 'Governance Challenges in Global Health', (2013) 368 *New England Journal of Medicine* 936.

[12] *Ibid.*, 940. [13] *Ibid.*

[14] Burci and Cassels, 'Health', have proposed a categorization including normative functions, technical collaboration, financing, coordination and coherence, humanitarian emergencies and development cooperation.

by the plethora of international institutions and actors influencing health outcomes. It also defines the relations, at times competitive while at others complementary or synergistic, among those actors. At the same time, the unprecedented devastation and long-term consequences of the COVID-19 pandemic may require adding emergency management as an additional function. COVID-19 goes beyond the management of externalities and requires a level of centralization and coordination that are for the moment absent in global health governance.

12.3 The World Health Organization

The creation of the WHO in 1946, as part of the construction of the UN system, marks a substantial shift both in the institutionalization process of health as well as the vision underpinning it as compared with the first generation of regional and global health organizations that emerged from the end of the nineteenth century largely to support international cooperation against the spread of epidemic diseases.[15] The preamble to the Constitution, building on the European tradition of social medicine, reads like a veritable universal declaration of global health that will have a deep influence on the development of international law and public health policy.[16] The preamble gives a positive definition of health as 'a state of complete physical, mental and social well-being and not merely the absence of disease or infirmity rather than the absence of disease'; most importantly, it defines for the first time health as a human right, a contributor to international peace and security and a matter of legitimate international concern. Also the objective of the WHO in Article 1 of the Constitution[17] and the long list of functions in Article 2 reveal the ambition of the WHO's founders to position it as the central organization in health governance endowed with directive, normative and coordinating powers as well as an expansive mandate covering most aspects of public health. It is telling that the first and overriding function under Article 2 requires the WHO to 'act as the directing and co-ordinating authority on international

[15] N. Howard-Jones, *The Scientific Background of the International Sanitary Conferences* (Geneva: WHO, 1975).

[16] Constitution of the World Health Organization (adopted 22 July 1946, entered into force 7 April 1948) 14 UNTS 185.

[17] 'The attainment by all peoples of the highest possible level of health'.

health work'.[18] Moreover, chapter XIV establishes a vertical system of accountability by requiring member states to report regularly to the WHO a broad range of information, including notably their compliance with the WHO's normative instruments. Even though those provisions have never been implemented very strictly, they reveal a 'managerial' approach to health governance that has acquired new relevance in the discussions around a post-COVID-19 health security architecture.

The WHO is the largest UN specialized agency, with 194 member states, a secretariat of about 7000 staff and its 2022–3 budget amounting to slightly more than US $6 billion. Its governance consists of a plenary World Health Assembly (WHA) with ultimate policy-setting powers, a thirty-four-member Executive Board (EB) with executive, preparatory and emergency powers, and a secretariat headed by a director-general. A defining feature of its governance is its uniquely regionalized structure and the ensuing tensions between global functions concentrated in its headquarters in Geneva, on the one hand, and 'regional' functions spread throughout its six 'regional organizations'.[19] A common but oversimplified description of that tension is that Geneva makes norms and global policies, while regions provide technical cooperation to their countries. Each regional organization consist of a regional committee comprising the member states of that region as well as a regional office headed by a regional director. Unlike the heads of the UN regional commissions – who are appointed by the Secretary-General – regional directors are in practice selected by the member states of their respective regions, thus ensuring that their allegiance is directed predominantly to their electors rather than the Director-General. This unusual structure, and the inevitable centrifugal forces and power struggles that it has produced, has defined the life of the WHO. It finds its cause in the uncertainties surrounding the regional health organizations pre-dating the WHO, and its most extreme manifestation is the status of the Pan-American Health Organization (PAHO). The PAHO was established in 1902 and embodies a distinct American experience and vision of public health. During the negotiation of the WHO Constitution, American states rejected a merger of the PAHO into the nascent WHO. While continuing to this day as a completely separate organization outside the UN system, the PAHO serves at the same time as the WHO's regional body for the Americas under a 1949

[18] *Ibid.* [19] This is the expression used in chapter XI of the Constitution, Articles 44–6.

agreement concluded between the two organizations. This situation was supposed to be transitional pending the PAHO's integration into the WHO, but it will almost certainly remain permanent and, despite a satisfactory level of programmatic integration, it generates constant ambiguities and occasional frictions.

The role of the WHO in a historical perspective spans the four functions mentioned above; it is characterized at the same time by a consistent core of activities and functions centred around disease control, coupled with significant shifts responding to evolving political and public health considerations. It has also been shaped by the coexistence and tension between two quite different visions of public health, neither of which entirely displaced the other but that alternatively prevailed under evolving political and epidemiological situations and continue to characterize the WHO's activities to this date. At the risk of oversimplifying more complex concepts, the first perspective sees health as the outcome of social and economic factors and postulates that improvements in public health also require social transformations taking place outside health care systems. From this perspective, which has also a strong ethical component, the pursuit of health with equity and justice is a fundamental duty of governments; persons and communities are not 'patients' but active participants in public health. The second perspective emphasizes a biomedical approach relying on technological and medical interventions and focuses on the control of specific diseases. Hospital-based health care plays a larger role in the latter approach, that also assess interventions from the perspective of improving economic productivity and national security. In this approach, the role of persons and communities affected by diseases inevitably becomes more passive.

Historically, the WHO was considered throughout the first two decades of the Cold War an essentially Western-dominated organization, with the USA exercising such a predominant influence that it led to the temporary withdrawal in the late 1940s of the Soviet Union and a number of Eastern European states.[20] Western dominance and a corresponding vision of public health was responsible for the WHO's image as an apolitical science-based organization with deeply shared goals and functions that promoted coordination through credible information, authoritative guidance and technical support for developing countries.

[20] G. L. Burci and C.-H. Vignes, *The World Health Organization* (The Hague: Kluwer, 2004) 29.

In its first decades, the WHO prioritized programmes targeting specific diseases and aiming at their eradication or elimination as a public health problem. This approach, that occasionally saw the United States and the Soviet Union joining forces across the Cold War divide, led to one of the WHO's main achievements, namely, the eradication of smallpox at the end of the 1970s. It also led, however, to embarrassing and costly failures (e.g. in the case of malaria, poliomyelitis and tuberculosis) that started generating doubts and resistance to a top-down biomedical approach, in particular by the growing ranks of newly independent states that used their numerical majority to try to change the rules of the game. This led to a shift towards the more horizontal and socially oriented approach of 'primary health care' championed by both the WHO and UNICEF that culminated in the adoption in 1978 of the 'Alma Ata Declaration' and the proclamation of 'health for all by 2000'.[21] That ambitious vision was soon reduced in scope to make it more realistic but also as a consequence of the profound geopolitical changes of the 1980s marked by the expansion of neoliberal market-based policies and a growing mistrust of multilateralism. Still, it represents one of the high marks of a more political approach to global health that focuses on social and economic determinants as well as considerations of justice and equity. This vision continues to influence global health thinking and practice and to generate substantial controversies within the WHO. While a more focused vertical and biomedical approach inevitably characterizes the WHO's efforts at disease control, the alternative perspective resurfaces as a consequence of the more complex and inequitable situations generated by globalization and neoliberal policies as well as by an increasingly divided membership, with emerging powers such as Brazil, India and South Africa challenging the prevailing neoliberal orthodoxy emerging from the end of the Cold War.

As a result of these dynamics, the functions and activities of the WHO have been varied and cover the whole spectrum of public health ranging from specific diseases, the strengthening of health systems and access to medicines to nutrition, food safety and current cutting-edge issues such as anti-microbial resistance. Despite recurring efforts to focus the work of the organization on areas and topics where there is the greatest need and the WHO offers a competitive advantage, priority-setting has traditionally

[21] M. Cueto, Th. Brown and E. Fee, *The World Health Organization: A History* (Cambridge University Press, 2019) 170.

suffered given diverging national agendas and internal competition within the secretariat. This problem has limited the WHO's role and impact in global health governance for a long time and at times has reflected the narrow strategic vision of key member states.

Particularly relevant for the purpose of this chapter are the normative functions of the WHO, that are generally considered both as a global public good and a stewardship tool aimed not only at developing countries but rather at setting effective and technically credible global standards at every level of development. Under its Constitution, the WHA can adopt (1) conventions with respect to any matter within the competence of the organization,[22] (2) legally binding regulations in five enumerated areas[23] that come into force automatically for all member states by a specified deadline except for states that object or file a reservation and (3) recommendations on any matter within the competence of the organization.[24] These powers, coupled with the reporting obligations mentioned above, testify to the ambitious vision of an organization with strong vertical powers of regulation and oversight. In fact, the WHO has exercised its lawmaking powers very sparsely, adopting a single convention in 2003 – the Framework Convention on Tobacco Control (FCTC)[25] – and two regulations – the Nomenclature Regulations (dealing with nomenclature of diseases and causes of death – adopted in 1948 and revised in 1967)[26] – and most importantly the International Health Regulations (IHR), adopted in 1951 and revised several times, most recently in 2005.[27] Such hesitation to use international law as part of the WHO's toolkit has been attributed to the rapid improvement in medical and public health conditions since the establishment of the organization, the different priorities of developing countries, reluctance in 'codifying science' and, maybe anecdotally, the discomfort and lack of familiarity of the medical epistemic community with legal instruments and processes.[28]

Even taking into account this quantitatively slim record, the WHO has adopted two groundbreaking instruments in contemporary global health

[22] WHO Constitution, Articles 19–20. [23] *Ibid.*, Articles 21–2. [24] *Ibid.*, Article 23.

[25] WHO Framework Convention on Tobacco Control (adopted 21 May 2003, entered into force 2005).

[26] WHO, Nomenclature Regulations, resolution WHA20/18 (22 May 1967), OR 13, Annex 1 349.

[27] International Health Regulations, Res. WHA58.3 (23 May 2005), WHA58/2005/REC/1 17.

[28] Burci and Vignes, *World Health Organization*, 153.

governance. The FCTC, which entered into force in 2005 and has currently 182 parties, is the first treaty regulating for health purposes the marketing, promotion and consumption of a lawful consumer product. It limits the supply as well as the demand for tobacco products and excludes the tobacco industry from any form of participation. Its adoption promoted the notion that the health impact of certain products or processes is such that they have to be carved out of normal regulatory and market mechanisms and subjected to dedicated rules and governance.[29] That consideration has broader implications for the fight against non-communicable diseases (NCD) (i.e. diabetes, cancer, respiratory and cardiovascular diseases) which are responsible for more than 65 per cent of global mortality and share common causal risk factors including, besides tobacco, alcohol, unhealthy diets, sedentary lifestyle and environmental factors. NCD are positioned at the intersection of the perspectives mentioned above and present particular challenges for the WHO: on the one hand the WHO supports countries on disease-specific technical interventions and research, but on the other it supports regulatory approaches that are crucial for decreasing exposure to risk factors caused or facilitated by market mechanisms and consumption models. This pits the WHO against the interests of powerful multinational corporations and explains the chronic underfunding of the WHO's NCD work and the so-far successful opposition to new treaties on acute transboundary risk factors such as, notably, alcohol.

The IHR, as drastically revised in 2005, represent the latest manifestation of the long history of international sanitary conventions and regulations. The pre-WHO conventions were eventually subsumed into a single instrument under the authority of the WHO, thereby centralizing and unifying international coordination and cooperation for the prevention and control of the international spread of diseases. Abandoning the previous approach relying on a set of rigid maximum measures applicable at the border to a short and exhaustive list of diseases, the 2005 IHR embody a dynamic and context-sensitive approach to globalized health risks that can arise not only from the natural spread of pathogens but also from accidental or intentional release of chemical and radioactive substances. The remarkable

[29] S. Zhou and J. Liberman, 'The Global Tobacco Epidemic and the WHO Framework Convention on Tobacco Control', in G. L. Burci and B. Toebes (eds.), *Research Handbook on Global Health Law* (Cheltenham: Edward Elgar, 2018) 340.

feature of the IHR is their managerial approach, whereby a global system of surveillance, alert and response is entrusted to the WHO secretariat without much intervention by member states. This approach to the management of externalities culminates in the authority of the Director-General (DG) to declare a 'public health emergency of international concern' (PHEIC) and issue time-limited temporary recommendations of urgent measures to control the outbreak and prevent its further spread. As part of its managerial and stewardship role, the secretariat can also rely on non-governmental sources of information and even keep information confidential under certain conditions to reassure notifying states against overreactions. While the WHA is supposed to exercise oversight over the implementation of the IHR, its role so far has been cursory and most authority rests on the secretariat. The DG has declared six PHEICs between 2009 and 2020, including notably in January 2020 with regard to the spread of COVID-19. While the innovative health governance model enshrined in the IHR has been repeatedly endorsed by member states, their implementation and the role of the WHO have pointed to several hurdles and flaws that have weakened the effectiveness of the IHR as a credible collective tool for global health security. These problems have been exacerbated by the chronic underfunding of WHO and have prompted much criticism, notably during the 2014–16 Ebola outbreak and the COVID-19 pandemic.

Such criticism has led to the establishment in 2016 of a WHO operational emergency programme that includes the management of the IHR as a component of a more holistic approach to global health security. The WHO has historically never been considered as an implementation or operational agency, mostly playing a normative and advisory role. The sudden addition of an operational component that had, inter alia, to incorporate jealously independent regional offices, has represented a major challenge for the organization but has also confirmed the fundamental confidence of member states in the WHO's central role in health security. The WHO's response to the 2019 Ebola outbreak in the Democratic Republic of the Congo and to the COVID-19 pandemic have been the baptism of fire for its enhanced role, including the shipment of large quantities of equipment and medical supplies and the aggressive use of the internet for the provision of information, analysis and most importantly constantly updated guidance. The response to COVID-19 (still ongoing as of the writing of this chapter) has tested the credibility and authority of the WHO in a complex political situation that grossly transcended purely health considerations. It has also shown the limits and rigidity of the IHR as the legal tool to guide and coordinate international response, with the WHO secretariat ironically not mentioning them at all in its guidance and outreach during the first months of the pandemic.

The perceived inadequacies of the IHR and, more generally, of the existing legal and institutional framework of global health security for managing the COVID-19 pandemic have led to widespread reflections and recommendations for reform by scholars, thinktanks and policy-makers. These findings and proposals have focused on areas and issues that have arguably contributed to the pandemic and its devastating consequences, from governance and lack of solidarity and equity, to financing and legal gaps such as with regard to the prevention of zoonotic diseases. With regard to the WHO, some of the main criticism focused on the inadequacy of the IHR and the secretariat's practice in their implementation as the main shields against the spread of disease, as well as on the fact that their limited scope under Article 21 of the WHO Constitution prevented them from covering crucial blind spots in international law such as equitable access to medicines.[30] This has led in turn to the proposal in late 2020 for a new WHO convention on pandemic preparedness and response as the best tool to ensure sustained political commitment and close existing normative gaps. The proposal, initially spearheaded by Western European countries as well as the WHO's DG Tedros, clashed with competing proposals to first focus on strengthening the IHR and other existing instruments. The WHA, meeting at the end of November 2020 in its second ever special session, eventually decided to both establish a new body to draft and negotiate 'a WHO convention, agreement or other international instrument' as well as to continue work on strengthening – and possibly amending – the IHR to increase their effectiveness.[31] This process had just been launched at the

[30] The most important contributions from this perspective came from the WHO-convened Independent Panel on Pandemic Preparedness and Response, 'COVID-19: Make it the Last Pandemic', https://theindependentpanel.org/mainreport/ (last accessed on 20 December 2021), and the IHR Review Committee equally convened by the DG pursuant to Article 50 of the IHR – 'Report of the Review Committee on the Functioning of the International Health Regulations (2005) during the COVID-19 response', WHO doc. A/74.9/Add.1 (5 May 2021).

[31] 'The World Together: Establishment of an intergovernmental negotiating body to strengthen pandemic prevention, preparedness and response' WHA decision SSA2(5) (1 December 2021).

time of writing, but if successful it will represent a dramatic development in the body of global health law and the WHO's role in it.

The final facet of the WHO's normative functions are its non-binding instruments and standards. This is certainly the most prolific and successful aspect of the WHO's practice. Such instruments fall into two broad categories: regulatory recommendations adopted by the WHA under Article 23 of the Constitution; and standards and recommendations issued by the secretariat. The former include instruments with a significant political weight and addressing controversial issues such as the 1981 International Code of Marketing of Breast-Milk Substitutes,[32] the 2010 Global Code of Practice on the International Recruitment of Health Personnel[33] and the 2011 Pandemic Influenza Pandemic Preparedness Framework.[34]

The adoption by the secretariat of recommendations, guidelines and standards, usually on the basis of standing authorizations by the WHA, is probably the most practically important aspect of the WHO's normative functions, in particular in the highly technical area of pharmaceutical regulation. The secretariat relies in turn on a large network of experts and external collaborating centres that carry out most of the analytical and preparatory work. The elaboration of the instruments in question, particularly those concerning medicines, drugs and biological products that are often of high technical complexity, require long and extensive preparations as well as strict quality control. Examples are the recommendations on the international control of narcotic drugs and psychotropic substances used by the UN Commission on Narcotic Drugs for international control; the Model List of Essential Medicines which has become an essential instrument for many countries at all levels of development to prioritize public procurement; and the International Non-Proprietary Names that protect the names of active ingredients of medicines from appropriation as trademarks. The secretariat in most cases seeks the views of member states and other stakeholders, but excludes them from participating in the elaboration of the instruments. This approach to

[32] International Code of Marketing of Breast-Milk Substitutes, Resolution WHA34.22, May 1981.

[33] Global Code of Practice on the International Recruitment of Health Personnel, Resolution WHA63.16, 21 May 2010.

[34] Pandemic Influenza Preparedness Framework for the Sharing of Influenza Viruses and Access to Vaccines and Other Benefits, Resolution WHA64/5, 24 May 2011.

standard-setting, very ingrained in the WHO's practice, conceptualizes technical standards as public goods based on evidence as well as reliable public health and scientific principles and methods, and shields them from the politics of an intergovernmental negotiation. However, the impact of standards and guidelines on the interests of powerful corporations has led to questions about the legitimacy of the WHO's methods of work and the power exercised by individual experts.

12.4 From Global Health Governance to Global Governance for Health

The traditional narrative that the WHO was the sole and unchallenged international health institution until the 1980s is unfounded. The WHO had to cooperate or contend since its inception with a number of UN agencies due to functional overlaps and the constraints of its mandate and resources. The most complex cooperative relationship has been established with UNICEF given its leadership on maternal and child health and its position globally as the main vaccine procurer for developing countries. UNICEF shared the WHO's evolving vision of global health governance in the 1970s, co-sponsored the Alma Ata Declaration and was instrumental in the run-up to the 1981 Code of Marketing of Breastmilk Substitutes. However, largely under US pressure, UNICEF broke ranks with the WHO on the implementation of primary health care.[35]

Another example of longstanding inter-agency collaboration is between the WHO and FAO in the field of food safety. The two organizations established in the early 1960s a joint food standard programme managed by an intergovernmental Codex Alimentarius Commission[36] with the dual purpose of protecting consumers while promoting fair practices in food trade. While initially conceived as an advisor to the two parent organizations in support of their policy-making functions, it has progressively turned into an independent standard-setter with a horizontal and non-hierarchical relationship with the FAO and WHO in order to preserve its

[35] Cueto, Brown and Fee, *World Health Organization*, 180.

[36] Codex Alimentarius, www.fao.org/fao-who-codexalimentarius/en/ (visited 25 February 2021). The Codex Commission currently has 189 members, including the European Commission. It has a complex structure with multiple thematic or regional committees and its governance includes numerous industry and consumer associations.

normative authority. Through an elaborate and slow consensual process mixing scientific evidence with risk management principles, the Commission adopts non-binding standards to facilitate international food trade while protecting human health (e.g. from pesticides, antibiotics, additives, genetically modified organisms and unfounded health claims). The role and power dynamics of Codex changed dramatically with the adoption in 1995 of the Agreements on Sanitary and Phytosanitary Measures (SPS) and on Technical Barriers to Trade as part of the World Trade Organization (WTO) package. In particular, the presumption of compliance with SPS obligations of trade restrictions conforming with Codex standards turned the latter into crucial components of agricultural trade policy, especially for developing countries reliant on commodity export. This has politicized the work of the Codex Commission to the point of dysfunction by placing divergent trade interests at the centre of its agenda, injected the WTO and its governance and dispute settlement system in health protection discourse and insulated Codex even more from the WHO's policy-making on food safety and nutrition.

The latter example is a graphic manifestation of the increasing political complexity of global health governance and of how health has become a factor in many other policy and legal regimes as well as in their respective institutions. Probably the most controversial aspect of this development is the role of health in international economic law and governance and the roles played in this connection by the WHO, WTO and UN. With regard to foreign investment law and policy, the lack of a dedicated international organization has focused attention on the role of international investment litigation in balancing public and private interests.[37] With regard to the WTO, the main controversies have raged around the protection of intellectual property rights on the one hand (mostly patent, data protection and trademarks), and on the other hand access to medicines or restrictions of the use of logos or displays on consumer products with the aim of reducing their appeal.

The controversial and disputed impact of patents and other proprietary rights on the availability and affordability of medicines, in particular, has been a constant source of frictions between the WTO and WHO literally since the establishment of the former. The Agreement on Trade-Related

[37] Ch. Giorgetti, 'Health and International Investment Law', in Burci and Toebes (eds.), *Research Handbook*, 164.

Aspects of Intellectual Property Rights (TRIPS) codifies and extends in principle to all industrial products and processes a western approach to innovation and was accepted with great reluctance by many emerging countries as part of the WTO package of agreements. The aggressive attitude of multinational pharmaceutical companies in enforcing those rights, in particular with regard to HIV antiretroviral medicines as well as expensive treatments for NCDs such as cancer and respiratory diseases, contributed to the deep and persistent polarization between framing life-saving medicines as public goods crucial for the realization of the rights to life and health, and the promotion of pharmaceutical innovation as well as the distinctive economic model of the pharmaceutical industry requiring high prices for innovative medicines as its bottom line.

WTO found itself in the crosshair of such an existential controversy, which led to the adoption in 2001 of the Doha Declaration on the TRIPS Agreement and Public Health as both an interpretive as well as a normative statement on how to balance such divergent public and private entitlements.[38] The Declaration provided a strong legitimization of the so-called 'TRIPS flexibilities', namely, national measures such as compulsory licensing limiting or correcting the effects of patents. References to the Doha Declaration and TRIPS flexibilities have become customary in resolutions by the WHA, the Human Rights Council and the UN General Assembly dealing even indirectly with access to medicines. Most importantly, the peculiar situation of developing countries without pharmaceutical manufacturing capacity led to the sole amendment of a WTO agreement thus far with the adoption in 2005 of an Article 31bis of TRIPS.[39] While WTO litigation on this issue has been relatively limited, the TRIPS Council has served as a forum to keep it alive but unresolved. In October 2020, India and South Africa proposed an unprecedented general waiver of intellectual property rights affecting access to COVID-19 treatments and vaccines.[40] This bold – and unsuccessful as of the time of writing – proposal confirms the emphasis on essential medicines as public goods as well as the legitimizing powers of the WTO. At the same time, the

[38] Declaration on the TRIPS Agreement and Public Health (14 November 2001), WT/MIN(01)/DEC/2.

[39] Amendment of the TRIPS Agreement, WT/L/641, 6 December 2005.

[40] Waiver from Certain Provisions of The TRIPS Agreement for the Prevention, Containment and Treatment of Covid-19 – Communication from India and South Africa, IP/C/W/669, 2 October 2020.

dogma of consensus decision-making within the WTO makes substantive changes elusive and shields western countries from serious risks in trade policy-setting.

The reaction to this stalemate, in institutional terms, has consisted of what has been theorized as 'regime shifting',[41] that is, opposing states moving the political debate to friendlier organizations for the purpose of contesting and weakening the 'hard law' of TRIPS. The WHO has been an organization of choice for such purpose; middle-income countries such as Brazil, India and South Africa have successfully built coalitions and pushed for 'soft' normative or policy instruments challenging the primacy of intellectual property rights, reviewing holistically the whole medicines cycle, insisting on transparency for pricing and patent landscapes, and exploring a range of options moving beyond sole reliance on patents and exclusivity rights. A prime example of this tactical shift is the 2008 Global Strategy and Plan of Action on Health, Innovation and Intellectual Property, that took four years of difficult negotiations, remains partly unimplemented and under review and was used as a political resource as much as an operative tool for the WHO and states alike.[42] A similar role has been played by the General Assembly and the Human Rights Council in their resolutions calling for equitable access to medicines either generally or in the context of the HIV/AIDS pandemic.[43] An important policy statement in this direction is provided by target 3.B of Sustainable Development Goal 3. The UN Secretary-General also played a controversial role in this field, by convening on his own initiative in 2015 a High-Level Panel on Access to Medicines that framed the problem in an unqualified manner as a matter of 'patents versus lives'.[44] This fragmented governance and functional landscape has facilitated a persistent policy stalemate on such an important aspect of global health. The multiplicity of normative and policy statements has 'softened' the interpretation and implementation of TRIPS but has also 'hardened soft law' and in particular made the

[41] G. Shaffer and M. Pollack, 'Hard and Soft Law', in J. Dunoff and M. Pollack (eds.), *Interdisciplinary Perspectives on International Law and International Relations* (Cambridge University Press, 2013) 197, 212.

[42] WHO Global Strategy and Plan of Action on Public Health, Innovation and Intellectual Property, Resolution WHA61.21 (Annex), 24 May 2008.

[43] HRC Resolution A/HRC/RES/17/14, 17 June 2011; Political Declaration on AIDS, UN General Assembly Resolution A/RES/60/262, 2 June 2006.

[44] Report of the United Nations Secretary-General's High-Level Panel on Access to Medicines (2016), www.unsgaccessmeds.org (visited 26 February 2021).

negotiation of broad strategic instruments long and difficult, with one of the paradoxical results being the ritualistic repetition of the same language without any visible policy progress.

Within this fragmented governance landscape (that I can only very summarily and incompletely exemplify within the limits of this chapter), the UN General Assembly has been playing since 2001 an important role in both strengthening the global governance for health discourse and ensuring a measure of policy coherence and division of labour within the UN system. While health-related issues were previously absent from its agenda, it was once again HIV/AIDS – and the WHO's failure in leading the international response – that moved health from the perceived 'technical' environment of WHO to the political level of the UN. With its 2001 Declaration of Commitment on HIV/AIDS and the subsequent five-year cycles of high-level reviews, the General Assembly took over the consolidation of political commitment and policy coordination for the international response to a fundamentally intersectoral problem that transcended a purely public health dimension. By doing so, the General Assembly also explicitly recognized the role of public health in foreign policy and global governance as well as the fact that global health issues increasingly go beyond the limits of public health and the WHO. Since 2001, the General Assembly has adopted resolutions and high-level declarations on the most diverse health questions, from complex and multidimensional problems such as NCD[45] and antimicrobial resistance[46] to narrower public health issues such as universal health coverage[47] and even specific diseases such as tuberculosis.[48] Some of the specific actions taken by the General Assembly are remarkable from a global health governance perspective and signal a trend that partially removes such governance from the WHO. In the case of HIV/AIDS and tuberculosis, for example, the Assembly has consolidated national commitments at a higher

[45] Political declaration of the High-level Meeting of the General Assembly on the Prevention and Control of Non-communicable Diseases, A/RES/66/2, 19 September 2011, subject also in this case to a cycle of periodic reviews.

[46] Political Declaration of the High-Level Meeting of the General Assembly on Antimicrobial Resistance, A/RES/71/3, 5 October 2016.

[47] Political Declaration of the High-level Meeting on Universal Health Coverage 'Universal Health Coverage: Moving Together to Build a Healthier World', A/RES/74/2, 10 October 2019.

[48] Political declaration of the High-Level Meeting of the General Assembly on the fight against tuberculosis, A/RES/73/3, 10 October 2018.

governmental level subject to periodic reporting and review requirements. In the case of antimicrobial resistance, the Assembly recognized the WHO's 2015 action plan as the 'blueprint' for international response and thus gave it a political endorsement that the WHA is arguably unable to provide. Still in the resolution on antimicrobial resistance as well as in the declaration on NCDs, the General Assembly divided labour and assigned implementation tasks to the WHO, FAO and World Organization for Animal Health, respectively. Even considering the non-hierarchical relations between the UN and other international organizations, including within the UN system, this approach signals a form of centralization and rationalization in global governance for health as a countertrend to the prevailing fragmentation.

12.5 The Institutional Complexification of Global Health Governance

As hinted in the introduction, the institutional landscape of global health governance has expanded beyond international organizations since the end of the twentieth century and has seen the emergence or increasing prominence of other international actors claiming a direct governance role unmediated from governmental legitimation: political and functional networks, public-private partnerships, non-state actors such as multinational corporation as well as philanthropic foundations (first and foremost the Bill and Melinda Gates Foundation) and hybrid standard-setting institutions such as the ISO.

While we can distinguish the origins, functions and impact of various groups and interests, a general explanation for this increasing complexity is, as noted above, the centrality and political prominence of health as a crucial input, output and indicator of other global agendas such as economic development, security, human rights, sustainable development and the management of globalization. The political and institutional dynamics shaping those agendas carry over into global health governance with particular regard to its participants. They are also coupled with equally significant structural and institutional developments as by-products of globalization: first, a relative retreat of the state as the sole source of authority and legitimacy – very visible in public health – and the increasing importance of non-state actors filling that void at national and international level. The second development is the disillusionment with the capacity of existing international organizations to effectively address stubborn developmental and societal problems and to bring to the table new stakeholders given their state-centred and vertical structure. This mistrust particularly affected the WHO that was emerging from a decade of challenges and setbacks at the end of the 1990s, and that had just lost the leadership in the fight against HIV/AIDS with the creation of UNAIDS. Third, the expansion of networked governance involving both public and private actors through forms of voluntary multi-stakeholder initiatives with substantial normative and policy impact.

All these actors aimed at filling what they perceived as gaps in global health governance or addressing systemic failures in the pharmaceutical market and the set of international rules supporting it. There was an emphasis across such an expanded governance landscape on the delivery of global public goods and the exercise of forms of stewardship to harmonize fragmented or uncoordinated areas of regulation and policy. In so doing, however, some of the initiatives characterizing this trend have added to the fragmentation, lack of coordination and competition that characterizes global health governance. From an institutional perspective, the emphasis was on voluntary and informal forms of organization, both to reduce transaction costs and facilitate both entry and exit as well as to stay away from the institutional model of 'classic' international organizations. The main exceptions are financing institutions for reasons of proper financial management and accountability.

An interesting example of voluntary trans-governmental network of a public nature is the International Conference of Drug Regulatory Authorities (ICDRA). The ICDRA is a voluntary forum of national drug regulatory authorities supported and convened by the WHO that has been meeting since 1980 on a biennial basis.[49] The ICDRA provides a platform for exchange of information and collaboration on issues of common concern to drug regulators, in particular given the increasing sophistication and complexity of the pharmaceutical market. As noted on its web page, '[t]he ICDRAs have been instrumental in guiding regulatory authorities, WHO and interested stakeholders and in determining priorities for action in national and international regulation of medicines, vaccines, biomedicines and herbals'. There is no doubt about the impact of this

[49] See www.who.int/medicines/areas/quality_safety/regulation_legislation/icdra/en/ (visited 26 February 2021).

voluntary and informal forum on national practices and increased transboundary harmonization.

Another important example is the Global Outbreak Alert and Response Network (GOARN), a voluntary network of over 270 institutions and other networks, convened by the WHO in 2000 for the purpose of providing 'technical support to WHO Member States experiencing a human health emergency due to various threats including disease outbreaks, food safety, chemical toxins, zoonosis, natural and manmade disasters'.[50] GOARN has played an invaluable role in supporting the WHO's emergency functions, given the gross disproportion between the level of demand and available resources. While loosely overseen by a Steering Committee and coordinated by the WHO Secretariat, GOARN is composed of a wide range of institutions and networks[51] that allow rapid deployment of human and technical resources and provide capacity building for local responders. Its highly networked model relies on self-organization by participating institutions and networks, that implement requests through their respective operating procedures rather than through a blueprint prescribed by the WHO.

It is ironic that the ICDRA incubated a more controversial experience of networked governance dedicated to harmonizing pharmaceutical safety, efficacy and quality standards to facilitate regulatory approval and international trade while protecting patients. The International Council for Harmonization of Technical Requirements for Pharmaceuticals for Human Use (ICH)[52] was initially established in 1990 as an unincorporated association of drug regulators and representative of the pharmaceutical industry from the then European Community, Japan and the USA, with public and private members enjoying the same authority for the adoption of harmonizing guidelines on important issues such as clinical trials and good manufacturing practices. The global spillover of the regulatory activities of a network that covers up to 85 per cent of the innovative pharmaceutical market generated criticism as a form of disguised protectionism through the introduction of regulatory standards unreasonably high and

[50] See https://extranet.who.int/goarn/ (visited 26 February 2021).

[51] Participants in GOARN range from Médecins sans Frontières, the African Field Epidemiology Network and the German Bundeswehr Institute of Microbiology to the Chinese Center for Disease Control and Prevention and the European Center for Disease Prevention and Control.

[52] See www.ich.org/ (visited 26 February 2021).

unachievable by developing countries. This legitimacy challenge was coupled by a threat from manufacturers of generic medicines and active pharmaceutical ingredients to adopt competing standards. Those reactions led the ICH in turn to substantially reform its governance in 2016, formalize its status into a Swiss non-profit corporation, open itself up to participation by a broader range of actors and establish the primacy of public regulators over corporate actors.[53]

The most visible and consequential aspect of these governance developments is the proliferation and (relative) success since the late 1990s of public–private partnerships (PPP). While health is not the only policy field where public and private actors have congregated into voluntary multistakeholder initiatives, it has been one of the main terrains of experimentation together with environment and education. The concept of PPP has been used in many different contexts with different understandings and functions. It has acquired a more institutionalized meaning in the field of health because of the relative consistency of a range of approaches, structures, purposes and participation.[54]

The proliferation of health PPPs mostly occurred between 1998 and 2008, a period that Jon Liden, adviser to former WHO DG Brundtland, defined as the 'grand decade for global health'[55] that lasted until the 2008 financial crisis put an end to new expensive multilateral experiments. Lidén notes insightfully that each new initiative knocked down metaphorical governance walls that created an ever-increasing space for new initiatives; that dynamic also shows the perceived need for innovative forms of governance to address old problems.[56] Three main groups of actors pushed or catalyzed the creation of health PPPs: political leaders, in particular from western European countries; activist organizations that saw in these

[53] A. Berman, 'The Role of Domestic Administrative Law in the Accountability of Informal International Lawmaking: The Case of the ICH', in J. Pauwelyn, R. Wessel and J. Wouters (eds.), *Informal International Lawmaking* (Oxford University Press, 2012) 468.

[54] Liliana Andonova defines them as 'voluntary agreements between public actors (IOs, states, or substate public authorities) and nonstate actors (nongovernmental organizations, companies, foundations, etc.) on a set of governance objectives and norms, rules, practices, or implementation procedures and their attainment across multiple jurisdictions and levels of governance'. L. Andonova, *Governance Entrepreneurs: International Organizations and the Rise of Global Public-Private Partnerships* (Cambridge University Press, 2017) 2.

[55] J. Lidén, *The Grand Decade for Global Health: 1998–2008* (London: Chatham House, 2013).

[56] *Ibid.*, 5.

new initiatives an unparalleled opportunity for shaping the agenda and raising the voice of the 'real stakeholders'; and senior executives in the WHO, UNICEF and World Bank. Liliana Andonova has dubbed these groups 'governance entrepreneurs', political actors seeking institutional changes and exploiting windows of opportunity brought by the symbolism of the new millennium and the systemic problems mentioned above.[57]

What is apparently surprising is that many of the PPPs in question were incubated or actively promoted by the same international organizations, in particular the WHO, whose alleged failures were the motivation for these new initiatives and with whom the latter were competing for governance space, funding and political attention. Even though tensions and rivalries are inevitable, the emergence of PPPs is largely endogenous to the multilateral system rather than an attempt to undermine it. The WHO is linked to health PPPs through a complex web of relations: as one of the governance entrepreneurs behind their creation, as a member of their governance, as a technical partner and at times as 'host' and provider of the secretariat of non-incorporated partnerships. That role can be explained in part by the role of WHO health economists that promoted a vision of health as an economic and developmental issue requiring new forms of governance. In part, however, it represents an effort by the WHO to remain relevant in a rapidly changing political environment; instead of seeing PPPs as unwanted rivals, it framed them as complementary partners or even as sources of funding.

Most health PPPs cluster in three broad groups from a functional perspective:[58] the first group aims at mobilizing and providing additional financial resources in innovative ways, tapping into the vastly increased public and philanthropic investments in health. The most prominent partnerships in this group are the Global Fund to fight AIDS, Tuberculosis and Malaria (Global Fund), the GAVI Alliance on immunization (GAVI), UNITAID and the more recent Coalition for Epidemic Preparedness Innovations (CEPI) focusing on vaccine development. The second group addresses one of the worst failures of global health governance, that is, the inability of the pharmaceutical market to produce new affordable medicines against neglected diseases that disproportionately affect poor

[57] Andonova, *Governance Entrepeneurs*, 21.

[58] G. L. Burci, 'Public/Private Partnerships in the Public Health Sector', (2009) 6 *International Organizations Law Review* 359, 373.

countries and populations and do not generate much profit for manufacturing companies. The PPPs falling in this group are often referred to as 'product development partnerships' since they aim in different ways at facilitating the development and introduction of new health products rather than providing funds. They include the Medicines for Malaria Venture (MMV), the Drugs for Neglected Diseases Initiatives (DNDI), the International AIDS Vaccine Initiative and the Foundation for Innovative New Diagnostics (FIND). PPPs in the third group coordinate the actions of diverse partners around diseases not receiving the required level of political attention and investments, raise awareness about them and advocate in favour of particular interventions. Some of them act like social mobilization initiatives and consequentially have a very open structure, being open to participation even by individuals. This group includes the Global Alliance for Improved Nutrition (GAIN), the Partnership for Maternal, Newborn and Child-health (PMNCH), the Roll-Back Malaria Partnership (RBM) and the Stop TB Partnership. It is not possible to review the foregoing given the limits of this chapter. I will limit myself to some more details on financing partnerships given their direct involvement in supporting the international response to the COVID-19 pandemic and in particular the development and equitable allocation of vaccines.

With the exception of UNITAID which is hosted by the WHO and protected under its legal status, the financing PPPs mentioned above have been established as non-profit corporations under national law. However, the Global Fund and GAVI have been granted by the Swiss government the status of international organizations and enjoy privileges and immunities. Both are invited as observers to the WHA and the Global Fund is an observer at the UN General Assembly. Their legal status is therefore not without ambiguities. The need to secure protection for its funds outside Switzerland has even led the Global Fund membership to adopt a convention on its privileges and immunities, which entered into force for ten states in 2019.[59] This unprecedented development, which so far has escaped the attention of international law scholars, blurs even more the differences between the formal legal status of the Global Fund and its role and perception. It is not exaggerated to state that highly institutionalized PPPs such as the Global Fund represent a new type of international

[59] See www.theglobalfund.org/en/news/2019-04-17-global-fund-agreement-on-privileges-and-immunities-enters-into-force/ (visited 4 February 2021).

organization. UNITAID raises different legal issues for WHO as its host, since the latter is extending its legal status and immunities to a separate governance structure linked to the organization by the provision of its secretariat and of administrative services on a contractual basis.[60] The PPPs in question have a multi-stakeholder horizontal structure, with governments, civil society organizations, philanthropic foundations and industry representatives participating on an equal footing. GAVI brings this concept to the extreme, with nine out of twenty-seven board seats allocated to independent individuals appointed in light of their professional position and contributions. GAVI and the Global Fund have implemented governance participation in the form of constituencies in order to keep their respective boards to a reasonable size while promoting inclusiveness. Constituencies are voluntary and self-organized groupings of members that share a single board seat.[61] This arrangement injects one more layer of voluntarism in PPPs already based on voluntary participation and administrative arrangements.

Financing partnerships operate in very different ways both upstream and downstream; while the Global Fund relies on contributions from its members, GAVI has also engaged in innovative experiments such as establishing a separate entity to float bonds on the financial market backed by sovereign pledges from some of its donor countries.[62] UNITAID is partly funded through an airline tax instituted by France and a few other countries as a fiscally neutral way to mobilize substantial additional resources. On the downstream side, the Global Fund and UNITAID follow a result-based approach with tight and sometimes complex monitoring of goals and targets; GAVI operates on a need basis without specific performance demands, but requires the establishment of a national coordinating committee including civil society representatives to ensure oversight, buy-in and broad stakeholder representation. GAVI has been experimenting with 'advance market commitment', whereby donors pledge to manufacturers that bring new vaccines to market a guaranteed price for a defined quantity and thus greatly reduce their risks.[63] UNITAID addresses the same three

[60] Burci, 'Public/Private Partnerships', 377.

[61] Those of the Global Fund Board are listed at www.theglobalfund.org/en/board/constituencies/ (visited on 20 December 2021).

[62] See https://iffim.org/ (visited 4 February 2021).

[63] See www.gavi.org/vaccineswork/what-advance-market-commitment-and-how-could-it-help-beat-covid-19 (visited 26 February 2021).

diseases as the Global Fund as well as hepatitis C but does not make direct grants to governments or other recipients, instead financing projects by partners such as UNICEF and the Bill Clinton Foundation. The WHO participates in all these PPPs either as an observer or a full member, for example in GAVI. In the latter case, the fact that GAVI is the largest funder of the WHO's immunization programme would normally constitute a conflict of interests. However, the philosophy underlying many partnerships reverses these governance principles and focuses instead on the comparative advantage of the various participants and their joint commitment to pursue a common goal.

12.6 Conclusions

Global health governance has been defined as a 'complex adaptive system' where different actors have emerged or evolved depending on political priorities and unfulfilled needs and functions.[64] These actors, only some of which could be included in this chapter, compete or cooperate with one another across multiple dimensions and increasingly compete for substantial but limited funding. In the absence of an accepted overarching framework defining roles and complementarities, this has produced fragmentation but also adaptation and innovation. The WHO, despite the periodic criticism against its structural weaknesses or ineffectiveness, remains in many respects the central organization in the health governance landscape. It suffers, however, from some significant systemic challenges, in particular its inadequate and inflexible funding as well as its inability to coordinate other actors. While other sectoral organizations may expand their specific role in the health field, for example the international financial institutions, the UN may be emerging as a political steward of disparate interests and a legitimizer of policies and strategies adopted by other institutions. While the informalization of global governance and the presence of hybrid bodies may be an irreversible phenomenon, it is a fact that the 'long wave' of public-private partnerships – at least in the health field – may have ended. The freewheeling experimentation of the end of the millennium may have shown the sustainability and resilience of a narrow range of structural and functional models, that tend

[64] Moon, 'Global Health', 13.

to become more institutionalized and similar to international organizations. The willingness of many actors to experiment and innovate to face new challenges has been confirmed during the COVID-19 pandemic. In the space of only a few months from the onset of the pandemic, the WHO, World Bank and the leading partnerships established with donor support the 'ACT Accelerator', a platform of remarkable institutional sophistication to coordinate development and allocation of COVID-19 'global public goods', in particular vaccines through the so-called COVAX facility.[65] Different actors assumed the lead on issues where they could bring comparative advantage and complementarity, and the WHO provided institutional space and normative functions, for example setting the principles for the global distribution of COVID-19 vaccines.[66] Even though the success of the initiative may be altogether moderate when compared with initial expectations, such spontaneous congregation and coordination is unprecedented and can offer a model for future complex intersectoral challenges, for example climate change and anti-microbial resistance.

[65] See www.who.int/initiatives/act-accelerator/about (visited 26 February 2021).
[66] WHO Concept for Fair Access and Equitable Allocation of COVID-19 Health Products.

13 Energy Provision

Volker Roeben

13.1 Concept and Problematique

Energy, in the broad sense of all sources and forms of energy, fossil, renewable, electricity and fuels, is a latecomer to the field of international organization. The twin principles of permanent sovereignty of producer states over their natural energy resources and the sovereignty of consumer states over their energy mix seemed to remove this matter from the realm of international law and to allocate it to domestic law. The organizational architecture reflects this. Different from other functional systems such as health or trade, there is no single, central international organization of universal membership for the energy sector. It is decentralized-plural. This plurality has historically developed. It has its origin in producer and consumer states organizing their cooperation in select membership organizations. Organizations and institutional arrangements deal with international pipelines and energy networks, fossil fuel resources and nuclear energy, and only recently with renewable energy. These are typically limited membership organizations which often escape public scrutiny. This layer of the organizational 'geology' of energy was marked by an antagonism for which the Organization of Petroleum Exporting Countries (OPEC) and the International Energy Agency (IEA) stood and to an extent still stand, serving the perspective of national energy security. The picture of antagonistic interests and a plural, decentralized organizational architecture is changing fast, though. This chapter describes how international institutions have expanded their hold on the provision of energy. It is about change in international organization, considered through the lens of energy provision.

Provision of energy has only recently arisen as a common concern of the international community of states. This concern is a focus of UN Agenda 2030 and the 2015 Sustainable Development Goals.[1] Goal 7 defines the priorities for the provision of energy. It is complemented by Goal 13 on protecting the climate, demanding the limiting of carbon emissions and hence fossil fuel consumption. The goal, which is reconfirmed by a range of international and regional strategy documents, has the strong normative impetus of a universal social welfare objective. Moving beyond the hitherto dominating rationale of security of supply (in oil and gas) defined from the perspectives of producer and of consumer states, the goal embodies the idea that all have access to sustainable, reliable and affordable energy, which is broken down into semi-quantified targets on renewable energy sources (RES) and energy efficiency. This means a pledge that energy be reliably available for consumption by all individuals in all states *and* that there should be a dynamic substitution in the sources of energy from fossil to RES and hence electrification. The international community of states assumes responsibility for designing a governance scheme covering the global value chain of energy and coordination between all states – producers and consumers – to achieve those goals. This responsibility has been acted upon in the 2020 global crisis and the unprecedented fall in the demand for energy. This collective responsibility complements the responsibility of each state towards its people to provide it with energy. Responsibility for the actual delivery of such energy rests iwith state-owned enterprises, private multinationals and generally the private sector in liberalized regimes. It is widely recognized that energy today is in transition globally, increasing the share of renewables and electricity and new kinds of energy in final consumption over fossil fuels, while at the same time meeting the growing demand for energy worldwide. This transition is not a market response. It is primarily driven by states' collective policies and evidences their effectiveness.

This common concern leads to a realignment of the extant decentralized-plural architecture, indicating autonomy and agency. The analytic device to make this realignment visible is the meta-norm. Meta-norms provide institutional actors with orientation in the management of complex governance schemes. The goal of sustainable energy has emerged as such a master-norm for this architecture and is driving a realignment across the organizational set-up. This

[1] UN Doc. A/RES/70/1: Transforming our world: the 2030 Agenda for Sustainable Development.

realignment is the result of separate autonomous processes responsive to the normative impetus of the meta-norm for energy provision in the twenty-first century. In these processes, each organization reinterprets its mandates, develops novel functions and makes available suitable instruments to achieve these. This has affected extant specialist organizations, has brought in new representative institutions of global reach, and has led to deepened cooperation on energy policies. What emerges is a much more streamlined architecture, that provides for infrastructure-based trade, standards and transboundary regulation. Eventually, this realignment is leading to institutionalized governance of the entire energy value-cycle, from generation through transportation to the consumption of energy.

As part of this realignment, a function of global governance of energy has been forming, making use of modern institutional developments and institutional models. These ensure representation in the decision-making of all or most relevant states on how to balance supply and demand in the transition to a sustainable and reliable global energy system. Representative institutions, the G7/G20 and the meeting of Parties to the Paris Agreement have now assumed universal governance functions for the global energy economy and the transition away from fossil fuels. Under the auspices of ECOSOC (i.e. the UN's Economic and Social Council), the High-Level Political Forum (HLPF) reviews the high-level SDGs and their implementation to this effect. The specialist international organizations become mandated with initiating such action and then also with follow-up and implementation. This leads to accountability of states for national energy policies. The mode of operation and the instruments that international organizations have in the energy sector have evolved to this effect. This mode aims to strategically direct national policy and law-making, with instruments deployed ranging from decision-making with recommendatory or binding quality to expert advice to best practice exchanges. The interlocutors are not just governments but also the private sector.

Regionalization is a third trend. Regional organizations, such as the European Energy Union, provide for the comprehensive institutionalization of energy regulation within transboundary energy markets and with interconnected infrastructure grids.

13.2 The Decentralized Architecture of Energy

The historically evolved organizational architecture of energy is decentralized and plural. It covers segments of the energy value-chain primarily in oil and gas and contains a range of organizational models.[2]

International trade in energy is necessarily bound to cross-border infrastructure, setting it apart from the trade in other commodities. Transboundary pipelines are essential infrastructure that transport oil and gas from the centres of production to the centres of consumption. This infrastructure is subject to a multilayered regime. This regime first comprises intergovernmental agreements (IGAs) on the construction and operation of the pipeline. Such IGAs are bilateral, serially bilateral or multilateral depending on the number of states through which the pipeline passes. An example of the latter is the Trans-Adriatic pipeline project that forms part of the Southern Gas Corridor transporting gas from the Black Sea to Europe.[3] Other pipeline agreements regulate the construction and operation of cross-border pipelines in the territories of the contracting states in general, setting forth the principles of non-discrimination with regard to their use and of non-interference with the flow. The IGA sets out the basic obligations of the sponsoring states and also the applicable international law, in particular the international law of the environment, including the treaty and customary obligations on environmental impact assessments for transboundary projects.[4] In addition, host government agreements under domestic law may be concluded between the state and the pipeline operator, the unit that actually runs the pipeline, which may be a company under foreign domestic law with multiple shareholders. Finally, transport through a pipeline usually is subject to contract

[2] K. Meyer, 'The Architecture of International Energy Governance', (2012) 106 *Proceedings of the American Society of International Law* 389; R. Leal-Arcas and A. Filis, 'The Fragmented Governance of the Global Energy Economy: A Legal-Institutional Analysis', (2013) 6 *Journal of World Energy Law and Business* 348.

[3] C. Vlachtis, 'Trans-Adriatic Pipeline Projects – Agreements and Energy Charter Model Texts', (2016) 38 *Comparative Law Yearbook of International Business* 185.

[4] D. Azaria, *Treaties on Transit of Energy via Pipelines and Countermeasures* (Oxford University Press, 2015). Submarine pipelines are governed by the law of the sea: see M. Roggenkamp, 'Petroleum Pipelines in the North Sea: Questions of Jurisdiction and Practical Status', (1998) 16 *Journal of Energy and Natural Resources Law* 92.

between the pipeline operator and the owner of the oil or gas.[5] The framework for pipelines, then, may be labelled as hybrid, comprised of an international and a domestic law element.[6] The sector lacks transparency as IGAs and host state agreements may not be published. International organizations have a role in providing harmonized and transparent standards and realigning the framework with the changing norms of global energy. The Energy Charter Secretariat to this effect has developed model IGAs and host state agreements. These models serve as standards and orientation for governments and pipeline entrepreneurs in designing the law – they are not binding themselves. While the 2006 model agreements[7] were largely designed to be enabling, the 2019 revision places a much greater emphasis on managing pipelines in a sustainable manner. Pipelines are only one part of the global energy infrastructure, though. Both oil and unconventional fossil energy sources such as LNG (i.e. liquefied natural gas) require maritime transportation that is governed by the International Maritime Organization (IMO). This maritime infrastructure of oil supertankers does not only transport but also stores oil. That maritime capacity adds to terrestrial storage capacity. Traders charter tankers for this purpose to mitigate temporal volatility in demand of oil. This insulates somewhat Brent crude, the international benchmark for the oil price, from turning negative, which would have negative consequences for the stability of the global oil market.

Energy is an internationally traded commodity. This applies to the traditional fossil fuels of oil and natural gas, but also to non-conventional (shale) oil and gas in liquified form. The production, trade and consumption of conventional oil rests on three organizations, the Organization of the Petroleum Exporting Countries (OPEC), the International Energy Agency (IEA) that organize antagonistic interests and the International Energy Forum (IEF) that seeks to bridge those interests.[8] OPEC is the organization

[5] K. Talus, S. Looper and S. Otillar, 'Lex Petrolea and the Internationalization of Petroleum Agreements: Focus on Host Government Contracts', (2012) 5 *Journal of World Energy Law and Business* 181.

[6] See Energy Charter Secretariat, Introductory Note to the Second Edition of the Intergovernmental and Host Government Model Agreements of the Energy Charter Secretariat, 2006, paras. 20 and 29.

[7] Model Host Government Agreement [2006]; Model Intergovernmental Agreement [2006].

[8] Further J. Colgan, R. Keohane and T. Van de Graaf, 'Punctuated Equilibrium in the Energy Regime Complex', (2012) 7 *Review of International Organisations* 117.

of oil-producing states, with a secretariat in Vienna. It was founded in 1960 by Iran, Iraq, Kuwait, Saudi Arabia and Venezuela. The organization now comprises the largest producer states on the Arab peninsula, in South America, Africa and South East Asia.[9] Membership requires a substantial output of crude oil.[10] OPEC is focused on the price of crude oil on the world market. The objective is a sustainable price that will not lead to a premature substitution by other energy sources. To this effect, OPEC observes the market and can intervene through coordinated production decisions, in particular production cuts. It may also discuss a preferred oil price level, as a way the group can guide market expectations. The organization has few formal powers: resolutions are recommendatory and cannot be enforced. It rests on the member states using their domestic powers to implement. The actions of OPEC are implemented by the national oil companies of the member states. The mode of operation is unanimity and consensus. Saudi Arabia, by far the biggest producer by scale and impact of its production decisions, carries more weight both in decision-making and effective implementation. OPEC's coverage is not comprehensive, though: important producers remain outside its formal membership circle, including the UK, Norway, the Netherlands and in particular Russia, China and the USA.[11] The response has been to seek to institutionalize cooperation with those non-members. OPEC+ was started in 2017 as a six-month agreement on production targets but worked for almost two years. Russia is the largest producer of that extended grouping. Under the 2019 open-ended cooperation agreement OPEC and non-OPEC are to work together to bring production up or down. It does not have fixed production targets, but foresees regular coordination and information sharing, inter alia on supply and demand, and what kind of intervention is needed, if any, and when. It

[9] Qatar (1961), Indonesia (1962), Libya (1962), the United Arab Emirates (1967), Algeria (1969), Nigeria (1971), Ecuador (1973), Gabon (1975), Angola (2007), Equatorial Guinea (2017) and Congo (2018). Indonesia suspended its membership in January 2009, reactivated it again in January 2016, but decided to suspend its membership once more at the 171st Meeting of the OPEC Conference on 30 November 2016.

[10] The Statute stipulates that 'any country with a substantial net export of crude petroleum, which has fundamentally similar interests to those of Member Countries, may become a Full Member of the Organization, if accepted by a majority of three-fourths of Full Members, including the concurring votes of all Founder Members'. A state that does not meet these requirements may become an associate member admitted under such special conditions as prescribed by the Conference.

[11] K. Hancock and V. Vivoda, 'International Political Economy: A Field Born of the OPEC Crisis Returns to Its Energy Roots', (2014) 1 *Energy Research and Social Science* 206.

has had a mixed record of success and in particular could not prevent a price war in 2020. But it still leaves out other major producers. The rise of non-conventional fossil fuel from shale has, at some point, turned the USA into the largest producer of oil. Others such as Canada have also become important. Different from the conventional situation, the market in these countries is in the hands of a competitive private sector, not of a national oil company.

Organized under the auspices of the Organisation for Economic Co-operation and Development (OECD) and hence assembling developed consumer states, the IEA has originally served to coordinate the response of major economies to shocks in supply. An IEA decision triggers the obligation to release reserve stocks. The IEA constituent document, the International Energy Programme, requires unanimity in the Governing Board for the activation of emergency measures.[12] The IEA has used this power on three occasions, lastly in response to the disruption caused by hurricane Katrina in the USA.

The International Energy Forum (IEF) is the only international organization that brings together producer and consumer states, including China and India, both heavyweight users outside of the IEA membership. A key objective is the provision of neutral and reliable data on energy. Data about oil and gas reserves are notoriously unreliable, with discrepancies between the sources, such as OPEC, IEA and the US Energy Information Administration (EIA). The JODI (Joint Organisation Data Initiative) was launched at the behest of the IEF Ministers in 2001 by six organisations (APEC, Eurostat, the IEA, OLADE, OPEC and the UN Statistics Division) and it is now managed by the IEF. Natural gas has become increasingly important in the energy mix, and it is the favoured substitute for coal and also oil in terms of carbon emissions. However, there is no comparable institutional structure on the producer side. Rather, the framework is set by bilateral IGAs between producer and consumer state governments.

In addition to these intergovernmental organizations, non-governmental organizations (NGOs) have an important function to address deep-seated problems of the sector. The Extractive Industries Transparency Initiative (EITI) is the global standard to promote the open and accountable management of oil, gas and mineral resources. The EITI Standard requires the

12 The IEA constituent treaty, the International Energy Programme (IEP Agreement), requires unanimity in the Governing Board for the activation of emergency measures. It also provides for weighted majority votes on the management of the IEA programme of work and recommendations.

disclosure of information along the extractive industry value chain from the point of extraction, to how revenues make their way through the government and how they benefit the public.

An interesting institutional model concerns the joint development of transboundary resources, particularly but not limited to maritime resources.[13] Joint development has the objective of reaching an efficient outcome that maximizes the social welfare of all states, transcending questions of sovereignty. Such joint development schemes presuppose institutional arrangements that administer the resource as a whole. They come about through the innovative use of non-confrontational dispute settlement mechanisms, as exemplified by the first conciliation under the UN Convention on the Law of Sea between Australia and Timor-Leste.[14]

Nuclear energy is the remit of the International Atomic Energy Agency (IAEA). It is an independent international organization, not a UN agency. Most of its tasks relate to developing a consensus on the safety standards to make nuclear energy safe to use for civilian purposes. Fissile material, minerals extraction and trade remain outside of its purview. This remit and structure of the IAEA is mirrored, regionally, by the European Community for Atomic Energy (Euratom). The European Union is competent to cover trade in the fissile material.

13.3 A Master-Norm of Sustainable Energy and the Realignment of the Institutional Architecture

This rise of a master-norm of sustainable energy has had a profound effect on this historically oil (and nuclear energy)-focused organizational architecture, which has been realigning itself with the novel meta-norm. Klabbers has introduced into that debate that international organizations are inevitably being autonomous through their actions vis-à-vis states or other actors.[15] But

[13] P. Cameron, 'The Rules of Engagement: Developing Cross-Border Petroleum Deposits in the North Sea and the Caribbean', (2006) 55 *International and Comparative Law Quarterly* 559.

[14] V. Roeben and R. Macatangay, 'Conciliation for Transboundary Energy Resources: A Law and Economics Approach', in Keyuan Zou, Shicun Wu and Qiang Ye (eds.), *The 21st Century Maritime Road: Challenges and Opportunities for Asia and Europe* (Abingdon: Routledge, 2019) 179.

[15] J. Klabbers, 'Interminable Disagreement: Reflections on the Autonomy of International Organisations', (2019) 88 *Nordic Journal of International Law* 111.

autonomy also assists in conceptualizing the transformation of the entire organizational architecture for the provision of energy. With the advent of the SDGs that constitute the consensus of states on their cooperation, the international community of states has fixed its priorities for global energy. These goals have a strong normative content, combining the provision of a fundamental human need with environmental, social and economic sustainability. The resulting master-norm of sustainable energy to which all have access has led to an autonomous realignment of the extant architecture. Intensified cooperation of states adds the new layer of institutions to carry forward the intended transition and absorbs an older layer of the fossil fuel age with little or no change to the formal legal bases.

The 2015 and 2017 meetings of IEA Ministerial, the organization's strategic decision-making organ, have laid down a modernization mandate, with three pillars: expanding the IEA's mandate on energy security beyond oil to natural gas and electricity; opening the agency's doors to emerging countries; and turning the IEA into a global clean energy hub, including for energy efficiency.[16] The IEA has added to its historic operational functions important energy-policy design functions and supporting capabilities. The flagship of that function is the Global Energy Outlook, an annual publication now in its most recent 2019 instalment. This Outlook, together with just a handful of others including that of the USA Energy Information Agency, lays out the factual baseline of transition planning.[17] It is not prescriptive but informative, constituting an essential element of transparency and hence accountability. It operates on the basis of scenarios, rather than forecasts. These scenarios have the SDGs and the Paris Agreement as a point of reference. They set out different assumptions about the energy policies and then explain their consequences over a time horizon, and ultimately against the parameter of global temperature rise. In its most recent 2019 edition, the Energy Outlook accordingly sets out three main scenarios. The first is business-as-usual with no change in policy. The second scenario extrapolates the change that will come about because of policies that states have already firmly committed to. The third, sustainable development scenario is normative. It takes the internationally

[16] H. Heubaum and F. Biermann, 'Integrating Global Energy and Climate Governance: The Changing Role of the International Energy Agency', (2015) 87 *Energy Policy* 229.

[17] X. Mu and D. Jena, 'Comparison of Outlooks and Implications for Energy Transition', in P. Cameron, X. Mu and V. Roeben (eds.), *Global Energy Transition* (Oxford: Hart, 2021).

binding objective of the Paris Agreement of limiting the global temperature rise to well below 2°C and charts those energy policies that would be needed to achieve it. This scenario is the clearest manifestation yet of the requisite shift in supply away from fossil fuels. The document's performance is of a normative quality, it is persuasive if not prescriptive for national decision-making. Underpinning this persuasiveness is the robustness and neutrality of the data used and the expertise of its staff in modelling techniques. The IEA's Policies and Measures Database aims at best practice dissemination concerning energy transition. It makes available information on past, existing or planned government policies and measures to reduce greenhouse gas emissions, improve energy efficiency and support the development and deployment of renewables and other clean energy technologies. The IEA has also realigned itself in terms of its membership. The meta-norm demands that organizations adopt a universal perspective on energy provision, rather than one of energy security from the point of view of a limited constituency. Consequently, the IEA has expanded beyond the original OECD circle towards a more universal membership, admittedly as associates rather than full members. This enables it to be representative and hence credible in its universal policy-recommendatory functioning. This enhanced representativeness underpins the agency's functionality in respect of the G20 and G7 as the global energy policy-makers (to be discussed below in Section 13.4). A re-alignment may also take place for OPEC. OPEC is developing a role in supporting its member states in transitioning to a larger share of renewables. This recognizes that the dependence of resource-endowed developing countries on those revenues can only be lessened over time.

Those realignments have been effectuated by the organizations infra-treaty – they have left the constitutive treaty unchanged. The Energy Charter may prove an exception in that the ongoing infra-treaty modernization of the Charter's mandate, functions and operation has entered the stage where parties embark on a re-negotiation of the treaty itself. Energy is now traded on a global market for all its forms whether fossil fuels or electricity, albeit to a different degree. In that market, energy is generated in one state and consumed in another, transported via transboundary infrastructure or vessel. The Energy Charter is the only organization to engage the value-chain of energy, from generation through trade and transit to consumption, comprising all forms of energy, inclusive of electricity, and all sources, including electricity, and also renewables although the textual basis is less clear. The Energy Charter rests on a multilateral treaty (Energy Charter Treaty, ECT). The treaty has three pillars: protection of foreign direct investment in production, rules for transboundary trade and transit in energy and cooperation on all matters including efficiency and environmental protection.[18] The membership comprises producer and consumer states. It now has fifty-one members from Europe, Asia and Africa, although the Russian Federation, one of the original signatories, in 2009 notified the depository of the treaty of its intention not to ratify it, terminating the provisional application of the treaty. This state remains bound, however, under Article 45 ECT to respect the investment protection provisions of the treaty for established investments for another twenty years following the date of termination.

The supreme decision-making body, the Energy Charter Conference, brings together the parties, candidates and observer states to implement and progressively develop the treaty to conform to the priorities of the post-2015 energy era. It has been realigning itself with the meta-norm through the 2015 International Energy Charter. This non-binding declaration modernizes the European Energy Charter, the document that preceded the ECT. Its expertise-based directional work on model agreements now accounts for the shift to environmental sustainability. This modernization process has now also shifted to amending the treaty base and hence the quasi-judicial function that the Energy Charter has acquired. This quasi-judicial function covers generation and hence a segment of the value-chain only, but within these limits it is highly effective. The energy industry is one of the heaviest users of investor-state arbitration to protect typically long-term and capital-intensive, transboundary investments. The ECT is unique in that it sets up a multilateral system of arbitration. Through the treaty, parties give their consent to the arbitration that investors with nationality of another party may institute. The protection standards are the usual: expropriation against compensation, non-discrimination and fair and equal treatment. These provide protection for investments admitted by and made in the host state, but do not open access for investments. They also protect investments in renewable energy projects. The energy transition has brought into focus that this restrains the space for regulatory

[18] T. Wälde (ed.), *The Energy Charter Treaty: An East-West Gateway for Investment and Trade* (London: Kluwer, 1996); Y. Selivanova, 'The Energy Charter and the International Energy Governance', (2012) 3 *European Yearbook of International Economic Law* 307.

change by host states. Treaty change driven by the EU will therefore aim to recognize that a state pursuing a legitimate objective will not trigger compensation obligations and retains discretion concerning which technologies it wishes to subsidize and whether to exit such support policy.

Energy transition is ultimately about decarbonizing the energy economy, and that means the substitution of fossil fuels. Ultimately, all technological offers to decarbonize the global economy – electrification through renewables, hydrogen – depend on the rollout of clean energy technologies at scale and globally.[19] A multi-faceted institutional framework is emerging to support this rollout. The cooperative provision of RES emerged as a novel concern in the 1990s as the potential of solar, wind, tidal and biomass became clearer. An obvious approach would have been to enlarge the mandate of the IEA, but for a number of reasons, states in 2009 decided to set up a new international organisation, the International Renewable Energy Agency (IRENA). The original signatories of the statute are all IEA members. But membership in the organization has expanded to non-OECD states, including China and India, and now is near-universal. The secretariat is based in the United Arab Emirates. The objective is for IRENA to promote rapid, widespread use of RES. The mandate includes promoting the use of all forms of renewable energy. The powers are determined by express text in the constitutive treaty, impliedly if necessary for the fulfilment of the organisation's functions, and by subsequent practice. Under Article IV(A)(1) of the statute, the IRENA Assembly has powers to recommend, but no power to establish legal obligations or targets for RES percentages. IRENA hence has been able to develop operational policies with two initiatives. In 2015, it launched Project Navigator, a new online tool to help develop renewable energy projects. It is designed to facilitate the development of bankable renewable energy projects by making the process more transparent. The second initiative, the Climate Investment Platform, is an online platform to enhance the development and financing of RES projects by pairing project owners with investors, with an initial focus on Africa, Latin America and the Caribbean. It also provides for a process of assessing national legislation.

Expansion of the share in renewables and clean energy policies is not the remit of IRENA alone, but is based on a multifaceted institutional system. The Financing for Development initiative under ECOSOC focuses on

[19] M. Citelli, M. Barassi and K. Belykh, 'Renewable Energy in the International Arena: Legal Aspects and Cooperation', (2014) 2 *Groningen Journal of International Law* 1.

multilateral investment. Clean technology transfer and financing is also the remit of the ECOSOC Forum on Financing for Development Follow-up (FfD Forum), an intergovernmental process with universal participation mandated to review the Addis Ababa Action Agenda (Addis Agenda) and other financing for development outcomes and the means of implementation of the Sustainable Development Goals. There is furthermore horizontal cooperation under the UN Framework Convention on Climate Change (UNFCCC) on clean energy. The Green Climate Fund and the UNFCC Clean Development Mechanism predominantly deal with such projects.

Finally, in a realignment with the meta-norm, flexible institutional models are forming for co-operation on transboundary electricity cables. There are the so-called interconnectors subject to organizational arrangements on a bilateral basis. But these cables can also build a large-scale grid infrastructure connecting several states. Such grids are more cost-effective the more states and markets they connect. These grids are necessarily subject to international organizational arrangements, which are, in contradistinction from pipelines, multilateral. An example is the North Sea Offshore Grid Initiative.[20] It brings together the littoral states of the Northern Seas, setting up an informal organizational structure of a steering group and several working groups for planning and implementation, including cost-sharing. The legal regime integrates international law, EU law and domestic laws. Similar forms of transboundary cooperation are developed in other parts of the world, for instance in Asia since 1990 there has been power trade in the Greater Mekong Subregion. China's Global Energy Interconnection (GEI) initiative for a global energy grid backbone by 2070 involves ultra-high-voltage transmission lines strung across vast distances and smart grid technology tapping large-scale renewable power sources. In 2016, GEI signed a collaboration memorandum of understanding with the UN Economic and Social Commission for Asia and the Pacific (UNESCAP).

13.4 Governing the Global Energy Economy

Again responding to the new master-norm, the most significant addition to the organizational architecture is a governance function, that is, collective

[20] V. Roeben, 'Governing Shared Offshore Electricity Infrastructure in the Northern Seas', (2013) 62 *International and Comparative Law Quarterly* 839.

decision-making on the energy value chain. To an extent, this function is assumed, within the UN system, by ECOSOC, which has always been concerned with energy. Under the auspices of ECOSOC, the HLPF reviews the high-level SDGs and their implementation to this effect. Energy is a horizontal matter and so UN programmes and specialized agencies address energy indirectly, from the perspectives of the environment (United Nations Environment Programme [UNEP]), development (United Nations Development Programme [UNDP]), and industrial innovation (United Nations Industrial Development Organisation [UNIDO]). UN-Energy is the mechanism for inter-agency collaboration in the field of energy specifically to support member states in their transition to sustainable energy. It is a subsidiary of the Chief Executives Board that coordinates UN bodies on social, economic and related matters, and reports to the High-Level Committee on Programmes. Former UN Secretary-General Ban Ki-moon launched the Sustainable Energy for All initiative in 2011 specific to advance on universal energy access through cooperation on best practices. It is now a non-governmental organization under Austrian law with close links with the UN under a relationship agreement and with UN agencies; the CEO acts as Co-Chair of UN-Energy. SE4All institutionally supports the coalition for energy transition that the 2019 UN Climate Summit adopted. This coalition of interested states and UN agencies as well as the World Bank Group is led by Denmark and Ethiopia. It will report to the next summit on deliverables including investment and public-private partnerships.

The UN Security Council has also come to address the international security dimension of energy. It has endorsed the Joint Comprehensive Programme of Action (JCPOA) and lifted sanctions.[21] While not a specialized UN agency, the IAEA has cooperated with the UN in the verification of the JCPOA (agreed between the USA, EU, China, Russia and Iran) under which Iran stops enriching uranium in exchange for a lifting of economic sanctions. The USA, when withdrawing from JCPOA, did not allege that the treaty had not been complied with or that verification had failed, but rather repudiated the basis and risk assessment underlying the treaty. The Security Council could in the future become more active and declare situations of serious energy shortages a threat to international security and call for international cooperation to address

[21] See also Nigel White, Chapter 14 in this volume.

them, following the precedent it has set for global health in cases of epidemics.

A global governance function for the energy economy has effectively been entrusted not to a formal international organization, but to a looser institutional set-up under the control of states. The international climate action regime anchored in the UNFCCC has emerged as the top-level driver of universal policy and lawmaking for states' energy policy, and hence the governance of energy. Adopted in 2015 to concretize and operationalize the UNFCCC, as well as SDG 13, the Paris Agreement assumes this function because it sets a legally binding objective for permissible anthropogenic temperature rise. The objective is to hold the temperature rise to well below 2°C and ideally to 1.5°C. This translates into a headline obligation to cut carbon emissions. But those cuts are not possible without a shift away from fossil fuels, which currently account for more than 60 per cent of global emissions. It is hence driving the rate and scale of deployment of clean energy technologies and electrification and thus of the fundamental shift in both supply and demand of energy. The spread of 0.5°C in the temperature rise implies radically different prescriptions of the speed and scale of decarbonizing the energy economy, with the lower objective requiring much faster and deeper changes to energy supply. The international climate regime also establishes a dynamic bottom-up and top-down lawmaking process based on Nationally Determined Contributions (NDCs) of each party and collective stocktaking. The stocktake leads to international objectives that must then be met through national implementing action, which can in turn be evaluated for aggregate progress against the objective.

The concretization of the temperature objective within the said spread and governance of the collective pathway of decarbonization is in the power of the Conference of the Parties to the UNFCCC serving as the meeting of the parties of the Paris Agreement (CMA). The meeting of the Parties receives the NDCs, it evaluates those in the Global Stocktake and it will issue any recommendations. It also provides the rules that harmonize NDCs such as the so-called Paris Rulebook. These and other rules concretize and make operational the treaty provisions couched at a high level of abstraction, which are directional rather than operational. Those rules are laid down formally in decisions of the meeting of parties. Even though the precise legal status of these CMA decisions may remain a matter for debate, they do have some legal value. Arguably, through these decisions, the Parties are authentically interpreting the Agreement within the meaning of Article 31(3)(a) of the Vienna Convention on the Law of Treaties. This view is supported by the conclusions of the International Law Commission on that provision.[22] As a consequence, obligations are now to be seen in the light of the decisions, and a party effectively must comply with them to satisfy its treaty obligations. This high-level governance by the meeting of parties is supported by the climate regime fund to bring about transformational change to the current fossil fuel base, through financing of disruptive projects. It is governed by a board of five experts elected in their personal capacity. The voting procedure of unanimity has been the subject of debate, as it will slow the process of decision-making. In October 2018, the board agreed on the first replenishment of the funds' resources, to be provided by the developed states parties to the Convention.

The interlocutors of this regime are not just states, but also the large multinationals that are dominating the field. It is true that the global oil market has evolved considerably since the 1970s when OPEC and the IEA were established. Physical trading comprises now both long-term bilateral supply agreements and spot deals and term contracts, backed by a deep, highly liquid futures market. Nevertheless the supply side remains in the hands of a few private international oil companies and state-owned companies in resource-endowed countries. The meta-norm seeks to directly address the conduct of these international companies, and not just indirectly through the home or host state, which is the traditional mode of operation of international law. International oil companies are indeed realigning themselves autonomously with the meta-norm, adopting corporate net zero carbon targets (BP, Shell), and therewith assume responsibility for sustainable energy. They will mirror targets and timetables for carbon neutrality adopted by states. This is ultimately grounded in developments in international law to extend human rights and sustainability beyond states. The UN Guiding Principles on Business and Human Rights lay the foundations within the framework of human rights, by identifying the secondary responsibility of companies to respect, protect and promote human rights, in addition to the primary responsibility of states.[23] The UN Global Compact creates voluntary commitments for signatory companies to respect and

[22] P. Minnerop, 'The Legal Effect of the 'Paris Rulebook' under the Doctrine of Treaty Interpretation', in Cameron, Mu and Roeben (eds.), *Global Energy Transition*.

[23] UN Doc A/HRC/17/31. The document also develops a set of guidelines for them to prevent, address and remedy human rights abuses committed in business operations.

promote sustainability principles. In so doing, energy multinationals align themselves with states as the holders of primary responsibility.

As was pointed out above, institutionalized cooperation in energy has historically evolved ad hoc for certain sectors and for antagonistic interests. There is no single organization with responsibility for and representation of all states. This creates a void for governance directly, specifically and comprehensively for the global energy system. This void is being filled by the G7/G20, which is representative in its membership for purposes of the global economy. With the normative perspective of sustainable and reliable energy, the G7/G20 has extended its remit for the global economy into energy. The G7/G20 has become the universal institutional arrangement with a policy-setting and oversight function over the energy market through self-coordination of the major energy producers and consumers. The G7/G20 has developed this function to drive the transition to a sustainable, low-carbon economy with a shift from fossil to renewable sources. This policy-making and indeed oversight function of the sister fora G7/G20 has manifested itself first for the transition to renewables. Meetings of the group have formulated the consensus on the meta-norm, the transition and means for its implementation.[24] Even though states' commitments are politically binding, not legally, there is a follow-up procedure through which actual compliance with these commitments is monitored.

The policy-making function-cum-national commitments extend to the stability of the global market in fossil fuels, under the master-norm of reliable energy and energy security for all countries. That security enables provision of essential services, in particular health care. Hence, the perspective on energy security changes. It is the common concern for energy security of all states, rather than the antagonistic securities of each individual state, that matters. Stability of the market is the means to provide this security during the transition. The comprehensive scope of cooperation for stability is provided by the G20, comprising the major consumer and producer economies. This grouping has ad hoc extended its mandate to support market stabilization

[24] See 2019 G20 Osaka leaders' declaration, para. 37. 'We acknowledge the importance of energy transitions that realize the "3E+S" (Energy Security, Economic Efficiency, and Environment + Safety) in order to transform our energy systems into affordable, reliable, sustainable and low GHG emissions systems as soon as possible, recognizing that there are different possible national paths to achieve this goal. ... We acknowledge the G20 Japanese Presidency's initiative called Research and Development 20 for clean energy technologies ("RD20")'.

through supply control. At the April 2020 extraordinary meeting in the context of oversupply and demand shock resulting from the coronavirus crisis, G20 energy ministers agreed a supply cut deal supported by producer and consumer states as 'necessary measures to ensure energy market stability'.[25] This deal is seven times bigger than action taken during the 2008 financial crisis, where the G20 first intervened for global oil-market stabilization. It also brings into play new instruments, such as side-payments for producers[26] and consumer states buying up oil for their strategic stockpiles.

13.5 Regionalization

The implementation of the master-norm and the concretizing Paris Agreement leave a large space to regional organizations, which can develop integrated climate and energy policies across the territory of their member states.

Sustainable (and secure) energy means electricity. Electricity can be traded across borders. It then falls under the world trading regime. Electricity is a good within the meaning of WTO law, and hence its general disciplines on market access and non-discrimination are applicable, as are rules on subsidies.[27] Through several argumentative devices that are very much aligned with the master-norm, WTO panels and the Appellate Body have refrained from preventing states from subsidizing the provision from renewables. But the European Union (EU) and other regional organizations such as the Energy Community have stepped in and driven forward the regulation of transboundary markets in electricity. The EU has created the project of a European Energy Union (EEU).[28] Under Article 194 TFEU, the EU has the competence to adopt the implementing legislation on carbon emission reductions, RES and EE percentages and the internal electricity market. The legislative packages of 2015 and 2016 serve to align the EU with the climate

[25] G20 extraordinary energy ministers meeting, 10 April 2020, statement, 'necessary measures to ensure energy market stability'. Available at www.canada.ca/en/natural-resources-canada/news/2020/04/g20-energy-ministers-statement.html?wbdisable=true (accessed 1 June 2020).

[26] For instance, the USA offered Mexico compensation for a 350K barrels per day cut.

[27] R. Leal-Arcas and A. Filis, 'Renewable Energy Disputes in the World Trade Organization', (2015) 12 *Transnational Dispute Management* 1.

[28] V. Roeben, *Towards a European Energy Union* (Cambridge University Press, 2018).

objectives of the Paris Agreement. But the process is circular, with the legislation enabling the EU to make pledges on the international level that drive the climate regime forward, motivating others to do more to achieve the collective goal. Objectives are set at the international level, but they depend for their implementation on action at the regional level. That implementation feeds back into the iterative objective setting at the international level. The EEU also contains a strong push to multilateralize the framework for pipelines. The EU has pushed for control over member states' IGAs against the EU Treaties. This requires legislation and does not come under the exclusive EU commercial competence, since these agreements are primarily commercial, not trade. The EU has also legislated to extend the principles of energy solidarity and of efficient, market-based affordable energy to import pipelines, legislation that was shaped in the controversies around the NordStream 2 pipeline. The Energy Union covers the EU member states. But it has connectivity beyond the territory of the member states. It extends to peripheral states organized within the Energy Community. Further expansion would ultimately connect several regional electricity markets, a connectivity that is also envisaged by the 2015 International Energy Charter.

Regional organization becomes the supplementary form of organizing transboundary international energy markets. In that space, regional organization provides an organizational programme that is potentially of universal application even if it is implemented to different degrees and at different times. In Africa, energy is an advanced sectoral policy of ECOWAS adopting policies and mechanisms to promote the efficient exploitation, development, joint research and utilization of various energy resources available within the region. Other relevant regional organizations include the Asia-Pacific Economic Cooperation and the Organization of Latin American Countries. Regional free trade agreements such as the North American Free Trade Agreement (NAFTA) are effective instruments to go much further than the WTO in liberalizing and regulating trade in energy aligned with the master-norm.

13.6 Conclusion

With the advent of the SDGs that constitute the consensus of states, the international community of states has fixed its priorities for global energy. These goals have a strong normative content, combining the provision of a fundamental human need with environmental, social and economic sustainability. The resulting master-norm of sustainable energy to which all have access has led to an autonomous realignment of the extant architecture. Intensified cooperation of states adds a new layer of institutions to carry forward the intended transition and absorbs an older layer of the fossil fuel age with little or no change to the formal legal bases. The Energy Charter may prove an exception in that the ongoing modernization of the Charter's mandate, functions and operation has now entered the stage where parties embark on a re-negotiation of the treaty itself.

This realignment results in a streamlining of the multifaceted architecture with a clearer definition of functionalities. There has, for the first time, emerged universal governance for the global energy system and value chain, supported by expertise-based initiative and implementation by specialist international organizations. Governance is assumed by several organizational fora that represent overlapping interests in energy, and critically, both consumer states and producer states. The overall governance of global energy hence rests with the G7/G20, then the COP to the UNFCCC, and also the HLPF for the SDG. Representative of the key states in the energy transition measured by the critical mass of their economies, the G7/G20 has emerged as a forum for governance of the global energy system with a dedicated energy ministers' segment. It establishes consensus on the objectives of the energy transition and the coordination of policies to be followed both at international and national level. The meetings result in commitments that are followed up at subsequent meetings. The international climate regime governs energy indirectly through climate and carbon targets. The UNFCCC and its conference of the parties is the universal forum for climate change negotiations and hence the key driver of the energy transition. G7/G20 are served by international organizations with energy expertise, such as the IEA, IRENA, OPEC and also the World Bank. The global governance function entails the autonomous reorientation of the capacity of these specialist international organizations towards policy-initiatives and policy-implementation. Their scenarios in energy production and consumption and the likely relative percentages of the different energy sources become a principal tool for governments to plan pathways towards the SDGs on energy.

Under the master-norm for energy, the idea of institutional governance as a process of strategic collective decision-making within a shared timeframe takes centre-stage. The emphasis lies on dynamic decision-making and the production of supportive rules infra-treaty towards the agreed objectives. Treaties only provide authorization of such governance processes, and the institutional home for them. Meetings of parties, either in the supreme decision-making body of an institutionalized treaty or in an organ of international organization, concretize the broad objectives and mechanism that the treaty lays down. They produce standards coordinating states' energy policy and lawmaking based on expertise, benchmarked and supported by standardized progressive best practices, supported by self-perception and ambition of the parties. These standards are improved through an iterative process that involves collective review of the standard and its implementation. All of this rests on a shared understanding of the methodology of delivery of strategic initiatives, monitoring, controlling and coordination, and ultimately of the combination of bottom-up and top-down decision-making governance techniques. On the basis of this strategic modus operandi, the institutional architecture can structure the value chain of energy, from generation through transportation to consumption.

In the architecture of energy, the dominant organizations of limited membership initially received little public scrutiny. Yet, the strategic focus on a decarbonized energy system has been changing this, and energy has become one of the more scrutinized fields. Such scrutiny of the work of the IEA by parliamentarians led to the creation of a new international organization, IRENA.[29] The point of the Paris Agreement was precisely to bring about that very public scrutiny and accountability of the work of governments, based on the independent scientific assessment of the universally legitimized IPCC and the policy scenarios of IEA. This has implications for enforcement. In addition to direct quasi-judicial enforcement means in the field of energy investment protection, the strategic modus operandi opens the possibility of indirect enforcement. Onto these standards can then be latched the general positive obligations to protect the environment and rights to life and health of individuals under regional human rights treaties that are underpinned by judicial machinery. This development can be exemplified in cases for Europe and for Africa. The crisis of climate change has turned the field of energy into a laboratory for the global governance of time-sensitive transition processes.

[29] T. Van de Graaf, 'Fragmentation in Global Energy Governance: Explaining the Creation of IRENA', (2013) 13 *Global Environmental Politics* 14.

14 International Organizations, Disarmament and State Behaviour

Nigel D. White

14.1 Introduction

In most international organizations there is a certain level of trust that basic commitments are being met by the member states. Disarmament organizations,[1] however, form a special case: they are often seen as subject to the motto 'trust, but verify' in ways that do not quite apply to others. This means that within disarmament organizations such as the International Atomic Energy Agency (IAEA) or the Organization for the Prohibition of Chemical Weapons (OPCW), different legal issues arise when compared to other organizations, rendering them of great theoretical importance in addition to their undoubted social relevance.

The focus of this chapter is on organizational efforts to regulate, supervise, control and possibly eliminate weapons of mass destruction (WMD). This involves gaining an initial understanding of state behaviour towards WMD in order to see how, if at all, organizations have shifted that behaviour. This is followed by an examination of how the UN through its plenary organ has tried to influence state behaviour, and then an exposition of the powers and practice of the technical organizations with competence over nuclear and chemical weapons – the IAEA and OPCW. The analysis then returns to the UN, but in the form of executive action by the Security Council and the turn to coercion in disarmament. The powers of these organizations in shaping norms and behaviour are assessed throughout. Does organizational law shape or control state behaviour, regularize state behaviour and by doing so make it more predictable, or simply reflect state

[1] 'Disarmament' includes 'arms control' and 'non-proliferation'; see L. Tabassi and O. Elias, 'Disarmament', in M. Bowman and D. Kritsiotis (eds.), *Conceptual and Contextual Perspectives on the Modern Law of Treaties* (Cambridge University Press, 2018) 578, 579.

behaviour? The overall question to be answered is: to what extent, if at all, do institutions and norms of disarmament influence state behaviour in the field of disarmament?

14.2 Understanding State Behaviour As Regards WMD

During the Cold War, '[n]either side really knew nor understood enough about the other's capability or strategy to be quite sure of their intentions, despite an extensive and expensive intelligence effort on both sides. Yet, at the same time, that mutual distrust could produce dialogue, cooperation and even agreement between the nuclear protagonists.'[2] The perception that arms control is predicated on mutual distrust helps explain why institutionalized arms control's main function is to try to achieve effective methods and mechanisms of verification to reassure the antagonists that they know enough about each other's capabilities and, importantly, intentions not to resort to such weapons. In other words, the aim of arms control is a pragmatic one: to reduce distrust or to increase the level of trust to a level that preserves world peace.

According to Schelling and Halperin, 'the essential feature of arms control is the recognition of the common interest, of the possibility of reciprocation and cooperation between common enemies with respect to their military establishments'. Modern weapons 'have inhumanely compressed the time available to make the most terrible decisions', with one side ready to use such weapons on the basis of a perception that the other side is about to use them – indeed the side that uses such weapons first has the clear advantage. Arms control is an effort 'by some kind of reciprocity or cooperation . . . to minimize, to offset, to compensate or to deflate some of the characteristics of modern weaponry and military expectations'. The idea of 'control' in 'arms control' is not control by an international organization, at least according to Schelling and Halperin, but is taken 'to mean induced or reciprocated "self-control", whether the inducements include negotiated treaties or just informal understandings and reciprocated restraints'.[3] To shift self-control by

[2] G. Bennett, review of *Armageddon and Paranoia: The Nuclear Confrontation*, (2018) 163 *RUSI Journal* 98.

[3] T. Schelling and M. Halperin, *Strategy and Arms Control* (New York: Twentieth Century Fund, 1961) 2–5.

states towards some form of control in the shape of supervision by an international organization is no easy task: '[d]isarmament obligations require a degree of precision and absolute predictability as they touch upon the very core of sovereignty'.[4]

When formal agreement is possible there may be a role for international organizations in 'regulating an arms agreement', in which 'getting the *facts* is only part of the examiner's task; the harder part is arguing over the interpretations, projections, forecasts, and evaluations of significance of the facts at hand'.[5] Regulation is by verification and verification is a judgement based on the facts, not a simple uncovering of the facts. This shows that for institutional arms control to work the parties must be convinced of the regulatory impartiality of the verification bodies. This clearly creates a tension in the existing institutional structures concerned with arms control and disarmament, especially in the apex organ in this regard – the UN General Assembly – where disarmament is a highly politicized subject.

Nonetheless, there may be room for the political organs of the UN to play a role in arms control if they reflect in their debates and resolutions on disarmament the balance of forces in international affairs.[6] According to Hedley Bull, 'the proper concern of arms control' is the 'preservation and perfection of the strategic nuclear balance, rather than as the attempt to dismantle it while leaving the world without security against nuclear war'. For Bull this meant that arms control 'will not have as its object the maximum disarmament, the reduction of armaments to the smallest quantities and most primitive kinds'. Rather, arms control 'will be concerned with discriminating between those kinds of forces and weapons that promote the stability of the balance of power, and those which do not: to tolerate or even to promote the former, and to restrict the latter'.[7]

Bull was dismissive of the UN having a controlling influence on the nuclear arms race. In criticizing ideas that the UN should control atomic power, which were very much debated in the 1950s,[8] he described the idea

[4] Tabassi and Elias, 'Disarmament', 582.

[5] Schelling and Halperin, *Strategy and Arms Control*, 108 (emphasis in original).

[6] Brezhnev as cited in G. Morozov, 'The Socialist Conception of International Organization', in G. Abi-Saab (ed.), *The Concept of International Organization* (Paris: UNESCO, 1981) 179.

[7] H. Bull, *The Control of the Arms Race* (New York: Praeger, 1961) 61–2.

[8] See, for example, P. Noel-Baker, *The Arms Race: A Programme for World Disarmament* (London: John Calder, 1958).

as appealing to many as the UN appeared to be free from the 'odour of tyranny', but pointed out that if the UN had such supreme power it would be tainted with that odour.[9] He concluded that in the condition of the world, at least in the 1960s, states were 'not only unlikely to conclude a general and comprehensive disarmament agreement, but are behaving rationally in refusing to do so'.[10] In sum, states behave with great jealously over ultimate weapons under their control, only grudgingly revealing their hand to other weaponized states and only then through self-interest. Organizations will only be able to influence that behaviour if they accommodate and regularize those behaviours.

14.3 The UN and Disarmament

Nonetheless, the UN may play a number of roles in arms control and disarmament. It may play an aspirational role – for example by calling for nuclear disarmament by majority vote if necessary. Or a normative role – by establishing the principles upon which arms control should be based either through resolutions or sponsoring treaties more often by consensus. And an institutional role – not as a supreme power but by helping establish impartial and autonomous arms control verification mechanisms, independent of the UN's political organs, such as the IAEA and OPCW.

The UN Charter is a long way from being a manifesto for disarmament,[11] having been drafted before the first use of nuclear weapons in August 1945 but coming into force ten weeks later. If the Charter had been drafted after the devastating effects of nuclear weapons became fully known, it might have been much stronger. In some ways, the Charter is weaker than the Covenant of the League of Nations, which declared that 'the maintenance of peace requires the reduction of national armaments to the lowest point consistent with national safety and the enforcement by common action of international obligations'.[12] In contrast, within the UN system the UN General Assembly 'may consider . . . the principles governing disarmament

[9] H. Bull, 'Disarmament and the International System', (1959) 9 *Australian Journal of Politics and History*, as reproduced in R. O'Neill and D. Schwartz (eds.), *Hedley Bull on Arms Control* (London: Macmillan, 1987) 39.

[10] *Ibid.* [11] Tabassi and Elias, 'Disarmament', 579.

[12] Article 8 League of Nations Covenant.

and the regulation of armaments' and make recommendations to member states thereon.[13] By 1959, the General Assembly 'had recognised the need for "general and complete disarmament" under effective international control as the most important question facing the world at that time'.[14] While the General Assembly has been active on disarmament,[15] the Security Council has not wielded its general powers of arms control. Article 26 provides that the Security Council 'shall be responsible for formulating, with the assistance of the Military Staff Committee ... plans ... for the establishment of a system of armaments'.[16] The extension of possession of nuclear weapons to all the permanent members of the Security Council, and the embodiment of this as a right in the Nuclear Non-Proliferation Treaty (NPT) in 1968, are the main reasons why this provision remains a dead letter. Any idea of pooling military power through the Military Staff Committee fell apart in the late 1940s.

The aspiration to disarm persists in the Conference on Disarmament, the UN General Assembly's First Committee and its subsidiary organ – the Disarmament Commission.[17] However, as Keith Krause notes, although the UN system has achieved some successes in arms control in terms of diplomacy, negotiation and norm setting, its main function in this area has been that of 'great power security governance'. In discussing the treaties governing WMD, including the Biological Weapons Convention (BWC) and the Chemical Weapons Convention (CWC) as well as the NPT, Krause explains that 'no concrete action by the UN was possible until Washington and Moscow agreed in the early 1960s to move forward on arms control discussions. All major achievements – the NPT, CWC, [BWC] – required great power consensus; when it did not exist, such as in the Comprehensive Test Ban Treaty, disarmament efforts stalled.'[18] Krause points out that the Ottawa

[13] Article 11(1) UN Charter.

[14] Tabassi and Elias, 'Disarmament', 580, citing UN Doc A/RES/1378 (1959).

[15] For example, the General Assembly has held three special sessions on disarmament in 1978, 1982 and in 1988. Only the first of these managed to produce a resolution by consensus in which the Assembly, inter alia, stated that '[r]emoving the threat of a world war – a nuclear war – is the most acute and urgent task of the present day. Mankind is confronted with a choice: we must halt the arms race and proceed to disarmament or face annihilation'. See UN Doc A/RES/S-10/2 (1978) para. 18.

[16] Article 26 UN Charter.

[17] K. Hailbronner and E. Klein, 'Article 11' in B. Simma (ed.), *The Charter of the United Nations: A Commentary*, 2nd ed. (Oxford University Press, 2002) 279.

[18] K. Krause, 'Disarmament', in T. G. Weiss and S. Daws (eds.), *Oxford Handbook on the United Nations* (Oxford University Press, 2007) 297.

Convention on land mines of 1997 worked around the great powers, but this was done 'deliberately and consciously outside the UN system'.[19] The same can be said of the Cluster Weapons Convention of 2008, both treaties coming into force without a significant part of the P5 (China, Russia and the United States) being on board. The trend towards negotiating and adopting major arms control treaties outside the UN system has the advantage of enabling norm setting and some implementation in arms control, but it does not provide for any great power security governance.

In this regard, the adoption in 2017 of a Treaty on the Prohibition of Nuclear Weapons, negotiated within the United Nations, should be considered. When it enters into force, the Treaty will ban the possession of nuclear weapons for all state parties. It will supplement the IAEA safeguards system that operates under the NPT for non-nuclear weapons states (NNWS), by requiring any nuclear weapons state (NWS) that becomes a party to the treaty to negotiate with a 'competent international authority' a plan for the verified and irreversible elimination of its nuclear weapons programme.[20] As of October 2019, seventy-nine states had signed the treaty, while thirty-two states out of the required fifty for it to come into force had ratified it. In a joint statement of 2017, the UK, France and the USA, noting that no NWS had taken part in the negotiations, stated that they would not become parties as it 'disregards the realities of the international security environment' being 'incompatible with the policy of nuclear deterrence, which has been essential to keeping the peace ... for over 70 years'.[21] For the UK, USA and France 'there will be no change in the legal obligations of our countries with respect to nuclear weapons', rejecting 'any claim that this treaty reflects or in any way contributes to the development of customary international law'. The Treaty reflects the frustrations, expressed in resolutions of the General Assembly, of many of the NNWS with the failure of NWS

[19] *Ibid.*

[20] Articles 1 and 4, Treaty on the Prohibition of Nuclear Weapons, 2017 (UN Doc A/CONF.229/2017/8).

[21] Joint Press Statement from the Permanent Representatives to the United Nations of the United States, the United Kingdom and France Following the Adoption of a Treaty Banning Nuclear Weapons, 7 July 2017.

to take seriously their obligations towards nuclear disarmament as contained in the NPT.[22]

14.4 'Atoms for Peace': Whose Atoms, Whose Peace?

In contrast to its recent resolutions on nuclear disarmament, which fit loosely into the Assembly performing its role as the 'conscience of humanity',[23] the very first resolution of the UN General Assembly in 1946 was more normative and institutional in its content. Prompted by fear of a second use of nuclear weapons, it established a UN Atomic Energy Commission.[24] This body consisted of members of the Security Council, plus Canada, and its terms of reference were to formulate proposals for: 'the exchange of basic scientific information for peaceful ends'; the 'control of atomic energy to the extent necessary to ensure its use only for peaceful purposes'; 'the elimination from national armaments of atomic weapons'; 'effective safeguards of inspection and other means to protect complying states against the hazards of violations and evasion'. Essentially this resolution contained the principles upon which nuclear weapons were to be subsequently managed – an inspection regime would be established under the supervision of the IAEA created in 1956, most states with nuclear technology would only use it only for peaceful purposes, but the 'grand bargain' that was finally hammered out in 1968 did not provide for the total elimination of nuclear weapons as envisaged by the General Assembly in 1946, but for their non-proliferation beyond a certain small club of NWS.

The 'grand bargain' on nuclear weapons achieved in 1968 was not what was envisaged in the UN in the immediate post-War period. Debate centred around the Baruch plan that envisaged an organization to be entrusted with the control of atomic energy in all its phases, endorsed by the General Assembly in 1948 at the instigation of the USA.[25] However, it was the USA that abandoned the plan until clear inspection methods and control arrangements were designed and adopted. US plans to retain a nuclear monopoly through institutional control had to be dropped as the Soviet

[22] See, for example, UN Doc A/RES/72/31, 11 December 2017, adopted by majority vote.
[23] *Yearbook of the United Nations* (1946–7), 51. [24] UN Doc A/RES/1(I) (1946).
[25] UN Doc A/RES/191 (III) (1948).

Union acquired atomic weapons in 1949, followed by the UK in 1952, France in 1960 and China in 1964.[26]

Ideas of UN control over nuclear power gave way to a proposal for great power management of nuclear technology by President Eisenhower in his famous 'Atoms for Peace' speech to the General Assembly in 1953;[27] a vision that foresaw the pooling of nuclear materials and technology in an International Atomic Energy Agency. According to Eisenhower, the Agency 'could be made responsible for the impounding, storage, and protection of the contributed fissionable and other materials', but its 'more important responsibility ... would be to devise methods whereby fissionable material would be allocated to serve the peaceful pursuits of mankind'. Moreover, 'a special purpose would be to provide abundant energy in the power-starved areas of the world'. This would 'allow all peoples of all nations to see that, in this enlightened age, the great powers of the earth, both of the East and West, are interested in human aspirations first, rather than in building up the armaments of war'. Parts of Eisenhower's speech suggested a 'reduction or elimination of atomic materials for military purposes', but the main concern was the production of 'peaceful power from atomic energy'.[28]

The adoption of the IAEA Statute in 1956 did not produce a 'common treasury for all' envisaged by Oppenheimer, the father of the bomb, after he realised the devastating effects of what he had helped to create in 1945,[29] and then to lesser extent by Eisenhower's 'Atoms for Peace'. However, parts of the Statute still foresaw that one of the functions of the IAEA would be to receive and establish control over special fissionable materials 'in order to ensure that these materials are used only for peaceful purposes'.[30] However, just as the idea to pool the military resources of the five permanent members of the Security Council in Chapter VII of the UN Charter remains unfulfilled, the idea of pooling the nuclear capabilities of the NWS failed to materialize.

The reality was that by 1956 three of the permanent members had developed nuclear weapons, while, by 1968, all five had. The NPT of 1968

[26] M. M. Bosch, 'The Non-Proliferation Treaty and Its Future', in L. Boisson de Chazournes and P. Sands (eds.), *International Law, the International Court of Justice and Nuclear Weapons* (Cambridge University Press, 1999) 375, 377.

[27] UN Doc A/PV/470, 8 December 1953, 450. [28] *Ibid.*

[29] P. J. Kuznick, 'A Tragic Life: Oppenheimer and the Bomb', available at www.armscontrol.org/print/1851 (accessed 18 October 2019).

[30] Article III.B.2, Article IX.A, Article IX.B, IAEA Statute 1956.

represented 'the maximum area of agreement ... obtainable', according to the US representative at the eighteen-nation Disarmament Committee.[31] The reality of nuclear weapons, and a precarious world peace based on their non-use through deterrence, meant that in 1968 the IAEA's functions were narrowed to ensuring through verification the non-proliferation or spread of nuclear weapons to other states. The system of IAEA safeguards agreements with member states was envisaged in the IAEA Statute of 1956,[32] amongst a number of functions, but its application was formally restricted to NNWS in 1968. In 1971, the IAEA laid down the structure and content of agreements between the IAEA and NNWS under the NPT.[33] Enforcement under the safeguards agreement (INFCIRC/153) is by means of suspension of assistance or other rights or privileges, or expulsion from the organization, and follows from the IAEA being unable to verify that there has been no diversion of nuclear material for military purposes. '[I]n other words: it is not the established violation of a treaty (e.g., the NPT or a NWFZ-treaty) that triggers the corrective/enforcement measures of INFCIRC/153, but the inability of the Agency, caused by the state concerned, to make a statement that diversion of nuclear material to military purposes has not taken place'.[34] Thus the IAEA inspectors, the Board of Governors and the General Conference,[35] have to make a judgement based on the verifiable facts and disclosure by the state about whether diversion to military uses has taken place.

After the Gulf War of 1991 and the imposition of disarmament conditions on Iraq by the Security Council,[36] IAEA inspectors uncovered a clandestine nuclear weapons programme. It was thus revealed that Iraq, a state party to the NPT since 1969, with an IAEA safeguards agreement in force since 1972, and a member of the IAEA since 1959, 'over many years had hidden its nuclear activities successfully from the Agency's inspections'.[37] This led to

[31] This Committee was established by agreement between the US and USSR and endorsed by the General Assembly in UN Doc A/RES/1722 (XVI) (1962). For discussion, see M. Willrich, 'The Treaty on Non-Proliferation of Nuclear Weapons: Nuclear Technology Confronts World Politics', (1968) 77 *Yale Law Journal* 1447.

[32] Article III.A.5, IAEA Statute 1956.

[33] IAEA Doc INFCIRC/153 (1971); IAEA Doc INFCRIC/153 (Corr.) (1972).

[34] G. Den Dekker, *The Law of Arms Control: International Supervision and Enforcement* (The Hague: Martinus Nijhoff, 2001) 295.

[35] Article VI.F IAEA Statute 1956 attributes the main competence for enforcement to the Board of Governors.

[36] UN Doc S/RES/687 (1991). [37] Den Dekker, *Arms Control*, 299.

the adoption of the 'Model Additional Protocol' of 1997,[38] which was 'designed to provide the Agency with access to more information and to additional locations as compared to the existing safeguards agreements'.[39] Hirsch assesses the purposes of the Additional Protocol as an attempt to 'transform IAEA inspectors from accountants to detectives'.[40] Joyner describes the additional powers of the inspectors on information gathering and inspections as 'significant improvements to the Agency's ability to verify not only the correctness, but also the completeness of the state's declaration', thereby allowing for 'increased confidence in the determinations of the IAEA that no undeclared nuclear-related activity is being carried out in the safeguarded territory'.[41]

As Murphy notes, in contrast to the obligations of NNWS to submit to a safeguards agreement and supervision by the IAEA, NWS 'are not under an obligation to submit peaceful nuclear activities within their territories' to the safeguards system. However, he notes that the USA and UK have submitted their peaceful nuclear activities to safeguards, and 'each of the five nuclear weapon-states has accepted IAEA safeguards on some of its civilian reactors to reduce the appearance of discrimination and encourage non-nuclear weapons parties to accept safeguards'.[42]

The UN General Assembly recommended the adoption of the NPT,[43] regularizing the balance of nuclear power and preventing the further spread of nuclear weapons pending nuclear disarmament. Under the 'grand bargain', embodied in the NPT,[44] NWS are obliged neither to supply nuclear weapons to NNWS nor to proliferate their own, and to negotiate disarmament to be achieved under strict and effective international control. NNWS, on their side, agree not to acquire or develop nuclear weapons, and subject themselves to supervision and verification by the IAEA. When adopted, the NPT was seen as a 'temporary contract between NWS and NNWS',[45] meant to last twenty-five years. The temporary nature of the NPT was insisted upon by certain NNWS that had the capability of developing

[38] IAEA Doc INFCRIC/540 (1997). [39] Den Dekker, *Arms Control*, 301.

[40] T. Hirsch, 'The IAEA Additional Protocol: What It Is and Why It Matters', (2004) 11 *Non-Proliferation Review* 140.

[41] D. Joyner, *International Law and the Proliferation of Weapons of Mass Destruction* (Oxford University Press, 2009) 23.

[42] J. F. Murphy, 'Force and Arms', in O. Schachter and C. Joyner (eds.), *United Nations Legal Order* (Cambridge University Press, 1995) 247, 311–12.

[43] UN Doc A/RES/2373 (XXII), 12 June 1968. [44] Joyner, *Proliferation*, 8.

[45] Bosch, 'Non-Proliferation Treaty', 377.

nuclear weapons (Germany, Italy, Japan and Switzerland), and were concerned about committing themselves to permanent nuclear disarmament before seeing evidence of progress towards nuclear disarmament by the NWS.[46] Despite little progress being made on general nuclear disarmament by NWS as required by Article VI of the NPT, a combined review and extension conference of NPT parties in 1995 decided to extend the NPT indefinitely.

No final declaration of any substance, and no commitment to nuclear disarmament as required by Article VI of the NPT,[47] could be agreed at the Review Conference in 2015. According to Wilfred Wan: '[t]he divide between the nuclear weapon states – the permanent five members of the UN Security Council – and the other parties to the treaty thus remains readily apparent. South Africa even invoked apartheid in describing the system in place.'[48] NNWS expressed their dissatisfaction both in the UN General Assembly and by supporting the adoption of the Treaty on the Prohibition of Nuclear Weapons in 2017.[49]

The IAEA's aim to 'promote and control the atom'[50] is ambitious, but it has been tempered by the 'grand bargain' contained in the NPT. The General Assembly has been both instrumental in legitimating this bargain on the basis that it represented a temporary freezing in the status quo in order to prevent further proliferation, but also in criticizing it for its apparent indelibility. Indeed, the NWS show no signs of giving up their weapons within a multilateral framework, treaty or organization – they will only negotiate bilaterally. Organizations have helped regularize the balance of nuclear power, but they exhibit no signs of control over it.

The safeguards system has held together to a large extent but its legitimacy is undermined by a number of factors including the lack of reciprocal

[46] *Ibid.*

[47] This was described as an obligation of result and not just of conduct in *Legality of the Threat or Use of Nuclear Weapons* (Advisory Opinion), [1996] ICJ Rep. 226, para. 105(2)(F). The Court declined a further opportunity to consider the obligation in Article VI of the NPT in *Obligations Concerning Negotiations Relating to the Cessation of the Nuclear Arms Race and to Nuclear Disarmament (Marshall Islands* v. *United Kingdom)*, Preliminary Objections, [2016] ICJ Rep. 833.

[48] W. Wan, 'Why the 2015 NPT Review Conference Fell Apart', UNU Centre for Policy Research, 28 May 2015, available at https://cpr.unu.edu/why-the-2015-npt-review-conference-fell-apart.html (accessed 18 October 2019).

[49] See the instruments referred to above, notes 20 and 22.

[50] IAEA website: www.iaea.org/about/overview/history (accessed 18 October 2019).

supervision of the obligations of the NWS and NNWS, as well as the uneven supervision of NNWS's obligations (contrast the treatment of South Korea and Iran in 2003–4).[51] Of further note is the role of the Nuclear Suppliers Group (NSG) of states in shaping export control guidelines outside of the IAEA, despite the latter's Statute containing an obligation on all parties not to export nuclear materials to NNWS for peaceful proposes unless such material is subject to the IAEA safeguards system.[52] Furthermore, there is the problem of the horizontal proliferation of nuclear weapons to India, Pakistan, Israel and North Korea, all states outside the NPT, and the fact that possession of nuclear weapons is not viewed as fundamentally contrary to international law as is the case with chemical and biological weapons.

14.5 'Chemistry for Peace'?[53] The OPCW and the Prohibition of Chemical Weapons

The NPT forms part of the grand bargain or social contract at the heart of the international legal and political order alongside the UN Charter. The BWC and CWC, on the other hand, are 'lawmaking treaties, providing a blanket prohibition upon development and possession, as well as proliferation, of their subject weapons technologies, binding upon all state parties'.[54] The CWC, like the NPT, has an institutional element in the form of the OPCW, which assists in the development of the treaty by interpreting and applying its obligations as well as by promoting 'chemistry for peace'.[55] As Williamson states, the potential 'dual-use' capability of both nuclear materials and chemicals requires a 'high degree of intrusiveness' by both the OPCW and the IAEA.[56]

[51] Joyner, *Proliferation*, 26.

[52] Article III.2 IAEA Statute. NSG guidelines have been adopted by the IAEA, for example, in IAEA Doc INFCIRC/254/Rev.1.Part.2 (2002) and IAEA Doc INFCIRC/405 1992. Non-Aligned States have argued that the NSG 'is essentially a supplier-state cartel whose policies unduly target states legitimately attempting to develop civilian power generation facilities'; see Joyner, *Proliferation*, 33.

[53] See OPCW, 'Promoting Chemistry for Peace' at www.opcw.org/our-work/promoting-chemistry-peace (accessed 18 October 2019).

[54] Joyner, *Proliferation*, 69.

[55] See OPCW, 'Promoting Chemistry for Peace' at www.opcw.org/our-work/promoting-chemistry-peace (accessed 18 October 2019).

[56] R. L. Williamson, 'Hard Law, Soft Law, and Non-Law in Multilateral Arms Control: Some Compliance Hypotheses', (2003) 4 *Chinese Journal of International Law* 59, 72.

Prior to the advent of the CWC in 1993, the BWC was adopted in 1972 following momentum in the General Assembly and associated bodies,[57] but without any agreement therein on a supervisory organization. Attempts in the 1990s to introduce a draft protocol failed due to the sudden withdrawal of US support in 2001: 'regime minimalist states, including the US and other powerful states, were the ultimate cause of the collapse of the additional protocol negotiations because they were unwilling to subject themselves to intrusive independent verification'.[58] The additional protocol would have created a similar verification regime and supporting organizational structure as found in the CWC of 1993.[59] The main means of supervision of the obligation in the BWC remains the review conferences of the parties, the production of state reports, and the creation of an Implementation Support Unit (ISU) to provide fairly low-level assistance to state parties in implementing the Convention at the Sixth Review Conference in 2007.[60] The General Assembly performs an oversight function in relation to the BWC, adopting annual resolutions that comment on progress being made under the Convention, and urging greater implementation and compliance.[61]

Clearly US attitudes to verification changed in 2001 with its rejection of the BWC's proposed additional protocol but, less than a decade earlier in 1993, the CWC was crafted in the light of the collapse of the USSR and the possibilities for international organization that this created.[62] Negotiations were difficult, taking place over twelve years in the Conference on Disarmament, and compromises were necessary even in this brief period of cooperation. Nevertheless, the CWC remains a significant accomplishment.[63]

[57] UN Doc A/RES/2662 (XXV) (1970); UN Doc A/RES/2827 (XXVI) (1971): UN Doc A/RES/2933 (XXVII) (1972).

[58] Joyner, *Proliferation*, 123, citing J. Littlewood, *The Biological Weapons Convention: A Failed Revolution* (Aldershot: Ashgate, 2005).

[59] Joyner, *Proliferation*, 98.

[60] See also the Secretary-General's Mechanism to carry out prompt investigations in response to allegations brought to his attention concerning the possible use of chemical and bacteriological (biological) and toxin weapons, which was developed in the late 1980s. Triggered by a request from any Member State, the Secretary-General is authorized to launch an investigation including dispatching a fact-finding team to the site(s) of the alleged incident(s) and to report to all United Nation Member States: UN Doc A/RES/42/37 (1987); UN Doc S/RES 620 (1988).

[61] See, for example, UN Doc A/RES/72/71 (2017). [62] See UN Doc A/RES/47/39 (1992).

[63] Joyner, *Proliferation*, 100; E. P. J. Myjer, 'The Organization for the Prohibition of Chemical Weapons: Closer Towards an International Arms Control Organization? A Quantum Leap in the Institutional Law of Arms Control', in E. P. J. Myjer (ed.), *Issues of Arms Control Law and the Chemical Weapons Convention* (The Hague: Martinus Nijhoff, 2001) 61.

Parties to the CWC are required to make a declaration of all chemical weapons and production facilities they possess; to be followed by a detailed plan for the destruction of both weapons and facilities; then their destruction according to the guidelines and schedules specified in the Convention. The OPCW is guaranteed access to all such materials and facilities for the purpose of on-site inspection and verification according to a schedule agreed between the OPCW and each member state. Ongoing monitoring by electronic detection methods is also provided for.[64]

Article IX of the CWC is a key provision that reflects a cooperative approach to weapons control by providing for reciprocal rights and duties of state parties. Paragraph 1 provides that state parties 'shall consult and cooperate, directly among themselves, or through the Organization or other appropriate international procedures', including within the framework of the United Nations, 'on any matter which may be raised relating to its object and purpose, or the implementation of the provisions, of this Convention'. Paragraph 2 provides that any state party should first of all, whenever possible, 'make every effort to clarify and resolve, through exchange of information and consultations among themselves, any matter which may cause doubt about compliance with this Convention, or which gives rise to concerns about a related matter which may be considered ambiguous'. Any state party which receives a request for such clarification from another state party shall provide the requesting state 'with information sufficient to answer the doubt or concern' within ten days of the request. This right to request information is supplemented by paragraphs 3 and 4: a state party has the right to request the Executive Council of the OPCW 'to assist in clarifying' or to 'obtain clarification from another State Party of . . . any situation which may be considered ambiguous or which gives rise to a concern about the possible non-compliance of another State Party with this Convention'. If the clarification is deemed unsatisfactory by the requesting state it can request a special session of the Executive Council, which 'may recommend any measure it deems appropriate to resolve the situation'. If doubts persist and have not been resolved within sixty days the requesting state can further request a special session of the Conference (of all state parties). In these circumstances, the Conference 'may recommend any measure it deems appropriate to resolve the situation'.[65]

[64] Articles III–XI, plus Verification Annex, CWC 1993. [65] Article IX(4)–(7), CWC.

None of these procedures is prejudicial to the right of a state party to request an 'on-site challenge inspection of any facility or location' within another party 'for the sole purpose of clarifying and resolving any questions concerning possible non-compliance with the provisions' of the CWC; 'and to have this inspection conducted anywhere without delay by an inspection team' designated by the Director General of the OPCW.[66] The challenge regime was directed at uncovering clandestine chemical weapons facilities not uncovered under the routine system of declarations and inspections by the OPCW. There have been no challenge inspections,[67] probably out of fear of 'retaliatory challenge inspections'.[68] The Executive Council will consider OPCW reports and, if applicable, 'take the appropriate measures to redress the situation and to ensure compliance with the Convention'.[69] Measures include the restriction or suspension of a state party's rights and privileges under the CWC. In addition, the Conference 'may recommend collective measures to State Parties in conformity with international law', envisaging 'sanctions' or, more accurately, collective countermeasures. Finally, the 'Conference shall, in cases of particular gravity, bring the issue, including relevant information and conclusions, to the attention' of the UN General Assembly and Security Council.[70] Although there has been some Security Council activity as regards chemical weapons especially in the Syrian conflict,[71] the General Assembly has taken a supervisory role.[72]

14.6 The Role of the Security Council: A Move from Cooperation to Coercion?

It has been argued as early as the 1980s that non-proliferation law is moving from a cooperative model of reducing distrust through impartial supervision and verification, towards one based on superiority and coercion.[73] US initiatives such as pulling out of the ABM Treaty of

[66] Article IX(8) CWC. The political and administrative functions of the Director General were discussed in the *Bustani* case of 2003; see J. Klabbers, 'The *Bustani* Case Before the ILOAT: Constitutionalism in Disguise', (2004) 53 *International and Comparative Law Quarterly* 455.

[67] T. Abe, 'Challenge Inspections under the Chemical Weapons Convention: Between Ideal and Reality' (2017) 24 *Nonproliferation Review* 167.

[68] Joyner, *Proliferation*, 116. [69] Article IX(23) CWC 1993. [70] Article XII CWC 1993.

[71] Reviewed in Section 14.6 below. [72] See, for example, UN Doc A/RES/72/43 (2017).

[73] R. O'Neill and D. N. Schwartz, *Hedley Bull on Arms Control* (London: Macmillan, 1987).

1972,[74] and its threat made in October 2018 to withdraw from the Intermediate-Range Nuclear Forces (INF) Treaty of 1987, suggest that it no longer fully subscribes to the 'most important goal of arms control', which is to stabilize the relationship of mutual deterrence between the superpowers.[75] In the post–Cold War period that strategic balance has to be achieved by all the nuclear powers, especially the recognized NWS, which was one of the US arguments for threatening to pull out of the INF Treaty in 2018 – that as a bilateral agreement between the US and Russia it did not cover China. That might suggest that the issue of control of WMD should return to the UN, specifically to the Security Council. However, rather than tackling WMD at a thematic level including the continued possession of nuclear weapons by the P5, the Security Council has focused on specific threats coming from North Korea as an unrecognized NWS, and Iran as a potential future unrecognized NWS. The Security Council has not taken action against all states that have acquired nuclear weapons outside of the five major powers; but has focused its coercive powers on the two 'rogue' states that the five major powers can agree represent the greatest threat. This illustrates that it is somewhat misleading to consider that the Security Council is enforcing non-proliferation law; rather it is responding to what it considers to be threats to the peace.

Following the news that North Korea had conducted an underground nuclear weapons test in October 2006, the Security Council acted under Chapter VII to condemn the test and determine that there was a threat to international peace, thereby justifying the imposition of non-forcible measures against North Korea under Article 41 of the Charter. It expressed its conviction that the non-proliferation regime embodied in the NPT of 1968 should continue and that North Korea did not (and could not) have the status of an NWS under that treaty. Since the proliferation of nuclear weapons to North Korea undermined peace it followed that the Security Council had competence to address the nuclear test not because it was a breach of the NPT (indeed North Korea had withdrawn from the NPT), but because it was

[74] R. Müllerson, 'The ABM Treaty: Changed Circumstances, Extraordinary Events, Supreme Interests and International Law', (2001) 50 *International and Comparative Law Quarterly* 509.

[75] H. Bull, 'The Classical Approach to Arms Control Twenty Three Years After', as summarized in O'Neill and Schwartz, *Bull on Arms Control*, 8.

a threat to the peace. Somewhat disingenuously, the Security Council decided that North Korea 'shall abandon all nuclear weapons and existing nuclear programmes in a complete, verifiable and irreversible manner, [and] shall act strictly in accordance with the obligations applicable to [NPT] parties'.[76]

In the case of Iran, the Security Council's initial concern was that the country was developing a nuclear programme involving the enrichment of uranium that was not entirely for peaceful purposes.[77] In Resolution 1737 (2006), the Security Council reaffirmed the right of NNWS states to develop nuclear energy for peaceful purposes, but expressed concern over the 'proliferation risks presented by the Iranian nuclear programme and, in this context, by Iran's continuing failure to meet the requirements of the IAEA Board of Governors and to comply with the provisions of Security Council resolution 1696 (2006)'. Then, 'mindful of its primary responsibility under the Charter of the United Nations for the maintenance of international peace and security', the Security Council imposed non-forcible measures under Article 41 (including targeted sanctions against nuclear scientists and others with nuclear expertise), mostly aimed at preventing Iran from acquiring the technology necessary to achieve a weapons programme, and established a Committee to oversee the implementation of those measures.

The lack of specific finding of a threat to the peace in the resolutions on Iran is probably a result of concern in at least a section of the P5 about the use of Chapter VII language as a way of opening up Iran to unilateral military action by Israel and possibly the United States, given the threats of force against Iran had already been issued by those countries. Indeed, at the meeting at which Resolution 1737 was adopted, the Russian representative expressed his conviction that the solution to the Iranian nuclear problem would be found exclusively within political, diplomatic and legal frameworks, meaning that the non-forcible measures adopted in the resolution should be taken in accordance with Article 41 and, therefore, should not

[76] UN Doc S/RES/1718 (2006); see more recently UN Doc S/RES/2094 (2013) condemning a further nuclear test by North Korea and imposing further non-forcible measures under Article 41 of the UN Charter.

[77] For detailed consideration of the institutional involvement of the IAEA and the Security Council regarding Iran, see Joyner, *Proliferation*, 50–5; M. ElBaradei, *The Age of Deception: Nuclear Diplomacy in Treacherous Times* (London: Bloomsbury, 2011) chs. 5, 9 and 12.

involve any use of force.[78] Further, in a follow-up resolution adopted in 2010, the preamble expressly stated that 'nothing in this resolution compels States to take measures or actions exceeding the scope of this resolution, including the use of force or the threat of force'.[79]

A reluctance in the Security Council as a whole to find a threat to the peace in the case of the Iran's nuclear programme remained evident in Resolution 1884 (2011). This found that the 'proliferation of weapons of mass destruction, as well as their means of delivery, continues to constitute a threat to international peace and security', but the resolution did not specifically mention Iran, although it did recall some of the resolutions against Iran and extended the mandate of the panel of experts working with the 1737 Committee. At the meeting at which the Resolution was adopted, it was clear that Iran was the focus of the Resolution.[80] Thus, the Security Council's measures against Iran slowly creep up the scale of measures it can adopt under Chapter VII, but has so far expressly fallen short of the threat or use of force under Article 42. Under the Joint Comprehensive Plan of Action, Iran's nuclear deal of 2015 with the P5 plus Germany and the EU, Iran agreed to restrict its nuclear activities and allow more stringent IAEA inspections. In December 2015, the IAEA Board of Governors voted to end its ten-year-long investigation into the possible military dimension of Iran's nuclear programme. Security Council sanctions would 'snap-back' if Iran violated the agreement. This positive diplomatic development revolved around the P5, showing that it is possible for the Security Council to operate within a cooperative model of arms control. However, this was undermined by the US withdrawal from the Plan in May 2018.

On chemical weapons, Syria has witnessed a more coercive approach to enforcing the prohibition, with threats or use of force by Western states leading to the Syrian government agreeing to disarm its chemical weapons in 2013 under the auspices of an OPCW-UN Joint Mission.[81] Further uses of chemical weapons in the conflict led to the establishment of an OPCW mission in 2014 to establish the facts, but not to identify who was responsible for alleged attacks. A joint OPCW-UN investigation panel (JIM, Joint Investigation Mechanism) looked into attacks in Syria and was set up to identify perpetrators,[82] but this

[78] UN Doc S/PV/5612 (2006) 2. [79] UN Doc S/RES/1929 (2010).
[80] UN Doc S/PV/6522 (2011).
[81] UN Doc S/RES/2118 (2013); OPCW Executive Council decision EC-M-33/DEC.1 (2013).
[82] UN Doc S/RES/2235 (2015).

was disbanded in November 2017 when members of the Security Council were unable to agree on an extension of its mandate. The Security Council's response to the chemical weapons attacks in Douma on 7 April 2018 illustrates the deadlock in that body.[83] On 10 April 2018 three draft resolutions were introduced, one by the US and two by Russia, each with the aim of investigating the attack but none were adopted due to opposition or the veto.[84]

The Security Council has also adopted general legislation under Chapter VII directed against WMD in Resolution 1540 of 2004, which supports the non-proliferation regime established by the NPT, BWC and CWC, by binding states not to provide or allow any WMD capabilities to non-state actors.[85] While the treaties aim to prevent proliferation of WMD to states, the resolution fills a perceived gap in the regulation of WMD by requiring states not to proliferate to non-state actors, and establishes a Committee of the Security Council to oversee that obligation.[86] This general legislative approach could be used to address the proliferation of nuclear weapons and the absence of a plan towards nuclear disarmament that would accommodate the security concerns of the P5.[87]

14.7 Conclusion

Joyner argues that the general prohibitive nature of the BWC and the CWC, providing for reciprocal and equal rights and duties among state parties, has worked against their effectiveness. Certainly in the case of the BWC, sovereign concerns have prevented any effective supervision or verification being developed,[88] while in the case of the CWC the lack of invocation of the challenge inspection regimes shows that inspection and verification

[83] Chemical weapons have been used on a number of occasions in the Syrian conflict most of which have been attributed to forces under the control of the Assad regime. See R. Barber, 'Uniting for Peace Not Aggression: Responding to Chemical Weapons in Syria without Breaking the Law', (2019) 24 *Journal of Conflict and Security Law* 71.

[84] UN Doc S/PV.8228 (2018). [85] UN Doc S/RES/1540 (2004).

[86] See also UN Doc S/RES 1810 (2008), UN Doc S/RES/1977 (2011).

[87] N. D. White, 'Understanding Nuclear Deterrence within the International Constitutional Architecture', in J. Black-Branch and D. Fleck (eds.), *Nuclear Non-Proliferation in International Law Volume V: Legal Challenges for Nuclear Security and Deterrence* (Berlin: Springer, 2020) 237.

[88] This has been undertaken to some extent outside the treaty by the Australia Group; see Joyner, *Proliferation*, 116–21, who draws parallels with the NSG.

can only go so far. Joyner points to the greater success of the NPT/IAEA regime, where the system of unequal rights and duties has meant that the NWS are 'more supportive of the strict implementation of the regime inclusive of intrusive verification procedures' for NNWS,[89] through the adoption of the IAEA Additional Protocol, and through resort to the UN Security Council where the NWS call the shots.

Despite considerable pressures on the arms control regime applicable to WMD, the premises underlying it remain those identified by the arms control thinkers of the early 1960s, which in legal terms translates to clear rights and duties, clear restrictions and prohibitions, and an agreed trusted independent verification mechanism (the IAEA, OPCW) to unearth the facts but also to make considered judgements on those facts. The General Assembly and associated bodies have proved vital in providing fora for negotiating key treaties, and in establishing general principles in advance of those treaties. The Assembly's normative function in arms control is not undermined by its parallel practice of adopting aspirational, but more divisive resolutions, aimed at nuclear disarmament. Given that arms control is predicated on common interest, reciprocity and cooperation, the General Assembly is the natural forum in which to try to achieve this, rather than the Security Council where the trend towards coercion could be said to be indicative of the weakening rather than the strengthening of arms control. Nevertheless, considering the confluence between the P5 under the UN Charter and the NWS under the NPT, solutions to nuclear disarmament can only be found in the Security Council.[90]

The struggle to establish new organizations in arms control especially in the area of WMD shows how difficult it is to create any sort of challenge to matters close to the heart of state sovereignty. The Comprehensive Nuclear Test Ban Treaty (CTBT) has not yet entered into force even though it was adopted by the UN General Assembly in 1996.[91] A Comprehensive Test Ban Treaty Organisation (CTBTO) is envisaged in that Treaty, indeed its preparatory commission has established a global network of facilities in anticipation of the CTBT coming into force and has created an international monitoring system to detect nuclear explosions.[92]

[89] Joyner, *Proliferation*, 123. [90] White, 'Understanding Nuclear Deterrence'.
[91] UN Doc A/RES/50/245 (1996).
[92] Tabassi and Elias, 'Disarmament', 586. See further M. Asada, 'CTBT: Legal Quagmire Arising from Its Non-Entry into Force', (2002) 7 *Journal of Conflict and Security Law* 85.

All of this demonstrates that organizations are not the 'control' element in arms control, but neither do they simply reflect the balance of power, although there is little doubt that arms control is dominated by pragmatism rather than principle. Despite this, organizations help to regulate the system of non-proliferation by increasing predictability and certainty in state behaviour, which reduces the chances of nuclear weapons being used precipitously, and prevents the re-emergence of the widespread use of bio-chemical weapons. The differential treatment of nuclear and bio-chemical weapons shows how arms control law is shot through with pragmatism, but the function of organizations is both to highlight the inconsistencies and to regulate them.

15 International Organizations and Stories of Development

Isabel Feichtner

Underdevelopment is really a sort of by-product of the development of the Western countries, or, if one prefers, the inevitable result of the development of the system of international economic relations.

Mohammed Bedjaoui[1]

Increasing the number of luxury resorts, capturing the retiree market, and basing cruise ships in the Pacific could increase the number of tourists visiting the Pacific by about 1 million, generate additional spending of more than US$1.6 billion, and create more than 110,000 additional jobs by 2040.

World Bank[2]

15.1 How to Write About International Organizations' Work on Development?

Writing about international organizations and development is a daunting task due to the elusiveness of the concept of development, the manifold international institutions, instruments and policies designed to promote development and the entanglement of the development discourse with colonial and imperial practices of domination and extraction. At this time of mass extinction, devastating climate events, increasing inequality and a global pandemic, much of international organizations' development work appears ever more an ill-suited answer to the urgency of finding new ways to cohabitate in 'capitalist ruins'.[3] How then to write about development and international organizations? This contribution is motivated by the recognition that '[i]t matters what

1 M. Bedjaoui, *Towards a New International Economic Order* (New York: UNESCO, 1979) 67.

2 World Bank, *Pacific Possible. Long-Term Economic Opportunities and Challenges for Pacific Island Countries* (Washington DC: World Bank, 2017) xvi.

3 A. Tsing, *The Mushroom at the End of the World. On the Possibility of Life in Capitalist Ruins* (Princeton University Press, 2015).

thoughts think thoughts; it matters what stories tell stories',[4] that we must rethink and change the story if we are to 'surviv[e] collaboratively in disturbance and contamination'.[5]

In the following section, I briefly (and incompletely) map international organizations' work for development (Section 15.2). Next, I zoom in on the dominant development story and draw attention to how the extractive industries, the site of some of the worst excesses of capitalist surplus value production, are integrated into this story (Section 15.3). I then turn to the only contemporary international organization primarily mandated to administer mineral extraction, the International Seabed Authority (ISA), and its role in managing and perpetuating exploitation, extraction and inequalities. I specify its development mandate and contrast its current implementation with Mohammed Bedjaoui's vision of the ISA as a new type of international institution central to a new law of development (Section 15.4). I end this chapter with some of the development stories that informed debates in the 1970s and 1980s on the future of international law and institutions, distinguishing between quests for radical transformation and moderate reform (Section 15.5).

15.2 Mapping International Organizations' Work towards Development

15.2.1 Note on Terminology

International organizations use the terms least-developed, developing and developed in order to categorize states – sometimes on the basis of objective criteria, sometimes self-designation.[6] Depending on how states are categorized, they incur differing responsibilities or are granted preferential or differential treatment. The terminology causes unease for the same reasons that inform critique of the prevalent concept of development: its connotations of

[4] D. Haraway, *Staying with the Trouble: Making Kin in the Chthulucene* (Durham NC: Duke University Press, 2016) 39. On utopian thinking and fabulation as method, see, moreover, R. Levitas, *Utopia as Method: The Imaginary Reconstitution of Society* (Basingstoke: Palgrave Macmillan, 2013); B. Massumi, *99 Theses on the Revaluation of Value: A Postcapitalist Manifesto* (Minneapolis MN: University of Minnesota Press, 2018).

[5] Haraway, *Making Kin*, 37, quoting Tsing.

[6] P. Dann, *The Law of Development Cooperation: A Comparative Analysis of the World Bank, the EU and Germany* (Cambridge University Press, 2013) 203–5.

hierarchy and progress and continuities with the distinction civilized/uncivilized that was crucial in legitimizing colonial domination and exploitation.[7] In 2016, the World Bank announced that in its World Development Indicators it no longer distinguished between developing and developed countries.[8] It reasoned that the categorization lacked analytical purchase and pointed to the fact that the Sustainable Development Goals (SDG) were development goals for all and not only for a group of states. Inequality, after all, not only existed within the so-called 'developing world'.[9]

While this is true, dismissing the distinction as an instance of 'development zeitgeist'[10] neglects the emancipatory history of the term '(under) developed'. As indicated by the quote from Bedjaoui at the outset of this chapter, the distinction underdeveloped/developed in the period of formal decolonization was used not only as a description of an economic state of affairs. It also invoked the responsibility of industrialized states for persisting exploitation, structural violence and resulting economic inequality.[11] In the following, I use the term developing states mindful of its ambivalence.

15.2.2 Mapping Work on Development

Development is omnipresent in the work of international organizations, including those of general jurisdiction. The EU has a development policy and concludes development agreements, the UN has its own Development Program (UNDP) and the General Assembly has adopted a number of development-related instruments, announcing a right to development in the 1980s,[12] and promulgating

[7] A. Anghie, *Imperialism, Sovereignty and the Making of International Law* (Cambridge University Press, 2005); S. Pahuja, *Decolonising International Law: Development, Economic Growth and the Politics of Universality* (Cambridge University Press, 2011); N. Tzouvala, *Capitalism as Civilization: A History of International Law* (Cambridge University Press, 2020).

[8] N. Fantom, T. Khokhar and E. Purdie, 'The 2016 Edition of World Development Indicators Is Out: Three Features You Won't Want to Miss', https://blogs.worldbank.org/opendata/2016-edition-world-development-indicators-out-three-features-you-won-t-want-miss (accessed 16 October 2020).

[9] T. Khokhar and U. Serajuddin, 'Should We Continue to Use the Term "Developing World"', https://blogs.worldbank.org/opendata/should-we-continue-use-term-developing-world (accessed 16 October 2020).

[10] *Ibid.*

[11] On the terms 'Third World', 'underdeveloped countries' and 'developing countries', see Bedjaoui, *New International Economic Order*, 25, 26.

[12] UN GA, 'Declaration on the Right to Development' (A/RES/41/128, 1986).

Millennium Development Goals (MDG) in 2000, succeeded by the Sustainable Development Goals (SDG) in 2015.[13]

Likewise, specialized international organizations like the World Trade Organization (WTO), the International Organization for Migration, the World Health Organization and the Food and Agricultural Organization have mandates relating to development, and particular bodies, programmes or bureaus dedicated to development. Finally, development banks, due to their specific development mandates, their organization as banks and weighted voting, can be categorized as a distinct group of development institutions.[14] One of the attractions of re-casting development in terms of MDG and SDG resides in the promise of harmonizing the vast variety of development activities of international organizations.

Despite attempts at harmonization, international organizations offer different understandings of development, the conditions and instruments required to achieve development. Some were created specifically to counter development agendas of existing organizations. The Asian Infrastructure Investment Bank (AIIB), for instance, was set up in 2015 as a counterweight to the International Bank for Reconstruction and Development (IBRD) and the International Monetary Fund (IMF). The United Nations Conference on Trade and Development (UNCTAD) was convened in the 1960s, when discussions on a Generalized System of Preferences had stalled under the General Agreement on Tariffs and Trade (GATT).

International law scholarship has addressed such politics of forum shifting,[15] the discrepancy between good intentions and the spectacular failure of development projects in practice, the changing styles and instruments of development and the role of law therein.[16] Recent works, moreover,

[13] UN GA, 'United Nations Millennium Declaration' (A/RES/55/2, 2000); UN GA, 'Transforming our World: The 2030 Agenda for Sustainable Development' (A/RES/70/1, 2015).

[14] For a categorization of development banks, see Dann, *Law of Development Cooperation*, 158, 202, 209.

[15] E. Benvenisti and G. W. Downs, 'The Empire's New Clothes: Political Economy and the Fragmentation of International Law', (2007) 60 *Stanford Law Review* 595; S. Ranganathan, *Strategically Created Treaty Conflicts and the Politics of International Law* (Cambridge University Press, 2014); M. Zürn, *A Theory of Global Governance: Authority, Legitimacy and Contestation* (Oxford University Press, 2018).

[16] See D. Trubek and M. Galanter, 'Scholars in Self-Estrangement. Some Reflections on the Crisis in Law and Development Studies in the United States', (1974) *Wisconsin Law Review* 1062; K. Rittich, 'The Future of Law and Development: Second-Generation Reforms and the Incorporation of the Social', in D. Trubek and A. Santos (eds.), *The New Law and Economic Development: A Critical Appraisal* (Cambridge University Press, 2006) 203; P. Dann, *Law of*

have examined organizations as bureaucracies with a tendency to act not merely as agents of states, but to develop agendas of their own that shape understandings of how a state should be organized and work for its population's development.[17]

To offer some orientation in the landscape of international organizations working towards development, I distinguish three areas of work: (1) the co-constitution and protection of markets and private property; (2) knowledge production, standard-setting and technical assistance; and (3) development finance. This mapping is not exhaustive. It departs from a narrow notion of 'development institution' that only encompasses international organizations engaged in transfers of funds and knowledge to poorer states[18] in order to draw attention to the close connection between the prevalent development story and the system of international economic relations – a system that is increasingly subjected to calls for a fundamental rethinking, also by economists, for its orientation towards continuous growth and the domination and destruction of life it produces.[19]

15.2.2.1 Co-constitution and Protection of Markets and Private Property

International organizations, in particular the WTO and the World Bank Group's International Center for the Settlement of Investment Disputes (ICSID), play an important part in co-constituting the legal infrastructure of a globalized liberal-capitalist market economy.[20] They do so through the protection of competition and private property, invoking a development narrative.

Development Cooperation; F. Johns, 'From Planning to Prototype: New Ways of Seeing Like a State', (2019) 82 *Modern Law Review* 833.

17 G. F. Sinclair, *To Reform the World: International Organizations and the Making of Modern States* (Oxford University Press, 2017).

18 For a mapping of development law and institutions based on a definition of 'law of development' as 'the law governing the actors, instruments and processes that organize the transfer of knowledge and funds to the South for development purposes', see P. Dann, 'The Law of International Development', in R. Buchanan, L. Eslava and S. Pahuja (eds.), *Oxford Handbook of International Law and Development* (Oxford University Press, forthcoming).

19 K. Raworth, *Doughnut Economics: Seven Ways to Think like a 21st-Century Economist* (White River Junction VT: Chelsea Green, 2017).

20 Instructive: Q. Slobodian, *Globalists. The End of Empire and the Birth of Neoliberalism* (Cambridge MA: Harvard University Press, 2018); see also N. Tzouvala, 'The Ordo-Liberal Origins of Modern International Investment Law: Constructing Competition on a Global Scale', in J. Haskell and A. Rasulov (eds.), *New Voices and New Perspectives in International Economic Law* (Dordrecht: Springer, 2020) 37.

Among the WTO's primary objectives are the incremental widening of market access for goods and services, the protection of competitive conditions from discrimination and the dismantling of government measures that restrict trade and do not meet the WTO's legal requirements. With the TRIPS Agreement the WTO, moreover, provides for the protection of intellectual property as the subject of 'private rights'. The WTO's dispute settlement system, which is to ensure compliance with this 'rules-based system', was considered one of the most effective international adjudication mechanisms before the Appellate Body became inoperational.

Investment protection, contained in bilateral investment treaties and regional trade agreements, is another building block of this legal order, protecting private investment inter alia against 'unfair and inequitable' government interference. Investors may bring claims for damages against host states in transnational investor-state dispute settlement (ISDS) proceedings, for which the ICSID provides a central forum.[21]

Both regimes, of trade and investment protection, are criticized for obstructing development by unduly limiting states' 'policy space' and fiscal leeway.[22] In the midst of the COVID-19 pandemic, a request supported by a group of developing WTO members for a waiver decision to suspend certain TRIPS rules to facilitate 'the prevention, containment and treatment of COVID-19'[23] was opposed by high-income WTO members. Investors continue to claim high amounts of damages, arguing that public policy measures, including in the areas of health and climate protection, violate standards of expropriation and fair and equitable treatment.

Even though the WTO and the institutional infrastructure of investment protection (which also includes the Multilateral Investment Guarantee Agency (MIGA)) are being critiqued for inadequately taking account of, and even counteracting, development needs, economic development is central to their legitimacy narrative. According to the self-understanding of these organizations, they contribute to maintaining the legal infrastructure of a liberal global

[21] T. St John, *The Rise of Investor State Arbitration* (Oxford University Press, 2014).

[22] D. Rodrik, *The Globalization Paradox: Democracy and the Future of the World Economy* (Oxford University Press, 2011). For an overview over critiques of investment law: R. Howse, 'International Investment Law and Arbitration: A Conceptual Framework', in H. Ruiz Fabri (ed.), *International Law and Litigation: A Look into Procedure* (Baden-Baden: Nomos, 2019) 363.

[23] Communication from India and South-Africa to the TRIPS Council, 2 October 2020, IP/C/W/669 (the original request has since been modified).

economic order into which all states are called to integrate for the benefit of their development.

15.2.2.2 Knowledge Production, Standard-Setting and Technical Assistance

A second area in which international organizations work towards development is the production of knowledge that informs standard-setting and technical assistance – since 2015 with a focus on realizing the SDG. Institutions active in this area include UNCTAD, UNDP, the United Nations Industrial Development Organization and many more.

The International Financial Institutions (IFI), that is, the IMF and the World Bank,[24] as well as the Organization for Economic Co-operation and Development (OECD) with its Development Assistance Committee, are particularly effective actors in this field. The World Bank refers to itself as a 'knowledge bank' and its staff produces highly influential 'knowledge products' such as the controversial Doing Business (discontinued in 2021) and the World Development Report.[25] During the decades leading up to the global financial crisis, policy advice and technical assistance by these organizations was informed by the so-called Washington Consensus, which, in the name of development, emphasized market liberalization, including the liberalization of global capital flows, and the privatization of the economy and cautioned against state intervention beyond the correction of market failures.[26]

15.2.2.3 Development Finance

Policy prescriptions by international organizations are particularly effective when they are formulated as conditions attached to development finance – taking the form of budget or project finance. From the Latin American debt crises in the 1980s to the Eurocrisis at the beginning of the twenty-first century, IFI have combined budget finance to indebted states with

[24] The term World Bank refers to the IBRD and the International Development Association (IDA), while the term World Bank Group further includes the International Finance Corporation that finances private sector investments, ICSID and MIGA.

[25] On governance of and through information by international institutions: M. Riegner, 'Towards an International Institutional Law of Information', (2015) 12 *International Organizations Law Review* 50.

[26] J. Williamson, 'Democracy and the "Washington Consensus"', (1993) 21 *World Development* 1329.

conditionality that prescribes public spending cuts, (re-)privatizations,[27] trade liberalization, tax, pension and labour market reforms in order to 'modernize' the recipient states' economies, render them 'competitive', promote private investment and place them on a growth trajectory.[28] Whether loans come with hard or soft conditions and preferential interest rates, they remain loans, which need to be paid back.[29] Even during the COVID-19 pandemic, when states struggle with mounting indebtedness, IFI granted some debt relief, yet no far-reaching debt forgiveness.

Together with numerous regional development banks, including the African Development Bank, the Asian Development Bank, the European Investment Bank, the European Bank for Reconstruction and Development and the Inter-American Development Bank, the World Bank is further engaged in project finance. These banks are set up in a roughly similar manner. Drawing on member state contributions and private capital (the better their credit rating, the better their chances to attract capital, providing a reminder of the power of credit rating agencies), they sponsor and finance capacity-building projects as well as investments (often large-scale infrastructure projects in transport, energy or telecommunications) and do so typically at rates that would be difficult to obtain on capital markets, and subject to conditionality.

In order to address environmental and human rights concerns and ensure the participation of local communities, the banks have devised procedural safeguards and performance standards.[30] The World Bank Group's

[27] Zambia is a case in point: see J. Craig, 'Putting Privatization into Practice: The Case of Zambia Consolidated Copper Mines Limited', (2001) 39 *Journal of Modern African Studies* 389; A. Fraser and J. Lungu, *For Whom the Windfalls? Winners & Losers in the Privatization of Zambia's Copper Mines* (CSTNZ/CCJDP, 2007).

[28] On structural adjustment conditionality, see E. Helleiner, *States and the Reemergence of Global Finance: From Bretton Woods to the 1990s* (Ithaca NY: Cornell University Press, 1994); on its successor policy, see C. Tan, *Governance through Development: Poverty Reduction Strategies, International Law and the Disciplining of Third World States* (London: Routledge, 2011).

[29] N. Woods, *The Globalizers: the IMF, the World Bank and Their Borrowers* (Ithaca NY: Cornell University Press, 2007).

[30] Attempts to make them more sensitive to human rights often meet with cultural obstacles. See G. Sarfati, *Values in Translation: Human Rights and the Culture of the World Bank* (Stanford CA: Stanford University Press, 2012); D. van den Meerssche, 'A Legal Black Hole in the Cosmos of Virtue: The Politics of Human Rights Critique Against the World Bank', (2021) 21 *Human Rights Law Review* 80.

environmental and social safeguard policies have become a decisive standard also for project finance by private financial institutions, inter alia through their incorporation into the Equator Principles, a voluntary code of conduct of the financial industry.[31] To further enhance its accountability, the World Bank in 1993 established the Inspection Panel to hear complaints by individuals affected by development projects.[32] Other development banks followed suit with similar mechanisms.

In the course of the global financial crisis, the Eurocrisis and the COVID-19 pandemic, international organizations have paid renewed attention to governments' 'policy space' and the important role of industrial policy in ensuring that investments benefit the public and do not harm future generations.[33] Yet, while the COVID-19 pandemic prompted massive government support measures, recent activities in the realm of development finance raise doubts about whether the IFI fundamentally are changing course to support a deprivatization of the economy.

Indeed, private investors and financial institutions may be primary beneficiaries of increased development finance to realize the SDG and protect against climate change risks. In order to limit public indebtedness, public finance is being combined – 'blended' – with finance provided by institutional investors,[34] who benefit from public guarantees, insurance and other public support that minimize their risk while ensuring significant returns.[35]

[31] P. Dann and M. Riegner, 'The World Bank's Environmental and Social Safeguards and the Evolution of Global Order', (2019) 32 *Leiden Journal of International Law* 537.

[32] A. Naudé Fourie, *The World Bank Inspection Panel and Quasi-Judicial Oversight* (Utrecht: Eleven, 2009).

[33] See, e.g., UNCTAD, 'Investment Policy Framework for Sustainable Development' (2015) UNCTAD/DIAE/PCB/2015/5, <https://unctad.org/system/files/official-document/diaepcb2015d5_en.pdf> (accessed 17 October 2020). Economist Mariana Mazzucato is a prominent advocate for a stronger role of the state in the economy: M. Mazzucato, *The Entrepreneurial State: Debunking Public vs Private Sector Myths* (London: Anthem Press, 2013); M. Mazzucato, *Mission Economy: A Moonshot Guide to Changing Capitalism* (London: Allen Lane, 2021).

[34] World Bank and IMF, 'From Billions to Trillions: Transforming Development Finance. Post-2015 Financing for Development: Multilateral Development Finance', Development Committee Meeting, DC2015-0002, 2 April 2015.

[35] Y. Dafermos, D. Gabor and J. Michell, 'The Wall Street Consensus in Pandemic Times: What Does It Mean for Climate-aligned Development?', (2021) 42 *Canadian Journal of Development Studies* 238; see also C. Tan, 'Creative Cocktails or Toxic Brews? Blended Finance and the Regulatory Framework for Sustainable Development', in C. Gammage and T. Novitz (eds.), *Sustainable Trade, Investment and Finance: Toward Responsible and Coherent Regulatory Frameworks* (Cheltenham: Edward Elgar, 2019) 300.

15.3 The Prevalent Development Story: Cruise Ships in the Pacific and Sustainable Extraction

Stories and conceptions of development in the work of international organizations are typically focused on economic growth, investment and competition, while recognizing the importance of the well-being and rights of individuals and protection of the environment. They form part of a development apparatus, which further includes epistemological devices, such as indicators to measure as well as legal and non-legal instruments to promote development.

One of the products of the World Bank functioning as a 'knowledge bank' is the Pacific Possible report. It illustrates how the contemporary development story is co-produced and continuously reproduced by international organizations, and – even though it does not endorse seabed mining as a development path – indicates how extraction can be integrated into this story.

15.3.1 The Development Story

> *The Pacific islands were settled by successive waves of intrepid seafarers who sailed boldly west to east across immense distances. Their incredible navigational skills, endurance and courage have shaped the Pacific's people and cultures. Pacific Possible has sought inspiration from these early seafarers to think outside the box and to propose bold solutions.*
>
> Epigraph to the World Bank's Pacific Possible Report

In 2017 the World Bank published *Pacific Possible*, a summary report on the 'long-term economic opportunities and challenges for Pacific Island Countries (PICs)'.[36] The report addresses the question of how PICs can achieve accelerated economic growth and improved standards of living. The authors present the report as departing from conventional development advice and the product of 'thinking outside the box' necessitated by the specific situation of PICs – their smallness, remoteness and particular exposure to the effects of climate change. Nonetheless, the report serves as an illustration of the dominant development story. It is instructive on four counts: first, the conventional view it alludes to; second, its actual proposals; third, the dystopian development path emerging from the report and fourth, the proposals it does *not* make.

[36] World Bank, *Pacific Possible.*

The report describes 'the conventional view' as follows:

One frequently held view is that low growth is due to a poor policy and institutional environment and that, with greater reform effort, higher economic growth would be possible. This view often comes with long lists of reforms that the PICs should pursue – covering broad reform areas such as governance, the business environment, and infrastructure, but also very specific issues such as land reform.[37]

This account represents a typical perspective with its focus on policy and institutions as well as good governance and business environment.[38]

Despite its self-characterization as 'out of the box thinking', the report's suggested policy options do not deviate much from the approach presented as 'conventional'. The report endorses expansion of the tourism sector and the fishing industry, integration into global value chains through improved internet access and connectivity and the use of 'expanded labor mobility opportunities' to enhance remittances and slow down the growth of a population threatened by climate change. The imagery becomes vivid as regards the suggestions for a tourism industry. The report tells the story of Chinese retirees travelling to the PICs on cruise ships and spending their money in luxury resorts.

Not only is the report's horizon – 'sustained high growth' and 'competitiveness' – very much in line with the conventional approach, but so are the instruments proposed. They include 'harmonized business regulations that make it easier for tourism operators to operate in multiple countries' and thus 'may increase the attractiveness of the region for international investors'.[39] In brief, the report sees promise in the further integration of PICs into the global capitalist economy – through global value chains, exports of primary commodities (fish) and labour and tourism. This development advice is largely compatible with the work of other organizations, directed at assisting developing countries in becoming 'investor-friendly' and integrating into global value chains.[40] As so often, this kind of policy advice presents development measures as producing mutual gain – for

[37] *Ibid.*, at xiv.

[38] On the World Bank's emphasis on governance reforms, see Sinclair, *To Reform the World.*

[39] World Bank, *Pacific Possible*, xxii.

[40] WTO, the Institute of Developing Economies (IDE-JETRO), OECD, the Research Center of Global Value Chains headquartered at the University of International Business and Economics (RCGVC-UIBE), the World Bank Group and the China Development Research Foundation, *Global Value Chain Development Report 2019. Technological Innovation, Supply Chain Trade, and Workers in a Globalized World* (Geneva: WTO, 2019).

developing states and their populations as well as foreign investors and their home states.[41]

Despite the promised gains, the envisaged development remains a bleak and dystopian affair. Two features in particular underline the urgency to change the story and think new concepts. First, the report does not hold a promise to overcome precarity. Rather, it seems to accept precarity as a feature of the contemporary formation of capitalism.[42] It thus differs from older 'modernization stories' of social progress. According to the report's advice, islanders should emigrate as a measure of 'population control' and to escape the consequences of climate change; the shores of the islands shall become the anchoring places of cruise ships to enable the population that remains to make a living by serving the vacationers. This scenario, second, illustrates how competitiveness and growth build on inequality – the wage gap enables retirees from neighbouring China to enjoy luxury vacations in the Pacific and turns the islanders into a cheap ('competitive') labour force.

Finally, the report is remarkable for what it does *not* propose. It 'recognizes that there are important interlinkages and tradeoffs between the pursuit of higher economic growth and other dimensions of wellbeing that need to be considered'. And that '[s]uch considerations would not only include distributional impacts, but also impacts on social cohesion, the environment, cultural and social preferences, equal opportunities for men and women and so forth'.[43] While it thus acknowledges the importance of questions of distribution, it does not contain proposals to address them. Similar reluctance to engage with distributive concerns can be observed in the work of other international organizations. The WTO, for example, recognizes that trade liberalization makes some social groups worse off, but leaves addressing this situation to its members.[44] Such restraint is being justified in the name of political autonomy. Yet, states' autonomy to take redistributive measures is frequently severely limited by a lack of resources and structural characteristics of the global economic order.

The report notes that PICs are 'competitive only in areas where natural resource rents outweigh the high costs of production' and consequently

[41] On the ideology of mutuality: S. Marks, 'Exploitation As an International Legal Concept', in S. Marks (ed.), *International Law on the Left. Re-Examining Marxist Legacies* (Cambridge University Press, 2009) 281, 302 ff.

[42] G. Standing, *The Precariat: The New Dangerous Class* (London: Bloomsbury, 2011).

[43] World Bank, *Pacific Possible*, 3.

[44] Rodrik, *Globalization Paradox.*

recommends expanding the fishing industry. Yet, it does *not* present mineral extraction from the seabed as a development opportunity for its uncertain, but potentially far-reaching effects on marine ecosystems, and the possibility that economic benefits remain insignificant.[45] It thus departs from the practice of other organizations to endorse PICs' engagement in seabed mining.

15.3.2 Integration of Extraction into the Development Story

> *About 3.5 billion people live in countries rich in oil, gas or minerals. With good governance and transparent management, the revenues from extractive industries can have an impact on reducing poverty and boosting shared prosperity, while respecting community needs and the environment.*
>
> World Bank[46]

As *Pacific Possible* acknowledges, extraction is not necessarily conducive to development even under the predominant development story. Not only is sustained economic growth in states with a large extractive sector potentially impeded by effects that development economists subsume under the term 'resource curse'. The objective of human development, as measured for example by UNDP's Human Development Index, is also endangered by the effects that large-scale extraction commonly has on health and habitats. Examples abound of extraction projects that required massive resettlements and contaminated water and soil.[47] From a perspective of underdevelopment, the history of colonial exploitation of natural wealth and ongoing unequal exchange provide further reasons against extraction-led development. Finally, in light of quickly progressing climate change, the extraction of fossil energy sources becomes increasingly unjustifiable as a contribution to development.[48]

At the same time, however, worldwide demand for primary commodities, raw materials and energy is still growing. For many resource-rich countries extraction thus becomes an opportunity to generate revenue and employment.

45 World Bank, *Pacific Possible*, 69 ff.

46 The World Bank, *Extractive Industries*, <www.worldbank.org/en/topic/extractiveindustries</int_i> (accessed 6 August 2020).

47 S. Sassen, *Expulsions: Brutality and Complexity in the Global Economy* (Cambridge MA: Harvard University Press, 2014); UNEP, *Environmental Assessment of Ogoniland* (Nairobi: UNEP, 2011).

48 The problem of 'stranded assets', however, poses a significant threat to economic and financial stability.

Even though this 'opportunity' follows inter alia from the demand in resource importing states, the interests of resource exporting and resource importing states do not necessarily align. Since the end of the formal colonial period, developing states have sought to increase control over their natural resources to secure a share in the gains from extraction. Central to this endeavour were the establishment of permanent sovereignty over natural resources as a legal principle,[49] cartelization, as well as (largely unsuccessful) demands for technology transfer and unconditional development finance expressed in the General Assembly resolutions on the New International Economic Order (NIEO).[50]

Nationalizations and other policies adopted by resource-rich developing states to enhance control, in turn prompted manifold reactions by importing states aiming to secure their access to raw materials and energy, among them the development of substitutes and of resource deposits in the importing states, the invention of transnational investment protection law, but also the creation of new international organizations, such as the International Energy Agency. The EU, as part of its raw materials strategy, engages in 'resource diplomacy' that seeks to promote 'free markets' for raw materials inter alia by including prohibitions of export restrictions in WTO accession protocols and regional trade agreements.[51]

Against this background, much of the work of international organizations on development can be understood as an attempt to reconcile these competing interests and make extraction work for development. While approaches differ with respect to the 'correct' market framework, there is strong agreement that 'good governance', 'rule of law' and 'corporate social responsibility' may ensure the sustainability of extraction, that is, contain the environmental and social costs while enhancing the economic benefits for the population of the resource state. SDG 12, 'sustainable consumption

[49] UN GA Resolution 1803 (XVII) (1962); N. Schrijver, *Sovereignty over Natural Resources: Balancing Rights and Duties* (Cambridge University Press, 1997).

[50] 'Declaration on the Establishment of the New International Economic Order' (Resolution 3201 (S-VI), 1974); 'Programme of Action on the Establishment of a New International Economic Order' (Resolution 3202 (S-VI), 1974); I. Feichtner, 'International (Investment) Law and Distribution Conflicts over Natural Resources', in S. Schill *et al.* (eds.), *International Investment Law and Sustainable Development* (Cheltenham: Edward Elgar, 2014) 256.

[51] EU Commission, 'Tackling the Challenges in Commodity Markets and on Raw Materials', COM (2011) 25 final.

and production', includes the target 'sustainable management of natural resources through the minimization of risks and maximization of shared benefits'. Instruments adopted or promoted by international organizations to make extraction work for development include the performance standards and safeguards mentioned above, multi-stakeholder initiatives (such as the Extractive Industries Transparency Initiative and the Voluntary Principles on Security and Human Rights) and codes of conduct (such as the UN Guidelines on Business and Human Rights and the OECD Due Diligence Guidance for Responsible Supply Chains of Minerals from Conflict-Affected and High-Risk Areas) that aim, inter alia, at enhancing transparency, combatting corruption and tax evasion, and protecting the environment, human rights and the rights of indigenous peoples.[52]

Global warming and the international consensus on the need to reduce carbon emissions have led to further prescriptions on how to render extraction sustainable. Moreover, the need for a 'low carbon future', has opened up yet another 'development opportunity', namely the extraction of minerals needed in the production of so-called 'clean energy technologies'. Thus, one can read on a World Bank blog: 'By working together, we can utilize the raw materials needed for clean-energy technologies and conserve forests at the same time – protecting the world's forests, reducing emissions and stepping up to the climate challenge.'[53]

Again, it is the idea of mutual gain that characterizes the story. Extraction is presented as potentially beneficial for everyone if only the necessary safeguards are adopted. If interest conflicts rise to the surface, they are addressed through procedures that seek to balance conflicting interests.[54] Where, however, extraction-based development not only affects interests, but does violence to life, value systems and cosmologies, resolution through balancing is no longer possible. As Sundhya Pahuja points out, international law and international organizations' work in the name of development efface international law's promise of justice and autonomy to the

[52] I. Feichtner, M. Krajewski and R. Rösch (eds.), *Human Rights in the Extractive Industries: Transparency, Participation, Resistance* (Berlin: Springer, 2019).

[53] K. Hund, E. Reed, *A Low-Carbon Future Must Protect the World's Forests*, https://blogs.worldbank.org/voices/low-carbon-future-must-protect-worlds-forests (accessed 3 August 2020).

[54] On the significance of 'interests' in capitalism, see A. Hirschmann, *The Passions and the Interests: Political Arguments for Capitalism before Its Triumph* (Princeton University Press, 1977).

postcolonial state and its people. Not only did the formerly colonized have to adopt the state form in order to participate as sovereign equals in international relations, but autonomy is further restricted as the parameters of development are being defined by international organizations.[55]

How international organizations – even if unintentionally – work to undermine the promise of overcoming underdevelopment, can be seen particularly well by tracing the history of the ISA, the only international organization that has resource extraction *and* development as its main mandates.

15.4 The ISA As a Development Organization

15.4.1 The ISA's Development Mandates

> *The International Seabed Authority is like no other international organization, it is here to run an industry – the deep seabed mining industry.*
>
> Delegate from Jamaica at the 25th Session of the ISA Council, March 2019

The ISA, which today has 168 member states, was established by the 1982 UN Law of the Sea Convention (LOSC) with the mandate to develop the mineral resources of and manage mineral exploration and exploitation in 'the Area' (Article 150 LOSC) – defined in Article 1(1)(a) LOSC as 'the seabed and ocean floor and subsoil thereof, beyond the limits of national jurisdiction'. According to Article 136 LOSC, the 'Area and its [mineral] resources are the common heritage of mankind'. As an agent of humankind, the ISA licenses and regulates mining activities in the Area. While it has adopted regulations on exploration, it currently negotiates the exploitation regulations to complete the Mining Code that is to govern large-scale commercial mineral extraction. Given this mandate, calling the ISA an international organization that runs a mining industry, as did the Jamaican delegate cited at the beginning of this section, seems very apt.

The ISA is further mandated to promote economic development and to do so in two ways. One is redistribution: The ISA shall 'provide for the equitable sharing of financial benefits derived from activities in the Area' (Article 140(2) LOSC) and in doing so take 'into particular consideration the interests and needs of developing States' (Article 160(2)(f)(i) LOSC). The

[55] Pahuja, *Decolonising International Law.*

other is ensuring the equal participation of developing states in the exploitation of seabed minerals. Both development objectives, redistribution and equal participation, have, however, been severely compromised.[56]

To ensure equal participation in deep seabed mining, developing states – organized in the G77 – during the LOSC negotiations first insisted that mining activities should be conducted by an international mining enterprise. Industrialized states objected, favouring a licensing system that would allow mining by private corporations.[57] On the basis of a proposal made in 1976 by US secretary of state Henry Kissinger, states ultimately agreed on what today is known as the 'parallel' or 'site banking' system. It was presented as a compromise that would allow private mining to go forward while ensuring that developing states also could participate in mining activities. Participation by developing states was to be enabled by the 'banking' of mining sites and the establishment of an international mining enterprise – the Enterprise. 'Site banking' means that when a (private or public) mining enterprise, under the sponsorship of a state,[58] is granted an exploration licence for a designated area of the seabed, a site of equal size and mineral worth is being reserved. These reserved areas may only be exploited by the Enterprise or by enterprises sponsored by developing states. The parallel system from its inception was criticized as inept to ensure equal participation. Elisabeth Mann Borgese called it an 'offer to pay with public funds for private profit',[59] as public funds would have financed the Enterprise in exchange for the right of commercial enterprises to exploit seabed minerals in competition with the Enterprise.[60]

The 1994 Implementation Agreement then significantly limited the scope for mining activities by the Enterprise. The agreement was to enhance the regime's 'market-orientation' and thus to appease a number

[56] For a more in-depth treatment: I. Feichtner, 'Sharing the Riches of the Sea: The Redistributive and Fiscal Dimension of Deep Seabed Exploitation', (2019) 30 *European Journal of International Law* 601.

[57] R. P. Anand, 'Common Heritage of Mankind: Mutilation of an Ideal', in R. P. Anand, *Studies in International Law and History* (Leiden: Martinus Nijhoff, 2004) 180.

[58] On the legal responsibilities of sponsoring states, see International Tribunal for the Law of the Sea, Seabed Disputes Chamber, *Responsibilities and Obligations of States Sponsoring Persons and Entities with Respect to Activities in the Area* (Advisory Opinion), 1 February 2011.

[59] E. Mann Borgese, 'The New International Economic Order and the Law of the Sea', (1977) 14 *San Diego Law Review* 584, 590.

[60] On the negotiations, see S. Ranganathan, 'The Common Heritage of Mankind: Annotation on a Battle', in J. von Bernstorff and P. Dann (eds.), *The Battle for International Law: South-North Perspectives on the Decolonization* (Oxford University Press, 2019) 35.

of industrialized states that had refrained from ratifying the LOSC because of its deep seabed mining regime. It scrapped mandatory financing and technology transfer and delayed operationalization of the Enterprise until its commercial viability.

The effects of the parallel system and lack of operationalization of the Enterprise on the economic development objectives are twofold: developing states cannot through the Enterprise actively participate in resource extraction, and the Enterprise does not generate any revenue for redistribution to developing states. As long as the Enterprise is not operationalized, any financial benefits to be redistributed must be generated from royalties or profit shares paid by individual enterprises to the ISA and developing states can only actively participate in seabed mining through the individual sponsorship of mining enterprises.

15.4.2 Development through Sponsorship of Commercial Deep Seabed Mining?

> *In 2011, [Nauru Ocean Resources Inc (NORI)] pioneered a pathway for developing states to directly participate in marine mineral development from the international seabed area. Through NORI, the Republic of Nauru – a small Pacific Island Country, became a Sponsoring State. This was the first time a developing state had partnered with a corporation to access the minerals of the International Seabed Area and in so doing will help to accomplish UNCLOS' vision of sharing benefits with developing states arising from activities related to the mineral resources in the Area.*
>
> Gerard Bannon, CEO of DeepGreen Metals, speaking as member of Nauru's Delegation at the 25th Session of the ISA Council.

One reason why the changes introduced by the 1994 Implementation Agreement found wide acceptance was 'that seabed exploitation of minerals [at the time was] only a distant dream not to be fulfilled until well into the next century'.[61] Since the financial crisis of 2008, interest in seabed mining has significantly increased. More generally, the ocean has drawn attention for the opportunities it offers to spur faltering economic growth. The EU Commission in its Blue Growth Initiative identifies growth potential in five 'focus areas', one of them being seabed mineral resources.[62]

[61] Anand, 'Common Heritage of Mankind', 194.

[62] European Commission, *Blue Growth*, https://ec.europa.eu/maritimeaffairs/policy/blue_growth_en (accessed 3 August 2020).

The policy handbook of the UN Economic Commission for Africa on Africa's Blue Economy states: 'If fully exploited and well managed, Africa's Blue Economy can constitute a major source of wealth and catapult the continent's fortunes'[63] and the African Union is promoting a Blue Economy, as the 'New Frontier of African Renaissance'.[64] Despite mounting ecological concerns and calls for a moratorium on seabed mining, the ISA's own Secretary General actively promotes seabed mining in the Area as a way to produce minerals needed to transition to a green economy and calls for the swift completion of the Mining Code.[65]

PICs have explored seabed mining, in their exclusive economic zones as well as in the Area, as a way to stimulate their economies. The Commonwealth Secretariat, the EU and the Pacific Community provided development support, assisting in drafting national mining legislation. To date, five PICs – Nauru, Tonga, Kiribati, the Cook Islands and Tuvalu – have sponsored corporations that seek to explore and eventually commercially exploit mineral resources in the Area. Such sponsorship is attractive to corporations due to the PICs' location, but also, and possibly more importantly, because it gives them access to the reserved areas. Again the contemporary development story unfolds, focused on growth opportunities for developing states and the mutually beneficial effects from what the CEO of mining corporation DeepGreen Metals (today The Metals Company) calls a 'partnership' between a developing state and a corporation. In his speech before the ISA's Council as part of Nauru's delegation, CEO Bannon further stressed that seabed mining was a 'good use of the common heritage' as it would produce metals needed to combat climate change.[66] He implied that the corporation would cease mining once *sufficient* minerals had been obtained – a highly unlikely postulation in a political economy driven not by need, but profit expectations.

It is also doubtful whether sponsorship will yield any economic development for Nauru and other PICs. Mining corporations will not establish

[63] United Nations Economic Commission for Africa, *Africa's Blue Economy: A Policy Handbook* (Addis Ababa: Economic Commission for Africa, 2016) x.

[64] N. D. Zuma (Chairperson of the African Union Commission), 'Key Note Address', https://au.int/sites/default/files/speeches/25437-sp-chairpersons_keynote_address_for_25_july_2015.pdf (accessed 6 August 2020).

[65] M. Lodge, 'How to Mine the Oceans Sustainably: Deep-Sea Minerals, Including Nickel, Copper, Manganese and Cobalt Are Crucial to Built Clean-energy Technologies', *Scientific American*, 11 August 2020.

[66] G. Bannon, 'Address to ISA Council 27 February 2019', <www.isa.org.jm/files/files/documents/nauru-gb.pdf> (accessed 4 August 2020).

processing plants on the islands that would generate employment. It is further unlikely that PICs will receive significant revenue, due to jurisdictional competition which finds expression in Nauru's International Seabed Minerals Act. It provides for a sponsorship application fee of merely US $15,000 (while the ISA's own application fee is currently set at US $ 500,000), and an annual administration fee of US $ 20,000. It further envisages seabed mineral recovery payments based on a percentage of the market value of mined metals.[67] Given that the ISA under its Mining Code will also collect royalties, it is not to be expected that this percentage will be significant. And yet, the ISA may be a reminder of more utopian stories and concepts, among them Bedjaoui's new law of development.[68]

15.4.3 The ISA As an Institution of a New Law of Development?

> *If the aim of the new international economic order is development, it must then be a comprehensive phenomenon, for development is itself a whole, a cultural process which transmits values and includes not only production, distribution and consumption, but also social relationships, education, the well-being and the natural environment of man.*
>
> ...
>
> *It [the NIEO] will call for the creation of direct international administrative bodies, i.e. operational institutions themselves responsible for managing an 'international civil service' or an intergovernmental or even supranational public enterprise of an economic or financial nature.*
>
> Mohammed Bedjaoui[69]

Bedjaoui, like many of his contemporaries, regarded underdevelopment as a product of the structure of the world economy. Development, to him, was a comprehensive pursuit, to be guided by human dignity and creatively build on each society's particular resources. To bring about development, the international law that had enabled and sustained imperial and neocolonial exploitation needed to change. International institutions had to be established that ultimately would work for the well-being and equality of all humankind.

For Bedjaoui, the concept of common heritage and its institutional operationalization held great promise, while he was conscious of the principle's

[67] International Seabed Minerals Act 2015 (No. 26 of 2015), Part 7 Fiscal Arrangements.

[68] For another re-engagement with Bedjaoui's work, see U. Öszu, 'In the Interests of Mankind As a Whole. Mohammed Bedjaoui's New International Economic Order', (2015) 6 *Humanity* 129.

[69] Bedjaoui, *New International Economic Order*, 74, 194.

colonial connotations and the danger that it could be co-opted by powerful economic interests and states.[70] He saw the possibility that designation of the seabed and its resources as common heritage would contribute to 'economic exploitation which could restore prosperity to all the peoples on Earth'. He argued for the extension of common heritage status to all resources, including knowledge and technology, thus turning humankind and the individual into the new subject of the future international law.[71] Like many of his contemporaries, he thought that the mineral riches of the seabed, designated as common heritage, could 'solve most of the world's problems of development and survival'.[72] Exploitation for the benefit of all states and with particular regard to the least privileged members of the international community, according to Bedjaoui, could forge a new kind of international relations based on solidarity and co-operation.[73] A 1971 report of the UN Secretary-General expresses well the new states' claim on revenue from deep seabed mining when it stresses that such revenue 'should not be confused with foreign aid' as it rightfully belonged to developing states.[74]

Bedjaoui envisaged the new international law of development to unfold in stages with the establishment of new institutions succeeding the setting of new norms. The ISA, not yet established when he wrote about it, held promise to become such a new organization. He envisaged it to be financially independent due to income from mining by the Enterprise and, thus, autonomously exercise jurisdiction over the seabed and to forge a new category of the 'international worker'. For these characteristics, Bedjaoui considered the ISA a para-state body.[75]

R. P. Anand recalls similar aspirations. Common heritage of the seabed was to result in common property and 'a centralized, democratically structured international regime and an international machinery with

[70] *Ibid.*, 222. [71] *Ibid.*

[72] *Ibid.*, 227; see also R. N. Cooper, 'The Oceans as a Source of Revenue', in J. N. Bhagwati, *The New International Economic Order: The North-South Debate* (Cambridge MA: MIT Press, 1977) 105; R. Katz, 'Financial Arrangements for Seabed Mining Companies: An NIEO Case Study', (1979) 13 *Journal of World Trade Law* 209, 211, fn. 3 (mentioning the estimate that individual 'developing states could expect to receive approximately $10m per year' from deep seabed mining).

[73] Bedjaoui, *New International Economic Order*, 227.

[74] United Nations Secretary-General, *Possible Methods and Criteria for the Sharing by the International Community of Proceeds and other Benefits Derived from the Exploitation of the Resources of the Area beyond the Limits of National Jurisdiction* (15 June 1971, A/AC.138/38) para. 47.

[75] Bedjaoui, *New International Economic Order*, 215–20.

comprehensive powers for the exploration and exploitation of the seabed and its resources' were to enable 'real participation' by developing countries. Yet, he concludes that this ideal of common heritage was mutilated: The 1994 Implementation Agreement had incapacitated the Enterprise and decreased the voice of developing states in the ISA.[76]

15.5 A New Law of Development or a Welfarist International Law?

The new international law envisaged by Bedjaoui for long has been considered a lost cause. Perceptions are changing, however. In recent years, many international lawyers have revisited the period of decolonization and its debates on a new international law in order to retell the story of international law and development.[77] In these debates, Bedjaoui's socialist-democratic position differs from a welfarist position held by Western international lawyers.[78] The latter's demands were less far-reaching, yet its promises of redistribution to address underdevelopment are also worth revisiting in the search of alternative stories of development.

15.5.1 A Socialist-Democratic Approach to Development

A socialist-democratic approach to development gained influence in the second half of the 1970s and 1980s.[79] Its prominence is attributed to unsuccessful initiatives to close the wealth gap between states and persisting extreme poverty. While initially states of the Third World had focused

[76] Anand, 'Common Heritage of Mankind'.

[77] L. Eslava, M. Fakhri and V. Nesiah (eds.), *Bandung, Global History, and International Law. Critical Pasts and Pending Futures* (Cambridge University Press, 2017); von Bernstorff and Dann (eds.), *The Battle*; I. Venzke, 'Possibilities of the Past: Histories of the NIEO and the Travails of Critique', (2018) 20 *Journal of the History of International Law* 263.

[78] Jouannet juxtaposes liberal and welfarist notions: E. Jouannet, *The Liberal-Welfarist Law of Nations: A History of International Law* (Cambridge University Press, 2012); for another distinction more similar to the one proposed here, see U. Öszu, 'Hydrocarbon Humanitarianism: Ibrahim Shihata, "Oil Aid", and Resource Sovereignty', (2020) 22 *Journal of the History of International Law* 1.

[79] For earlier debates on postcolonial political economy, see L. Eslava, 'The Developmental State: Independence, Dependency, and the History of the South', in von Bernstorff and Dann (eds.), *The Battle*, 71.

on political independence and equality, they increasingly formulated demands for economic equality.[80]

Many proposals for transformation towards a more egalitarian global economic system were informed by dependency or world system theorists, including André Gunder Frank, Fernando Henrique Cardoso, Samir Amin and Immanuel Wallerstein. They questioned the theorem of comparative advantage, which still today serves prominently as justification for trade liberalization. Frank stresses how classical presentations ignore that the international division of labour, which forms the basis of comparative advantage, was brought about by violence and results in dependency of the underdeveloped states from the imperial centre.[81] 'Unequal exchange' is a central tenet: if states at the periphery (developing states) exchange goods with states at the centre (industrialized states), then – despite equality in prices indicating an equal exchange – more value, measured in labour and natural resources, is transferred from the periphery to the centre. Unequal exchange is attributed to dependency, resource extraction in the periphery and the wage gap between North and South. Further integration into the capitalist society was not seen as a solution to inequality, as this would only benefit the bourgeoisie of the underdeveloped state. Instead, South-South co-operation was a preferred path to self-reliant development.[82]

The ultimate horizon of these writings was not only a transformation of the world capitalist economy. They also aimed at democratizing society (national and international) and ending exploitation.[83] They recognized ecological devastation caused by capitalist production and consumption, exacerbated by a growing world population.[84] They were conscious, however, of the racism inherent in calls for population control addressed to developing states. In response to such calls, Bedjaoui writes: 'The first and basic cause of a population explosion does indeed reside in the underdevelopment,

[80] H. Addo (ed.), *Transforming the World Economy? Nine Critical Essays on the New International Economic Order* (London: Hodder and Stoughton, 1984). For an incisive analysis of different positions, see Bhagwati, 'Introduction', in Bhagwati (ed.), *New International Economic Order* 1.

[81] A. G. Frank, *Dependent Accumulation and Underdevelopment* (London: Macmillan, 1978).

[82] J. Bockman, 'Socialist Globalization against Capitalist Neocolonialism: The Economic Ideas behind the New International Economic Order', (2015) 6 *Humanity* 109.

[83] R. Preiswerk, 'Hidden Dimensions of the So-Called New International Economic Order', in Addo (ed.), *Transforming the World Economy?* 32.

[84] These ecological concerns can be traced back to Marx; see K. Saito, *Karl Marx's Ecosocialism* (New York: Monthly Review Press, 2017).

depredation and exploitation of the riches of the Third World.'[85] The 'development' he postulated as the objective of an anti-imperialist and anti-capitalist new law of development was to be receptive to ecological concerns. Bedjaoui envisaged designating carbon sinks like the Amazon forest as common heritage, but also insisted that industrialized states may not employ the concept to socialize the riches of the Third World and at the same time use it to exploit common riches (such as ocean minerals) for private profit.[86]

To Bedjaoui, international law is not mere superstructure. While influenced by material relations it can be an agent of change in its own right. The European international law had been permissive and supportive of imperialist acquisitions as well as formalist in securing the co-existence of states that were part of the club and their freedom to exploit. The new law of development by contrast would no longer be formalist, it would not only ensure formal political sovereignty, but also pursue economic sovereignty through material equality.[87] The new institutions of international law were to secure equal participation and be operational actors in administration and economy. A prime example, as noted, was the ISA with its operational arm, the Enterprise, indicating a trajectory with international institutions serving not states but the well-being of humankind and 'the law of solidarity' taking the place of 'the law of competition'.[88]

Other international lawyers in this tradition (understood widely) supported the establishment of UNCTAD's Integrated Programme for Commodities and international commodity organizations to address dependency and unequal exchange through the indexing of primary commodity prices to prices of manufactured goods and other market interventions.[89] Producer associations such as OPEC were assigned an important role in bringing about the new order. Cartelization of oil production through OPEC was partially successful as it allowed developing states to exercise what was called 'commodity power' (or 'oil weapon' by Western international lawyers)[90] and to engage in 'third world trade unionism'.[91]

85 Bedjaoui, *New International Economic Order*, 45. 86 *Ibid.*, 224.

87 On the distinction between formal and material law, see D. Kennedy, 'Three Globalizations of Law and Legal Thought, 1850–2000', in Trubek and Santos (eds.), *New Law and Economic Development* 19.

88 Bedjaoui, *New International Economic Order*, 224.

89 B. Chimni, *International Commodity Agreements: A Legal Study* (London: Croom Helm, 1986).

90 J. Paust and A. Blaustein, 'The Arab Oil Weapon: A Threat to International Peace', (1974) 68 *American Journal of International Law* 410.

91 Bhagwati, 'Introduction'.

15.5.2 A Welfarist Approach to Development

Western international lawyers also recognized the need to change international law to accommodate the interests of new states and alleviate poverty. Many were inspired by the welfare state and endorsed the desirability (and obligation) of transfers from the rich to the poor.[92] Calls to democratize international institutions and to turn the General Assembly into a world legislator, as proposed by Bedjaoui, were, however, met with hesitation or rejected. A shared sensitivity to ecological concerns by progressive lawyers from the Third World and the West, moreover, could lead to very different positions. This becomes apparent when comparing Bedjaoui's stance with that of German international lawyer Wolfgang Vitzthum. While an outspoken critic of the industrial states' endeavour to commodify and plunder the seabed, Vitzthum dismissed the developing states' position as ideological and an impediment to the successful conclusion of the Third UN Conference on the Law of the Sea.[93] A similar plea for moderation is Oscar Schachter's 1977 monograph *Sharing the World's Resources*, which endorses the parallel system for deep seabed mining as 'a classic equitable solution'.[94]

Economist Jagdish Bhagwati, too, accepted the need for a redistribution of wealth from the North to the South, yet called for pragmatic recognition that US support was critical for any reform of the global order. Reform proposals he considered both economically sensible and politically practicable included taxation of international seabed mining and fisheries for the benefit of developing states.[95] He was highly critical of the Integrated Programme for Commodities as far as it provided for price indexing, but thought that commodity price stabilization could be considered a 'mutual gain bargain'.

15.6 Development on a Damaged Planet

> *New Gauley compostists soon found that storytelling was the most powerful practice for comforting, inspiring, remembering, warning,*

[92] B. V. A. Röling, *International Law in an Expanded World* (Amsterdam: Djambatan, 1960); C. W. Jenks, *Social Justice in the Law of Nations* (Oxford University Press, 1970).

[93] W. Vitzthum, 'Die Bemühungen um ein Régime des Tiefseebodens: Das Schicksal einer Idee', (1978) 38 *Zeitschrift für ausländisches öffentliches Recht und Völkerrecht* 745.

[94] O. Schachter, *Sharing the World's Resources* (New York: Columbia University Press, 1977) 56.

[95] He also endorsed proposals for a brain drain tax: Bhagwati, 'Introduction'.

nurturing compassion, mourning-with each other in their differences, hopes, and terrors.

Donna Haraway[96]

Most of the proposals to make international law and relations more social(ist) have not been implemented. That underdevelopment nonetheless did not cause a major crisis of international law and institutions may be attributed to generally strong rates of economic growth.[97] Today, prosperity loses ground as a stabilizer. Economic precarity, together with ecological crises, make development stories sound increasingly dystopian.

It matters which stories tell stories and which concepts think concepts. Which story can be told about the development of states and populations whose lands are slowly submerged by the sea with a story populated with cruise ships and machines with 'huge spikes like medieval cudgels to tear through the seabed to mine gold and copper ore'?[98] The stories about a new development law and new international organizations sounded more hopeful, utopian rather than dystopian. Recall, for example, the story of a common enterprise in which international workers in solidarity develop and mine deep seabed resources and distribute the revenue to the world's poorest populations.

Past stories and concepts provide an important repertoire and toolbox to draw on for institutional imagination. A number of institutional proposals and concepts have been revisited during past and present crises. Price stabilization mechanisms and commodity agreements were rediscovered during the last financial crisis and the International Resource Panel in its report *Re-Defining Value* addresses the unequal exchange (not using the term) resulting from the exploitation of natural resources in developing states for production and consumption in high-income states.[99] COVID-19 draws attention to

96 Haraway, *Making Kin*, 50.

97 S. Amin, *Capitalism in the Age of Globalization* (London: Zed Books, 1997).

98 Thus a description of deep-sea mining machines in Tighe, *Nautilus Minerals Steps Up Deep-Sea Mining Plans* (*Financial Times*, 11 November 2015) <www.ft.com/content/0fe538d2-8895-11e5-90de-f44762bf9896> (accessed 6 August 2020).

99 N. Nasr *et al.*, *Re-Defining Value. The Manufacturing Revolution. Remanufacturing, Refurbishment, Repair and Direct Reuse in the Circular Economy*, Report of the International Resource Panel (Nairobi: UNEP, 2018).

(old) warnings against further value chain integration and to the concept of self-reliant development. This repertoire will hardly be enough, however. If international organizations are to support a development that overcomes (neo)colonial exploitation and does justice to human beings' entanglements and interdependence with other species, they must join the telling of new stories.

16 Food Security and International Organizations

Why Not Global? Why Not Now?

Mónica García-Salmones Rovira

16.1 Introduction

The strangest thing about international organizations is that for all the appearance that they have of bringing about a dulling rationalization of life, they are enmeshed in global politics as deeply as any other actor, if not more deeply. The very existence of international organizations in a world order founded on the equal sovereignty of states defies fundamental logic and possibly confirms that they exist both as instruments of policy and as political agents. International organizations have a complex history of their own, and ascertaining their politics is, arguably, in the eyes of the beholder. However, some progressivist and functionalist narratives about the rise of international organizations may 'be doing an injustice to the topic'.[1] International organizations are frequently created in order to act politically on an issue that otherwise states would pursue. However, they may also see the light so that other agents may appropriate what should have been the organization's functions. The organization is hence born, in a way, sterile. International organizations are also like angels, each a species of its own.[2] They constitute legal personalities and each is unique.[3] Therefore, it is hardly possible to generalize beyond a bare minimum about the why and how of their coming into being. These principles of vexed origins and uniqueness are well exemplified by the international organizations working with food security.

[1] J. Klabbers, 'International Institutions', in J. Crawford and M. Koskenniemi (eds.), *Cambridge Companion to International Law* (Cambridge University Press, 2012) 228.

[2] T. Aquinas, *Summa theologiae*, First Part, q. 50, art. 4, www.newadvent.org/summa/1050.htm.

[3] F. Bordin, *The Analogy between States and International Organizations* (Cambridge University Press, 2018).

The food security approach, originally known as the nutrition approach, changed the world order in the 1940s. The reason for this did not lie in its paramount importance. In the midst of the political, military and economic forces, which were simultaneously tremendously divisive and tremendously unifying in effect, that played out between 1935 and 1945, the fact that the issue of food was deemed fairly irrelevant was instrumental in its coming to the fore in international terms. This chapter narrates, first, how in a world distorted by World War II the new science of nutrition and the principle of 'freedom from want' managed the unthinkable for the organization of the world economy: the first unifying efforts made by way of policies for common consumption, production and trade of (food) commodities under the guidance of the United States (USA). Notwithstanding the role of the USA in pushing the matter forward, the approach taken in respect of food security was not of North American, Eurocentric, or even European origin. Perhaps the most remarkable feature of the first international organization dealing with food security is its roots in the Pacific Dominions of the British Empire. Food security was the instrument devised by a couple of clever individuals in order to boost the economy of a country dependent on the export of food: Australia. Ultimately, food security served the Dominion's aspiration of acting independently from Great Britain.

As a concept, food security has been reinvented several times over the last eighty years or so. It appeared with its main characteristics of securing enough nutrition for all people throughout the world in the short writings of Frank Lidgett McDougall (1884–1958) in the 1930s. McDougall himself later dubbed it one of President Franklin D. Roosevelt's four freedoms – 'freedom from want' – and quickly thereafter the expression 'freedom from hunger' spread.[4] Currently the most widely accepted notion of food security, with its origins in the 1996 World Food Summit convened by the Food and Agriculture Organization (FAO), incorporates the coverage of basic physical needs as well as aspects relating to human happiness and cultural, social and anthropological dimensions, in terms of diet and taste.[5]

[4] 'Hot Springs Final Act', United Nations Conference on Food and Agriculture, Hot Springs, Virginia, 18 May to 3 June 1943. Final Act and Section Reports (Washington DC: US Government Printing Office, 1943); R. Jachertz and A. Nützenadel, 'Coping with Hunger? Visions of a Global Food System, 1930–1960', (2011) 6 *Journal of Global History* 99.

[5] Rome Declaration on World Food Security and World Food Summit Plan of Action: World Food Summit, 13–17 November 1996, FAO (063)/F688; reproduced in (1996) 22 *Population and Development Review* 807.

Further features that complement the concept of food security have been added in subsequent World Summits on Food Security. These include social access, stability and sustainability, referring to access to food at any level of economic capacity; for example, the access enjoyed by an elderly person. However, the normative principle of equality behind the inception of the first international organizations dealing with world hunger places particular emphasis on 'people under the most disadvantaged conditions'.[6] That is to say, people suffering from hunger and malnutrition due to natural or human-caused disasters, such as war or economic exploitation, receive special consideration under the umbrella of food security. Moreover, the larger framework of development present in relation to food matters, and generally in the majority of international organizations since the 1950s, agrees with Amartya Sen's argument. It is not only scarcity of food that provokes undernourishment, since access to food is also vital, and extreme poverty, as a rule, means hunger even if the village market has a bountiful supply of food commodities.[7]

The topic of food security per se is not generally conceived as an issue of the primary responsibility of international organizations, but rather securing food at each level, individual, household, regional and global, is a concern mostly of the state, and states ought to cooperate to achieve it.[8] McDougall was the first real promoter of an international organization for food, and envisaged a union of consumption and production and of food and agriculture that entailed a radical change in global economic and political structures towards greater interdependence.[9] His major success was to change the mindset of politicians before the end of World War II towards working together within this broad constellation of ideas. McDougall spearheaded the idea that the best method by which to collaborate worldwide in economy and trade was to aim at securing food and nutrition for every human being. However, when the

[6] W. Peng and E. Berry, 'The Concept of Food Security', in P. Ferranti *et al.* (eds.) *Encyclopedia of Food Security and Sustainability*, vol. 2 (Amsterdam: Elsevier, 2019) 1.

[7] A. Sen, *Poverty and Famines: An Essay on Entitlement and Deprivation* (Oxford University Press, 1983). For a study on the politics of hunger from after the 1950s postcolonial period with an emphasis on the 'financialization' of food commodities, see A. Chadwick, *Law and the Political Economy of Hunger* (Oxford University Press, 2019).

[8] *Rome Declaration.*

[9] This is the argument of W. Way, *A New Idea Each Morning: How Food and Agriculture Came Together in One International Organisation* (Canberra: Australian National University E-Press, 2013). On the perception of that representing Australian self-interest, see W. J. Hudson, *Australia and the League of Nations* (Sydney University Press, 1980) 176.

moment arrived to establish a dedicated organization, food consumption and food production were decoupled. Since the establishment in 1945 of the first international organization with a mandate related to food security (the FAO), the core of the internationalist spirit has been embodied in the attempts made to establish an international food reserve. As we shall see, the goal of creating a world food reserve has also proven too ambitious and powerful countries have regarded sovereignty over food as being too sensitive a topic to allow for compromise. In fact, the issue of food has followed the same internationalist shocks of expansion and restriction as are described for other international organizations dealing with issues of vital interest, evolving in step with the rhythm of international geopolitics. The international organizations involved have seen their mandates expanded or restrained accordingly.

It has been clear for a century or more that the supply of food, as one of the three material essentials of individual human life together with water and oxygen, should be secured at international level.[10] Although famines were known in the nineteenth century and before, World War I – during which food blockade was one of the main weapons used by the Allies against Germany – raised awareness of how important it was for the survival of nations to control food supplies.[11] In recent years, the widespread use of corn-based ethanol for gasoline additive has further complicated the interrelations between food and international markets. In food security terms, food prices and oil prices are interconnected now to a dangerous level.[12]

Food also has a paradoxical spiritual dimension, which may also help explain why passions and emotions run high, and why there is an almost absolute refusal of states to give away their sovereignty on vital issues of food, unless there is 'hunger in the balance'.[13] In his critique of the inefficient international system of food aid in the early 1980s, John Cathie described what was in his view an important obstacle to changing things some forty years ago: the 'moral conviction' engrained in the system 'that giving food to hungry people is right'.[14] At the outset it seems to be a sound

[10] Jachertz and Nützenadel, 'Coping with Hunger?'

[11] C. P. Vincent, *The Politics of Hunger: The Allied Blockade of Germany, 1915–1919* (Athens OH: Ohio University Press, 1985).

[12] F. Avalos and M. Lombardi, 'The Biofuel Connection: Impact of US Regulation on Oil and Food Prices', (2015) *Bank for International Settlements Working Papers* No. 487.

[13] J. Clapp, *Hunger in the Balance: The New Politics of International Food Aid* (Ithaca NY: Cornell University Press, 2012).

[14] To be sure, Cathie agreed with that principle, but criticized the ideology of food aid without commitment to social, economic and political reform: 'In retrospect the scope and quixotic

moral principle to try to avoid at any cost that human beings, not to say pregnant women or children, suffer hunger, malnutrition or want, and to do so, if necessary, by giving them food. Binay Ranjan Sen, Director General of FAO from 1956 to 1967, famously noted that 'hunger has a unique universal appeal. Nothing touches the consciousness as much as hunger'.[15] Interestingly, the old tradition of natural law framed the problem both in terms of feeding the poor and of enabling the poor to use their right to self-preservation. And almost every theologian and canon lawyer for many centuries has written that when those suffering hunger have taken what they needed from people who have plenty, they have simply used their right. This did not constitute theft, because necessity made all things common.[16] The later tradition of natural lawyers was also careful to point out that to deny the rest of mankind food was against 'the great Design of God', and neither could a sovereign justly exploit another's need.[17] Dwight Furrow studies another perspective of the spiritual dimension of food describing 'the food truck as vehicle of salvation', and he does not refer to situations of emergency or famine but to the American Foodie culture. In a society of mass production and its resulting dehumanization, the food revolution, he writes 'is fundamentally an aesthetic revolution driven by a felt need to reconnect with reality'.[18]

Food security intersects with the work of many international organizations.[19] The most central of these is the FAO, which took over the assets and mandate of the International Institute of Agriculture (IIA), founded in 1905. The IIA was probably the first international institution that had the goal of achieving fair prices for

ambition underlying the promotion of one agency to combat "world hunger" seem quite utopian and politically naïve'; J. Cathie, *The Political Economy of Food Aid* (Aldershot: Gower, 1982) 35, 70.

[15] Quoted in D. J. Shawn, *World Food Security: A History since 1945* (New York: Palgrave Macmillan, 2007) 1.

[16] B. Tierney, *The Idea of Natural Rights* (Grand Rapids MI: Eerdmans Publishing, 1997) 69.

[17] J. Locke, *Two Treatises of Government* (Cambridge University Press, 1967 [1689]) 169–70.

[18] D. Furrow, *American Foodie: Taste, Art, and the Cultural Revolution* (Lanham MD: Rowman & Littlefield, 2016) 30.

[19] K. Mechlem, 'Food and Agriculture Organization of the United Nations', *Max Planck Encyclopedia of Public International Law* (online); G. van Zutphen *et al.*, 'The Role of International Agencies in Achieving Food Security', in P. Ferranti, E. Berry and A. Jock (eds.), *Encyclopedia of Food Security and Sustainability* (Amsterdam: Elsevier, 2017) 1; B. Reinalda, *Routledge History of International Organizations: From 1815 to Present Day* (Abingdon: Routledge, 2009).

grain by associating scientific knowledge with legislative power.[20] The World Food Program (WFP) works together with the FAO, and is tasked with agriculture and food delivery per se.[21] The Consortium of International Agricultural Research Centers promotes innovation in contributing to food security in partnership with the FAO. Other key international organizations working with food security are those involved in providing funds, such as the International Bank for Reconstruction and Development (IBRD) and the International Fund for Agricultural Development (IFAD). The International Union for the Protection of New Varieties of Plants (UPOV) is tasked with the protection of intellectual property rights concerning new plant varieties.

Food security constitutes a broad and constantly evolving agenda in which many players from the international political and economic order participate in order to promote national and private interests under the umbrella topic of food security. One example, among hundreds, of the rapid proliferation of entities in the framework of operation of food security and international organizations may illustrate the creative, fluid, sometimes obscure, sometimes fleeting agenda of those engaged with this topic and, above all, the complex dimensions of the challenge. Following the World Food Summit of 1996, and with a view to implementing the food security agenda, the FAO and a number of other partners established the joint Soil Fertility Initiative (SFI), which focused on sub-Saharan Africa and later took shape as the land and water investment priority of the African Union Comprehensive Africa Agriculture Development. The other partners were the International Food Policy Research Institute, the World Agroforestry Centre (ICRAF),[22] the IBRD, the US Agency for International Development (USAID), the International Fertilizer Development Center (IFDC)[23] and the International Fertilizer Association (IFA).[24]

[20] L. Luzzati, 'The International Institute of Agriculture', (1906) 182 *North American Review* 651.

[21] Described as the 'food aid arm of the UN system'. K. Mechlem, 'World Food Programme WFP' in *Max Planck Encyclopedia.*

[22] ICRAF was founded in 1977 to prevent deforestation, rural poverty and land depletion. Its seat is in Nairobi, Kenya.

[23] The IFDC was founded in 1974 in Muscle Shoals, Alabama (US) to research, produce and market sustainable fertilizers. See Open Yearbook of the Union of International Associations (UIA) at https://uia.org/s/or/en/1100049256. It was set up as a non-profit entity, and while it has no member states, it has the status of a public international organization under US law. See *ibid.*, at https://uia.org/s/or/en/1100049256.

[24] The IFA was founded in London in 1927 and is an association of interested industries active in the fertilizer business. *Ibid.*, https://uia.org/s/or/en/1100049256.

Concrete research projects ensued after this initiative. For instance, the Food Security Research Project (FSRP), set up to improve the fertilization of crops, was a collaborative partnership between key Zambian organizations working together in the Agricultural Consultative Forum, as well as Zambia's Ministry of Agriculture and Cooperatives and Michigan State University's Department of Agricultural Economics. The Project's activities aimed to improve capacity for agricultural policy analysis in Zambia through in-service capacity building, applied research and analysis, and policy outreach. The FSRP was co-funded by USAID and the Swedish International Development Agency. The FSRP has now become an innovation laboratory for food security policy at Michigan State University in conjunction with the US government's Feed the Future project. A scholar writing several years after the SFI was launched, placed it squarely within the context of FAO's efforts, since its inception, to support initiatives for freedom from hunger. In the light of the resistance it encountered locally, he also noted that rural people have 'a deep understanding' of their land, and that the criterion to assess the initiative ought to be the political acceptance of SFI in each country.[25] A 2007 Report submitted to the Council Committee for the Independent External Evaluation of FAO noted that the evaluators could not find any information on the outcomes of the SFI, 'but it appears to have had limited investment or policy impact'.[26]

Resistance to alien intervention seems to have been a recurring attitude experienced by the FAO.[27] The reason for this seems to be that peoples' and countries' paths may be disrupted by means of external intervention through food aid or agricultural policy; radically so in the context of an armed conflict.[28] And yet, scientists, NGOs and international organizations, which have planning capacity, organizational structures and the ability to carry out reforms concerning basic physical human needs, may

[25] R. Dudal, 'Forty Years of Soil Fertility Work in Sub-Saharan Africa', in B. Vanlauwe *et al.* (eds.), *Integrated Plant-Nutrient Management in Sub-Saharan Africa: From Concept to Practice* (Wallingford: Cabi Publishing, 2001) 1.

[26] *FAO: The Challenge of Renewal: An Independent External Evaluation of the Food and Agriculture Organisation.* Working Draft for Consultation (July 2007), available at www.fao.org/unfao/bodies/IEE-Working-Draft-Report/K0489E.pdf, 144.

[27] Cathie, *Political Economy of Food Aid*; T. A. Wise, *Eating Tomorrow: Agribusiness, Family Farmers and the Battle for the Future of Food* (New York: New Press, 2019).

[28] S. Jaspers, *Food Aid in Sudan: A History of Power, Politics and Profit* (London: Zed Books, 2018).

save many millions of lives by providing the appropriate technical expertise, mediation and actual food in emergencies and famines. The FAO reported in 2019 that hunger is on the rise in almost all African sub-regions, in Latin America, in the Caribbean and in Western Asia, that 20.5 million babies globally suffered from low birthweight in 2015, and that in 2018 more than 820 million people suffered from hunger.[29] At any rate, in the midst of general puzzlement towards the inability of international organizations working in the field of food security to end hunger, a faint note of optimism appears, always linked to the need to redesign contemporary governance. This involves, for example, tackling the different and multilayered factors causing poverty and attributing real authority to a single central international organization.[30] However, the bulk of literature attributes a mystifying agency to globalization, producing 'emergent priorities' and 'conflicting interests'. In parallel, contemporary food security appears not as the outcome of how economies are organized, but as an abstract theme dominated by scientific experts.[31] It is presented as an externality that international organizations and, increasingly other agents, such as NGOs or the private sector, must cope with.[32] In her recent book *Food Aid in Sudan*, Susanne Jaspers criticizes the current approach to resilience. This promotes the depolitization of food aid by medicalizing it by reference to nutritional content and expectations that populations suffering from severe food crises ought to change their patterns of behaviour. She criticizes the *fantasies* of science that make social and economic problems invisible and make the poor responsible for their own hunger. The political economy of food aid still appears to be the Achilles' heel of the global economy.[33]

[29] FAO, IFAD, UNICEF, WFP and WHO, 2019, *The State of Food Security and Nutrition in the World 2019. Safeguarding against Economic Slowdowns and Downturns* (Rome: FAO, 2019), vii–viii.

[30] A. Sen, 'Why Is There So Much Hunger in the World', Twenty-Eighth McDougall Memorial Lecture, Food and Agriculture Organisation, C 2013/INF/1, 2013; Van Zutphen *et al.*, 'International Agencies'.

[31] See, however, Chadwick, *Political Economy of Hunger*, 2019.

[32] H. Page, *Global Governance and Food Security as Global Public Good* (New York: NYU Center on International Cooperation, 2013); Van Zutphen *et al.*, 'International Agencies'.

[33] Jaspers, *Food Aid in Sudan*, 154–5; see also Lord Boyd Orr, *As I Recall: The 1880's to the 1960's* (London: Macgibbon and Kee, 1967); Cathie, *World Food Security*; Clapp, *Hunger in the Balance.*

For all their utopian proposals, the first promoters of international organizations working with food security shared the realist insight that food was a fundamental commodity in national and international economies. Therefore, they understood that the goal of greater distribution of food required massive structural economic reforms and truly global collaboration, starting with trade relations. Their nutrition approach was fundamentally a movement for free trade, advocating a single world economy and a single international organization devoted to the economy, combined with the wish to secure a certain structural hierarchy among countries, articulated in turn as a programme for the (gradual) development of poorer economies. Their political realism was apparent in their wish for a hierarchical organization of countries; and their utopianism in the idea that this hierarchy would eventually disappear. The nutrition approach also entailed a vision for a common economy and for growing political unity among countries, either on a regional or global basis, although sovereign nations resisted it and it did not materialize in the form they envisaged it. The chapter also suggests that food security projects are entrenched in an imperial mindset, usually conceived in terms of the existence of a centre and a periphery. Finally, the failure to establish an international organization with authority to adopt economic decisions for the world has cemented the position of private international corporations as free riders, contributing to precariousness.

16.2 Hot Springs

'All men on earth are consumers of food. More than two thirds are also producers of it.' Thus summarized Judge Marvin Jones, the Secretary General of the United Nations Conference on Food and Agriculture (Hot Springs, Virginia, 1943), on why the matter of food was the best start for a common project of the United Nations. Food was eminently an economic issue and every single individual on this earth was implicated in it. Moreover, at the outset it looked like something 'positive' to start with. A Norwegian delegate at the Hot Spring Conference, K. Evang, asked rhetorically in a presentation at the British Nutrition Society after the conference, why the conference was called just at that time. His answer was as follows:

> The feeling amongst the delegates was that the Allied leaders, and especially Mr. Roosevelt, had felt that although the United Nations had been fighting together

very well for a long time, yet they did not feel themselves to be a working organisation or team, and it would be a good thing if they could get together on some positive work.[34]

Organized at the initiative and under the auspices of US President Roosevelt, Hot Springs was the first meeting of the UN after the course of the war was decided in Leningrad, and one that apparently set the tone. When in the autumn of 1944 the Minister of Finance of New Zealand, Walter Nash (1882–1968), explained the 'United Nations Relief and Rehabilitation Administration Bill' to his Parliament, he detailed the money and resources the country had to commit for relief of the hunger of the war zones when the conflict ended, and the advantages that would accrue to New Zealand's economy. He also reported on the different 'historical' meetings he had attended during his sixteen months as resident minister in Washington. Most important was the Pacific War Council (PWC), a body chaired by Roosevelt consisting of representatives from the Philippines, Australia, New Zealand, Britain, Canada, China, the Netherlands and the Free French. The PWC had thirty-six formal meetings during its lifetime between April 1942 and February 1944. T. P. Maga explains that due to experiences with relief by the USA and Britain relating to famines in American and British Samoa, on 28 October 1942, when addressing the PWC, Roosevelt remarkably took up the topic of food and its equitable distribution in the Pacific. Roosevelt underlined that food distribution merited a special conference at the end of the war that would 'demonstrate to the world the present solidarity of the United Nations and their intention to hold together after the war'.[35] The conference would also show that an international solution on food was an efficient way to improve living conditions in the Pacific.[36] As well as the Hot Springs Conference, Nash also attended the UN Relief and Rehabilitation Administration Conference (UNRRA),[37] the International Labour Office Conference (with its declaration 'that poverty anywhere endangers

[34] K. Evang, 'The United Nations Conference on Food and Agriculture, Hot Springs, Virginia, 18th May-3rd June, 1943', in M. Lyon, 'The Hot Springs Conference', (1944) 2 *Proceedings of the Nutrition Society* 163.

[35] Roosevelt quoted in T. P. Maga, 'Vision and Victory: Franklin Roosevelt and the Pacific War Council, 1942–1944', (1991) 21 *Presidential Quarterly* 351, 358.

[36] B. Currey, 'Famine in the Pacific: Losing the Chances for Change', (1980) 4 *GeoJournal. Pacific Affairs* 447; Maga, 'Vision and Victory'.

[37] Atlantic City, 9 November 1943.

prosperity everywhere'),[38] and the UN Monetary and Financial Conference.[39] In his address to the New Zealand Parliament, Nash also explained the latter meeting through the lens of food: 'That was the first invasion of the nations of the world into the financial field. That work had to be controlled, organized and operated if we were to reach the objectives in regard to everybody getting enough to eat.'[40]

Nash might have been inclined to see Bretton Woods through rose-tinted spectacles. As a socialist, internationalist, pacifist and committed Anglican Christian, he had an impressive record of efficient work on social questions.[41] As finance minister in 1936, the first thing he did was to nationalize the Reserve Bank of New Zealand, taking control from the private bankers and working to solve the disastrous underemployment in the countryside. Housebuilding, cheap loans to farmers, guaranteed prices for butter and cheese and provision of free milk in schools were among the measures he brought in. And in 1938, as minister in charge of social security, he devised a universal pension scheme. Against the backdrop of the biography of individuals like Nash or Roosevelt, the odd rhetoric among the Allies of 'feeding the other half of the world' while suffering a world war, comes into focus.

Of course, geopolitical interests concerning the reorganization of the post-War world with the *right* states were also at stake; this is perhaps why food appears in international politics always entangled in, and masking, contradictory principles of *Realpolitik*. The Interim Commission for Food and Agriculture that arose from the Hot Springs meeting, envisaged a threefold classification of the world (in 1943!) in plans for assistance in relation to nutrition and agriculture by the future food organization. There would be, first, 'countries of Western civilization which are already organized and will not need direct assistance'; second, 'countries lacking organization in which population already presses severely on the present means of subsistence, e.g. India, China and many others', and third, the Commission identified the 'rest of the world in which also organization is lacking'. This group literally comprised *the rest of the world* where there was no pressure of population on the soil, such as 'the Latin Americas, the

[38] Philadelphia, 20 April–12 May 1944. [39] Bretton Woods, 1 July–22 July 1944.

[40] Parliamentary Debates, First Session, Twenty-Seventh Parliament, 12 October to 15 December 1944 (Wellington: E. V. Paul Government Printer, 1945), vol. 267, 305.

[41] B. Gustafson, 'Walter Nash (1882–1968)', *Dictionary of New Zealand Biography* (1998).

Middle East and Africa'.[42] In this light, the inclusion of Argentina in this latter category, a member of the International Wheat Council (established a year earlier in 1942) is especially striking.[43] Despite the notorious combination of food surpluses and widespread hunger and malnutrition during the Great Depression of the 1930s in Europe and the USA, 'Western civilization' felt itself to be exempt from any need of assistance in the governance of matters of nutrition and agriculture beyond the workings of the UNRRA, considered a strictly 'temporal' arrangement. That fact alone showed that food touched a vital nerve of the nations in the West.[44] At the same time, food was the new ideal that promised to unite the world. Could one possibly get more practical about it, and yet manage to remain peculiarly moral?

The plans for the new organization of the world in the context of food started well before the Hot Springs conference, and have been identified by scholars as the origin of development economics.[45] An authentic sense of a new beginning for the world may be detected in the documents emanating from Hot Springs, as opening 'a door of hope for mankind'.[46]

16.3 McDougall and (International) Organizations

'Realism', Duncan Bell writes, 'is the silent shadow of the debates over global justice, the spectre that haunts them'.[47] This certainly applies to the food approach to economy created by the brilliant Frank L. McDougall, visionary, adventurer and above all, one of the finest actors of politics through (international) organization that the past century produced. The accounts of his persona are contradictory: ranging from 'perhaps the most

[42] F. L. McDougall, 'The United Nations Interim Commission for Food and Agriculture', in Lyon, 'Hot Springs Conference', 169. See also Way, *A New Idea Each Morning*, 237.

[43] In addition, the IWC was composed of Australia, Canada, the UK and the USA. 'International Wheat Council', (1948) 1 *International Organization*, 386–7.

[44] Shawn, *World Food Security*.

[45] N. Lamoreaux and I. Shapiro (eds.), *The Bretton Woods Agreements: Together with Scholarly Commentaries and Essential Historical Documents* (New Haven CT: Yale University Press, 2019) 10, 170; D. Rimmer, 'Some Origins of Development Economics', (1979) 10 *Development and Change* 33.

[46] Evang, 'The United Nations Conference on Food and Agriculture', 166.

[47] D. Bell, 'Security and Poverty: On Realism and Global Justice', in M. Sleat (ed.), *Politics Recovered: Realist Thought in Theory and Practice* (New York: Columbia University Press, 2018) 296, 298.

underestimated man in twentieth century Australian history' to 'an amateur economist'.[48] The British Foreign Office labelled him in 1943 as 'an extremist', a 'ginger man' leader of a 'ginger group' on nutrition and, more accurately perhaps, others have called him an 'eminence grise'.[49] In a letter to his half-brother in 1925, McDougall reported a conversation with the Prime Minister of Australia, later his associate and lifelong collaborator, Stanley Bruce (1883–1967), who had asked him something amounting to 'what are you?'. He replied: an 'expert on Empire Trade and an artist at propaganda' who would be most useful in London 'to work for preference and for Empire Development'.[50]

In order to grasp what McDougall understood by 'Empire development', it is worth quoting at length from a letter to the Prime Minister written the following year:

> 'I am convinced that the one permanent road to British prosperity is through Empire Development. It will be a slow road but a sure one. If I am right in assuming that 1926 is going to be another year of overseas trade depression, then in October it will be easier to preach the necessity for a bold, sustained and comprehensive policy of Empire development. The West African per capita purchases, which I have quoted to you before, are a most striking example of how Imperial schemes assist Great Britain. The 22, 000, 000 natives of the West African Colonies buy 12/- per head from Great Britain, whereas the citizens of the U.S.A. only buy 8/8d.[51]

Increasing the flow of trade in commodities within the limits of the Empire was done more easily through intra-imperial organizations. McDougall had started working in London in the early 1920s within the ambit of the Dried Fruits Export Control Board, which was probably the first organization that he established, and which focused on one single food commodity of Australian origin. That position gave him an understanding of the importance of the complementarity of products in fostering

[48] The former in Hudson, *Australia and the League of Nations*, 7; the latter in S. Turnell, 'F. L. McDougall: Eminence Grise of Australian Economic Diplomacy', (2000) 40 *Australian Economic History Review* 51, 64.

[49] S. Turnell, *Monetary Reformers, Amateur Idealists and Keynesian Crusades: Australian Economists' International Advocacy, 1925–1950* (PhD, Macquarie University, 1999) 144; Way, *A New Idea Each Morning*, 286; Turnell, 'Eminence Grise'.

[50] Way, *A New Idea Each Morning*, 55.

[51] F. L. McDougall, letter of 8 April 1926, in W. J. Hudson and W. Way, *Letters from a 'Secret Service Agent': F L. McDougall to S.M. Bruce, 1924–1929* (Canberra: Australian Government Publishing Service, 1986) 199.

a successful commercial economy and thus expanded his view to an imperial outlook. Considering that Australia, along with Argentina and Canada, were the most significant global food exporters during those decades it is quite natural that he concentrated on food commodities. In essence, the trajectory of his participation in imperial organizations began with his active participation as a member of the Imperial Economic Committee and the Empire Marketing Board (EMB). The EMB, which existed from 1926 to 1933, was a government-funded body with a 'materialist understanding of the British Empire', focusing on education of the public, publicity, funding scientific and economic research, and marketing. It worked on the simple principle that increasing consumption would stimulate employment throughout the empire.[52] Through his work in Australia's Council for Scientific and Industrial Research (CSIR), McDougall would meet John Boyd Orr, who facilitated McDougall's introduction to the science of nutrition. Boyd Orr was instrumental in the creation of the FAO in 1945 and was its first Secretary-General. He was later knighted and awarded the Nobel Peace Prize. His studies on the nutrition of British children during the 1920s had demonstrated the relationship of illnesses and undernourishment. McDougall's encounter with Boyd Orr, another amateur economist, sparked probably the most creative idea of his life: that of solving undernourishment by increasing food production.[53] The increase of production on which the nutrition approach was founded resulted from McDougall's keen perception that in moments of high food prices and undersupply in Great Britain, the distributors of food had become rich – exactly as still happens nowadays in places affected by grave food insecurity. He continued his work at the Development and Migration Commission, the Federation of British Industries (a failed 'tariff advisory committee', drafting work for which took up much of his time), the Imperial Agricultural Bureau and the Skelton Committee on Economic Cooperation, among others.[54] While instrumental in achievements gained for Australia at the Ottawa Conference – something he was proud of – McDougall realized the limitations of sheltered markets when Britain, soon after its signature, dismantled an agreement

[52] E. Rappaport, *A Thirst for Empire: How Tea Shaped the Modern World* (Princeton University Press, 2017) 235.

[53] Way, *A New Idea Each Morning*; Turnell, *Monetary Reformers*.

[54] See Way, *A New Idea Each Morning*, and Turnell, 'Eminence Grise'.

that was perceived as detrimental for its world exports.[55] Officially from then on, but presumably earlier, McDougall grasped that the future of Australian food production was wider in scope than the Empire, and that only free trade would serve the purpose of maintaining healthy economies.

The jump to the League of Nations was an obvious next step. Since 1928 McDougall had been delegate of the Economic Consultative Committee of the Economic and Financial Organisation of the League, in which capacity he lobbied, among other things, for reform of the IIA, whose work he found unsatisfactory. On the whole, he considered the League's work on agriculture 'Eurocentric' and tried to influence its reorientation.[56] During the 1930s, a period of severe world crisis of wheat harvests and prices, McDougall worked with characteristic zeal on the Wheat Advisory Committee (now the International Grains Council). After a revolutionary speech by Bruce, Australian High Commissioner at the time, to the plenary of the League of Nations, in which the need 'to marry health and agriculture' was declared, a new Mixed Committee was established to report to the plenary of the League in 1936, of which McDougall was one of the most active members. The core proposal conveyed in Bruce's speech was to divert national production away from energy food such as wheat towards protective food, such as milk, vegetables and meat that were expensive and difficult for the poor to afford, since the latest scientific studies indicated that these were the most nutritious for human beings. Money then spent in maintaining an illusory self-sufficiency in the production of agricultural products that could be easily imported ought to be spent on the national production of protective food. In this manner, international agricultural production would be greatly simplified.[57]

Bruce became President of the Assembly of the League in 1936,[58] by which point many considered the League politically 'dead'. McDougall and

[55] Recalling the aftermath of the Ottawa Conference, see 'The Imperial Economic Conference with Particular Reference to the United-Kingdom-Canada Agreement', (1934) 13 *International Affairs* 245; J. O'Brien, 'Empire v. National Interests in Australian-British Relations during the 1930s', (1987) 22 *Historical Studies* 569; B. P. Attard, *The Australian High Commissioner's Office Politics and Anglo-Australian Relations, 1901–1939* (PhD, Oxford University, 1991).

[56] Way, *A New Idea Each Morning.*

[57] S. M. Bruce, 'Speech by the Rt. Hon. S.M. Bruce (Australia), 1935'; see also F. L. McDougall, 'The Agricultural and the Health Problem' (1935), both in *The McDougall Memoranda* (Rome: FAO, 1956), 18 and 2 respectively,

[58] H. Radi, 'Bruce, Stanley Melbourne' (1883–1967), in *Australian Dictionary of Biography* (Melbourne University Publishing, 1979).

Bruce, with the collaboration of Joseph Avenol, Secretary-General of the League from 1933 to 1940, moved on to promote the production of the Bruce Report. Circumventing highly political questions, the main proposal of the Bruce Report was to establish a new Central Committee for Economic and Social Questions within the League. This was meant to supervise the work of all the committees, uniting all social and economic issues under a single agency, hoping to instil 'efficiency and vigour' in international economic collaboration.[59] William James Hudson considered that 'the potential radical significance' of these steps was already understood. He quotes a letter to Bruce from Sean Lester, High Commissioner for the Free City of Danzig and after Avenol's resignation in 1940, acting Secretary-General, in which he expressed his vision for the Central Committee: 'Apart from the immediate importance of the subject matter of the Committee, great as that is, I have in mind the possibility that it might lead to still more important developments in the whole field of international organisation.'[60]

Although McDougall had always been careful to indicate allegiance to the International Labour Organization (ILO), to all intents and purposes the new Central Committee clearly overlapped with the ILO's sphere of action. This fact was perceived, with much anxiety, by the ILO, whose director general, John G. Winant, demanded, and obtained, from Avenol, assurances of respect for ILO's autonomy and competences.[61] It was, in any case, too late for reform. However, despite the outbreak of World War II, McDougall's work on food commodities had become significant, and would be even more so in the future.

16.4 The Final Struggle for an International Food Organization: The USA

After holding the office of Prime Minister of Australia in the 1920s, McDougall's mentor Bruce was Resident Minister in the United Kingdom (1930–2), and Australian High Commissioner to the United Kingdom (1932–45). In Australia, Bruce and McDougall gained a reputation as

[59] M. D. Dubin, 'Toward the Bruce Report: The Economic and Social Programs of the League of Nations in the Avenol Era', in *The League of Nations in Retrospect/La Société des Nations: Retrospective* (Berlin: de Gruyter, 1983) 42, 58.

[60] Hudson, *Australia and the League of Nations*, 179.

[61] Dubin, 'Toward the Bruce Report'.

tremendously skilled and tough economic negotiators and subtle strategists who managed to unite the issue that was vital to them, Australian food exports – to the point of being suspected of having 'xenophobic nationalist instincts' – with the ideal of 'feeding the other half'.[62] McDougall was clearly the creative element of the team, while Bruce was the diplomat. Both were respected in their own areas of expertise and observed with the curiosity that accompanies internationalists. John O'Brien perceptively described them as 'a government in exile', only 'far more effective'.[63] In his *History of Food Security*, Shawn remarked that 'the greatest success belonged to McDougall who sold the idea of an international agency to Franklin D. Roosevelt, which led to the Hot Springs Conference'.[64]

Indeed, Wendy Way's substantial biography of McDougall studies the ideological union of food and agriculture, including his dealings with the US government in order to prepare the new organization of the world immediately following the beginning of World War II.[65] Sean Turnell quotes some excerpts from a memorandum on a 'peace settlement' written by McDougall and sent to the British government, but neither he nor other scholars writing on McDougall and the FAO mention the visit that Bruce paid on 12 March 1940 to Sumner Welles, US Undersecretary of State.[66] The latter reported to President Roosevelt:

> I received at the Embassy [in London], at 12, the visit of Mr. Bruce, the Australian High Commissioner. Bruce said that he had come to let me know that the Dominion governments held views with regard to an eventual peace settlement, and to the policy to be followed at that time with regard to Germany, which were widely divergent from the opinions held by the majority of the members of the British Government. He was providing me with a memorandum setting forth the views of his own Government in that regard. A copy of this memorandum is attached here too.[67]

62 J. O'Brien, 'F.L. McDougall and the Origins of the FAO', (2000) 46 *Australian Journal of Politics and History* 164, 165.

63 O'Brien, 'Empire v. National Interests', 575.

64 Shawn, *World Food Security*, 8. See also Lamoreaux and Shapiro, *The Bretton Woods Agreements*, 164.

65 Way, *A New Idea Each Morning*.

66 Turnell, *Monetary Reformers*, 138.

67 Welles, 12.3.1940: Reports Sumner Welles, Assistant and Undersecretary of State and Ambassador to Cuba, box 6, Safe files, *Franklin D. Roosevelt Presidential Library and Museum*.

Part of McDougall's obligation in Australia House consisted of political warfare. This is probably the context of the memorandum – in fact two memoranda, A and B, also included in Welles's diplomatic correspondence. Turnell mentions that memorandum B had been sent the previous month to Anthony Eden, Secretary of State for the Dominions (reaching also the First Lord of the Admiralty, Winston Churchill), and R. G. Menzies, Australia's Prime Minister. In a letter to Menzies (who supported wholeheartedly the idea of a new 'World Organisation for Economic and Social Affairs') in early February 1940, Bruce reported 'cautious support from Chamberlain and the British Foreign Secretary, Lord Halifax, polite rejection from Eden and outright hostility from Churchill'.[68] Churchill, for once, did not want to change anything in the world order after the war. In the memoranda on 'The Peace Settlement', McDougall, through Bruce, presented a radical proposal for organizing the world, following the pattern of his idea of a Central Committee for Economic and Social Questions, and yet less ambitious than the future UN. The documents brought together McDougall's thinking on world trade, nutrition and economic appeasement.[69] The result was something close to the future twentieth-century developmental *Weltanschauung*, at once touching and appalling in denying 'the other half' a political status. Indeed, political realism lurked behind McDougall's claims to distributive justice. However, the political claim also held the other way about: social and economic equality pushed the movement of trade and capital forward. Bruce's visit to Welles, and his and McDougall's subsequent multiple contacts with the US administration, also marked the moment when they moved on to new pastures: America. According to Way, in the phase of contacts with America they acted with the full support of the Australian government.[70]

From the outset, memorandum A handed over to Welles stressed that a 'more equitable share of national incomes' was needed in order to avoid

[68] Turnell, *Monetary Reformers*, 138. Interestingly Sumner Welles met later the same day with Eden. Probably impressed by Bruce's detailed ideas on postwar policy, he concluded his report about their meeting by stating: 'Mr. Eden impressed me as even more superficial than he had impressed me as being in Washington. He seems to have given no thought to any alternative to war, nor to what any eventual peace terms should be'. Welles, 12.3.1940: Reports Sumner Welles, Assistant and Undersecretary of State and Ambassador to Cuba, box 6, Safe files, *Franklin D. Roosevelt Presidential Library and Museum.*

[69] Before the war, some had suggested that Hitler could be appeased by economic concessions.

[70] Way, *A New Idea Each Morning.*

world revolution and the danger of communism.[71] Care for the 'forgotten man' of Roosevelt's New Deal was to be undertaken on a global scale, and the Allies should treat Germany better than after the previous war. To the Dominions 'an expanding world demand is even more important than it is to U.S.A' and German participation in that endevour was crucial. In the words of the memorandum, probably the greatest contribution to world recovery would be produced 'through a freeing of the channels of international trade'; despite the efforts made by 'Mr. Cordell Hull' it was evident that 'sectional interests' were working against it. McDougall proposed an 'international economic co-operation on a scale never previously envisaged' in which 'more attention to the interests of consumers' would be paid, and which was to result in a 'great international movement for increased prosperity based on freer trade'. McDougall (and Bruce) proposed a series of four remarkable agreements that anticipate much of what happened in the following decades, (a) for a 'co-ordinated attack upon the problems of poverty', in which nutrition was to figure prominently; (b) '[i]nternational solutions of commodity problems (such as the world wheat problem)'; (c) '[i]nternational agreement on the reduction of trade barriers'; (d) '[i]nternational agreement on monetary and financial policy and systems of assistance from the creditor nations in the solution of the financial difficulties of other nations'.[72]

The question of the colonies was handled in a somewhat fuzzy manner. On the one hand, it was discussed in terms of the need to suspend preferential trade agreements for those countries that possessed colonies in order to avoid the old jealousy of the 'haves' (referring to possession of colonies) and 'have nots' that in McDougall's view had been an important cause of the war. This proposal combined an approach to progressive self-government of territories when possible, with the need for an international political economy entailing an 'open door' to the territories of 'non-self-governing peoples' and 'a progressive internationalization of responsibility for the welfare of all such peoples'.[73]

At the same time, McDougall himself was somewhat sceptical about achieving the creation of a global international organization. In the

[71] 'The Peace Settlement: Which Is the Most Practical – A Co-Operative or an Enforced Peace Settlement?' (Memorandum A) in Welles 1940: Reports Sumner Welles, Assistant and Undersecretary of State and Ambassador to Cuba, box 6, Safe files, *Franklin D. Roosevelt Presidential Library and Museum.*

[72] *Ibid.*, 12. [73] *Ibid.*, 12–13.

memorandum B, which dealt mainly with security and economic questions, he affirmed that 'the nations will have to be prepared for radical changes in their conceptions of national sovereignty', but doubted that the 'forces of reaction' and 'the natural conservatism of mankind' would allow these changes to take place. Moreover, 'in the light of the experience of 1919–1935' and the 'failures of the political side of the League of Nations', with each state 'jealously safeguarding her sovereign rights', he proposed two things.[74] First, he suggested the abolition of national armies and the creation of an international police force. Second, in lieu of a worldwide political organization, he advocated regional political pacts, dividing the world into four regions: Europe, including the Mediterranean; the two Americas; USSR; and a Pacific region. He also suggested the possibility of adding a fifth region – the Near and Middle East – and envisaged India as the leader when gaining full Dominion status after some years of experience with complete self-government. He added to this the suggestion that several interesting combinations of great powers might participate in several regions. These fundamentally amounted to bringing Europe to the Pacific, but not the other way round. Within the regional pact, complete national disarmament ought to happen and responsibility for security at regional level would be the norm. The coordination of the regional pacts could be done through a regional council with similar 'political functions to the Council of the League'.[75] In fact, McDougall wrote that a United States of Europe and a European Parliament were ideas that were already being considered seriously. Rather presciently he noted that: 'From the standpoint of the British Commonwealth the idea of a European Federation has many difficulties of which the greatest is that it might involve the United Kingdom in increased European responsibilities with results which would seriously affect the relationship of the United Kingdom to the Dominions.'[76] But the international organization was needed anyway. 'The foregoing considerations indicate that whereas political problems may be best dealt with on a regional basis, there is need for a world organisation to secure international action on economic and social affairs, including the problems of the non-self-governing territories.'[77]

[74] 'The Peace Settlement. Methods for Securing a Co-Operative Peace' (Memorandum B), in Welles 1940: Reports Sumner Welles, 2.

[75] *Ibid.*, 11. [76] *Ibid.*, 3–4. [77] *Ibid.*, 6–7.

In short, he repeated the ideas set out in the earlier memorandum A. While 'the creditor nations should assist the other nations to reorganize their finances and to develop their resources', the peace settlement ought to be the 'starting point of an internationally concerted attack upon the problems of poverty within each country'. Evidently, 'some international machinery' was needed for all this and McDougall suggested that, together with the ILO, he had in mind something akin to the League's Central Committee on Economic and Social Questions, embodying the separation of political from economic questions.[78]

The nutrition approach had gone a long way by that point. Starting with a commodity (dried fruit), and accompanied by McDougall's gradual acquisition of enormous and detailed knowledge of individual food and agricultural commodities, McDougall and Bruce fought for the organization of the world around nutrition, trade and development. An important account of the larger economic planning for peace written in the 1950s acknowledged Bruce and McDougal's role in achieving a prominent function for food in post-war reconstruction. But its author, E. F. Penrose, was far from describing the broad scope of their efforts in the organization of the world. Penrose reported Keynes's perplexity when Roosevelt announced the conference of Hot Springs and on the whole attributed the failure to establish Keynes's proposal of buffer stocks of commodities to internal strife, within the US and UK governments, between agricultural extremists (opposed to any concession on the matter) and other ministries and departments dealing with trade.[79] The idea of a multilateral organization with authority over production, trade in and distribution of food commodities would remain utopian.

16.5 Development of the World through Food

Both Wendy Way and Sean Turnell relate in detail Bruce and McDougall's close collaboration with the US administration in the years leading up to the Hot Springs conference. A memorandum dated October 1942 which

[78] *Ibid.*, 10–11.

[79] E. F. Penrose, *Economic Planning for the Peace* (Princeton University Press, 1953) 119. E. F. and Edith Penrose had been economic advisors to Winant during his time as Ambassador to the UK, 1941–6. See A. Penrose, *No Ordinary Woman: The Life of Edith Penrose* (Oxford University Press, 2017).

discusses the topic of freedom from want at length probably represents the culmination of McDougall's many years of drafting ideas on food, economy and international organizations. In disregard of his earlier ideas, even those of the early 1940s, McDougall now proposed a 'World Authority' with 'both political and economic functions'. In his own words: '[t]he Need is to establish a United Nations Organization such as an Economic Council' which should appoint 'Technical Commissions'.[80] Among them a 'Technical Commission on Food and Agriculture' should set up programmes to help states to bring food problems to an end. These momentous words, conceiving of the future organization as a development organization, followed:

> Its recommendation should include ways and means of setting up an International Agricultural Authority and the methods whereby such an Authority would work in close liaison with the suggested International Bank and its subsidiary International Agricultural Credit Bank and International Raw Materials Authority and an International Authority established to assist in the development of backward areas throughout the world.[81]

The FAO's mandate did not come to encompass real economic measures of food, trade and agriculture reform. Indeed, the FAO never became the 'International Authority' that McDougall conceived of, and this was largely the result of opposition on the part of the USA and the UK; the former a leading wheat exporter, the latter mainly an importer of food. The USA, instead, monopolized food aid for the world for around twenty years, using it to solve its dramatic agricultural problems stemming from excess supply. In this light, the thought presents itself that the US government utilized McDougall, taking advantage, for its own purposes, of the ideas that he so lavishly shared.

Naomi Lamoreux and Ian Shapiro rightly highlight the complementarity of goals that explain why McDougall and Bruce's collaboration with the US government went so well up to a point.[82] A review of the Roosevelt papers on agriculture from the 1930s shows that oversupply of corn was a pressing concern for the administration, while farmers also formed a crucial part of the electorate. Moreover, by 1937 the Secretary of Agriculture, Henry A. Wallace, was quite aware of the need to develop agricultural policy

[80] F. L. McDougall, 'Draft Memorandum on a United Nations Program for Freedom from Want of Food', in *The McDougall Memoranda*, 26, 35.

[81] *Ibid.* [82] Lamoreaux and Shapiro, *Bretton Woods*, 167.

and integrate farms into the economic life of the country. Wallace would be one of Bruce and McDougall's main interlocutors during their trips to America. According to Wallace, the support of agriculture demanded government intervention but also collaboration with business and labour. In this triumvirate, 'the contribution the farmers' could make 'to a continuing balanced abundance at fair prices' was what Wallace called 'the ever-normal granary'.[83] He used this term to refer to a situation of stable supply of corn at a stable price (reached presumably by buffer stocks), to prevent situations of oversupply or underproduction (through heat, pestilences or other nature related causes) while maintaining farm purchasing power.[84] Again, if farmers, business and labour would not collaborate, the danger existed, in Wallace's view, that foreign ideologies might tear democracy apart. In a young democracy characterized by population growth and the availability of land, economic action would entail 'freedom to exploit natural resources and to grab profit without regard to the welfare of others'. But in a mature nation, Wallace argued, 'license must give way to law and order', to prevent democracy from turning into anarchy. In essence Wallace put forward a call 'to decency and tolerance'.[85]

While there was indeed a complementarity of interest between the USA's oversupply problem and McDougall's agriculture and health approach, his conception of an international organization that had international authority did not match with US strategy in the mid-1940s. Rather than having an international organization coordinating the externalization of its economic problems, the USA took total control of the idea.[86] However, while Boyd Orr grew increasingly frustrated with the FAO, Wendy Way notes that McDougal seemed quite content with how the FAO evolved.[87] Perhaps McDougall understood the magnitude of the impending Cold War. Moreover, while McDougall's increasing idealism is a fact, his nutrition approach, though fundamental, had been always secondary, dependent on increases in production, consumption and economic growth. It is certain that McDougall's career had started promoting the development of

[83] Henry A. Wallace, 'Agriculture, Business, Labor and Government' (12.6.1937) in Franklin D. Roosevelt, Papers as President: (PSF), 1933–1945; Agriculture, 1934–1938; Box 53. *Franklin D. Roosevelt Presidential Library and Museum*, 5.

[84] *Ibid.* [85] *Ibid.*, 6.

[86] Cathie, *Political Economy of Food Aid*; Clapp, *Hunger in the Balance.*

[87] Boyd Orr, *As I Recall*; Way, *A New Idea Each Morning*, 290–9.

Australia within what he took to be, although it was not, an economic unity, the British Empire.[88] Not all Australians felt that way. On the event of the termination of the EMB, the respected chemist and science administrator David Rivett (1885–1961), who was CSIR's chief executive and good friend of McDougall, expressed his relief: 'that Great Britain should finance research in the Dominions was always, to my mind, rather a scandal and we need not regret the passing of that little bit of charity'.[89] By contrast, McDougall, a naturalized Australian who did not arrive in his new country until he was twenty-five years old, remained impervious to other moral considerations when he saw a need 'of being developed'. After all, he had been a developer of a dominion within the Empire during an important part of his life. And in the end, though vague in its conclusions, and apparently lacking teeth in practice, Hot Springs was fundamentally a conference on development for the world that put in motion a whole new international machinery to achieve it.[90]

The long list of delegates at Hot Springs, most of whom had backgrounds in agriculture, commerce, finance and (mining) banking, peppered with three or four members of health administrations, confirmed the suggestion that the goal of nutrition was the tip of the iceberg. Reading the report of the conference one gets a real sense of vertigo. Its ambition to transform the world economy and trade through food, agriculture and an enormous increase in production is breathtaking. The logic was simple but powerful. One of Roosevelt's 'four freedoms', the freedom from want, could be achieved if enough attention was paid to the interdependence between consumption and production. Malnutrition (resulting in diseases and child mortality) was in effect the consequence of low consumption of food, and it was imperative that governments of the world *committed* themselves to the obligation to free their citizens from want. McDougall probably felt that the new cluster of organizations arising from Hot Springs, in particular the World Bank and the FAO, would eventually do the job of fostering nutrition and development.

[88] O'Brien, 'Origins of the FAO'. On this issue, see also Michael Fakhri, *Sugar and the Making of International Trade Law* (Cambridge University Press, 2014).

[89] In a letter to the Cambridge physiologist and director of the Lister Institute of Preventive Medicine, Sir Charles Martin (1866–1955), who had spent more than a decade at the University of Melbourne. See Way, *A New Idea Each Morning*, 119–20.

[90] See Article XXI of the 1943 Hot Springs Final Act, *United Nations Conference on Food and Agriculture*, 22.

Indeed, in a sense it were McDougall and Bruce who utilized the US government to put Australia on the map of international politics, using the USA as an instrument to advance their internationalist ideas on political economy. The Australians arguably pressed the Roosevelt administration into action. In this regard, a report sent to Secretary of State Cordell Hull from the US ambassador in London, John G. Winant (earlier the ILO's Secretary-General, and in 1946 delegate of the USA to the UN Economic and Social Council), among Roosevelt's papers is illuminating. Winant asked Hull to present the summary to the three men mentioned in the text, adding that he would send the entire article by mail.

The report is a three-page summary, sent by telegram the same day, of the main editorial that appeared in *The Times* on 26 May 1942, titled 'An American Lead'. The editorial reflected recent statements by Hull, Wallace and Milo Perkins. Perkins was Wallace's deputy at the Board of Economic Warfare and President of the Federal Surplus Commodities Corporation, in charge of carrying out the Food Stamp Act, 'the first thoroughgoing attempt of the department of Agriculture directly to increase effective economic demand for food among the underfed'.[91] The editorial aimed to amplify the messages of the three American officials, and possibly to unify the American State Department torn apart by factions. In substance, the editorial endorsed McDougall's food approach. In the words of Winant, quoting the editorial:

> Times declares that while each approaches problems of peace from a different angle, 'all agree in proclaiming that these problems cannot be solved by any nation, even the United States, acting by itself and seeking its own advantage'. It cites secretary's call for immediate acts of collaboration to show American readiness to shoulder full share of responsibility for building a better world; Mr. Wallace's proclamation that peace objective must be freedom from want for all peoples, and Mr. Perkins' warning that if the United States does not help to promote all-out worldwide production, it will face isolation in a world where men are growing closer together.[92]

The editorial next pointed out that Perkins's idea of increased world consumption and Wallace's aim of world freedom from want were

[91] S. Herman, 'The Food Stamp Plan: a Study in Law and Economics', (1940) 13 *Journal of Business of the University of Chicago* 331, 332.

[92] Quoted from J. G. Winant, 'Summary of Editorial in Times, 26.5.1942', in *Franklin D. Roosevelt, Papers as President: The President's Secretary's File (PSF, 1933–1945), Diplomatic Correspondence, Box 38, Great Britain, Winant, John G, Franklin D. Roosevelt Presidential Library and Museum*, 1–2.

connected with Hull's ideal of revival of international trade. The editorial attributed meaning to international trade only if it was capable of ministering 'to human needs by making the resources of the whole world available to all the peoples of the world.'[93] The anonymous author showed admiration for those ideas, employing at some points practically the same terms as those in McDougall's 1940 report.[94]

16.6 Aftermath: The Reign of Private Companies

Hot Springs saw a struggle between two groups. The first of these was in favour of a powerless organization with only fact-finding and advisory functions and a limited budget. The second favoured a strong organization with authority to work on production increase and price stabilization. The first group turned out to be victorious. In the Quebec meeting to set up the FAO in 1945 a disappointed Boyd Orr famously stated that '[t]he hungry people of the world wanted bread, and they were to be given statistics'.[95] Surprisingly, he was elected Secretary-General of the FAO. He immediately put forward a plan for a World Food Board in 1946, which was to have encompassed a world food reserve, a mechanism through which to stabilize prices of agricultural commodities and the means to finance the distribution worldwide of food surpluses.[96] However, these efforts came to nothing. During the Washington conference of the FAO in 1947, the US delegate, speaking first, openly expressed the refusal of the great powers to give 'any authority or funds to any international organisation for the purpose set out in the proposal for a World Food Board'.[97]

Over the next twenty years, the USA became the world's granary.[98] In 1947, it helped Europe with the European Recovery Plan or Marshall Plan,

[93] J. G. Winant, 'Summary of Editorial in Times, 26.5.1942', 2.

[94] It is well known that McDougall often wrote in *The Times* and many other newspapers, not always under his own name.

[95] Boyd Orr, *As I Recall*, 162. [96] Cathie, *Political Economy of Food Aid*, 32–3.

[97] Boyd Orr, *As I Recall*, 191.

[98] On these years see also, Clapp, *Hunger in the Balance*; S. Salvatici, 'Writing for the History of Food Security', (2015) 18 *Contemporanea* 347; H. Wieters, 'The World's Hungry: American NGOs and New Private-Public Partnerships after World War II', (2015) 18 *Contemporanea* 355; R. Jachertz, 2015. 'The World Food Crisis of 1972-1975', (2015) 18 *Contemporanea*, 425; A. Mann, 'Food Sovereignty: Alternatives to Failed Food and Hunger Policies', (2015) 18 *Contemporanea* 445.

while 1954 saw the enactment of the Agricultural Trade Development and Assistance Act (also known as 'PL 480' and 'Food for Peace') that legislated the future policy on food aid for developing countries. No more steps towards a multilateral agency on food aid were taken until 1963, when the USA controlled 96 per cent of all international food aid.[99] With the creation in 1958 of the European Economic Community's Common Agricultural Policy marking the emergence of serious competition to US agriculture, the idea of a multilateral food aid agency was finally accepted by the American government. Thus, 1963 saw the creation of the WFP in Rome as a formal venture between the FAO and UN.[100] The donors' commitments were concretized in the negotiations that took place at the Wheat Trade Convention and the International Grains Agreement, which became part of the Kennedy Round of the GATT Negotiations.

Today the WFP tries to manage the most challenging famines, in many cases with the help of private donors. The FAO Report 2019's commonsense conclusion, which advocated large structural economic reforms worldwide to strengthen the economic resilience of countries, is nevertheless valuable: '[e]nsuring that this transformation (of food and agriculture systems) is pro-poor and inclusive will not be possible by focusing on economic growth alone'.[101] Commentators on international organizations working with food security sometimes refer to overlaps between the activities of various organizations, and to human flaws.[102] Another critique describes how international organizations appear to support the agendas of private companies and developed countries, rather than the needs of developing countries facing food emergencies. This applies to the protection of breeders' rights to plant varieties, UPOV, as well as agricultural negotiations taking place within the WTO.[103] Graham Dutfield notes that the current system for protecting plant breeding, disconnected from actual farming and focusing on commercialization, concentrates investment in a few crop species and displaces traditional farming necessary

[99] Reported in Cathie, *Political Economy of Food Aid*, 15.

[100] Over time the WFP has established itself as independent from the FAO, though in collaboration with it, and presents itself as such: www.wfp.org/un-agencies-and-international-institutions.

[101] FAO *et al.*, *Food Security and Nutrition*, 119.

[102] A. Heucher, 'Reconsidering Overlap in Global Food Security Governance', (2019) 11 *Food Security*, 555–8.

[103] T. Gebrehiwot, S. Cornelius and L. Korsten, 'Impact of Global Food and Agriculture Laws on Africa's Food Security', (2019) 52 *De Jure Law Journal* 85.

for the food security of very large populations.[104] Likewise, Timothy Wise describes how international organizations working with food security have displaced individuals and communities on the ground in favour of agribusiness. Wise notes the disconnect between the real needs of local farmers and the climate-smart conferences that only have 'one consistent winner: agribusiness, the conglomerates that dominate the production of seeds, fertilizers and other farm inputs'.[105] Against claims that capital-intensive food production must increase dramatically, Wise recalls the fact that 70 per cent of developing countries' food is produced by small-scale farmers. It is to them, he argues, that support must be directed.

The most prominent complaint against international organizations relates to their dependence on their member states. The history of the relationship between organizations and member states on a topic such as food clarifies much with regard to responsibility.[106] Certainly, the FAO ought not to be blamed for the lack of political commitment on the part of governments. In the case of other organizations, such as UPOV, states have left food security in the hands of private interests: food-processing companies, supermarket chains, agribusiness, conglomerate seed and chemical companies. There are increasing calls for international organizations to play a more prominent role that balances cooperation with governments and the private sector in developing countries and with independence from developed countries in framing agricultural projects.[107] In short, international organizations working with food (and their member states) need to carve out a political space (of law and order) in the international economic arena where currently private corporations reign. The only way, as McDougall knew well, to marry health and agriculture, economy and food, and to realize the welfare of all, is to allow the global order to mature politically.

[104] G. Dutfield, 'Farmers, Innovation, and Intellectual Property: Current Trends and their Consequences for Food Security', in F. Girard and C. Frison (eds.), *The Commons, Plant Breeding and Agricultural Research. Challenges for Food Security and Agrobiodiversity* (Abingdon: Routledge, 2018), ch. 1.

[105] Wise, *Eating Tomorrow*, 3–4. [106] Klabbers, 'International Institutions'.

[107] O. M. Ashe, 'International Agencies and the Quest for Food Security in Nigeria, 1970–2015' (2019) 8 *Ubuntu: Journal of Conflict and Social Transformation* 251.

Financial Stability 17

Matthias Goldmann

17.1 Introduction

This chapter addresses the role of international organizations in securing financial stability. Regulating financial stability is a chief concern of capitalist economies. Like in other fields of economic law, the challenge is to strike a balance between protecting a jurisdiction against overspill risks emanating from other jurisdictions, and containing risks across jurisdictions by shifting regulation to the international level. This results in two modes of regulation, which I call sovereignty and cooperation.

Since the demise of the Bretton Woods system in the early 1970s, the financial sector has been characterized by an increasingly complex pattern of interaction protecting sovereignty and facilitating cooperation alike. At first sight, the regulatory framework looks highly fragmented, with lots of different actors sharing at times overlapping regulatory competencies. Upon closer inspection, though, it appears that there is method in the present system. It features a hierarchical structure controlled by the governments of the big capital-exporting countries and the upper echelons of the financial industry. This hierarchy rests on carefully designed access restrictions, privileges and mechanisms of exclusion. In this respect, not only private actors, but also the law of international organizations,[1] participate in the codification of capital.[2]

[1] I use the law of international organizations in a broad sense here, referring to formal and informal institutions as well as their relations with private and hybrid actors. See A. von Bogdandy, Ph. Dann and M. Goldmann, 'Developing the Publicness of Public International Law: Towards a Legal Framework for Global Governance Activities', (2008) 9 *German Law Journal* 1375, 1393.

[2] This complements the private-law focus in K. Pistor, *The Code of Capital: How the Law Creates Wealth and Inequality* (Princeton University Press, 2019).

The financial sector is characterized by a plethora of international legal instruments. Its hierarchical structure rests on both binding and non-binding rules and also includes spheres of private self-regulation and contractual activity. The delimitation of spheres of sovereignty usually relies on hard international law, while the instruments deployed for regulatory purposes at the international level are typically of non-binding character, including soft law and governance by information. The field of financial regulation is a prime example of their effectiveness, which justifies classifying them as international public authority.[3] The root cause of this effectiveness is market power – it is in governments' best interest to implement soft legal agreements in order to avoid detrimental effects for financial stability and competition.[4] This goes against key descriptions of the law as a necessary requirement for enforcing the interests of the owners of capital.[5] While this might hold true for contractual relationships, the law of public finance, with the notable exception of tax law, has never relied on top-down enforcement structures but is, like constitutional law, voluntarily observed.[6] In fact, as this chapter will elaborate, binding and non-binding law fulfil a variety of functions. Binding law, to the extent it plays a role, entrenches hierarchy, but also protects sovereignty; non-binding rules may serve community interests, or isolate hierarchical relationships against legal attack. The role of binding and non-binding rule is therefore essentially ambiguous. The financial sector provides a laboratory of different instruments of international organizations.

Despite its incoherent character, some formal and substantive principles have emerged particularly since the financial crisis. While respect for human rights is notoriously underwhelming, the principle of sustainability seems to enjoy greater acceptance. But its impact is rather marginal – it aims at nothing more than the survival of the system as a whole and the people affected by it. To anyone unenthused by this prospect, the principle of equality may provide greater relief.

[3] A. von Bogdandy, M. Goldmann and I. Venzke, 'From Public International to International Public Law: Translating World Public Opinion into International Public Authority', (2017) 28 *European Journal of International Law* 115, 131 ff.

[4] Comprehensively C. Brummer, 'Why Soft Law Dominates International Finance – And Not Trade', (2010) 13 *Journal of International Economic Law* 623.

[5] Pistor, *Code of Capital*, 17–18.

[6] Cf. H. Kelsen, *Pure Theory of Law* (Berkeley CA: University of California Press, 1967) 51.

17.2 Between Sovereignty and Community

17.2.1 Capitalism and Financial Stability

Contemporary capitalism as it emerged gradually during the modern age in Europe and North America as well as in their overseas territories and relationships is an economic and social order characterized by dynamic development and periodic crisis.[7] In this regard, capitalism bears the traits of modernity's unleashed subjectivism and its difficult relationship with society.[8] Growth tends to produce crises, usually in the financial sector. One can understand crisis as an event where the allocation of capital is severely disrupted on a systemic level, driving aggregate performance of the economy away from equilibrium.[9] Crises range from asset crises to crises of public or private debt, or currency crises. Often enough, one type of crisis subsequently morphs into another. Not infrequently, such cascades of crises culminate in sovereign debt crises as the government or the central bank shoulders the burden of easing other types of crisis.[10] Chief examples include the Great Depression at the turn of the 1930s and the Great Recession at the turn of the 2010s.

The international legal framework relating to the financial sector has the purpose of ensuring financial stability, characterized as the absence of crisis, while facilitating international investment and trade. Undergirding this objective is for the most part an idea of development and growth bequeathed from post-war modernization theories as modified by financial liberalism in the so-called Washington Consensus. Accordingly, development and growth require capital investments, and opening the borders for capital flows fosters the efficient allocation of capital, ideally through private investment and free from government intervention.[11]

[7] In the context of the financial sector: H. Minsky, *Stabilizing an Unstable Economy* (New York: MacGraw-Hill, 2008), see also K. Polanyi, *The Great Transformation: The Political and Economic Origins of Our Time* (Boston MA: Beacon Press, 2001 [1944]) 147.

[8] On crisis and modernity generally cf. J. Habermas, *The Structural Transformation of the Public Sphere: An Inquiry into a Category of Bourgeois Society* (Cambridge MA: MIT Press 1991); R. Koselleck, *Critique and Crisis: Enlightenment and thePpathogenesis of Modern Society* (Cambridge MA: MIT Press, 1988).

[9] F. Mishkin, 'Anatomy of a Financial Crisis', (1992) 2 *Journal of Evolutionary Economics* 115.

[10] R. Aliber and Ch. Kindleberger, *Manias, Panics, and Crashes*, 7th ed. (New York: Palgrave 2015) 260ff.

[11] The significance of modernization as a frame for postwar development economics is apparent in J. Sadie, 'The Social Anthropology of Economic Underdevelopment', (1960)

17.2.2 Two Modes of Regulation

There are two modes of regulation governing the international framework for ensuring financial stability, following different ideas of risk management each. The first one could be called the sovereigntist mode. It has the purpose of isolating jurisdictions against each other to the extent possible, to contain the spread of crises. Historically, this mode of regulation represents the older layer. It is reflected in rules such as sovereign immunities; restrictions on the recognition and enforcement of foreign judgments, regulation, and debts held by foreign nationals; or in rules dividing the right to tax specific activities among different jurisdictions.[12]

Of more recent heritage is the second mode of regulation, which one might call the community mode. It is based on the idea that common standards may contain risks of contagion while enabling international financial interconnectedness. Early predecessors of this regulatory mode include the Latin monetary union and the emergence of an international gold standard on the basis of a gentlemen's agreement in the nineteenth century.[13] The Bretton Woods regime established a binding legal framework for money. Globalization has boosted this regulatory mode, notably in the field of banking regulation, where the Basel Committee on Banking Supervision (BCBS) established a level playing field. Binding rules relating to macroeconomic policy are few and far between; most macroeconomic policy coordination has a soft character, or relies on information such as

Economic Journal 294. On the neoliberal transformation, see J. Williamson, 'A Short History of the Washington Consensus', (2009) 15 *Law and Business Review of the Americas* 7. On the continuing relevance of modernization theory, see R. Marsh, 'Modernization Theory, Then and Now', (2014) 13 *Comparative Sociology* 261. Mapping these paradigm changes in development economics: Ph. Dann, 'Ideengeschichte von Recht und Entwicklung', in Ph. Dann, S. Kadelbach and M. Kaltenborn (eds), *Entwicklung und Recht: eine systematische Einführung* (Baden-Baden: Nomos 2014) 19. Modernization theory resonates with functionalism as a chief undercurrent of post-war international organizations law, see J. Klabbers, 'The Emergence of Functionalism in International Institutional Law: Colonial Inspirations', (2014) 25 *European Journal of International Law* 645.

12 See, e.g., the Convention on the Limitation of Employment of Force for Recovery of Contract Debts of 18 October 1907; or the Calvo Doctrine, see A. Freeman, 'Recent Aspects of the Calvo Doctrine and the Challenge to International Law', (1946) 40 *American Journal of International Law* 121. For contemporary examples, see below Section 17.4.1.

13 A. Redish, 'The Latin Monetary Union and the Emergence of the International Gold Standard', in N. Tamaki (ed.), *Monetary Regimes in Transition* (Cambridge University Press, 1993) 63.

Article IV surveillance. Only the European Monetary Union has been equipped with a framework of binding fiscal rules.[14]

17.2.3 The Evolution of Financial Regulation

The balance between the two modes of regulation has changed over time with the evolution of the financial sector.[15] In the post-war era, the Bretton Woods regime established in 1944 had set up a common framework for money, complementing GATT rules for trade liberalization. Moreover, the Paris Club, established in 1956, constituted at the time a fairly comprehensive, though informal, framework for addressing debt crises, which were at the time predominantly seen as shortages of foreign currency. Beyond this framework, financial regulation followed the sovereigntist mode of regulation. Capital controls were commonplace, in line with the (unchanged) Articles of Agreement of the International Monetary Fund (IMF). While many jurisdictions had established some form of banking and capital market regulation after the Great Financial Crisis, standards differed, and providers of financial services focused their operations on their home jurisdictions as they were frequently prevented from offering them abroad. Investment treaties constituted the exception rather than the rule. A regime of double taxation treaties aimed at a fair delineation of tax regimes.

The transformation of financial regulation since the early 1970s has profoundly unsettled this arrangement to the extent that it represents now almost the exact opposite state. A comprehensive international monetary regime shrunk into a rule against currency manipulation too general to be applied effectively.[16] The possibility to restructure debt comprehensively in the frame of the Paris Club evaporated when the Baker Plan of 1989 ushered in a profound shift from public to private, bonded debt for developing and emerging economies.[17] Attempts to

[14] Cf. Article 126(2) TFEU; Protocol (No. 12) on the excessive deficit procedure, OJ C 115, 9. May 2008, pp. 279–80.

[15] Comprehensively: C. Brummer, *Minilateralism: How Trade Alliances, Soft Law and Financial Engineering are Redefining Economic Statecraft* (Cambridge University Press, 2014) 22ff.

[16] Article IV(1)(iii), IMF Articles of Agreement.

[17] M. Frenkel, 'The International Debt Problem: An Analysis of the Brady Plan', (1989) 24 *Intereconomics* 110.

re-establish a comprehensive restructuring framework failed serially.[18] As a consequence, belated and insufficient debt restructurings sent countries into spirals of crisis and austerity, leading to severe human rights violations.[19] On the other hand, the frequent phase-out of capital controls since the 1970s and the spread of international investments made it necessary to establish a common level playing field for financial regulation. Otherwise, diverging regulatory requirements would have massively distorted competition between banks and other financial service providers from different jurisdictions. Financial liberalization therefore resulted in the Basel Accord on regulatory capital for banks, and a range of other regulatory standards for different actors. A considerable part of capital markets still remains in the shadow of international standards, though. However, companies in search of capital and investors with plenty of it available can easily move to different jurisdictions to issue securities, or invest their money in such instruments. This has resulted in the emergence of the equivalent of 'flags of convenience' in capital market law, that is, jurisdictions where regulation and supervision follow a more lenient approach, to the extent possible. Much of the shift to such jurisdictions is also motivated by the desire to evade higher tax burdens.

Compared to the post-1970 transformation of financial sector regulation, the changes occurring in the aftermath of the Global Financial Crisis almost pale by comparison. The most significant institutional development during this period has been the emergence of an institutional hierarchy with the G20 at the top. On substance, the IMF temporarily relaxed its lending conditions to address systemic crises, notably on the pressure of developed members to be able to lend to Greece, but later backtracked faced with criticism arising from the handling of the Greek crisis.[20] The human rights impact of austerity again reached deplorable levels.[21] Meanwhile, there have been some laudable signs that the IMF may have

[18] Cf. K. Rogoff and J. Zettelmeyer, 'Bankruptcy Procedures for Sovereigns: A History of Ideas, 1976–2001', (2002) 49 *IMF Staff Papers* 470.

[19] Cf. D. Bradlow, 'The World Bank, the IMF, and Human Rights', (1996) 6 *Transnational Law and Contemporary Problems* 47.

[20] See IMF, The Fund's Lending Framework and Sovereign Debt—Further Considerations, 9 April 2015, www.imf.org/external/np/pp/eng/2015/040915.pdf.

[21] T. Stubbs and A. Kentikelenis, 'Conditionality and Sovereign Debt: An Overview of Human Rights Implications', in I. Bantekas and C. Lumina (eds.), *Sovereign Debt and Human Rights* (Oxford University Press, 2018) 359.

changed course, although experiences have been mixed.[22] Moreover, a post-crisis reassessment eased the Fund's critical stance towards capital controls.[23]

The regulation of financial firms has become tighter in the crisis aftermath. Concern for systemic risk drove the evolution, both on substance and institutionally.[24] But on the whole, regulation evolved incrementally rather than fundamentally.[25] The new role of central banks as providers of ample liquidity is not reflected in new institutional settings, despite legal challenges to this effect.[26] Nor did the largest debt crisis in developed countries in recent history facilitate the creation of a comprehensive debt restructuring mechanism. The fiscal constraints in the aftermath of the Global Financial Crisis only prompted a number of initiatives to curb tax evasion. One might speculate about the reasons for this development. It seems plausible that the political will to scale back financial liberalization was lacking. Rather, much of the crisis response was based on the hope that the status quo ante would someday return and that private finance would ultimately fix problems of growth. Only the Covid-19 crisis may have effectively toppled this idea.

To date, the spread of autocracy in many parts of the world has had only a marginal impact upon the financial sector only for a number of reasons. First, contemporary autocratic governments are essentially capitalist, or rather, follow a peculiar model of state capitalism that relies on close ties with the private capital market. Unlike during the Cold War, there is no principled ideological barrier preventing autocracies from participating in international financial institutions. Second, due to its fragmented nature, the international regulation of the financial sector is flexible enough to accommodate new actors with new agendas, such as the Asian Infrastructure Investment Bank. A third and related point is that the

[22] M. Goldmann, 'Financial Institutions and Social Rights: From the Washington Consensus to the Lagarde Concord?', in C. Binder *et al.* (eds.), *Research Handbook on International Law and Social Rights* (Cheltenham: Edward Elgar, 2020) 440.

[23] K. Gallagher, 'Contesting the Governance of Capital Flows at the IMF', (2015) 28 *Governance* 185.

[24] P.-H. Verdier, 'The Political Economy of International Financial Regulation', (2013) 88 *Indiana Law Journal* 1405, 1459ff.

[25] D. Zaring, 'International Institutional Performance in Crisis Symposium: International Law and the Economic Crisis', (2009) 10 *Chicago Journal of International Law* 475.

[26] See, recently, BVerfG, Judgment of the Second Senate of 5 May 2020 – 2 BvR 859/15 -, paras. 1–237, www.bverfg.de/e/rs20200505_2bvr085915en.html.

reliance of the financial sector on soft and private forms of regulation enables autocratic governments to redesign financial regulation to some extent without changing the existing international institutional framework.

17.3 Between Fragmentation and Hierarchy

The financial sector is a hierarchical order.[27] At its apex are states as the entities creating money. This holds even in times of cryptocurrencies, not only because states hold the power to regulate such activities, but also because they decide which kinds of money to accept as tax payments.[28] Moreover, the apex role of states even increases if one follows Modern Monetary Theory, which ascribes the regulation of the quantity of money to fiscal and tax policy.[29] Not all states sit at the apex, though. There are considerable differences between the centre of the financial sector, the United States of America due to the role of the US dollar as a global anchor currency; the halo consisting of the governments issuing highly convertible currencies including Yuan, Euro, Yen, Swiss Franc, and the British Pound, and the more peripheral states, which often try to improve their credibility by pegging their currency to the dollar or another lead currency. Moreover, a number of states may not issue a comparable currency, but sit close to the centre due to the large size of their financial sector over which they yield considerable regulatory authority, including the power of taxation.

The situation of the private sector defies simple characterizations. On the one hand, private wealth and the provision of financial services depend on public institutions like currency, licenses, regulation, supervision and, last but not least, effective taxation as an ultimate backstop of financial risk. On the other hand, the financial prowess of private capital may make

[27] K. Pistor, 'A Legal Theory of Finance', (2013) 41 *Journal of Comparative Economics* 315.

[28] For a sobering account in historical perspective: B. Eichengreen, *From Commodity to Fiat and Now to Crypto: What Does History Tell Us?*, (2019) NBER Working Paper 25426.

[29] S. Bell, 'Do Taxes and Bonds Finance Government Spending?', (2000) 34 *Journal of Economic Issues* 603. The theory goes back to G. F. Knapp, *The State Theory of Money* (London: MacMillan, 1924, Lucas and Bonar transl.). For a critique, see G. Mankiw, 'A Skeptic's Guide to Modern Monetary Theory', (2020) 110 *AEA Papers and Proceedings* 141.

public authority dependent on it. This dependency ranges from the public sector's dependence on private actors for issuing debt and conducting monetary policy, to campaign finance, and, in the worst scenario, cases of outright corruption. This puts the hierarchy of the financial sector in perspective. One might actually describe it as a situation of co-dependence.

However, the public-private distinction only works on the proviso that political and economic powers are actually separated. The recent decades have witnessed the emergence of hybrid forms which, in the long run, might call this distinction into question, with considerable consequences for the operation and understanding of the financial sector. One such phenomenon is the spread of sovereign wealth funds among resource-rich countries. These funds absorb excess liquidity generated by extractive industries that constitutes a major risk for the diversification of the economy due to the pressure it may exert on the exchange rate (the so-called 'Dutch disease').[30] The downside of this welcome effect is that they transform the state into a private investor, and not one of the least significant ones. The political economy of sovereign wealth funds markedly differs from the one of public investments paid by taxes and approved by parliament. In case of sovereign wealth funds, states become investors with the ability to undercut the rules applicable to fiscal policy and to control economic activity in accordance with the rules applicable to private capital. The temptation for autocratic leaders seems irresistible.[31] Moreover, autocratic governments attempt to control considerable parts of the economy independently of sovereign wealth funds. But even among non-autocratic governments, the recent move towards public investment in the aftermath of the Covid-19 pandemic calls the distinction between public and private actors in the financial sector into question. If anything, the financial sector is getting even more hierarchical as a consequence of governments' increasing yield over the financial sector.

Another major reshuffle, this time within the private sector, is related to the pull towards digital finance (Fintech). One can distinguish three partly

[30] Cf. W. Corden, 'Booming Sector and Dutch Disease Economics: Survey and Consolidation', (1984) 36 *Oxford Economic Papers* 359.

[31] Cf. K. Hatton and K. Pistor, 'Maximizing Autonomy in the Shadow of Great Powers: The Political Economy of Sovereign Wealth Funds', (2011) 50 *Columbia Journal of Transnational Law* 1. For a more optimistic view, see G. Gilligan, J. O'Brien and M. Bowman, 'Sovereign Wealth Funds: The Good Guy Investment Actors?', (2014) *UNSW Law Research Paper* 14.

contradictory trends in this regard. First, digital finance offers opportunities for new start-ups to challenge the position of established financial firms. Their interests align with those of some jurisdictions seeking to attract a considerable share of this business, such as Luxembourg, Switzerland, Singapore, and many other common law jurisdictions. They offer regulatory 'sandboxes' and other measures relieving Fintech start-ups of some of their regulatory burden in the hope of obtaining a competitive advantage over other financial centres.[32] The risk of a regulatory race to the bottom is more than merely theoretical, as the Wirecard bankruptcy in Germany amply demonstrated.[33] Second, companies established in different branches seek to enter the market for financial services through their usage of digital technologies. This concerns primarily established players in the platform economy, who recognized the potential of financial services for their data-driven business model, and vice versa. One might think of Facebook's attempt to establish a digital stable coin in this regard, that is, a cryptocurrency whose value depends on a carefully hedged basket of actual currencies and debt instruments.[34] Third, new regulation might prefer established financial firms due to excessive hurdles for entering the market.[35] The outcome of these different trends is yet to be expected. It is, however, unlikely to change the hierarchical structure of the financial sector per se – it will only reshuffle the seating chart at the apex.

The current seating chart among international organizations is characterized by the G20 serving as an overarching bridge. Much of the legwork on macro policies is carried out by the International Financial Institutions (IFIs, i.e. the IMF and the World Bank Group) and the Organisation for Economic Co-operation and Development (OECD). Micro policies are in the hands of regulatory institutions. The international regulation of money and debt, by contrast, constitutes an almost deliberate void.

[32] L. Bromberg, A. Godwin and I. Ramsay, 'Fintech Sandboxes: Achieving a Balance between Regulation and Innovation', (2017) 28 *Journal of Banking and Finance Law and Practice* 314.

[33] This case has been amply documented by the *Financial Times*. See www.ft.com/wirecard (accessed 25 April 2021).

[34] Libra Association, *An Introduction to Libra* (Geneva: Libra, 2019).

[35] E.g. Proposal for a Regulation of the European Parliament and of the Council on Markets in Crypto-assets, COM(2020) 593 final, 24 September 2020.

17.3.1 The Bridge: G20

The G20 has been at the apex since the market turmoil triggering the Great Recession.[36] It overtook this function from the G7 at the time, which proved unable to play the apex of the financial system any longer, due to shrinking market shares of its members and the increasing regulatory significance and financial prowess of formerly emerging economies like the so-called BRICS states (Brazil, Russia, India, China, South Africa). The G20 was charged with coordinating both the immediate crisis response and the long-term regulatory change.

As the name says, the G20 has twenty members, including the European Union. Membership is based not only on the size of the respective economies, but also on geographic representation. From a financial sector perspective, the failure to include important financial hubs like Switzerland or Singapore is a potential impediment to the effectiveness of the group. This exclusion is understandable, though, since other G20 members would consider certain aspects of these two countries' past or present tax policies as harmful to global public interests. In fact, however, both countries are frequently involved in the work of the G20 as guests.

The G20 meets at the levels of the Heads of State and Government, the ministers of finance, and the central bank governors. Its main function is to take decisions at the highest policy level, which are to be implemented by the IFIs and the OECD to the extent that they concern macroeconomic policies, and by the main regulatory institutions described below in respect of (predominantly) micro-prudential regulation. One could therefore describe the G20 as a catalyst for change for the entire regulatory field.[37] The G20 meets in the form of summits convened by rotating member states acting as G20 presidency. This structure reflects its intergovernmental character and lack of legal personality. Its bureaucratic backbone therefore chiefly relies on member state governments.

The G20 has established a bureaucratic backbone in the form of the Financial Stability Board (FSB). It is charged with carrying out systemic supervision at a global level. Like the G20, the FSB is an informal group, composed by the G20 members, the IFIs and the main regulatory institutions. Different from the G20, the FSB does have a statute, which specifies

[36] A. Cooper and R. Thakur, *The Group of Twenty (G20)* (Abingdon: Routledge, 2013) 69ff.

[37] M. Larionova, 'G20: Engaging with International Organizations to Generate Growth', (2017) 12 *International Organisations Research Journal* 54.

its non-legal character.[38] Its secretariat is hosted by the Bank of International Settlements (BIS) in Basel.

On the whole, the G20 represents predominantly the interests of industrialized economies and the heavyweights among the emerging economies. It may lack the power and the legitimacy to steer the financial sector effectively at a global level. Its power deficits arise from its network character, lacking the legal means necessary to constrain powerful actors and overcome power asymmetries.[39]

Its legitimacy deficits are due to the dynamics of exclusion and inclusion intrinsic to its restrictive approach to membership. On the one hand, the G20 has frequently been under the influence of established financial firms from the G20 countries and their representatives. The G20 has regularly engaged with proposals by organizations like the International Institute of Finance (IIF), a lobby group of the banking industry, or the International Capital Market Association (ICMA), a private standard setter and lobby group for service providers on the capital market. For example, the model aggregation clauses for sovereign debt instruments proposed by ICMA in 2014 were approved by the IMF after endorsement by the G20.[40]

On the other hand, the perspective of developing countries is hardly represented within the G20. Even international organizations with a focus on the Global South like UNCTAD have a difficult time to be recognized as a stakeholder. This would be justified if the small size of the financial sector of many developing countries and their limited impact on the world economy made them bystanders rather than actors. However, this appears doubtful as developing countries have regularly absorbed considerable risks emanating from the financial policies of the industrialized economies. Examples abound. Developing countries have repeatedly experienced inflows of capital motivated by excess liquidity in developed states. The 'petrodollars' channelled predominantly into large scale, long-term infrastructure projects during the 1970s are one example. As soon as interest rates rose in the United States in the early 1980s, capital flows reversed and the 'Volcker Shock' set in, triggering a debt crisis in the developing world

[38] Article 16, Financial Stability Board Charter, www.fsb.org/wp-content/uploads/r_090925d.pdf?page_moved=1 (accessed 25 April 2021).

[39] Zaring, 'International Institutional Performance', 485 (comparing it to the Concert of Europe).

[40] Mark Sobel, 'Strengthening Collective Action Clauses: Catalysing Change–The Back Story', (2016) 11 *Capital Markets Law Journal* 3.

that lasted for over a decade.[41] Given this impact, it is therefore difficult to fathom how an oversight body like the G20 could be considered as legitimate without substantially including the developing world. Legitimacy ordinarily requires the inclusion of all those regularly affected.[42]

17.3.2 The Upper Deck: The International Financial Institutions

17.3.2.1 The Historical Framework

Historically, the IFIs formed the apex of the post-war institutional framework of essentially the Western hemisphere. Reflecting the community mode in a strong sense, they were charged with ensuring stable financial conditions for their members and avoid the disruptions characteristic of the interwar period.

The gold standard prevalent during much of the interwar period had become a main cause of contagion during the Great Depression, facilitating capital flight from Europe to the USA and thereby the import of deflation. The IMF changed course and established a common system for the management of stable exchange rates and for avoiding capital flight. Under the Articles of Agreement of the IMF, the US dollar played the role of an anchor currency, instead of an independent anchor as proposed by John Maynard Keynes.[43] The US Federal Reserve pledged to exchange dollars into gold at a price of 35 dollars per ounce. Other central banks committed to buy and sell their currency in order to maintain stable exchange rates. The IMF's original function was to serve as a fund for currencies, which countries lacking the requisite currencies for complying with their commitments for exchange rate stabilization could draw on. Periodic adjustments should ensure that the system remained in place even as the economic weights between the participating countries changed. Countries were, and still are, in principle at liberty to impose capital controls to avoid contagion and capital flight.[44] By contrast, restrictions on payments are allowed only in narrowly defined exceptional situations, as they would disrupt international trade.[45]

[41] Aliber and Kindleberger, *Manias, Panics, and Crashes*, 354–5.

[42] For many: S. Wheatley, 'A Democratic Rule of International Law', (2011) 22 *European Journal of International Law* 525, 536.

[43] J. Boughton and D. Moggridge, 'Why White, not Keynes? Inventing the Post-War International Monetary System', in A. Arnon and W. Young (eds.), *The Open Economy Macromodel: Past, Present and Future* (Berlin: Springer, 2002) 73.

[44] Article VI, Section 3, IMF Articles of Agreement.

[45] Article VIII, Section 2, IMF Articles of Agreement.

The World Bank and initially also the Organization of European Economic Cooperation (OEEC), the predecessor of the OECD, had the purpose of disbursing funds needed for development. In case of the World Bank, the member states had pooled their resources, while the OEEC and the now-defunct Economic Cooperation Administration administered the US-funded European Recovery Program, the so-called Marshall Plan.

The IFIs and the OECD have been characterized by highly differentiated hierarchical structures. Before 1990, large parts of the communist block choose not to become members of any of these organizations. That made them the institutional backbone of the Western hemisphere. Increasing membership in the IFIs on the part of the developing world did not change this situation, as the IFIs have in place a system of weighed voting. Votes are composed by basic votes equal to each member, and quota-based votes.[46] Quotas reflect a country's contribution to the fund.[47] The determination of quotas is essentially a political issue. The Articles of Agreement do not precisely describe the criteria. Currently, the size of GDP and the openness and diversification of the economy are the most important factors. Like in the case of the G20, this voting structure does not adequately reflect the distribution of risks emanating from the past or current global financial order.

17.3.2.2 The Age of Financial Capitalism

The role of the IFIs took a major turn in the course of the 1970s.[48] The Bretton Woods regime collapsed in the early 1970s as the United States' persistent trade deficit and high debt due to the Vietnam War undermined trust in the US dollar. Country after country stopped pegging their exchange rate and discontinued capital controls to allow for marked-based exchange rates. In 1973, the United States discontinued the convertibility promise of the US dollar.

In the following decade, the IFIs recalibrated their tasks. They extended the reach of their activities under the community mode of regulation far

[46] Article XII, Section 5, IMF Articles of Agreement; see A. Viterbo, *International Monetary Fund (IMF)* (London: Kluwer, 2019), Chapter 6 § 1.

[47] Article III, IMF Articles of Agreement.

[48] Comprehensively from the perspective of the IMF: J. Boughton, *Silent Revolution: The International Monetary Fund 1979-1989* (Washington DC: IMF, 2001). On the World Bank, see G. F. Sinclair, *To Reform the World: International Organizations and the Making of Modern States* (Oxford University Press, 2017) 236ff.

beyond money and investments into many sensitive policy areas. The IMF shifted from an institution ensuring the liquidity of convertible currencies to one charged with the management of macroeconomic balance, including debt crises and developmental issues. Countries applying for IMF emergency funding saw themselves compelled to adopt so-called structural adjustment programmes and to overhaul their social and economic policies including their institutional frameworks in accordance with the preferences of the IMF. The World Bank changed from facilitating large-scale infrastructure projects and the deployment of industrial policy into an institution concerned with the governance structures of developing states.[49] 'Good governance' became the catchphrase of development policy.[50] In imposing such conditionalities, the IFIs concurred in their dislike for state intervention in economic policy and their preference for market-based solutions – a set of policies that should become known as the 'Washington Consensus'.[51] This change was meticulously orchestrated by the United States and involved a new generation of staff and ideas inspired by the Chicago School in economics, a veritable hub of neoliberal thinking.[52] The OECD joined the bandwagon by advocating policies like capital account liberalization,[53] or approaches to education focusing on human capital.[54]

While the spillover to the developing world made the weighed voting mechanism of the IFIs difficult to justify even during the Bretton Woods era, it became even more untenable under the Washington Consensus as the IFIs extended their activities more and more into core fields of domestic economic and social policies.[55] This is all the more astonishing if one

[49] R. Wade, 'Agenda Change in Western Development Organizations: From Hard Production to Soft, Timeless, Placeless Policy', (2015) 20 *Lahore Journal of Economics* 1; Sinclair, *To Reform the World*, 251ff.

[50] Cf. Th. Weiss, 'Governance, Good Governance and Global Governance: Conceptual and Actual Challenges', (2000) 21 *Third World Quarterly* 795.

[51] Williamson, 'Washington Consensus'.

[52] A. Kentikelenis and S. Babb, 'The Making of Neoliberal Globalization: Norm Substitution and the Politics of Clandestine Institutional Change', (2019) 124 *American Journal of Sociology* 1720.

[53] D. Howarth and T. Sadeh, 'In the Vanguard of Globalization: The OECD and International Capital Liberalization', (2011) 18 *Review of International Political Economy* 622.

[54] A. von Bogdandy and M. Goldmann, 'The Exercise of Public Authority through National Policy Assessment: The OECD's PISA Policy as a Paradigm for a New International Standard Instrument', (2008) 5 *International Organizations Law Review* 241.

[55] A. Buira, 'The Bretton Woods Institutions: Governance without Legitimacy' in A. Buira (ed.), *Reforming the Governance of the IMF and the World Bank* (London: Anthem Press, 2005) 7.

considers that in this period, the symbolic significance of IFI funding may have surpassed its financial value. IFI funding became a signal of trust that opened other sources' funding, whether private or public. This reduced the importance of capital contributions, the basis of IFI voting, for the discharge of the IFI's mission, and increased the need for democratic, non-quota based legitimacy. However, no significant steps in this direction have been taken, apart from increases in transparency, especially since the Global Financial Crisis. Adjustments to the quotas only reflected changing economic weights among states. The hierarchy of international finance has remained intact.

17.3.3 The Middle Deck: BITs and DTAs

By contrast, a sovereignty mode of regulation governs international investments and taxation. While bilateral investment treaties (BITs) and double taxation agreements (DTA) have existed for many decades, their numbers increased significantly during the recent phase of globalization and liberalization. Both fields are famous for avoiding any explicit institutional hierarchy in favour of a bilateral, network-like structure, despite there being a high degree of convergence among BITs and DTAs. However, this apparently fragmented structure allows for a different type of hierarchy, as it puts states into competition against each other. While an isolated, bilateral treaty might be the perfect tool to protect a state's sovereignty, in a context in which states compete for investments it became a tool for trading away one's public interests. While World Trade Law points to harmonization as a way of preventing a downward spiral in a comparable situation, investment law and tax law lacked any explicit reference to such standards. Regulation and taxation therefore have become open to attack before domestic and international courts.[56] The OECD has established a running commentary to its model convention that is to prevent such divergence, but, like most instruments adopted by the OECD in the field of taxation, it lacks binding force.[57] This setting makes

[56] Insightful in the context of domestic environmental regulation: Y. Zhu, 'Fair and Equitable Treatment of Foreign Investors in an Era of Sustainable Development', (2018) 58 *Natural Resources Journal* 319, 327ff.

[57] Insightful in this respect is the failure of the OECD in the early 2000s to define harmful tax practices. See J. Sharman, *Havens in a Storm: The Struggle for Global Tax Regulation* (Ithaca NY: Cornell University Press, 2006).

public interests highly vulnerable. Skirting an institutional hierarchy entrenches the hierarchical impact of market power.

Only in the aftermath of the Global Financial Crisis and in the face of public outcry against the power of investment tribunals and the dimensions of tax avoidance and evasions, boosted by the transformation towards a digitalized economy, there have been efforts in both fields to better protect public interests. The OECD has launched an ambitious action plan on Base Erosion and Profit Shifting (BEPS), while UNCITRAL has launched an initiative aiming at investment arbitration reform. Both initiatives are still to be completed and to take effect, but it seems that in the long run, there is a realistic chance that both fields will shift towards a community mode of regulation.

17.3.4 The Machine Room: The Standard-Setting Bodies

While the IFIs are concerned with public finance, the regulation of financial markets is in the hands of an array of administrative networks.[58] Each of them functions as a standard-setter and monitoring agency in a specified field, operating under the community mode of regulation. The FSB ensures coordination among the standard-setting bodies, inter alia by issuing a compendium of key standards, and connects the standard-setting bodies with the political level via the G20.

The most important standard-setting bodies are the BCBS, the International Organization of Securities Commission (IOSCO), and the International Association of Insurance Supervisors (IAIS). Together, they form the Joint Forum for the regulation of cross-cutting issues. BCBS, IOSCO, and IAIS are each composed of domestic regulatory authorities, but their composition varies significantly. The BCBS is the most exclusive one with still only twenty-eight members after two rounds of expansion in 2009 and 2014. Lacking legal personality, it has been hosted by the BIS, and, unusual for an informal forum, adopted a charter in 2013. Its primary responsibility is the drafting and revision of the Basel Accord on banking supervision, which sets out rules and principles for the calculation of the regulatory capital banks must hold to back up different investments. By contrast, the IAIS has a much broader membership base with supervisors

[58] A list is available at www.fsb.org/work-of-the-fsb/about-the-compendium-of-standards/wssb/ (accessed 25 April 2021).

from 140 countries. Supervisors from an even larger number of countries are represented in IOSCO. Membership requires the government of each country to sign the IOSCO Multilateral Memorandum of Understanding Concerning Consultation and Cooperation and the Exchange of Information (MMoU). Drafted in the aftermath of September 2001, it focuses on information exchange in order to allow the tracing of financial flows. This fact alone underscores the significance of the USA and the UK as the principal markets for securities.[59] Representation thus does not need amount to equal power.

Another group of standard-setting bodies consists in boards of independent experts chosen by professional organizations. This selection mechanism prevails in the field of accounting, with the International Accounting Standards Board (IASB) in a leading role. Interestingly, the FSB considers the IFIs and the OECD as standard-setting bodies as they have contributed to standard-setting in specific areas, such as financial reporting, and are involved in the monitoring of compliance. By contrast, not among the official standard-setting bodies recognized by the FSB are industry associations like the International Swaps and Derivatives Association or ICMA, despite their standard-setting functions.[60] Another white elephant in the standard-setting bodies room are the Credit Rating Agencies (CRA). While their original function was to provide information on securities for investors willing to pay, under the Basel Accord, they could seek supervisory accreditation for issuing ratings determinative of the credit risk to be assigned to the rated securities. This gives their rating methodology the function of quasi-standards, despite their lack of transparency.[61] The crisis has not changed their role in a significant way, even though they have been subjected to more stringent supervisory examination. But to quit with ratings altogether would require an incisive regulatory turn away from regulatory capital requirements. Alternatives are available, such as a portfolio approach, but the political will to impose this change is missing.

[59] Instructive: B. Simmons, 'The International Politics of Harmonization: The Case of Capital Market Regulation', (2003) 55 *International Organization* 589.

[60] See J. Horst, 'Lex Financiaria: Das transnationale Finanzmarktrecht der International Swaps and Derivatives Association (ISDA)', (2015) 53 *Archiv des Völkerrechts* 461.

[61] Cf. M. Richardson and L. White, 'The Rating Agencies: Is Regulation the Answer?', in V. Acharya and M. Richardson (eds.), *Restoring Financial Stability* (Hoboken NJ: Wiley 2009) 101.

The legitimacy of the standard-setting bodies rests on a mix of technocratic expertise, representativeness, and the idea of self-regulation. Their composition does not encourage the politicization of regulatory issues. Even though public consultations on their policies became a common feature after the financial crisis, expertise-driven bodies tend to attract expert opinions only. They do not necessarily provide a forum for debates on public interests like environmental issues.[62] The community mode after all requires a forum for the community to articulate itself.[63] Moreover, the under-inclusive composition or power asymmetry among the members further decreases their legitimacy.[64] Nevertheless, the connection with the G20 establishes at least some form of political oversight.

The lack of legitimacy is met by a lack of rigour in implementation, hampering the effectiveness of coordination. The soft nature of the regulatory frameworks leaves governments and regulators with a large margin of discretion, both as to the content and the timing. The United States were still in the process of implementing Basel II when the Global Financial Crisis occurred. As a result, countries have been reluctant to open their markets for financial services from other jurisdictions, allowing them access often only on the basis of a unilateral recognition of equivalence.[65] The impact of this fragmented market structure is, however, sizeable as capital possesses a high degree of mobility and financial firms have the possibility of establishing local branches and subsidiaries.

17.3.5 The Voids: Monetary and Debt Regimes

17.3.5.1 Monetary Coordination

Since the demise of the Bretton Woods system, there has not been any comprehensive institutional framework for monetary coordination any more. The prohibition of exchange rate manipulation is only marginally

[62] K. Alexander, *Stability and Sustainability in Banking Reform: Are Environmental Risks Missing in Basel III?* (Cambridge: CSIL, 2014).

[63] On the forum function of international institutions cf. J. Klabbers, 'Two Concepts of International Organization', (2005) 2 *International Organizations Law Review* 277.

[64] R. M. Lastra, *International Financial and Monetary Law*, 2nd ed. (Oxford University Press, 2015), para. 14.57ff.

[65] L. Quaglia, 'The Politics of "Third Country Equivalence" in Post-Crisis Financial Services Regulation in the European Union', (2015) 38 *West European Politics* 167; P.-H. Verdier, 'Mutual Recognition in International Finance', (2011) 52 *Harvard International Law Journal* 55, 101ff.

kept in check by the IMF Articles of Agreement, which in principle allows member states to choose an exchange rate arrangement of their liking.[66] GATT rules on exchange arrangements refer back to IMF rules,[67] and exchange rate manipulations do not meet the definition of subsidies.[68]

Beyond the forlorn quest for preventing exchange rate manipulations, monetary coordination is highly informal and dispersed, relying on institutions like the Jackson Hole meetings. At least, it has been effective, as the ample and generous provision of central bank liquidity during the Global Financial Crisis and the Covid-19 crisis amply demonstrates. However, given the cross-border impact of monetary policy,[69] its general redistributive impact,[70] and the recent politicization of central banks,[71] it seems apposite to call for an international forum and common standards.[72]

17.3.5.2 Sovereign Debt Restructuring

The absence of a sovereign debt restructuring mechanism is the second, much more frequently deplored void in the architecture of financial stability. The need for such a forum has increased in recent decades. For much of the time before the Second World War, sovereigns borrowed from private creditors and were protected by their jurisdictional and enforcement immunities.[73] When bilateral loans from developed countries became a major source of funding in the post-war era, the Paris Club established itself as a venue for necessary restructurings. Even though its operations remained rather

66 Article IV(1)(iii), (2)(b), IMF Articles of Agreement.

67 Article XV(1), (2), and (3), GATT 1947.

68 M. Waibel, 'Retaliating Against Exchange-Rate Manipulation under WTO Rules', in S. Evenett (ed.), *The US-Sino Currency Dispute: New Insights from Economics, Politics, and Law* (London: CEPR, 2010) 133.

69 K. Bagchi, 'Revisiting the Taper Tantrum: A Case for International Monetary Policy Coordination', (2017) 3 *Journal of Financial Regulation* 280.

70 I. Feichtner, 'Public Law's Rationalization of the Legal Architecture of Money: What Might Legal Analysis of Money Become?', (2016) 17 *German Law Journal* 875.

71 Ch. Goodhart and R. Lastra, 'Populism and Central Bank Independence', (2018) 29 *Open Economies Review* 49; Feichtner, 'Legal Architecture'.

72 D. Bradlow and S. Park, 'A Global Leviathan Emerges: The Federal Reserve, COVID-19, and International Law', (2020) 114 *American Journal of International Law* 657.

73 Overview of the evolution in A. Gelpern, 'Sovereign Debt: Now What?' (2016) 42 *Yale Journal of International Law Online* 45. For a detailed analysis see H. Feldmann, *Internationale Umschuldungen im 19. Und 20. Jahrhundert. Eine Analyse ihrer Ursachen, Techniken und Grundprinzipien* (Berlin: Duncker & Humblot 1991).

secret for a long time, it was fairly effective in addressing debt crises in close co-ordination with the IMF.[74] The emergence of syndicated loans in the 1970s led to the creation of the London Club, an informal venue of private banks. As all participants were repeat players, the informal system was working fairly reliably, even though the developing countries rejected the influence it assigned to foreign creditors over their economic and social policies.[75]

Things took a decisive turn with the debt crisis hitting the developing world in the 1980s in the wake of rising interest rates in the developed countries.[76] The crisis was too deep to be addressed by restructurings that did not reduce the stock of the bond, but only changed payment conditions. At the end of a decade of serial restructurings, the time was ripe for a decisive change in course. The end of the Cold War also ushered in a new relation between the capital exporting countries in the Western hemisphere and the Global South. As capitalism seemed to have won over communism, the need to keep defaulting developed economies within one's camp evaporated, and the interest in liberalizing financial relations with them grew. This resulted in the Brady Plan of 1989. It transformed sovereign loans into bonds and sold them off on the market. To entice investors, sovereign debtors had to waive their immunities. The consequent privatization of sovereign debt saw debtor states confronted not only with an array of bondholders much more difficult to coordinate in case of a restructuring. It also exposed them to increasing litigation before domestic[77] and international courts.[78]

For the poorest countries, the IFIs initiated the Heavily Indebted Poor Countries Initiative (HPIC Initiative) in the mid-1990s, which

[74] L. Grard, 'Le Club de Paris et les dettes publiques des Etats', in D. Carreau and M. Shaw (eds.), *La dette extérieure* (Dordrecht: Martinus Nijhoff, 1995) 197.

[75] I am tracing the contours of this development in M. Goldmann, 'Contesting Austerity: Genealogies of Human Rights Discourse', (2020-09) Max Planck Institute for Comparative Public Law & International Law Research Paper.

[76] The following draws on J. Bohoslavsky and M. Goldmann, 'An Incremental Approach to Sovereign Debt Restructuring: Sovereign Debt Sustainability as a Principle of Public International Law', (2016) 42 *Yale Journal of International Law Online* 13.

[77] J. Schumacher, C. Trebesch and H. Enderlein, 'Sovereign Defaults in Court', (2018) ECB Working Paper 2135).

[78] M. Waibel, *Sovereign Defaults before International Courts and Tribunals* (Cambridge University Press, 2011).

resulted in the effective reduction of their debt.[79] Richer countries were less lucky, though, as their private creditors pulled them before courts, even though they may have acquired the debt instrument at a huge discount. The development culminated in the Argentinean crisis and its legal aftermath that saw creditors and judges go to unprecedented lengths to seek enforcement.[80] Again, the sovereignty mode had become an entry gate for highly intrusive power. The apparent lack of international coordination triggered a number of initiatives, notably in the frame of the United Nations and UNCTAD,[81] culminating in General Assembly resolution 69/319.[82] Human rights bodies also addressed the matter, mostly with a view to attenuating the social consequences of debt crises.[83] On the whole, there is thus a range of developments pointing in the direction of an emerging community mode of regulation.[84]

But a binding framework is still not in sight. Its creation has been thwarted by capital-exporting states, at times with the doubtful claim that the IMF had primary responsibility.[85] In fact, however, the UN has addressed the problem of external debt for nearly sixty years in the frame of UNCTAD and regional debt commissions. This excuse therefore

[79] L. Guder, *The Administration of Debt Relief by the International Financial Institutions* (Berlin: Springer 2009).

[80] Overview in P. López and C. Nahón, 'The Growth of Debt and the Debt of Growth: Lessons from the Case of Argentina', (2017) 44 *Journal of Law and Society* 99; see also M. Weidemaier and A. Gelpern, 'Injunctions in Sovereign Debt Litigation', (2014) 31 *Yale Journal on Regulation* 189.

[81] See UNCTAD, *Sovereign Debt Workouts: Going Forward. Roadmap and Guide* (2015), http://unctad.org/en/PublicationsLibrary/gdsddf2015misc1_en.pdf.

[82] UN General Assembly, 'Basic Principles on Sovereign Debt Restructuring Processes', UN Doc A/RES/69/319 of 29 September 2015.

[83] Human Rights Council, 'Guiding principles on foreign debt and human rights', Annex to the Report of the Independent Expert on the effects of foreign debt and other related international financial obligations of States on the full enjoyment of all human rights, particularly economic, social and cultural rights, Cephas Lumina (hereinafter Guiding Principles), UN Doc. A/RES/20/23 of 10 April 2011. The Human Rights Council endorsed the Guiding Principles by majority with Resolution 20/10 of 18 July 2012, UN Doc. A/HRC/RES/20/10; see A. Nolan and J. Bohoslavsky, 'Human Rights and Economic Policy Reforms', (2020) 24 *International Journal of Human Rights* 1247; M. Goldmann, 'Human Rights and Sovereign Debt Workouts', in J. Bohoslavsky and J. Cernic (eds.), *Making Sovereign Financing and Human Rights Work* (Oxford: Hart 2014) 79.

[84] Bohoslavsky and Goldmann, 'An Incremental Approach'.

[85] This was the content of a statement by Italy on behalf of the European Union in the UN General Assembly on 9 September 2014 on the subject of a multilateral framework for sovereign debt restructuring.

constitutes a formidable example of how fragmentation is used strategically and how the pretence to foster coordination actually entrenches the existing hierarchy.

17.4 Between Soft and Hard Regulation

17.4.1 Legal Rules

The Bretton Woods regime was based on a binding legal framework following the community mode of regulation. Since then, the use of 'hard' law has been mostly limited to fields like tax law and investment law, characterized by the sovereignty mode of regulation. Hard law continues to play a role for the IFIs, though, yet in a different sense. Instead of regulating common interests, it serves as a barrier against human rights and other public interests deemed overly political and therefore as falling outside the respective mandates.[86] For example, the requirement of the IMF to receive 'adequate assurance' that a member state will repay a loan allegedly prevents it from excluding corruption debt from the calculation of outstanding debt for that purpose.[87] Conspicuously, conditionalities have never been a problem for the mandates, despite their highly political, highly intrusive character.

17.4.2 Soft Regulation

The regulation of financial stability is replete with different types of soft law and instruments falling into the category of governance by information. In fact, the community mode of regulation relies almost exclusively on these types of instruments.

This begins with IMF loans. The IMF decides on eligibility on the basis of a Debt Sustainability Assessment, a complex framework including a host of different economic and circumstantial factors, many of which comprise a discretionary element. In case a country is eligible, the loan is usually based on stand-by arrangements, or on concessional instruments for low-

[86] F. Gianviti, *Economic, Social, and Cultural Human Rights and the International Monetary Fund* (Washington DC: IMF, 2001).

[87] M. Goldmann, 'The Law and Political Economy of Mozambique's Odious Debt', (2019) available at SSRN 3513651.

income countries. Lending under any such instrument requires the requesting country to adopt a structural adjustment programme, submitted after consultations to the IMF in a letter of intent, often specified in Memoranda of Understanding. None of these instruments has binding legal force, and each of them is highly discretionary. The IMF wants to avoid legal responsibility and relies on its power of the purse instead.[88] Moreover, one is inclined to suspect that soft law has the advantage of skirting parliaments and the public attention that comes with a ratification process,[89] although negotiations recently tend to take place under the watchful eye of the public.

The bilateral and multilateral surveillance of the IMF is based on Article IV(3) of the Articles of Agreement. It takes place on a regular basis and allows the IMF, like the World Bank, to collect statistical data and gain insight knowledge of a country's economy.[90] The recommendations issued in this process gain high significance in case a country needs to apply for a loan.

Many activities of the IFIs are determined by their internal rules. The IMF maintains a compendium of executive board decisions adopting fund policies. Below this level, the IMF also follows its 'practices', that is, normative rules lacking executive board decisions, which are often only known to insiders. The World Bank has a more transparent system of Operational Policies and Procedures. As is well-known, the inspection panel checks Bank-funded projects for their compliance with these rules.[91]

Sovereign debt restructurings are also predominantly conducted on the basis of soft legal instruments. The Paris Club bases them on standard terms, follows soft legal principles that guide its discretion, and settles individual cases in 'agreed minutes'. Negotiations with institutional creditors remain informal until all or the requisite majority of creditors accepts

88 Instructive: J. Gold, 'The rule of law in the International Monetary Fund', (1980) 32 IMF Pamphlet Series (1980).

89 J. Klabbers, 'The Changing Image of International Organizations', in J.-M. Coicaud and V. Heiskanen (eds.), *The Legitimacy of International Organizations* (Tokyo: UNU Press, 2001) 221, 237.

90 On the IFI's information management, see M. Riegner, *Informationsverwaltungsrecht internationaler Institutionen: Dargestellt am Entwicklungsverwaltungsrecht der Weltbank und Vereinten Nationen* (Tübingen: Mohr Siebeck, 2018).

91 Ph. Dann, 'Accountability in Development Aid Law: The World Bank, UNDP and Emerging Structures of Transnational Oversight', (2006) 44 *Archiv des Völkerrechts* 381.

a restructuring offer. Only the London Agreement on German debts and the UN resolution on Iraqi debt had a binding international legal nature.[92]

Moreover, financial standards adopted by the standard-setting bodies are soft law without exception. This is puzzling because their massive distributive impact suggests that only binding rules might work. However, the regulatory authorities usually lack the capacity to adopt binding international legal rules. The need to frequently adapt financial standards also makes binding legal rules less convenient than in the case of trade law. On the assumption that capital markets are efficient, one may also assume a preference of investors for compliant supervisors and financial firms.[93] One should also not forget that some financial standards, such as the anti-money laundering standards developed by the Financial Action Task Force, can be implemented via surveillance and conditionality, or by way of incorporation into trade law like the Export Credits Arrangement facilitated by the OECD.[94] One further factor are differences in the market structure, as a result of which universal standards would by necessity favour some jurisdictions over others. A certain flexibility in the implementation therefore seems adequate, but bears the risk of undermining common standards to obtain competitive advantages.[95] For these reasons, one should therefore not expect financial regulation to 'harden' anytime soon.[96]

Coherent with this view is the trend to use principles in international finance. For example, the BCBS has proposed Core Principles for Effective Bank Supervision in 2012. The FSB has

[92] For details, see A. von Bogdandy and M. Goldmann, 'Sovereign Debt Restructurings as Exercises of Public Authority: Towards a Decentralized Sovereign Insolvency Law', in C. Espósito, J. Bohoslavsky and Y. Li (eds.), *Responsible Sovereign Lending and Borrowing: The Search for Common Principles* (Oxford University Press, 2013) 39.

[93] Cf. Brummer, 'Why Soft Law Dominates', 636ff.

[94] J. Levit, 'A Bottom-Up Approach to International Lawmaking: The Tale of Three Trade Finance Instruments', (2005) 30 *Yale Journal of International Law* 125.

[95] Cf. J. Klabbers, 'The Undesirability of Soft Law', (1998) 67 *Nordic Journal of International Law* 381.

[96] See, however, Lastra, *International Financial and Monetary Law*, para. 14.88ff.; M. Giovanoli, 'A New Architecture for the Global Financial Market: Legal Aspects of International Financial Standard Setting', in M. Giovanoli (ed.), *International Monetary Law-Issues for the New Millenium* (Oxford University Press, 2000) 3, 51; D. Zaring, 'Finding Legal Principle in Global Financial Regulation', (2011) 52 *Virginia Journal of International Law* 683.

assembled a number of Key Standards for Sound Financial Systems.[97] These principles provide guidance in a field that seems to assume a certain level of heterogeneity among jurisdictions even if they apply in principle the identical standards.

A more recent layer of soft law is composed of instruments adopted mainly within the UN system and specifically by human rights bodies addressing questions of debt restructuring and austerity, as discussed above. However, market powers are unlikely to sustain them. It is therefore safe to assume that the choice of soft or hard law is not indicative of the effectiveness or legitimacy of financial regulation.

17.4.3 Private Law

The regulation of financial stability relies to no small extent on private law instruments. This category comprises industry self-regulation like accounting standards. Their legitimacy is debatable, even though their regulatory function entails higher levels of public scrutiny.[98] A special case are credit ratings, which enjoy journalistic privileges in the United States, never mind their quasi-regulatory function.[99] Standard terms of securities also play an immensely important role for the prevention of systemic risk and the management of financial crises. This is especially acute in the field of sovereign debt, where public interests depend on the effectiveness of restructuring clauses developed with the guidance of industry associations.[100] The reliance of financial regulation on private law comes with an invitation for extensive forum shopping, both in respect of the applicable law and the forum state. The *Ara Libertad* case represents an extreme case, where efforts of US creditors to enforce Argentinean debt governed by US law led to the enforcement

[97] Lastra, *International Financial and Monetary Law*, para. 14.29.

[98] M. De Bellis, 'Public Law and Private Regulators in the Global Legal Space', (2011) 9 *International Journal of Constitutional Law* 425.

[99] T. Nagy, 'Credit Rating Agencies and the First Amendment: Applying Constitutional Journalistic Protections to Subprime Mortgage Litigation', (2009) 94 *Minnesota Law Review* 140.

[100] M. Weidemaier and M. Gulati, 'A People's History of Collective Actions Clauses', (2013) 54 *Virginia Journal of International Law* 51.

of a UK judgment via the attachment of an Argentinean navy ship in Ghana.[101] On the whole, the prevalence of private law in the regulation of the financial sector, justified often by ideas of subsidiarity and efficiency, is more often than not yet another coffin nail to both the legitimacy and effectiveness of such regulation.

17.5 Between Form and Substance

17.5.1 Formal Principles

17.5.1.1 Consent

Much of financial sector regulation is based on consent and voluntary compliance, including structural adjustment programmes, adherence to regulatory standards, and tax and investment treaties. Consent in international law is normally the expression of state sovereignty. In the regulation of financial stability, consent has degenerated into a mere formal requirement that disguises power asymmetries. In fact, consent has become a means of shifting responsibility from creditor to debtor states or from home states to host states, concealing the absence or insufficiency of rules to safeguard important public interests. It seems preferable to understand such modes of regulation as authoritative acts.[102]

17.5.1.2 Transparency and Participation

Transparency and participation are now widespread among the different actors of the financial hierarchy and especially the IFIs.[103] Respect for these principles increases the accountability and capacity for self-correction of regulatory bodies.[104] It is not entirely implausible to argue that certain policy shifts, for example the renewed concern of the IMF for social spending, are due to this organizational openness. Nevertheless, access is not always granted on an equal level.

[101] *Ara Libertad* (*Argentina* v. *Ghana*), International Tribunal for the Law of the Sea, Case No. 20, Order of December 2012.

[102] Cf. von Bogdandy and Goldmann, 'Sovereign Debt Restructurings'.

[103] L. Hinojosa, 'Transparency in International Financial Institutions', in A. Bianchi and A. Peters (eds.), *Transparency in International Law* (Cambridge University Press, 2013) 77.

[104] C. Kaufmann and R. Weber, 'The Role of Transparency in Financial Regulation', (2010) 13 *Journal of International Economic Law* 779.

17.5.2 Substantive Principles

17.5.2.1 Technocratic Legitimacy

Traditionally, much of the work of the IFIs and the standard-setting bodies operates under the premise of technocratic, expert-driven legitimacy. This idea of legitimacy goes back to the post-war concept of functionalism that considers international institutions as a way of depoliticizing decision-making by moving them above the minefield of domestic politics and into the orderly structures of bureaucratic rationality.[105] The underlying idea of objectivity survived the demise of the post-war world in the 1970s, as it was replaced by another objectivity stemming from law and economics, which replaced bureaucratic rationality with the idea of efficiency measured in microeconomic perspective.[106] The political salience and distributive repercussions of financial regulation, whether it concerns public finance, investments or financial markets, has brought this line of thinking into crisis. Nevertheless, to replace it with democratic forms of decision-making is easier said than done, absent a global polity. Transparency and participation may partly compensate for democratic deficits, but will not fully replace democratic structures.

17.5.2.2 Human Rights

In recent decades, civil society has mostly relied on human rights in order to address legitimacy deficits of the IFIs and financial regulation generally. The argument goes that the IFIs are bound by human rights due to their mandate, their membership in the UN family of international organizations, customary law, or as a consequence of the human rights obligations of their member states.[107] These efforts received a rather cold response from the IFIs. The IMF has deemed human rights issues as too political, reaching therefore beyond the scope of its mandate.[108] Nevertheless, in practice, it has attempted to address

[105] J. Klabbers, 'The EJIL Foreword: The Transformation of International Organizations Law', (2015) 26 *European Journal of International Law* 9; J. Steffek, 'Max Weber, Modernity and the Project of International Organization', (2016) 29 *Cambridge Review of International Affairs* 1502.

[106] Many of these themes are elaborated in P. Kjaer, 'The Law of Political Economy: An Introduction', in P. Kjaer (ed.), *The Law of Political Economy: Transformation in the Function of Law* (Cambridge University Press, 2020) 1, 4–5; J. Britton-Purdy *et al.*, 'Building a Law-and-Political-Economy Framework: Beyond the Twentieth-Century Synthesis', (2019) 129 *Yale Law Journal* 1784.

[107] For many: S. Skogly, *The Human Rights Obligations of the World Bank and the International Monetary Fund* (London: Cavendish, 2001).

[108] Gianviti, 'Economic, Social, and Cultural Human Rights'.

some of the concerns by focusing on poverty reduction, social spending, et cetera. The 2017 report on social protection by the IMF's Independent Evaluation Office, otherwise a rather sobering stocktaking, suggests a relation between these policies and a human rights-based approach.[109] Whether such theory will eventually converge with practice is, of course, a different question. The World Bank, by contrast, has been more open towards human rights. According to the so-called Shihata formula, the mandate of the World Bank comprises the promotion of human rights as long as economic considerations prevail in case of a conflict.[110] In line with this formula, the World Bank has insisted that its developmental mission advances human rights.[111] Investment tribunals have approached human rights issues predominantly from an investor's perspective,[112] and the discussion in tax law is still at the beginning.[113]

Common to all these conceptual moves is, however, a propensity to favour a minimalistic approach to human rights that focuses on minimum core requirements instead of equality in a broader sense.[114] Litigation against austerity measures in the aftermath of the Global Financial Crisis achieved to make some inroads into the human rights responsibilities of international institutions,[115] but hardly reached beyond minimum requirements.[116] Austerity-related human rights issues might therefore better be addressed

[109] IMF Independent Evaluation Office, *The IMF and Social Protection* (Washington DC: IMF, 2017), 13 (footnote 40); see also V. Engström, 'The IMF and Protection of Vulnerable Groups', (2020) 89 *Nordic Journal of International Law* 209.

[110] I. Shihata, *The World Bank in a Changing World: Selected Essays and Lectures*, vol. 2 (Dordrecht: Martinus Nijhoff, 1991) 70ff.

[111] World Bank, *Development and Human Rights: The Role of the World Bank* (Washington DC: World Bank, 1998).

[112] S. Steininger, 'What's Human Rights Got To Do With It? An Empirical Analysis of Human Rights References in Investment Arbitration', (2017) 31 *Leiden Journal of International Law* 26.

[113] P. Alston and N. Reisch, *Tax, Inequality, and Human Rights* (Oxford University Press, 2019).

[114] In detail Goldmann, 'Contesting Austerity'. On the ambivalence between sufficiency and equality in human rights law, see S. Moyn, *Not Enough: Human Rights in an Unequal World* (Cambridge MA: Harvard University Press, 2018).

[115] E.g. ECJ, Case C-8/15 P, *Ledra Advertising* v. *Commission and ECB*, ECLI:EU:C:2016:701, 6.

[116] Overview in C. Kilpatrick, 'Constitutions, Social Rights and Sovereign Debt States in Europe: A Challenging New Area of Constitutional Inquiry', in B. de Witte, C. Kilpatrick and T. Beukers (eds.), *Constitutional Change through Euro-Crisis Law* (Cambridge University Press, 2017), 279.

by procedural approaches that aim at strengthening domestic democratic decision-making.[117]

17.5.2.3 Sustainability

Complementing and corroborating human rights approaches is the principle of sustainability. It is no newcomer to the field of financial regulation. The IMF uses debt sustainability to assess a country's eligibility for a loan. However, it understands debt sustainability in a purely economic sense as the ability to roll over existing debt in the medium term without major policy changes.[118] An alternative understanding would consider debt sustainability as inspired by the idea of development and human rights.[119] Nevertheless, sustainability may not lead to greater equality. On substance, the Sustainable Development Goals aim at poverty eradication, rather than at a state of relative equality within and across societies. Moreover, sustainability may also be used to entrench a managerial attitude to development that favours the interests of investors rather than effective emancipation.[120] For the latter purpose, resort to the principle of equality *tout court* might be the better alternative.[121]

17.6 Outlook

Predictions are notoriously difficult. For the issue at hand, this applies with particular force, as there are two countervailing trends to be kept in mind. On the one hand, in the wake of the Covid-19 crisis, monetary and fiscal policy is playing an ever more important role. In the long run, this will require new forms of policy coordination, as it would otherwise undermine the idea of fair competition. Complicating the

[117] For such a framework, see Nolan and Bohoslavsky, 'Economic Policy Reforms'. On the connection between human rights and democracy, see M. Goldmann, 'Human Rights and Democracy in Economic Policy Reform: The European COVID-19 Response under Scrutiny', (2020) 24 *International Journal of Human Rights* 1290.

[118] IMF, 'Assessing Sustainability' (IMF Policy Paper, May 2002), 4.

[119] Bohoslavsky and Goldmann, 'An Incremental Approach'.

[120] M. Riegner, 'The Equator Principles on Sustainable Finance Assessed from a Critical Development and Third World Perspective', (2014) 5 *Transnational Legal Theory* 489, 496ff.

[121] See, e.g., J. Bohoslavsky, 'Economic Inequality, Debt Crises and Human Rights', (2016) 42 *Yale Journal of International Law Online* 177.

situation is the fact that with the rise of China, the connection between capitalism and liberal democracy, which has been formative for the current institutional framework, is no longer the only game in town. On the other hand, the evolution of digital finance has added a new, competitive edge to a field hitherto dominated by a few, increasingly global and state-like, financial firms. Platform providers and blockchain-based services are roughing up a saturated market, often defying regulatory structures or evoking regulatory leniency as the competition among jurisdictions intensifies. It is difficult to fathom which trend will prevail. However, looking at the history of financial market regulation, it would be the exception that markets revolutionize politics. Financial market liberalization was a deliberate effort, in which international institutions played key roles. As things stand, they seem to hold the keys to a reversal of this trend.

Epilogue

Jan Klabbers

The chapters collected in this *Cambridge Companion* together demonstrate a few things about the law of international organizations – and law generally perhaps – that may not always be realized. A first point to note is that international organizations are active in nigh-on all walks of life, as these chapters suggest. There are few human activities with which international organizations have no point of contact. Whether it concerns energy provision or the movement of persons across the globe; whether it concerns disarmament or financial stability or the governance of resource extraction, international organizations are often involved in one way or another. And even in those policy domains where there is no single overarching international organization (most conspicuously perhaps the heavily fragmented domain of environmental protection), there are nonetheless entities active which may not generally be considered international organizations (largely because their founding fathers shy away from using that label), but which are remarkably similar to international organizations in all but name. Environmental regimes tend to be governed by means of Conferences or Meetings of the Parties (COPs or MOPs), supported by a secretariat, and tend to do the things that international organizations tend to do.

International organizations are not only omnipresent, they are also very influential, despite a dearth of formal legislative powers. Few international organizations can actually formally enact abstract rules of general application – the sort of rules that are normally associated with lawmaking. Not even the UN can do this, although it is fair to say that the Security Council on occasion has come close. But many organizations are engaged in standard-setting in one way or another, whether in the form of formal lawmaking procedures or through operational and related activities. Partly because the staff of international organizations is often selected on the basis of professional expertise (economists at financial institutions, engineers at the International Telecommunications Union (ITU), et cetera), their output is often highly authoritative. It may need to stay within formal legal parameters, in the sense that a migration processing manual produced by the International Organization for Migration (IOM) should not advocate widespread transgressions of human rights conventions, for example, but it is more than likely that what the migration officials of states have on their desk are not copies of the International Covenant on Civil and Political Rights, but are copies of the IOM's handbooks and manuals. Confronted with practical questions, their first impulse is to reach for those documents emanating from the IOM, rather than for the (more abstract, less directly applicable) international treaties and conventions. And what applies to migration applies to other policy areas as well.

International lawyers – lawyers generally – have a hard time making sense of this. International lawyers are accustomed to analyzing normative output in one of two, maybe three categories: something should either fit the box marked 'treaty', or the box marked 'customary international law',[1] as these are generally considered the two main, generally accepted sources of international law. Yet, it is contested whether international organizations can easily contribute to the making of customary international law; and much of their normative output consists of more elusive standard-setting, emerges from their operational activities, takes the form of conditional support for member states (conditional, that is, on meeting standards set by the organization) or consists of setting examples, developing benchmarks or indicators or generally formulating 'best practices'. It is fair to say international lawyers are struggling to come to terms with these developments.[2] The textbook patterns of authority (with diplomats who represent states concluding treaties based on approval by domestic authorities) no longer accurately describe the process by which international law is made – if they ever did. Indeed, the stronger claim is even that the law still struggles to come to terms with the very existence of international organizations.

As so often, the terminology invoked has done more to obscure than to clarify things. For a few decades, the discipline of international organizations rested content with the fact that international organizations were

[1] The third 'box' would consist of instruments, such as resolutions, that derive their force from a treaty.

[2] See also J. Klabbers, 'Law-Making and Constitutionalism', in J. Klabbers, A. Peters and G. Ulfstein, *The Constitutionalization of International Law* (Oxford University Press, 2009) 81.

deemed a subject of international law by no lesser authority than the ICJ. What was conveniently forgotten was that the ICJ was the first to acknowledge that this term ('subject') did not come with a very specific meaning. The ICJ was happy to conclude that the UN was an international person ('a subject of international law') but this, so it continued, only meant that the UN was 'capable of possessing international rights and duties'. Beyond this, the Court only hinted that the UN was not on a par with a state, let alone that it would be a super-state, 'whatever that expression may mean'.[3] The notion of subject, it turns out, is a capacious box, but one of uncertain, nondescript, contents.

Many of the activities of international organizations, it turns out, have but a slender or uncertain legal basis. International organizations may often have a competence to collect information, but turning this information into a manual or a set of guidelines is usually not specifically provided for – even if not expressly prohibited either. They may often be allowed to collaborate with other organizations working in related fields, but without being specifically instructed by constitutional authority to enter into joint projects, or work with organizations in different domains. This highlights, yet again, the erosion or redundancy of our old notions of authority – involving diplomats concluding treaties and aiming to secure domestic political approval. In fact, the normative landscape bears little resemblance to the textbook description. This may be substantively justifiable in individual cases. Surely, it is not a bad thing if several international organizations work together to provide humanitarian assistance, or develop facilities to use mobile phones aboard aircraft. Equally surely, there would be little inclination on the part of states these days to update and upgrade the Refugee Convention, so it may also be preferable to let this happen organically or through the work of UNHCR.[4] And yet, it also entails that such Rule of Law elements as democratic control and judicial review of policy become rare.[5]

The chapters in this *Cambridge Companion* also suggest – and rather strongly so – that authority can take on various manifestations and can stem from a variety of actors. This is, as such, not a particularly novel

[3] *Reparation for Injuries Suffered in the Service of the United Nations* (Advisory Opinion), [1949] ICJ Rep. 174, 179.

[4] See generally I. Venzke, *How Interpretation Makes International Law: On Semantic Change and Normative Twists* (Oxford University Press, 2012).

[5] See also J. Klabbers, 'The Cheshire Cat That Is International Law', (2020) 31 *European Journal of International Law* 269.

observation, but still, it remains noteworthy to what extent authority devolves on international organizations, internationally operating private associations, networks of states and other interested actors (including NGOs), public-private partnerships, assemblies or conferences of states parties, and much, much besides. The landscape has become so varied, and the boundaries between actors so porous, that it is difficult to locate global governance with any degree of precision.[6] Whether in energy provision or health or financial matters, it would be mistaken to claim that the world is 'run' by international organizations – and to be sure, few would go that far. But it would be equally mistaken to discount the role of international organizations, whether as lawmakers or standard-setters, as independent operators, as intermediaries, as facilitators or as venues for debate and discussion. Understanding the world around us requires a basic idea about the role(s) of international organizations – this may complicate theorizing (in that it is easier to present a model only comprising one kind of actor, such as the state), but is indispensable for a proper understanding. And properly understanding the role(s) of international organizations is impossible without some understanding of the legal structures, the legal concepts and the legal vocabularies relating to international organizations.

The typical *Cambridge Companion* is, by its very definition, not a traditional research work. It does not enquire into a specific research question, nor does it set out to prove or demonstrate a set of hypotheses, axioms and theorems. This *Cambridge Companion* is no exception. It aims to illuminate, from various perspectives, different aspects of the role(s) of international organizations in global affairs, and to offer different views on some of these aspects. Some of the contributors to this volume probably see themselves predominantly as doctrinal legal scholars; some others may view themselves mostly as law and society scholars, and yet others draw inspiration from critical approaches, perhaps sprinkled with insights from diplomatic and intellectual history. Together they demonstrate the richness of an immense, and still underexplored, field of study, politically perhaps even more important in light of Covid-19 than ever before.

[6] Compulsory reading includes D. Avant, M. Finnemore and S. Sell (eds.), *Who Governs the World?* (Cambridge University Press, 2010), and E. Benvenisti, *The Law of Global Governance* (The Hague: Hague Academy of International Law, 2014).

Bibliography

Blogposts, online papers and the like are not listed, and neither are publications and documents stemming from international organizations, states or similar sources.

Abbott K., and D. Snidal, 'Why States Act through Formal International Organizations', (1998) 42 *Journal of Conflict Resolution* 3

Abbott, K., J. Green and R. Keohane, 'Organizational Ecology in World Politics: Institutional Density and Organizational Strategies', (2016) 70 *International Organization* 247

Abe, T., 'Challenge Inspections under the Chemical Weapons Convention: Between Ideal and Reality', (2017) 24 *Nonproliferation Review* 167

Addo, H. (ed.), *Transforming the World Economy? Nine Critical Essays on the New International Economic Order* (London: Hodder and Stoughton, 1984)

Adler, E., *Communitarian International Relations: The Epistemic Foundations of International Relations* (Abingdon: Routledge, 2005)

Adler, E. and V. Pouliot (eds.), *International Practices* (Cambridge University Press, 2011)

Ahn, D., 'Linkages between International Financial and Trade Institutions', (2000) 34 *Journal of World Trade* 1

Akande, D., 'International Organizations', in M. Evans (ed.), *International Law*, 5th ed. (Oxford University Press, 2018) 227

Alexander, K., *Stability and Sustainability in Banking Reform: Are Environmental Risks Missing in Basel III?* (Cambridge: CSIL, 2014)

Aliber, R. and C. Kindleberger, *Manias, Panics, and Crashes*, 7th ed. (New York: Palgrave, 2015)

Alston, P. and N. Reisch, *Tax, Inequality, and Human Rights* (Oxford University Press, 2019)

Alter, K., *The New Terrain of International Law* (Princeton University Press, 2014)

Alter, K. and S. Meunier, 'The Politics of International Regime Complexity', (2009) 7 *Perspectives on Politics* 13

Alter, K., C. Romano and Y. Shany (eds.), *Oxford Handbook of International Adjudication* (Oxford University Press, 2014)

Alvarez, J. E., 'International Organizations and the Rule of Law', (2016) 14 *New Zealand Journal of Public and International Law* 3

International Organizations as Law-Makers (Oxford University Press, 2005)

'Judging the Security Council', (1996) 90 *American Journal of International Law* 1

'Nuremberg Revisited: The *Tadić* Case', (1996) 7 *European Journal of International Law* 245

The Boundaries of Investment Arbitration (Huntington: JurisNet, 2018)

The Impact of International Organizations on International Law (Leiden: Martinus Nijhoff, 2017)

Amerasinghe, C. F., *Principles of the Institutional Law of International Organizations*, 2nd ed. (Cambridge University Press, 2005)

Amin, S., *Capitalism in the Age of Globalization* (London: Zed Books, 1997)

Amrith, S., *Unruly Waters: How Mountain Rivers and Monsoons Have Shaped South Asia's History* (New York: Basic Books, 2018)

Amtenbrink, F. and R. Repasi, 'G7, G20 and Global Summits', in R. Wessel and J. Odermatt (eds.), *Research Handbook on the European Union and International Organizations* (Cheltenham: Edward Elgar, 2019) 338

Anand, R. P., 'Common Heritage of Mankind: Mutilation of an Ideal', in R. P. Anand, *Studies in International Law and History* (Leiden: Martinus Nijhoff, 2004) 180

Andonova, L., *Governance Entrepreneurs: International Organizations and the Rise of Global Public-Private Partnerships* (Cambridge University Press, 2017)

Andrijasevic, R. and W. Walters, 'The International Organization for Migration and the International Government of Borders', (2010) 28 *Society and Space* 977

Anghie, A., *Imperialism, Sovereignty and the Making of International Law* (Cambridge University Press, 2004)

'Time Present and Time Past: Globalization, International Financial Institutions, and the Third World', (2000) 32 *New York University Journal of International Law and Politics* 243

d'Argent, P., 'La personnalité juridique internationale', in E. Lagrange and J.-M. Sorel (eds.), *Droit des organisations internationals* (Paris: LGDJ, 2013) 439

Asada, M., 'CTBT: Legal Quagmire Arising from Its Non-Entry into Force', (2002) 7 *Journal of Conflict and Security Law* 85

Ashe, O. M., 'International Agencies and the Quest for Food Security in Nigeria, 1970–2015' (2019) 8 *Ubuntu: Journal of Conflict and Social Transformation* 251

Attard, B. P., *The Australian High Commissioner's Office Politics and Anglo-Australian Relations, 1901–1939* (doctoral thesis, Oxford University, 1991)

Auby, B., *Globalisation, Law and the State* (Oxford: Hart, 2017)

Avalos, F. and M. Lombardi, 'The Biofuel Connection: Impact of US Regulation on Oil and Food Prices', (2015) *Bank for International Settlements Working Papers* 487

Avant, D. D., M. Finnemore and S. Sell (eds), *Who Governs the Globe?* (Cambridge University Press, 2010)

Azaria, D., *Treaties on Transit of Energy via Pipelines and Countermeasures* (Oxford University Press, 2015)

Babb, S. and N. Chorev, 'International Organizations: Loose and Tight Coupling in the Development Regime', (2016) 51 *Studies in Comparative International Development* 81

Bagchi, K., 'Revisiting the Taper Tantrum: A Case for International Monetary Policy Coordination', (2017) 3 *Journal of Financial Regulation* 280

Barber, R., 'Uniting for Peace Not Aggression: Responding to Chemical Weapons in Syria without Breaking the Law', (2019) 24 *Journal of Conflict and Security Law* 71

Barnett, M. and R. Duvall (eds.), *Power in Global Governance* (Cambridge University Press, 2005)

Barnett, M. and M. Finnemore, *Rules for the World: International Organizations in Global Politics* (Ithaca NY: Cornell University Press, 2004)

Bederman, D., 'The Souls of International Organizations: Legal Personality and the Lighthouse at Cape Spartel', (1996) 36 *Virginia Journal of International Law* 275

Bedjaoui, M., *Towards a New International Economic Order* (New York: UNESCO, 1979)

Bell, D., 'Security and Poverty: On Realism and Global Justice' in M. Sleat (ed.), *Politics Recovered: Realist Thought in Theory and Practice* (New York: Columbia University Press, 2018) 296

Bell, S., 'Do Taxes and Bonds Finance Government Spending?', (2000) 34 *Journal of Economic Issues* 603

de Bellis, M., 'Public Law and Private Regulators in the Global Legal Space', (2011) 9 *International Journal of Constitutional Law* 425

Bennett, G., 'Review of *Armageddon and Paranoia*: The Nuclear Confrontation', (2018) 163 *RUSI Journal* 98

Benvenisti, E., *The International Law of Occupation*, 2nd ed. (Oxford University Press, 2012)

The Law of Global Governance (The Hague: Hague Academy of International Law, 2014)

Benvenisti, E. and G. Downs, 'The Empire's New Clothes: Political Economy and the Fragmentation of International Law', (2007) 60 *Stanford Law Review* 595

Berman, A., 'The Role of Domestic Administrative Law in the Accountability of Informal International Lawmaking: The Case of the ICH', in J. Pauwelyn, R. Wessel and J. Wouters (eds.), *Informal International Lawmaking* (Oxford University Press, 2012) 468

Berman, N., '"But the Alternative Is Despair": European Nationalism and the Modernist Renewal of International Law', (1993) 106 *Harvard Law Review* 1792

Berman, P. S., 'Can Global Legal Pluralism Be Both "Global" and "Pluralist"', (2019) 29 *Duke Journal of Comparative and International Law* 381

Bernstorff, J. von and P. Dann (eds.), *The Battle for International Law: South-North Perspectives on the Decolonization Era* (Oxford University Press, 2019)

Bhagwati, J., 'Introduction', in J. Bhagwati (ed.), *New International Economic Order: The North-South debate* (Cambridge MA: MIT Press, 1977) 1

Bhuta, N. and G. F. Sinclair (eds.), *Technologies of Stateness: International Organizations and the Making of States* (2020) 11 *Humanity Journal*

Binder, C., 'The Prohibition of Amnesties by the Inter-American Court of Human Rights', (2011) 12 *German Law Journal* 1203

Bingham, T., *The Rule of Law* (London: Penguin, 2010)

Bjola, C., 'Legitimizing the Use of Force in International Politics', (2005) 11 *European Journal of International Relations* 266

Blackburn, G., 'International Control of the River Danube', (1930) 32 *Current History and Forum* 1154

Blackett, A. and A. Trebilcock, 'Conceptualizing Transnational Labour Law', in A. Blackett and A. Trebilcock (eds.), *Research Handbook on Transnational Labour Law* (Cheltenham: Edward Elgar, 2015) 3

Block-Lieb, S. and T. Halliday, *Global Lawmakers* (Cambridge University Press, 2017)

Blokker, N., 'International Organizations and Customary International Law – Is the International Law Commission Taking International Organizations Seriously?', (2017) 14 *International Organizations Law Review* 1

Blokker, N. and R. Wessel, 'Revisiting Questions of Organisationhood, Legal Personality and Membership in the OSCE: The Interplay between Law, Politics and Practice', in M. Steinbrück Platise, C. Moser and A. Peters (eds.), *The Legal Framework of the OSCE* (Cambridge University Press, 2019) 135

Blutman, L., 'In the Trap of a Legal Metaphor: International Soft Law', (2010) 59 *International and Comparative Law Quarterly* 605

Bockman, J., 'Socialist Globalization against Capitalist Neocolonialism: The Economic Ideas behind the New International Economic Order', (2015) 6 *Humanity* 109

Bogdandy, A. von and M. Goldmann, 'Sovereign Debt Restructurings as Exercises of Public Authority: Towards a Decentralized Sovereign Insolvency Law', in C. Espósito, J. Bohoslavsky and Y. Li (eds.), *Responsible Sovereign Lending and Borrowing: The Search for Common Principles* (Oxford University Press, 2013) 39

Bogdandy, A. von and M. Goldmann, 'The Exercise of Public Authority through National Policy Assessment: The OECD's PISA Policy as a Paradigm for a New International Standard Instrument', (2008) 5 *International Organizations Law Review* 241

Bogdandy, A. von and I. Venzke, 'Beyond Dispute: International Judicial Institutions as Lawmakers', (2011) 12 *German Law Journal* 979

Bogdandy, A. von and I. Venzke, 'The Spell of Precedents: Lawmaking by International Courts and Tribunals' in C. Romano *et al.* (eds.), *Oxford Handbook of International Adjudication* (Oxford University Press, 2014) 503

Bogdandy, A. von, P. Dann and M. Goldmann, 'Developing the Publicness of Public International Law: Towards a Legal Framework for Global Governance Activities', in A. von Bogdandy *et al.* (eds.), *The Exercise of Public Authority by International Institutions: Advancing International Institutional Law* (Heidelberg: Springer, 2010) 3

Bogdandy, A. von, M. Goldmann and I. Venzke, 'From Public International to International Public Law: Translating World Public Opinion into International Public Authority', (2017) 28 *European Journal of International Law* 115

Bogdandy, A. von *et al.* (eds.), *The Exercise of Public Authority by International Institutions: Advancing International Institutional Law* (Heidelberg: Springer, 2010)

Bohoslavsky, J., 'Economic Inequality, Debt Crises and Human Rights', (2016) 42 *Yale Journal of International Law Online* 177

Bohoslavsky, J. and M. Goldmann, 'An Incremental Approach to Sovereign Debt Restructuring: Sovereign Debt Sustainability as a Principle of Public International Law', (2016) 42 *Yale Journal of International Law Online* 13

Boisson de Chazournes, L., *Interactions between Regional and Universal Organizations: A Legal Perspective* (Leiden: Martinus Nijhoff, 2017)

'Relations with Other International Organizations', in J. Cogan, I. Hurd and I. Johnstone (eds.), *Oxford Handbook of International Organizations* (Oxford University Press, 2016) 691

Boisson de Chazournes, L. and A. Gadkowski, 'A Critical Appraisal of the Human Rights Council Advisory Committee', in P. Alston and F. Mégret (eds.), *The United Nations and Human Rights: A Critical Appraisal* (Oxford University Press, 2020) 239

Bordin, F., *The Analogy between States and International Organizations* (Cambridge University Press, 2018)

Borzyskowski, I. von and F. Vabulas, 'Credible Commitments? Explaining IGO Suspensions to Sanction Political Backsliding', (2019) 63 *International Studies Quarterly* 139

'Hello, Goodbye: When Do States Withdraw from International Organizations?', (2019) 14 *Review of International Organizations* 335

Bosch, M. M., 'The Non-Proliferation Treaty and Its Future', in L. Boisson de Chazournes and P. Sands (eds.), *International Law, the International Court of Justice and Nuclear Weapons* (Cambridge University Press, 1999) 375

Boughton, J., *Silent Revolution: The International Monetary Fund 1979–1989* (Washington DC: IMF, 2001)

Boughton, J. and D. Moggridge, 'Why White, Not Keynes? Inventing the Post-War International Monetary System', in A. Arnon and W. Young (eds.), *The Open Economy Macromodel: Past, Present and Future* (Berlin: Springer, 2002)

Boyd Orr, Lord, *As I Recall: The 1880's to the 1960's* (London: MacGibbon and Kee, 1967)

Bradlow, D., 'The World Bank, the IMF, and Human Rights', (1996) 6 *Transnational Law and Contemporary Problems* 47

Bradlow, D. and A. Naude Fourie, 'The Operational Policies of the World Bank and the International Finance Cooperation', (2014) 10 *International Organizations Law Review* 3

Bradlow, D. and S. Park, 'A Global Leviathan Emerges: The Federal Reserve, COVID-19, and International Law', (2020) 114 *American Journal of International Law* 657

Britton-Purdy, J. *et al.*, 'Building a Law-and-Political-Economy Framework: Beyond the Twentieth-Century Synthesis', (2019) 129 *Yale Law Journal* 1784

Brölmann, C., *The Institutional Veil in Public International Law: International Organisations and the Law of Treaties* (Oxford: Hart, 2007)

Brölmann, C., R. Collins and R. Wessel, 'Exiting International Organizations: A Brief Introduction', (2018) 15 *International Organizations Law Review* 243

Bromberg, L., A. Godwin and I. Ramsay, 'Fintech Sandboxes: Achieving a Balance between Regulation and Innovation', (2017) 28 *Journal of Banking and Finance Law and Practice* 314

Bromley, P. and W. Powell, 'From Smoke and Mirrors to Walking the Talk: Decoupling in the Contemporary World', (2012) 6 *Academy of Management Annals* 483

Brosig, M., 'The Interplay of International Institutions in Kosovo between Convergence, Confusion and Niche Capabilities', (2011) 20 *European Security* 185

Broude, T., 'Keep Calm and Carry On: Martti Koskenniemi and the Fragmentation of International Law', (2013) 27 *Temple International and Comparative Law Journal* 279

Brown Weiss, E., 'On Being Accountable in a Kaleidoscopic World', (2010) 104 *Proceedings of American Society of International Law* 477

Brownlie, I., *Principles of Public International Law*, 7th ed. (Oxford University Press, 2008)

Brummer, C., *Minilateralism: How Trade Alliances of Law and Financial Engineering Are Redefining Economic Statecraft* (Cambridge University Press, 2014)

'Why Soft Law Dominates International Finance – And Not Trade', (2010) 13 *Journal of International Economic Law* 623

Brunnée, J. and S. Toope, *Legitimacy and Legality in International Law: An Interactional Account* (Cambridge University Press, 2010)

Buchanan, A., and R. Keohane, 'The Legitimacy of Global Governance Institutions', (2006) 20 *Ethics and International Affairs* 405

Bueger, C. and F. Gadinger, *International Practice Theory*, 2nd ed. (New York: Palgrave Macmillan, 2018)

Buira, A., 'The Bretton Woods Institutions: Governance without Legitimacy', in A. Buira (ed.), *Reforming the Governance of the IMF and the World Bank* (London: Anthem Press, 2005) 7

Bull, H. , 'Disarmament and the International System', reproduced in R. O'Neill and D. Schwartz (eds.), *Hedley Bull on Arms Control* (London: Macmillan, 1987) 39

The Control of the Arms Race (New York: Praeger, 1961)

Burci, G. L., 'Ebola, the Security Council and the Securitization of Health', (2014) 20 *Questions of International Law* 27

'Public/Private Partnerships in the Public Health Sector', (2009) 6 *International Organizations Law Review* 359

'The Legal Response to Pandemics', (2020) *Journal of International Humanitarian Legal Studies* 1

Burci, G. L. and A. Cassels, 'Health', in J. Cogan, I. Hurd and I. Johnstone (eds.), *Oxford Handbook of International Organizations* (Oxford University Press, 2016) 447

Burci, G. L. and C.-H. Vignes, *The World Health Organization* (The Hague: Kluwer, 2004)

Burdeau, G., 'Les organisations internationales: Entre gestion publique et gestion privée', in J. Makarczyk (ed.), *Essays in Honour of Krzysztof Skubiszewski* (The Hague: Kluwer, 1996) 611

Burgorgue-Larsen, L., 'La structure institutionnelle de l'organisation internationale', in E. Lagrange and J.-M. Sorel (eds.), *Droit des organisations internationales* (Paris: LGDJ, 2013) 375

Byrne, R., G. Noll and J. Vedsted-Hansen, 'Understanding Refugee Law in an Enlarged European Union', (2004) 15 *European Journal of International Law* 355

Cahier, P., 'L'ordre juridique interne des organisations internationales', in R.-J. Dupuy (ed.), *Manuel sur les organisations internationales* (Dordrecht: Martinus Nijhoff, 1998) 377

Cahn, J., 'Challenging the New Imperial Authority: The World Bank and the Democratization of Development', (1993) 6 *Harvard Human Rights Journal* 159

Cameron, P., 'The Rules of Engagement: Developing Cross-Border Petroleum Deposits in the North Sea and the Caribbean', (2006) 55 *International and Comparative Law Quarterly* 559

Caron, D., 'The ILC Articles of State Responsibility: The Paradoxical Relationship between Form and Authority', (2002) 96 *American Journal of International Law* 857

Cassese, S., 'Administrative Law without the State? The Challenge of Global Regulation', (2005) 37 *New York University Journal of International Law and Politics* 663

(ed.), *Research Handbook on Global Administrative Law* (Cheltenham: Edward Elgar, 2016)

Cathie, J., *The Political Economy of Food Aid* (Aldershot: Gower, 1982)

Chadwick, A., *Law and the Political Economy of Hunger* (Oxford University Press, 2019)

Chahrour, M., '"A Civilizing Mission"? Austrian Medicine and the Reform of Medical Structures in the Ottoman Empire, 1838–1850', (2007) 38 *Studies in History and Philosophy of Biological and Biomedical Sciences* 687

Charlesworth, H. and C. Chinkin, *The Boundaries of International Law: A Feminist Analysis* (Manchester: Manchester University Press, 2000)

Charnovitz, S., 'Nongovernmental Organizations and International Law', (2006) 100 *American Journal of International Law* 348

Chaumont, C., 'L'équilibre des organes politiques des Nations Unies et la crise de l'Organisation', (1965) 11 *Annuaire Français de Droit International* 428

Chayes, A. and A. Handler Chayes, *The New Sovereignty: Compliance with International Regulatory Agreements* (Cambridge MA: Harvard University Press, 1995)

Chen, R., 'Precedent and Dialogue in Investment Treaty Arbitration', (2019) 60 *Harvard International Law Journal* 47

Chesterman, S., *You, the People: The United Nations, Transitional Administration, and State-Building* (Oxford University Press, 2004)

(ed.), *Secretary or General? The UN Secretary-General in World Politics* (Cambridge University Press, 2017)

Chesterman, S., D. Malone and S. Villalpando, 'Introduction', in S. Chesterman, D. Malone and S. Villalpando (eds.), *Oxford Handbook of United Nations Treaties* (Oxford University Press, 2019) 1

Chesterman, S., D. Malone and S. Villalpando (eds.), *Oxford Handbook of United Nations Treaties* (Oxford University Press, 2019)

Chetail, V., *International Migration Law* (Oxford University Press, 2019)

'The Global Compact for Safe, Orderly and Regular Migration: A Kaleidoscope of International Law', (2020) 16 *International Journal of Law in Context* 253

'The Human Rights of Migrants in General International Law: From Minimum Standards to Fundamental Rights', (2013) 28 *Georgetown Immigration Law Journal* 225

'The Transnational Movement of Persons under General International Law: Mapping the Customary Law Foundations of International Migration Law', in V. Chetail and C. Bauloz (eds.), *Research Handbook on International Law and Migration*, (Cheltenham: Edward Elgar, 2014) 1

Chevallier-Govers, C. , 'Article 13 [The Institutions]', in H.-J. Blanke and S. Mangiameli (eds.), *The Treaty on European Union (TEU): A Commentary* (Berlin: Springer, 2013) 529

Chimni, B. S., 'Co-Option and Resistance: Two Faces of Global Administrative Law', (2006) 37 *New York University Journal of International Law and Politics* 799

'History of International Organizations: 1945-2013', in J. Cogan, I. Hurd and I. Johnstone (eds.), *Oxford Handbook on International Organizations* (Oxford University Press, 2016) 113

International Commodity Agreements: A Legal Study (London: Croom Helm, 1986)

'International Institutions Today: An Imperial Global State in the Making', (2004) 15 *European Journal of International Law* 1

'The Limits of the All Affected Principle: Attending to Deep Structures', (2018) 3 *Third World Thematics: A TWQ Journal* 807

Chinkin, C., *Third Parties in International Law* (Oxford University Press, 1993)

Choi, S. and M. Gulati, 'Customary International Law: How Do Courts Do It?', in C. Bradley (ed.), *Custom's Future* (Cambridge University Press, 2016) 117

Churchill, R. and G. Ulfstein, 'Autonomous Institutional Arrangements in Multilateral Environmental Agreements: A Little-Noticed Phenomenon in International Law', (2000) 94 *American Journal of International Law* 623

Chwieroth, J., *Capital Ideas: The IMF and the Rise of Financial Liberalization* (Princeton University Press, 2010)

Citelli, M., M. Barassi and K. Belykh, 'Renewable Energy in the International Arena: Legal Aspects and Cooperation', (2014) 2 *Groningen Journal of International Law* 1

Clapham, A. , *Human Rights Obligations of Non-State Actors* (Oxford University Press, 2006)

Clapp, J., *Hunger in the Balance: The New Politics of International Food Aid* (Ithaca NY: Cornell University Press, 2012)

Claude, I. L., *Swords into Plowshares: The Problems and Progress of International Organization* (New York: Random House, 1956)

Clavin, P., *Securing the World Economy* (Oxford University Press, 2013)

Cogan, J., 'The Regulatory Turn in International Law', (2011) 52 *Harvard International Law Journal* 322

Cohen, H. G. , 'Fragmentation', in J. d'Aspremont and S. Singh (eds.), *Concepts of International Law: Contributions to Disciplinary Thought* (Cheltenham: Edward Elgar, 2019) 315

Cohen, J., 'Democracy's Reason, Global Reason', *Tanner Lecture on Human Values* II, 2007

Colgan, J., R. Keohane and T. van de Graaf', 'Punctuated Equilibrium in the Energy Regime Complex', (2012) 7 *Review of International Organisations* 117

Common, R., 'The New Public Management and Policy Transfer: The Role of International Organizations', in M. Minogue, C. Polidano, and D. Hulme (eds.), *Beyond the New Public Management* (Cheltenham: Edward Elgar, 1998) 59

Conforti, B. and C. Focarelli, *The Law and Practice of the United Nations*, 5th ed. (Leiden: Martinus Nijhoff, 2016)

Cooper, A. and R. Thakur, *The Group of Twenty (G20)* (Abingdon: Routledge, 2013)

Cooper, R. N. , 'The Oceans as a Source of Revenue', in J. N. Bhagwati, *The New International Economic Order: The North-South Debate* (Cambridge MA: MIT Press, 1977) 105

Corden, W., 'Booming Sector and Dutch Disease Economics: Survey and Consolidation', (1984) 36 *Oxford Economic Papers* 359

Cox, R. W., 'Gramsci, Hegemony and International Relations: An Essay in Method', (1983) 12 *Millennium* 162

Craig, J., 'Putting Privatization into Practice: The Case of Zambia Consolidated Copper Mines Limited', (2001) 39 *Journal of Modern African Studies* 389

Crawford, J., *Brownlie's Principles of Public International Law*, 9th ed. (Oxford University Press, 2019)

'*Marbury v. Madison* at the International Level', (2004) 36 *George Washington International Law Review* 505

Crema, L., 'Testing Amici Curiae in International Law: Rules and Practice', (2012) 22 *Italian Yearbook of International Law* 91

Crépeau, F. and I. Atak, 'Global Migration Governance. Avoiding Commitments on Human Rights, yet Tracing a Course for Cooperation', (2016) 34 *Netherlands Quarterly of Human Rights* 113

Cueto, M., T. Brown and E. Fee, *The World Health Organization: A History* (Cambridge University Press, 2019)

Currey, B., 'Famine in the Pacific: Losing the Chances for Change', (1980) 4 *GeoJournal: Pacific Affairs* 447

Curtin, D. and A. Nollkaemper, 'Conceptualizing Accountability in International and European Law', (2005) 36 *Netherlands Yearbook of International Law* 3

Dafermos, Y., D. Gabor and J. Michell, 'The Wall Street Consensus in Pandemic Times: What Does It Mean for Climate-aligned Development?', (2021) 42 *Canadian Journal of Development Studies* 238

Dann, P. , 'Accountability in Development Aid Law: The World Bank, UNDP and Emerging Structures of Transnational Oversight', (2006) 44 *Archiv des Völkerrechts* 381

'Ideengeschichte von Recht und Entwicklung', in P. Dann, S. Kadelbach and M. Kaltenborn (eds.), *Entwicklung und Recht: eine systematische Einführung* (Baden-Baden: Nomos, 2014) 19

The Law of Development Cooperation: A Comparative Analysis of the World Bank, the EU and Germany (Cambridge University Press, 2013)

'The Law of International Development', in R. Buchanan, L. Eslava and S. Pahuja (eds,), *Oxford Handbook of International Law and Development* (Oxford University Press, forthcoming)

Dann, P. and M. Riegner, 'The World Bank's Environmental and Social Safeguards and the Evolution of Global Order', (2019) 32 *Leiden Journal of International Law* 537

Darrow, M., *Between Light and Shadow: The World Bank, the International Monetary Fund and International Human Rights Law* (Oxford: Hart, 2003)

Dastyari, A. and A. Hirsch, 'The Ring of Steel: Extraterritorial Migration Controls in Indonesia and Libya and the Complicity of Australia and Italy', (2019) 19 *Human Rights Law Review* 435

Daugirdas, K., 'How and Why International Law Binds International Organizations', (2016) 57 *Harvard International Law Journal* 325

Davis, K. *et al.* (eds.), *Governance by Indicators* (Oxford University Press, 2012)

Decorzant, Y. , 'Internationalism in the Economic and Financial Organization of the League of Nations', in D. Laqua (ed.), *Internationalism Reconfigured* (London: Tauris, 2011) 115

Dekker, G. den, *The Law of Arms Control: International Supervision and Enforcement* (The Hague: Martinus Nijhoff, 2001)

Delbrück, J. (ed.), *New Trends in International Lawmaking: International 'Legislation' in the Public Interest* (Berlin: Duncker & Humblot, 1997)

Delmas-Marty, M., 'Comparative Law and International Law: Methods of Ordering Pluralism', (2006) 3 *University of Tokyo Journal of Law and Politics* 44

Dingwerth, K. and P. Nanz, 'Participation', in J. Cogan, I. Hurd and I. Johnstone (eds.), *Oxford Handbook of International Organizations* (Oxford University Press, 2016) 1126

Donaldson, M., 'The League of Nations, Ethiopia and the Making of States', (2020) 11 *Humanity Journal* 6

Donaldson, M. and B. Kingsbury, 'The Adoption of Transparency Policies in Global Governance Institutions: Justifications, Effects, and Implications', (2013) 9 *Annual Review of Law and Social Science* 119

Drezner, D., 'The Power and Peril of International Regime Complexity', (2009) 7 *Perspectives on Politics* 65

Dryzek, J., *Deliberative Global Politics: Discourse and Democracy in a Divided World* (Cambridge: Polity, 2006)

Dubin, M., 'Toward the Bruce Report: The Economic and Social Programs of the League of Nations in the Avenol Era', in *The League of Nations in Retrospect/La Société des Nations: Retrospective* (Berlin: de Gruyter, 1983) 42

'Transgovernmental Processes in the League of Nations', (1983) 37 *International Organization* 469

Dubnick, M. J., 'Accountability as a Cultural Keyword', in E. Ferlie, L. Lynn Jr and C. Pollitt (eds.), *Oxford Handbook of Public Management* (Oxford University Press, 2014) 23

Ducasse-Rogier, M., *The International Organization for Migration 1951–2001* (Geneva: IOM, 2002)

Dudal, R., 'Forty Years of Soil Fertility Work in Sub-Saharan Africa', in B. Vanlauwe *et al.* (eds.), *Integrated Plant-Nutrient Management in Sub-Saharan Africa: From Concept to Practice* (Wallingford: Cabi Publishing, 2001) 1

Dunoff, J., 'A New Approach to Regime Interaction', in M. Young (ed.), *Regime Interaction in International Law: Facing Fragmentation* (Cambridge University Press, 2012) 136

'The Politics of International Constitutions: The Curious Case of the World Trade Organization', in J. Dunoff and J. Trachtmann (eds.), *Ruling the World? Constitutionalism, International Law and Global Governance* (Cambridge University Press, 2009) 178

Dunoff, J. and M. Pollack, 'The Judicial Trilemma', (2017) 111 *American Journal of International Law* 225

Dunoff, J. and J. Trachtman (eds.), *Ruling the World? Constitutionalism, International Law and Global Governance* (Cambridge University Press, 2009)

Dutfield, G., 'Farmers, Innovation, and Intellectual Property: Current Trends and their Consequences for Food Security', in F. Girard and C. Frison (eds.), *The Commons, Plant Breeding and Agricultural Research. Challenges for Food Security and Agrobiodiversity* (Abingdon: Routledge, 2018) 1

Duxbury, A., *The Participation of States in International Organizations: The Role of Human Rights and Democracy* (Cambridge University Press, 2011)

Dzehtsiarou, K. and D. Coffey, 'Suspension and Expulsion of Members of the Council of Europe: Difficult Decision in Troubled Times', (2019) 68 *International and Comparative Law Quarterly* 443

Eagleton, C., 'International Organizations and the Law of Responsibility', (1950–I) 76 *Recueil des Cours* 319

Eagleton, T., *Ideology: An Introduction* (London: Verso, 2007)

Eichengreen, B., *From Commodity to Fiat and Now to Crypto: What Does History Tell Us?*, (2019) NBER Working Paper 25426

ElBaradei, M., *The Age of Deception: Nuclear Diplomacy in Treacherous Times* (London: Bloomsbury, 2011)

Elias, O., 'Who Can Make Treaties? International Organizations', in D. Hollis, *The Oxford Guide to Treaties* (Oxford University Press, 2012) 73

Engström, V., 'The IMF and Protection of Vulnerable Groups', (2020) 89 *Nordic Journal of International Law* 209

Eslava, L., *Local Space, Global Life: The Everyday Operation of International Law and Development* (Cambridge University Press, 2015)

'The Developmental State: Independence, Dependency, and the History of the South', in J. von Bernstorff and P. Dann (eds.), *The Battle for International Law: South-North Perspectives on the Decolonization Era* (Oxford University Press, 2019) 71

Eslava, L. , M. Fakhri and V. Nesiah (eds.), *Bandung, Global History, and International Law: Critical Pasts and Pending Futures* (Cambridge University Press, 2017)

Evang, K., 'The United Nations Conference on Food and Agriculture, Hot Springs, Virginia, 18th May–3rd June, 1943', in M. Lyon, 'The Hot Springs Conference', (1944) 2 *Proceedings of the Nutrition Society* 163

Everling, U., 'Sind die Mitgliedstaaten der Europäischen Gemeinschaft noch Herren der Verträge? Zum Verhältnis von Europäischem Gemeinschaftsrecht und Völkerrecht', in R. Bernhardt *et al.* (eds.), *Völkerrecht als Rechtsordnung: Festschrift für Hermann Mosler* (Berlin: Springer, 1983) 173

Eysinga, W. J. M. van, *Ontwikeling en inhoud der Nederlandsche tractaten sedert 1813* (The Hague: Martinus Nijhoff, 1916)

Fagbayibo, B., 'Why the Pan-African Parliament Must Clean Up Its Act if It Wants to Survive', *The Conversation*, May 24, 2018

Fakhri, M., *Sugar and the Making of International Trade Law* (Cambridge University Press, 2014)

Farrall, J. M., *United Nations Sanctions and the Rule of Law* (Cambridge University Press, 2007)

Faude, B., *Von Konkurrenz zu Arbeitsteilung: Komplexität und Dynamik im Zusammenspiel internationaler Institutionen* (Frankfurt am Main: Campus, 2015)

Feichtner, I., 'International (Investment) Law and Distribution Conflicts over Natural Resources', in S. Schill *et al.* (eds.), *International Investment Law and Sustainable Development* (Cheltenham: Edward Elgar, 2014) 256

'Public Law's Rationalization of the Legal Architecture of Money: What Might Legal Analysis of Money Become?', (2016) 17 *German Law Journal* 875

'Sharing the Riches of the Sea: The Redistributive and Fiscal Dimension of Deep Seabed Exploitation', (2019) 30 *European Journal of International Law* 601

Feichtner, I., M. Krajewski and R. Rösch (eds.), *Human Rights in the Extractive Industries: Transparency, Participation, Resistance* (Berlin: Springer, 2019)

Feldmann, H., *Internationale Umschuldungen im 19. und 20. Jahrhundert. Eine Analyse ihrer Ursachen, Techniken und Grundprinzipien* (Berlin: Duncker & Humblot 1991)

Ferguson, J. and A. Gupta (eds.), 'Spatializing States: Toward an Ethnography of Neoliberal Governmentality', (2002) 29 *American Ethnologist* 981

Ferstman, C., *International Organizations and the Fight for Accountability: The Remedies and Reparations Gap* (Oxford University Press, 2017)

Fidler, D., 'Architecture amidst Anarchy: Global Health's Quest for Governance', (2007) 1 *Global Health Governance* 1

Finnemore, M., *National Interests in International Society* (Ithaca NY: Cornell University Press, 1996)

'Norms, Culture, and World Politics: Insights from Sociology's Institutionalism', (1996) 50 *International Organization* 325

Fiore, P., 'L'organisation juridique de la société internationale', (1899) 2 *Revue de droit international et de législation comparée* 105

Fletcher, E. R., 'Swelling Bloc of WHO Member States Propose Invitation to Taiwan for May 18 World Health Assembly', *Health Policy Watch*, 11 May 2020

Follesdal, A., R. Wessel and J. Wouters (eds.), *Multi-level Regulation and the EU: The Interplay between Global, European and National Normative Processes* (Leiden: Martinus Nijhoff, 2008)

Foucault, M., *Security, Territory, Population* (New York: Palgrave Macmillan, 2007, Burchell tr.)

Fox, J. and L. D. Brown (eds.), *The Struggle for Accountability: The World Bank, NGOs and Grassroots Movements* (Cambridge MA: MIT Press, 1998)

Franchino, F., *The Powers of the Union: Delegation in the EU* (Cambridge University Press, 2007)

Franck, T., *The Power of Legitimacy among Nations* (Oxford University Press, 1990)

Frank, A. G., *Dependent Accumulation and Underdevelopment* (London: Macmillan, 1978)

Fraser, A. and J. Lungu, *For Whom the Windfalls? Winners & Losers in the Privatization of Zambia's Copper Mines* (CSTNZ/CCJDP, 2007)

Freeman, A., 'Recent Aspects of the Calvo Doctrine and the Challenge to International Law', (1946) 40 *American Journal of International Law* 121

Frenk, J., and S. Moon, 'Governance Challenges in Global Health', (2013) 368 *New England Journal of Medicine* 936

Frenk, J., O. Dantés and S. Moon, 'From Sovereignty to Solidarity: A Renewed Concept of Global Health for an Era of Complex Interdependence', (2014) 383 *The Lancet* 9

Frenkel, M., 'The International Debt Problem: An Analysis of the Brady Plan', (1989) 24 *Intereconomics* 110

Frey, M., S. Kunkel and C. R. Unger (eds.), *International Organizations and Development, 1945–1990* (New York: Palgrave Macmillan, 2014)

Fröhlich, M., and A. Williams (eds.), *The UN Secretary-General and Security Council: A Dynamic Relationship* (Oxford University Press, 2018)

Furrow, D., *American Foodie: Taste, Art, and the Cultural Revolution* (Lanham MD: Rowman & Littlefield, 2016)

Gallagher, K., 'Contesting the Governance of Capital Flows at the IMF', (2015) 28 *Governance* 185

Gardner, R., *Sterling-Dollar Diplomacy in Current Perspective: The Origins and the Prospects of Our International Economic Order* (New York: Columbia University Press, 1980)

Garritsen de Vries, M. and J. K. Horsefield, *The International Monetary Fund 1945–1965: Twenty Years of International Monetary Cooperation* (Washington DC: IMF, 1969)

Gebrehiwot, T., S. Cornelius and L. Korsten, 'Impact of Global Food and Agriculture Laws on Africa's Food Security', (2019) 52 *De Jure Law Journal* 85

Gelpern, A., 'Sovereign Debt: Now What?', (2016) 42 *Yale Journal of International Law Online* 45

Gianviti, F., *Economic, Social, and Cultural Human Rights and the International Monetary Fund* (Washington DC: IMF, 2001)

Giddens, A., *The Constitution of Society: Outline of the Theory of Structuration* (Cambridge: Polity, 1984)

Gilbert, M., *Official Biography of Winston Churchill: Never Despair*, vol. 8. (London: Heinemann, 1988)

Gilligan, G., J. O'Brien and M. Bowman, 'Sovereign Wealth Funds: The Good Guy Investment Actors?', (2014) *UNSW Law Research Paper* 14

Giorgetti, C., 'Health and International Investment Law', in G. L. Burci and B. Toebes (eds.), *Research Handbook on Global Health Law* (Cheltenham: Edward Elgar, 2018) 164

Giovanoli, M., 'A New Architecture for the Global Financial Market: Legal Aspects of International Financial Standard Setting', in M. Giovanoli (ed.), *International Monetary Law-Issues for the New Millenium* (Oxford University Press, 2000) 3

Gold, J., 'The Rule of Law in the International Monetary Fund', (1980) 32 *IMF Pamphlet Series* (1980)

Goldmann, M., 'Contesting Austerity: Genealogies of Human Rights Discourse', (2009–20) Max Planck Institute for Comparative Public Law & International Law Research Paper

'Financial Institutions and Social Rights: From the Washington Consensus to the Lagarde Concord?', in C. Binder *et al.* (eds.), *Research Handbook on International Law and Social Rights* (Cheltenham: Edward Elgar, 2020) 440

'Human Rights and Democracy in Economic Policy Reform: The European COVID-19 Response under Scrutiny', (2020) 24 *International Journal of Human Rights* 1290.

'Human Rights and Sovereign Debt Workouts', in J. Bohoslavsky and J. Cernic (eds.), *Making Sovereign Financing and Human Rights Work* (Oxford: Hart 2014) 79

Internationale öffentliche Gewalt (Heidelberg: Springer 2015)

'The Law and Political Economy of Mozambique's Odious Debt', (2019) *available at SSRN 3513651*

Goodhart, C. and R. Lastra, 'Populism and Central Bank Independence', (2018) 29 *Open Economies Review* 49

Goodin, R., 'Enfranchising All Subjected, Worldwide', (2016) 8 *International Theory* 365

Goodman, R. and D. Jinks, *Socializing States: Promoting Human Rights through International Law* (Oxford University Press, 2013)

Goodrich, L., *The United Nations in a Changing World* (New York: Columbia University Press, 1974)

Gowlland-Debbas, V., 'The Relationship between the International Court of Justice and the Security Council in the Light of the Lockerbie Case', (1994) 88 *American Journal of International Law* 643

Graaf, T. van de, 'Fragmentation in Global Energy Governance: Explaining the Creation of IRENA', (2013) 13 *Global Environmental Politics* 14

Gram-Skjoldager, K. , H. Ikonomou and T. Kahlert (eds.), *Organizing the 20th-Century World: International Organizations and the Emergence of International Public Administration, 1920–1960s* (London: Bloomsbury, 2020)

Grant, R. W. and R. O. Keohane, 'Accountability and Abuses of Power in World Politics', (2005) 99 *American Political Science Review* 29

Grant, T., *Admission to the United Nations: Charter Article 4 and the Rise of Universal Organization* (Leiden: Martinus Nijhoff, 2009)

Grard, L. , 'Le Club de Paris et les dettes publiques des Etats', in D. Carreau and M. Shaw (eds.), *La dette extérieure* (Dordrecht: Martinus Nijhoff, 1995) 197

Gregoratti, C. , 'UN-Business Partnerships', in T. Weiss and R. Wilkinson (eds.), *International Organization and Global Governance* (Abingdon: Routledge, 2013) 309

Guilfoyle, D., 'Counter-Piracy Law Enforcement and Human Rights', (2010) 59 *International and Comparatively Law Quarterly* 141

Gustafson, B., 'Walter Nash (1882–1968)', *Dictionary of New Zealand Biography* (1998)

Gutmann A. and D. Thompson, *Democracy and Disagreement* (Cambridge MA: Harvard University Press, 1998)

Gutmann A. and D. Thompson, *Why Deliberative Democracy?* (Princeton University Press, 2004)

Guzman, A., 'Against Consent', (2012) 52 *Virginia Journal of International Law* 747

'International Common Law: The Soft Law of International Tribunals', (2009) 9 *Chicago Journal of International Law* 515

Habermas, J., *Between Facts and Norms* (Cambridge MA: MIT Press, 1996)

The Structural Transformation of the Public Sphere: An Inquiry into a Category of Bourgeois Society (Cambridge MA: MIT Press 1991)

Hacking, I., *The Taming of Chance* (Cambridge University Press, 1990)

Hafner, G., 'Accountability of International Organizations', (2003) 97 *Proceedings of the American Society of International Law* 236

Hailbronner, K. and E. Klein, 'Article 11', in B. Simma (ed.), *The Charter of the United Nations: A Commentary*, 2nd ed. (Oxford University Press, 2002) 279

Halliday, T. and G. Shaffer (eds.), *Transnational Legal Orders* (Cambridge University Press, 2015)

Hancher, L. and M. Moran, 'Organizing Regulatory Space', in L. Hancher and M. Moran (eds.), *Capitalism, Culture, and Economic Regulation* (Oxford: Clarendon, 1989) 271

Hancock, K. and V. Vivoda, 'International Political Economy: A Field Born of the OPEC Crisis Returns to its Energy Roots', (2014) 1 *Energy Research and Social Science* 206

Hansen, T. and F. Stepputat (eds.), *States of Imagination* (Durham NC: Duke University Press, 2001)

Haraway, D., *Staying with the Trouble: Making Kin in the Chthulucene* (Durham NC: Duke University Press, 2016)

Hatton, K. and K. Pistor, 'Maximizing Autonomy in the Shadow of Great Powers: The Political Economy of Sovereign Wealth Funds', (2011) 50 *Columbia Journal of Transnational Law* 1

Heldt, E., 'Lost in Internal Evaluation? Accountability and Insulation at the World Bank', (2018) 24 *Contemporary Politics* 568

Heldt, E. and H. Schmidtke, 'Global Democracy in Decline? How Rising Authoritarianism Limits Democratic Control over International Institutions', (2019) 25 *Global Governance* 231

Helleiner, E., *Forgotten Foundations of Bretton Woods* (Ithaca NY: Cornell University Press, 2014)

States and the Re-emergence of Global Finance: From Bretton Woods to the 1990s (Ithaca NY: Cornell University Press, 1994)

Herman, S., 'The Food Stamp Plan: A Study in Law and Economics', (1940) 13 *Journal of Business of the University of Chicago* 331

Herren, M., *Internationale Organisationen seit 1865: Eine Globalgeschichte der internationalen Ordnung* (Darmstadt: WBG, 2009)

Heubaum, H. and F. Biermann, 'Integrating Global Energy and Climate Governance: The Changing Role of the International Energy Agency', (2015) 87 *Energy Policy* 227

Heucher, A., 'Reconsidering Overlap in Global Food Security Governance', (2019) 11 *Food Security* 555

Higgins, R., *Problems and Process: International Law and How We Use It* (Oxford: Clarendon, 1995)

Higgins, R. *et al.*, *Oppenheim's International Law: United Nations* (Oxford University Press, 2017)

Hinojosa, L., 'Transparency in International Financial Institutions', in A. Bianchi and A. Peters (eds.), *Transparency in International Law* (Cambridge University Press, 2013) 77

Hirsch, A. and C. Doig, 'Outsourcing Control: The International Organization for Migration in Indonesia', (2018) 22 *International Journal of Human Rights* 681

Hirsch, T., 'The IAEA Additional Protocol: What It Is and Why It Matters', (2004) 11 *Non-Proliferation Review* 140

Hirschmann, A., *The Passions and the Interests: Political Arguments for Capitalism before Its Triumph* (Princeton University Press, 1977)

Hix, S., 'The Study of the European Union II: The "New Governance" Agenda and Its Rival', (1998) 5 *Journal of European Public Policy* 38

Holcombe Henley, P. and N. Blokker, 'The Group of 20: A Short Legal Anatomy from the Perspective of International Institutional Law', (2014) 14 *Melbourne Journal of International Law* 550

Hooghe, L., T. Lenz and G. Marks, *A Theory of International Organization* (Oxford University Press, 2019)

Hornstein, D., 'Complexity Theory, Adaptation and Administrative Law', (2005) 54 *Duke Law Journal* 913

Horst, J., 'Lex Financiaria: Das transnationale Finanzmarktrecht der International Swaps and Derivatives Association (ISDA)', (2015) 53 *Archiv des Völkerrechts* 461

Hovary, C. la, 'The ILO's Supervisory Bodies' Soft Law Jurisprudence', in A. Blackett and A. Trebilcock (eds.), *Research Handbook on Transnational Labour Law* (Cheltenham: Edward Elgar, 2015) 316

Howard-Jones, N., *The Scientific Background of the International Sanitary Conferences* (Geneva: WHO, 1975)

Howarth, D. and T. Sadeh, 'In the Vanguard of Globalization: The OECD and International Capital Liberalization', (2011) 18 *Review of International Political Economy* 622

Howse, R., 'International Investment Law and Arbitration: A Conceptual Framework', in H. Ruiz Fabri (ed.), *International Law and Litigation: A Look into Procedure* (Baden-Baden: Nomos, 2019) 363

Hudson, W. J., *Australia and the League of Nations* (Sydney University Press, 1980)

Hudson, W. J. and W. Way, *Letters from a "Secret Service Agent": F L. McDougall to S.M. Bruce, 1924–1929* (Canberra: Australian Government Publishing Service, 1986)

Irmscher, T., 'The Legal Framework for the Activities of the United Nations Interim Administration Mission in Kosovo: The Charter, Human Rights, and the Law of Occupation', (2001) 44 *German Yearbook of International Law* 353

Jachertz, R., 2015. 'The World Food Crisis of 1972–1975', (2015) 18 *Contemporanea* 425

Jachertz, R. and A. Nützenadel, 'Coping with Hunger? Visions of a Global Food System, 1930–1960', (2011) 6 *Journal of Global History* 99

Jacqué, J.-P., 'The Principle of Institutional Balance', (2004) 41 *Common Market Law Review* 383

Jain, N., 'Judicial Lawmaking and General Principles of Law in International Criminal Law', (2016) 57 *Harvard International Law Journal* 111

James, A., 'The Peacekeeping Role of the League of Nations', (1999) 6 *International Peacekeeping* 154

Janmyr, M., *Protecting Civilians in Refugee Camps: Unable and Unwilling States, UNHCR and International Responsibility* (Leiden: Martinus Nijhoff, 2014)

Jaspers, S., *Food Aid in Sudan: A History of Power, Politics and Profit* (London: Zed Books, 2018)

Jellinek, G., *Die Lehre von den Staatenverbindungen* (Berlin: Hölder, 1882)

Jenks, C. W., 'Due Process of Law in International Organizations', (1965) 19 *International Organization* 163

Social Justice in the Law of Nations (Oxford University Press, 1970)

The Proper Law of International Organisations (London: Stevens and Co, 1962)

Jia, B. B., 'The Crime of Aggression as Custom and the Mechanisms for Determining Acts of Aggression', (2015) 109 *American Journal of International Law* 569

Joerges, C., and J. Neyer, 'From Inter-governmental Bargaining to Deliberative Political Process: The Constitutionalization of Comitology', (2002) 3 *European Law Journal* 273

Johns, F., 'From Planning to Prototype: New Ways of Seeing Like a State', (2019) 82 *Modern Law Review* 833

Johnson, T., *Organizational Progeny* (Oxford University Press, 2014)

Johnstone, I., 'Law-Making by International Organizations: Perspectives from International Law/International Relations Theory', in J. Dunoff and M. Pollack (eds.), *Interdisciplinary Perspectives on International Law and International Relations: The State of the Art* (Cambridge University Press, 2013) 266

'Law-making through the Operational Activities of International Organizations', (2008) 40 *George Washington International Law Review* 87

'Security Council Deliberations: The Power of the Better Argument', (2002) 14 *European Journal of International Law* 437

The Power of Deliberation: International Law, Politics and Organization (Oxford University Press, 2011)

'The UN Charter and Its Evolution' in S. Chesterman, D. Malone and S. Villalpando (eds.), *Oxford Handbook on United Nations Treaties* (Oxford University Press, 2019) 23

'US-UN Relations after Iraq: The End of the World (Order) as We Know It', (2004) 15 *European Journal of International Relations* 813

Joseph, J., *The Social in the Global: Social Theory, Governmentality and Global Politics* (Cambridge University Press, 2012)

Jouannet, E., *The Liberal-Welfarist Law of Nations: A History of International Law* (Cambridge University Press, 2012)

Joyner, D., *International Law and the Proliferation of Weapons of Mass Destruction* (Oxford University Press, 2009)

Karns, M., and A. Mingst, *International Organizations: The Politics and Processes of Global Governance*, 3rd ed. (Boulder CO: Lynne Rienner, 2015)

Katz, R., 'Financial Arrangements for Seabed Mining Companies: An NIEO Case Study', (1979) 13 *Journal of World Trade Law* 209

Kaufmann, C. and R. Weber, 'The Role of Transparency in Financial Regulation', (2010) 13 *Journal of International Economic Law* 779

Kazansky, P., 'Les premiers éléments de l'organisation universelle', (1897) 29 *Revue de Droit International et de Législation Comparée* 238

'Théorie de l'administration internationale', (1902) 9 *Revue Générale de Droit International Public* 353

Kelly, M., *Restoring and Maintaining Order in Complex Peace Operations* (The Hague: Kluwer, 1999)

Kelsen, H., *The Law of the United Nations: A Critical Analysis of Its Fundamental Problems* (London: Stevens & Sons, 1951)

Pure Theory of Law (Berkeley CA: University of California Press, 1967)

Reine Rechtslehre (Vienna: Deuticke, 1934)

Reine Rechtslehre, 2nd ed. (Tübingen: Mohr Siebeck, 1960)

Kennedy, D., *A World of Struggle* (Princeton University Press, 2016)

'One, Two, Three, Many Legal Orders: Legal Pluralism and the Cosmopolitan Dream', (2007) 31 *New York University Review of Law and Social Change* 641

'The Move to Institutions', (1987) 8 *Cardozo Law Review* 841

Kennedy, D., 'Three Globalizations of Law and Legal Thought, 1850–2000', in D. Trubek and A. Santos (eds.), *The New Law and Economic Development* (Cambridge University Press, 2010) 19

Kentikelenis, A. and S. Babb, 'The Making of Neoliberal Globalization: Norm Substitution and the Politics of Clandestine Institutional Change', (2019) 124 *American Journal of Sociology* 1720

Kentikelenis, A., T. Stubbs and L. King, 'IMF Conditionality and Development Policy Space', (2016) 23 *Review of International Political Economy* 543

Keohane, R. and D. Victor, 'The Regime Complex for Climate Change', (2011) 9 *Perspectives on Politics* 7

Kilpatrick, C., 'Constitutions, Social Rights and Sovereign Debt States in Europe: A Challenging New Area of Constitutional Inquiry', in B. de Witte, C. Kilpatrick and T. Beukers (eds.), *Constitutional Change through Euro-Crisis Law* (Cambridge University Press, 2017) 279

Kingsbury, B., 'Frontiers of Global Administrative Law in the 2020s', in J. Varuhas and S. Wilson Stark (eds.), *The Frontiers of Public Law* (Oxford: Hart, 2020), 41

'Operational Policies of International Institutions as Part of the Law-Making Process: The World Bank and Indigenous Peoples', in G. Goodwin-Gill and S. Talmon (eds.), *The Reality of International Law* (Oxford University Press, 1999) 323

'The Concept of "Law" in Global Administrative Law', (2009) 20 *European Journal of International Law* 23

Kingsbury, B. and L. Casini, 'Global Administrative Law Dimensions of International Organizations Law', (2009) 6 *International Organizations Law Review* 319

Kingsbury, B., N. Krisch and R. Stewart, 'The Emergence of Global Administrative Law', (2005) 68 *Law and Contemporary Problems* 15

Kirgis, F. Jr., *International Organizations in Their Legal Setting*, 2nd ed. (Eagan MN: West, 1993)

'Specialized Law-Making Processes', in O. Schachter and C. Joyner (eds.), *United Nations Legal Order* (Cambridge University Press, 1995) 109

Kjaer, P., 'The Law of Political Economy: An Introduction', in P. Kjaer (ed.), *The Law of Political Economy: Transformation in the Function of Law* (Cambridge University Press, 2020) 1

Klabbers, J., 'An Accidental Revolution: The ILO and the Opening Up of International Law', in T. Halonen and U. Liukkunen (eds.), *International Labour Organization and Global Social Governance* (Dordrecht: Springer, 2020) 123

An Introduction to International Institutional Law, 2nd ed. (Cambridge University Press, 2009)

An Introduction to International Organizations Law, 3rd ed. (Cambridge University Press, 2015)

'Checks and Balances in the Law of International Organizations', in M. Sellers (ed.), *Autonomy in the Law* (Dordrecht: Springer, 2007) 141

'Contending Approaches to International Organizations: Between Functionalism and Constitutionalism', in J. Klabbers and Å. Wallendahl (eds.), *Research Handbook on the Law of International Organizations* (Cheltenham: Edward Elgar, 2011) 3

'Interminable Disagreement: Reflections on the Autonomy of International Organisations', (2019) 88 *Nordic Journal of International Law* 111

'International Institutions', in J. Crawford and M. Koskenniemi (eds.), *Cambridge Companion to International Law* (Cambridge University Press, 2012) 228

'International Organizations and the Problem of Privity: Towards a Supra-Functionalist Approach', in G. Politakis *et al.* (eds.), *ILO 100: Law for Social Justice* (Geneva: ILO, 2019) 629

'Notes on the Ideology of International Organizations Law: The International Organization for Migration, State-making, and the Market for Migration', (2019) 32 *Leiden Journal of International Law* 383

'Sources of International Organisations' Law: Reflections on Accountability', in S. Besson and J. D'Aspremont (eds.), *Oxford Handbook on the Sources of International Law* (Oxford University Press, 2017) 987

'The *Bustani* Case before the ILOAT: Constitutionalism in Disguise', (2004) 53 *International and Comparative Law Quarterly* 455

'The Changing Image of International Organizations', in J.-M. Coicaud and V. Heiskanen (eds.), *The Legitimacy of International Organizations* (Tokyo: UNU Press, 2001) 221

'The Cheshire Cat That is International Law', (2020) 31 *European Journal of International Law* 269

'The EJIL Foreword: The Transformation of International Organizations Law', (2015) 26 *European Journal of International Law* 9

'The Emergence of Functionalism in International Institutional Law: Colonial Inspirations', (2014) 25 *European Journal of International Law* 645

'The Normative Gap in International Organizations Law: The Case of the World Health Organization', (2019) 16 *International Organizations Law Review* 272

'The Paradox of International Institutional Law', (2008) 5 *International Organizations Law Review* 151

'The Undesirability of Soft Law', (1998) 67 *Nordic Journal of International Law* 381

'Transforming Institutions: Autonomous International Organisations in Institutional Theory', (2017) 6 *Cambridge International Law Journal* 105

'Two Concepts of International Organization', (2005) 2 *International Organizations Law Review* 94

'Unity, Diversity, Accountability: The Ambivalent Concept of International Organization', (2013) 14 *Melbourne Journal of International Law* 149

'What Role for International Organizations in the Promotion of Community Interests? Reflections on the Ideology of Functionalism', in E. Benvenisti and G. Nolte (eds.), *Community Interests across International Law* (Oxford University Press, 2018) 86

Klabbers, J. and G. Palombella (eds.), *The Challenge of Inter-Legality* (Cambridge University Press, 2019)

Klabbers, J., A. Peters and G. Ulfstein, *The Constitutionalization of International Law* (Oxford University Press, 2009)

Klabbers, J. and T. Piiparinen, 'Normative Pluralism: An Explanation', in J. Klabbers and T. Piiparinen (eds.) *Normative Pluralism and International Law: Exploring Global Governance* (Cambridge University Press, 2013) 13

Klabbers, J. and Å. Wallendahl (eds.), *Research Handbook on the Law of International Organizations* (Cheltenham: Edward Elgar, 2011)

Klein, E. and S. Schmahl, 'Article 12', in B. Simma *et al.* (eds.), *The Charter of the United Nations: A Commentary*, 3rd ed. (Oxford University Press, 2012) 507

Klein, P., 'International Organizations or Institutions, Internal Law and Rules', in *Max Planck Encyclopedia of Public International Law* (online)

'Responsibility', in J. Cogan, I. Hurd and I. Johnstone (eds.), *Oxford Handbook of International Organizations* (Oxford University Press, 2016) 1026

Knapp, G. F., *The State Theory of Money* (London: MacMillan, 1924, Lucas and Bonar transl.)

Koch, A., 'The Politics and Discourse of Migrant Return: The Role of UNHCR and IOM in the Governance of Return', (2014) 40 *Journal of Ethnic and Migration Studies* 905

Koenig-Archibugi, M., 'Accountability', in J. Cogan, I. Hurd and I. Johnstone (eds.), *Oxford Handbook of International Organizations* (Oxford University Press, 2016) 1146

Koh, H., 'Transnational Legal Process', (1996) 75 *Nebraska Law Review* 181

Koh, H. and T. Buckwald, 'The Crime of Aggression: The United States' Perspective', (2015) 109 *American Journal of International Law* 257

Kolb, R., 'L'article 103 de la Charte des Nations Unies', (2013) 367 *Recueil des Cours* 9

Koremenos, B., C. Lipson and D. Snidal, 'The Rational Design of International Institutions', (2001) 55 *International Organization* 761

Koselleck, R., *Critique and Crisis: Enlightenment and the Pathogenesis of Modern Society* (Cambridge MA: MIT Press, 1988)

Koskenniemi, M., *Fragmentation of International Law: Difficulties Arising from the Diversification and Expansion of International Law* (Helsinki: Erik Castrén Institute, 2007)

From Apology to Utopia: The Structure of International Legal Argument, 2nd ed. (Cambridge University Press, 2005)

'Hegemonic Regimes', in M. Young (ed.), *Regime Interaction in International Law: Facing Fragmentation* (Cambridge University Press, 2012) 305

'The Police in the Temple', (1995) 6 *European Journal of International Law* 325

Kothari, A. and R. Bhartari, 'Narmada Valley Project – Development or Destruction?', (1984) 19 *Economic and Political Weekly* 907

Koutrakos, P., 'Institutional Balance and Sincere Cooperation in Treaty-Making under EU Law', (2019) 68 *International and Comparative Law Quarterly* 1

Krasner, S., 'Structural Causes and Regime Consequences: Regimes as Intervening Variables', in S. Krasner (ed.), *International Regimes* (Ithaca NY: Cornell University Press, 1983) 1

Krause, K., 'Disarmament', in T. G. Weiss and S. Daws (eds.), *Oxford Handbook on the United Nations* (Oxford University Press, 2007) 297

Krisch, N., *Beyond Constitutionalism: The Pluralist Structure of Postnational Law* (Oxford University Press, 2010)

'The Decay of Consent: International Law in an Age of Global Public Goods', (2014) 108 *American Journal of International Law* 1

Kuijper, P.-J., 'Recent Tendencies in the Separation of Powers in EU Foreign Relations: An Essay', in E. Neframi and M. Gatti (eds.), *Constitutional Issues of EU External Relations Law* (Baden-Baden: Nomos, 2018) 199

'WTO Institutional Aspects', in D. Bethlehem *et al.* (eds.), *Oxford Handbook of International Trade Law* (Oxford University Press, 2009) 79

Kuo, M., 'Inter-Public Legality or Post-Public Legitimacy? Global Governance and the Curious Case of Global Administrative Law as a New Paradigm of Law', (2012) 10 *International Journal of Constitutional Law* 1050

'The Concept of "Law" in Global Administrative Law: A Reply to Benedict Kingsbury', (2009) 20 *European Journal of International Law* 997

Lagrange, E. , 'La catégorie "organisation internationale"', in E. Lagrange and J-M. Sorel (eds.), *Droit des Organisations Internationales* (Paris: LGDJ, 2013) 25

Lamoreaux, N. and I. Shapiro (eds.), *The Bretton Woods Agreements: Together with Scholarly Commentaries and Essential Historical Documents* (New Haven CT: Yale University Press, 2019)

Larionova, M., 'G20: Engaging with International Organizations to Generate Growth', (2017) 12 *International Organisations Research Journal* 54

Larner, W. and W. Walters (eds.), *Global Governmentality: Governing International Spaces* (Abingdon: Routledge, 2004)

Lastra, R. M., *International Financial and Monetary Law*, 2nd ed. (Oxford University Press, 2015)

Lauterpacht, E., 'The Development of the Law of International Organization by the Decisions of International Tribunals', (1976-IV) 152 *Recueil des Cours* 377

Lave, J. and E. Wenger, *Situated Learning: Legitimate Peripheral Participation* (Cambridge University Press, 1991)

Leal-Arcas R. and A. Filis, 'Renewable Energy Disputes in the World Trade Organization', (2015) 12 *Transnational Dispute Management* 1

'The Fragmented Governance of the Global Energy Economy: A Legal-Institutional Analysis', (2013) 6 *Journal of World Energy Law and Business* 384

Legg, S., '"The Life of Individuals as well as of Nations": International Law and the League of Nations' Anti-Trafficking Governmentalities', (2012) 25 *Leiden Journal of International Law* 647

Levit, J., 'A Bottom-Up Approach to International Lawmaking: The Tale of Three Trade Finance Instruments', (2005) 30 *Yale Journal of International Law* 125

Levitas, R., *Utopia as Method: The Imaginary Reconstitution of Society* (Basingstoke: Palgrave Macmillan, 2013)

Lidén, J., *The Grand Decade for Global Health: 1998–2008* (London: Chatham House, 2013)

Lippold, M. and A. Paulus, 'Article 7', in B. Simma *et al.* (eds.), *The Charter of the United Nations: A Commentary*, 3rd ed. (Oxford University Press, 2012) 388

Livermore, M. A., 'Authority and Legitimacy in Global Governance: Deliberation, Institutional Differentiation, and the Codex Alimentarius', (2006) 81 *New York University Law Review* 766

Lloyd, R., 'Promoting Global Accountability: The Experiences of the Global Accountability Project', (2008) 14 *Global Governance* 273

Locke, J., *Two Treatises of Government* (Cambridge University Press, 1967 [1689])

Lodge, M., 'How to Mine the Oceans Sustainably: Deep-sea Minerals, Including Nickel, Copper, Manganese and Cobalt are Crucial to Build Clean-energy Technologies', *Scientific American*, 11 August 2020

Loewenthal, P.-J., 'Article 13 TEU', in M. Kellerbauer, M. Klammert, J. Tomkin (eds.), *The EU Treaties and the Charter of Fundamental Rights: A Commentary* (Oxford University Press, 2019), 126

López, P. and C. Nahón, 'The Growth of Debt and the Debt of Growth: Lessons from the Case of Argentina', (2017) 44 *Journal of Law and Society* 99

Louis, M. and L. Maertens, *Why International Organizations Hate Politics: Depoliticizing the World* (Abingdon: Routledge, 2021)

Luzzati, L., 'The International Institute of Agriculture', (1906) 182 *North American Review* 651

Lynch, C., 'WHO becomes Battleground as Trump chooses Pandemic Confrontation over Cooperation', *Foreign Policy*, 29 April 2020

Maâ, A., 'Manufacturing Collaboration in the Deportation Field: Intermediation and the Institutionalisation of the International Organisation for Migration's "Voluntary Return" Programmes in Morocco', (2020) 25 *Journal of North African Studies* 1

MacMillan, M., *Paris 1919* (New York: Random House, 2001)

Maga, T., 'Vision and Victory: Franklin Roosevelt and the Pacific War Council, 1942–1944', (1991) 21 *Presidential Quarterly* 351

Magliveras, K. , 'Membership in International Organizations', in J. Klabbers and Å. Wallendahl (eds.), *Research Handbook on the Law of International Organizations* (Cheltenham: Edward Elgar, 2011) 84

Mankiw, G., 'A Skeptic's Guide to Modern Monetary Theory', (2020) 110 *AEA Papers and Proceedings* 141

Mann, A., 'Food Sovereignty: Alternatives to Failed Food and Hunger Policies', (2015) 18 *Contemporanea* 445

Mann Borgese, E., 'The New International Economic Order and the Law of the Sea', (1977) 14 *San Diego Law Review* 584

Marks, G., L. Hooghe and K. Black, 'European Integration for the 1980s: State-Centric and Multi-level Governance', (1996) 34 *Journal of Common Market Studies* 341

Marks, S., 'Big Brother is Bleeping Us – With the Message That Ideology Doesn't Matter', (2001) 12 *European Journal of International Law* 109

'Exploitation as an International Legal Concept', in S. Marks (ed.), *International Law on the Left: Re-Examining Marxist Legacies* (Cambridge University Press, 2009) 281

'Naming Global Administrative Law', (2004) 37 *New York University Journal of International Law and Politics* 995

Marsh, R., 'Modernization Theory, Then and Now', (2014) 13 *Comparative Sociology* 261

Massumi, B., *99 Theses on the Revaluation of Value: A Postcapitalist Manifesto* (Minneapolis MN: University of Minnesota Press, 2018)

Mathias, S., 'UN Peacekeeping Today: Legal Challenges and Uncertainties', (2017) 17 *Melbourne Journal of International Law* 138

Maul, D., *Human Rights, Development and Decolonization: The International Labour Organization, 1940–1970* (New York: Palgrave Macmillan, 2012)

Mayer, P., 'Civil Society Participation in International Security Organizations: The Cases of NATO and the OSCE', in J. Steffek *et al.* (eds.), *Civil Society Participation in European and Global Governance: A Cure for the Democratic Deficit?* (Basingstoke: Palgrave MacMillan, 2008) 116

Mazower, M., *Governing the World* (London: Allen Lane, 2012)

No Enchanted Palace: The End of Empire and the Ideological Origins of the United Nations (Princeton University Press, 2009)

Mazzucato, M., *Mission Economy: A Moonshot Guide to Changing Capitalism* (London: Allen Lane, 2021)

The Entrepreneurial State: Debunking Public vs Private Sector Myths (London: Anthem Press, 2013)

McDougal, M. S. and R. Goodman, 'Chinese Participation in the United Nations: The Legal Imperative of a Negotiated Solution', (1966) 60 *American Journal of International Law* 671

McDougal, F. L., *The McDougall Memoranda* (Rome: FAO, 1956)

McLachlan, C., 'The Assault on International Adjudication and the Limits of Withdrawal', (2019) 68 *International and Comparative Law Quarterly* 499

McNeely, C. L., *Constructing the Nation-State: International Organization and Prescriptive Action* (Westport CT: Greenwood Press, 1995)

Mearsheimer, J., 'Bound to Fail: The Rise and Fall of the Liberal International Order', (2019) 43 *International Security* 7

'The False Promise of International Institutions', (1994–5) 19 *International Security* 5

Mechlem, K., 'Food and Agriculture Organization of the United Nations', *Max Planck Encyclopedia of Public International Law* (online)

'World Food Programme WFP', *Max Planck Encyclopedia of Public International Law* (online)

Meerssche, D. van den, 'A Legal Black Hole in the Cosmos of Virtue: The Politics of Human Rights Critique against the World Bank', (2021) 21 *Human Rights Law Review* 80

Mégret, F., and F. Hoffman, 'The UN as a Human Rights Violator? Some Reflections on the United Nations Changing Human Rights Responsibilities', (2003) 25 *Human Rights Quarterly* 314

Meron, T., 'The Humanization of Humanitarian Law', (2000) 94 *American Journal of International Law* 239

Merry, S. E., K. Davis and B. Kingsbury (eds.), *The Quiet Power of Indicators* (Cambridge University Press, 2015)

Meyer, J. W. *et al.*, 'World Society and the Nation-State', (1997) 103 *American Journal of Sociology* 144

Meyer, K., 'The Architecture of International Energy Governance', (2012) 106 *Proceedings of the American Society of International Law* 389

Michaels, R., 'Global Legal Pluralism', (2009) 5 *Annual Review of Law and Social Sciences* 243

Micinski, N. and T. Weiss, 'International Organization for Migration and the UN System: A Missed Opportunity', (2016) 42 *Future United Nations Development System Briefing* 4

Miller, P., 'On the Interrelations between Accounting and the State', (1990) 15 *Accounting, Organizations and Society* 317

Minnerop, P., 'The Legal Effect of the "Paris Rulebook" under the Doctrine of Treaty Interpretation', in P. Cameron, X. Mu and V. Roeben (eds.), *Global Energy Transition* (Oxford: Hart, 2021) 101

Minsky, H., *Stabilizing an Unstable Economy* (New York: MacGraw-Hill, 2008)

Mishkin, F., 'Anatomy of a Financial Crisis', (1992) 2 *Journal of Evolutionary Economics* 115

Missbach, A., *Troubled Transit: Asylum Seekers Stuck in Indonesia* (Singapore: ISEAS Yusof Ishak Institute, 2015)

Mitchell, T., 'Society, Economy, and the State Effect' in G. Steinmetz (ed.), *State/Culture: State-Formation after the Cultural Turn* (Ithaca NY: Cornell University Press, 1999) 7

Monaco, R., 'Les principes régissant la structure et le fonctionnement des organisations internationales', (1977-III) 156 *Receuil des Cours* 81

Moon, S., 'Global Health: A Centralized Network Searching for Hierarchy', in M. Barnett, J. Pevehouse and K. Raustiala (eds.), *Global Governance in a World of Change* (Cambridge University Press, 2021) 234

Morlino, E., *Procurement by International Organizations: A Global Administrative Law Perspective* (Cambridge University Press, 2019)

Morozov, G., 'The Socialist Conception of International Organization' in G. Abi-Saab (ed.), *The Concept of International Organization* (Paris: UNESCO, 1981) 179

Moyn, S., *Not Enough: Human Rights in an Unequal World* (Cambridge MA: Harvard University Press, 2018)

Mu, X. and D. Jena, 'Comparison of Outlooks and Implications for Energy Transition', in P. Cameron, X. Mu and V. Roeben (eds.), *Global Energy Transition* (Oxford: Hart, 2021) 11

Müllerson, R., 'The ABM Treaty: Changed Circumstances, Extraordinary Events, Supreme Interests and International Law', (2001) 50 *International and Comparative Law Quarterly* 509

Murphy, C., *International Organization and Industrial Revolution: Global Governance since 1850* (Cambridge: Polity, 1994)

'Private Sector', in T. Weiss and S. Daws (eds.), *Oxford Handbook on the United Nations* (Oxford University Press, 2007) 264

The United Nations Development Programme: A Better Way (Cambridge University Press, 2006)

Murphy, J. F., 'Force and Arms', in O. Schachter and C. Joyner (eds.), *United Nations Legal Order* (Cambridge University Press, 1995) 247

Murphy, S., 'Identifying the Rules for Identifying Customary International Law', (2014) 108 *AJIL Unbound* 169

Myjer, E. P. J., 'The Organization for the Prohibition of Chemical Weapons: Closer towards an International Arms Control Organization? A Quantum Leap in the Institutional Law of Arms Control', in E. P. J. Myjer (ed.), *Issues of Arms Control Law and the Chemical Weapons Convention* (The Hague: Martinus Nijhoff, 2001) 61

Naert, F., *International Law Aspects of the EU's Security and Defence Policy, with a Particular Focus on the Law of Armed Conflict and Human Rights* (Antwerp: Intersentia, 2010)

Naffine, N., 'Who Are Law's Persons? From Cheshire Cats to Responsible Subjects', (2003) 66 *Modern Law Review* 346

Nagy, T., 'Credit Rating Agencies and the First Amendment: Applying Constitutional Journalistic Protections to Subprime Mortgage Litigation', (2009) 94 *Minnesota Law Review* 140

Nandan, S., 'Administering the Mineral Resources of the Deep Seabed', in D. Freestone, R. Barnes and D. Ong (eds.), *The Law of the Sea: Progress and Prospects* (Oxford University Press, 2006) 75

Naudé Fourie, A., *The World Bank Inspection Panel and Quasi-judicial Oversight* (Utrecht: Eleven, 2009)

Nelson, P., 'Agendas, Accountability, and Legitimacy among Transnational Networks Lobbying the World Bank', in S. Khagram, J. Riker and K. Sikkink (eds.), *Restructuring World Politics* (Minneapolis MN: University of Minnesota Press, 2002) 131

N. N., 'Interview with Robert W. Cox', (2003) 1 *Globalisation, Societies and Education* 22

Noel-Baker, P., *The Arms Race: A Programme for World Disarmament* (London: John Calder, 1958)

Nolan, A. and J. Bohoslavsky, 'Human Rights and Economic Policy Reforms', (2020) 24 *International Journal of Human Rights* 1247

Oberthür, S. and T. Gehring, 'Institutional Interaction: Ten Years of Scholarly Development', in S. Oberthür and O. Stokke (eds.), *Managing Institutional Complexity: Regime Interplay and Global Environmental Change* (Cambridge MA: MIT Press, 2011) 25

Okonjo-Iweala, N., 'Finding a Vaccine Is Only the First Step: No-one Will Be Safe without the Whole World Being Safe', *Foreign Affairs*, 30 April 2020

O'Brien, J., 'Empire v. National Interests in Australian-British Relations during the 1930s', (1987) 22 *Historical Studies* 569

'F.L. McDougall and the Origins of the FAO', (2000) 46 *Australian Journal of Politics and History* 164

O'Neill, R. and D. N. Schwartz, *Hedley Bull on Arms Control* (London: Macmillan, 1987)

Orford, A., *International Authority and the Responsibility to Protect* (Cambridge University Press, 2011)

Oswald, B., H. Durham and A. Bates, *Documents on the Law of UN Peace Operations*, 2nd ed. (Oxford University Press, 2019)

Özsu, U., *Formalizing Displacement: International Law and Population Transfers* (Oxford University Press, 2014)

'Hydrocarbon Humanitarianism: Ibrahim Shihata, "Oil Aid" and Resource Sovereignty', (2020) 22 *Journal of the History of International Law* 1

'In the Interests of Mankind as a Whole: Mohammed Bedjaoui's New International Economic Order', (2015) 6 *Humanity* 129

Page, H., *Global Governance and Food Security as Global Public Good* (New York: NYU Center on International Cooperation, 2013)

Pahuja, S., *Decolonising International Law* (Cambridge University Press, 2011)

'Technologies of Empire: IMF Conditionality and the Reinscription of the North/South Divide', (2000) 13 *Leiden Journal of International Law* 749

Paust, J. and A. Blaustein, 'The Arab Oil Weapon: A Threat to International Peace', (1974) 68 *American Journal of International Law* 410

Pauwelyn, J., *Conflict of Norms in Public International Law: How WTO Law Relates to Other Rules of International Law* (Cambridge University Press, 2003)

Pauwelyn, J., R. Wessel and J. Wouters (eds.), *Informal International Lawmaking* (Oxford University Press, 2012)

Pauwelyn, J., R. Wessel and J. Wouters, 'When Structures Become Shackles: Stagnation and Dynamics in International Lawmaking', (2014) 25 *European Journal of International Law* 733

Pécoud, A., 'What Do We Know about the International Organization for Migration?', (2017) 44 *Journal of Ethnic and Migration Studies* 1621

Pedersen, S., *The Guardians: The League of Nations and the Crisis of Empire* (Oxford University Press, 2015)

Pellet, A., 'Le glaive et la balance. Remarques sur le rôle de la C.I.J. en matière de maintien de la paix et de la sécurité internationales', in Y. Dinstein (ed.), *International Law at a Time of Perplexity: Essays in Honour of Shabtai Rosenne* (Dordrecht: Kluwer, 1989) 539

Peng, W. and E. Berry, 'The Concept of Food Security', in P. Ferranti *et al.* (eds.) *Encyclopedia of Food Security and Sustainability*, vol. 2. (Amsterdam: Elsevier, 2019) 1

Penrose, A., *No Ordinary Woman: The Life of Edith Penrose* (Oxford University Press, 2017)

Penrose, E. F., *Economic Planning for the Peace* (Princeton University Press, 1953)

Périgord, P., *The International Labor Organization* (New York: Appleton and Co., 1926)

Perruchoud, R., 'From the Intergovernmental Committee for European Migration to the International Organization for Migration', (1989) 1 *International Journal of Refugee Law* 501

'Persons Falling under the Mandate of the International Organization for Migration (IOM) and to Whom the Organization May Provide Migration Services', (1992) 4 *International Journal of Refugee Law* 205

Peters, A., 'Constitutionalisation', in J. d'Aspremont and S. Singh (eds.), *Concepts for International Law: Contributions to Disciplinary Thought* (Cheltenham: Edward Elgar 2019) 141

'International Organizations and International Law', in J. Cogan, I. Hurd and I. Johnstone (eds.), *Oxford Handbook of International Organizations* (Oxford University Press, 2016) 33

'The Constitutionalisation of International Organisations', in N. Walker, J. Shaw and S. Tierney (eds.), *Europe's Constitutional Mosaic* (Oxford: Hart, 2011)

Peters, A. and S. Peter, 'International Organizations: Between Technocracy and Democracy', in B. Fassbender and A. Peters (eds.), *Oxford Handbook of the History of International Law* (Oxford University Press, 2012) 170

Peters, A. and A. Petrig, *Völkerrecht*, 5th ed. (Zürich: Schulthess, 2020)

Pistor, K., 'A Legal Theory of Finance', (2013) 41 *Journal of Comparative Economics* 315

The Code of Capital: How the Law Creates Wealth and Inequality (Princeton University Press 2019)

Polanyi, K., *The Great Transformation: The Political and Economic Origins of Our Time* (Boston MA: Beacon Press, 2001 [1944])

Pollack, M., *The Engines of European Integration: Delegation, Agency and Agenda-Setting in the EU* (Oxford University Press, 2003)

Porretto, G. and S. Vité, 'The Application of International Humanitarian Law and Human Rights Law to International Organisations', University Centre for International Humanitarian Law, Research Paper No. 1 (2006)

Portmann, R., *Legal Personality in International Law* (Cambridge University Press, 2010)

Poulantzas, N., *Classes in Contemporary Capitalism* (London: Verso, 1978)

Preiswerk, R., 'Hidden Dimensions of the So-called New International Economic Order', in H. Addo (ed.), *Transforming the World Economy? Nine Critical Essays on the New International Economic Order* (London: Hodder and Stoughton, 1984) 32

Pugach, N., *Paul S. Reinsch: Open Door Diplomat in Action* (Millwood NY: KTO Press, 1979)

Quaglia, L., 'The Politics of "Third Country Equivalence" in Post-Crisis Financial Services Regulation in the European Union', (2015) 38 *West European Politics* 16

Quigley, J., *The Statehood of Palestine: International Law in the Middle East Conflict* (Cambridge University Press, 2012)

Qureshi, A., *Interpreting WTO Agreements: Problems and Perspectives* (Cambridge University Press, 2015)

Radbruch, G., 'Rechtsphilosophie', in G. Radbruch, *Gesamtausgabe Band 2: Rechtsphilosophie II* (Heidelberg: Müller, 1987/1993) 363

Radi, H., 'Bruce, Stanley Melbourne' (1883–1967), in *Australian Dictionary of Biography* (Melbourne University Publishing, 1979)

Rajagopal, B., *International Law from Below* (Cambridge University Press, 2003)

Ramcharan, B., 'Lacunae in the Law of International Organizations: The Relations between Subsidiary and Parent Organs with Particular Reference to the Commission and Sub-Commission on Human Rights', in M. Nowak, D. Steurer and H. Tretter (eds.), *Progress in the Spirit of Human Rights: Festschrift Ermacora* (Kehl am Rhein: Engel, 1988) 37

(ed.), *The Principle of Legality in International Human Rights Institutions: Selected Legal Opinions* (Dordrecht: Martinus Nijhoff, 1997)

Randeria, S. and C. Grunder, 'The (Un)Making of Policy in the Shadow of the World Bank: Infrastructure Development, Urban Resettlement and the Cunning State in India', in C. Shore, S. Wright and D. Però (eds.), *Policy Worlds: Anthropology and the Analysis of Contemporary Power* (New York: Berghahn Books, 2011) 201

Ranganathan, S., *Strategically Created Treaty Conflicts and the Politics of International Law* (Cambridge University Press, 2014)

'The Common Heritage of Mankind: Annotation on a Battle', in J. von Bernstorff and P. Dann (eds.), *The Battle for International Law: South-North Perspectives on the Decolonization Era* (Oxford University Press, 2019) 35

Rappaport, E., *A Thirst for Empire: How Tea Shaped the Modern World* (Princeton University Press, 2017)

Raustiala, K., 'Institutional Proliferation and the International Legal Order', in J. Dunoff and M. Pollack (eds.), *Interdisciplinary Perspectives on International Law and International Relations: The State of the Art* (Cambridge University Press, 2013) 293

Raustiala, K. and D. Victor, 'The Regime Complex for Plant Genetic Resources', (2004) 58 *International Organization* 277

Raworth, K., *Doughnut Economics: Seven Ways to Think like a 21st-Century Economist* (White River Junction VT: Chelsea Green, 2017)

Redish, A., 'The Latin Monetary Union and the Emergence of the International Gold Standard', in N. Tamaki (ed.), *Monetary Regimes in Transition* (Cambridge University Press, 1993) 63

Reinalda, B., *Routledge History of International Organizations: From 1815 to Present Day* (Abingdon: Routledge, 2009)

Reinicke, W., 'The Other World Wide Web: Global Public Policy Networks', (1999) 117 *Foreign Policy* 44

Reinisch, A. , 'Sources of International Organizations' Law: Why Custom and General Principles are Crucial', in S. Besson and J. d'Aspremont (eds.), *Oxford Handbook of the Sources of International Law* (Oxford University Press, 2017) 1007

Reinsch, P., *Public International Unions, Their Work and Organization: A Study in International Administrative Law* (Boston: McGinn, 1911)

Reisman, W. M. and D. Stevick, 'The Applicability of International Law Standards to United Nations Economic Sanctions Programmes', (1998) 9 *European Journal of International Law* 86

Reuter, P., 'Les organes subsidiaires des organisations internationales', in *Hommages d'une génération de juristes au Président Basdevant* (Paris: Pedone, 1960) 415

'Principes de droit international public', (1961-II) 103 *Recueil des Cours* 425

Richardson, M. and L. White, 'The Rating Agencies: Is Regulation the Answer?', in V. Acharya and M. Richardson (eds.), *Restoring Financial Stability* (Hoboken NJ: Wiley 2009) 101

Riegner, M., *Informationsverwaltungsrecht internationaler Institutionen: Dargestellt am Entwicklungsverwaltungsrecht der Weltbank und Vereinten Nationen* (Tübingen: Mohr Siebeck, 2018)

'The Equator Principles on Sustainable Finance Assessed from a Critical Development and Third World Perspective', (2014) 5 *Transnational Legal Theory* 489

'Towards an International Institutional Law of Information', (2015) 12 *International Organizations Law Review* 50

Rimmer, D., 'Some Origins of Development Economics', (1979) 10 *Development and Change* 33

Risse, T., *A Community of Europeans: Transnational Identities and Public Spheres* (Ithaca NY: Cornell University Press, 2010)

Rittberger, V., B. Zangl and A. Kruck, *International Organization*, 2nd ed. (New York: Palgrave Macmillan, 2012)

Rittich, K., 'The Future of Law and Development: Second-Generation Reforms and the Incorporation of the Social', in D. Trubek and A. Santos (eds.), *The New Law and Economic Development: A Critical Appraisal* (Cambridge University Press, 2006) 203

Rivier, R., *Droit international public*, 2nd ed. (Paris: PUF, 2013)

Roberts, A. *et al.*, (eds.), *Comparative International Law* (Oxford University Press, 2018)

'Conceptualizing Comparative International Law', in A. Roberts *et al.* (eds.), *Comparative International Law* (Oxford University Press, 2018) 3

Is International Law International? (Oxford University Press, 2017)

Roberts, I., *Satow's Diplomatic Practice*, 7th ed. (Oxford University Press, 2016)

Rockwood, L., *Legal Framework for IAEA Safeguards* (Vienna: IAEA, 2013)

Rodiles, A., *Coalitions of the Willing and International Law* (Cambridge University Press, 2018)

Rodrik, D., *The Globalization Paradox: Democracy and the Future of the World Economy* (Oxford University Press, 2011)

Roeben, V., 'Governing Shared Offshore Electricity Infrastructure in the Northern Seas', (2013) 62 *International and Comparative Law Quarterly* 839

Towards a European Energy Union (Cambridge University Press, 2018)

Roeben, V. and R. Macatangay, 'Coalition for Transboundary Energy Resources: A Law and Economics Approach', in K. Zou, S. Wu and Q. Ye (eds.), *The 21st Century Maritime Road: Challenges and Opportunities for Asia and Europe* (Abingdon: Routledge, 2019) 117

Roggenkamp, M., 'Petroleum Pipelines in the North Sea: Questions of Jurisdiction and Practical Status', (1998) 16 *Journal of Energy and Natural Resources Law* 92

Rogoff, K. and J. Zettelmeyer, 'Bankruptcy Procedures for Sovereigns: A History of Ideas, 1976–2001', (2002) 49 *IMF Staff Papers* 470

Röling, B. V. A., *International Law in an Expanded World* (Amsterdam: Djambatan, 1960)

Ruffert, M., 'The Administration of Kosovo and East Timor by the International Community', (2001) 50 *International and Comparative Law Quarterly* 613

Ruffert, M. and C. Walter, *Institutionalised International Law* (Munich: Beck, 2015)

Sabel, R., *Procedure at International Conferences*, 2nd ed. (Cambridge University Press, 2009)

Sadie, J., 'The Social Anthropology of Economic Underdevelopment', (1960) *Economic Journal* 294

Saito, K., *Karl Marx's Ecosocialism* (New York: Monthly Review Press, 2017)

Salminen, J., 'The Accord on Fire and Building Safety in Bangladesh: A New Paradigm for Limiting Buyer's Liability in Global Supply Chains?', (2018) 66 *American Journal of Comparative Law* 411

Salvatici, S., 'Writing for the History of Food Security', (2015) 18 *Contemporanea* 347

Sander, G., 'International Organization for Standardization (ISO)', in *Max Planck Encyclopedia of Public International Law* (online)

Sands, P. and P. Klein, *Bowett's Law of International Institutions*, 5th ed. (London: Sweet and Maxwell, 2001)

Sands, P. and P. Klein, *Bowett's Law of International Institutions*, 6th ed. (London: Sweet & Maxwell, 2009)

Santulli, C., 'Retour à la theorie de l'organe commun', (2012) 116 *Revue Générale de Droit International Public* 565

Sarfaty, G., *Values in Translation: Human Rights and the Culture of the World Bank* (Stanford University Press, 2012)

'Why Culture Matters in International Institutions: The Marginality of Human Rights at the World Bank', (2009) 103 *American Journal of International Law* 647

Sarooshi, D., *The United Nations and the Development of Collective Security: The Delegation by the UN Security Council of Its Chapter VII Powers* (Oxford University Press, 1999)

Sassen, S., *Expulsions: Brutality and Complexity in the Global Economy* (Harvard University Press, 2014)

Sato, T., 'Constituent Instruments of International Organizations and Their Interpretative Framework – Introduction to the Principal Doctrines and Bibliography', (1986) 14 *Hitotsubashi Journal of Law and Politics* 1

Saul, B., 'Legislating from a Radical Hague: The United Nations Special Tribunal for Lebanon Invents an International Crime of Transnational Terrorism', (2011) 24 *Leiden Journal of International Law* 677

Sayre, F. B., *Experiments in International Administration* (New York: Harper, 1919)

Schachter, O., *Sharing the World's Resources* (New York: Columbia University Press, 1977)

'The Invisible College of International Lawyers', (1977) 72 *Northwestern University Law Review* 217

Schäfer, A., 'A New Form of Governance? Comparing the Open Method of Coordination to Multilateral Surveillance by the IMF and the OECD', (2006) 13 *Journal of European Public Policy* 70

Scharf, M., *Customary International Law in Times of Fundamental Change* (Cambridge University Press, 2013)

Scharpf, F., *Governing in Europe: Effective and Democratic?* (Oxford University Press, 1999)

Schauer, F., 'The Convergence of Rules and Standards', (2003) *New Zealand Law Review* 303

Schelling, T. and M. Halperin, *Strategy and Arms Control* (New York: Twentieth Century Fund, 1961)

International Institutional Law: Unity within Diversity, 4th ed. (Dordrecht: Martinus Nijhoff, 2003)

International Institutional Law: Unity within Diversity, 5th ed. (Leiden: Martinus Nijhoff, 2011)

International Institutional Law: Unity within Diversity, 6th ed. (Leiden: Martinus Nijhoff, 2018)

'International Organizations or Institutions, Financing of', in *Max Planck Encyclopedia of Public International Law* (online)

Schifano, A., 'Distribution of Power within International Organizations', (2017) 14 *International Organizations Law Review* 346

Schill, S., 'Sources of International Investment Law: Multilateralization, Arbitral Precedent, Comparativism, Soft Law', in S. Besson and J. d'Aspremont (eds.), *Oxford Handbook on the Sources of International Law* (Oxford University Press, 2017) 1095

Schmalenbach, K., 'International Organizations or Institutions: General Aspects', *Max Planck Encyclopedia of Public International Law* (online)

Schofer, E. *et al.*, 'Sociological Institutionalism and World Society', in E. Amenta *et al.* (eds.), *The Wiley-Blackwell Companion to Political Sociology* (Hoboken NJ: Blackwell, 2012) 57

Schrijver, N., *Sovereignty over Natural Resources: Balancing Rights and Duties* (Cambridge University Press, 1997)

Schücking, W., 'Die Organisation der Welt', in W. van Calker and P. Laband (eds.), *Staatsrechtliche Abhandlungen* (Tübingen: Mohr, 1908)

Schumacher, J., C. Trebesch and H. Enderlein, 'Sovereign Defaults in Court', (2018) *ECB Working Paper* 2135

Selivanova, Y., 'The Energy Charter and the International Energy Governance', (2012) 3 *European Yearbook of International Economic Law* 307

Sen, A., *Poverty and Famines: An Essay on Entitlement and Deprivation* (Oxford University Press, 1983)

'Why Is There so Much Hunger in the World', *Twenty-eighth McDougall Memorial Lecture* (Rome: FAO, 2013)

Seyersted, F., 'Applicable Law in Relations between Intergovernmental Organizations and Private Parties', (1967) 122 *Recueil des Cours* 529

Common Law of International Organizations (Leiden: Martinus Nijhoff, 2008)

'Objective International Personality of Intergovernmental Organizations: Do Their Capacities Really Depend upon the Conventions Establishing Them?' (1964) 34 *Nordisk Tidsskrift for International Ret* 3

United Nations Forces in the Law of Peace and War (Leiden: Sijthoff, 1966)

Shaffer, G., *Transnational Legal Ordering and State Change* (Cambridge University Press, 2013)

Shaffer, G. and M. Pollack, 'Hard and Soft Law', in J. Dunoff and M. Pollack (eds.), *Interdisciplinary Perspectives on International Law and International Relations* (Cambridge University Press, 2013) 197

Sharma, A. and A. Gupta (eds.), *The Anthropology of the State: A Reader* (Hoboken NJ: Blackwell, 2006)

Sharma, P., *Robert McNamara's Other War: The World Bank and International Development* (Philadelphia PA: University of Pennsylvania Press, 2017)

Sharman, J., *Havens in a Storm: The Struggle for Global Tax Regulation* (Ithaca NY: Cornell University Press, 2006)

Shawn, D. J., *World Food Security: A History since 1945* (New York: Palgrave Macmillan, 2007)

Shihata, I., *The World Bank in a Changing World: Selected Essays and Lectures*, vol. 2. (Dordrecht: Martinus Nijhoff, 1991)

The World Bank Inspection Panel (Oxford University Press, 1994)

The World Bank Inspection Panel, 2nd ed. (Oxford University Press, 2000)

Sicilianos, L.-A., 'L'autorisation par le Conseil de sécurité de recourir à la force: une tentative d'évaluation', (2002) 106 *Revue Générale de Droit International Public* 5

Sikkink, K., 'Human Rights Advocacy Networks and the Social Construction of Legal Rules', in Y. Dezalay and B. Garth (eds.), *Global Prescriptions: The Production, Exportation and Importation of a New Legal Orthodoxy* (Ann Arbor MI: University of Michigan Press, 2002) 37

Sikkink, K. and M. Keck, *Activists beyond Borders* (Ithaca NY: Cornell University Press, 1998)

Sikkink, K. and T. Risse, 'The Socialization of International Human Rights Norms into Domestic Practices', in T. Risse, M. Sikkink and S. Ropp (eds.), *The Power of Human Rights: International Norms and Domestic Politics* (Cambridge University Press, 1999) 1

Sikkink, K. and C. Walling, 'The Justice Cascade and the Impact of Human Rights Trials in Latin America', (2007) 44 *Journal of Peace Research* 427

Simma, B., 'NATO, the UN and the Use of Force: Legal Aspects', (1999) 10 *European Journal of International Law* 1

Simma, B. and A. Paulus, 'The Responsibility of Individuals for Human Rights Abuses in Internal Conflicts: A Positivist View', (1999) 93 *American Journal of International Law* 93

Simma, B. and D. Pulkowski, 'Of Planets and the Universe: Self-Contained Regimes in International Law', (2006) 17 *European Journal of International Law* 483

Simmons, B., 'The International Politics of Harmonization: The Case of Capital Market Regulation', (2003) 55 *International Organization* 589

Sinclair, G. F., 'A Battlefield Transformed: The United Nations and the Struggle over Postcolonial Statehood', in J. von Bernstorff and P. Dann (eds.), *The Battle for International Law: South–North Perspectives on the Decolonization Era* (Oxford University Press, 2019) 257

'A "Civilizing Task": The International Labour Organization, Social Reform, and the Genealogy of Development', (2018) 20 *Journal of the History of International Law* 145

'Forging Modern States with Imperfect Tools: United Nations Technical Assistance for Public Administration in Decolonized States', (2020) 11 *Humanity Journal*

'State Formation, Liberal Reform and the Growth of International Organizations', (2015) 26 *European Journal of International Law* 445

To Reform the World: International Organizations and the Making of Modern States (Oxford University Press, 2017)

'Toward a Postcolonial Genealogy of International Organizations Law', (2018) 31 *Leiden Journal of International Law* 841

Singer, M., 'Jurisdictional Immunities of International Organizations: Human Rights and Functional Necessity Concerns', (1995) 36 *Virginia Journal of International Law* 5

Skogly, S., *The Human Rights Obligations of the World Bank and the International Monetary Fund* (Abingdon: Routledge, 2001)

Skubiszewski, K., 'Enactment of Law by International Organizations', (1965–6) 41 *British Yearbook of International Law* 198

Slaughter, A.-M., *A New World Order* (Princeton University Press, 2004)

Slobodian, Q., *Globalists: The End of Empire and the Birth of Neoliberalism* (Harvard University Press, 2018)

Sly, J., 'The Genesis of the Universal Postal Union', (1927) 233 *International Conciliation* 393

Sobel, M., 'Strengthening Collective Action Clauses: Catalysing Change–The Back Story', (2016) 11 *Capital Markets Law Journal* 3

Sohn, L. B., 'Expulsion or Forced Withdrawal from an International Organization', (1964) 77 *Harvard Law Review* 1381

Sovacool, B., 'Cooperative or Inoperative? Accountability and Transparency at the World Bank's Inspection Panel', (2017) 1 *Case Studies in the Environment* 900

Staden, A. von, 'No Institution Is an Island: Checks and Balances in Global Governance', in J. Mendes and I. Venzke (eds.), *Allocating Authority: Who Should Do What in European and International Law?* (Oxford: Hart, 2018) 115

Stahn, C., *The Law and Practice of International Territorial Administration* (Cambridge University Press, 2008)

Standing, G., *The Precariat: The New Dangerous Class* (London: Bloomsbury, 2011)

Steffek, J., 'Max Weber, Modernity and the Project of International Organization', (2016) 29 *Cambridge Review of International Affairs* 1502

Steinbrück Platise, M., 'Legitimate Governance as a Privilege and Price for the Autonomy of International Organisations', in M. Steinbrück Platise, C. Moser and A. Peters (eds.), *The Legal Framework of the OSCE* (Cambridge University Press, 2019) 297

Steinbrück Platise, M., C. Moser and A. Peters (eds.), *The Legal Framework of the OSCE* (Cambridge University Press, 2019)

Steininger, S., 'What's Human Rights Got to Do With It? An Empirical Analysis of Human Rights References in Investment Arbitration', (2017) 31 *Leiden Journal of International Law* 26

Steinmetz, G. (ed.), *State/Culture: State-Formation after the Cultural Turn* (Ithaca NY: Cornell University Press, 1999)

Stephan, P., 'Comparative International Law, Foreign Relations Law and Fragmentation: Can the Center Hold?', in A. Roberts *et al.* (eds.), *Comparative International Law* (Oxford University Press, 2018) 53

Stephen, M., 'Legitimacy Deficits of International Organizations: Design, Drift, and Decoupling at the UN Security Council', (2018) 31 *Cambridge Review of International Affairs* 96

Stewart, R., 'Remedying Disregard in Global Regulatory Governance: Accountability, Participation, and Responsiveness', (2014) 108 *American Journal of International Law* 211

St John, T., *The Rise of Investor State Arbitration* (Oxford University Press, 2014)

Stubbs, T. and A. Kentikelenis, 'Conditionality and Sovereign Debt: An Overview of Human Rights Implications', in I. Bantekas and C. Lumina (eds.), *Sovereign Debt and Human Rights* (Oxford University Press, 2018) 359

Sundaram, L., 'The International Status of India', (1931) 17 *Transactions of the Grotius Society* 35

Suzuki, E. and S. Nanwani, 'Responsibility of International Organizations: The Accountability Mechanisms of Multilateral Development Banks', (2005) 27 *Michigan Journal of International Law* 50

Sybesma-Knol, N., *The United Nations* (The Hague: Kluwer, 2012)

Szasz, P., 'General Law-Making Processes', in O. Schachter and C. Joyner (eds.), *United Nations Legal Order* (Cambridge University Press, 1995) 35

Tabassi, L. and O. Elias, 'Disarmament', in M. Bowman and D. Kritsiotis (eds.), *Conceptual and Contextual Perspectives on the Modern Law of Treaties* (Cambridge University Press, 2018) 578

Tallberg, J., 'Transparency', in J. Cogan, I. Hurd and I. Johnstone (eds.), *Oxford Handbook of International Organizations* (Oxford University Press, 2016) 1170

Tallberg, J. and M. Zürn, 'The Legitimacy and Legitimation of International Organizations: Introduction and Framework', (2019) 14 *Review of International Organizations* 581

Tallberg, J. *et al.*, *The Opening Up of International Organizations: Transnational Access in Global Governance* (Cambridge University Press, 2013)

Talus, K., S. Looper and S. Otillar, 'Lex Petrolea and the Internationalization of Petroleum Agreements: Focus on Host Government Contracts', (2012) 5 *Journal of World Energy Law and Business* 181

Tamanaha, B., 'Understanding Legal Pluralism: Past and Present, Local to Global', (2008) 30 *Sydney Law Review* 375

Tan, C., 'Creative Cocktails or Toxic Brews? Blended Finance and the Regulatory Framework for Sustainable Development', in C. Gammage and T. Novitz (eds.), *Sustainable Trade, Investment and Finance: Toward Responsible and Coherent Regulatory Frameworks* (Cheltenham: Edward Elgar 2019) 300

Governance through Development: Poverty Reduction Strategies, International Law and the Disciplining of Third World States (London: Routledge, 2011)

Teitel, R., *Humanity's Law* (Oxford University Press, 2011)

Teubner, G., '*Quod Omnes Tangit*: Transnational Constitutions Without Democracy?', (2018) 45 *Journal of Law and Society* 5

Teubner, G. and A. Fischer-Lescano, 'Regime-Collisions: The Vain Search for Legal Unity in the Fragmentation of Global Law', (2004) 25 *Michigan Journal of International Law* 999

Teubner, G. and P. Korth, 'Two Kinds of Legal Pluralism: Collisions of Transnational Regimes in the Double Fragmentation of World Society', in M. Young (ed.), *Regime Interaction in International Law: Facing Fragmentation* (Cambridge University Press, 2012) 23

Thornburgh, D., 'Today's United Nations in a Changing World', (1993) 9 *American University International Law Review* 215

Thorstensen, V., D. Ramos and C. Muller, 'The "Missing Link" between the WTO and the IMF', (2013) 16 *Journal of International Economic Law* 353

Tierney, B., *The Idea of Natural Rights* (Grand Rapids MI: Eerdmans Publishing, 1997)

Trebilcock, A., 'Why the Shift from International to Transnational Law Is Important for Labor Standards', in H. Gött (ed.), *Labour Standards in International Economic Law* (Dordrecht: Springer 2018) 57

Trubek, D. and M. Galanter, 'Scholars in Self-Estrangement: Some Reflections on the Crisis in law and Development Studies in the United States', (1974) *Wisconsin Law Review* 1062

Trubek, D. and A. Santos (eds.), *The New Law and Economic Development* (Cambridge University Press, 2010)

Tsing, A., *The Mushroom at the End of the World: On the Possibility of Life in Capitalist Ruins* (Princeton University Press, 2015)

Turnell, S., 'F. L. McDougall: Eminence Grise of Australian Economic Diplomacy', (2000) 40 *Australian Economic History Review* 51

Monetary Reformers, Amateur Idealists and Keynesian Crusades: Australian Economists' International Advocacy, 1925–1950 (doctoral thesis, Macquarie University, 1999)

Twining, W., 'Normative and Legal Pluralism: A Global Perspective', (2010) 20 *Duke Journal of Comparative and International Law* 473

Tzouvala, N., 'The Ordo-Liberal Origins of Modern International Investment Law: Constructing Competition on a Global Scale', in J. Haskell and A. Rasulov (eds.), *New Voices and New Perspectives in International Economic Law* (Dordrecht: Springer, 2020) 37

Ukpabi, U. C., 'Juridical Substance or Myth over Balance-of-Payment: Developing Countries and the Role of the International Monetary Fund in the World Trade Organization', (2004) 26 *Michigan Journal of International Law* 701

Unger, C., 'Development Projections: The World Bank in Calcutta in the 1970s', (2020) 11 *Humanity Journal*

Urueña, R., *No Citizens Here: Global Subjects and Participation in International Law* (Leiden: Martinus Nijhoff, 2012)

'Prosecutorial Politics: The ICC's Influence in Colombian Peace Processes, 2003–2017', (2017) 111 *American Journal of International Law* 104

'Temporariness and Space in Global Governance', (2014) 45 *Netherlands Yearbook of International Law* 19

Vallat, F., 'The General Assembly and the Security Council of the United Nations', (1952) 29 *British Yearbook of International Law* 63

Venturas, L. (ed.), *International 'Migration Management' in the Early Cold War: The Intergovernmental Committee for European Migration* (Corinth: University of the Peloponnese, 2015)

Venzke, I., *How Interpretation Makes International Law* (Oxford University Press, 2012)

'Possibilities of the Past: Histories of the NIEO and the Travails of Critique', (2018) 20 *Journal of the History of International Law* 263

Verdier, P.-H., 'Mutual Recognition in International Finance', (2011) 52 *Harvard International Law Journal* 55

'The Political Economy of International Financial Regulation', (2013) 88 *Indiana Law Journal* 1405

Verdirame, G., *The UN and Human Rights: Who Guards the Guardians?* (Cambridge University Press, 2011)

Vincent, C. P., *The Politics of Hunger: The Allied Blockade of Germany, 1915–1919* (Athens OH: Ohio University Press, 1985)

Virally, M., 'Definition and Classification: A Legal Approach', (1977) 39 *International Social Sciences Journal* 58

'La notion de fonction dans la théorie de l'organisation internationale', in *Le droit international en devenir: essais écrits au fil des ans* (Paris: PUF, 1990) 271

Viterbo, A., *International Monetary Fund (IMF)* (London: Kluwer, 2019)

Vitzthum, W., 'Die Bemühungen um ein Régime des Tiefseebodens: Das Schicksal einer Idee', (1978) 38 *Zeitschrift für ausländisches öffentliches Recht und Völkerrecht* 745

Vlachtis, C., 'Trans-Adriatic Pipeline Projects – Agreements and Energy Charter Model Texts', (2016) 38 *Comparative Law Yearbook of International Business* 185

Voeten, E., 'Making Sense of the Design of International Institutions', (2019) 22 *Annual Review of Political Science* 147

Wade, R., 'Accountability Gone Wrong: The World Bank, Non-governmental Organisations and the US Government in a Fight over China', (2009) 14 *New Political Economy* 25

'Agenda Change in Western Development Organizations: From Hard Production to Soft, Timeless, Placeless Policy', (2015) 20 *Lahore Journal of Economics* 1

Waibel, M., 'Retaliating against Exchange-Rate Manipulation under WTO Rules', in S. Evenett (ed.), *The US-Sino Currency Dispute: New Insights from Economics, Politics, and Law* (London: CEPR, 2010) 133

Sovereign Defaults before International Courts and Tribunals (Cambridge University Press, 2011)

Wälde, T. (ed.), *The Energy Charter Treaty: An East-West Gateway for Investment and Trade* (London: Kluwer, 1996)

Ward, M., *Quantifying the World: UN Ideas and Statistics* (Bloomington IN: Indiana University Press, 2004)

Way, W., *A New Idea Each Morning: How Food and Agriculture Came Together in One International Organisation* (Canberra: Australian National University E-Press, 2013)

Webber, F., 'How Voluntary Are Voluntary Returns?', (2011) 52 *Race and Class* 98

Weidemaier, M. and A. Gelpern, 'Injunctions in Sovereign Debt Litigation', (2014) 31 *Yale Journal on Regulation* 189

Weidemaier, M. and M. Gulati, 'A People's History of Collective Actions Clauses', (2013) 54 *Virginia Journal of International Law* 51

Weil, P., 'Towards Relative Normativity in International Law?' (1983) 77 *American Journal of International Law* 413

Weisband, E. and A. Ebrahim, 'Introduction: Forging Global Accountabilities', in A. Ebrahim and E. Weisband (eds.), *Global Accountabilities: Participation, Pluralism, and Public Ethics* (Cambridge University Press, 2007) 3

Weiss, T., 'Governance, Good Governance and Global Governance: Conceptual and Actual Challenges', (2000) 21 *Third World Quarterly* 795

Wenger, E., *Communities of Practice: Learning, Meaning, and Identity* (Cambridge University Press, 1998)

Wheatley, S., 'A Democratic Rule of International Law', (2011) 22 *European Journal of International Law* 525

White, N., 'Lawmaking', in J. Cogan *et al.* (eds.), *Oxford Handbook of International Organizations* (Oxford University Press, 2016)

'Understanding Nuclear Deterrence within the International Constitutional Architecture', in J. Black-Branch and D. Fleck (eds.), *Nuclear Non-Proliferation in International Law Volume V: Legal Challenges for Nuclear Security and Deterrence* (Berlin: Springer, 2020) 237

Wieters, H., 'The World's Hungry: American NGOs and New Private-Public Partnerships after World War II', (2015) 18 *Contemporanea* 355

Wilde, R., '*Quis Custodiet Ipos Custodes?* Why and How UNHCR Governance of 'Development' Refugee Camps Should be Subject to Human Rights Law', (1998) 1 *Yale Human Rights and Development Law Journal* 107

Williamson, J., 'A Short History of the Washington Consensus', (2009) 15 *Law and Business Review of the Americas* 7

'Democracy and the "Washington Consensus"', (1993) 21 *World Development* 1329

Williamson, R. L., 'Hard Law, Soft Law, and Non-Law in Multilateral Arms Control: Some Compliance Hypotheses', (2003) 4 *Chinese Journal of International Law* 59

Willrich, M., 'The Treaty on Non-Proliferation of Nuclear Weapons: Nuclear Technology Confronts World Politics', (1968) 77 *Yale Law Journal* 1447

Wise, T. A., *Eating Tomorrow: Agribusiness, Family Farmers and the Battle for the Future of Food* (New York: New Press, 2019)

Witte, B. de, 'The Role of the Court of Justice in Shaping the Institutional Balance in the EU', in J. Mendes and I. Venzke (eds.), *Allocating Authority: Who Should Do What in European and International Law?* (Oxford: Hart, 2018) 143

Woeste, P. and T. Thomma, 'Article 17', in B. Simma *et al.* (eds.), *The Charter of the United Nations: A Commentary*, 3rd ed. (Oxford University Press, 2012) 576

Wolfrum, R., 'Chapter I: Purposes and Principles', in B. Simma *et al.* (eds.), *The Charter of the United Nations: A Commentary*, 3rd ed. (Oxford University Press, 2012) 107

Woods, N., *The Globalizers: the IMF, the World Bank and Their Borrowers* (Ithaca NY: Cornell University Press, 2007)

Wouters, J. and D. Coppens, 'International Economic Policy-Making: Exploring the Legal Linkages between the World Trade Organization and the Bretton Woods Institutions', (2006) 3 *International Organizations Law Review* 267

Wouters, J. and J. Odermatt, 'Certain Expenses of the United Nations', in C. Ryngaert *et al.* (eds.), *Judicial Decisions of the Law of International Organizations* (Oxford University Press, 2016) 91

Wouters, J. *et al.* (eds), *Accountability for Human Rights Violations by International Organisations* (Antwerp: Intersentia, 2010)

Zalcberg, J., 'The World Bank Inspection Panel: A Tool for Ensuring the World Bank's Compliance with International Law?', (2012) 8 *Macquarie Journal of International and Comparative Environmental Law* 1

Zanasi, M., 'Exporting Development: The League of Nations and Republican China', (2007) 49 *Comparative Studies in Society and History* 143

Zaring, D., 'Finding Legal Principle in Global Financial Regulation', (2011) 52 *Virginia Journal of International Law* 683

'International Institutional Performance in Crisis Symposium: International Law and the Economic Crisis', (2009) 10 *Chicago Journal of International Law* 475

Zaum, D., 'Legitimacy', in J. Cogan, I. Hurd and I. Johnstone (eds.), *Oxford Handbook of International Organizations* (Oxford University Press, 2016) 1107

Zhou, S. and J. Liberman, 'The Global Tobacco Epidemic and the WHO Framework Convention on Tobacco Control', in G. L. Burci and B. Toebes (eds.), *Research Handbook on Global Health Law* (Cheltenham: Edward Elgar, 2018) 340

Zhu, Y., 'Fair and Equitable Treatment of Foreign Investors in an Era of Sustainable Development', (2018) 58 *Natural Resources Journal* 319

Zieck, M., *UNHCR's Worldwide Presence in the Field: A Legal Analysis of UNHCR's Cooperation Agreements* (Nijmegen: Wolf, 2006)

Zürn, M., *A Theory of Global Governance* (Oxford University Press, 2018)

'Democratic Governance beyond the Nation-State: The EU and Other International Institutions', (2000) 6 *European Journal of International Relations* 183

Zutphen, G. van *et al.*, 'The Role of International Agencies in Achieving Food Security' in P. Ferranti, E. Berry and A. Jock (eds.), *Encyclopedia of Food Security and Sustainability* (Amsterdam: Elsevier, 2017) 1

Index